AF323955

GUERRILLA GIRLS

THE ART OF BEHAVING BADLY

CHRONICLE BOOKS
SAN FRANCISCO

CONTENTS

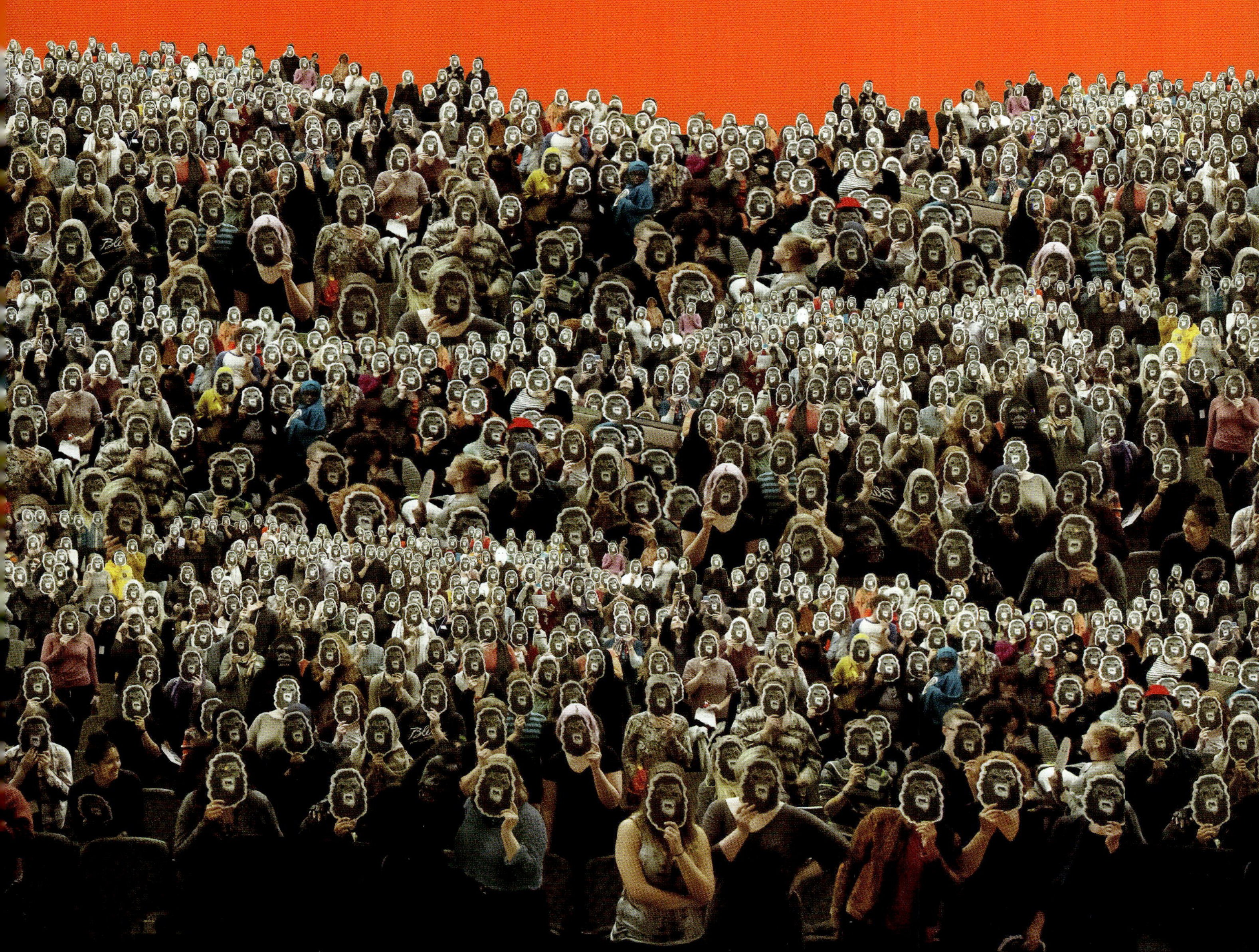

Dedicated to each amazing member of the
Guerrilla Girls, 1985 to today; to our friends
and supporters worldwide; and to everyone
who uses art to create change. #resist

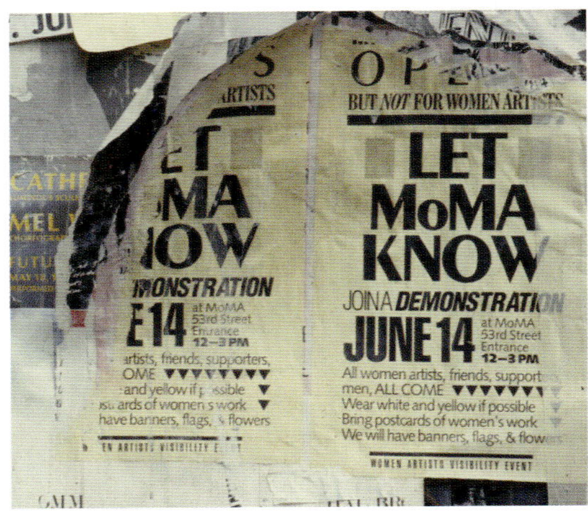 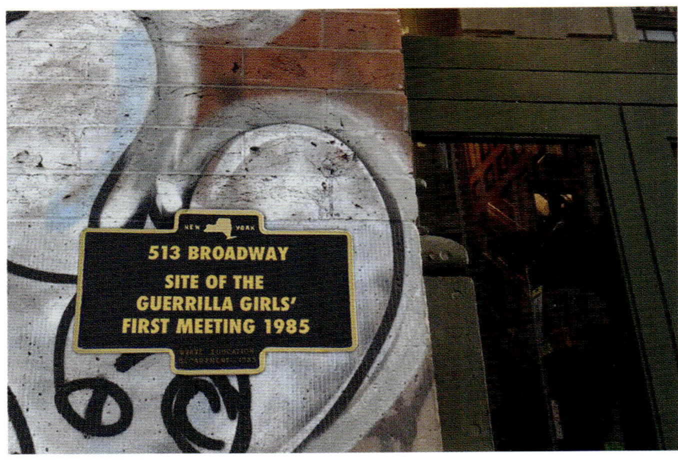

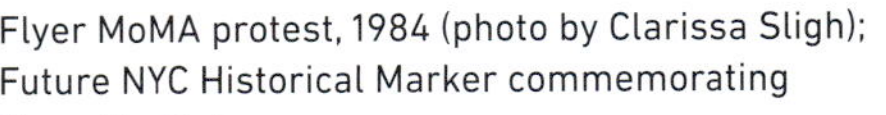
Flyer MoMA protest, 1984 (photo by Clarissa Sligh);
Future NYC Historical Marker commemorating
Guerrilla Girls

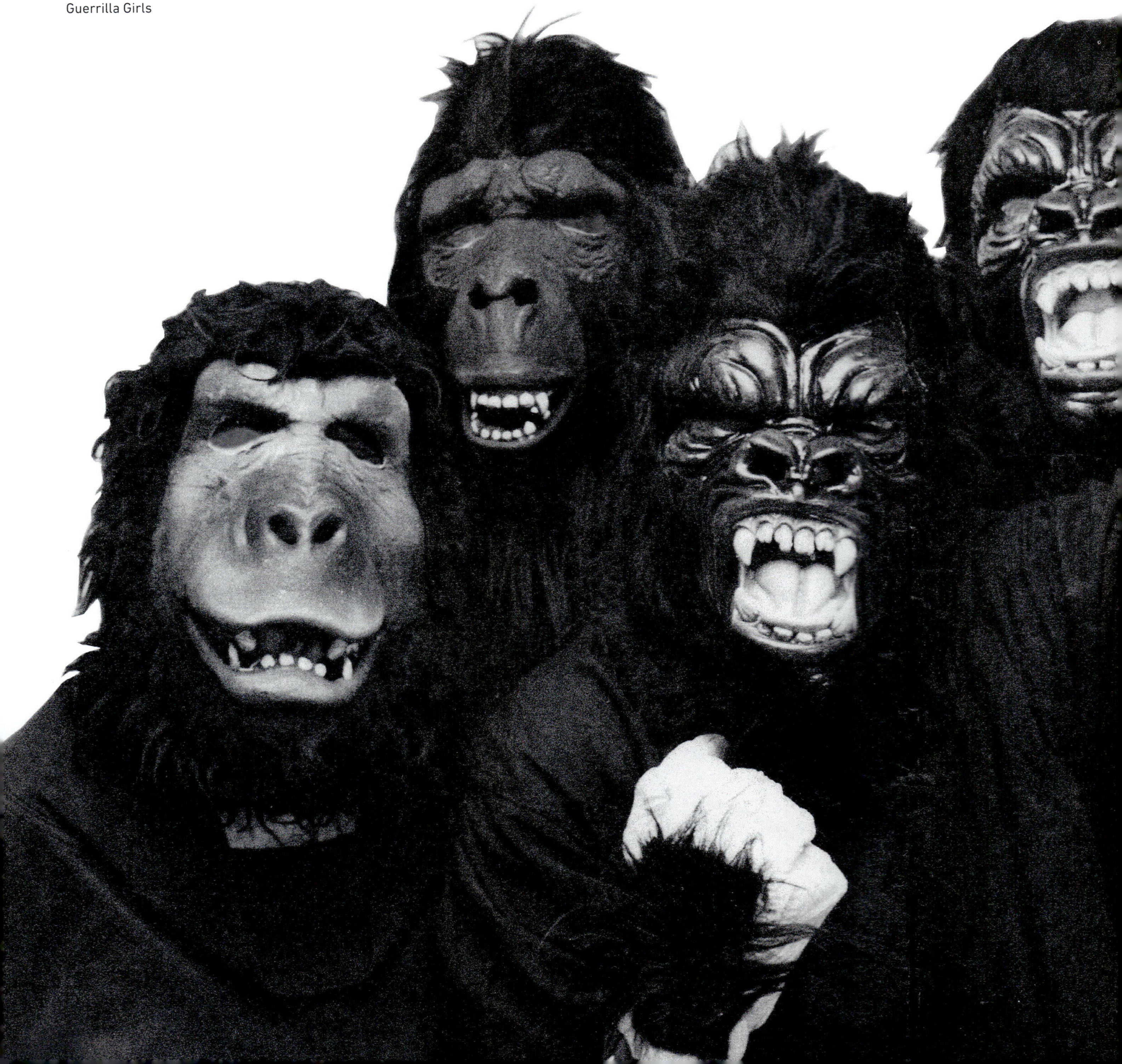

Imagine you're artists pissed off that almost all the opportunities in the artworld go to white men. Imagine you go to a protest outside the Museum of Modern Art after it opens an "international" exhibition in 1984 with 169 artists but only 13 women and 8 artists of color. You see immediately no museum goer even cares! Imagine you have an aha moment and realize there HAS to be a better way — an in-your-face, unforgettable way — to break through people's preconceptions and prove to them that the art system isn't a meritocracy where museums, galleries, critics and collectors always know best.

Imagine you dream up a new kind of street poster to wake people up to the pathetically low number of women artists shown in galleries and museums. You call a meeting, decide to be anonymous and name yourselves Guerrilla Girls. You pass the hat around to print the first posters. Within weeks you're sneaking around New York in the middle of the night, carrying stacks of posters and buckets of glue. Your work ignites a public argument about racism and sexism in the artworld. What follows? Two hundred posters, billboards, street banners, video projections, exhibitions, performances, workshops and books — not just about the lack of gender and ethnic diversity in art, but also in film, politics and pop culture. You get thousands of messages from people all over the world, aged 8 to 80, saying your crazy kind of activism is a model for them.

Over 60 individuals become members of the Guerrilla Girls. Some stay for months, some for decades, a few for just a single meeting. They're cis, lesbian and transgender; diverse in age, sexual orientation and class; and from many ethnic backgrounds — South Asian, African American, Latinx and European, and so on. Each takes on the name of a dead woman artist as a pseudonym.

These days we feel in our gut that something important has changed. No longer can anyone claim that the history of art and culture can be written without including all the diverse voices of that culture. But museums, galleries and art collecting are still dominated and controlled by big money and white men. For the history of art to be more than the story of wealth and power, that must change.

Our work is not finished. We invite you to look through these pages, get mad and keep up the fight. Creative complaining works!

Photo by Jack Mitchell, 1990

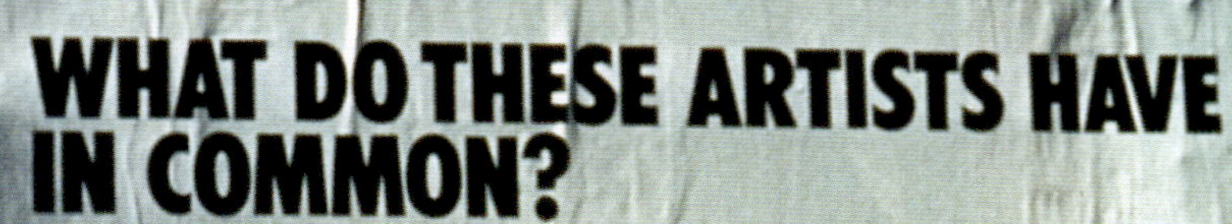

WHAT DO THESE ARTISTS HAVE IN COMMON?

Arman
Jean-Michel Basquiat
James Casebere
John Chamberlain
Sandro Chia
Francesco Clemente
Chuck Close
Tony Cragg
Enzo Cucchi
Eric Fischl
Joel Fisher
Dan Flavin
Futura 2000
Ron Gorchov

Keith Haring
Bryan Hunt
Patrick Ireland
Neil Jenney
Bill Jensen
Donald Judd
Alex Katz
Anselm Kiefer
Joseph Kosuth
Roy Lichtenstein
Walter De Maria
Robert Morris
Bruce Nauman
Richard Nonas

Claes Oldenburg
Philip Pearlstein
Robert Ryman
David Salle
Lucas Samaras
Peter Saul
Kenny Scharf
Julian Schnabel
Richard Serra
Mark di Suvero
Mark Tansey
George Tooker
David True
Peter Voulkos

THEY ALLOW THEIR WORK TO BE SHOWN IN GALLERIES THAT SHOW NO MORE THAN 10% WOMEN ARTISTS OR NONE AT ALL.

SOURCE ART IN AMERICA ANNUAL 1984-85

A PUBLIC SERVICE MESSAGE FROM **GUERILLA GIRLS** CONSCIENCE OF THE ART WORLD

THESE GALLERIES SHOW NO MORE THAN 10% WOMEN ARTISTS OR NONE AT ALL.

Blum Helman
Mary Boone
Grace Borgenicht
Diane Brown
Leo Castelli
Charles Cowles
Marisa Del Re
Dia Art Foundation
Executive
Allan Frumkin

Fun
Marian Goodman
Pat Hearn
Marlborough
Oil & Steel
Pace
Tony Shafrazi
Sperone Westwater
Edward Thorp
Washburn

A PUBLIC SERVICE MESSAGE FROM **GUERILLA GIRLS** CONSCIENCE OF THE ART WORLD

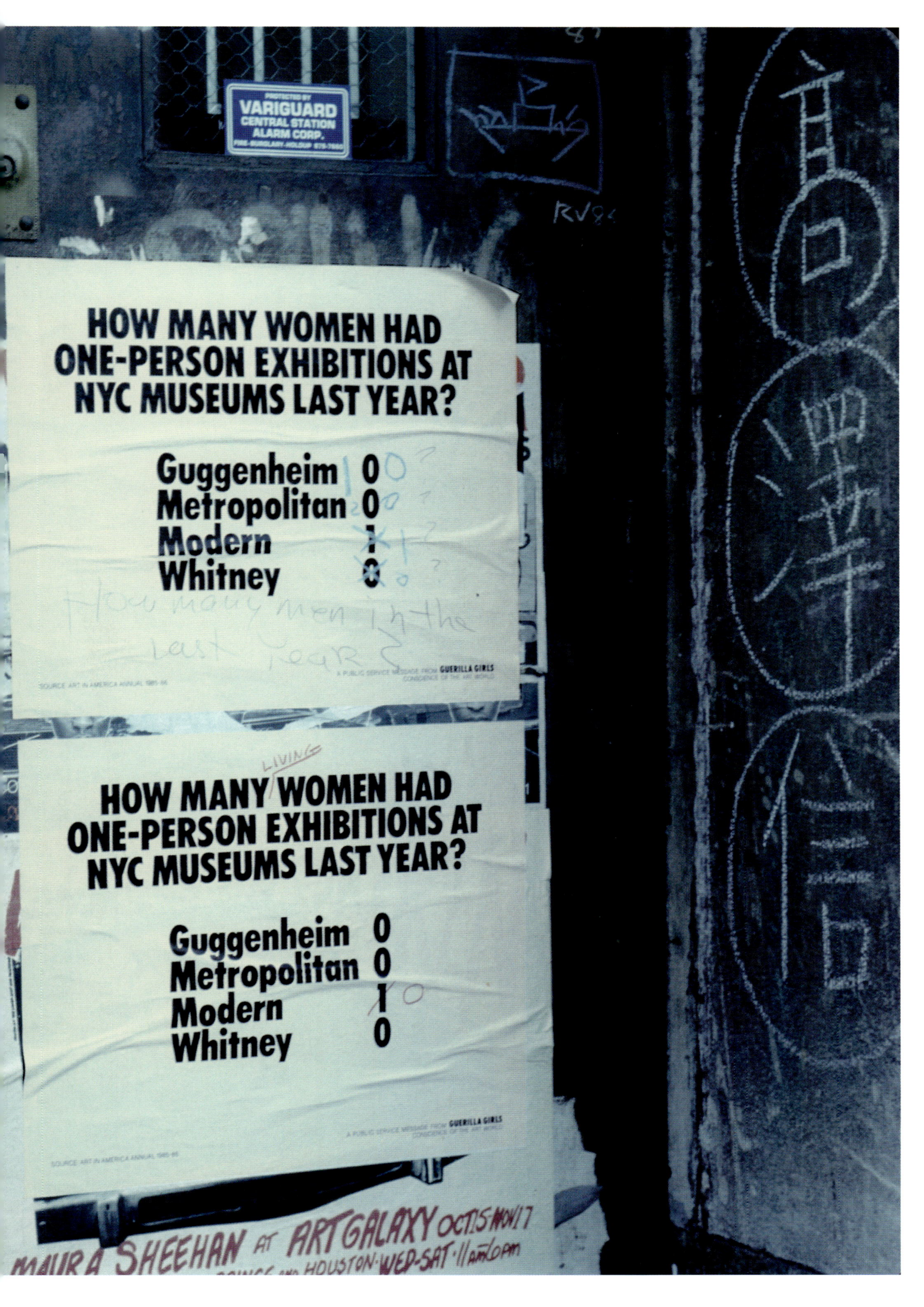
HOW MANY WOMEN HAD
ONE-PERSON EXHIBITIONS AT
NYC MUSEUMS LAST YEAR?
Guggenheim 0
Metropolitan 0
Modern 1
Whitney 0
A PUBLIC SERVICE MESSAGE FROM GUERILLA GIRLS CONSCIENCE OF THE ART WORLD
SOURCE ART IN AMERICA ANNUAL 1985-86
HOW MANY LIVING WOMEN HAD
ONE-PERSON EXHIBITIONS AT
NYC MUSEUMS LAST YEAR?
Guggenheim 0
Metropolitan 0
Modern 1
Whitney 0
A PUBLIC SERVICE MESSAGE FROM GUERILLA GIRLS CONSCIENCE OF THE ART WORLD
SOURCE ART IN AMERICA ANNUAL 1985-86
MAURA SHEEHAN AT ART GALAXY OCT15-NOV17
PRINCE AND HOUSTON · WED-SAT · 11am-6pm

GUERRILLA GIRLS
CONSCIENCE OF THE ART WORLD

WHAT DO THESE ARTISTS HAVE IN COMMON?

Arman
Jean-Michel Basquiat
James Casebere
John Chamberlain
Sandro Chia
Francesco Clemente
Chuck Close
Tony Cragg
Enzo Cucchi
Eric Fischl
Joel Fisher
Dan Flavin
Futura 2000
Ron Gorchov

Keith Haring
Bryan Hunt
Patrick Ireland
Neil Jenney
Bill Jensen
Donald Judd
Alex Katz
Anselm Kiefer
Joseph Kosuth
Roy Lichtenstein
Walter De Maria
Robert Morris
Bruce Nauman
Richard Nonas

Claes Oldenburg
Philip Pearlstein
Robert Ryman
David Salle
Lucas Samaras
Peter Saul
Kenny Scharf
Julian Schnabel
Richard Serra
Mark di Suvero
Mark Tansey
George Tooker
David True
Peter Voulkos

THEY ALLOW THEIR WORK TO BE SHOWN IN GALLERIES THAT SHOW NO MORE THAN 10% WOMEN ARTISTS OR NONE AT ALL.

SOURCE: ART IN AMERICA ANNUAL 1984-85

A PUBLIC SERVICE MESSAGE FROM GUERRILLA GIRLS CONSCIENCE OF THE ART WORLD

THESE GALLERIES SHOW NO MORE THAN 10% WOMEN ARTISTS OR NONE AT ALL.

Blum Helman
Mary Boone
Grace Borgenicht
Diane Brown
Leo Castelli
Charles Cowles
Marisa Del Re
Dia Art Foundation
Executive
Allan Frumkin

Fun
Marian Goodman
Pat Hearn
Marlborough
Oil & Steel
Pace
Tony Shafrazi
Sperone Westwater
Edward Thorp
Washburn

SOURCE: ART IN AMERICA ANNUAL 1984-85

A PUBLIC SERVICE MESSAGE FROM GUERRILLA GIRLS CONSCIENCE OF THE ART WORLD

FOR IMMEDIATE RELEASE 6 MAY 1985

Contact 925-2587

Posters pointing to the inadequate numbers of women artists
represented in leading New York galleries are appearing in
SoHo streets, on walls, streetlamps and telephone booths.
Two strongly worded posters drawing attention to the con-
tinuing discrimination against women artists are the work
of a newly formed group calling itself Guerrilla Girls and
preferring to conduct its campaign of information and public
exposure without identifying its individual members.
Guerrilla Girls plans to continue its campaign throughout
the next weeks and next season, drawing attention to the
retrograde attitudes toward women artists that characterize
certain segments of the art world of the mid-80's. Simple
facts will be spelled out; obvious conclusions can be drawn.

BOX 766 CANAL STREET STATION · NEW YORK 10013

Press release for the first two Guerrilla Girls posters, 1985

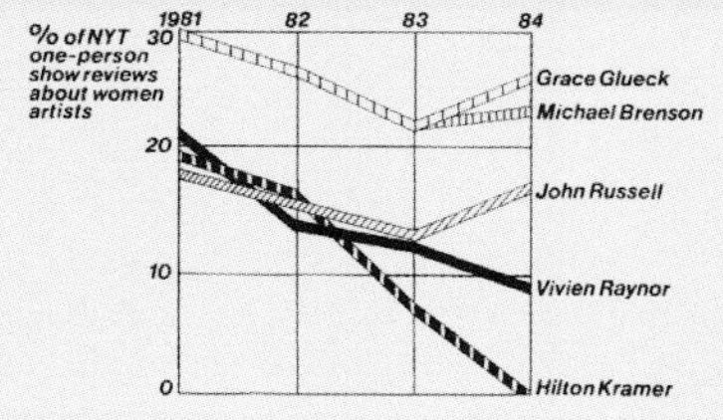

HOW MANY WOMEN HAD ONE-PERSON EXHIBITIONS AT NYC MUSEUMS LAST YEAR?

Guggenheim	0
Metropolitan	0
Modern	1
Whitney	0

SOURCE: ART IN AMERICA ANNUAL 1985-86

A PUBLIC SERVICE MESSAGE FROM **GUERRILLA GIRLS**
CONSCIENCE OF THE ART WORLD

THESE CRITICS DON'T WRITE ENOUGH ABOUT WOMEN ARTISTS:

John Ashbery	*Robert Pincus-Witten
*Dore Ashton	*Peter Plagens
Kenneth Baker	Annelie Pohlen
Yves-Alain Bois	*Carter Ratcliff
*Edit de Ak	Vivien Raynor
Hilton kramer	John Russell
Donald Kuspit	Peter Schjeldahl
Gary Indiana	Roberta Smith
*Thomas Lawson	Valentine Tatransky
*Kim Levin	Calvin Tomkins
*Ida Panicelli	John Yau

Between 1979 & 1985, less than 20% of the feature articles & reviews of one-person shows by these critics were about art made by women. Those asterisked wrote about art by women less than 10% of the time or never.

SOURCE: ART INDEX, READERS GUIDE, ARTFORUM, ART IN AMERICA
ARTNEWS, VILLAGE VOICE, NEW YORK TIMES

A PUBLIC SERVICE MESSAGE FROM **GUERRILLA GIRLS**
CONSCIENCE OF THE ART WORLD

JOHN RUSSELL THINKS THINGS ARE GETTING BETTER FOR WOMEN ARTISTS:

It is a matter of fact, and not of opinion, that in NY in the Eighties shows by women artists have been just as rewarding and just as widely remarked as shows by men artists.
—John Russell, NY Times, 8/24/83

GUERRILLA GIRLS THINKS HE SHOULD READ HIS OWN PAPER:

A PUBLIC SERVICE MESSAGE FROM **GUERRILLA GIRLS**
CONSCIENCE OF THE ART WORLD

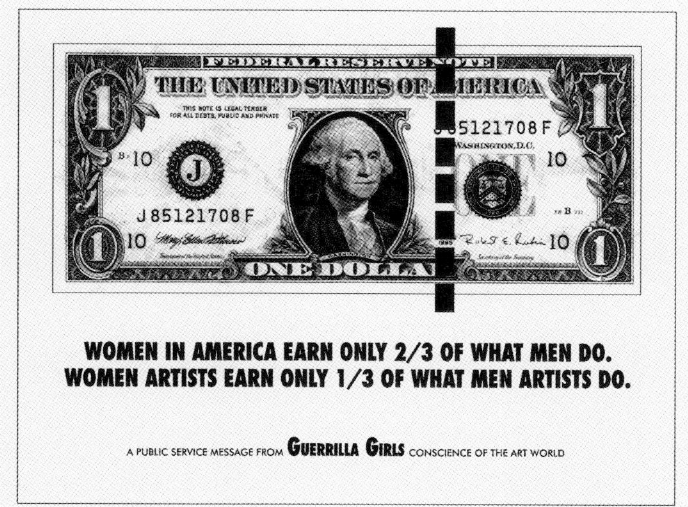

**WOMEN IN AMERICA EARN ONLY 2/3 OF WHAT MEN DO.
WOMEN ARTISTS EARN ONLY 1/3 OF WHAT MEN ARTISTS DO.**

A PUBLIC SERVICE MESSAGE FROM **GUERRILLA GIRLS** CONSCIENCE OF THE ART WORLD

The powers that be in the artworld claimed discrimination wasn't their fault, so we pointed fingers at all of them for contributing to a biased system. Our first two posters targeted fellow artists and their galleries, accompanied by a press release. Next, we went after museums, critics and the *New York Times*. Whenever we put up new posters, we would lurk on the streets nearby, overhear what people had to say and get ideas for the next ones.

Posters, 1985

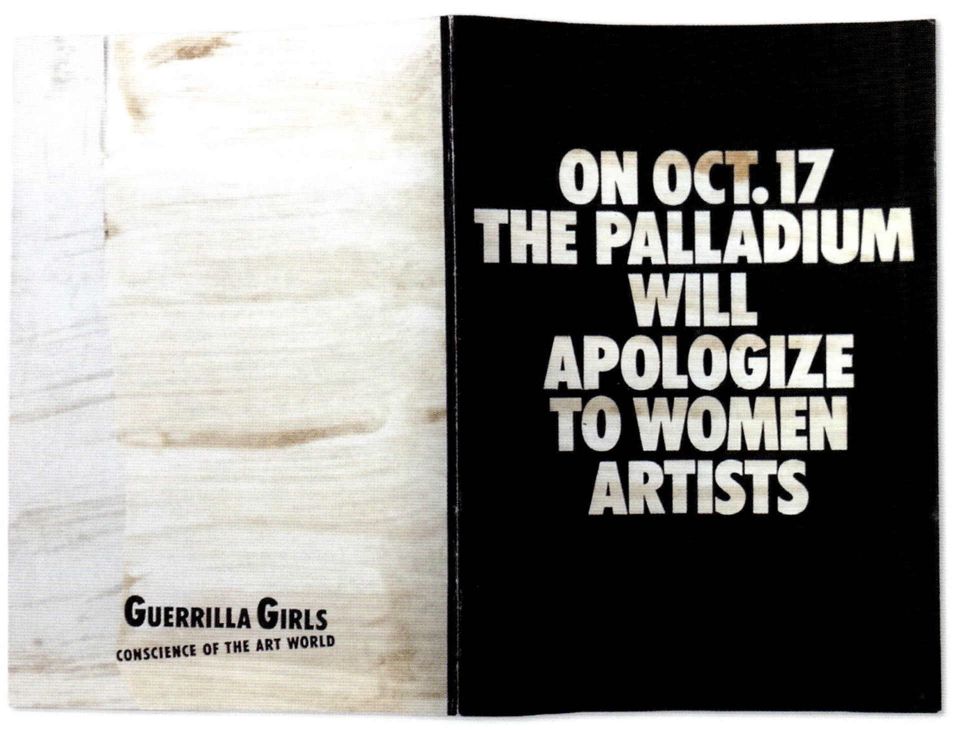

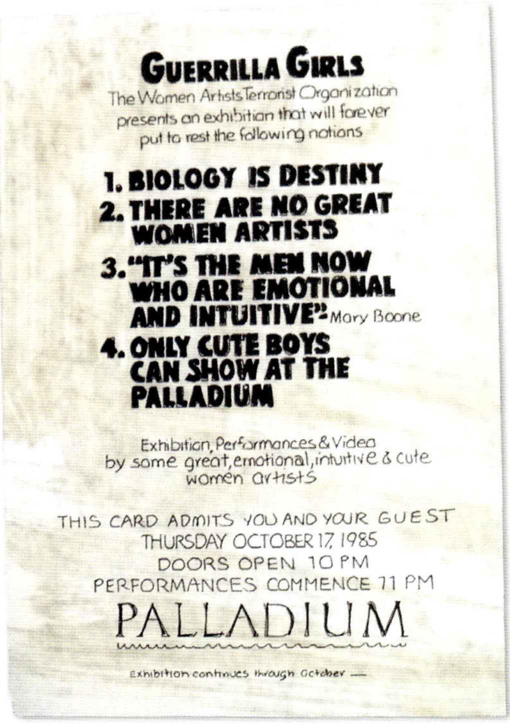

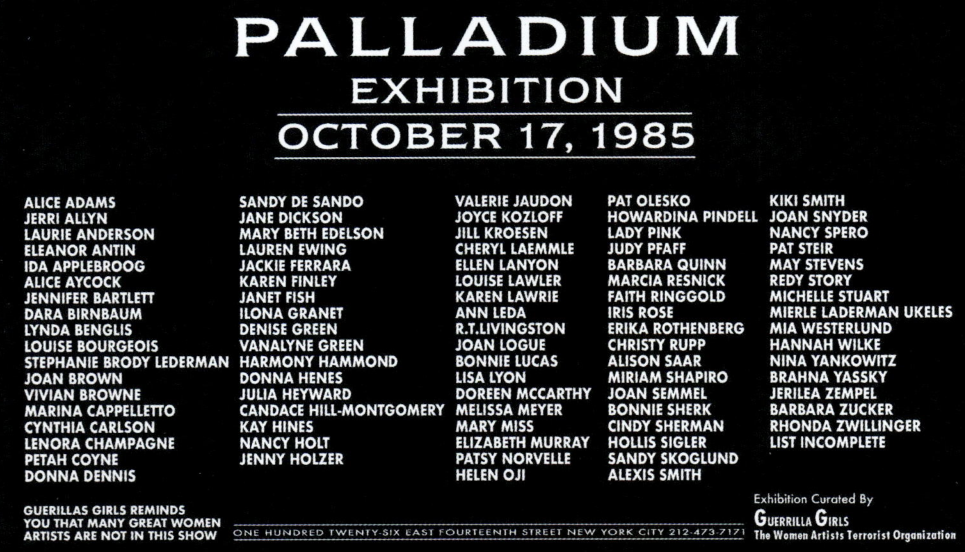

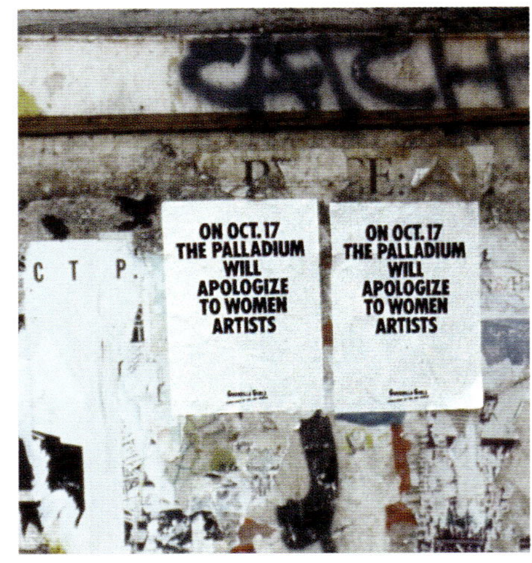

The Palladium, a hot downtown New York club, was loaded with contemporary art. Problem was, all of it was by men. Provoked by our first posters, the owners invited us to organize an all-women exhibition. We posted flyers announcing the show as their apology, and that pissed them off. The show was a runaway success, but a bitter lesson for us. Making choices left too many artists out. We haven't curated anything since.

Palladium Will Apologize to Women Artists, announcement design, exhibition poster, and flyers on street, 1985

ONLY 4 COMMERCIAL GALLERIES IN N.Y. SHOW BLACK WOMEN.*

ONLY 1 SHOWS MORE THAN 1.**

*Cavin-Morris, Condeso/Lawler, Bernice Steinbaum, Shreiber/Cutler
**Cavin-Morris

SOURCE: ART IN AMERICA ANNUAL 1986-7

A PUBLIC SERVICE MESSAGE FROM **GUERRILLA GIRLS** CONSCIENCE OF THE ART WORLD

These statistics were shocking, and no one could deny the racism, sexism and tokenism at work.

Poster, 1986

GUERRILLA GIRLS' 1986 REPORT CARD

GALLERY	NO. OF WOMEN 1985-6	NO. OF WOMEN 1986-7	REMARKS
Blum Helman	1	1	No improvement
Mary Boone	0	0	Boy crazy
Grace Borgenicht	0	0	Lacks initiative
Diane Brown	0	2	Could do even better
Leo Castelli	4	3	Not paying attention
Charles Cowles	2	2	Needs work
Marisa del Rey	0	0	No progress
Allan Frumkin	1	1	Doesn't follow directions
Marian Goodman	0	1	Keep trying
Pat Hearn	0	0	Delinquent
Marlborough	2	1	Failing
Oil & Steel	0	1	Underachiever
Pace	2	2	Working below capacity
Tony Shafrazi	0	1	Still unsatisfactory
Sperone Westwater	0	0	Unforgivable
Edward Thorp	1	4	Making excellent progress
Washburn	1	1	Unacceptable

A PUBLIC SERVICE MESSAGE FROM **GUERRILLA GIRLS** CONSCIENCE OF THE ART WORLD

WHICH ART MAG WAS WORST FOR WOMEN LAST YEAR?

% of features, projects and one-person show reviews on women artists Sept 1985-Summer 1986

Flash Art	13%
Artforum	16
ArtNews	22
Art in America	24
Arts	25

Box 1056 Cooper Sta. NY, NY 10276 **GUERRILLA GIRLS** CONSCIENCE OF THE ART WORLD

GUERRILLA GIRLS HITS LIST:

Pam Adler	Lawrence Campbell
A.I.R.	Ronny Cohen
Brooke Alexander	April Kingsley
Ave. B	Barbara Kruger
Baskerville & Watson	Lisa Liebman
Paula Cooper	Kate Linker
Ronald Feldman	Lucy Lippard
Monique Knowlton	Thomas McEvilley
Kathryn Markel	John Perreault
Robert Miller	Jeff Perrone
Deborah Sharpe	Ann Sargent Wooster
SOHO 20	Jeanne Silverthorne
Bernice Steinbaum	Judd Tully
Barbara Toll	Steven Westfall

THESE PEOPLE ARE MAKING THINGS BETTER FOR WOMEN ARTISTS The above galleries and critics devoted at least 30% of their shows (1984-5) one-person reviews and feature articles (1979-85) to women.

SOURCES: Art in America Annual 1985-6
Art Index & others

GUERRILLA GIRLS CONSCIENCE OF THE ART WORLD

Posters, 1986

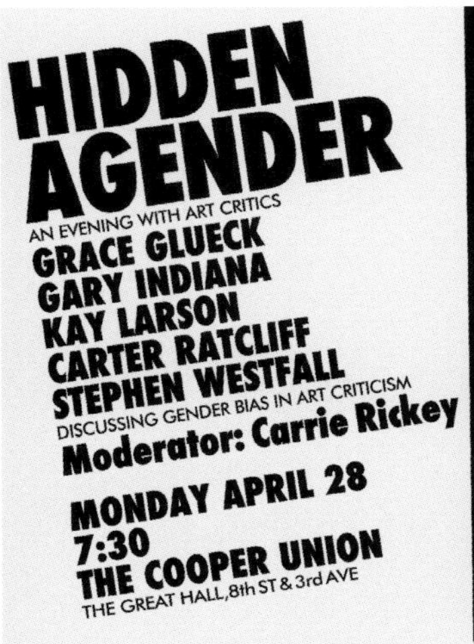

Posters, 1986

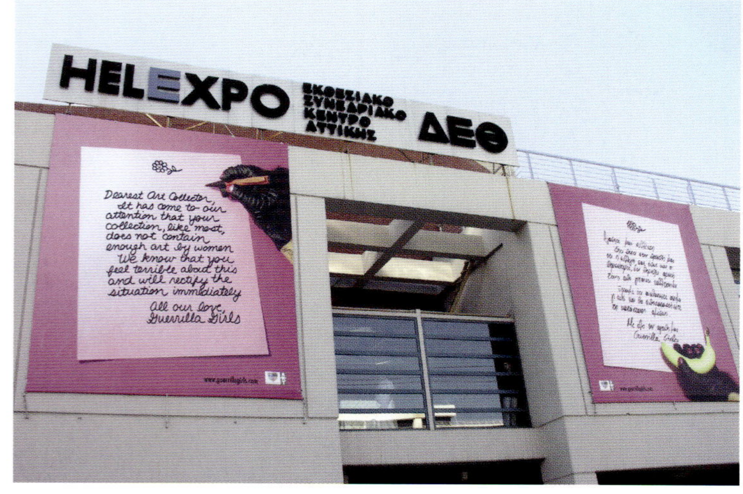

When it came to criticizing art collectors we pretended to be nice, but not too nice.

Poster, 1986. Banners in English and Greek, Art Athina, 2007

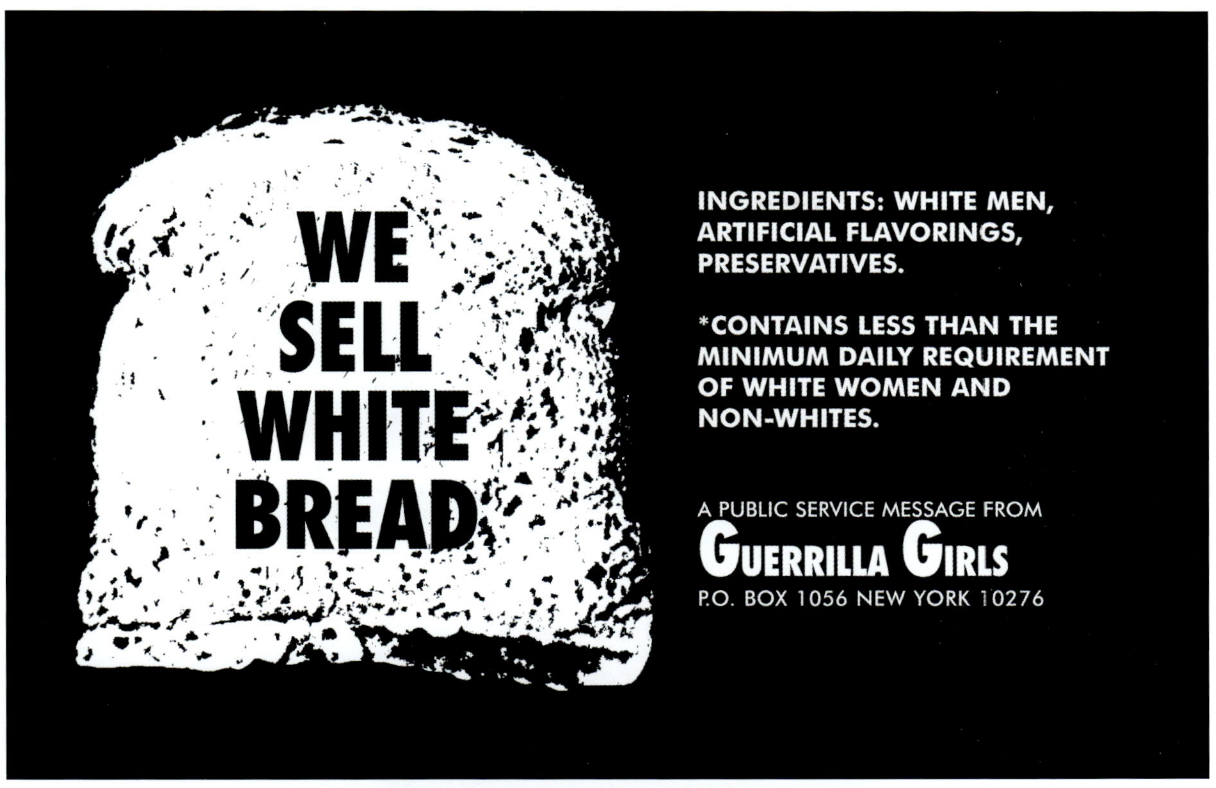

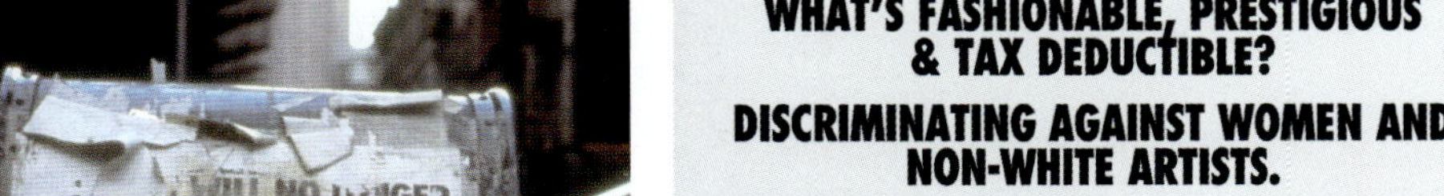

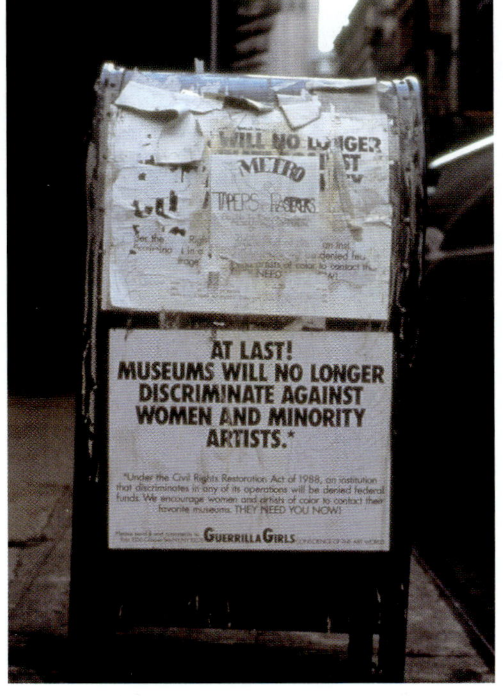

WHAT'S FASHIONABLE, PRESTIGIOUS & TAX DEDUCTIBLE?

DISCRIMINATING AGAINST WOMEN AND NON-WHITE ARTISTS.

THESE CORPORATIONS & FOUNDATIONS SPONSORED...	THESE EXHIBITIONS...	CONTAINING THESE PERCENTAGES:
Owen Cheatham Foundation; The National Endowment for the Arts (NEA)	"Transformations in Sculpture: Four Decades" 1985. Guggenheim Museum. Diane Waldman, curator	95% men 96% white
Exxon; Grand Marnier Foundation; Enichem Americus, Inc; the NEA	"Emerging Artists 1978-1986: Selection from the Exxon Series" 1987. Guggenheim Museum. Diane Waldman, curator	75% men 98% white
McGraw-Hill Foundation	"Printed Art: A View of Two Decades: 1980. The Museum of Modern Art. Riva Castleman, curator	95% men 96% white
The New York State Council on the Arts; the NEA	"Monumental Drawings: Works by Twenty-two Americans" 1986. Brooklyn Museum. Charlotta Kotik, curator	94% men 93% white
A.T.&T; the NEA	"International Survey of Recent Painting and Sculpture" 1984. The Museum of Modern Art. Kynaston McShine, curator	82% men 98% white
Phillip Morris Companies, Deutsche Bank; Bohen Foundation; The Federal Republic of Germany; the NEA	"BerlinArt 1961-1987" 1987. The Museum of Modern Art. Kynaston McShine, curator	95% men 100% white
Kaufman Foundation; Lauder Fund; Lipman Foundation; Rose Foundation	"Blam! The Explosion of Pop, Minimalism and Performance 1958-1964" 1984. Whitney Museum. Barbara Haskell, curator	85% men 91% white
Chase Manhattan Bank; the NEA	"High Styles: Twentieth Century American Design" 1986. Whitney Museum. Lisa Phillips, curator	87% men 97% white

A PUBLIC SERVICE MESSAGE FROM GUERRILLA GIRLS CONSCIENCE OF THE ART WORLD

Clockwise from top: Sticker, 1987; Card distributed at Documenta, 1987; Poster, 1988; Poster, 1987

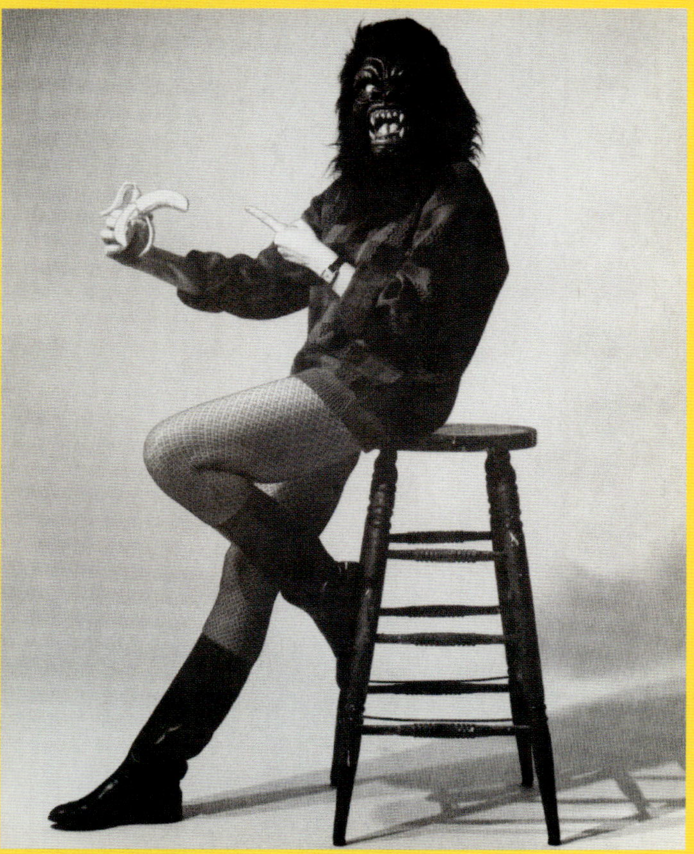

The Clocktower/PS1 asked us to do an exhibition during the
Whitney Biennial, so we did a show about the Biennial's history,
using stats from the museum's publications. We documented
its worsening record for showing and collecting women and
artists of color.

Poster, 1987

Right: Exhibition view, 1987

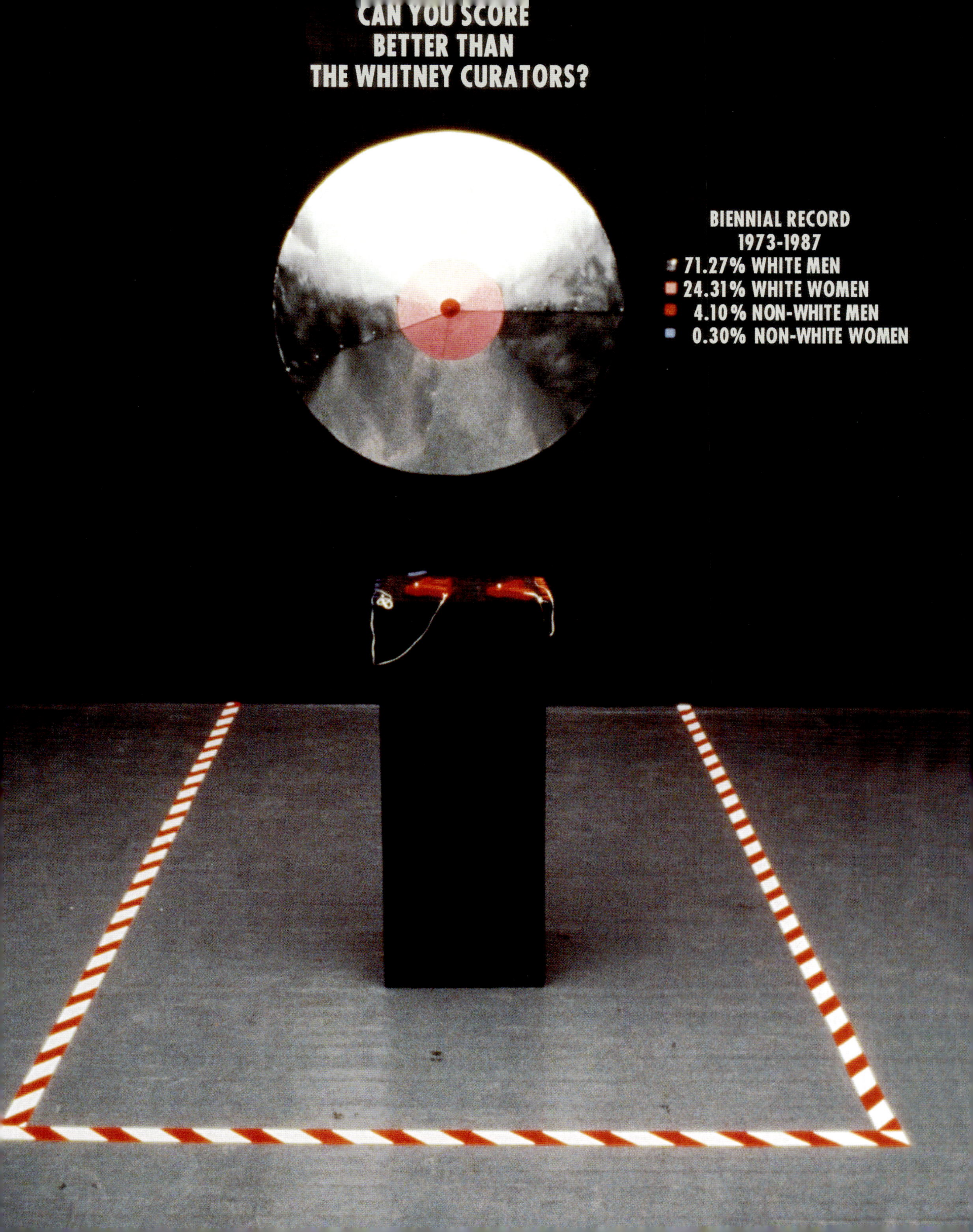

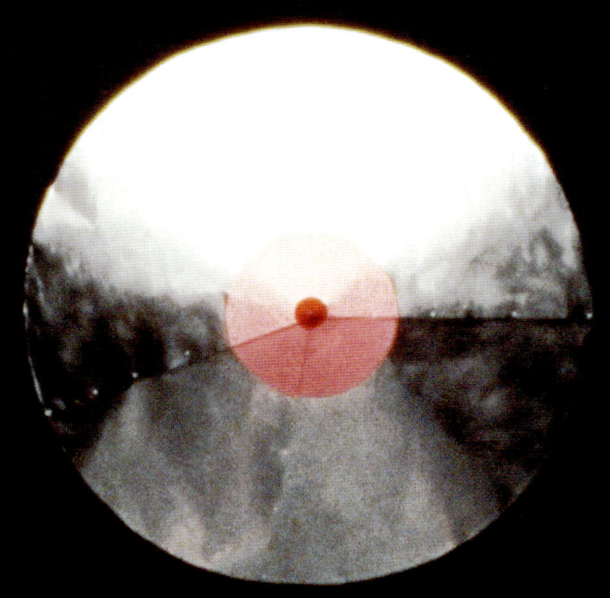
CAN YOU SCORE
BETTER THAN
THE WHITNEY CURATORS?

BIENNIAL RECORD
1973-1987
71.27% WHITE MEN
24.31% WHITE WOMEN
4.10% NON-WHITE MEN
0.30% NON-WHITE WOMEN
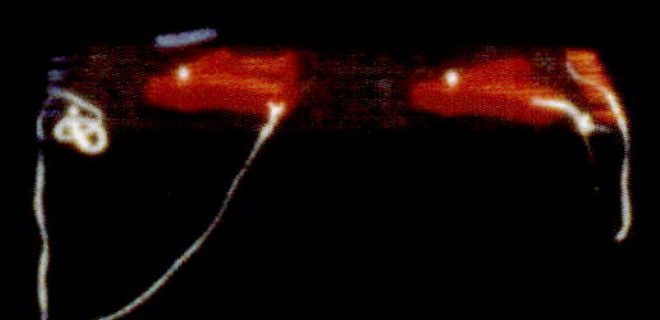

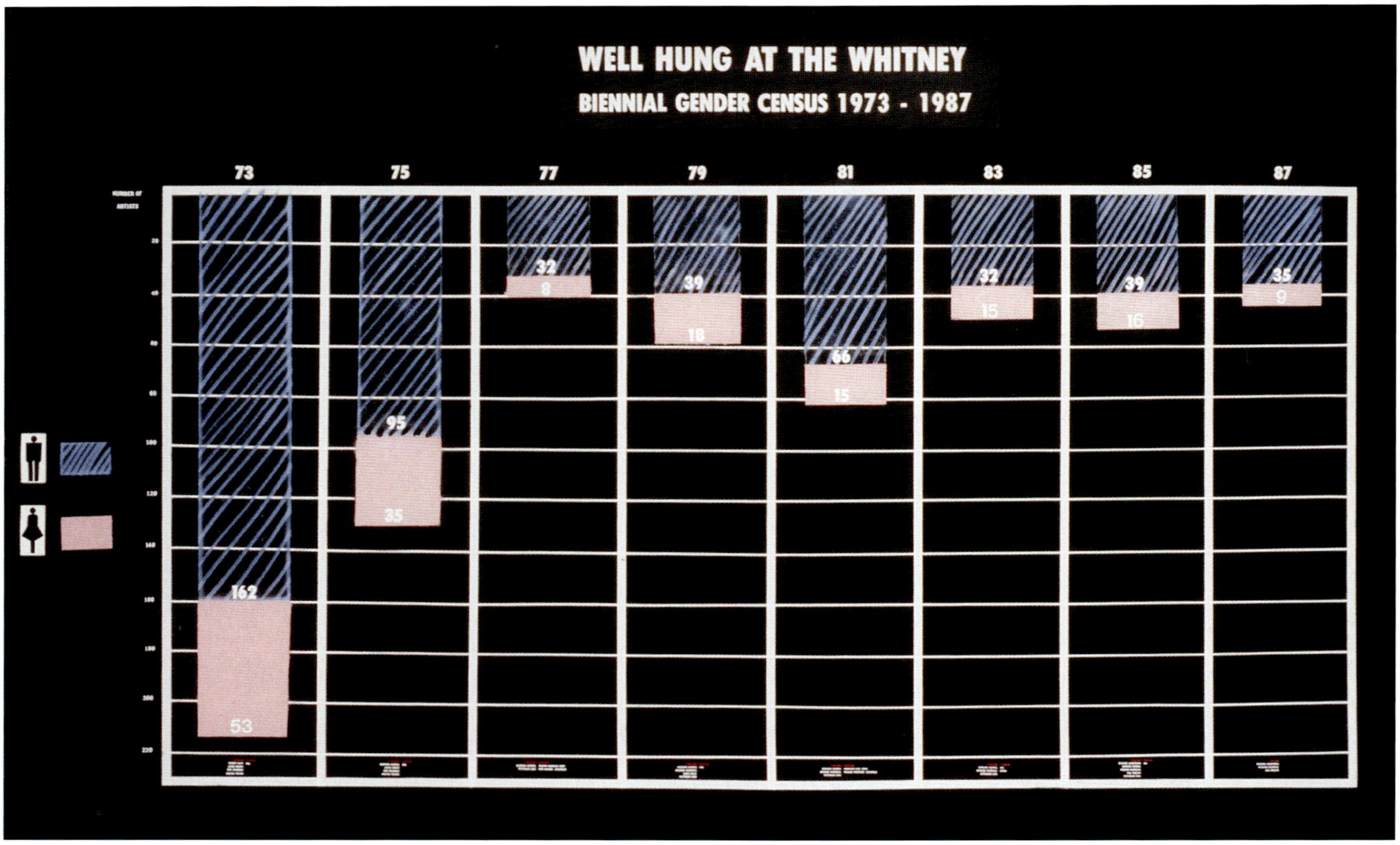

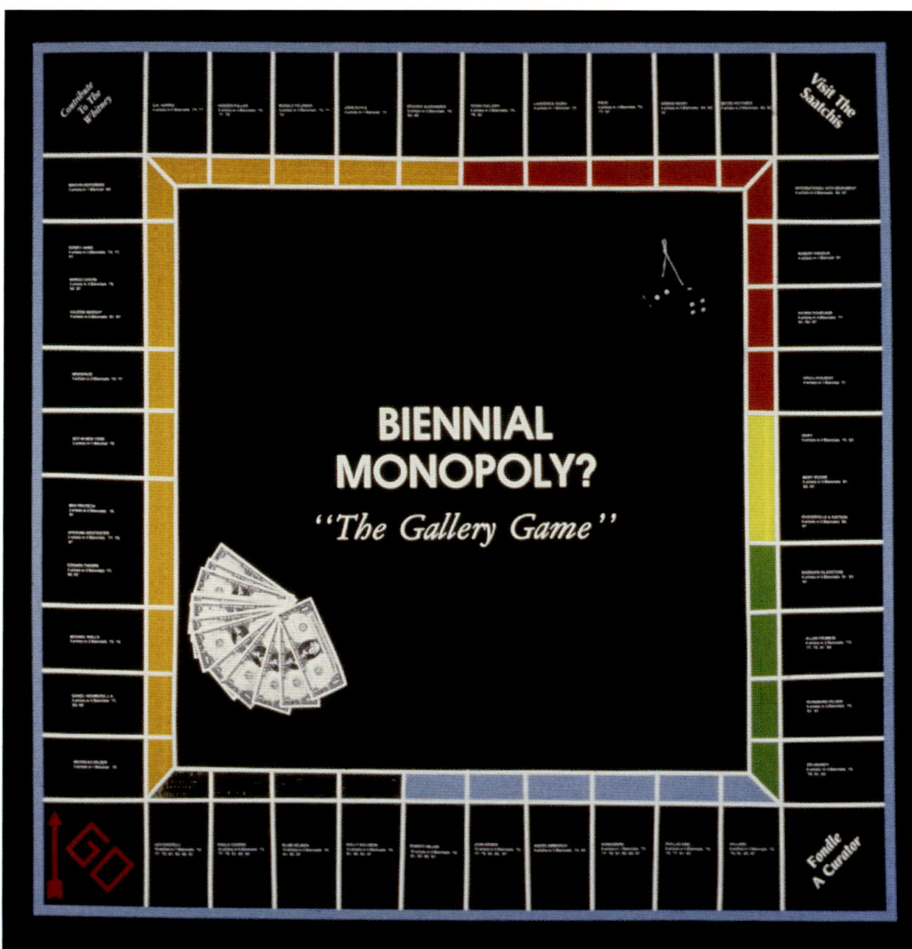

Left: Most of the artists chosen for the Biennial came from a handful of galleries with bad records for diversity.

Right: Ironically, some museum trustees ran businesses that catered to women and communities of color.

Exhibition views, 1987

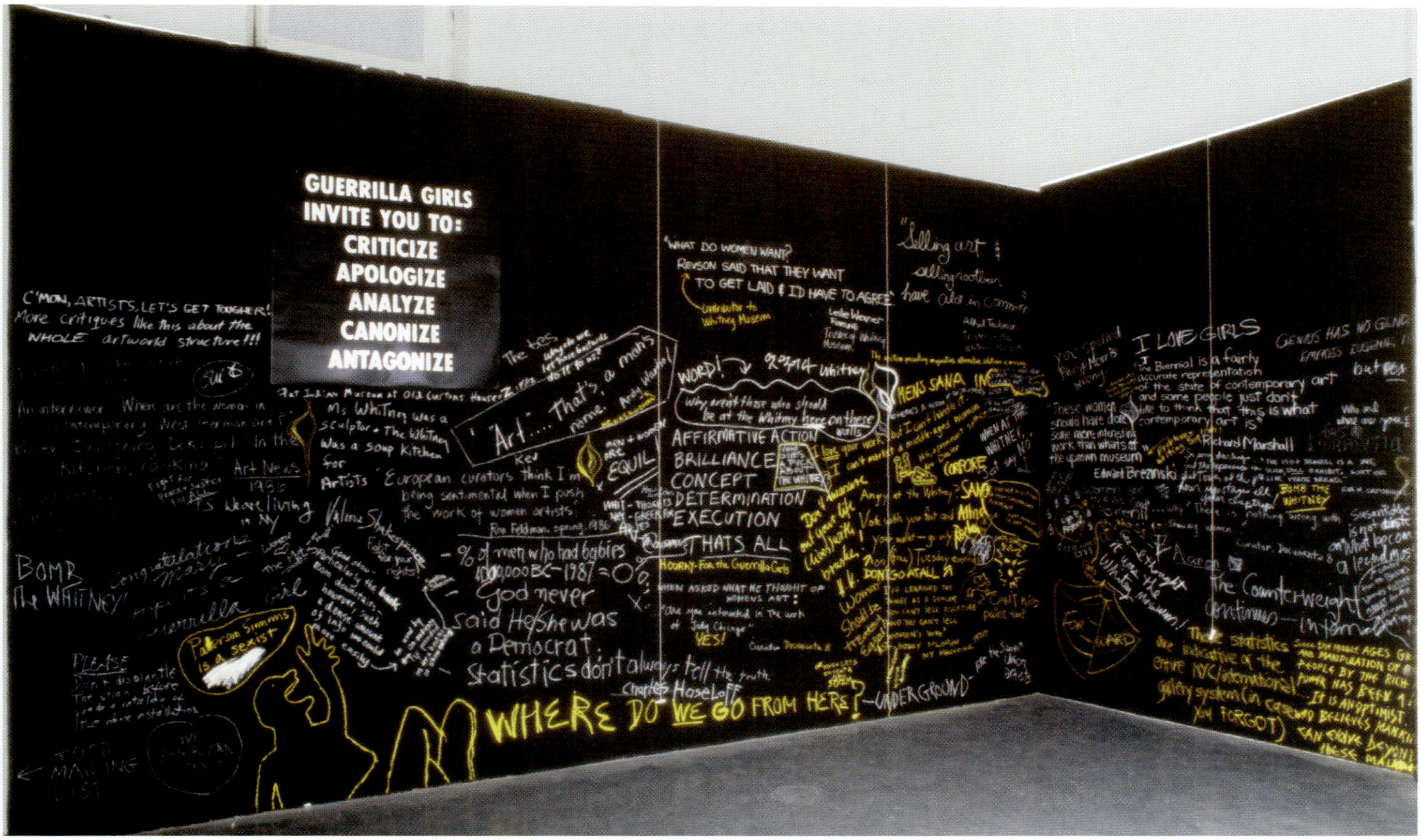

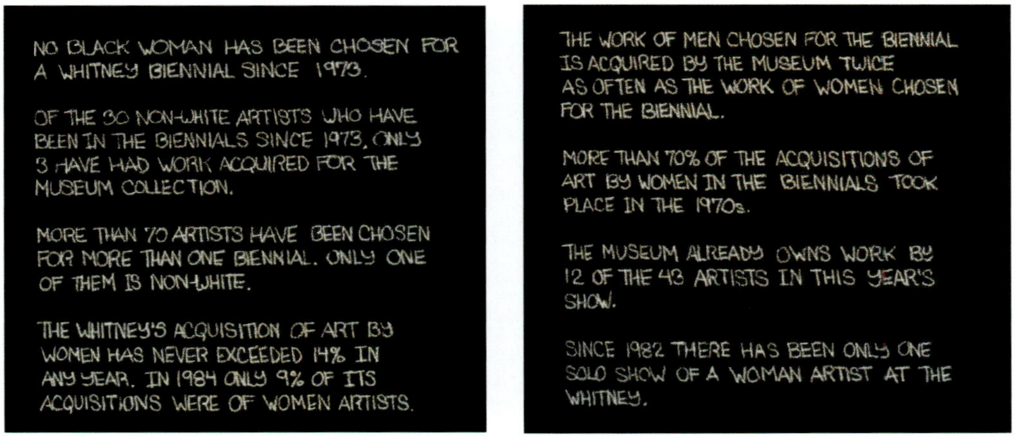

NO BLACK WOMAN HAS BEEN CHOSEN FOR A WHITNEY BIENNIAL SINCE 1973.

OF THE 30 NON-WHITE ARTISTS WHO HAVE BEEN IN THE BIENNIALS SINCE 1973, ONLY 3 HAVE HAD WORK ACQUIRED FOR THE MUSEUM COLLECTION.

MORE THAN 70 ARTISTS HAVE BEEN CHOSEN FOR MORE THAN ONE BIENNIAL. ONLY ONE OF THEM IS NON-WHITE.

THE WHITNEY'S ACQUISITION OF ART BY WOMEN HAS NEVER EXCEEDED 14% IN ANY YEAR. IN 1984 ONLY 9% OF ITS ACQUISITIONS WERE OF WOMEN ARTISTS.

THE WORK OF MEN CHOSEN FOR THE BIENNIAL IS ACQUIRED BY THE MUSEUM TWICE AS OFTEN AS THE WORK OF WOMEN CHOSEN FOR THE BIENNIAL.

MORE THAN 70% OF THE ACQUISITIONS OF ART BY WOMEN IN THE BIENNIALS TOOK PLACE IN THE 1970s.

THE MUSEUM ALREADY OWNS WORK BY 12 OF THE 43 ARTISTS IN THIS YEAR'S SHOW.

SINCE 1982 THERE HAS BEEN ONLY ONE SOLO SHOW OF A WOMAN ARTIST AT THE WHITNEY.

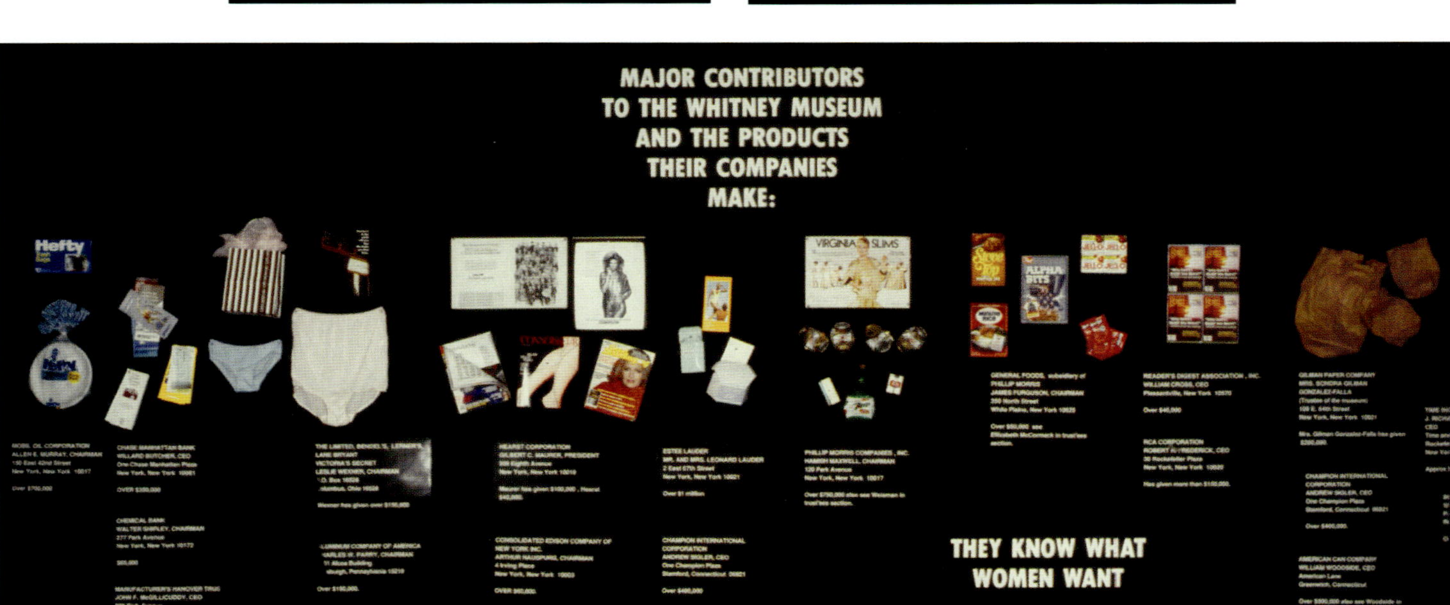

THE ADVANTAGES OF BEING A WOMAN ARTIST:

Working without the pressure of success
Not having to be in shows with men
Having an escape from the art world in your 4 free-lance jobs
Knowing your career might pick up after you're eighty
Being reassured that whatever kind of art you make it will be labeled feminine
Not being stuck in a tenured teaching position
Seeing your ideas live on in the work of others
Having the opportunity to choose between career and motherhood
Not having to choke on those big cigars or paint in Italian suits
Having more time to work when your mate dumps you for someone younger
Being included in revised versions of art history
Not having to undergo the embarrassment of being called a genius
Getting your picture in the art magazines wearing a gorilla suit

A PUBLIC SERVICE MESSAGE FROM **GUERRILLA GIRLS** CONSCIENCE OF THE ART WORLD

After being described as whiny and negative, we decided it was time to help women look on the positive side of their situation. We turned the disadvantages of being a woman artist into advantages. Workers in physics, veterinary medicine, cartooning, music, even mortuary science — as well as a male columnist for the *New York Times* — wrote us that this poster was the story of their lives, too. An artist sent us money to run it as an ad in *Artforum*.

Poster, 1987–88
Right: Advantages poster in Spanish; Chinese; French; Greek; Swedish; Basque; German; Japanese; Russian; Malayalam (Kochi Biennale, 2018); Italian (Cheap Festival, Bologna, 2017); Portuguese (Museum of Art São Paulo, 2016)

LAS VENTAJAS DE SER MUJER ARTISTA:

Trabajar sin la presión del éxito
No tener que coincidir con hombres en las exposiciones
Poder desconectar del mundo artístico tras tus 4 trabajos como autónoma
Saber que tu carrera profesional puede repuntar cumplidos los ochenta años
Tener la garantía de que, no importa el tipo de arte que hagas, se etiquetará siempre como femenino
No verte atrapada en un puesto fijo en la enseñanza
Ver tus ideas perpetuadas en las obras de los demás
Tener la oportunidad de elegir entre una carrera profesional y la maternidad
No tener que ahogarte con esos puros enormes ni pintar ataviada con trajes italianos
Tener más tiempo para trabajar cuando tu compañero(a) te deje tirada por otra persona más joven
Que te incluyan en versiones revisadas de la historia del arte
No tener que pasar por el bochorno de que te llamen genio
Que tu imagen salga en las revistas de arte disfrazada de gorila

A PUBLIC SERVICE MESSAGE FROM **GUERRILLA GIRLS** CONSCIENCE OF THE ART WORLD

做女性藝術家有咩著數

唔駛背負住成功既包袱去做嘢
唔駛同嗰佢同場展出
用四份 *freelance* 去逃開藝術界
八張幾嘢或者有機會升上神枱
可以放心無做咩都會被標籤為女人嘢
唔駛煩點解要成世做嘢
轉頭嗰人地作品中見到自己既諗頭
有得揀返工定保衛個阿媽
唔駛抽大雪茄或者著住件老西畫畫
Partner 為左俾後生啲既女人飛咗妳，於是更得開專心做嘢
被編埋入修正過既藝術史
唔駛因為比人叫 *genius* 而老羞
著到成隻猩猩咁比人登上上藝術雜誌—

由藝術界良知 **Guerrilla Girls** 發出既公共服務公告

LES AVANTAGES D'ETRE UNE FEMME ARTISTE:

Être sûre que le succès ne vous montera pas à la tête.
Ne pas être en compétition avec les hommes.
S'évader du monde de l'art en ayant 4 petits boulots.
Savoir que votre carrière peut exploser dés 80 ans.
Être assurée que quelque soit l'art que vous produisez, il sera taxé de féminin.
Ne pas être prisonnière d'une carrière dans l'enseignement.
Voir ses propres idées reprises dans le travail des autres.
Pouvoir choisir entre sa carrière et sa maternité.
Ne pas avoir à fumer un gros cigare ou s'écraser devant les costards
        3 pièces-machos et les hipsters.
Avoir plus de temps pour travailler, après que votre mec vous ait virée
        pour quelqu'un de plus jeune.
Être citée dans une édition révisée de l'histoire de l'art.
Ne pas avoir à éviter le désagrément d'être appelée un génie.
Avoir vos photos dans les magazines d'art vêtue d'un costume de gorille.

GUERRILLA GIRLS CONSCIENCE DU MONDE DE L'ART
www.guerrillagirls.com

ΤΑ ΠΛΕΟΝΕΚΤΗΜΑΤΑ ΤΟΥ ΝΑ ΕΙΣΑΙ ΓΥΝΑΙΚΑ ΚΑΛΛΙΤΕΧΝΙΔΑ:

Να δουλεύεις χωρίς πίεση να επιτύχεις
Να μη χρειάζεται να συμμετέχεις σε εκθέσεις με άνδρες
Να ξεφεύγεις από τον κόσμο της τέχνης μέσα από τις 4 ελεύθερες επαγγελματικές του δουλειές
Να ξέρεις ότι η καριέρα σου μπορεί να ανθίσει μετά τα 80
Να είσαι βέβαιη ότι όποιο τέχνη κι αν υπηρετείς, η δουλειά σου θα ονομαστεί φεμινιστική
Να μην ταλαιπωρείσαι σε μια μόνιμη θέση εκπαίδευσης
Να βλέπεις τις ιδέες σου να ζουν μέσα από τη δουλειά των άλλων
Να έχεις την ευκαιρία να διαλέξεις ανάμεσα σε καριέρα και μητρότητα
Να μην αναγκάζεσαι να καπνίζεις εκείνα τα χοντρά πούρα ή να ζωγραφίζεις με ιταλικά κοστούμια
Να έχεις περισσότερο χρόνο να δουλεύεις, όταν ο σύντροφός σου σε εγκαταλείπει για κάποια νεότερη
Να αναφέρεσαι στις αναθεωρημένες εκδόσεις της ιστορίας της τέχνης
Να μη χρειάζεται να αποφεύγεις το ξεβόλεμα του να σε αποκαλούν μια ιδιοφυΐα
Να βλέπεις τη φωτογραφία σου να δημοσιεύεται σε περιοδικά τέχνης φορώντας στολή γορίλα.

ΕΝΑ ΚΟΙΝΩΝΙΚΗ ΠΡΟΣΦΟΡΑ ΤΩΝ **GUERRILLA GIRLS** CONSCIENCE OF THE ART WORLD

FÖRDELARNA MED ATT VARA KVINNLIG KONSTNÄR:

Att arbeta utan pressen av succé
Att inte behöva ställa ut tillsammans med män
Att ha en tillflykt från konstvärlden i 4 free-lance jobb
Att veta att din karriär kanske kommer igång efter du fyllt åttio.
Att vara försäkrad om att vilken slags konst du än skapar kommer den att stämplas som kvinnlig.
Att inte vara hindrad av en fast lärartjänst.
Att se dina idéer leva vidare i andras verk.
Att ha möjligheten att välja mellan karriär och moderskap.
Att inte behöva storkna av de där feta cigarrerna eller måla iklädd italienska kostymer.
Att få mer tid att arbeta när din partner dumpat dig för någon yngre.
Att komma med i reviderade upplagor av konsthistorien.
Att slippa det genanta med att bli geniförklarad.
Att bli avbildad i konstmagasin iförd gorilladräkt.

EMAKUMEZKO ARTISTA IZATEAREN ABANTAILAK

Arrakastu izateko presiorik gabe lan egitea
Erakusketetan gizonekin batera agertu behar ez izatea
Autonomo modura egindako zure 4 lanetan mundu artistikotik ihes egin ahal izatea
Zure ibilbide artistikoaren altortza leurogei urte beteta dituzula jaso ahal izatea
Egiten duzun artea egiten dezula ere, lan femenino gisa izendatuko duton bermea edukitzea
Ez goldituen etengabeko irakaskuntzan harrapatute
Zure ideiak besteen obretan ikustea
Esperientziaren eta amatasunaren arteko hautua egiteko aukera
Ez ibili behar izatea zigarro puru erraldoi horiekin erdi itota, eta italiar jantziak eraman behar izan gabe margotu ahal izatea
Laneko denbora gehiago edukitzea, zure bikotekideak zu baino gazteago den norbaitengatik uzten zaltuenean
Artearen historiako bertsio zuzenduetan agertzea
Ez pasatu behar izatea jelnau zarela entzuteko lotsa
Gorilaz jantzita agertzea arte aldizkarietan

DIE VORTEILE EINES KÜNSTLERINNEN-DASEINS

Du arbeitest ohne Erfolgsdruck.
Du mußt nicht gemeinsam mit Männern ausstellen.
Deine vier Nebenjobs bieten dir eine Abwechslung zur Kunstwelt.
Du weißt, daß deine Karriere mit achtzig richtig losgehen könnte.
Ganz egal welche Art von Kunst du machst: du kannst sicher sein, daß diese als feminin bezeichnet wird.
Du sitzt nicht auf einem unbefristeten Lehrstuhl fest.
Du siehst, wie deine Ideen in den Arbeiten anderer weiterleben.
Du hast die Möglichkeit, zwischen Karriere und Mutterschaft zu wählen.
Du mußt nicht an einer dieser dicken Zigarren kauen oder in italienischen Anzügen malen.
Du hast mehr Zeit zu arbeiten, nachdem dein Freund dich für eine Jüngere fallengelassen hat.
Du wirst in überarbeiteten Fassungen der Kunstgeschichte erwähnt.
Du kommst nicht in die Verlegenheit, als Genie bezeichnet zu werden.
Du wirst in Kunstzeitungen abgebildet - als Gorilla verkleidet.

Bitte schickt $ und Kommentare an die **GUERILLA GIRLS** Das Gewissen der Kunstwelt

女性芸術家として有利な点

成功の圧迫感なしで仕事が出来る
男性と美術界に属をしなくてすむ
四つのフリーランスの仕事に芸術の世界から逃げることが出来る
八十才過に専門家として認められるかもしれないことを、限待出来る
どんな芸術を制作しても、その作品はきっとフェミニスト的だと呼ばれることはまちがいない
大学の教授としてしばられるおそれはない
他人の作品の中に自分の考えが見い出せる
仕事をするお弟子になるか、選ぶことが出来る
あの大きな黒巻タバコに咥えることもないし、イタリア製のスーツを着て絵を描かなくてもいい
遅れあいが若い子とつきあって逃げてから、仕事をする時間がもっとふえる
女性を認める美術界に、芸術を観せてもらえる
天才と呼ばれてはずかしい思いをすることはないでしょう
ゴリラのスーツを着た写真が美術雑誌に載せてもらえる

どうぞ寄付金の意見を下記の住所宛に送って下さい。
GUERRILLA GIRLS CONSCIENCE OF ART WORLD
（ゴリラ・ガール・美術界の良性意識）
BOX 237, 532 LaGuardia Pl., NY 10012

Гориллы-Партизанки
ХОРОШО БЫТЬ ХУДОЖНИЦЕЙ—У ЖЕНЩИН СТОЛЬКО ПРИВИЛЕГИЙ!

Работай-- и не надейся на успех.

Не обязательно выставляться с мужчинами.

Художественный рынок на тебя не давит-- ты в нем по совместительству.

Сейчас ты можешь не беспокоиться, слава придет не раньше восьмидесяти.

Не сомневайся, твое искусство всегда будет называться женским.

Ты никогда не завязнешь в номенклатурной должности профессора.

Не правда ли приятно вдруг встретить свои идеи в картине подписанным чужим именем?

Ты свободна в выборе между детьми и карьерой.

Необязательно попыхивать артистической трубкой и носить дорогой костюм маэстро.

Со временем ты сможешь полностью отдаться искусству, когда твой муж уйдет к молодой.

Тебе обеспечено место в истории искусств которую напишут ревизионисты.

Тебе не придется краснеть оттого, что тебя назвали гением.

Твоя фотография будет опубликована в художественных журналах под маской гориллы-партизанки.

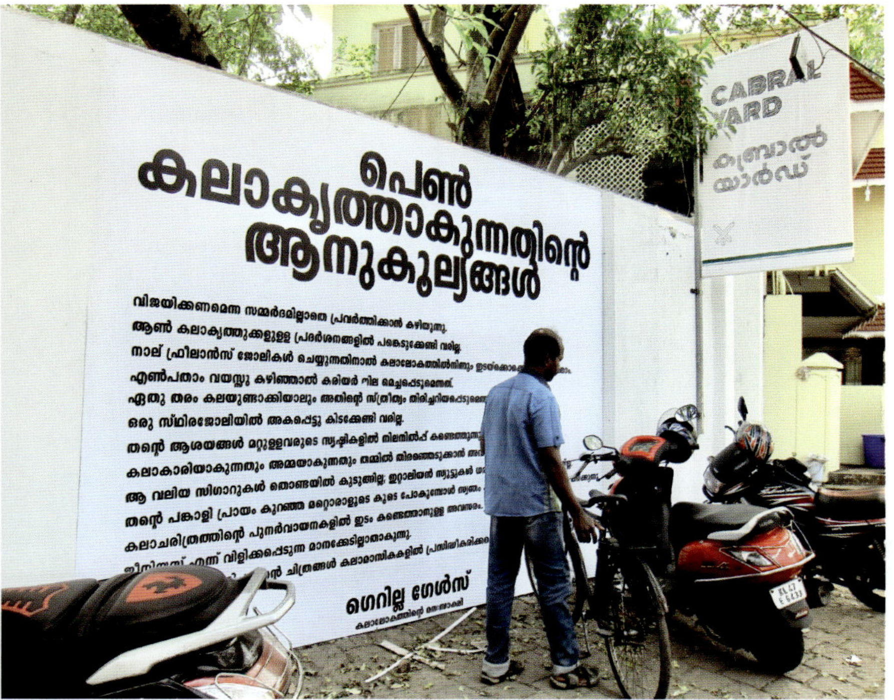

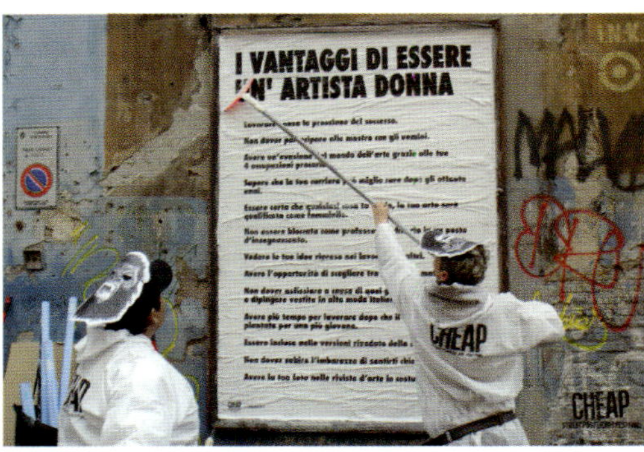

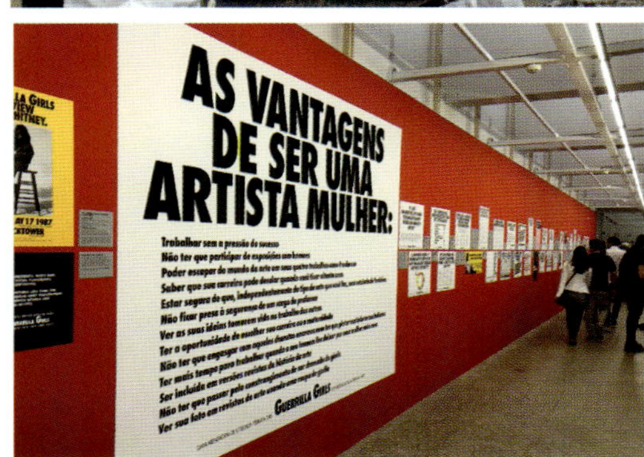

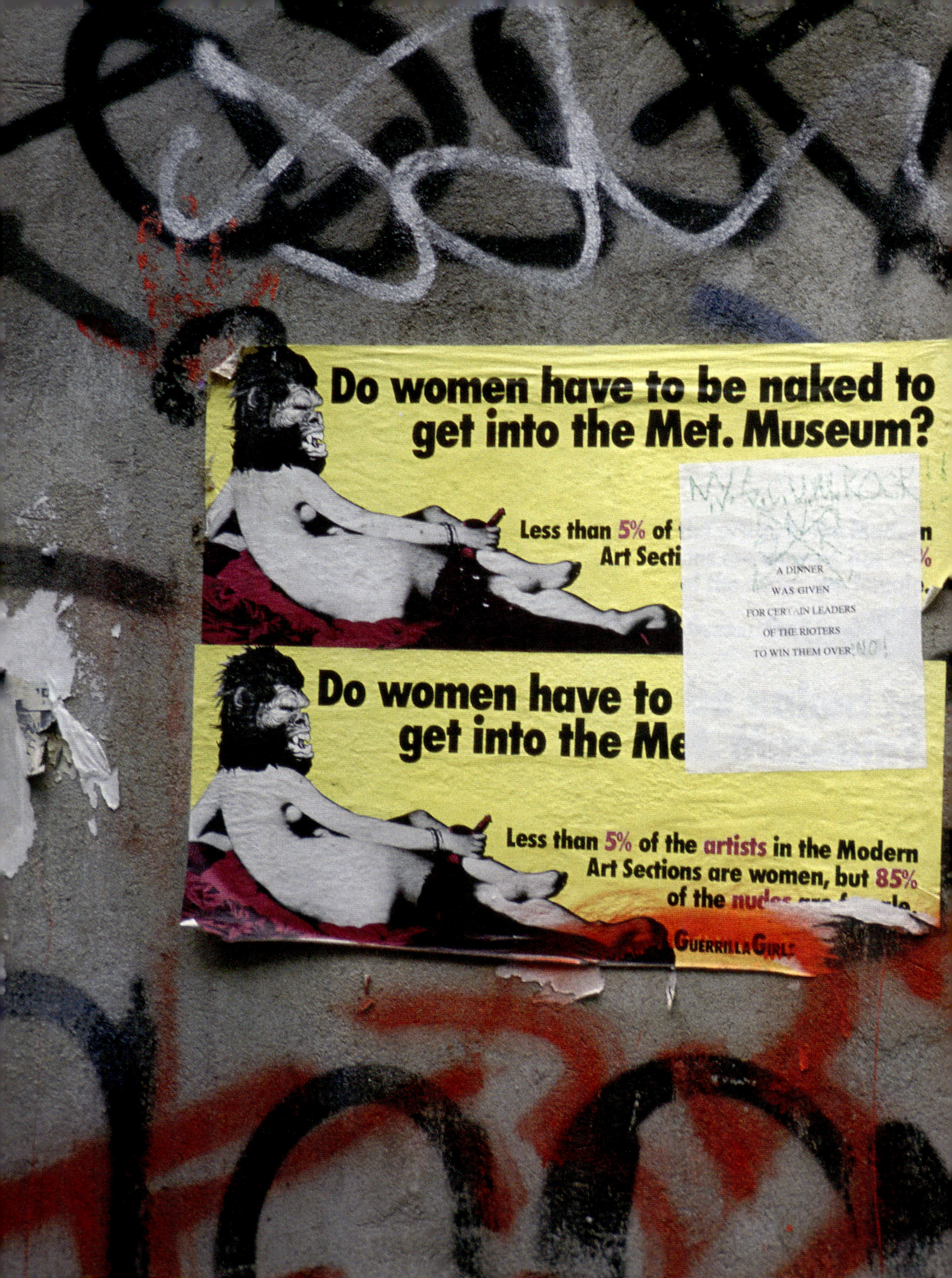

Do women have to be naked to get into the Met. Museum?
Less than 5% of the artists in the Modern Art Sections are women, but 85% of the nudes are female.
Do women have to get into the Me
Less than 5% of the artists in the Modern Art Sections are women, but 85% of the nudes are female.
GUERRILLA GIRLS
A DINNER WAS GIVEN FOR CERTAIN LEADERS OF THE RIOTERS TO WIN THEM OVER.

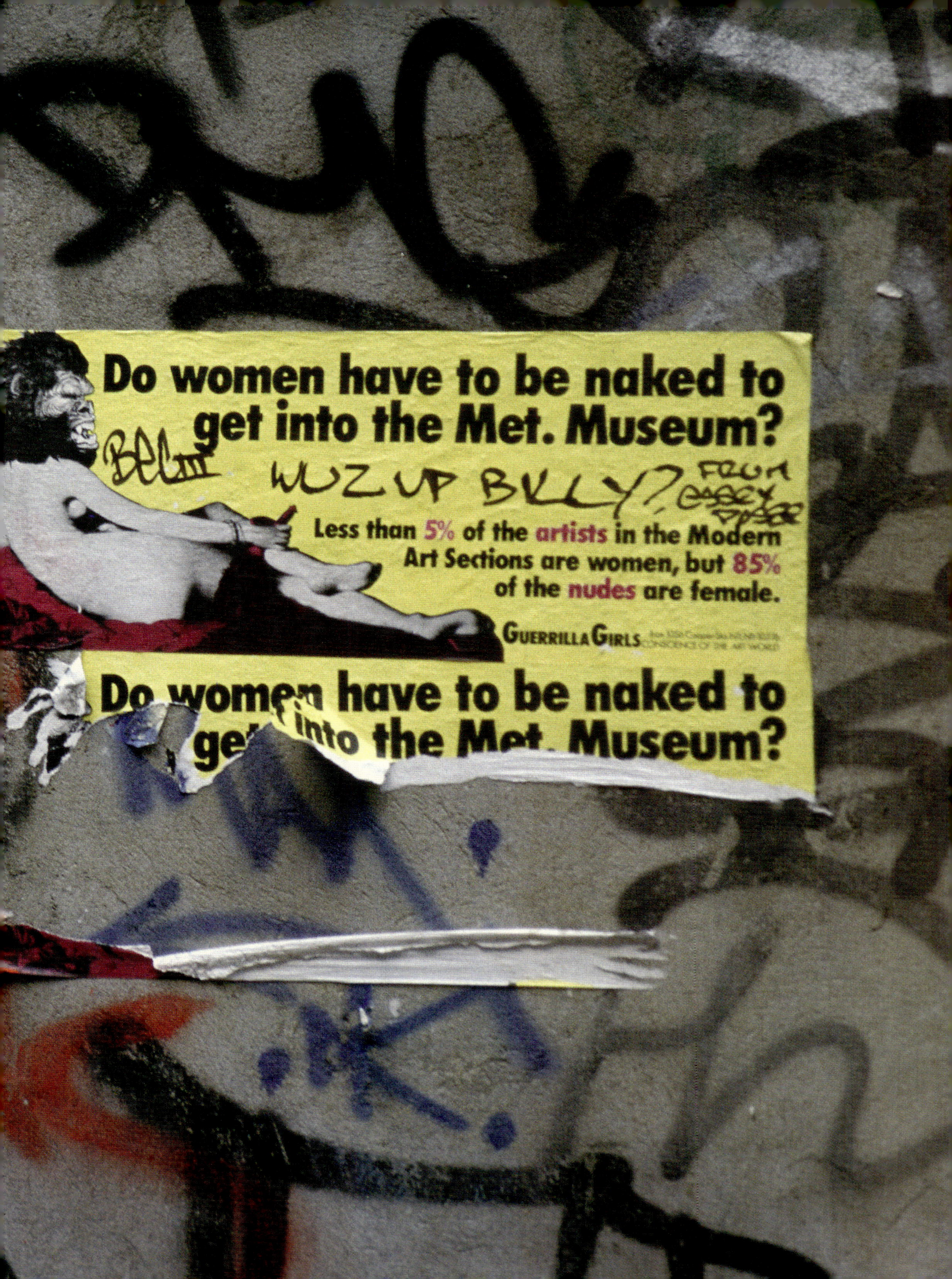

Do women have to be naked to get into the Met. Museum?
Less than 5% of the artists in the Modern Art Sections are women, but 85% of the nudes are female.
GUERRILLA GIRLS
CONSCIENCE OF THE ART WORLD
Do women have to be naked to get into the Met. Museum?

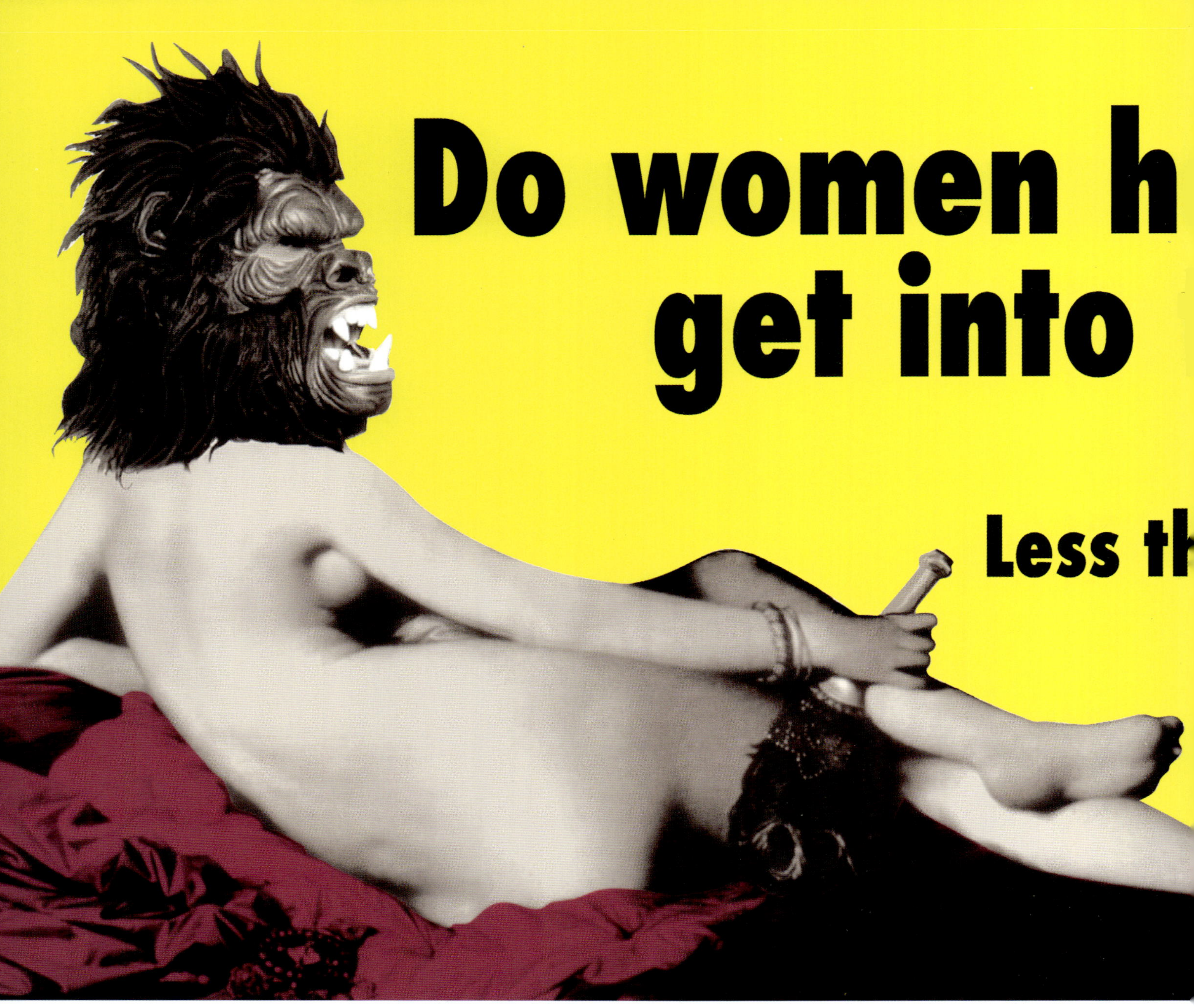

Above: We went to the Metropolitan Museum of Art to count the number of women artists on exhibit compared to the number of naked female bodies in the artworks. The results were very revealing. The Public Art Fund had asked us to do a billboard but rejected our proposal saying it wasn't "clear enough." We ran it as an ad in New York City buses instead. Since then, it's been reproduced thousands of times and traveled all over the world.

Right: From time to time we go back to the Met to do a recount. Here's our latest.

Poster, 1989; Right: Poster, 2012

ve to be naked to
he Met. Museum?

n **5%** of the **artists** in the Modern Art sections are women, but **85%** of the **nudes** are female

Statistics from the Metropolitan Museum of Art, New York City, 1989

GUERRILLA GIRLS CONSCIENCE OF THE ART WORLD

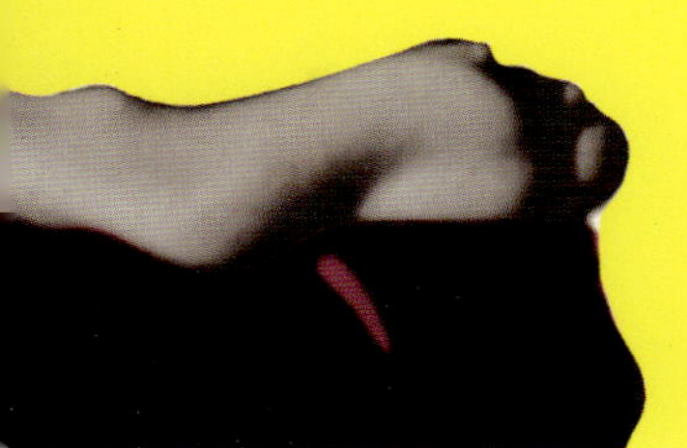

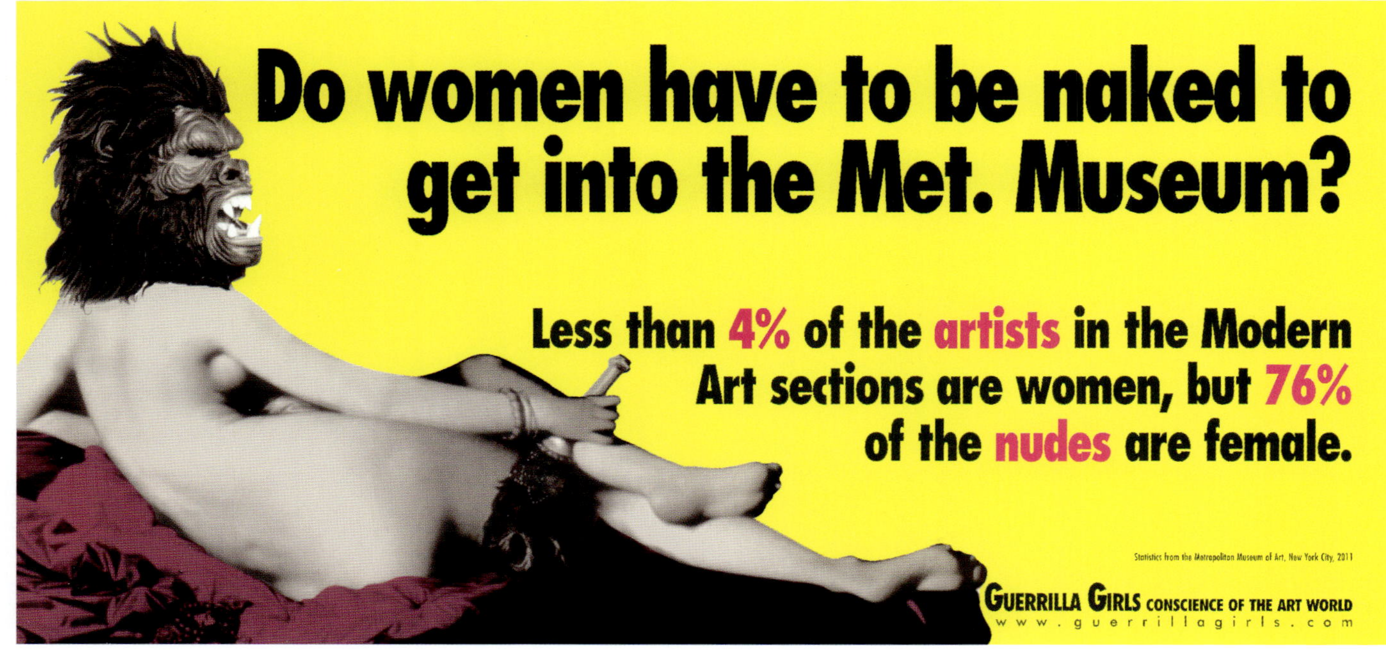

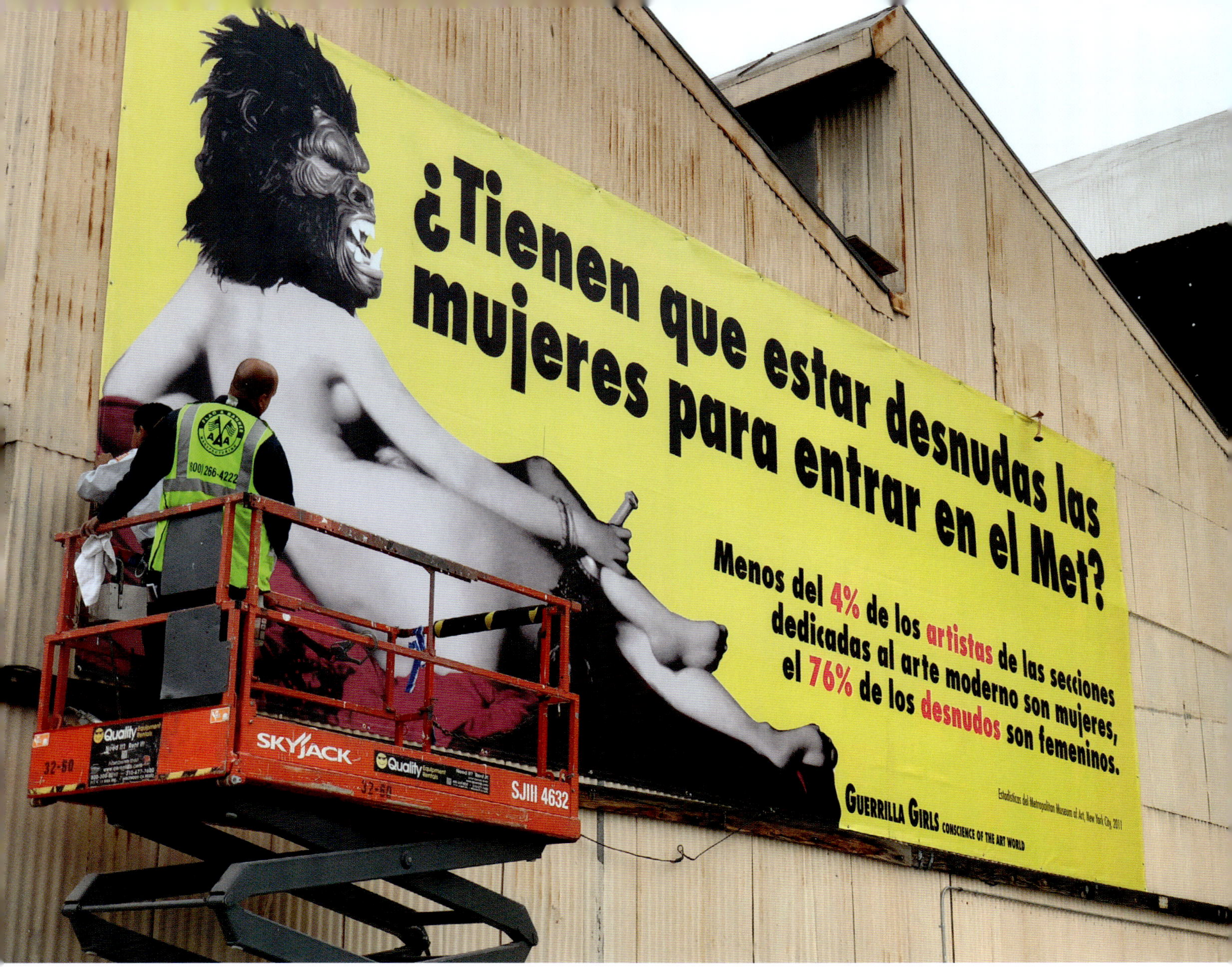

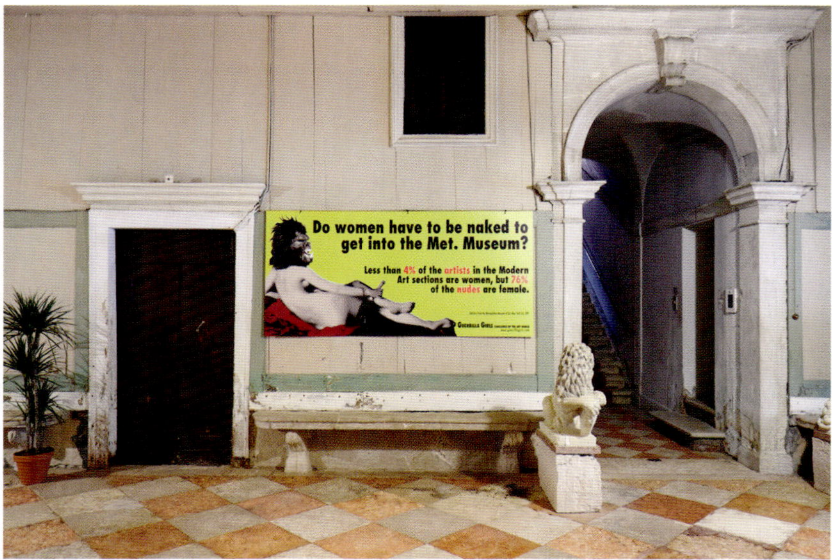

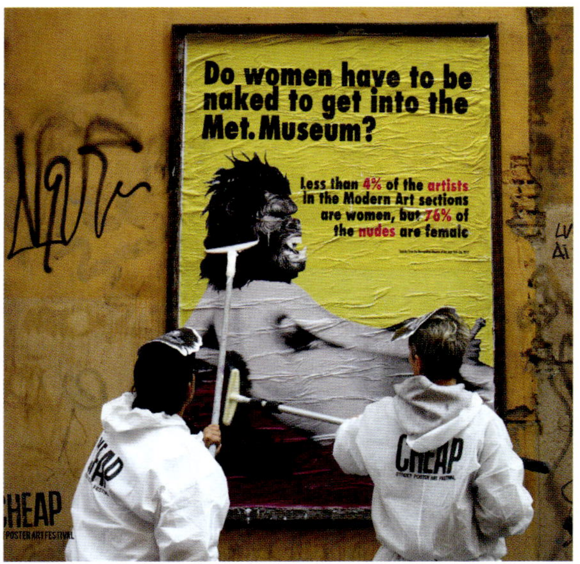

Since *Naked* first appeared on NYC buses, it's graced hundreds of books, streets, museums and countless dormitory rooms. Above, clockwise from top: *Beyond the Streets*, Los Angeles, 2018; Cheap Festival, Bologna, 2017; Heist Gallery, Venice, Italy, 2019. Right, clockwise from top: *Late Show with Steven Colbert*, 2016; Montalban, France, 2009; *Public Viewing*, Shanghai, 2010; Boston, 2012; São Paulo, 2018–19; Madrid, 2015

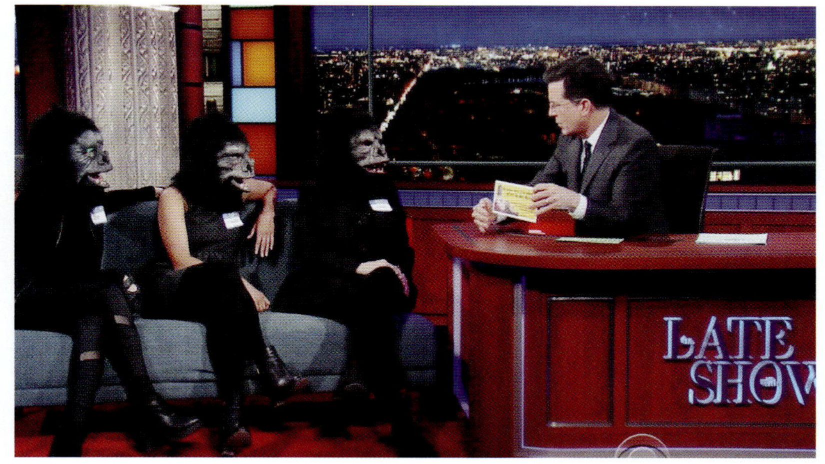

LATE
SHOW

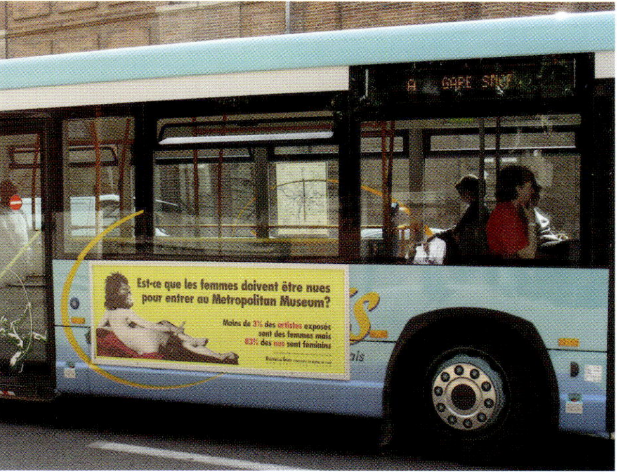

Est-ce que les femmes doivent être nues
pour entrer au Metropolitan Museum?
Moins de 3% des artistes exposés
sont des femmes mais
83% des nus sont féminins

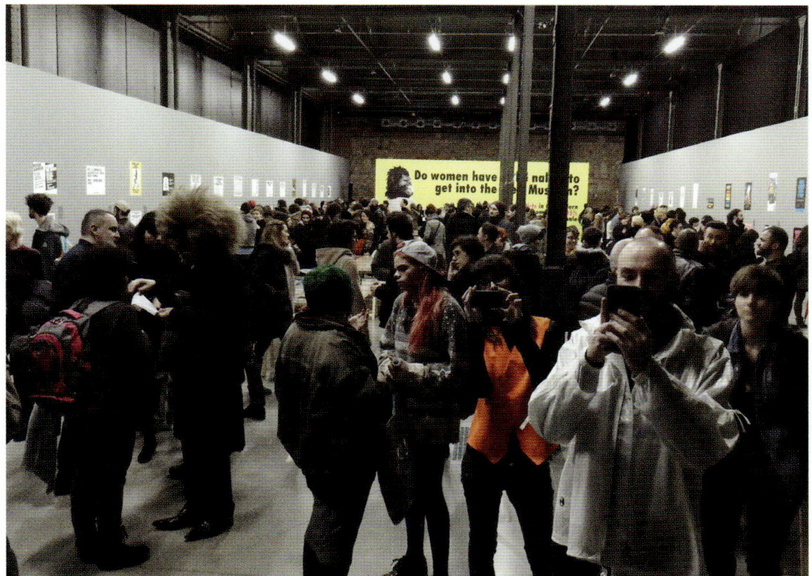

Do women have to be naked to
get into the Met. Museum?

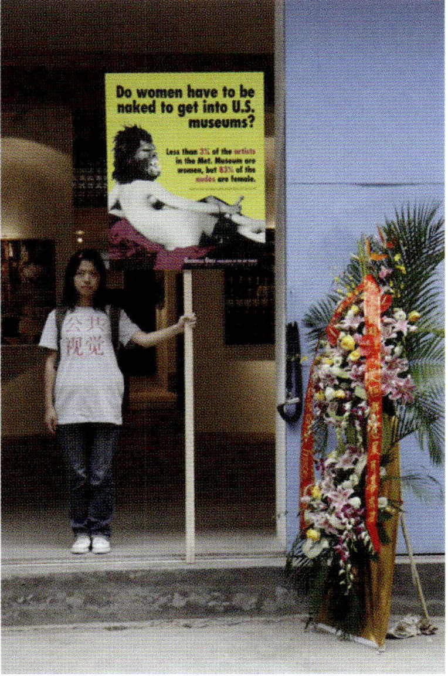

Do women have to be
naked to get into U.S.
museums?
Less than 3% of the artists
in the Met. Museum are
women, but 83% of the
nudes are female.

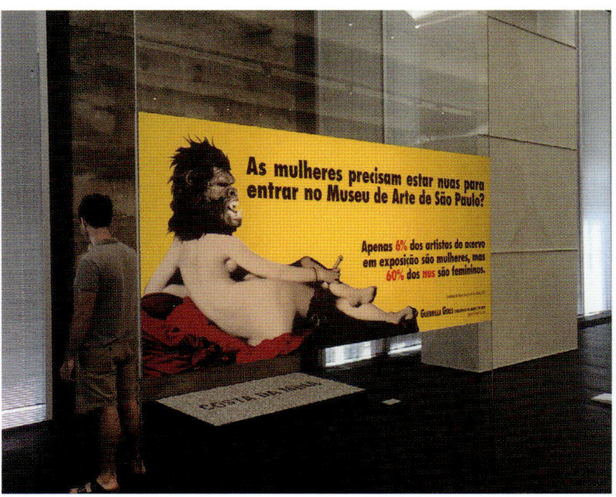

As mulheres precisam estar nuas para
entrar no Museu de Arte de São Paulo?
Apenas 6% dos artistas do acervo
em exposição são mulheres, mas
60% dos nus são femininos.

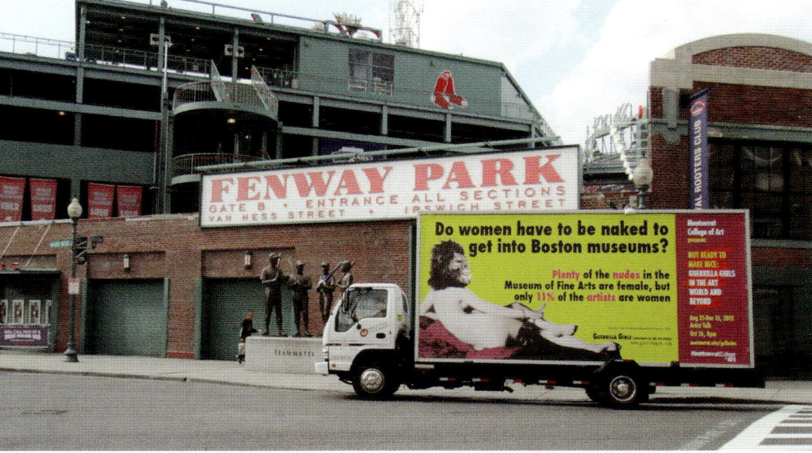

FENWAY PARK
GATE B · ENTRANCE ALL SECTIONS
VAN NESS STREET   IPSWICH STREET
Do women have to be naked to
get into Boston museums?
Plenty of the nudes in the
Museum of Fine Arts are female, but
only 11% of the artists are women

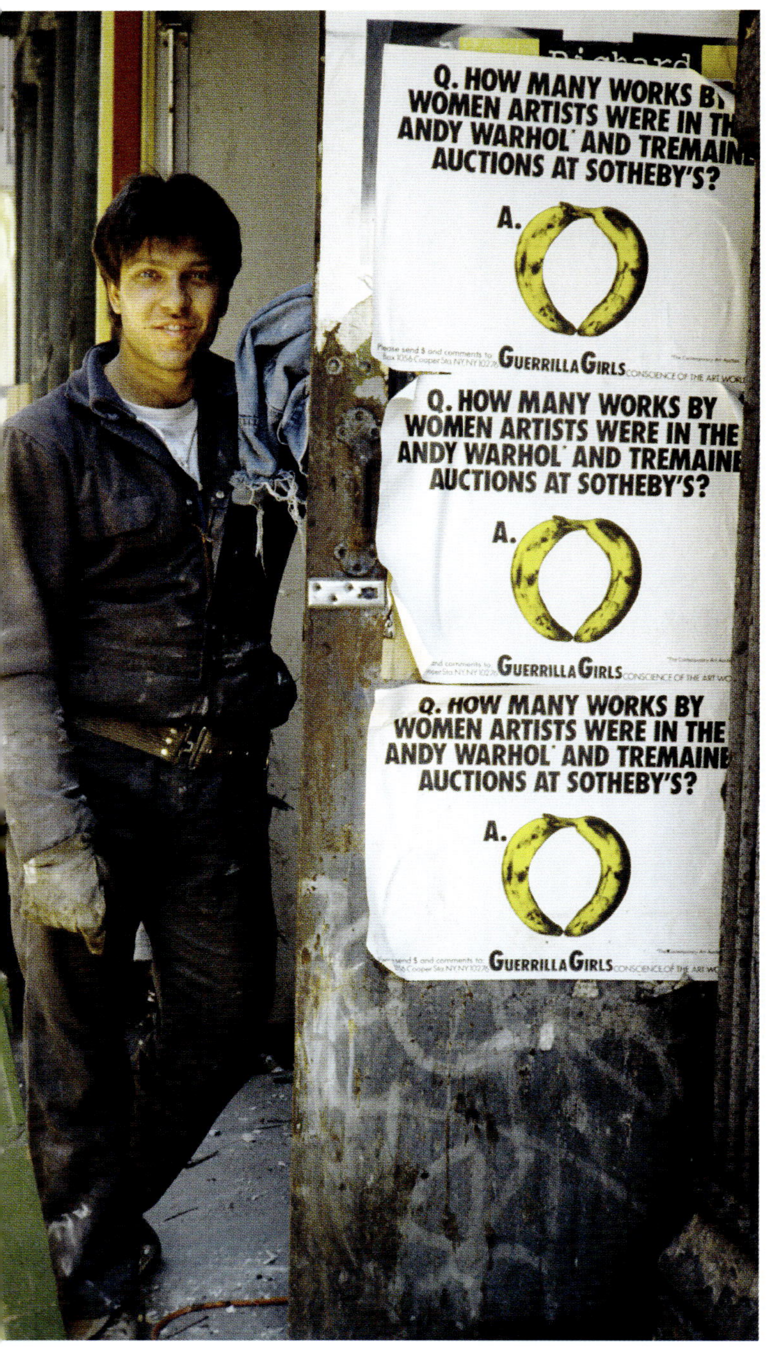

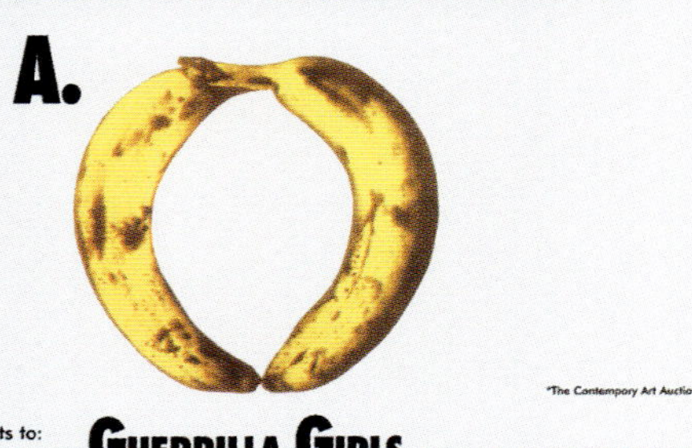

Posters, 1989

GUERRILLA GIRLS
conscience of the art world

March 1, 1988

Dear ______________

Guerrilla Girls invites you to participate in a collaborative poster to encourage white male artists to voice concern about sexual and racial bias in the New York art world. We plan to distribute a poster this spring listing male artists with prominent gallery affiliations who have agreed to speak with their dealer about the male-female, white-non-white balance in his or her stable of artists. We intend this poster to be positive in contrast to many of our previous posters which have focused on the bad news about the art world.

We would like to include your name, with your permission and assistance. All you have to do is speak with your dealer, or any other in case yours has a good record, and let us know by returning the enclosed post card with signatures. Then you can be assured that your name will be included on a Guerrilla Girls Honor Roll for 1989. Any contributions you can make will help us print and distribute the poster nationally and internationally. We look forward to your response.

XXOO,

GUERRILLA GIRLS

P.S. If we don't hear from you by April 15, we will assume you don't want to be on the Honor Roll. We are considering another poster of these artists.

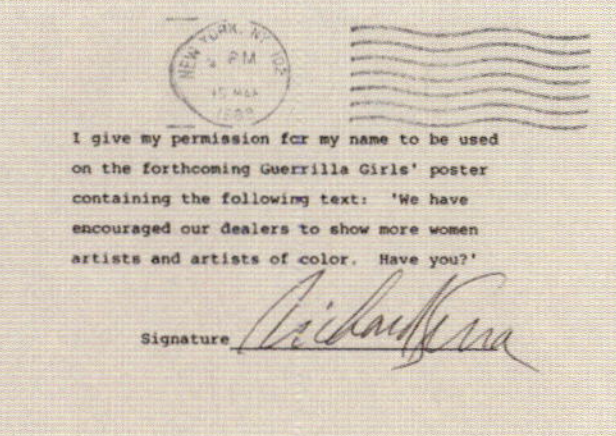

WE'VE ENCOURAGED OUR GALLERIES TO SHOW MORE WOMEN & ARTISTS OF COLOR. HAVE YOU?

Vito Acconci	Sam Gilliam	Joseph Kosuth	Irving Petlin
Dennis Adams	Glenn Goldberg	Robert Kushner	Lucio Pozzi
Mac Adams	Michael Goldberg	Les Levine	David Reed
Benny Andrews	Ron Gorchov	Sol Lewitt	Bruce Robbins
John Baldessari	Peter Halley	Donald Lipski	James Rosenquist
Bill Beckley	David Hammons	Robert Longo	Juan Sanchez
Jake Berthot	Jene Highstein	David Mach	Richard Serra
Howard Buchwald	Bill Jensen	Brice Marden	Ned Smyth
William Conlon	Alex Katz	Joseph Nechvatel	Robert Stackhouse
David Diao	Steve Keister	John Newman	Mark Tansey
Rackstraw Downes	Alain Kirili	Richard Nonas	Lawrence Weiner
Peter Drake	Komar and Melamid	Jim Nutt	Robin Winters
Carroll Dunham	Mark Kostabi	Claes Oldenburg	Michael Zwack

Please send $ and comments to:
Box 1056 Cooper Sta. NY, NY 10276 **GUERRILLA GIRLS** CONSCIENCE OF THE ART WORLD

It was time to get men on our side. We wrote letters to established male artists asking them to convince their art dealers to show more women and artists of color. We put the guys who agreed on a poster, and threatened to expose those who didn't. We still have that list.

Letter to male artists; Postcards from male artists; Poster, 1989

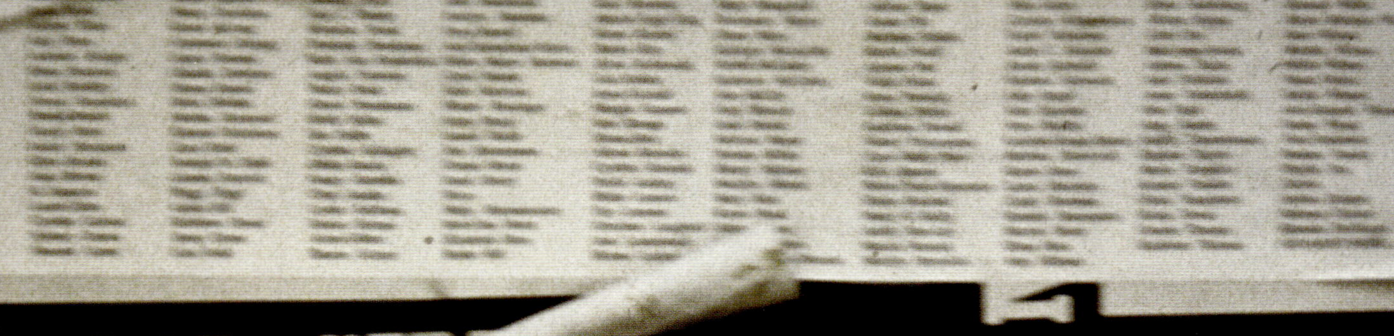

RELAX SENATOR HELMS, THE ART WORLD IS YOUR KIND OF PLACE!

- The number of blacks at an art opening is about the same as at one of your garden parties.

- Many museum trustees are at least as conservative as Ronald Lauder.

- Because aesthetic quality stands above all, there's never been a need for Affirmative Action in museums or galleries.

- Most art collectors, like most successful artists, are white males.

- Women artists have their place. After all, they earn less than 1/3 of what male artists earn.

- Museums are separate but equal. No female black painter or sculptor has been in a Whitney Biennial since 1973. Instead, they can show at the Studio Museum in Harlem or the Women's Museum in Washington.

- Since most women artists don't make a living from their work and there's no maternity leave or childcare in the art world, they rarely choose both career and motherhood.

- The sexual imagery in most respected works of art is the expression of wholesome heterosexual males.

- Unsullied by government interference, art is one of the last unregulated markets. Why, there isn't even any self-regulation!

- The majority of exposed penises in major museums belong to the Baby Jesus.

Please send $ and comments to: **GUERRILLA GIRLS** CONSCIENCE OF THE ART WORLD
Cooper Sta. NY, NY 10276

WHEN RACISM & SEXISM ARE NO LONGER FASHIONABLE, WHAT WILL YOUR ART COLLECTION BE WORTH?

The art market won't bestow mega-buck prices on the work of a few white males forever. For the 17.7 million you just spent on a single Jasper Johns painting, you could have bought at least one work by all of these women and artists of color.

<table>
<tr><td>Bernice Abbott</td><td>Elaine de Kooning</td><td>Dorothea Lange</td><td>Sarah Peale</td></tr>
<tr><td>Anni Albers</td><td>Lavinia Fontana</td><td>Marie Laurencin</td><td>Ljubova Popova</td></tr>
<tr><td>Sofonisba Anguisolla</td><td>Meta Warwick Fuller</td><td>Edmonia Lewis</td><td>Olga Rosanova</td></tr>
<tr><td>Diane Arbus</td><td>Artemisia Gentileschi</td><td>Judith Leyster</td><td>Nellie Mae Rowe</td></tr>
<tr><td>Vanessa Bell</td><td>Marguérite Gérard</td><td>Barbara Longhi</td><td>Rachel Ruysch</td></tr>
<tr><td>Isabel Bishop</td><td>Natalia Goncharova</td><td>Dora Maar</td><td>Kay Sage</td></tr>
<tr><td>Rosa Bonheur</td><td>Kate Greenaway</td><td>Lee Miller</td><td>Augusta Savage</td></tr>
<tr><td>Elizabeth Bougereau</td><td>Barbara Hepworth</td><td>Lisette Model</td><td>Vavara Stepanova</td></tr>
<tr><td>Margaret Bourke-White</td><td>Eva Hesse</td><td>Paula Modersohn-Becker</td><td>Florine Stettheimer</td></tr>
<tr><td>Romaine Brooks</td><td>Hannah Hoch</td><td>Tina Modotti</td><td>Sophie Taeuber-Arp</td></tr>
<tr><td>Julia Margaret Cameron</td><td>Anna Huntingdon</td><td>Berthe Morisot</td><td>Alma Thomas</td></tr>
<tr><td>Emily Carr</td><td>May Howard Jackson</td><td>Grandma Moses</td><td>Marietta Robusti Tintoretto</td></tr>
<tr><td>Rosalba Carriera</td><td>Frida Kahlo</td><td>Gabriele Münter</td><td>Suzanne Valadon</td></tr>
<tr><td>Mary Cassatt</td><td>Angelica Kauffmann</td><td>Alice Neel</td><td>Remedios Varo</td></tr>
<tr><td>Constance Marie Charpentier</td><td>Hilma of Klimt</td><td>Louise Nevelson</td><td>Elizabeth Vigée Le Brun</td></tr>
<tr><td>Imogen Cunningham</td><td>Kathe Kollwitz</td><td>Georgia O'Keeffe</td><td>Laura Wheeling Waring</td></tr>
<tr><td>Sonia Delaunay</td><td>Lee Krasner</td><td>Meret Oppenheim</td><td></td></tr>
</table>

A PUBLIC SERVICE MESSAGE FROM **GUERRILLA GIRLS** CONSCIENCE OF THE ART WORLD

Left: The artworld thinks itself progressive and liberal, but we've always thought it more "derriere" than "avant." This poster called out all the ways it resembled the world of conservative politics.

Above: Women have always been way undervalued in the art market. We offered some investment advice for art collectors.

Posters, 1989

GUERRILLA GIRLS' IDENTITIES EXPOSED!

"We've signed up to fight discrimination in the art world. Call us Guerrilla Girls."

Cecile Abish
Pat Adams
Alice Adams
Edna Andrade
Suzanne Anker
Emma Amos
Kary Arimoto-Mercer
Susan Anderson
Eleanor Antin
Polly Apfelbaum
Ida Applebroog
Marl Lee Ataie
Dotty Attie
Julie Ault
Nancy Azara
Lillian Ball
Susan Ball
Poni Baptiste
Barbara Berg
Priscilla Barton
Jennifer Bartlett
Linda Bastian
Jackie Battenfield
Arlyne Bayer
Susan Bee
Andrea Belag
Diane Burko
Stephanie Bernheim
Betty Beaumont
Gretchen Bender
Judith Bernstein
Dara Birnbaum
Mariella Bisson
Darla Bjork
Andrea Blum
Judy Blum
Lorraine Bodger
Elena Borstein
Leah Bradley
Teresa Bramlette
Brenda Branch
Nancy Brett
Jackie Brookner
Ellen Brooks
Joan Brown
K. Caraccio
Lauric Carlos
Cynthia Carlson
Sydney Carson
Nanette Carter

Ivy Cartier
Joscly Carvalho
Zehnep Celik
Whitney Chadwick
Amy Chaiklin
Lenora Champagne
Emily Cheng
Hsienli Chia
Abigail Child
Lindy Lois Churchill
Maureen Clavel
Wendy Coad
Margaret Cogswell
Nancy Cohen
Carolyn Cole
Colette
Angela Collins
Maureen Connor
Linda S. Connor
Petah Coyne
Eileen Cowin
Kathy Constantinides
Susan Crile
Dana Cranmer
Ann Craven
Judith Croce
Jody Culkin
Virginia Cuppaidge
Jessica Cusick
Peggy Cyphers
Annette Cyr
Betsy Damon
Susan Daykin
Nancy Davidson
Karen deLong
Constance DeJong
Laura Demme
Claudia DeMonte
Donna Dennis
Daria Deshuk
Martha Diamond
Eleanor Dickinson
Carol Diehl
Georgia M. Diehl
Linnea Dietrich
Peggy Diggs
Leslie Dill
Kathleen Dinan
Jenny Dixon
Lois Dodd

Jerrilynn Dodds
Michele Oka Doner
Beverly Donofrio
Judith dos Santos
Ellen Driscoll
Orshi Drozdik
Loretta Dunkelman
Fontaine Dunn
Anne Doran
Elizabeth Dworkin
Nancy Dwyer
Cynthia Eardley
Martha Edelheit
Sally S. Eckhopf
Mary Beth Edelson
Elizabeth Egbert
Diane Elmeer
Laura Emrick
Carol Engelson
Alix Euwer
Jan Evans
Lauren Ewing
Heide Fasnacht
Nan Feinberg
Frieda Fehrenbacher
Rochelle Feinstein
Sandy Fellman
Jackie Ferrara
Angelika Festa
Janet Fish
Bruria Finkel
Mary Fish
Audrey Flack
Gail C. Flanery
Hermine Freed
Deborah Freedman
Ruth Ann Fredenthal
Angela Fremont
Nancy Fried
Gloria Friedmann
Emily Fuller
Sue Fuller
Cynthia Gallagher
Ofelia Garcia
Nancy Garruba
Cheri Gaulke
Lynne Gelfman
Danita Geltner
Aimee Gilbert
Sharon Gilbert

Gitta Gisell
Ann Gillen
Dorothy Gillespie
Sandy Gellis
Kate Gleason
Eunice Golden
Pennelope Goodfriend
Sharon Gold
Kathy Goodell
Jewelle Gomez
April Gornik
Christiane Graham
Ilona Granet
Grace Graupe-Pillard
Nancy Graves
Renee Green
Mary Grigoriadis
Nancy Grossman
Wendy Good
Julie Gross
Mimi Gross
Vanalyne Green
Kathy Grove
Karen Gunderson
Freda Guttman
Marcia Hafif
Jessica Hagedorn
Eb Haggerty
Samia Palestinian Halaby
Nade Haley
Susan Hall
Mary Hambleton
Jane Hammond
Jerelyn Hanrahan
Freya Hansell
Ann Sutherland Harris
Helen Mayer Harrison
Carol Haerer
Julie Harrison
Maren Hassinger
Anne Healy
Laurel Hecht
Sue Heinemann
Donna Henes
Janet Henry
Hera
Mary Hermansader
Betti-Sue Hertz
Elizabeth Hess
Burke Hill

Gilah Yelin Hirsch
Rosalind Hodgkins
Robin Holland
Robin Holder
Wopo Holup
P. Holt
Pat Horner
Jenny Holzer
Mei-Ling Hom
Rebecca Howland
Holly Hughes
Nene Humphrey
Nancy Chunn
Marian Hunter
Carrie Inoshita
Joy Jacobs
Yvonne Jacquette
Valerie Jaudon
Canela Jaramillo
Suzanne Jay
Christine Jederyki
Corrine Jennings
Kristin Jones
Daile Kaplan
Deborah Kass
Barbara Kasten
Peggy Katz
Jane Kaufman
Darra Keeton
Tatana Kellner
Flo Kennedy
Kate Kennedy
Marcia Gygli King
Karen Kitchel
Sherie Kley
Silvia Kolbowski
Lisa Koklin
Joyce Kozloff
Margia Kramer
Ann Kresge
Diana Kurz
Alison Knowles
Cynthia Karasek
Stella Lackey
Blake Lannon
Fay Lansner
Gretchen Langheld
Ann Lauterbach
Helene Leclerc

Cheryl Laemmle
Ann Leda
Annette Lemieux
Bibi Lencek
Mary McLeod
Susan Leopold
Ora Lerman
Marilyn Lerner
Jill Levine
Kim Levin
Susan Leurig
Vered Lieb
Claire Lieberman
Jacqueline Lima
Valborg Linn
Lucy R. Lippard
Eunice Lipton
Jackie Lipton
Ann Litke
Liz of Liz+Val
Catherine Lord
Arlene Love
Margot Lovejoy
Ellen Lubell
Bonnie Lucas
Mary Lucier
Toby MacLennan
Sarah Wells
Virginia Maksymowicz
Phyllis Mark
Deborah Masters
Mary Maughelli
Rosemary Mayer
Diane Mayo
Kathryn McAuliffe
Robbie McCauley
Kathleen McCarthy
Ann McCoy
Ivey Minsch
Josie Merck
Melissa Meyer
Brenda Miller
Sherry Millner
Marilyn Minter
Mary Miss
Karen Moak
Sabra Moore
Linda Montano
Carmen Gloria Morales

Maria Morganti
Kathy Muehlemann
Susanne Mueller
Elizabeth Murray
Rita Myers
Florence Neal
Melanie Neilson
Laura Newman
Linda Nochlin
Larissa Noon
Janet Nolan
Linda Norden
Linda Novak
Jeanne O'Connor
Melanie O'Harra
Helen Oji
Annette Oko
Lorraine O'Grady
Anna O'Sullivan
Nancy Ostrovsky
Grace Paley
Ida Panicelli
Patricia Patterson
Andrea Pedersen
Linda Peer
Alice Phillips
Cara Perlman
Judy Pfaff
Ellen Phelan
Emily T. Phillips
Howardena Pindell
Jody Pinto
Adrian Piper
Suzan Pitt
Barbara Pollack
Reeva Potoff
Alyson Pou
Vicki Polon
Rona Pondick
Liliana Porter
Kathleen Powell
Nancy Princenthal
Carol Molly Prior
E.A. Racette
Helen Evans Ramsaran
Elaine Reichek
Nancy O. Reilly
Judith Ren-Lay
Marcia Resnick
Marilyn Reynolds

Shelley Rice
B. Ruby Rich
Judy Rifka
Faith Ringgold
Marie Ringwald
Carole Robb
Joyce Robins
Charlotte Robinson
Abby Robinson
Therese Rolland
Jane Rosen
Lynn Rosenfeld
Betsy Rosenwald
Ce Roser
Martha Rosler
Erika Rothenberg
Ann Marie Rousseau
Beth T. Rowe
Meridel Rubenstein
Christy Rupp
Ellen Rumm
Alison Saar
Aleya Saad
Barbara Sahlman
Christina Salusti
Barbara Sandler
Hope Sandrow
Joan Semmel
Margo Sawyer
Miriam Schapiro
A.C. Schatzie
Christina Schlesinger
Mira Schor
Carolee Schneemann
Sarah Schulman
Sarah C. Schuster
Susan Schwalb
Barbara Schwartz
Judy Seigel
Ann Sgarlata
Fern Shaffer
Lucinda Knaus Shanos
Barbara Shawcroft
Karen Shaw
Laura Shechter
Cindy Sherman
Pamela Shoemaker
Harriet Shorr
Elena Sisto
Amy Sillman

Laurie Simmons
Coreen Simpson
Sharon Siskin
Sandy Skoglund
Arlene Slavin
Dumriegbe Slawson
Cynthia Smith
Roberta Smith
Sylvia Sleigh
Clarissa Sligh
Terise Slotkin
Alexis Smith
Mimi Smith
Susan Smith
Valerie Smith
Jenny Snider
Joan Snyder
Kit-Yin Snyder
Katherin Sokolnikoff
Elke Solomon
Michelle Spark
Nancy Spero
Ann Sperry
Eileen Spikol
Annie Sprinkle
Susan Stein
Carla Stellweg
May Stevens
Sandy Strauss
Elizabeth Streb
Marjorie Strider
Sylvia de Swaan
Erika Suderburg
Altoon Sultan
Carol Sun
B.th Ames Swartz
Athena Tacha
Jude Tallichet
Anne Tabachnick
Rea Tajiri
Amy Taubin
Judith Tannenbaum
Daphne Taylor
Merle Tempkin
Ronnie Tendler
Fiona Templeton
Robin Tewes
Gwenn Thomas
Kathleen Thomas

Jeannie Thurston
Regina Tierney
Betty Tompkins
Carole Tormollan
Diana Tornado
Selina Trieff
Marcia Tucker
Susan Tunick
Lisa Tuttle
Patty Tyrol
Mierle Laderman Ukeles
Lynn Umlauf
Mary Ann Unger
Bonnie Van Allen
Regina Vater
Nora Vest
Jill Viney
Ursula Von Rydingsvaard
Kay Walkingstick
Dawn Walnut
June Wayne
Sarah Wells
Lilly Wei
Rebecca Welz
Debra Weisberg
Ruth Weisberg
René Westbook
Mia Westerlund Roosen
Barbara Westermann
Ada Whitney
Betty Wilde
Faith Wilding
Hannah Wilke
Helen Miranda Wilson
Jane Wilson
Martha Wilson
Millie Wilson
Paula Winot
Jackie Winsor
Ann-Sargent Wooster
Susan Wyatt
Nina Yankowitz
Brahna Yassky
Phyllis Yes
Zarina
Jerilea Zempel
Barbara Zucker
Rhonda Zwillinger
AND MANY MORE........

GUERRILLA GIRLS
CONSCIENCE OF THE ART WORLD

February, 1989

Dear

Will you be our Valentine? GUERRILLA GIRLS are planning a poster of names of women artists who support the issues we raise. We would like you to be one of them. The poster will read "CALL US GUERRILLA GIRLS....we've signed up to fight discrimination in the artworld, have you?" Thousands of letters like this are being sent all over the country.

If you don't want to be left out, please return the enclosed card by March 15 and your name will be on the streets soon.

Love and kisses,
THE GUERRILLA GIRLS

P.S. Please pass this letter to a friend

PO BOX 1056 COOPER STATION NY 10276

We sent a valentine to a long list of artists and asked them to publicly call themselves Guerrilla Girls. The response was overwhelming. Are the real Guerrilla Girls on the poster? We'll never tell.

Poster, 1990; Sign-up flyer, 1989

GUERRILLA GIRLS' POP QUIZ

Q. If February is Black History Month and March is Women's History Month, what happens the rest of the year?

A. discrimination

A PUBLIC SERVICE MESSAGE FROM **GUERRILLA GIRLS** CONSCIENCE OF THE ART WORLD

Above: Assigning commemorative months to the struggles of marginalized groups is important, but it is not enough. See our update on page 135 and Trump version on page 154.

Poster, 1990

Next spread: In 1990, many museums didn't have a Code of Ethics, so we wrote one for them. We used biblical language to condemn their egregious behavior. See our 2019 update on page 179.

Poster, 1990

GUERRILLA G
ETHICS FOR A

I. Thou shalt not be a Museum Trustee and also the Chief Stockholder of a Major Auction House.

II. A Curator shalt not exhibit an Artist, or the Artists of a Dealer, with whom he/she has had a sexual relationship, unless such liaison is explicitly stated on a wall label 8" from the exhibited work.

III. Thou shalt not give more than 3 retrospectives to an Artist whose Dealer is the brother of the Chief Curator.

IV. Thou shalt not limit thy Board of Trustees to Corporate Officers, Wealthy Entrepreneurs and Social Hangers-on. At least 2% must be Artists representing the racial and gender percentages of the U.S. population.

V. Thou shalt not permit Corporations to launder their public images in Museums until they cleaneth up their Toxic Waste Dumps and Oil Slicks.

RLS' CODE OF
RT MUSEUMS:

VI. Thou shalt provide lavish funerals for Women and Artists of Color who thou planeth to exhibit only after their death.

VII. If thou art an Art Collector sitting on the Acquisitions or Exhibitions Committee, thou shalt useth thy influence to enhance the value of thine own collection not more than once a year.

VIII. Thy Corporate Benefactors who earneth their income from products for Women and People of Color shalt earmark their Museum donations for exhibits and acquisitions of art by those groups.

IX. Thou shalt keepeth Curatorial Salaries so low that Curators must be Independently Wealthy, or willing to engage in Insider Trading.

X. Thou shalt admit to the Public that words such as genius, masterpiece, seminal, potent, tough, gritty and powerful are used solely to prop up the Myth and inflate the Market Value of White Male Artists.

GIRLS CONSCIENCE OF THE ART WORLD

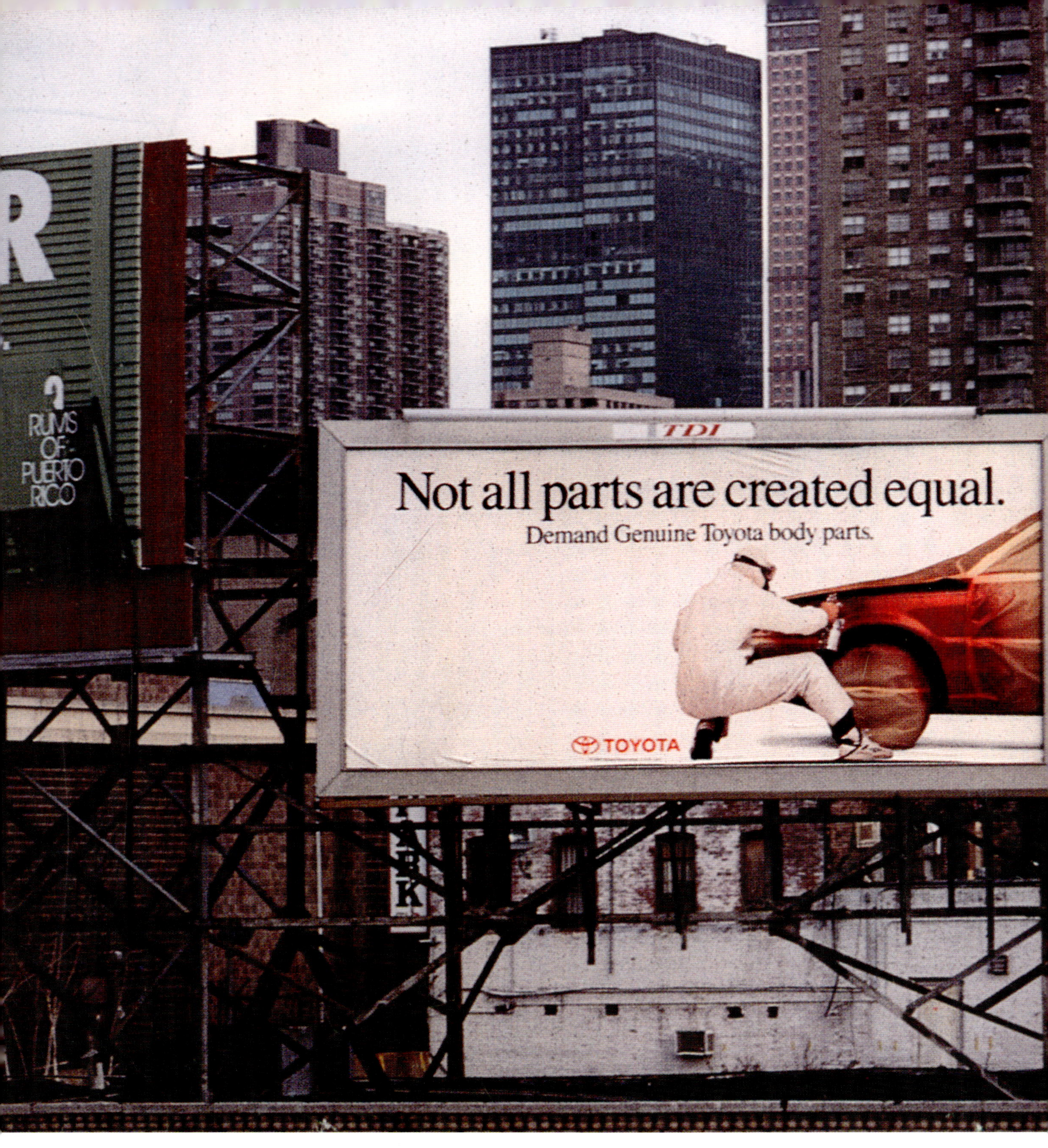
TDI
Not all parts are created equal.
Demand Genuine Toyota body parts.
TOYOTA

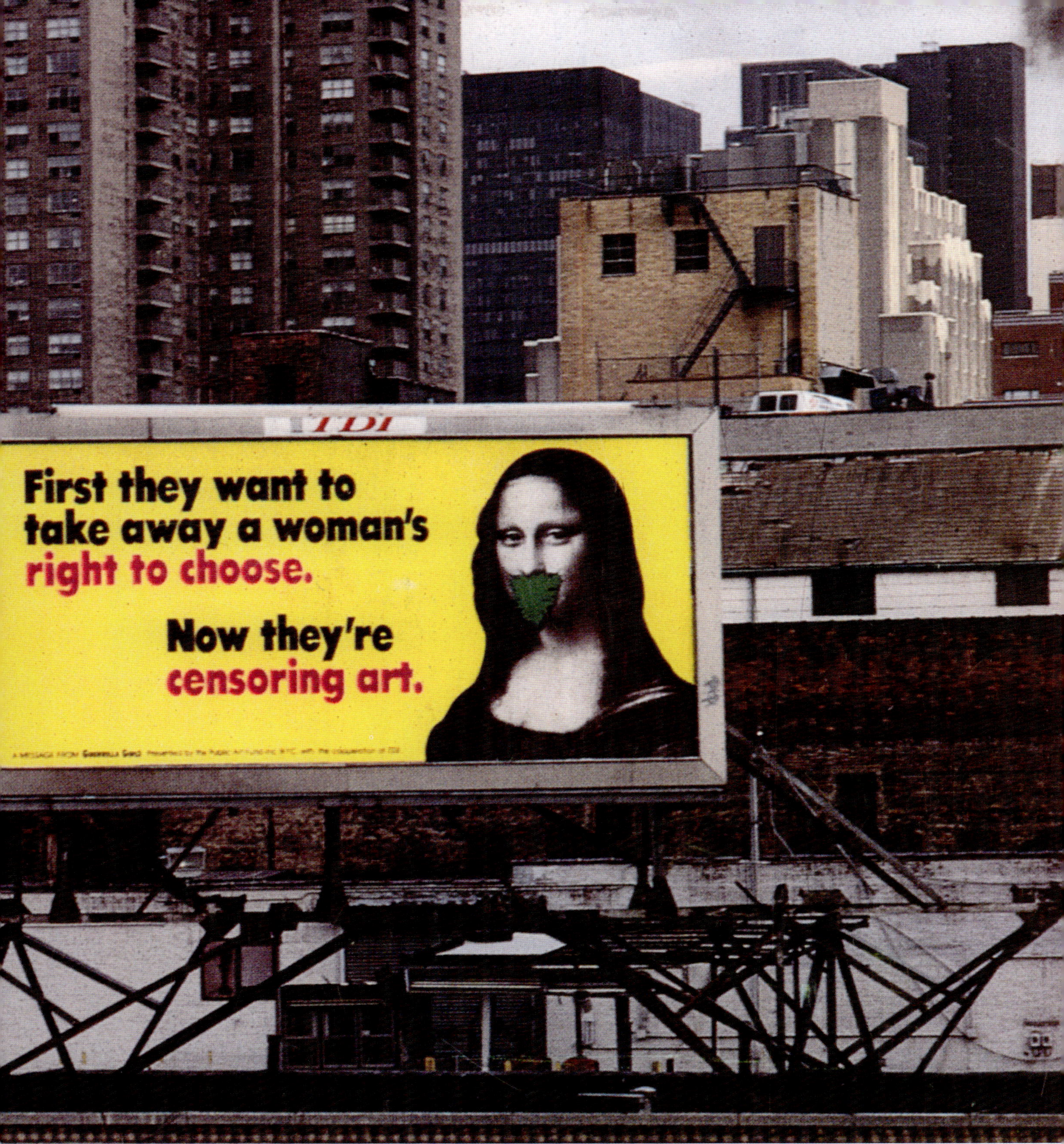

Our first billboard appeared in Manhattan during the
Congressional fight over public funding of an exhibition
of sexually explicit photographs by Robert Mapplethorpe.
We connected right wing attempts to censor art with
right wing attacks on women's reproductive rights. We
had absolutely nothing to do with the ad that ran next to it!

Billboard, 1990 (photo by Timothy P. Karr for the Public Art Fund)

"I can survive on the street."

"I know what church will give me
a hot meal.
I know where to go to keep
warm and dry.
I know where to get clothes.
I know a place to get cleaned up at.

But, I know I can't live on the
street because
MEN RAPE ME."

"I've begged."

"Yes, I have eaten out of garbage cans.
I've had coffee thrown in my face.
They tell me to get a job.
They don't know your problem.
If you stand in a food place looking
pitiful enough, someone will
buy you a sandwich.
I've had people buy me a meal and
bring it back to me, throw it in
the garbage and tell me to get it."

"What I want for Mother's Day:"

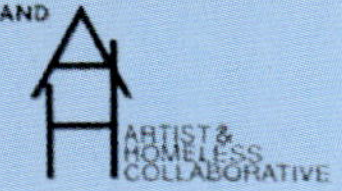

"I don't want candy.
I don't want flowers.
I want a lease
and
keys."

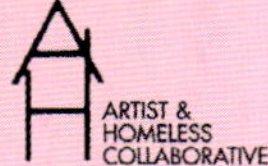

We collaborated with residents of a New York homeless shelter, and they expressed the problems they
faced as women and mothers.

Posters, 1991

THESE ARE THE MOST BIGOTED GALLERIES IN NEW YORK.

Why? Because they show the fewest women & artists of color.

GALLERY	No. of women 1989-90	Artists of Color 89-90
Blum Helman	2	0
Diane Brown	3	1
Leo Castelli	0	0
Charles Cowles	3	1
Larry Gagosian	0	0
Gemini G.E.L.	2	1
Marian Goodman	2	0
Jay Gorney	2	*
Hirschl & Adler Modern	1	0
Kent	1	0
Knoedler	1	0
Koury Wingate	1	0
David McKee	1	0
Pace	3	1
Tony Shafrazi	0	1
Holly Solomon	3	1
Sperone Westwater	1	1
Stux	0	1

Source: *Art In America Annual* 1990-91

*Tim Rollins and K.O.S.

Please send $ and comments to: **GUERRILLA GIRLS** CONSCIENCE OF THE ART WORLD
Box 237, 496 LaGuardia Pl, NY 10012

Some of the fanciest galleries in New York just didn't get it. We called them what they were.

Poster, 1991

250,000

Dear Uncle Sam and the News Media,
        The way we WON that WAR was a
BLAST, but compared to Rambo or
even Vietnam, it was a REAL SNORE.
What I like about war IS ACTION —
seeing BLOOD AND GUTS! Come on,
man, 250,000 PEOPLE GOT BLOWN AWAY!
Why couldn't we see the PIECES???
        Next time we get to KICK ASS,
you'd better show some COLLATERAL
DAMAGE, or else DON'T HOG PRIME
TIME!!!!!!!
                Yours,
                A REAL American!

250,000

The devastating Gulf War of the the first Bush presidency set the clock back on everything: women's rights, press freedom, educational policy, the environment and the hope for world peace.

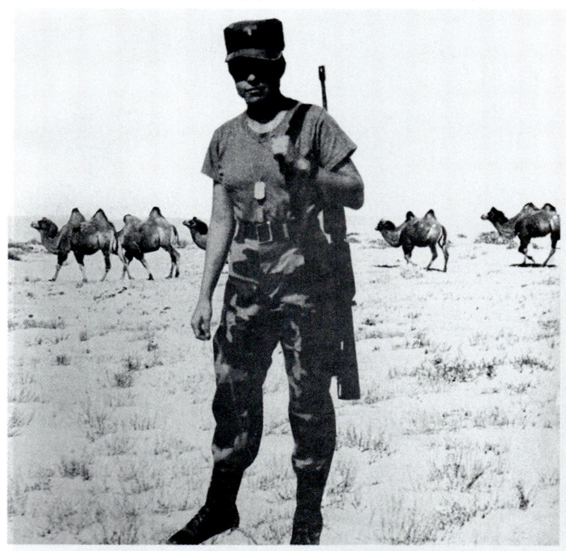

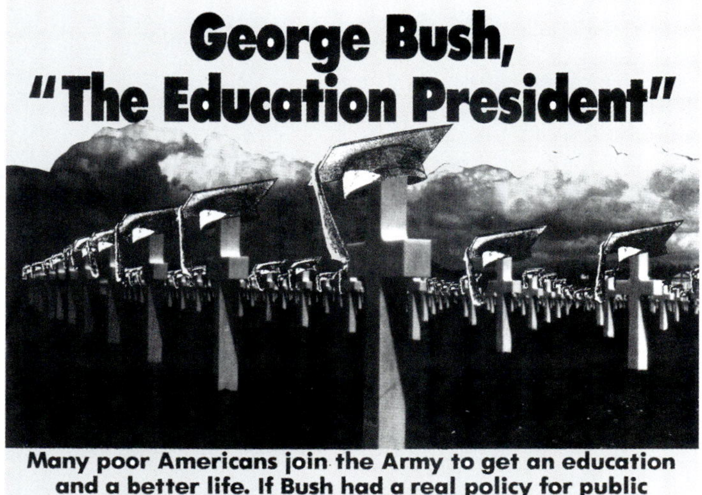

Posters, 1991

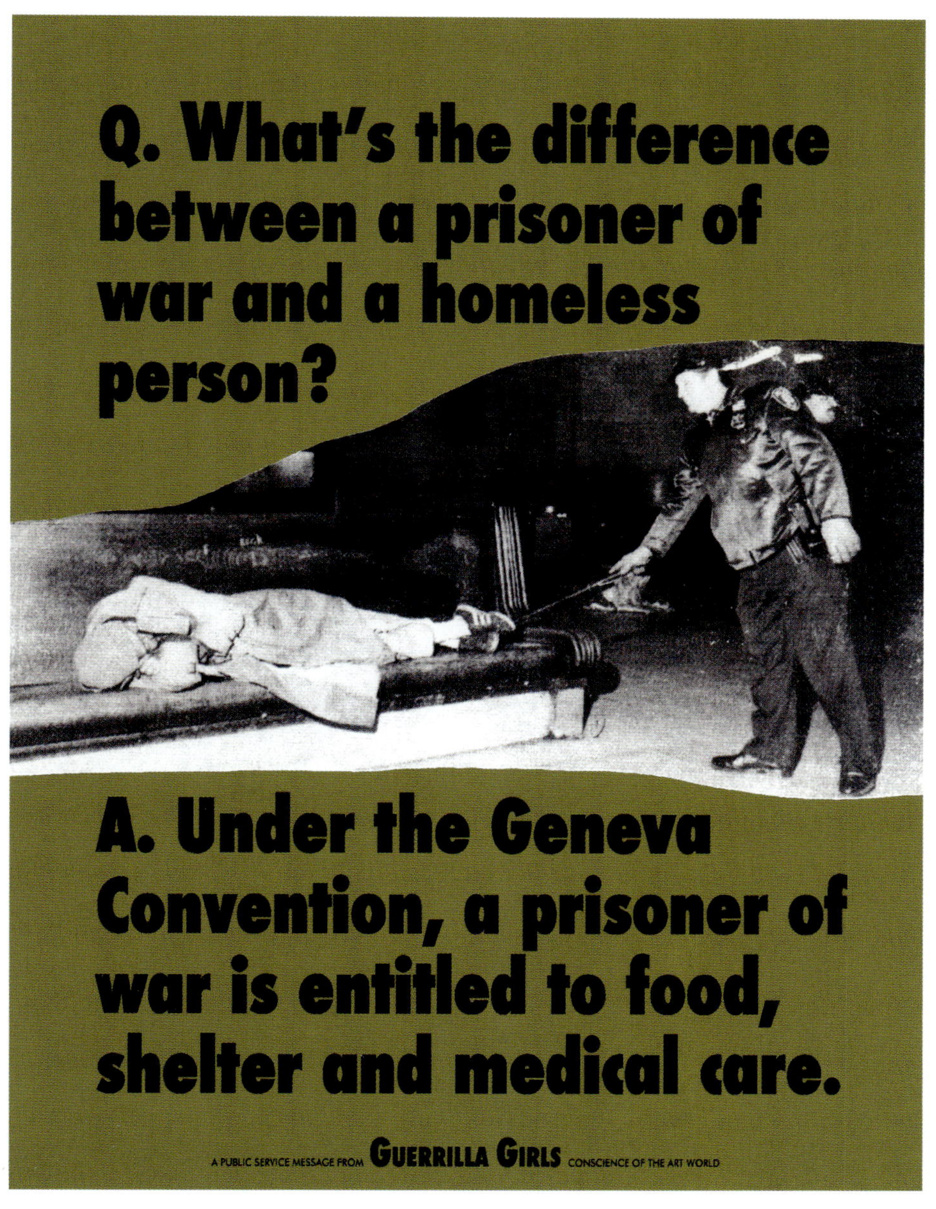

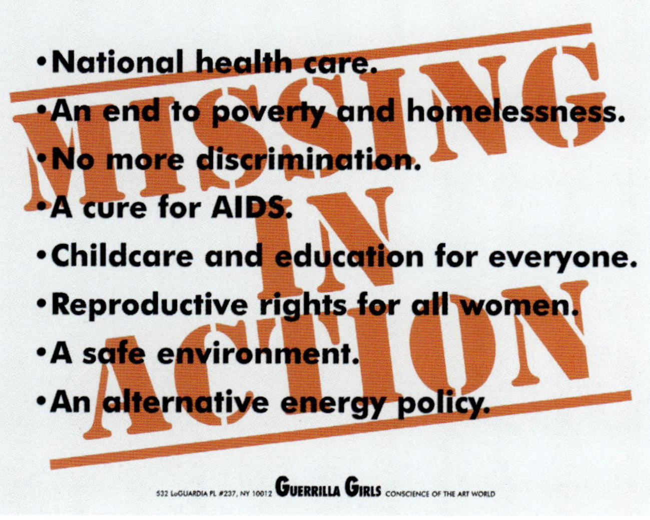

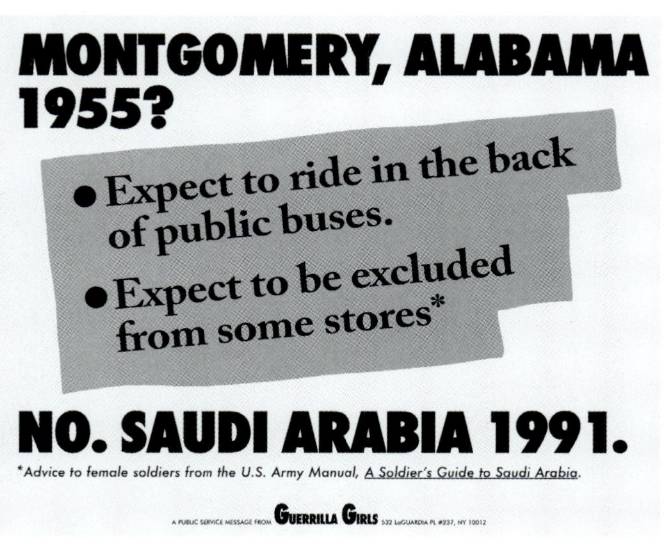

Posters, 1991

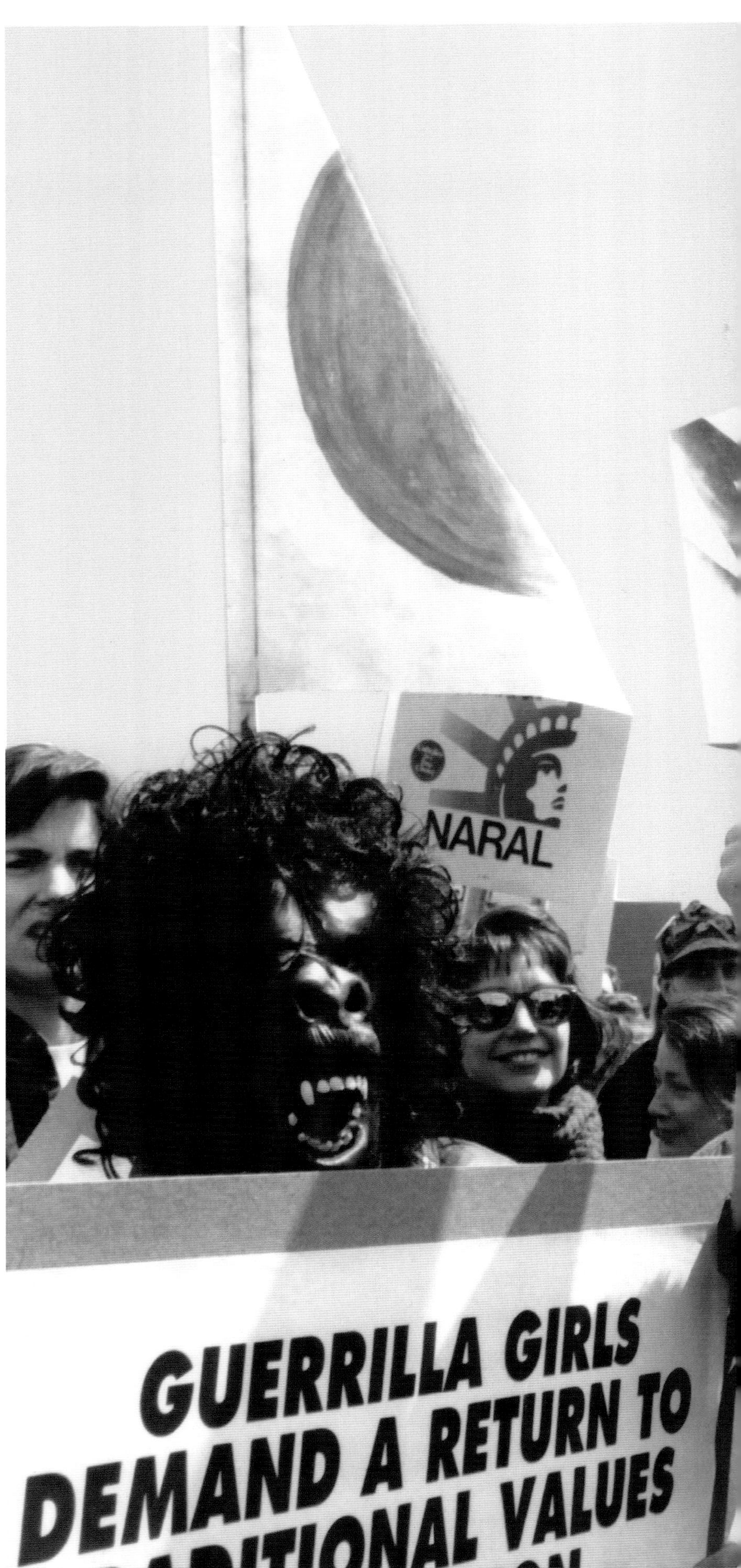

Right: Before the 20th century, abortion was legal in the U.S. This fact surprised lots of marchers at a Pro-Choice rally in Washington, D.C.

Page 44: "Natural Law" was the warped logic used by the right wing to justify sexism and homophobia.

Pro-Choice March, Washington, D.C., 1992. Photo by Teri Slotkin. Next page: *Mirabella* magazine, July 1992

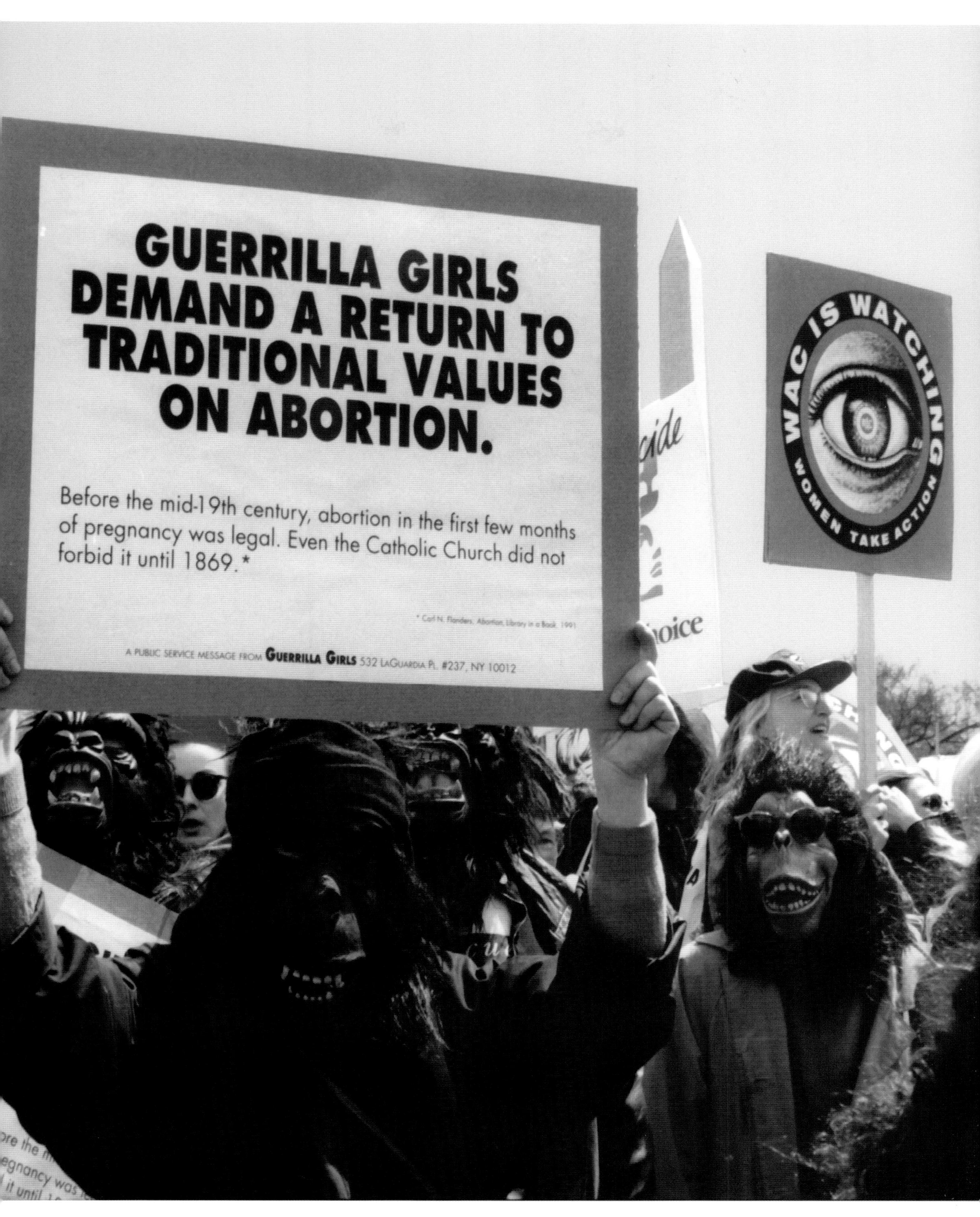

GUERRILLA GIRLS DEMAND A RETURN TO TRADITIONAL VALUES ON ABORTION.
Before the mid-19th century, abortion in the first few months of pregnancy was legal. Even the Catholic Church did not forbid it until 1869. *
* Carl N. Flanders, Abortion, Library in a Book, 1991
A PUBLIC SERVICE MESSAGE FROM GUERRILLA GIRLS 532 LaGuardia Pl. #237, NY 10012
WAC IS WATCHING
WOMEN TAKE ACTION

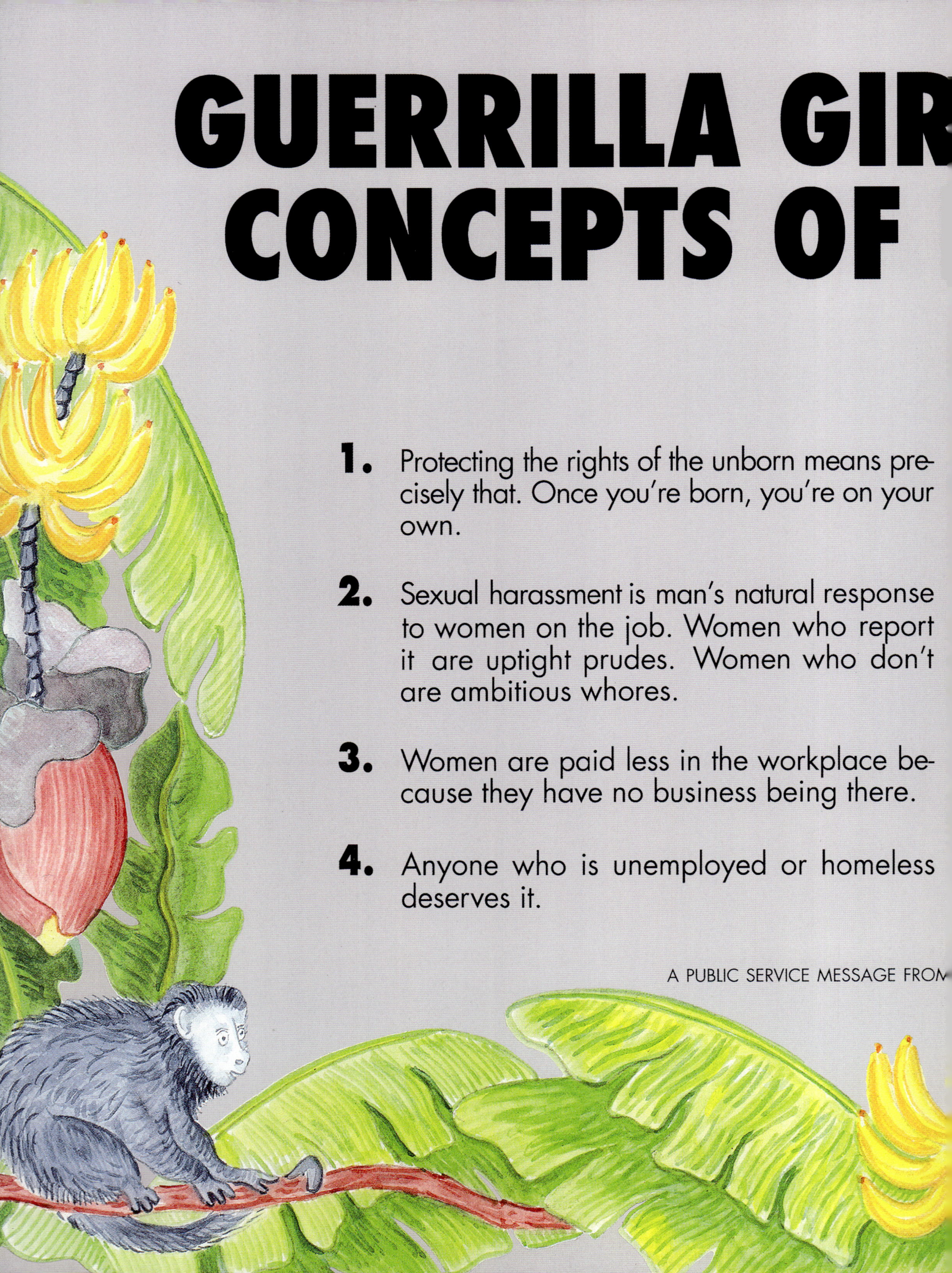

GUERRILLA GIR
CONCEPTS OF

1. Protecting the rights of the unborn means pre-cisely that. Once you're born, you're on your own.

2. Sexual harassment is man's natural response to women on the job. Women who report it are uptight prudes. Women who don't are ambitious whores.

3. Women are paid less in the workplace be-cause they have no business being there.

4. Anyone who is unemployed or homeless deserves it.

A PUBLIC SERVICE MESSAGE FROM

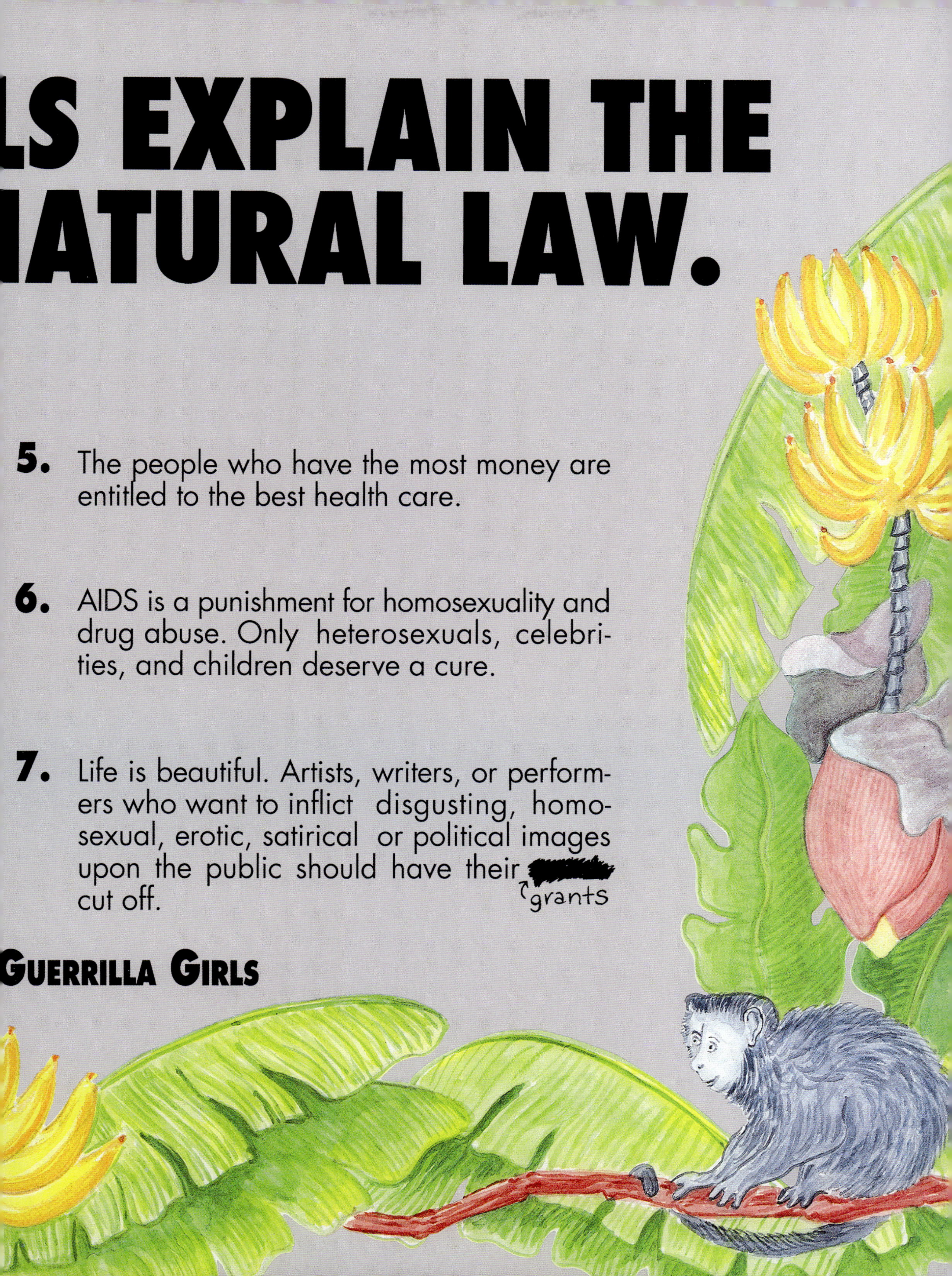
LS EXPLAIN THE
NATURAL LAW.

5. The people who have the most money are entitled to the best health care.

6. AIDS is a punishment for homosexuality and drug abuse. Only heterosexuals, celebrities, and children deserve a cure.

7. Life is beautiful. Artists, writers, or performers who want to inflict disgusting, homosexual, erotic, satirical or political images upon the public should have their grants cut off.

GUERRILLA GIRLS

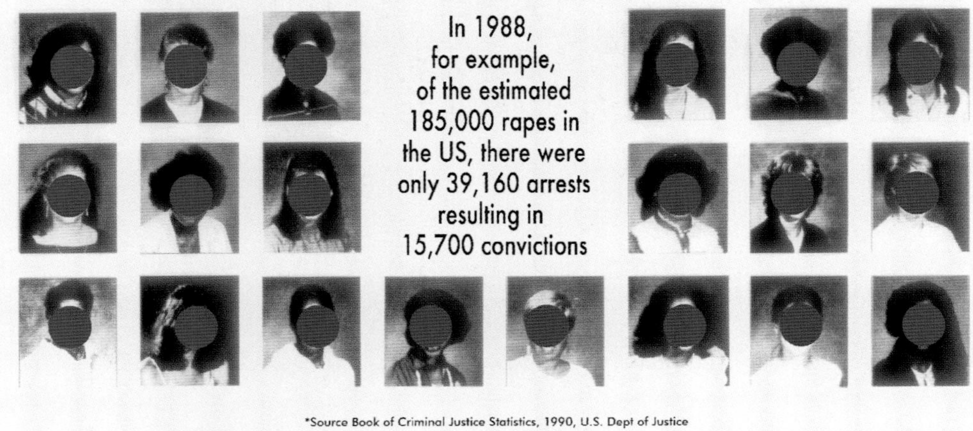

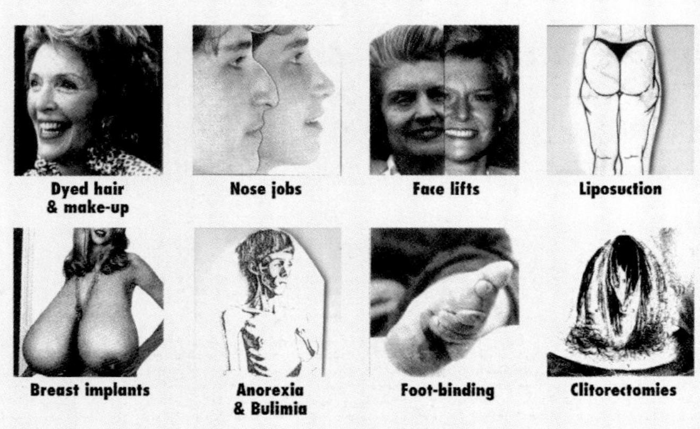

Top: In 1988, women who accused their attackers were discredited and shamed. That's still true today on college campuses, in the workplace, during Supreme Court confirmation hearings and everywhere else.

Bottom: The same people who want to deny women reproductive rights are okay with lots of other procedures done to women's bodies.

Posters, 1992

After the 1992 Los Angeles riots/rebellion, we declared that communities of color had been looted for years by racism.

Posters, 1992

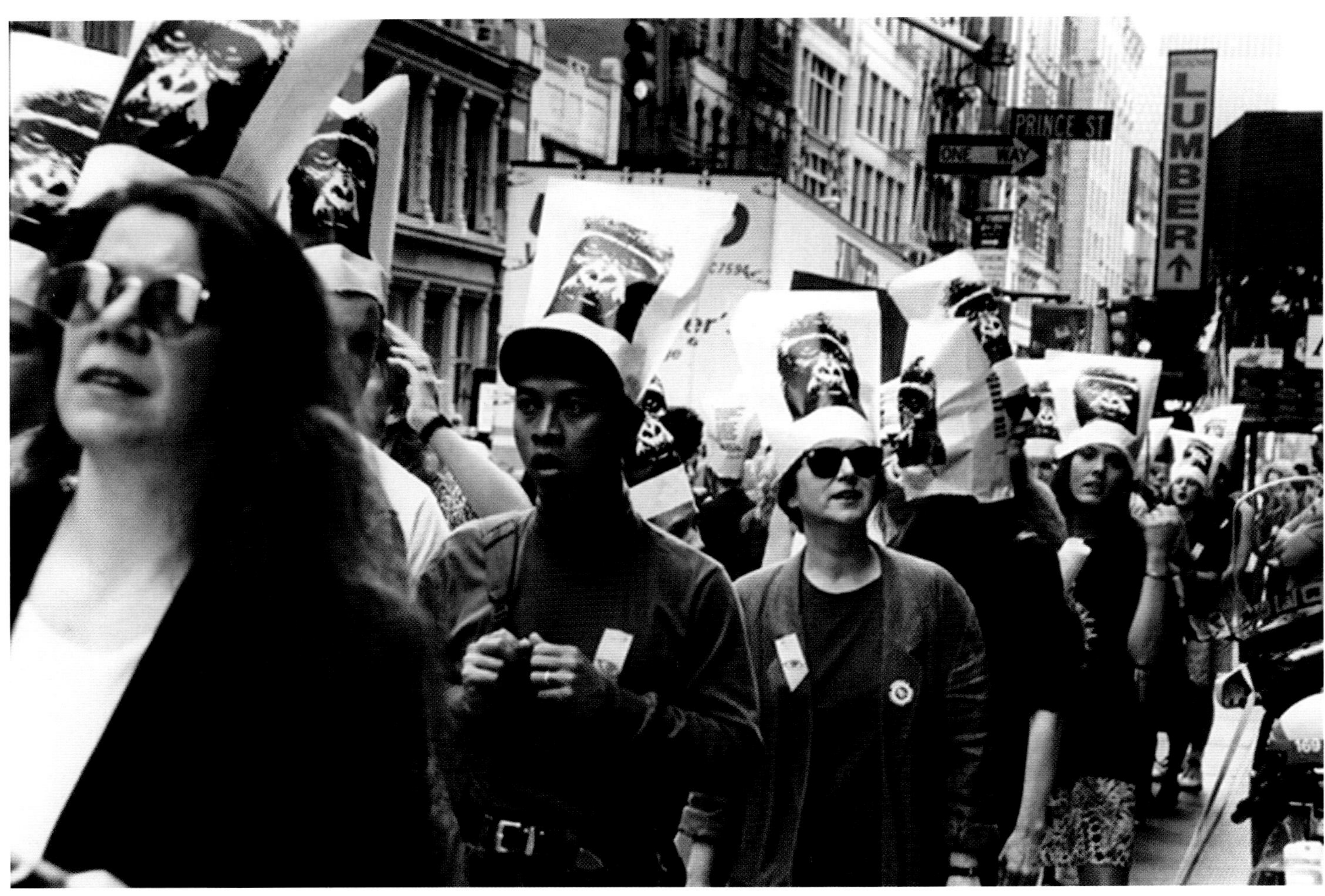

The Guggenheim Museum tried to open a downtown branch in
New York with an inaugural exhibition of four white men. With the
Women's Action Coalition (WAC), we sent thousands of threatening
postcards to director Thomas Krens. At the last minute, he added
Louise Bourgeois, but that wasn't enough. WAC staged a noisy
street demo at the opening, and hundreds of protesters wore our
gorilla mask bags. Even Louise put one on.

Protest, Guggenheim Museum, New York, 1988 (photo by Terri Slotkin)

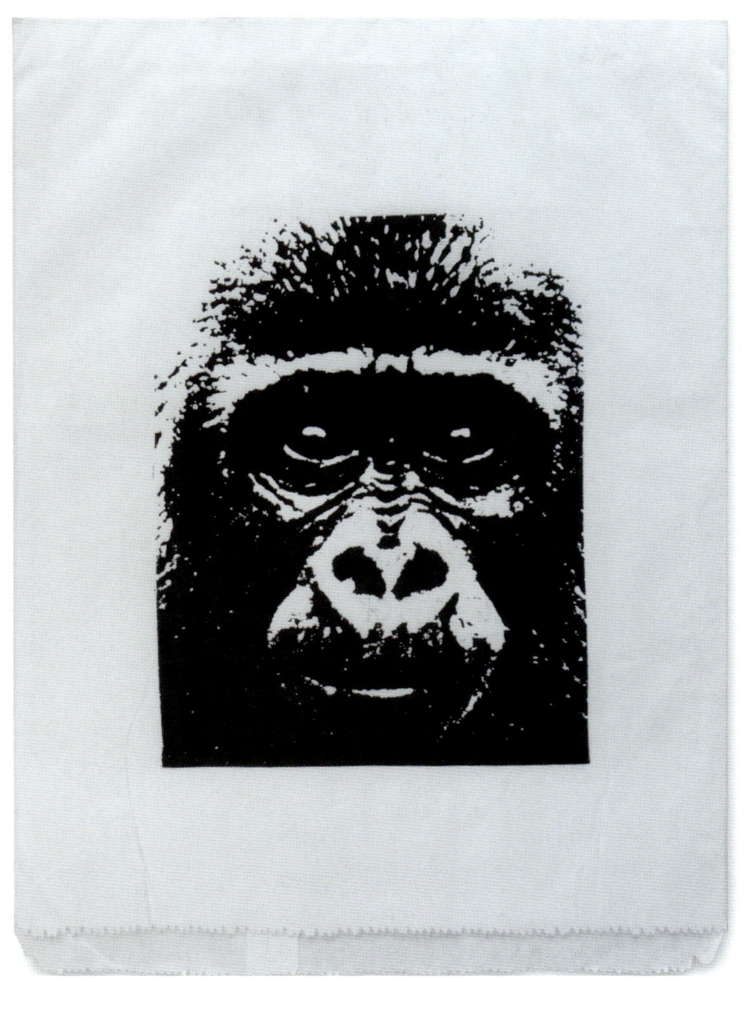

Guggenheim mask bag and postcard, 1992

SUPREME COURT JUSTICE SUPPORTS RIGHT TO PRIVACY FOR GAYS AND LESBIANS.

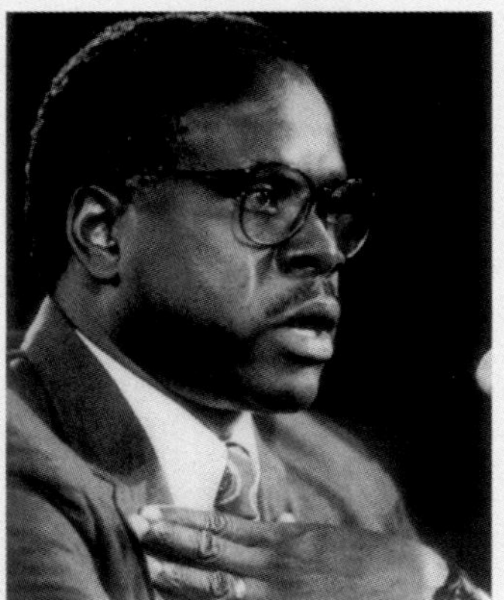

Clarence Thomas claims that a person's sex life is none of the government's business.

"I'm not going to engage in discussions of what goes on in the most intimate parts of my private life or the sanctity of my bedroom. They are the most intimate parts of my privacy and will remain just that."

—Clarence Thomas, quoted in the New York Times, 11/12/91.

A PUBLIC SERVICE MESSAGE FROM **GUERRILLA GIRLS** 532 LA GUARDIA PL #237, NY 10012

We used Clarence Thomas's own words to claim he supported LGBTQ rights. Wrong. His court decisions have reinforced discrimination, and he opposed marriage equality in 2015.

Poster, 1992

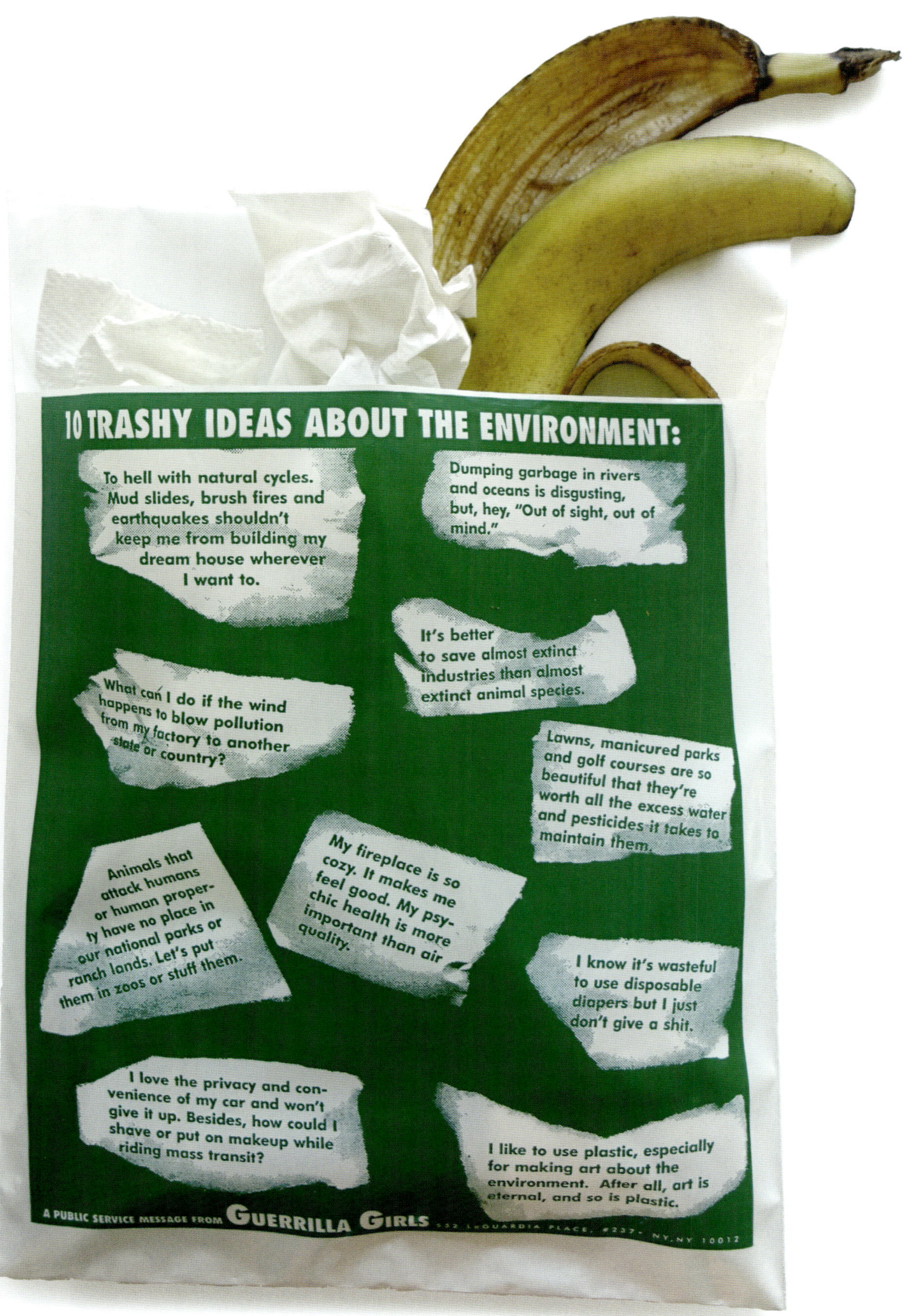

Corporate greed and consumer culture have always undermined environmentalism.

Plastic bag, 1994

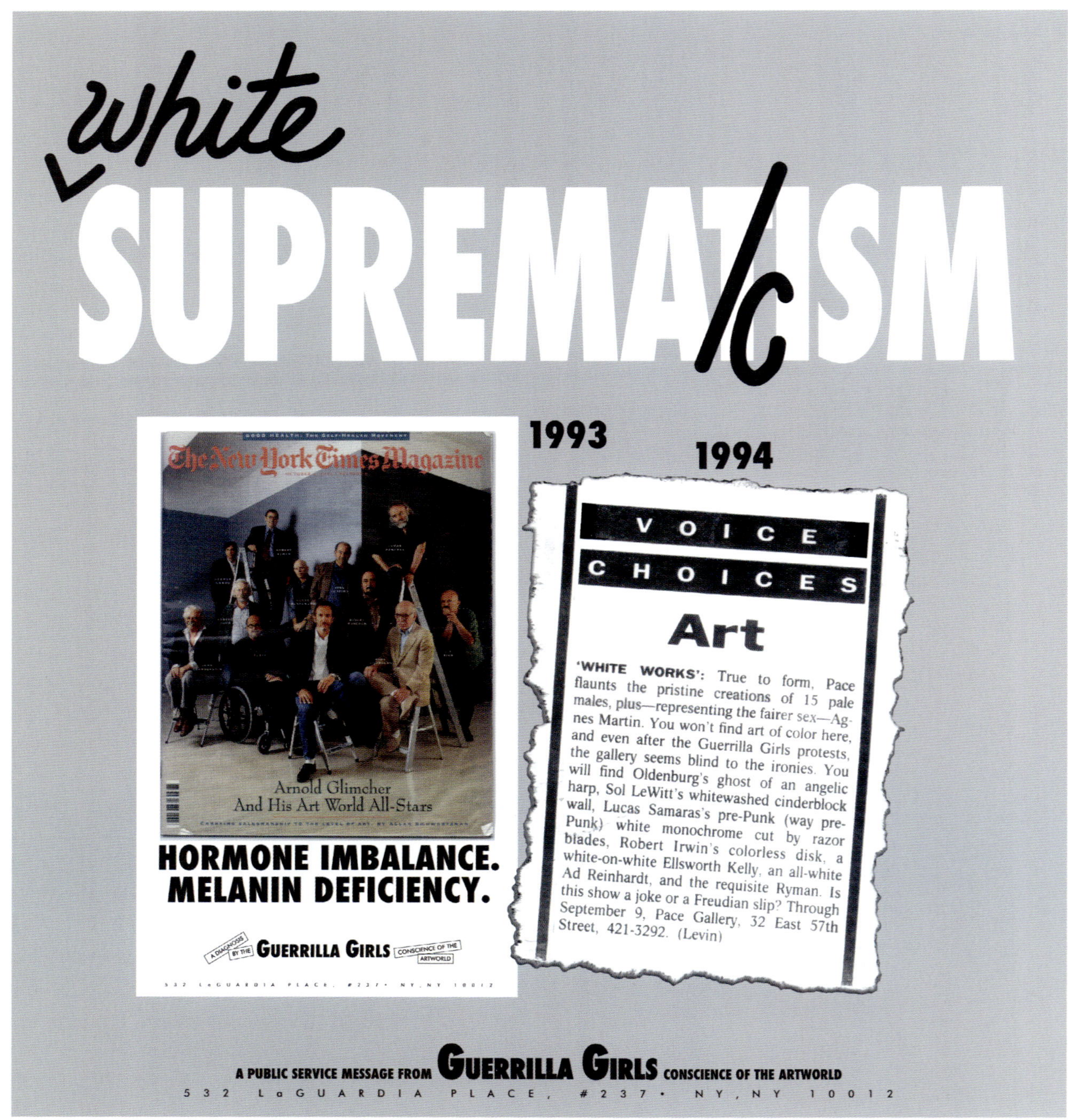

When the *New York Times Magazine* fawned over the Pace Gallery and its white male art stars, we offered a diagnosis. Pace then mounted a show of all white artworks by all white artists. We ridiculed the gallery, and art history, by turning the early-20th-century art movement Suprematism into a word to describe the artworld.

World Art magazine, 1993

ARTFORHIM

Ingrid
Editor of *Artforhim* 1985-87

	Covers	Articles*
white men	91%	80%
white women	6%	15%
men of color	3%	4%
women of color	0%	1%

Ida
Editor of *Artforhim* 1988-92

	Covers	Articles*
white men	72%	71%
white women	26%	22%
men of color	0%	5%
women of color	2%	2%

& Jack
Editor of *Artforhim* 1992-present

	Covers	Articles*
white men	67%	75%
white women	28%	21%
men of color	5%	1%
women of color	0%	3%

*We counted only feature articles on a single artist, not articles about groups of artists, not reviews.

A PUBLIC SERVICE MESSAGE FROM GUERRILLA GIRLS CONSCIENCE OF THE ARTWORLD

When we examined the record of glossy *Artforum* magazine, we gave it a new name, more in line with its content. Ida Panicelli sent a letter promising to do better. We never heard from Ingrid or Jack.

Poster, 1994

Newsletter, Vol. 1, No. 1, front and back, 1993

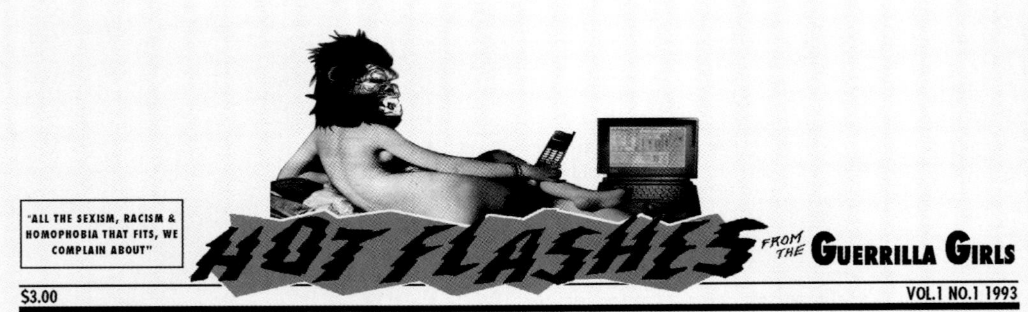

GUERRILLA GIRLS PROBE THE NEW YORK TIMES

TIMES LINE

A BRIEF HISTORY OF THE PAPER THAT'S TOO MALE, TOO PALE, TOO STALE AND TOO YALE!

1963
Ada Louise Huxtable, 42, respected architectural historian, with major books to her credit, is made Architecture Critic at *NYT*, first such position in the country.

1970
Huxtable is second woman to win Pulitzer Prize, first given for criticism.

1973
Female employees sue *NYT* for salary and promotion discrimination. Grace Glueck, Culture Editor, 1972-3, plays major role.

Paul Goldberger, student writer fresh from Yale (AB, '72), replaces Huxtable after less than a year as a copy editor. Rumor is he was pushed by Philip Johnson, who differed with Huxtable's progressive views and criticism of developers.

1974
Huxtable, who chose not to support women's lawsuit, is promoted to Editorial Board.

1976
Editor-in-Chief Abe Rosenthal creates separate daily culture section (Section C) to attract more advertisers and *New York Magazine*-style readers. Art coverage expands.

1978
Lawsuit settled. Times agrees to hire more women in top positions. But art coverage remains dominated by male Chief Critics. And no reviewers of color are hired.

1981
Staff:
Hilton Kramer, Chief Critic; Grace Glueck, Reviewer; Helen A. Harrison, Reviewer; John Russell, Reviewer; Paul Goldberger, Architecture Critic; Rita Reif, Reporter.

1982
Kramer leaves to start even more conservative journal, *The New Criterion*, funded by Olin Foundation, right-wing think tank. John Russell replaces him.

1984
Pulitzer Board overrules own jury to give prize to Goldberger. *NYT* fails to mention unusual circumstances of award in its announcement.

1985
Art market boom. Auction houses flourish. Coverage of art expands again. Staff: William Honan, Culture Editor; John Russell, Chief Critic; Vivian Raynor, Reviewer; Grace Glueck, Reviewer; Helen A. Harrison, Reviewer; Michael Brenson, Reviewer; Paul Goldberger, Architecture Critic; Rita Reif, Reporter.

1988
Michael Kimmelman arrives as an art reviewer after attending Yale and Harvard and winning second prize in a piano competition.

1990
Yalie Goldberger becomes Culture Editor. Honan demoted to writing about the NEA. Goldberger promotes Yalie Kimmelman to Chief Critic over veteran critic and Johns Hopkins Ph.D. Brenson, who wrote too many articles on sculpture, women, artists of color and alternative spaces.

Richard Bernstein denounces multiculturalism in Sunday Arts and Leisure article, "The Arts Catch Up With a Society in Disarray."

1991
Rita Reif, Auction Reporter, exposes Sotheby's scheme to quietly finance auction purchases and inflate market prices. Sotheby's, major *NYT* advertiser, is forced to discontinue practice. Reif is removed from auction beat.

1992
Art market crashes. *NYT* covers auction collapse gingerly. Number of reviews half of 1985 coverage. Public funding and NEA crises mentioned only in passing.

Staff: See "Scientific Study...", *at right.*

1993 AND BEYOND
Goldberger depressed, secretly believing wrong Yalie won Presidential election, ushers in new age of Reluctant Liberalism and allows a bit more coverage of women and artists of color. Hiring practices, however, remain the same: male reviewers are given powerful positions fresh from Yale; women must prove themselves in the field and never become Chief Critic; people of color need not apply.

DEEP DISHING: WHO GOT THE BIGGEST PIECE OF THE CRITICS PIE?

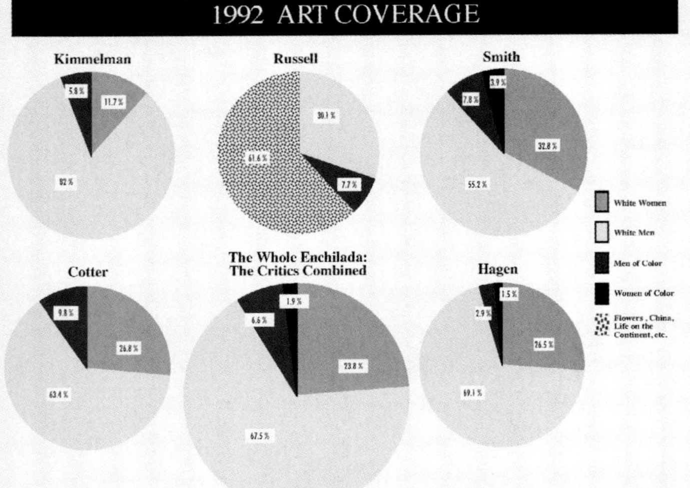

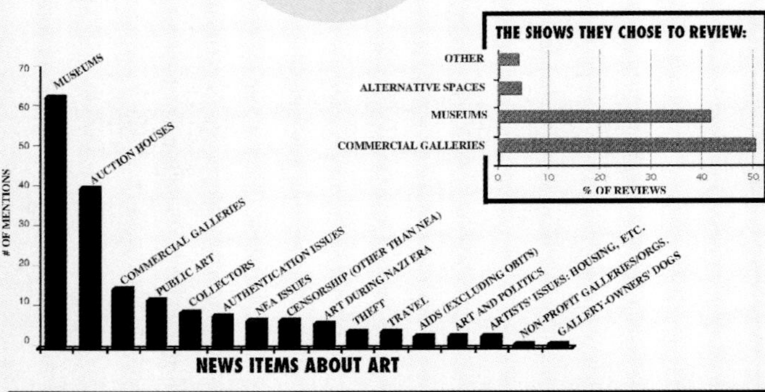

SCIENTIFIC STUDY PROVES NYT ART WRITERS ARE CHANNELERS FOR THE CULTURAL ELITE!

Guerrilla Girls researched the present *Times* art writers. Seldom having reputations outside the paper and allowing their writing to be so tightly edited that it cannot have an individual voice, we concluded that they are Messengers of Good Taste, anointed by the *Times* establishment out of loyalty, persistence or connections. What they say is not as important as who and what they cover. A profile and analysis of each follows:

Paul Goldberger, Culture Editor. 40 ish white male, powerbroker of the cultural page, began as architecture critic one year out of Yale(see *Times* line). Won Pulitzer Prize in 1984 under suspicious circumstances (see *Times* line). Ambitious follower, not leader. Is uncritical of social and political issues in own field. Thought to be cozy with big real estate interests and small group of chosen architects, all white and mostly male. Most penetrating 1992 feature: "25 Years of Unabashed Elitism, the Design of Ralph Lauren". Sponsored Richard Bernstein's attack on multiculturalism in 1990, then allowed increased coverage of women and artists of color in 1992. Out of tune with the times but in step with the *Times.*

Michael Kimmelman, Chief Art Critic. 30 ish white Yale wunderkind, considered "Renaissance Man" by editors. Once wrote about music and was made chief Art Critic in 1990 despite lack of experience or distinction as an art writer. Covers establishment beat and specializes in white males. Friday reviews are more conservative than Sunday features. Only reviews women who are famous or dead, providing their work appears in a major museum. Was he revolted by 1993 Whitney Biennial *because* it had the best representation ever of women and artists of color?

John Russell, Retired Chief Critic. White Eminence Gris, wrote as many Sunday features in 1992 as Kimmelman. Chatty anglophile, subscribes to Laura Ashley school of writing, covering all the bright and beautiful aspects of culture. Ignored women artists in 1992, did occasional features on males of color, when they showed in museums. Can even write about Russian Constructivism without mentioning politics. *(cont'd on back)*

Roberta Smith, Staff Art Critic.
40ish white female, only full time reviewer besides Kimmelman. Earned position after long career in galleries and art criticism. Most adventurous, has best record for covering women. Rumored to call shots at *Times* on current art. Feminist, but writes about women artists as a group, often as victims, or as appropriators of male art. Guerrilla Girls wouldn't think of saying anything bad about her: she wrote favorable article about us in 1991.

Holland Cotter, Non-staff Reviewer.
White male "stringer," paid by the article. Came to *NYT* from art mags. Did the most Friday reviews in '92. Interesting pattern in writing: worst record for women, but best record for artists of color, especially males, and best record for alternative spaces. Not trusted to do Sunday features on contemporary art; covers historical and non-Western subjects instead.

Charles Hagen, Non-staff Reviewer.
Another white male "stringer," rumored to moonlight to support his habit of writing for the *Times*. Came from photography world. Can write about politics, but deferred to Kimmelman to trash Serrano. Worst record for covering alternative spaces, but second best on women.

Vicki Goldberg, Photography Reviewer.
50ish white female stringer, established writer with reputation outside *NYT*. Didn't write enough reviews in '92 for pie chart, but was allowed to write about pop culture: article on the politics of Benetton ads and review of Madonna's *Sex*.

William Honan, Cultural Correspondent, former Culture Editor.
White old-boy newsman. Deposed by Goldberger in 1990 (see *Times* Line.) Consolation prize: covering art news, in particular NEA and censorship issues. Rumored not to have heard of the Guerrilla Girls as late as Spring, 1992.

Rita Reif, Reporter.
60ish white female, seasoned art market maven at *Times* since 1948, starting as clerk. Developed auction coverage through the 80's boom, but was abruptly removed from beat in 1991 (see *Times* Line.) Subject of scathing story in *Art and Antiques*, January, 1991.

Carol Vogel, Reporter.
White female, up and coming author of Art Market column, which has prospered as reviews have shrunk. Avoids controversial subjects like insider trading and conflicts of interest in favor of chatter about prominent collectors, lawsuits and gallery closings.

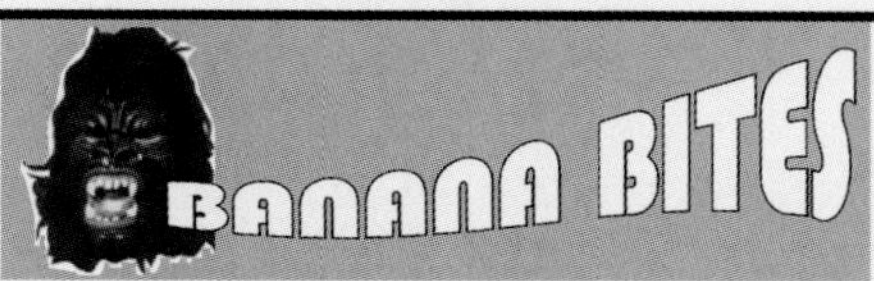

In an average month last year, the *NYT* reviewed 25 art exhibitions. (There are over 575 listed per month in the *Gallery Guide*.) In 1985, the *NYT* reviewed over 60 shows a month.

Ellsworth Kelly was the subject of 2 Sunday feature articles in 1992, surpassed only by Picasso, who got 3, 2 from John Russell alone.

There were not less than 5 NYT articles on the Matisse opening at MOMA.

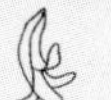

The *Times* covered Dan Flavin's wedding in the Guggenheim Museum, during its opening, rather than a demonstration organized by WAC at the same time to protest the museum's exclusion of women and artists of color. More people attended the demonstration than the wedding.

No *Times* writer is allowed to accept a gift worth over $15. If you've ever visited John Russell, you may wonder how he managed to acquire his extensive art collection on a critic's salary.

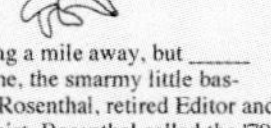

The word "Ms." was not permitted until 1986 and can only be applied to a woman born in the U.S.

Larry Gagosian, one of the *NYT's* largest gallery advertisers, was granted Most-Favored-Gallery Status in '92, with several lengthy feature articles.

Sotheby's and Christie's spent over $750,000. on *NYT* ads in 1992. Is it any wonder that the Times created a special column just to cover auctions?

In June, 1992, the Art Market column reported that Sotheby's went public. It did not mention the $275. million windfall profit that Alfred Taubman, Sotheby's CEO and Whitney Museum Trustee, earned in the deal. That tidbit appeared only in the Business section.

While many museums and public institutions engaged in questionable practices during the past year, the *NYT* singled out the Barnes Foundation, controlled by African American Lincoln University, at least 3 times. No other institution received such bad press.

"I can spot a fag a mile away, but ______ really fooled me, the smarmy little bastard." -- A.M. Rosenthal, retired Editor and current columnist. Rosenthal called the '70s sex discrimination suit against the *NYT* an infringement of his First Amendment rights.

The word "gay" was banned until 1975, the word "anal-intercourse" until 1985. Same-sex couples were not acknowledged in obituaries until 1983.

If you want to read about AIDS in the artworld, you'll find more on the obituary page than in the culture section.

At least 3 times in 199: a woman artist was identified in a review as "the wife of..." In 2 of the reviews, the fact was mentioned in the second line. In the third, her work was compared unfavorably to his.

During all of 1992, the *NYT* made no mention of women or artists of color in it's auction coverage.

GUERRILLA GIRLS RECIPE FOR A NEW, IMPROVED NYT:

1. Bring back Michael Brenson; find a critic of color; put a hiring freeze on young white men from the Ivy League.

2. To achieve gender and racial parity in reviews, devote the next 100 years to covering only women and artists of color.

3. Print fewer authoritative opinions from uninteresting, over-edited writers, and feature more articles where artists speak for themselves.

4. Make more connections between High Culture and Culture-at-large, not just between High Culture and High Money.

5. Pay the same attention to ethical issues in the artworld as the *Times* does in politics and business, including conflicts of interest, insider trading, price-fixing, discrimination, harassment, unfair hiring practices, civil rights violations, etc.

EDITORIAL STATEMENT: GUERRILLA GIRLS are devoting the premiere issue of our new quarterly, *Hot Flashes*, to an examination of the U.S. newspaper of record, *The New York Times*. And what a record it is! Future issues will explore the national picture, multiculturalism and social class in the artworld. Ideas, articles and comments are welcomed.

SUBSCRIPTIONS (4 issues) are $9. for women and people of color, $12. for white males.

Funded in part with a grant from the National Endowment for the Arts, a Federal Agency.

c/o GUERRILLA GIRLS, 532 LaGuardia Pl. #237, New York, NY 10012

HOT FLASHES

OBITCHUARY DEPT.

GUERRILLA GIRLS REVISIONIST HISTORY QUIZ:

One of the following obituaries really appeared in the *NYT*. One was written by the Guerrilla Girls, with the help of a well-known art historian. Can you tell which is which?

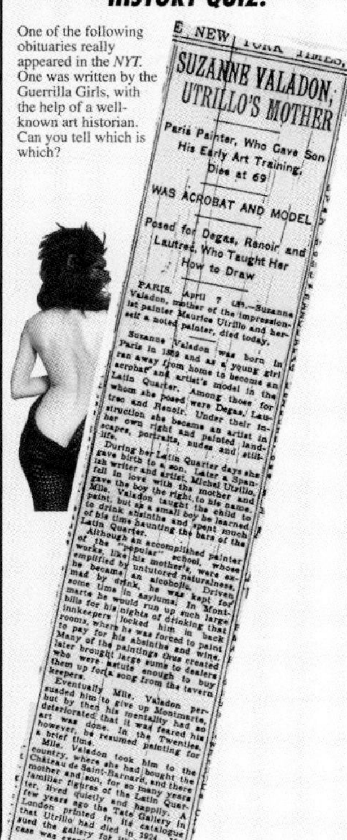

THE NEW YORK TIMES

SUZANNE VALADON, UTRILLO'S MOTHER

Paris Painter, Who Gave Son His Early Art Training, Dies at 69

WAS ACROBAT AND MODEL

Posed for Degas, Renoir and Lautrec, Who Taught Her How to Draw

PARIS, April 7 (AP)—Suzanne Valadon, mother of the impressionist painter Maurice Utrillo and herself a noted painter, died today.

MARY CASSATT, IMPRESSIONIST PAINTER, IS DEAD AT 81

PARIS, JULY, 1926- Mary Cassatt, the American painter who fled Philadelphia in 1866 to escape resistance to both women artists and modern ideas about painting, died yesterday in Paris, at the age of 81. While the earlier deaths of Whistler and Sargent, American artists who lived in Europe and built their reputations there, received elaborate coverage in the New York Times, the paper was silent on Cassatt's death and ignored her contributions to art, and to art collecting in the U.S.

Cassatt was the only American artist and the second woman painter whose work was given the respect and admiration of the Almost-All-Male Club of Impressionists. This was a feat, considering the fact that she was never known to have posed nude for any of them, or borne their illegitimate children.

While Cassatt's sex was not in her favor as a painter, her social class was. She was able to use her position as the daughter of a wealthy industrialist to navigate the sexism of her age. Able to leave the U.S. and its intolerance, and denied entrance to the free Ecole des Beaux Arts in Paris because she was a woman, Cassatt had the means to afford private instruction. This separated her from her less-monied sister-artists, who had little choice but to take off their clothes to gain access to the "master" painters of the time.

Cassatt put her private fortune to good use, especially in 1898 when she returned to the U.S. to promote her work and encourage wealthy friends to collect the new art from Europe. Undaunted by the rejection of her own painting because of prejudice, she was still able to influence the formation of a major American collection, the Havemeyer Collection, housed at the Philadelphia Museum of Art, which initiated an era of collecting in this country. Cassatt's persistence was responsible for the extensive collections of Impressionism in American Museums. No other artist of her time could claim that kind of influence.

While the political lives of male artists like Courbet and Pissarro were touted in the writing of art history, little has been mentioned about Cassatt, who was an early feminist, involved in the Suffrage movement. She encouraged many women artists who sought careers in France.

Standard art history, following Victorian social values, dismissed Cassatt as a childless, frustrated spinster who compensated for her own maternal lack by painting portraits of women and children. In fact, Cassatt did not lack a family life, helping to raise a number of nieces and nephews who came to live with her in Paris in the 1870's. What's more, the scenes of domestic life for which Cassatt is best known comprise less than a third of her output. While her male colleagues were hailed at the Painters of Modern Life for their depictions of the commonplace, a double standard was applied to Cassatt, whose use of similar subject matter was judged less important and trivial.

A closer examination of Cassatt's work shows that she depicted women actively, at work, at women's work, not as passive models or mere spectacle as did many of the male Impressionists. Her use of shifting perspective and planar spatial representation, based on her study of Japanese prints, was a radical revision in the history of European painting. Her scenes of women in domestic situations, especially a 10-print series in 1891, influenced the young painter Matisse, who, all the same, continued to paint women as delectable, passive objects.

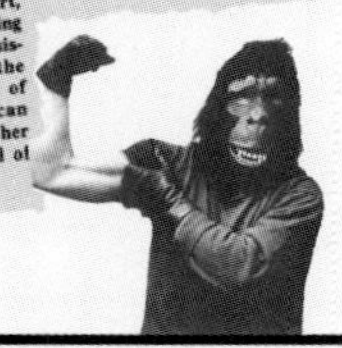

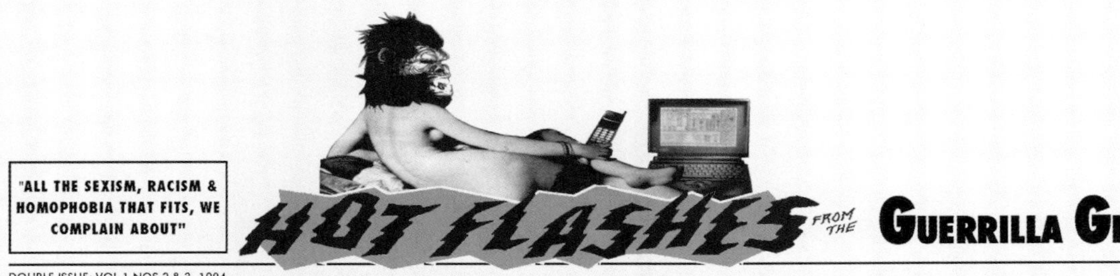

GUERRILLA GIRLS PREDICT THAT MUSEUMS IN THE EAST WILL HAVE A WHITE MALE WINTER. AND A WHITE MALE SPRING, SUMMER & FALL.

% OF SOLO EXHIBITS FEATURING WOMEN AND ARTISTS OF COLOR AT A SAMPLING OF MUSEUMS FROM EACH REGION.

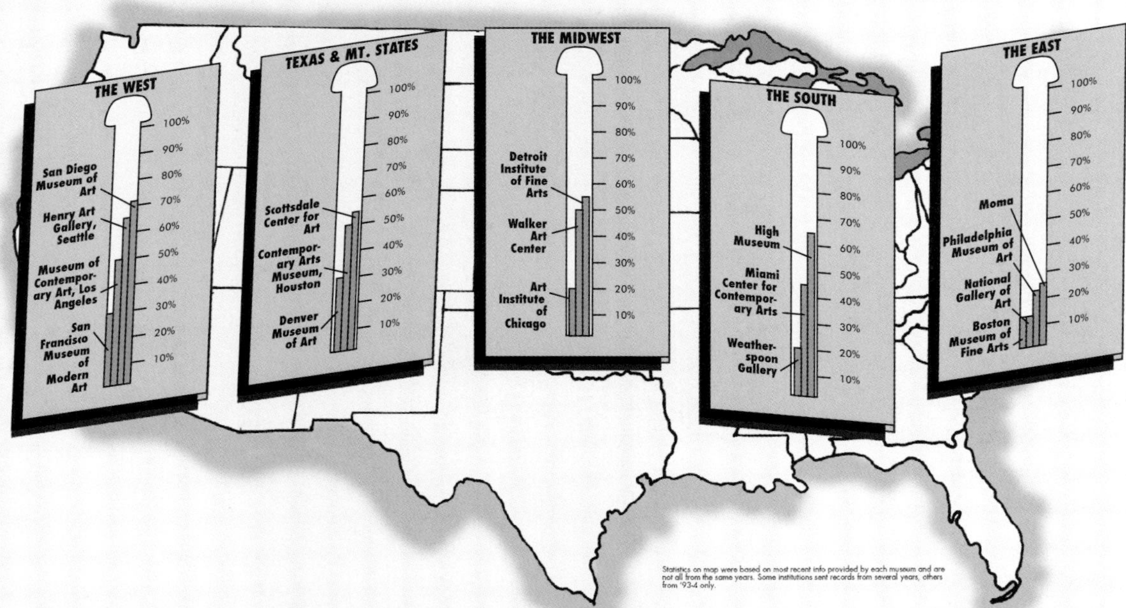

SUMMARY: The West is best, the East is worst. Women of color have a hard time everywhere.

Editorial Statement: .
It is an indisputable fact that over the years American museums have presented only a part of the story of our culture. The systematic exclusion of women and artists of color from exhibitions and acquisitions should not continue.
Some museums are working toward change; others are resolute. For this special double issue of *Hot Flashes,* Guerrilla Girls asked museums around the U.S. to tell us what they're doing.*

*All information contained in this issue of *HF* was taken from promotional materials provided by the museums.

Newsletter, Vol. 1, Nos. 2 & 3, pages 1–3, 1994

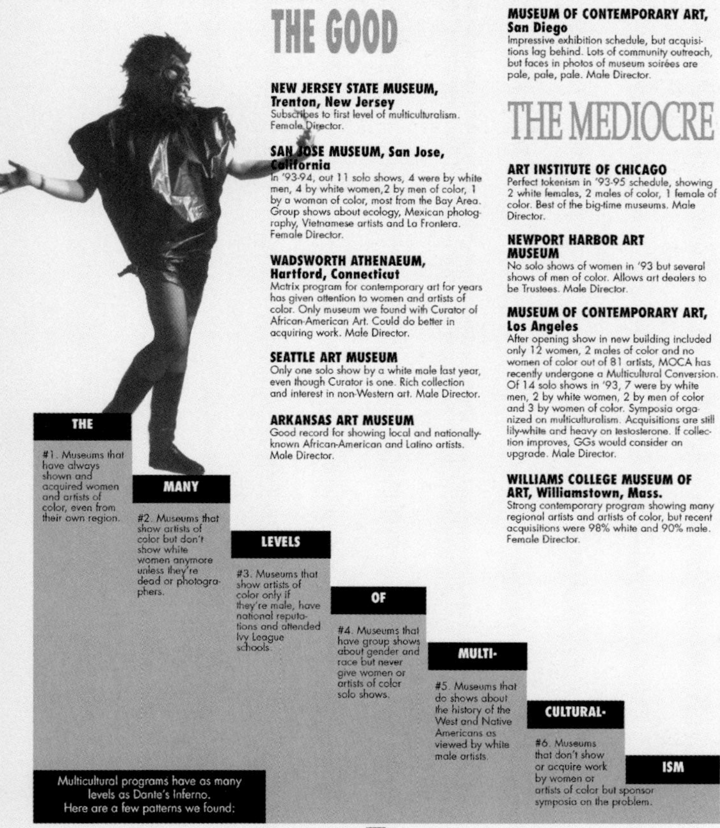

THE GOOD

NEW JERSEY STATE MUSEUM, Trenton, New Jersey
Subscribes to first level of multiculturalism. Female Director.

SAN JOSE MUSEUM, San Jose, California
In '93-94, out 11 solo shows, 4 were by white men, 4 by white women, 2 by men of color, 1 by a woman of color, most from the Bay Area. Group shows about ecology, Mexican photography, Vietnamese artists and La Frontera. Female Director.

WADSWORTH ATHENAEUM, Hartford, Connecticut
Matrix program for contemporary art for years has given attention to women and artists of color. Only museum we found with Curator of African-American Art. Could do better in acquiring work. Male Director.

SEATTLE ART MUSEUM
Only one solo show by a white male last year, even though Curator is one. Rich collection and interest in non-Western art. Male Director.

ARKANSAS ART MUSEUM
Good record for showing local and nationally-known African-American and Latino artists. Male Director.

MUSEUM OF CONTEMPORARY ART, San Diego
Impressive exhibition schedule, but acquisitions lag behind. Lots of community outreach, but faces in photos of museum soirées are pale, pale, pale. Male Director.

THE MEDIOCRE

ART INSTITUTE OF CHICAGO
Perfect tokenism in '93-95 schedule, showing 2 white females, 2 males of color, 1 female of color. Best of the big-time museums. Male Director.

NEWPORT HARBOR ART MUSEUM
No solo shows of women in '93 but several shows of men of color. Allows art dealers to be Trustees. Male Director.

MUSEUM OF CONTEMPORARY ART, Los Angeles
After opening show in new building included only 12 women, 2 males of color and no women of color out of 81 artists, MOCA has recently undergone a Multicultural Conversion. Of 14 solo shows in '93, 7 were by white men, 2 by white women, 2 by men of color and 3 by women of color. Symposia organized on multiculturalism. Acquisitions are still lily-white and heavy on testosterone. If collection improves, GGs would consider an upgrade. Male Director.

WILLIAMS COLLEGE MUSEUM OF ART, Williamstown, Mass.
Strong contemporary program showing many regional artists and artists of color, but recent acquisitions were 98% white and 90% male. Female Director.

WALKER ART CENTER, Minneapolis
Shows women, but weak on women of color. Prestigious sculpture garden is 72% white and male. Female Director.

MUSEUM OF CONTEMPORARY ART, Chicago
Generous to white women, stingy on multiculturalism: artists of color ghettoized into group and/or summer shows. Male Director.

HENRY ART GALLERY, UNIV. OF WASHINGTON, Seattle
Commendable schedule for artists of color in '93, but white women paid the price. Acquisitions still white and male. Male Director.

THE BAD

HARVARD UNIVERSITY MUSEUMS
Solo shows are exclusively by white males. Women are allowed in group shows and may give gallery talks. No visible multicultural programs. Historical shows heavy on connoisseurship and light on new ideas. Wins GG Award for the Richest, Deadist Museum in the U.S. Male Director.

BOSTON MUSEUM OF FINE ARTS
Only one white female solo show in '93-4, none by artists of color. Lumps non-Western art into group shows. Acquires paintings by white men only, but will accept some photographs by women. Speaker program, however, is primarily female. Has Committee on Connections to try to make things better. Male Director.

THE SAN FRANCISCO MUSEUM OF MODERN ART
Only women to get solo shows are photographers and they don't get collected by the museum. Artists of color must have national reputations and their shows are imported from other places. Acquires painting and sculpture by white males only. Has task force for multicultural programming. Male Director.

ALBRIGHT-KNOX MUSEUM, Buffalo
Family affair for the Knoxes of Buffalo, despite fact that nearly 30% of income is from government sources. Specializes in exhibits about sports, ignores issues of diversity. Solo male shows get catalogs; lone woman in '91-3 got brochure. Recent acquisitions and Board of Trustees are both 87% male. Worst multicultural record in the Rust Belt. Male Director.

THE PITS: MUSEUMS IN NEW YORK CITY

The most shocking discovery was how rotten museums are in the Big Apple. Run by Directors, Curators and Trustees who wheel and deal in the art market, we created this special category just for them.

THE GUGGENHEIM:
All shows but 1 in '92-94 went to white males. Lots of dead white women were included in Russian Constructivist show (which the Guggie did NOT organize) none could be found in "Italian Art from 1943-68" and most of the women in a show of Contemporary German Photography were members of husband-wife teams. Consistently ignores artists of color. Is recipient of the GG Award for the Most Eurocentric Art Museum in the New World; even hires German artist to do show about Native Americans. Exhibition titled "Total Risk" is 100% white and 89% male. Acquisition record even worse. Only major Manhattan art museum without an African-American Curator.

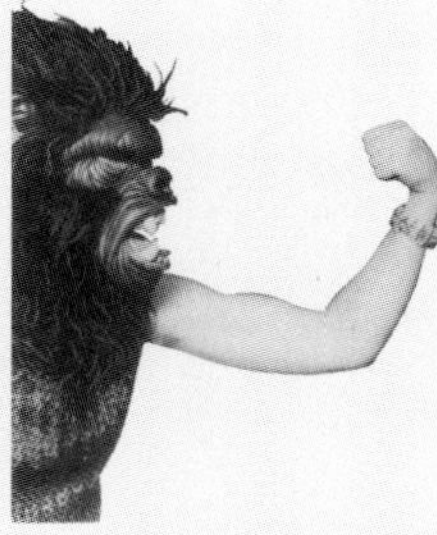

MUSEUM OF MODERN ART, New York
Has shown recent interest in the art of Latin America but no interest in art by Latinas or Latinos in America. Recently gave one retrospective to a woman and one to a male of color; both are over 70. The woman's show (Louise Bourgeois) was of prints; she already had a sculpture show at MOMA in the '80's. She was also only female acquired in the area of painting and sculpture and the acquisition was a gift from her! Drawing and Prints Department occasionally purchases white women (20% of acquisitions) but never women of color. To avoid conflicts of interest no artist serves as a Trustee, but Trustees' Painting and Sculpture Committee (overseeing acquisitions and exhibition schedule) is riddled with Hollywood art investors like David Geffen, Douglas Cramer and Michael Ovitz.

THE WHITNEY(Whitey) MUSEUM OF AMERICAN ART
Main branch only shows aging white women and dead male artists of color (25% of solo shows, '91-94). Rest devoted to white males. Except for group shows and the Biennial no women of color have been seen since the '70's at the main branch of this museum, charged with preserving American Art. Instead, African-American female curator's strong program of non-white, non-male art has been ghettoized at branch museum sponsored by Phillip Morris (corporation best known for targeting woman and African-Americans in their advertising campaigns for smoking.) Recent acquisitions of big-ticket items like painting and sculpture 84% white and male. Conflicts of interest on Board of Directors include one auction house owner and the wife of at least one art dealer. Courageous program in film and video, recent Biennial and upcoming main branch show on Black masculinity could earn Whitey an upgrade. But acquisitions must improve, Black girls must get shows and Board must clean up its act.

THE METROPOLITAN MUSEUM OF ART
Receives $15 million a year from the ethnically diverse taxpayers of New York City, yet has worst record for solo shows of women and artists of color. 20th century collection shows some diversity due to progressive African-American female curator, but sculpture court remains all white and male. Women were seen in group show, "The Nude" but only as bodies, not artists. Trustees more from the world of big time power and money than from the art market: Arthur Ochs Sulzberger (NYTimes), Mrs. Vincent Astor, etc. Despite above, more color on Board of Trustees than at any other Manhattan museum.

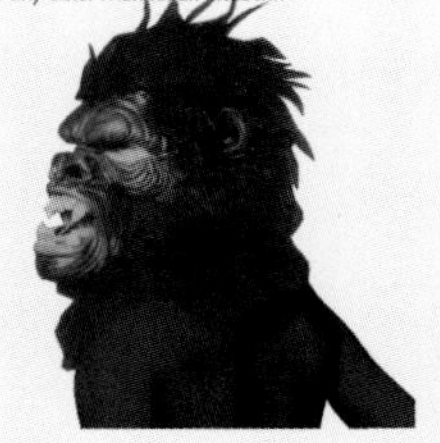

Hot Flashes issue Nos. 2 & 3 examined multiculturalism in museums. We sent letters to hundreds of museums from an imaginary grad student, asking for statistics. We discovered that the farther women and artists of color were from New York, the better their chances for a bright, sunny career.

FOR SALE:

The Guggenheim just sold its name for $10 million to Samuel J. and Ethel LeFrak and someone bought the directorship of the Whitney for only $2 million.

PLEASE SEND MONEY TO THE GGs

so we can buy part of a major museum and have it named after us.

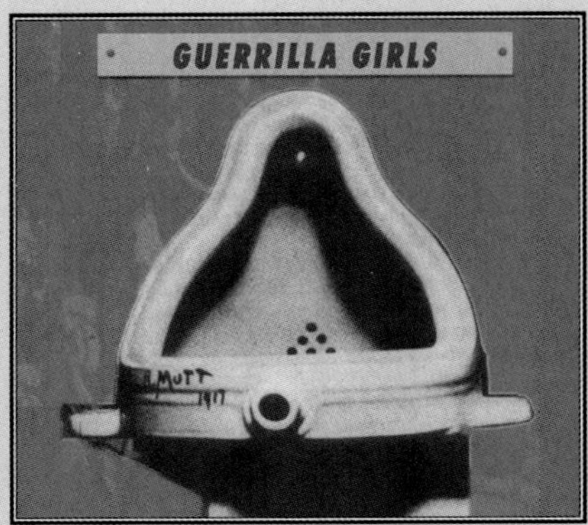

(Maybe the urinals at the Guggenheim)

4

MORE MUSEUM MISFIRES.

White women artists often pay the price when a museum plays multi-cultural catch-up.

The number of museums headed by women is declining across the US. Museums with women in charge show more women and artists of color.

MULTICULTURAL BUT PHALLOCENTRIC: The High Museum in Atlanta has an excellent record for showing and collecting artists of color, mostly male.

If museums call someone who doesn't go to the right schools, show with the right dealer and in general doesn't bother with the world of High Art an "Outsider Artist," why doesn't it call the rest "Insider Artists?"

The Museum of Modern Art is so politically enlightened that it doesn't give its staff Martin Luther King Day off as a holiday.

Alfred Taubman, Trustee of the Whitey Museum and member of its Painting and Sculpture Committee, is also Chairman of Sotheby's auction house.

The Chair of the Met Museum's Exhibition Committee is the great art expert Henry Kissinger.

How many times did the GGs mispell the Whitney Museum as the Whitey museum? The first ten people who send us the right answer will receive a free subscription to *Hot Flashes*.

Most American art museums were founded by guilty rich industrialists who became philanthropists out of a desire to educate the masses. Now that the art market is an exciting, sexy way to make money, there is a whole new crop of trustees who use their position to enhance the value of their own art investments.

Several practicing architects are members of the Architecture Committee of The Museum of Modern Art. Several film producers are on the Film Committee. No artists serve on any committees.

Two New York Art Investors, Raymond Learsy and Emily Fisher Landau, are not satisfied to be on the Board of just one art museum but have influence at both the Modern and the Whitney.

MALEFACE PALEFACE ART OF THE WEST: The Fred Jones Jr. Museum at the University of Oklahoma 'mounted' a Festival in '93 of "the history and culture of the American Indian as seen through the eyes of the White Man, both past and present."

Publicity sent out by the Metropolitan Museum in New York makes frequent use of the words "master" and "masterpiece." Considering the small number of African-Americans on its Board of Trustees, the Guerrilla Girls suggest changing these terms to "The Massa" and "The Massa's Piece."

TAXATION WITHOUT REPRESENTATION: The National Gallery received $54 million in tax money in '92 and spent $22 million in the art market. Acquisitions during the same year were 95% white and 80% male; contemporary exhibitions were 100% white and 87% male.

With the exception of the San Francisco Museum of Modern Art, the further a museum is from New York, the better its record for showing and collecting women and artists of color.

5

Newsletter, Vol. 1, Nos. 2 & 3, pages 4–8, 1994

Letter to a would-be curator

The GGs received this letter from an irate female relative of a Director of a major NYC museum. She wrote him about a job. We share his response with our readers:

PHILLIPPE D. MOUNTBEAUTIFUL
1000 FIFTH AVENUE
NEW YORK, NEW YORK 10019

Ma chère enfante:

How flattered I was to receive your letter about a career for yourself in museum work. While your Ivy League education and social class (being related to me) are in your favor, I must state bluntly, your gender is not.

If you really want to become a power at a prestigious art museum, you have no chance unless you leave town. (Or, if you have the money or chutzpah, start your own place like Gertrude Vanderbilt Whitney did years ago or Marcia Tucker more recently.)

You're right, three of the four major art museums in Manhattan were founded by women, but keep in mind that they were all close to the money. Gertrude paid the Whitney's bills and made a woman, Juliana Force, its first Director.

Abby Aldrich Rockefeller, Mary Sullivan and Lizzie Bliss put up the money to start MOMA and, yes, several of the early departments were run by women, Iris Barry started the film department when no real connoisseur gave a horse's behind for the flickers. Dorothy Miller was allowed to be the Curator of American Art when everyone thought the Abstract Expressionists were just a bunch of drunken degenerates. Hasn't been a female head of a big department there since.

Solomon started the Guggenheim. He made her the first Director him interested in European modernism. He made her the first Director but his family kicked her out after Solomon died and put a man in her place. Even though she was responsible for the impressive collection and that Wright building, she was ridiculed in the press for her connections to the old man.

Katharine Kuh at the Art Institute of Chicago was pilloried in the press for her support of avant-garde art and Adelyn Breeskin was permitted to be Acting Director of the Baltimore Museum while the boys were off at war. Then she snagged the Cone Collection because no one else knew how to talk to the surviving sister. The San Francisco Museum of

Modern Art had a female Director early on when no one cared about the place and Isabella Stewart Gardner did her own thing in Boston. I heard that femi-nazi group Guerrilla Girls appeared there last year.

You must understand, women have had their place in the history of American museums. They are good at taking some risks, setting the places up and getting them in order, but when the museums enter the big leagues then it becomes a man's job.

I'm afraid it's too late for you in this town. Unless you want to head a museum that specializes in art that's a tad out of the mainstream like The Studio Museum in Harlem or the Museo del Barrio. What about the National Museum of Women in the Arts in D.C.? No white male would ever want to be Director at those places. If you want to be at a big New York museum, why not be happy with a job in Education or PR? Or better yet, come be a volunteer. Or move to the suburbs; lots of stylish, suburban museums are run by unpaid and underpaid females.

That's just the way things are in the world of High Art. But, cheer up, at least you're white. Otherwise, you wouldn't have a chance.

Your loving uncle,

Phil

P.S. Do let me know how this letter sounds. So many of us museum people were saying such old-fashioned things about diversity that the National Organization of Museum Directors made us take sensitivity training sessions. How am I doing?

AN UPDATED MUSEUM

The Guerrilla Girls demand the immediate substitution of the following new words to more accurately describe the current art situation:

ART INVESTOR: replacement for the term Art Collector.

CONFLICT OF INTEREST: when a Museum Trustee also invests large sums of money in artworks.

GENIUS: a white male artist chosen by a very small group of tastemakers to make lots of money for an equally small number of art dealers and art investors.

GENIUS SYSTEM: the economic system in which scarcity is manufactured by all of the above, leading to inflated prices for a few white male artists and peanuts for the rest of us; results in the preservation of a grossly inaccurate record of the cultural production of our era.

GOVERNMENT-FUNDED MARKET SUBSIDY: NEA grants given to museums to finance shows of artists whose work sells in the 6 figures.

INSIDE TRADER: an Art Investor who is simultaneously a museum trustee; can also refer to a Museum Curator who also advises art collectors.

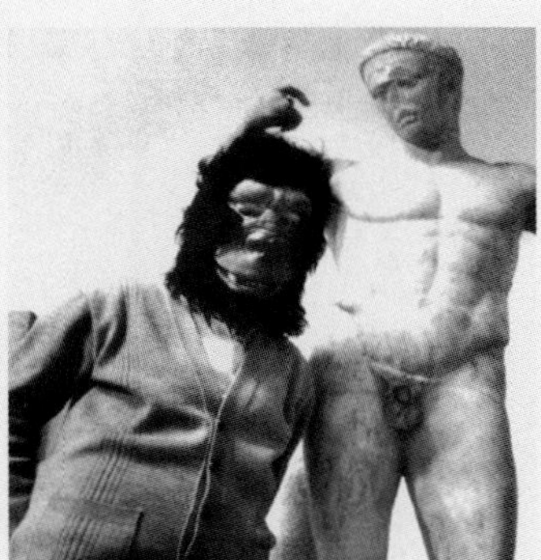

GLOSSARY OF TERMINOLOGY

RESTRAINT OF TRADE: when museums show women and artists of color but never acquire their work.

ABANDONMENT OF PUBLIC TRUST: when a museum in a diverse, urban area such as New York, Buffalo, Philadelphia or Boston ignores the culture of its own region and continues to promote White Male High Art.

PORNOGRAPHY: when the exhibition schedule and/or acquisitions record of a museum follows a direct path to a curator's or trustee's bedroom.

MILD ABUSE: the look one is given by the receptionist upon entering a chic art gallery in New York such as Mary Boone's.

QUOTA SYSTEM: when museums give only 1 show a year to a woman or artist of color.

FAMILY VALUES: when Frank Stella, whose dealer is the brother of Bill Rubin, Chief Curator Emeritus of MOMA, is given 3 retrospectives at MOMA before he's fifty.

PRO-LIFE: when the exhibition schedule and acquisition record of major art institutions reflects the diversity in our culture.

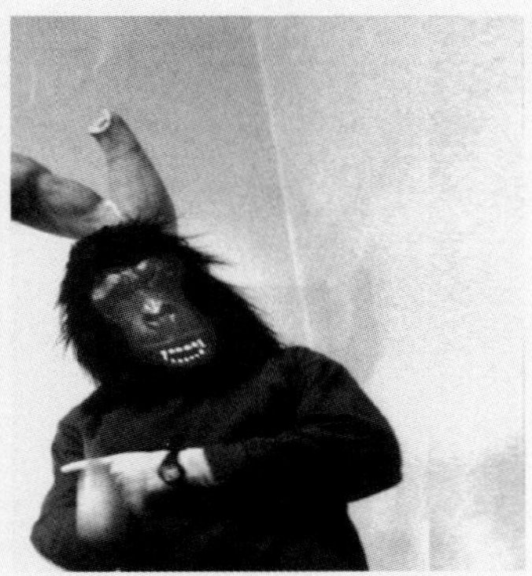

Rx for the future

OUTLAW THE CULT OF GENIUS. IN A CULTURE OF MORE THAN 250 MILLION, WHY SHOULD MUSEUMS ACROSS THE U.S. ALL SHOW AND COLLECT THE SAME FEW MARKET-VALIDATED ARTISTS?

REQUIRE ARTISTS WHO ARE GIVEN RETROSPECTIVES TO TITHE A PERCENTAGE OF THE INCREASED VALUE OF THEIR WORK TO ARTISTS WHO AREN'T SO LUCKY.

MAKE IT AS ACCEPTABLE TO SHOW SEXUALLY EXPLICIT GAY AND LESBIAN ART AS IT IS TO SHOW SEXUALLY EXPLICIT HETEROSEXUAL ART.

AFRICAN-AMERICAN ART DIDN'T START WITH WHITE CURATORS' FORCED DISCOVERY OF A FEW TOKEN GENIUSES. MUSEUMS SHOULD DO THEIR DUTY AND DISCOVER WHAT OTHER ROSES HAVE BEEN BLOOMING IN THE DESERT.

MAKE CURATORS AND BOARD MEMBERS FOLLOW ETHICAL STANDARDS LIKE GOVT. OFFICIALS AND AVOID CONFLICTS OF INTEREST.

SUE MUSEUMS THAT DON'T SHOW AND COLLECT ENOUGH ART BY WOMEN AND ARTISTS OF COLOR.

THROW ALL ART COLLECTORS OFF MUSEUM BOARDS; REPLACE THEM WITH ARTISTS.

ALLOW ALL ARTISTS TO 'EMERGE' AT THE SAME AGE. WHY SHOULD WOMEN AND ARTISTS OF COLOR HAVE TO WAIT UNTIL THEY'RE OLD OR DEAD TO GET RETROSPECTIVES WHEN WHITE BOYS GET THEM IN THEIR 30'S AND 40'S?

LETTERS TO THE GIRLS

The following letters were sent to us about the first issue of Hot Flashes. The first two express concern about our subscription rate of $12. for white males and $9. for women and people of color.

Dear GGs:
Thank you very much for sending me the first issue of Hot Flashes, which is fabulous – so much so that I was willing to swallow my gay pride and pay the 12 bucks. However, given the mission statement on the masthead: "All the sexism, racism & homophobia that fits, we complain about," I just can't bring myself to subscribe at the same rate that –let's say – A.M.Rosenthal would pay. I support everything that you do (and I feel that I have a pretty good track record, which I ascribe to my youth, which allows me to accept as completely natural the fact that the best artists working today about 6-7 times out of 10 are women), but I just can't write the check.

What's the deal? Is this a symptom of the kind of thinking that believes that since I, unlike a woman or a person of color, can "pass" in the power game that I'm one of them? Or is it based on some sort of point system where the "one strike" against me is not as great as the one against –oh, maybe someone like Roberta Smith? Whatever the reasons, do they really wash?

So why is the word "homophobia" on your mission statement if you're not as committed to complaining about it as you are racism or sexism?
Truly yours,

Terry R. Myers
New York

Ed. note: See change in subscription rate, below.

Dear GGs:
May we suggest a more politically correct subscription rate scale? Something along the lines of what follows:

SEX	Male	$5.
	female	2.
	other	1.
RACE	white	5.
	person of color	2.
	bi-racial	1.
EDUCATION	Ivy League	5.
	small liberal arts college	4.
	state university	3.
	community college	2.
	none	1.
INCOME	above $40,000	5.
	below $40, 000	1.
SEXUAL ORIENTATION	heterosexual	4.
	gay/lesbian	3.
	bisexual	2.
	other	1
HAIR COLOR	natural blonde	5.
	other	1.
OTHER	(check at least 3)	
	ugly	1.
	attractive	5.
	non-gym body	1.
	gym body	4.
	eating disorder	1.
	abused child	1.
	non-abused child	5.
	child of gay/lesbian parent	1.
	elitist substance abuser	5.
	non-elitist substance abuser	1.
	physically handicapped	1.
	smoker	1.
	non-smoker	2.
	reformed smoker	3.
	oppressed by body hair	2.

Add up the dollar amount and send check to the Guerrilla Girls.

Li García-Mambuka IV
New York

Dear GGs:
Kindest of hurrahs for sticking it to the Slime at the *New York Times. We have all felt the sting of that backlash –"grey old lady" my ass – there lurks a white Yale male under that Mother Bates drag – butcher knife in hand...keep up the good work!*

Name withheld

BLACK MARKET WHITE SALE

GET YOUR OWN RED HOT GG POSTERS SUITABLE FOR FRAMING (OR FRAMING SOMEONE ELSE)
$20. will bring you one of our all-time favorites:
GUERRILLA GIRLS' CODE OF ETHICS FOR MUSEUMS,
THE ADVANTAGES OF BEING A WOMAN ARTIST,
DO WOMEN HAVE TO BE NAKED TO GET INTO THE MET MUSEUM?
GUERRILLA GIRLS EXPLAIN NATURAL LAW
RELAX, SENATOR HELMS, THE ARTWORLD IS YOUR KIND OF PLACE,
GUERRILLA GIRLS' IDENTITIES REVEALED.
For any other of our 45+ posters, please write to us. Payment should be sent by check to 532 LaGuardia Place, NY, NY 10012. **POSTERS WILL BE MAILED IN PLAIN BROWN WRAPPERS.**

ATTENTION HIGH ROLLERS:
Complete portfolios of our posters are available to individuals and to the institutions we are trying to reform. Please contact us regarding details.

HAVE MASK, WILL TRAVEL
ESCAPE THE ART WORLD JUNGLE BY INVITING THE GUERRILLA GIRLS TO SPEAK AT YOUR SCHOOL, ORGANIZATION OR MUSEUM. FOR A REASONABLE FEE, YOU CAN HAVE THE GIRLS DISCUSS THEIR LIFE, TIMES AND THEIR WORK OVER THE PAST 10 YEARS.

GUERRILLA GIRLS IS AN ALL-VOLUNTEER ORGANIZATION. ALL PROCEEDS GO TOWARD FUTURE PROJECTS AND PAST DEBTS.

SUBSCRIBE TO HOT FLASHES! SUGGESTED DONATION : $12./STRAIGHT WHITE MALES WITH SUPERIOR EARNING POWER; $9./EVERYONE ELSE.

BULK RATE
U.S. POSTAGE
PAID
NEW YORK, N.Y.
Permit No. 6198

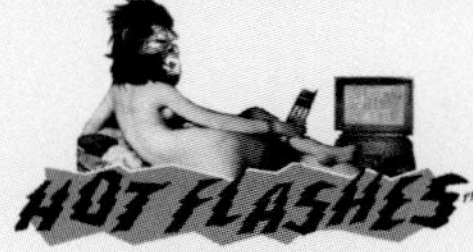

c/o GUERRILLA GIRLS, 532 LaGuardia Pl. #237
New York, NY 10012

SUBSCRIBE TO *HOT FLASHES!* SUGGESTED DONATION FOR FUTURE ISSUES:
____ **$12. FOR STRAIGHT WHITE MALES WITH SUPERIOR EARNING POWER**
____ **$9. FOR EVERYONE ELSE**
PLEASE START MY SUBSCRIPTION WITH ISSUE #__.

NAME____________________
ADDRESS____________________
CITY__________STATE___ZIP______

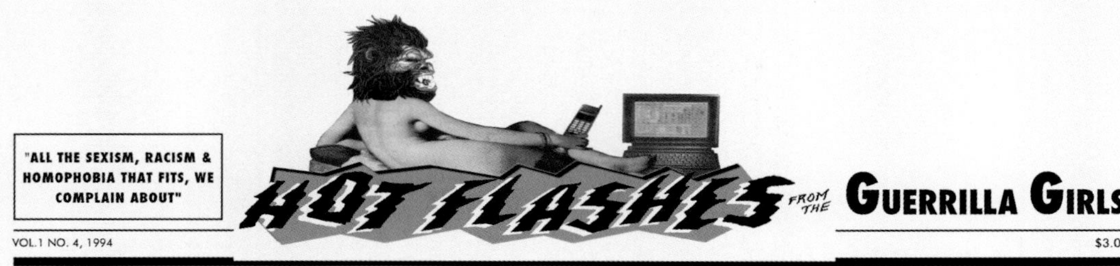

TOP TEN SIGNS YOU'RE BEING TOKENIZED:

10. Your busiest months are February (Black History Month), March (Women's History), April (Asian-American Awareness), June (Stonewall Anniversary) and September (Latino Heritage).

9. At openings and parties, the only other people of color are serving drinks.

8. Everyone knows your race, gender and sexual preference even when they don't know your work.

7. A museum that won't show your work gives you a prominent place in its lecture series.

6. Your last show got a lot of publicity, but no cash.

5. You're a finalist for a non-tenure-track teaching position at every art school on the east coast.

4. No collector ever buys more than one of your pieces.

3. Whenever you open your mouth, it's assumed that you speak for "your people," not just yourself.

2. People are always telling you about their interracial and gay sexual fantasies.

1. A curator who never gave you the time of day before calls you right after a Guerrilla Girls demonstration.

Hot Flashes 4 explored the practice of hiring or exhibiting one or two individuals from a marginalized group, then pretending the entire system had miraculously become diverse.

Newsletter, Vol. 1, No. 4, 1994

EDITORIAL STATEMENT:

A few moments had to come together to get the tokenism project underway. The first was when Frida Kahlo was working on the museum stats for *Hot Flashes #2*. She noticed that, at several museums, whenever shows and acquisitions for minorities went up, the numbers for white women went down. This wasn't something we had anticipated, we just found that it was there. Subliminally, I flashed back to when Starrett City offered integrated middle-class housing in Brooklyn: the pent-up demand by blacks was so great that, though the developers were political radicals, they had to reimpose a quota so the complex wouldn't "tip." They thought even progressive whites would move out of an area when they sensed blacks becoming a majority, no matter what showed up on polls or was even consciously thought, so they limited blacks to a proportion of 30-40%.

You couldn't help but wonder: what would be the corresponding figure for the art world? Lurking about in those museum figures was a hint that, at a certain point, the hold of white-male, art-as-usual assumptions might be "tipped." A conscious, or unconscious, defense against this possibility could keep white women and artists of color combined within set limits.

Shortly afterwards, on a speaking gig for the Girls, when I announced that underneath my mask I was a black artist, an African-American women in the rear asked, didn't I think it was a mistake to combine our issues that those of white women? In my head, I heard the warning notes of several bits of African-American folk wisdom echoing simultaneously: don't trust anybody, don't collaborate, don't share your ideas, just remember when you make your move that there's room for only one of you at any time in any office, any grad school, any gallery, any art magazine. It seemed like the 50s redux in the 90's. Perhaps in the meantime nothing had changed? But if we as African-Americans knew all there was to know about tokenism, about being "the spook who sat by the door," then perhaps sharing that with white women could help us both. Because white women are certainly tokens themselves, though on a larger scale, and we couldn't dislodge the structures of power alone. When the tokenism campaign was proposed, it was one on which we all could agree.

–Alma Thomas

[Individual Guerrilla Girls use the names of dead women artists as pseudonyms. Alma Thomas (1892-1978) was an African-American abstract painter who came to prominence, when she was in her 70's, as one of the Washington, D.C. color field painters.]

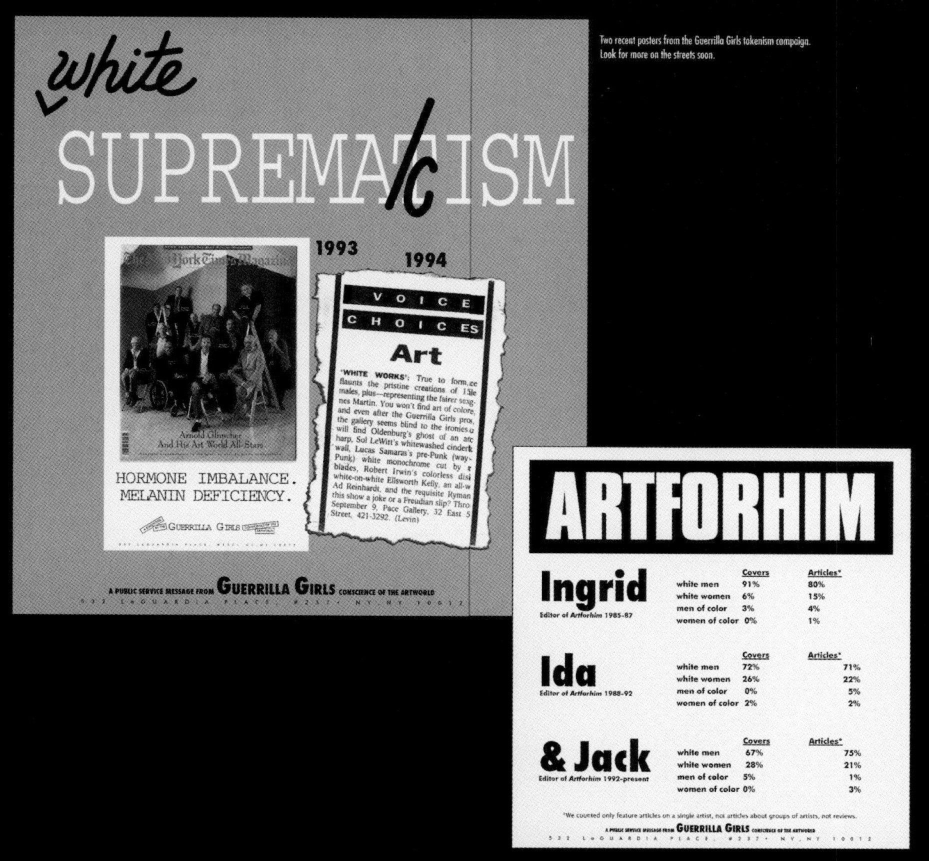

Two recent posters from the Guerrilla Girls tokenism campaign. Look for more on the streets soon.

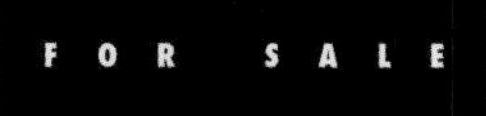

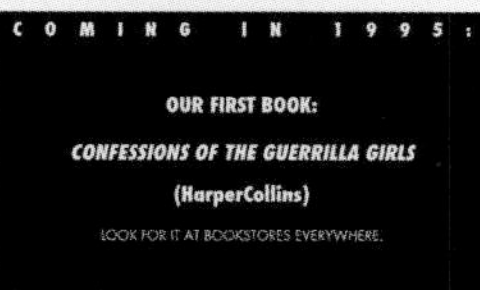

Ingrid		Covers	Articles*
Editor of Artforhim 1985-87	white men	91%	80%
	white women	6%	15%
	men of color	3%	4%
	women of color	0%	1%

Ida		Covers	Articles*
Editor of Artforhim 1988-92	white men	72%	71%
	white women	26%	22%
	men of color	0%	5%
	women of color	2%	2%

& Jack		Covers	Articles*
Editor of Artforhim 1992-present	white men	67%	75%
	white women	28%	21%
	men of color	5%	1%
	women of color	0%	3%

*We counted only feature articles on a single artist, not articles about groups of artists, not reviews.

A PUBLIC SERVICE MESSAGE FROM GUERRILLA GIRLS CONSCIENCE OF THE ARTWORLD
532 LaGUARDIA PLACE #237 NY, NY 10012

Dear Girls:
Recently I visited the Metropolitan Museum of Art's exhibit of "Picasso and The Weeping Women." The wall texts accompanying the various drawings and paintings contained what I thought were very negative characterizations. Some exerpts appear below:

"Picasso's most constant subjects were the women he successively possessed."

On Olga Picasso: "As her classic beauty faded, Olga's erratic disposition increased. Vain and vapid, she was also extremely conventional and socially pretentious, and she became a jealous shrew."

On Marie-Therese: "Young, complacent and unwordly, Marie-Therese offered him refuge and calm as well as ecstasy. For several yeasrs her voluptuous compliance inspired many of his tender works."

What misogynist wrote these awful descriptions? Has anyone in your group seen this show? Perhaps I am a bit late in realizing the extent of the art world's exploitation of women, so any comments, thoughts that anyone there might have on the topic would be greatly appreciated. I applaud all the great work you all do.
In Sisterhood,
Maryann Calendrille

ANSWER:
The misogynist is Bill Lieberman, the Met's chief curator of 20th Century Art, who "improved" the material submitted to him by Judi Freeman, the show's curator. The Guerrilla Girls declare him The Dirty Old Art Historian of 1994 for espousing the seminal theory that male artists paint better after fucking.

To Whom it May Concern:
I am writing to respond to your action at the College Art Association Conference which called attention to the predominance of male faculty in art schools across the United States. While I applaud what I assume is your intent–to raise consciousness about gender discrimination in the arts, I would like to call into question the source of your data.

Your flyer quotes your source as the CAA Guide to MFA Programs in the Visual Arts…The only faculty listed in the CAA Guide are those who happen to be teaching in a given year. In the case of Massachusetts College of Art, that mix changes every semester…

In fact, our faculty statistics are something to brag about in terms of gender issues…

Full Time:	Male	Female
Professor	24	16
Associate Professor	6	7
Assistant Professor	6	5
Instructor	2	0
Total:	38	28

Part Time:	Male	Female
Professor	1	4
Associate Professor	2	4
Assistant Professor	4	9
Instructor	1	3
Total:	8	20

While it is true that a higher percentage of female faculty are part-time, in many cases this is by choice and women are well represented in all ranks…
Sincerely,
Patricia Doran
Pat Doran, Dean

ANSWER:
The information you submitted to the CAA Guide listed Mass College of Art's Faculty as being 86% male. We've heard that some art schools hire women for one-year appointments so that over a five year period they can report all of them as faculty members. We're sure that Mass isn't that kind of art school. And we're relieved to hear that your part time female faculty members, unlike adjuncts at other schools, have chosen that status.

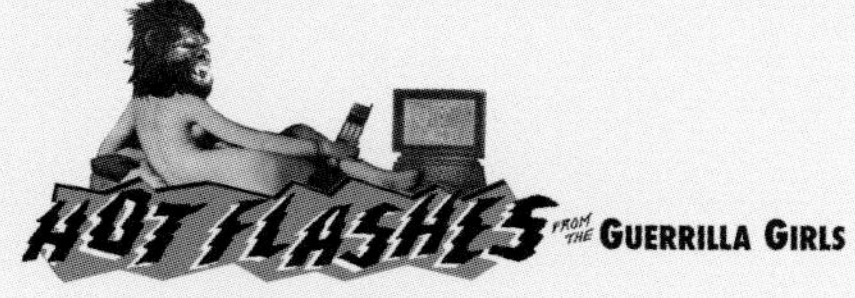

c/o GUERRILLA GIRLS, 532 LaGuardia Pl. #237
New York, NY 10012

ART DEPARTMENT	% FACULTY WHO ARE FEMALE	% OF HIGHER-RANKING FACULTY WHO ARE FEMALE
University of South Carolina	0	0
Utah State	10	0
Western Michigan U	10	11
Notre Dame	11	0
Michigan State	11	13
Colorado State	12	10
New Mexico State	13	0
Louisiana State	13	17
U of Tulsa	14	0
Massachusetts College of Art	14	won't tell
New York Academy of Art	15	0
U of Wisconsin, Milwaukee	16	16
University of Georgia	18	5
U of Washington, Seattle	19	14
U of Florida, Gainesville	19	27
U of Kansas	19	12
U of Wisconsin, Madison	20	14
U of Idaho	23	15
U of Kentucky	23	25
Cornell	24	28
School of Visual Arts, NYC	25	won't tell
U of Texas, Austin	26	13
Hunter College	26	40
UCLA	30	0
USC	30	25
Yale	32	11
U of Houston	33	34
U of Pennsylvania	40	50

ART DEPARTMENT	% FACULTY WHO ARE MALE	% OF HIGHER-RANKING FACULTY WHO ARE MALE
U of South Carolina	100	100
Utah State	90	100
Western Michigan U	90	89
Notre Dame	89	100
Michigan State	89	87
Colorado State	88	90
New Mexico State	87	100
Louisiana State	87	83
University of Tulsa	86	100
Massachusetts College of Art	86	won't tell
New York Academy of Art	85	100
U of Wisconsin, Milwaukee	84	84
U of Georgia	82	95
U of Washington, Seattle	81	86
U of Florida, Gainesville	81	73
U of Kansas	81	88
U of Wisconsin, Madison	80	86
U of Idaho	77	85
U of Kentucky	77	75
Cornell	76	72
School of Visual Arts, NYC	75	won't tell
U of Texas, Austin	74	87
Hunter College	74	60
UCLA	70	100
USC	70	75
Yale	68	89
U of Houston	67	66
U of Pennsylvania	60	100

For decades, the majority of art students were women while the professors were almost all white men. The schools were happy to take women's tuition, but not to hire them. We decided to give job applicants at the College Art Association conference some color-coded advice. One school recruiting at CAA had an all-female student body and all-male faculty!

Flyers, 1994

TRADITIONAL VALUES AND QUALITY RETURN TO THE WHITEY MUSEUM.

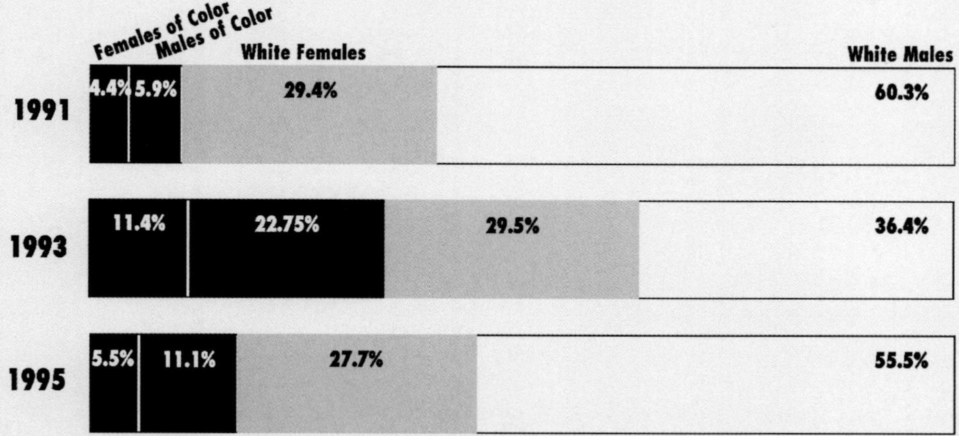

In 1993 the Whitney Biennial tried something different: diversity. The show got trashed in the press, and the next Biennial went back to whiteness as usual. Oops. We misspelled the museum's name.

Poster, 1995

THE Token Times

CLASSIFIED

HELP WANTED, ART WORLD

OUTSTANDING CAREER OPPORTUNITY: CURATORIAL ASST TO ASST-CURATOR AT MAJOR MUSEUM. ENTRY LEVEL POSITION.
Ph.D from Top School, publications & 10 years experience required.
Must know Word Processing, answer own phone, conduct own research.
Possibility of curating shows at branch museum, providing you can raise the money. EOE; Women and minorities encouraged to apply.

WELL-DRESSED ART HISTORY MAJOR?
Blue chip NYC art gallery, wanting to change male, pale image; seeks multicultural receptionist with drop-dead appear. & clothes to match; ivy league education & attitude a must; NO ETHNIC ACCENTS. Minimum wage, no health insurance. Fringe benefits include: attending fancy parties and meeting the right people.

$$$$$$$$$$SMILE$$$$$$$$$$$$$$

DEVELOPMENT ASSISTANT: person of color needed to intimidate foundations, corporations, and collectors into giving large amounts of money. Successful candidate must relish being only minority staff member. High visibility in public, silence at staff meetings required. Photogenic a plus.

EARN A GREAT P/T INCOME !!!!

MAJOR MUSEUM seeks 1 artist of color EVERY year for next five years (or as long as multicult. lasts) for solo shows. Prefer artist already discovered by major galleries, collectors and other museums. Must restrict artistic output to ethnic issues: FORMALIST NEED NOT APPLY.

GRAND OPENING! ARTIST CALL!
Female African-American, Latina, Asian or Lesbian artists wanted for large summer group show in out of the way location.
No honorarium, no sales.
Must deliver own work.

A PUBLIC SERVICE MESSAGE FROM GUERRILLA GIRLS CONSCIENCE OF THE ARTWORLD
532 LaGUARDIA PLACE, #237 • NY, NY 10012

Poster, 1995

The buzzword in the artworld was "multiculturalism," and institutions started playing catch-up, showing one or two tokens. Is tokenism a solution, or part of the problem?

Poster, 1995

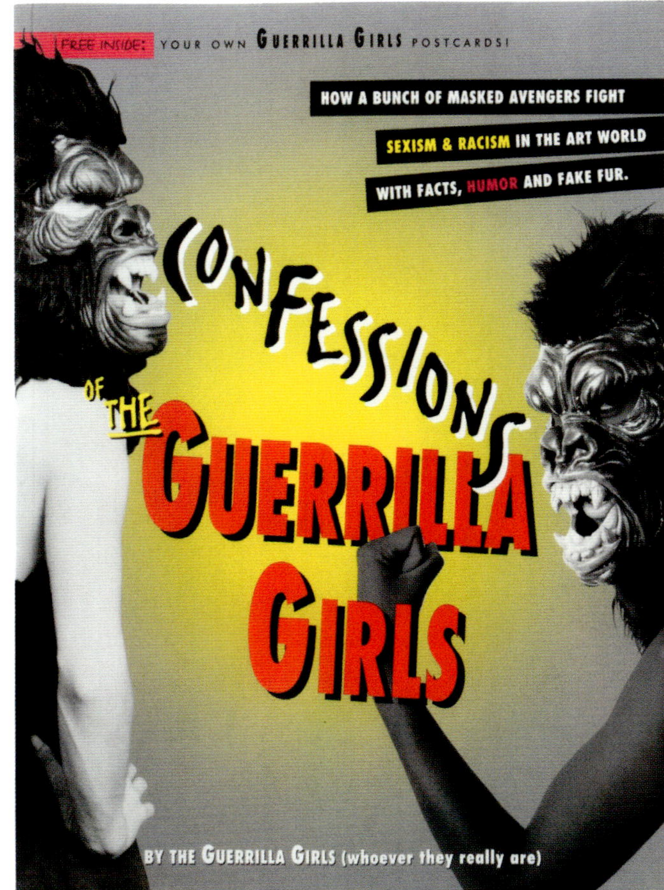

Our first book included posters, a self-interview, members' stories, shout-outs to other activist groups, love letters, hate mail, and tributes from bell hooks, Faith Ringgold, Gloria Steinem and others.

Book, 1995, cover and some interior pages

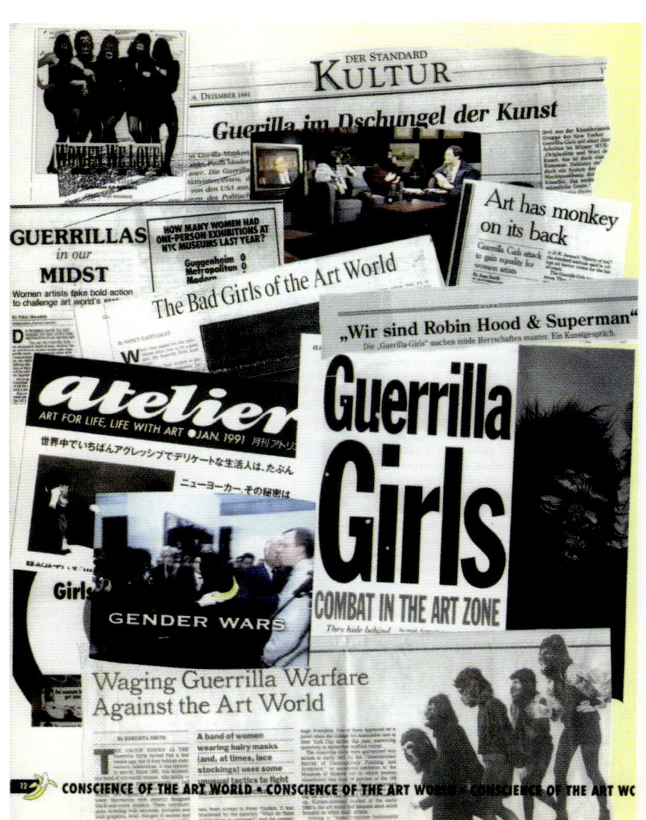

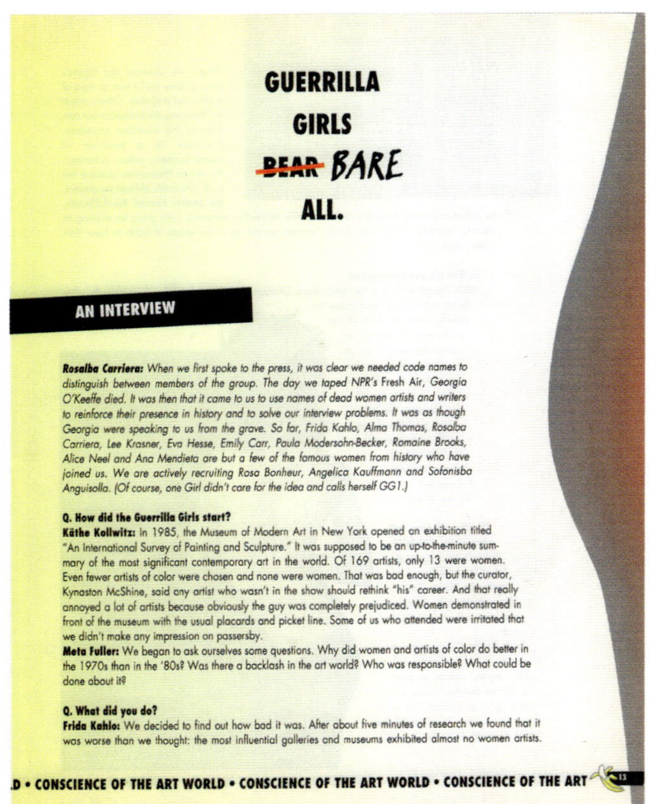

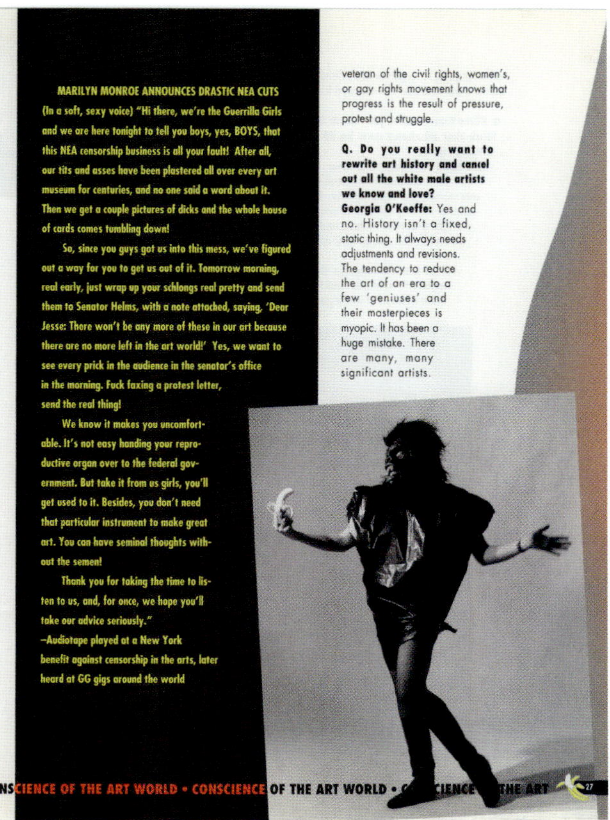

MARILYN MONROE ANNOUNCES DRASTIC NEA CUTS

(In a soft, sexy voice) "Hi there, we're the Guerrilla Girls and we are here tonight to tell you boys, yes, BOYS, that this NEA censorship business is all your fault! After all, our tits and asses have been plastered all over every art museum for centuries, and no one said a word about it. Then we get a couple pictures of dicks and the whole house of cards comes tumbling down!

So, since you guys got us into this mess, we've figured out a way for you to get us out of it. Tomorrow morning, real early, just wrap up your schlongs real pretty and send them to Senator Helms, with a note attached, saying, 'Dear Jesse: There won't be any more of these in our art because there are no more left in the art world!' Yes, we want to see every prick in the audience in the senator's office in the morning. Fuck faxing a protest letter, send the real thing!

We know it makes you uncomfortable. It's not easy handing your reproductive organ over to the federal government. But take it from us girls, you'll get used to it. Besides, you don't need that particular instrument to make great art. You can have seminal thoughts without the semen!

Thank you for taking the time to listen to us, and, for once, we hope you'll take our advice seriously."
—Audiotape played at a New York benefit against censorship in the arts, later heard at GG gigs around the world

veteran of the civil rights, women's, or gay rights movement knows that progress is the result of pressure, protest and struggle.

Q. Do you really want to rewrite art history and cancel out all the white male artists we know and love?
Georgia O'Keeffe: Yes and no. History isn't a fixed, static thing. It always needs adjustments and revisions. The tendency to reduce the art of an era to a few 'geniuses' and their masterpieces is myopic. It has been a huge mistake. There are many, many significant artists.

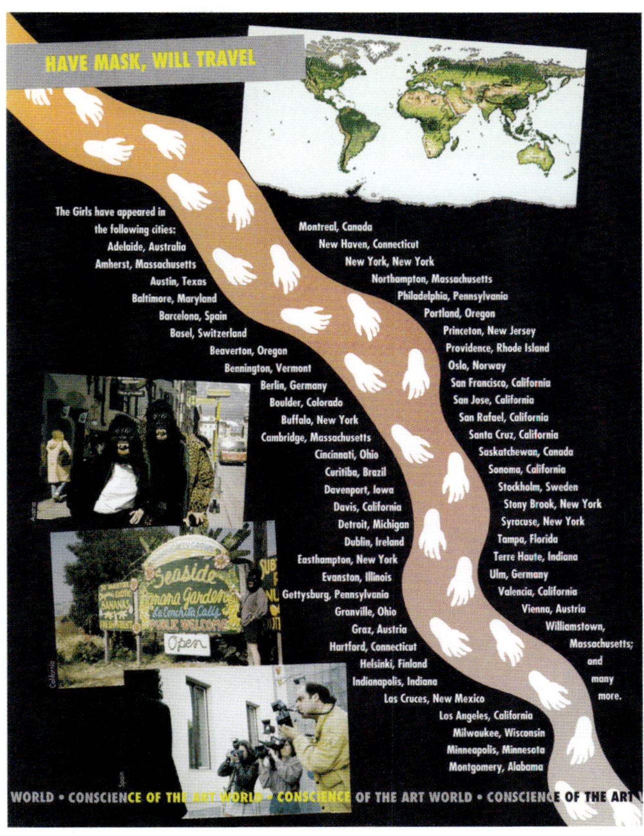

HAVE MASK, WILL TRAVEL

The Girls have appeared in the following cities:
Adelaide, Australia
Amherst, Massachusetts
Austin, Texas
Baltimore, Maryland
Barcelona, Spain
Basel, Switzerland
Beaverton, Oregon
Bennington, Vermont
Berlin, Germany
Boulder, Colorado
Buffalo, New York
Cambridge, Massachusetts
Cincinnati, Ohio
Curitiba, Brazil
Davenport, Iowa
Davis, California
Detroit, Michigan
Dublin, Ireland
Easthampton, New York
Evanston, Illinois
Gettysburg, Pennsylvania
Granville, Ohio
Graz, Austria
Hartford, Connecticut
Helsinki, Finland
Indianapolis, Indiana
Las Cruces, New Mexico
Los Angeles, California
Milwaukee, Wisconsin
Minneapolis, Minnesota
Montgomery, Alabama
Montreal, Canada
New Haven, Connecticut
New York, New York
Northampton, Massachusetts
Philadelphia, Pennsylvania
Portland, Oregon
Princeton, New Jersey
Providence, Rhode Island
Oslo, Norway
San Francisco, California
San Jose, California
San Rafael, California
Santa Cruz, California
Saskatchewan, Canada
Sonoma, California
Stockholm, Sweden
Stony Brook, New York
Syracuse, New York
Tampa, Florida
Terre Haute, Indiana
Ulm, Germany
Valencia, California
Vienna, Austria
Williamstown, Massachusetts;
and many more.

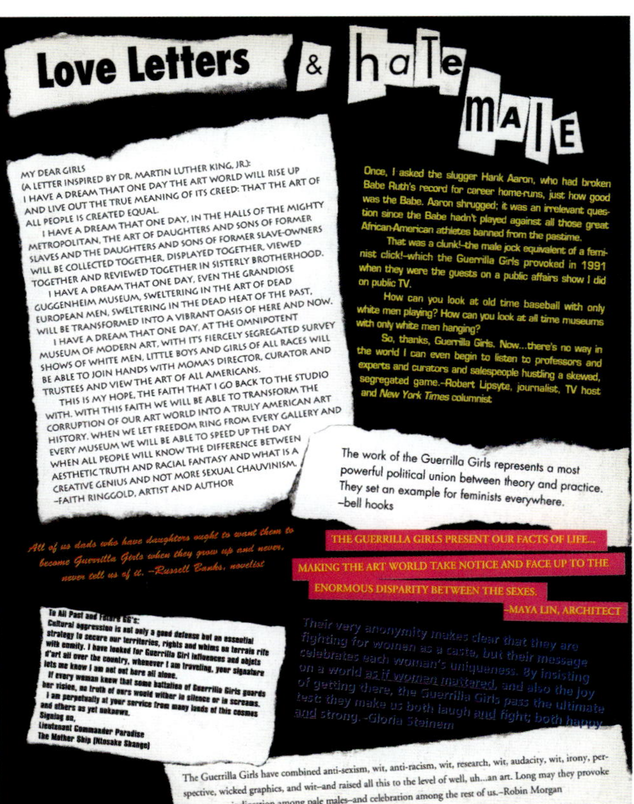

Love Letters & hate male

MY DEAR GIRLS
(A LETTER INSPIRED BY DR. MARTIN LUTHER KING, JR.):
I HAVE A DREAM THAT ONE DAY THE ART WORLD WILL RISE UP AND LIVE OUT THE TRUE MEANING OF ITS CREED: THAT THE ART OF ALL PEOPLE IS CREATED EQUAL.
I HAVE A DREAM THAT ONE DAY, IN THE HALLS OF THE MIGHTY METROPOLITAN, THE ART OF DAUGHTERS AND SONS OF FORMER SLAVES AND THE DAUGHTERS AND SONS OF FORMER SLAVE-OWNERS WILL BE COLLECTED TOGETHER, DISPLAYED TOGETHER, VIEWED TOGETHER AND REVIEWED TOGETHER IN SISTERLY BROTHERHOOD.
I HAVE A DREAM THAT ONE DAY, EVEN THE GRANDIOSE GUGGENHEIM MUSEUM, SWELTERING IN THE ART OF DEAD EUROPEAN MEN, SWELTERING IN THE DEAD HEAT OF THE PAST, WILL BE TRANSFORMED INTO A VIBRANT OASIS OF HERE AND NOW.
I HAVE A DREAM THAT ONE DAY, AT THE OMNIPOTENT MUSEUM OF MODERN ART, WITH IT'S FIERCELY SEGREGATED SURVEY SHOWS OF WHITE MEN, LITTLE BOYS AND GIRLS OF ALL RACES WILL BE ABLE TO JOIN HANDS WITH MOMA'S DIRECTOR, CURATOR AND TRUSTEES AND VIEW THE ART OF ALL AMERICANS.
THIS IS MY HOPE, THE FAITH THAT I GO BACK TO THE STUDIO WITH. WITH THIS FAITH WE WILL BE ABLE TO TRANSFORM THE CORRUPTION OF OUR ART WORLD INTO A TRULY AMERICAN ART HISTORY. WHEN WE LET FREEDOM RING FROM EVERY GALLERY AND EVERY MUSEUM WE WILL BE ABLE TO SPEED UP THE DAY WHEN ALL PEOPLE WILL KNOW THE DIFFERENCE BETWEEN AESTHETIC TRUTH AND RACIAL FANTASY AND WHAT IS A CREATIVE GENIUS AND NOT MORE SEXUAL CHAUVINISM.
—FAITH RINGGOLD, ARTIST AND AUTHOR

Once, I asked the slugger Hank Aaron, who had broken Babe Ruth's record for career home-runs, just how good was the Babe. Aaron shrugged; it was an irrelevant question since the Babe hadn't played against all those great African-American athletes banned from the pastime.
That was a clunk!—the male jock equivalent of a feminist click!—which the Guerrilla Girls provoked in 1991 when they were the guests on a public affairs show I did on public TV.
How can you look at old time baseball with only white men playing? How can you look at all time museums with only white men hanging?
So, thanks, Guerrilla Girls. Now...there's no way in the world I can even begin to listen to professors and experts and curators and salespeople hustling a skewed, segregated game.—Robert Lipsyte, journalist, TV host and *New York Times* columnist

The work of the Guerrilla Girls represents a most powerful political union between theory and practice. They set an example for feminists everywhere.
—bell hooks

All of us dads who have daughters ought to want them to become Guerrilla Girls when they grow up and never, never tell us of it. —Russell Banks, novelist

THE GUERRILLA GIRLS PRESENT OUR FACTS OF LIFE...
MAKING THE ART WORLD TAKE NOTICE AND FACE UP TO THE ENORMOUS DISPARITY BETWEEN THE SEXES.
—MAYA LIN, ARCHITECT

To All Past and Future GG's:
Cultural segregation is not only a good defense but an essential strategy to secure our territories, rights and whims on terrain rife with enmity. I have looked for Guerrilla Girl influences and objets d'art all over the country, whenever I am traveling, your signature lets me know I am not out here all alone.
If every woman knew that some battalion of Guerrilla Girls guards her vision, no truth of ours would wither in silence or in screams. I am perpetually at your service from many lands of this cosmos and others as yet unknown.
Signing on,
Lieutenant Commander Paradise
The Mother Ship [Ntozake Shange]

Their very anonymity makes clear that they are fighting for women as a caste, but their message celebrates each woman's uniqueness. By insisting on a world in which women mattered, and also the joy of getting there, the Guerrilla Girls pass the ultimate test: they make us both laugh and fight; both happy and strong. —Gloria Steinem

The Guerrilla Girls have combined anti-sexism, wit, anti-racism, wit, research, wit, audacity, wit, irony, perspective, wicked graphics, and wit—and raised all this to the level of well, uh...an art. Long may they provoke indigestion among pale males—and celebration among the rest of us.—Robin Morgan

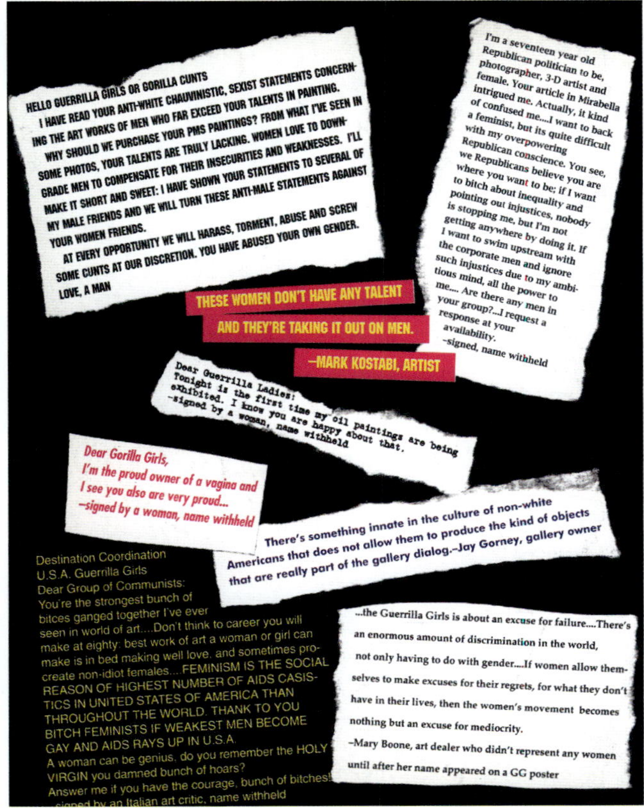

HELLO GUERRILLA GIRLS OR GORILLA CUNTS
I HAVE READ YOUR ANTI-WHITE CHAUVINISTIC, SEXIST STATEMENTS CONCERNING THE ART WORKS OF MEN WHO FAR EXCEED YOUR TALENTS IN PAINTING. WHY SHOULD WE PURCHASE YOUR PMS PAINTINGS? FROM WHAT I'VE SEEN IN SOME PHOTOS, YOUR TALENTS ARE TRULY LACKING. WOMEN LOVE TO DOWNGRADE MEN TO COMPENSATE FOR THEIR INSECURITIES AND WEAKNESSES. I'LL MAKE IT SHORT AND SWEET: I HAVE SHOWN YOUR STATEMENTS TO SEVERAL OF MY MALE FRIENDS AND WE WILL TURN THESE ANTI-MALE STATEMENTS AGAINST YOUR WOMEN FRIENDS.
AT EVERY OPPORTUNITY WE WILL HARASS, TORMENT, ABUSE AND SCREW SOME CUNTS AT OUR DISCRETION. YOU HAVE ABUSED YOUR OWN GENDER.
LOVE, A MAN

I'm a seventeen year old Republican politician to be, photographer, 3-D artist and female. Your article in Mirabella intrigued me. Actually, it kind of confused me....I want to back with my overpowering Republican conscience. You see, we Republicans believe you are where you want to be; if I want to bitch about inequality and pointing out injustices, nobody is stopping me, but I'm not getting anywhere by doing it. If I want to swim upstream with the corporate men and ignore such injustices due to my ambitious mind, all the power to me.... Are there any men in your group?...I request a response at your availability.
—signed, name withheld

THESE WOMEN DON'T HAVE ANY TALENT AND THEY'RE TAKING IT OUT ON MEN.
—MARK KOSTABI, ARTIST

Dear Guerrilla Ladies:
Tonight is the first time my oil paintings are being exhibited. I know you are happy about that.
—signed by a woman, name withheld

Dear Gorilla Girls,
I'm the proud owner of a vagina and I see you also are very proud...
—signed by a woman, name withheld

There's something innate in the culture of non-white Americans that does not allow them to produce the kind of objects that are really part of the gallery dialog.—Jay Gorney, gallery owner

Destination Coordination
U.S.A. Guerrilla Girls
Dear Group of Communists:
You're the strongest bunch of bitces ganged together I've ever seen in world of art....Don't think to career you will make at eighty: best work of art a woman or girl can make is in bed making well love. and sometimes pro-create non-idiot females... FEMINISM IS THE SOCIAL REASON OF HIGHEST NUMBER OF AIDS CASISTICS IN UNITED STATES OF AMERICA THAN THROUGHOUT THE WORLD. THANK TO YOU BITCH FEMINISTS IF WEAKEST MEN BECOME GAY AND AIDS RAYS UP IN U.S.A. A woman can be genius. do you remember the HOLY VIRGIN you damned bunch of hoars? Answer me if you have the courage, bunch of bitches.
—signed by an Italian art critic, name withheld

...the Guerrilla Girls is about an excuse for failure....There's an enormous amount of discrimination in the world, not only having to do with gender....If women allow themselves to make excuses for their regrets, for what they don't have in their lives, then the women's movement becomes nothing but an excuse for mediocrity.
—Mary Boone, art dealer who didn't represent any women until after her name appeared on a GG poster

WHAT DO THESE MEN HAVE IN COMMON?

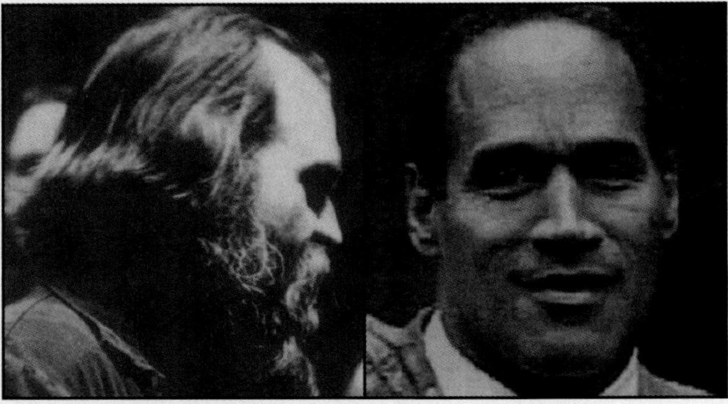

The murder of Nicole Brown Simpson in 1994 reminded us of the death nine years earlier of artist Ana Mendieta. In both cases their rich and successful husbands were acquitted. We used these deaths to call attention to all women who suffer violence at the hands of a partner.

Poster, 1995

WHO IS THIS SLIMY CREATURE?

Raised by a single mom, but wants to put other fatherless children in orphanages.

Smoked pot in college, but seeks harsher penalties for drug use.

Dodged the draft, but plans to increase military spending.

Rants about government corruption, but agreed to a $4.5 million book advance/bribe from a company under investigation by Congress.

Divorced wife number one while she was in the hospital with cancer and is a deadbeat dad, but supports "traditional family values."

IT'S NEWT!

A PUBLIC SERVICE MESSAGE FROM **GUERRILLA GIRLS**
532 LaGUARDIA PLACE, #237 • NY, NY 10012

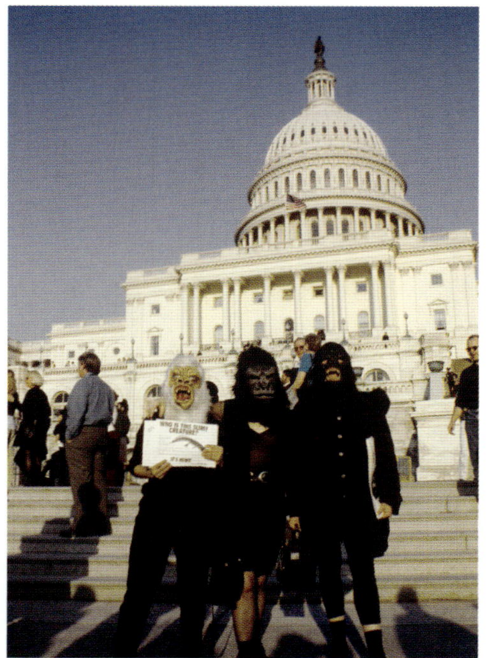

Newt Gingrich, former speaker of the house, built his political career promoting traditional family values. But when we dissected his life we found hypocrisy after hypocrisy. It's poetic justice that his name is synonymous with another cold-blooded creature.

Poster, 1995; Washington, D.C., 1995

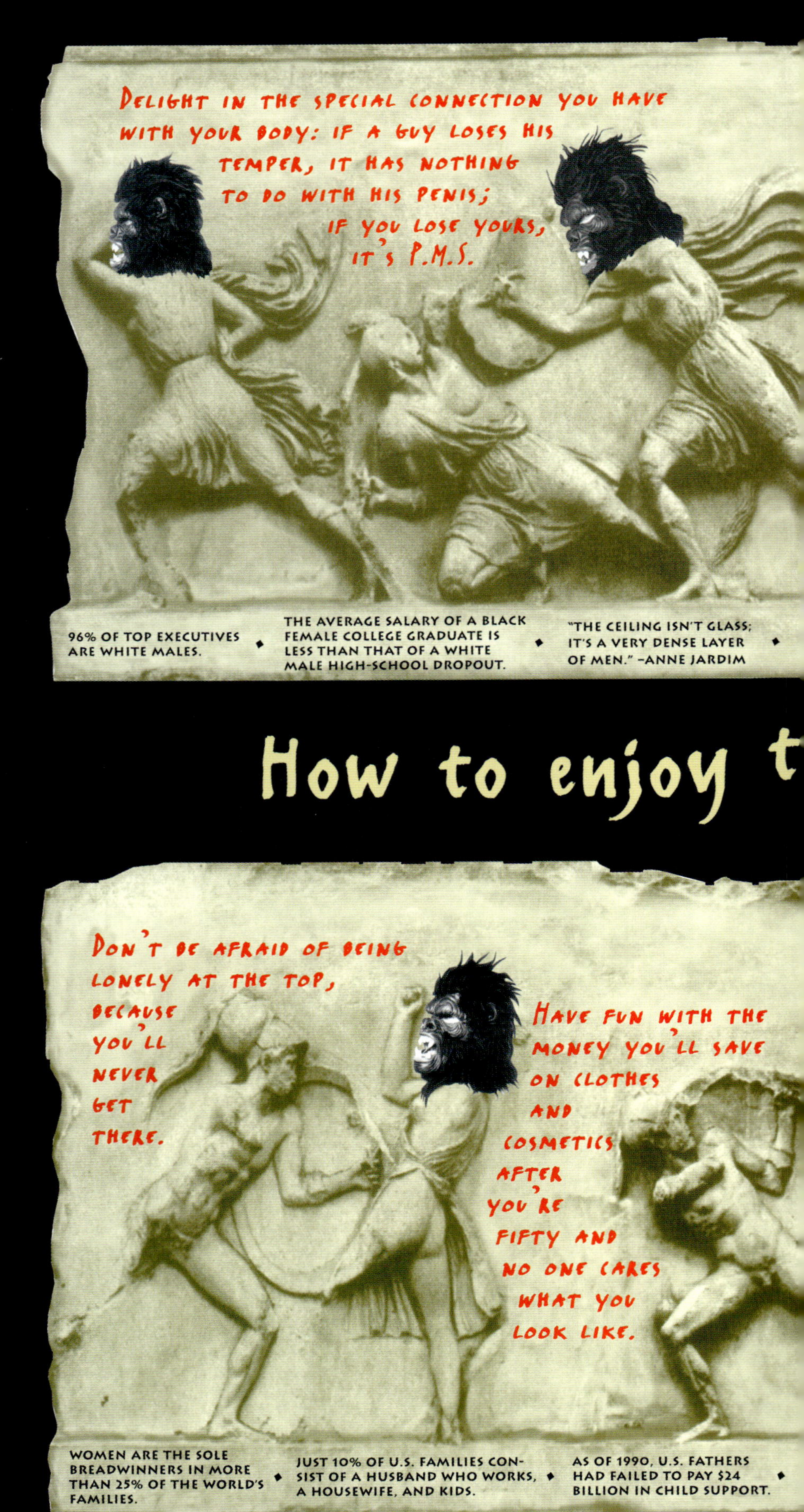

The New Yorker did its first issue on women under its first and only female editor. We used the mythical battle between the Greeks and Amazons to give women advice, backed up by some harsh realities.

The New Yorker, February 26 and March 4, 1996

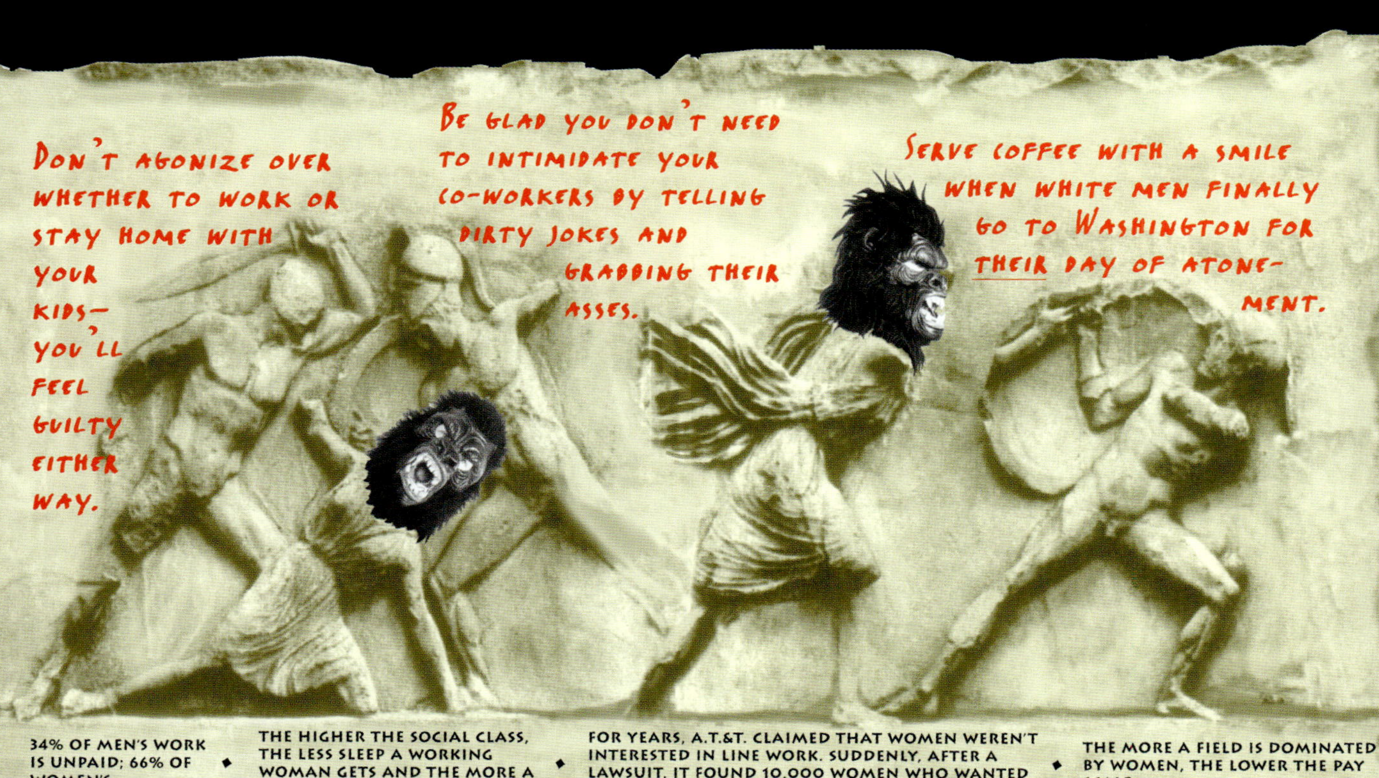

battle of the sexes

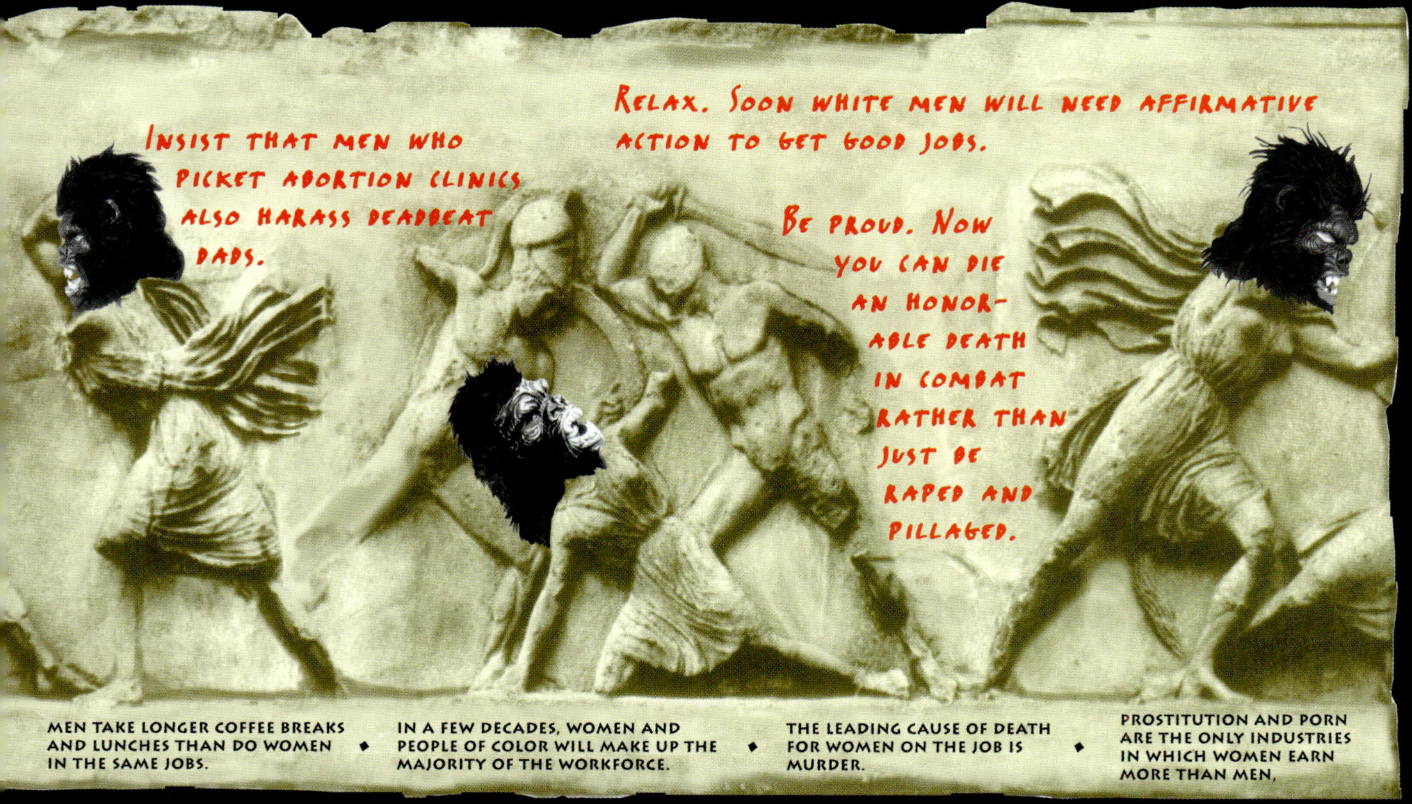

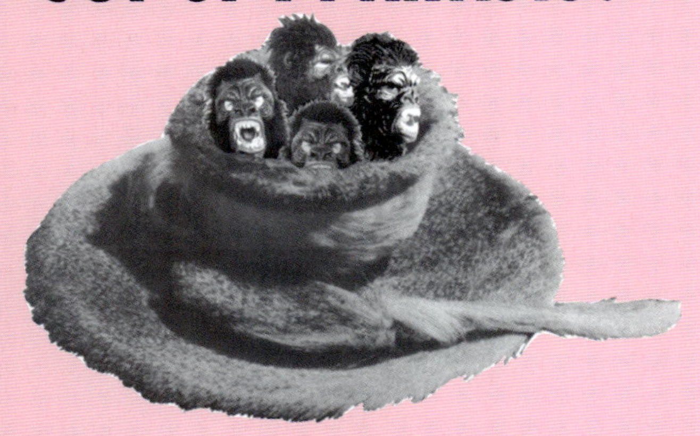

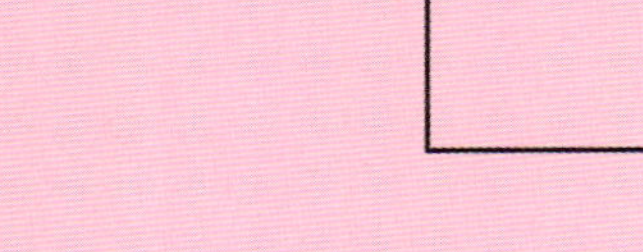

Postcard, 1997

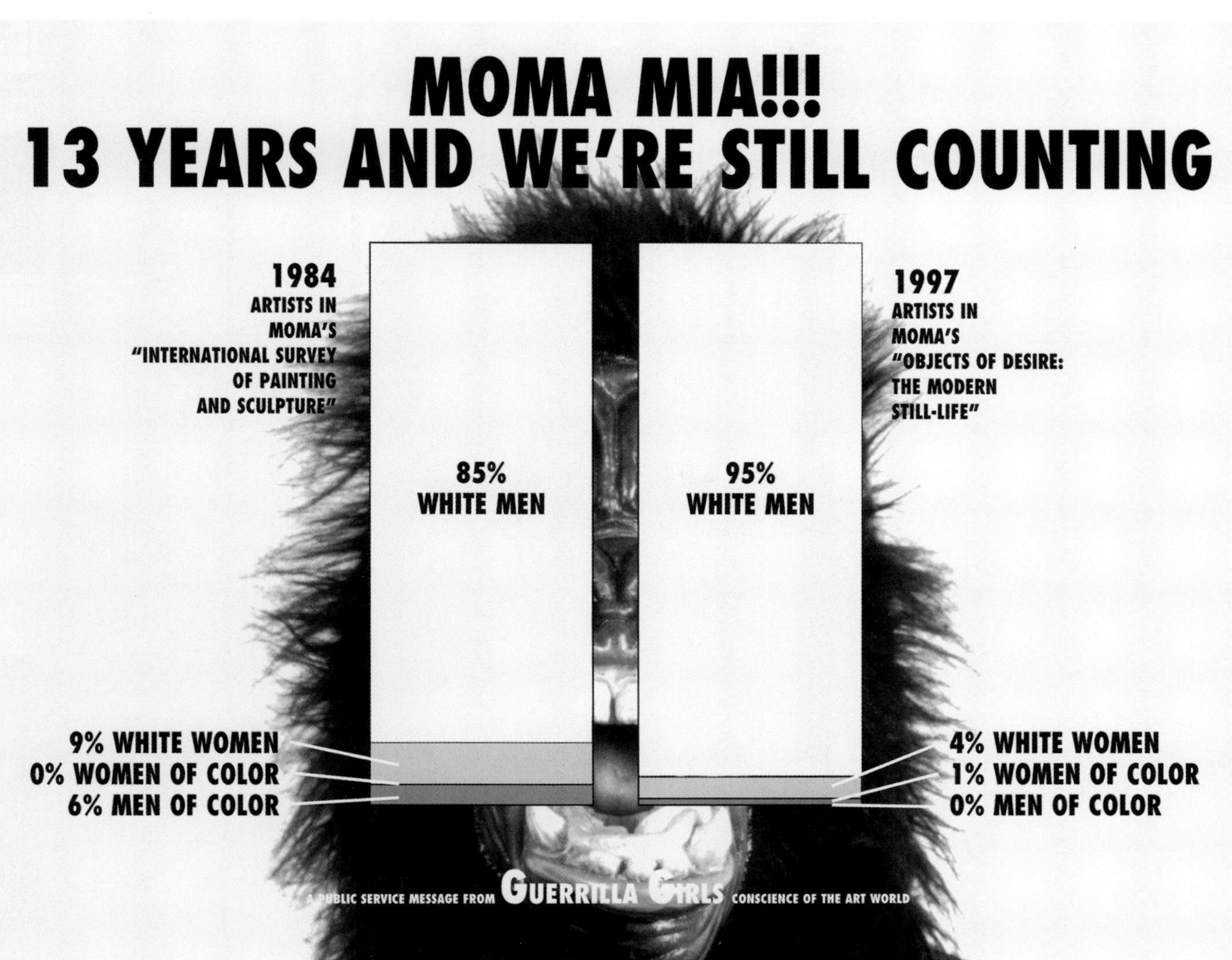

A MoMA curator managed to serve up a very white and male history of still life, when for centuries it was one of few genres open to women. Our supporters sent her thousands of postcards (page 72). Every review panned the show for its pale maleness. Above: The stats were even worse than the 1984 MoMA show that incited us to invent a new kind of activist art.

Poster, 1997

Why do people have trouble naming more than one or two women artists? Against all odds, women have always been artists, many with productive and successful careers. Historians dismissed, ignored or forgot them in a relentless drive to define the Western canon through the work of white male "geniuses." We decided to tell the story of women artists who should never be forgotten.

Book, 1998, cover and some interior pages

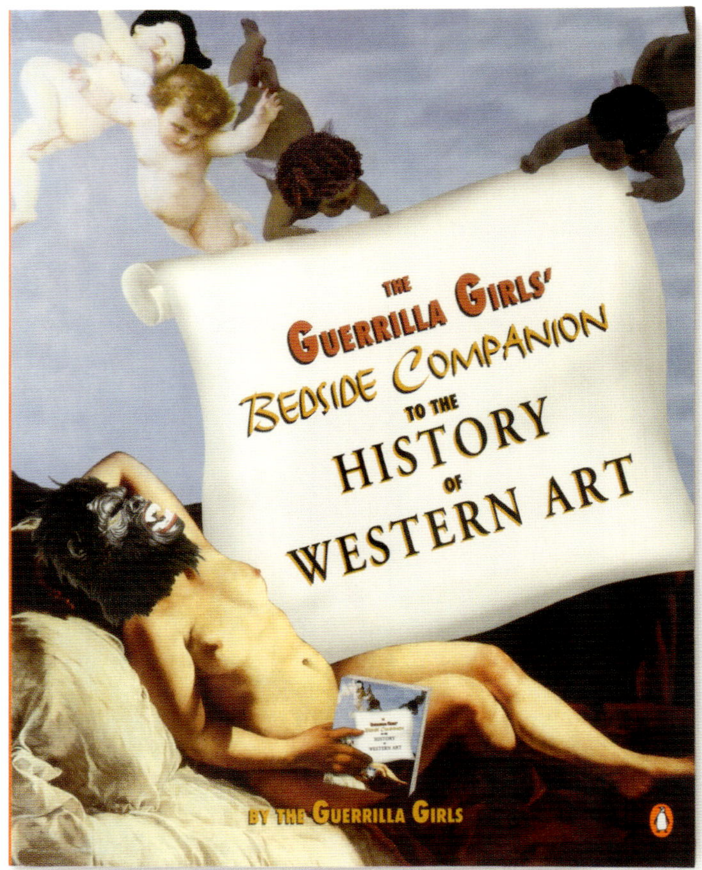

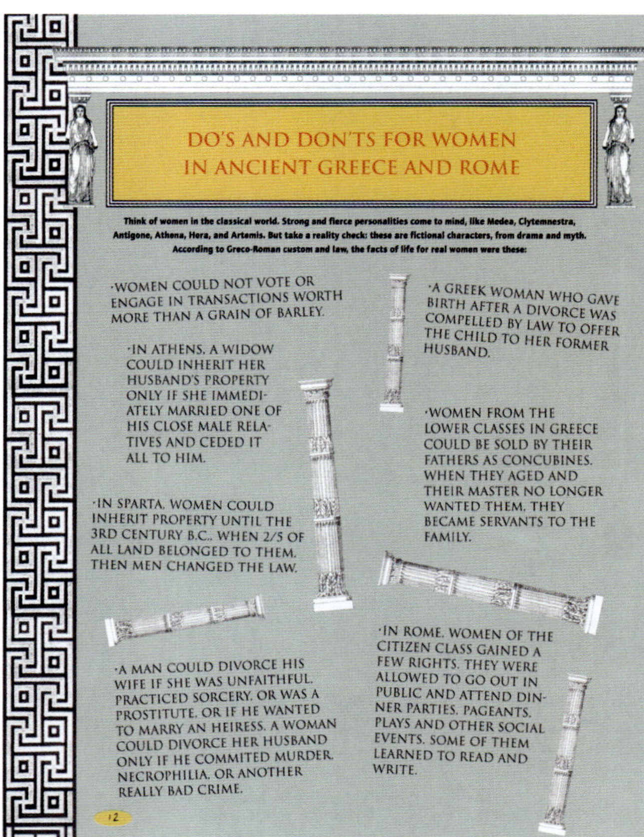

DO'S AND DON'TS FOR WOMEN
IN ANCIENT GREECE AND ROME

Think of women in the classical world. Strong and fierce personalities come to mind, like Medea, Clytemnestra, Antigone, Athena, Hera, and Artemis. But take a reality check: these are fictional characters, from drama and myth. According to Greco-Roman custom and law, the facts of life for real women were these:

·WOMEN COULD NOT VOTE OR ENGAGE IN TRANSACTIONS WORTH MORE THAN A GRAIN OF BARLEY.

·IN ATHENS, A WIDOW COULD INHERIT HER HUSBAND'S PROPERTY ONLY IF SHE IMMEDIATELY MARRIED ONE OF HIS CLOSE MALE RELATIVES AND CEDED IT ALL TO HIM.

·IN SPARTA, WOMEN COULD INHERIT PROPERTY UNTIL THE 3RD CENTURY B.C., WHEN 2/5 OF ALL LAND BELONGED TO THEM. THEN MEN CHANGED THE LAW.

·A MAN COULD DIVORCE HIS WIFE IF SHE WAS UNFAITHFUL, PRACTICED SORCERY, OR WAS A PROSTITUTE. OR IF HE WANTED TO MARRY AN HEIRESS, A WOMAN COULD DIVORCE HER HUSBAND ONLY IF HE COMMITED MURDER, NECROPHILIA, OR ANOTHER REALLY BAD CRIME.

·A GREEK WOMAN WHO GAVE BIRTH AFTER A DIVORCE WAS COMPELLED BY LAW TO OFFER THE CHILD TO HER FORMER HUSBAND.

·WOMEN FROM THE LOWER CLASSES IN GREECE COULD BE SOLD BY THEIR FATHERS AS CONCUBINES. WHEN THEY AGED AND THEIR MASTER NO LONGER WANTED THEM, THEY BECAME SERVANTS TO THE FAMILY.

·IN ROME, WOMEN OF THE CITIZEN CLASS GAINED A FEW RIGHTS. THEY WERE ALLOWED TO GO OUT IN PUBLIC AND ATTEND DINNER PARTIES, PAGEANTS, PLAYS AND OTHER SOCIAL EVENTS. SOME OF THEM LEARNED TO READ AND WRITE.

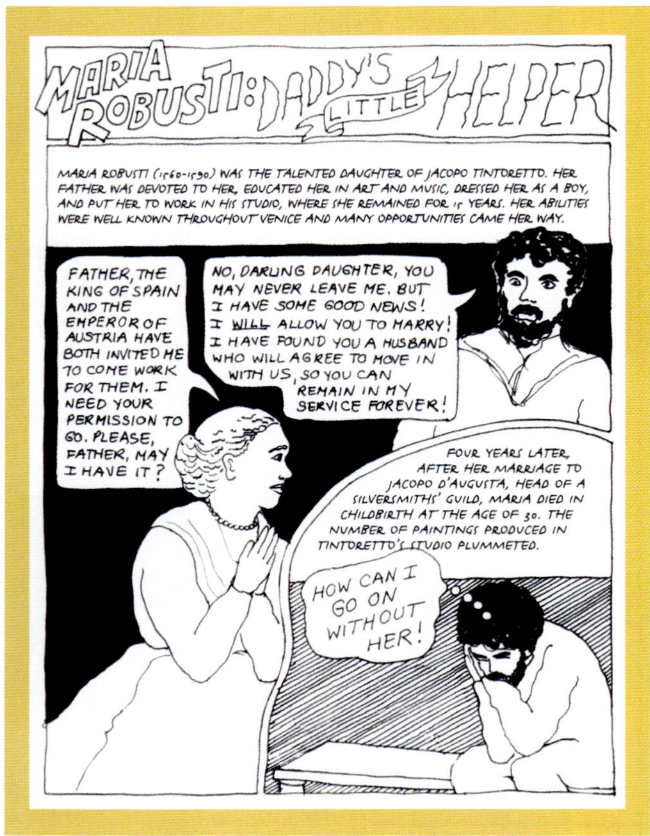

EDMONIA LEWIS: ROME VS. HOME

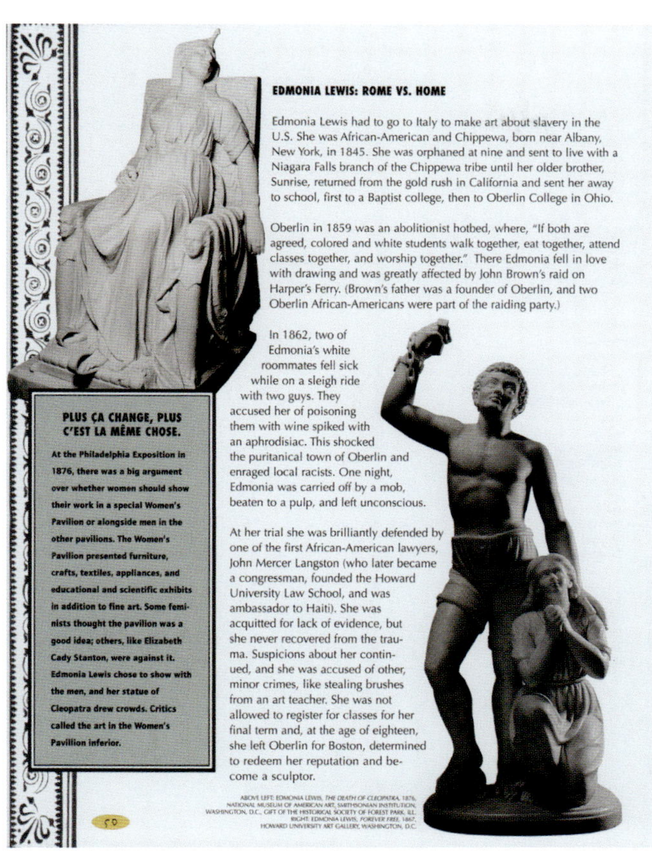

Edmonia Lewis had to go to Italy to make art about slavery in the U.S. She was African-American and Chippewa, born near Albany, New York, in 1845. She was orphaned at nine and sent to live with a Niagara Falls branch of the Chippewa tribe until her older brother, Sunrise, returned from the gold rush in California and sent her away to school, first to a Baptist college, then to Oberlin College in Ohio.

Oberlin in 1859 was an abolitionist hotbed, where, "If both are agreed, colored and white students walk together, eat together, attend classes together, and worship together." There Edmonia fell in love with drawing and was greatly affected by John Brown's raid on Harper's Ferry. (Brown's father was a founder of Oberlin, and two Oberlin African-Americans were part of the raiding party.)

In 1862, two of Edmonia's white roommates fell sick while on a sleigh ride with two guys. They accused her of poisoning them with wine spiked with an aphrodisiac. This shocked the puritanical town of Oberlin and enraged local racists. One night, Edmonia was carried off by a mob, beaten to a pulp, and left unconscious.

At her trial she was brilliantly defended by one of the first African-American lawyers, John Mercer Langston (who later became a congressman, founded the Howard University Law School, and was ambassador to Haiti). She was acquitted for lack of evidence, but she never recovered from the trauma. Suspicions about her continued, and she was accused of other, minor crimes, like stealing brushes from an art teacher. She was not allowed to register for classes for her final term and, at the age of eighteen, she left Oberlin for Boston, determined to redeem her reputation and become a sculptor.

> **PLUS ÇA CHANGE, PLUS C'EST LA MÊME CHOSE.**
>
> At the Philadelphia Exposition in 1876, there was a big argument over whether women should show their work in a special Women's Pavilion or alongside men in the other pavilions. The Women's Pavilion presented furniture, crafts, textiles, appliances, and educational and scientific exhibits in addition to fine art. Some feminists thought the pavilion was a good idea; others, like Elizabeth Cady Stanton, were against it. Edmonia Lewis chose to show with the men, and her statue of Cleopatra drew crowds. Critics called the art in the Women's Pavilion inferior.

ABOVE LEFT: EDMONIA LEWIS, THE DEATH OF CLEOPATRA, 1876, NATIONAL MUSEUM OF AMERICAN ART, SMITHSONIAN INSTITUTION, WASHINGTON, D.C., GIFT OF THE HISTORICAL SOCIETY OF FOREST PARK, ILL. RIGHT: EDMONIA LEWIS, FOREVER FREE, 1867, HOWARD UNIVERSITY ART GALLERY, WASHINGTON, D.C.

> WOMEN DON'T WANT TO BE GRANTED EQUALITY; THEY WANT TO WIN IT, WHICH IS NOT THE SAME THING AT ALL.
> —SIMONE DE BEAUVOIR.
>
> IN OUR CULTURE, WOMEN OF ALL RACES AND CLASSES WHO STEP OUT ON THE EDGE, COURAGEOUSLY RESISTING CONVENTIONAL NORMS FOR FEMALE BEHAVIOR, ARE ALMOST ALWAYS PORTRAYED AS CRAZY, OUT OF CONTROL, MAD.
> —BELL HOOKS
>
> WHAT DO WOMEN WANT? THEY WANT THE HUMAN TO BE NEITHER MAN NOR WOMAN.
> —JEAN-FRANÇOIS LYOTARD

From the end of the 19th century to the first half of the 20th, revolution was on everyone's mind, including artists. Some wanted to change the world, others just wanted to change art. In Western art, movements and "isms" appeared, one after another: impressionism, postimpressionism, fauvism, cubism, futurism, constructivism, dada-ism, surrealism, expressionism, abstract expressionism, etc. Put them all together and what do we get? "Modernism."

Paris, Berlin, Moscow, and New York—each had its own stereotypical white male artist (see below). So where were the women? As usual, they didn't fit the stereotypes, but they were there, working away. Often they came up with innovations that their husbands got credit for. Sometimes they sublimated their careers so as not to outshine the men in their lives. Sometimes they could make art only when they retired from their day jobs. There was still lots of discrimination, still lots of critics nagging that women's work was not as good as men's. But there was also more opportunity than ever before for a woman to live her life and make art on her own terms. In the 20th century, women won rights never given to them before, including the right to vote. With more freedom, more women have become artists.

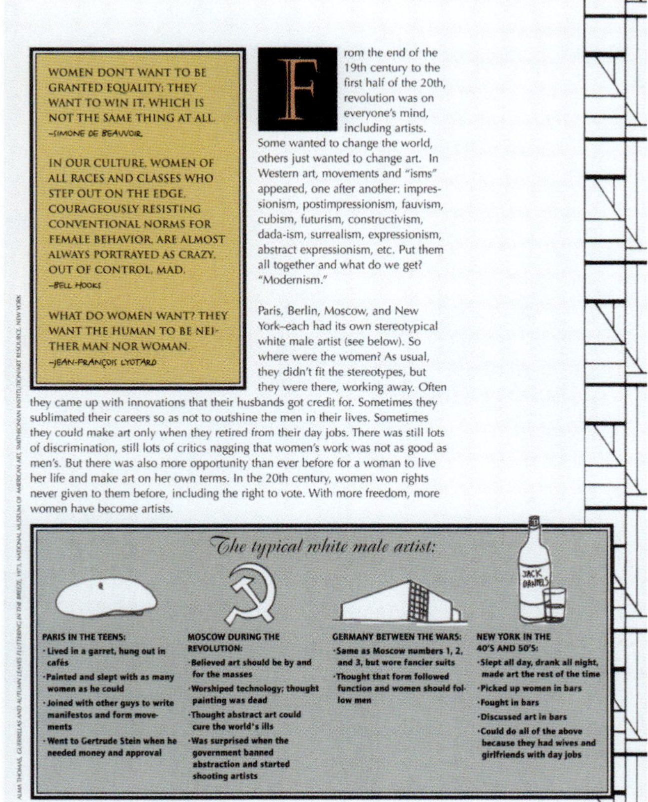

ALMA THOMAS, GUERABELAS AND AUTUMN LEAVES FLUTTERING IN THE BREEZE, 1973, NATIONAL MUSEUM OF AMERICAN ART, SMITHSONIAN INSTITUTION/ART RESOURCE, NEW YORK

CLAUDE CAHUN: BOY AND GIRL TOGETHER

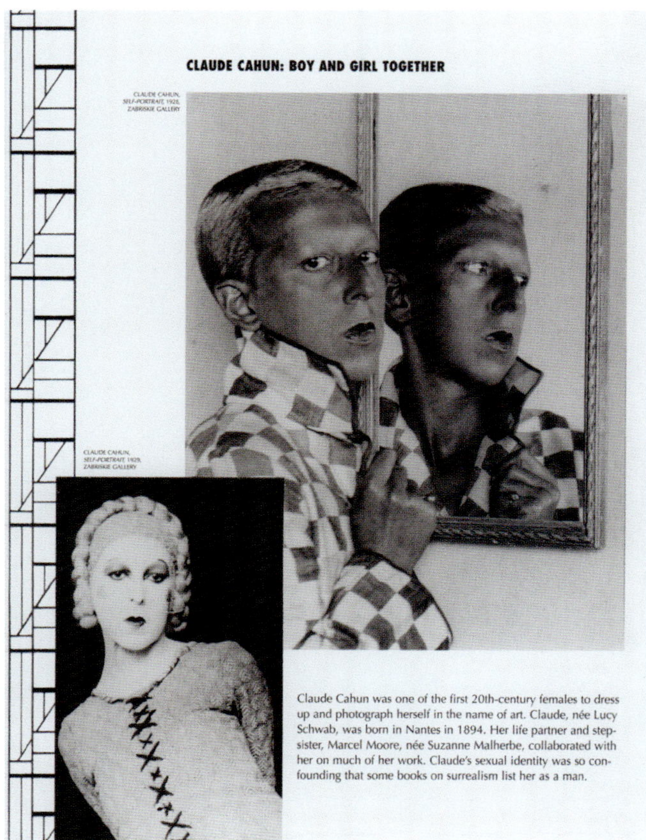

CLAUDE CAHUN, SELF-PORTRAIT, 1928, ZABRISKIE GALLERY

CLAUDE CAHUN, SELF-PORTRAIT, 1928, ZABRISKIE GALLERY

Claude Cahun was one of the first 20th-century females to dress up and photograph herself in the name of art. Claude, née Lucy Schwab, was born in Nantes in 1894. Her life partner and stepsister, Marcel Moore, née Suzanne Malherbe, collaborated with her on much of her work. Claude's sexual identity was so confounding that some books on surrealism list her as a man.

ANA MENDIETA: GIRL INTERRUPTED TOO

ANA MENDIETA, UNTITLED (FROM THE 'SILUETA' SERIES), 1978, COURTESY THE ESTATE OF ANA MENDIETA AND GALERIE LELONG, NEW YORK

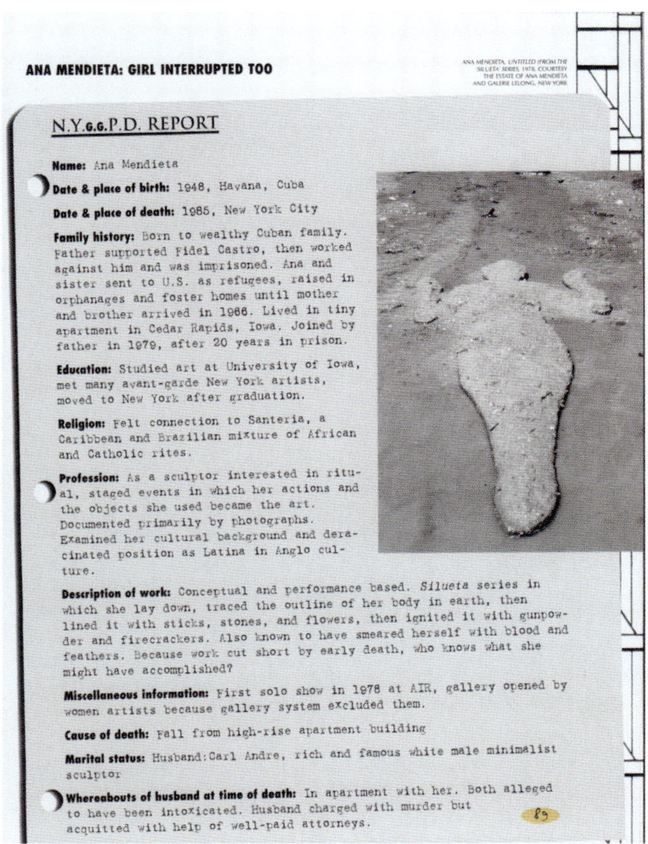

N.Y.G.G.P.D. REPORT

Name: Ana Mendieta

Date & place of birth: 1948, Havana, Cuba

Date & place of death: 1985, New York City

Family history: Born to wealthy Cuban family. Father supported Fidel Castro, then worked against him and was imprisoned. Ana and sister sent to U.S. as refugees, raised in orphanages and foster homes until mother and brother arrived in 1966. Lived in tiny apartment in Cedar Rapids, Iowa. Joined by father in 1979, after 20 years in prison.

Education: Studied art at University of Iowa, met many avant-garde New York artists, moved to New York after graduation.

Religion: Felt connection to Santeria, a Caribbean and Brazilian mixture of African and Catholic rites.

Profession: As a sculptor interested in ritual, staged events in which her actions and the objects she used became the art. Documented primarily by photographs. Examined her cultural background and deracinated position as Latina in Anglo culture.

Description of work: Conceptual and performance based. *Silueta* series in which she lay down, traced the outline of her body in earth, then lined it with sticks, stones, and flowers, then ignited it with gunpowder and firecrackers. Also known to have smeared herself with blood and feathers. Because work cut short by early death, who knows what she might have accomplished?

Miscellaneous information: First solo show in 1978 at AIR, gallery opened by women artists because gallery system excluded them.

Cause of death: Fall from high-rise apartment building

Marital status: Husband: Carl Andre, rich and famous white male minimalist sculptor

Whereabouts of husband at time of death: In apartment with her. Both alleged to have been intoxicated. Husband charged with murder but acquitted with help of well-paid attorneys.

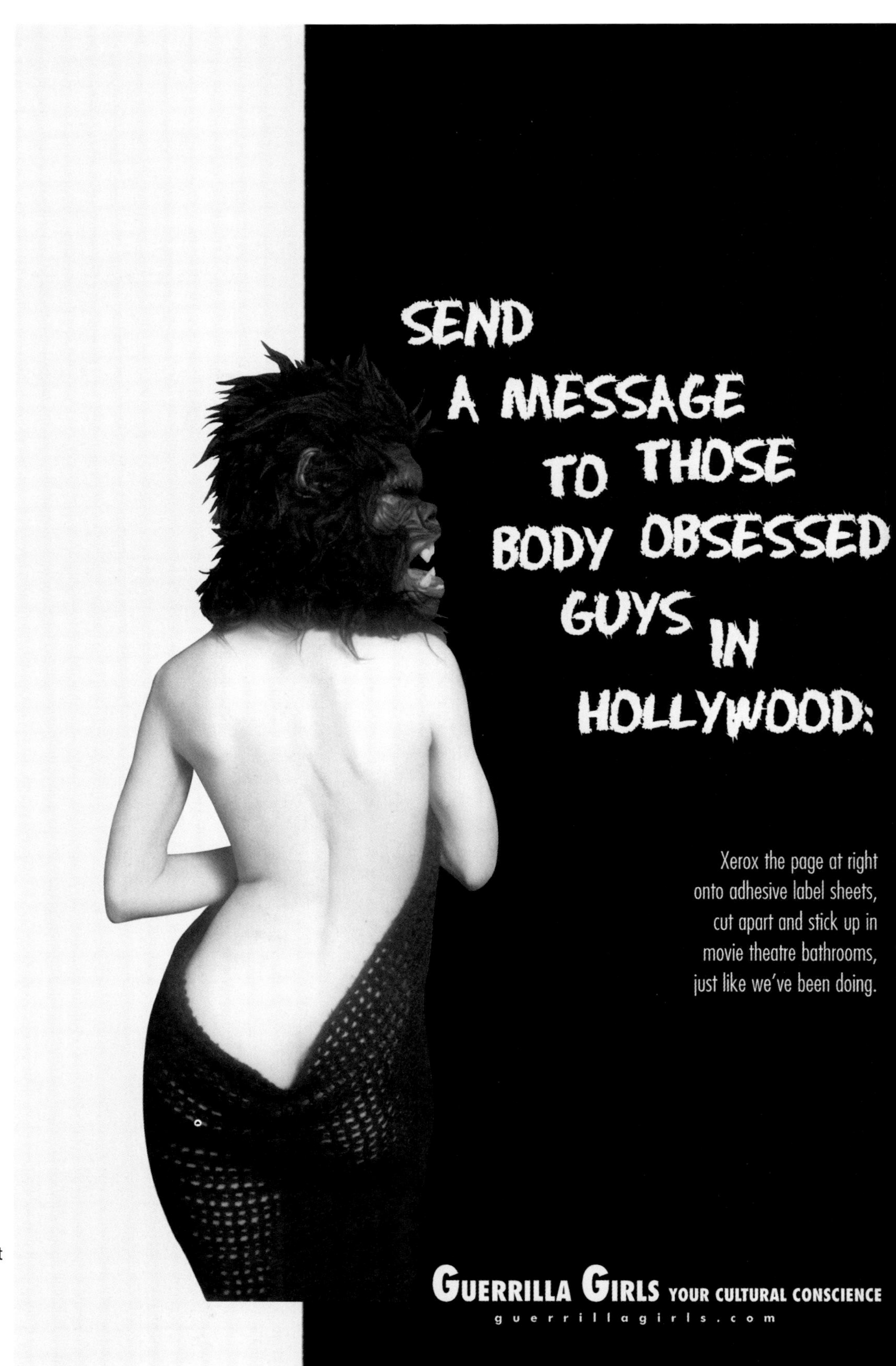

The Hollywood film industry is even worse than the artworld! We began a campaign to expose the lack of diversity in film, with street banners, billboards, magazine spreads and stickers.

Bitch magazine spread, 2000

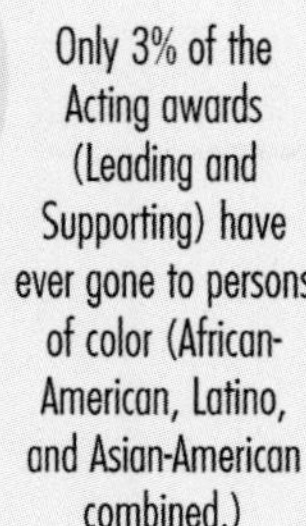

THE
ANATOMICALLY CORRECT
OSCAR
HE'S WHITE AND MALE, JUST LIKE
THE GUYS WHO WIN!

No woman has
ever won an Oscar
for Direction,
Cinematography or
Sound.

94% of the Writing
awards have gone to
men.

Only 3% of the
Acting awards
(Leading and
Supporting) have
ever gone to persons
of color (African-
American, Latino,
and Asian-American
combined.)

A MESSAGE
FROM THE
GUERRILLA
GIRLS
YOUR CULTURAL
CONSCIENCE
guerrillagirls.com

FOR MORE OF THESE PATHETIC STATISTICS, CHECK OUT WWW.OSCARS.COM

©GUERRILLA GIRLS FOR BITCH MAGAZINE #13

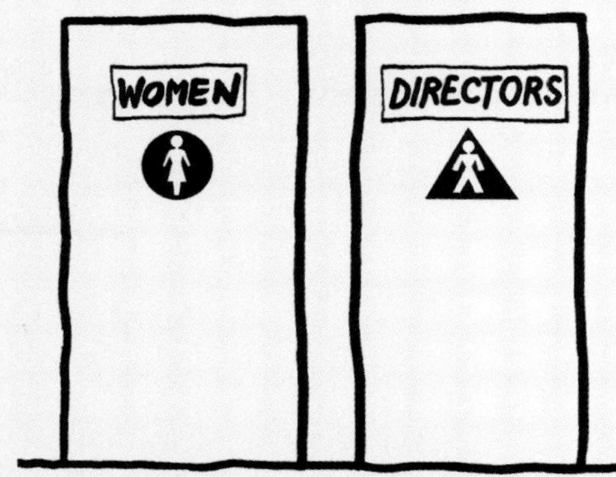

WANNA DIRECT?
YOU'RE IN THE WRONG
BATHROOM.

WOMEN

DIRECTORS

In 1987, 2.4% of major films were directed by women.
By 1999, that number rose to a whopping 4%.

A MESSAGE FROM THE GUERRILLA GIRLS YOUR CULTURAL CONSCIE
guerrillagirls.com

©GUERRILLA GIRLS FOR BITCH MAGAZINE #13

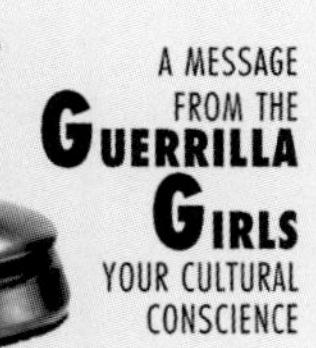

THIN

THINNER

THINNEST

The earnings of female actors peak
from age 20 to 29,
then drop permanently after 30.

Only 27% of roles for actors over 40
go to women.

African-Americans get only 13.4% of acting jobs,
Latinos 3.5%, Asians 2.1%

A MESSAGE FROM THE GUERRILLA GIRLS YOUR CULTURAL CONSCIENCE
guerrillagirls.com

©GUERRILLA GIRLS FOR BITCH MAGAZINE #13

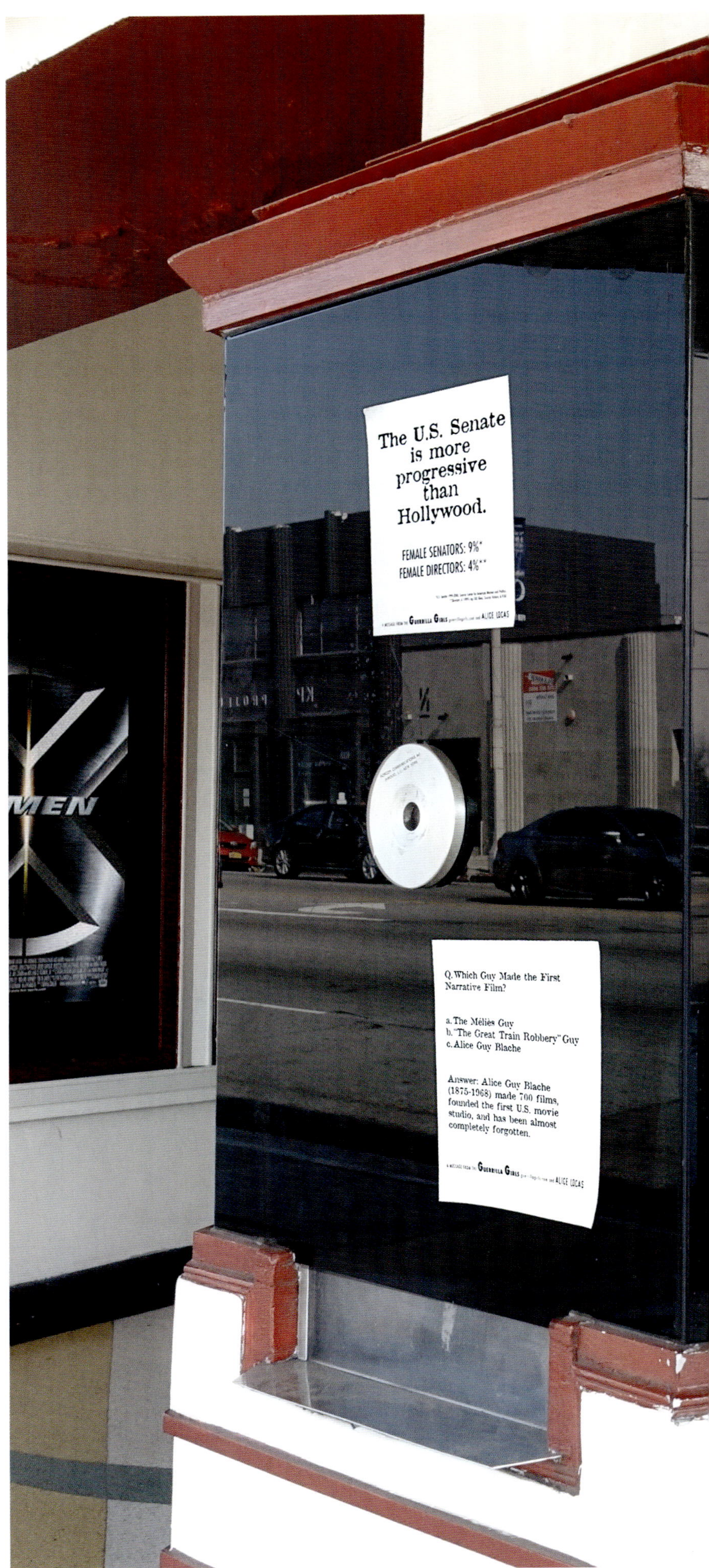

We worked with an anonymous group of women
directors to create stickers that traveled to the
Sundance Film Festival, the Academy Awards
ceremony and movie theatre bathrooms everywhere. See our 2019 update (page 174) to see
if anything changed.

Stickers, 2000

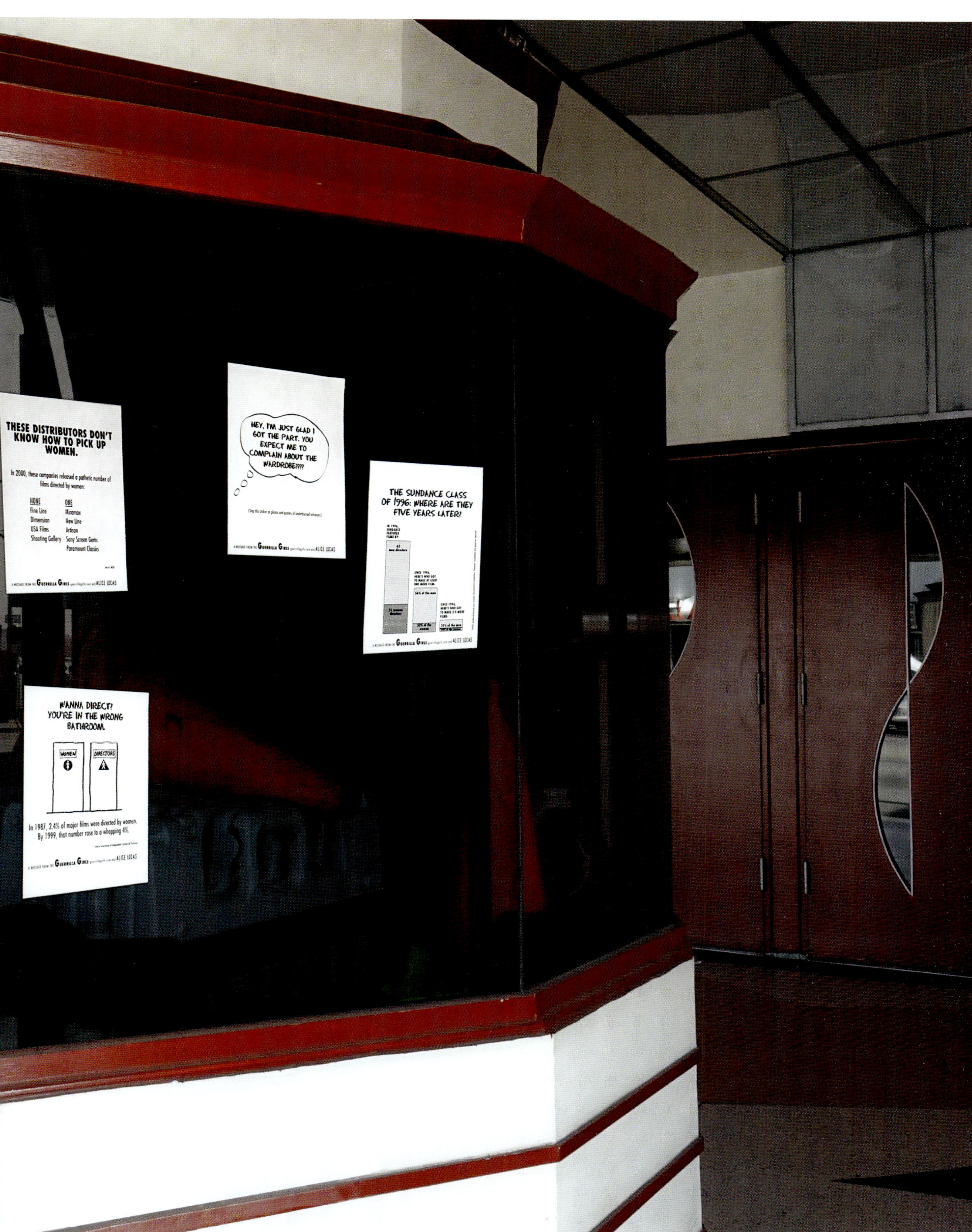
THESE DISTRIBUTORS DON'T
KNOW HOW TO PICK UP
WOMEN.

NONE
Fine Line
Dimension
USA Films
Shooting Gallery

ONE
Miramax
New Line
Artisan
Sony Screen Gems
Paramount Classics

A MESSAGE FROM THE GUERRILLA GIRLS and ALICE LOCAS
HEY, I'M JUST GLAD I
GOT THE PART. YOU
EXPECT ME TO
COMPLAIN ABOUT THE
WARDROBE????

A MESSAGE FROM THE GUERRILLA GIRLS and ALICE LOCAS
THE SUNDANCE CLASS
OF 1996: WHERE ARE THEY
FIVE YEARS LATER?

A MESSAGE FROM THE GUERRILLA GIRLS and ALICE LOCAS
WANNA DIRECT?
YOU'RE IN THE WRONG
BATHROOM

WOMEN   DIRECTORS

In 1987, 2.4% of major films were directed by women.
By 1999, that number rose to a whopping 4%.

A MESSAGE FROM THE GUERRILLA GIRLS and ALICE LOCAS

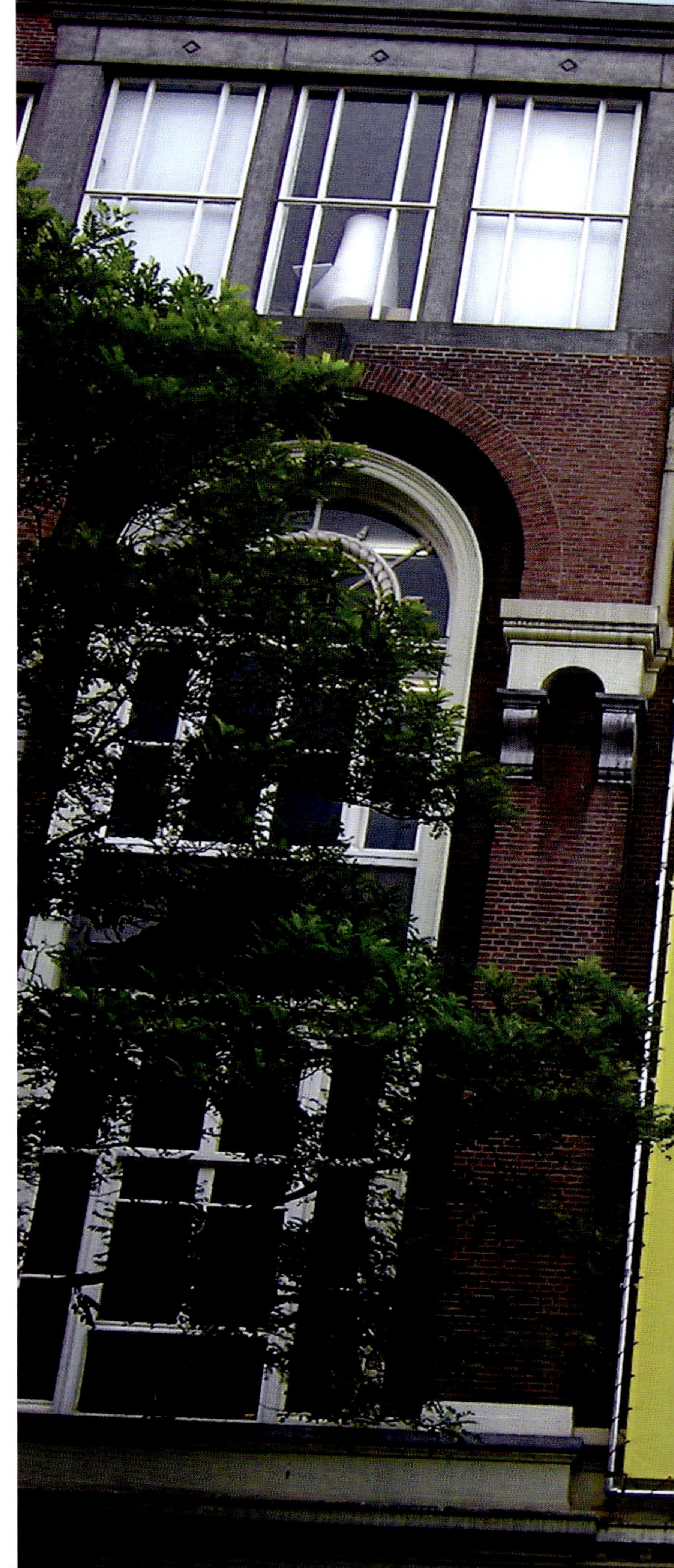

What kind of movie would Hollywood concoct
about the history of feminism? We made a movie
poster for the film we hope never gets made the
Hollywood way.

Poster, 2001/Banner, 2006, at Witte de With, Rotterdam

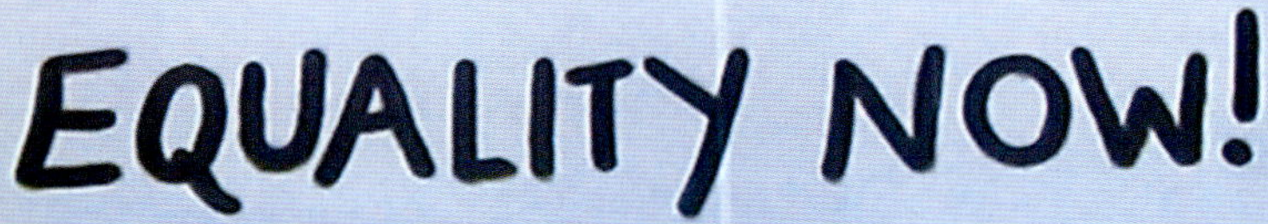

A Major Hollywood Studio presents

the BIRTH of FEMINISM

EQUALITY NOW!

PAMELA ANDERSON
AS FEMINIST LEADER
GLORIA STEINEM

HALLE BERRY
AS CIVIL RIGHTS LAWYER
FLO KENNEDY

CATHERINE ZETA-JONES
AS CONGRESSWOMAN
BELLA ABZUG

They made women's rights look good. Really good.

A JERRY BRUCKHEIMER PRODUCTION   CATHERINE ZETA-JONES   HALLE BERRY   PAMELA ANDERSON "THE BIRTH OF FEMINISM"
DIRECTED BY OLIVER STONE   SCREENPLAY BY JOE ESZTERHAS   GET THE SOUNDTRACK ALBUM FEATURING EMINEM   POSTER BY THE GUERRILLA GIRLS

www.guerrillagirls.com

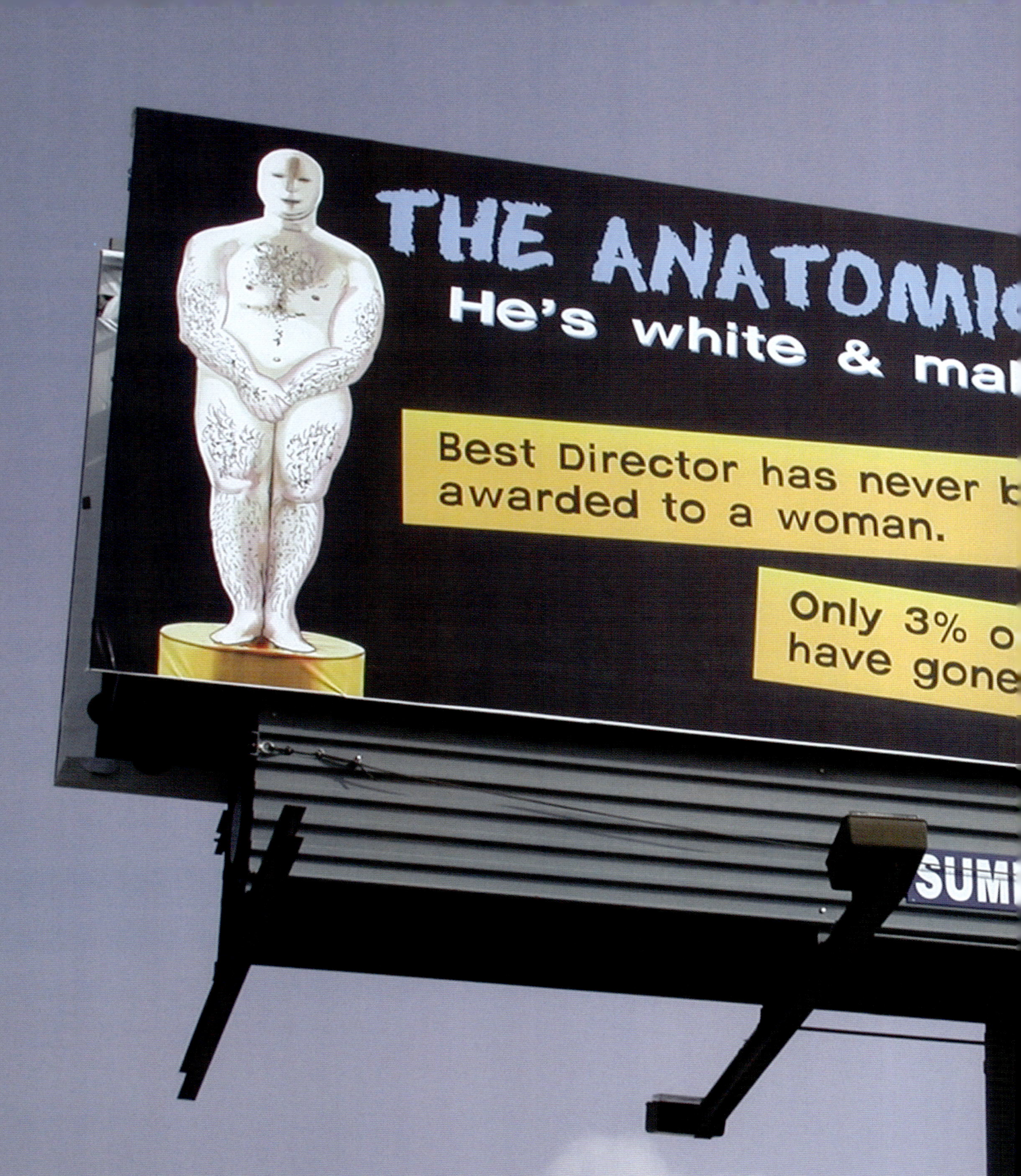

For several years we rented a billboard in Hollywood during
Academy Awards season. The first year, Halle Berry and
Denzel Washington won Oscars. Coincidence?

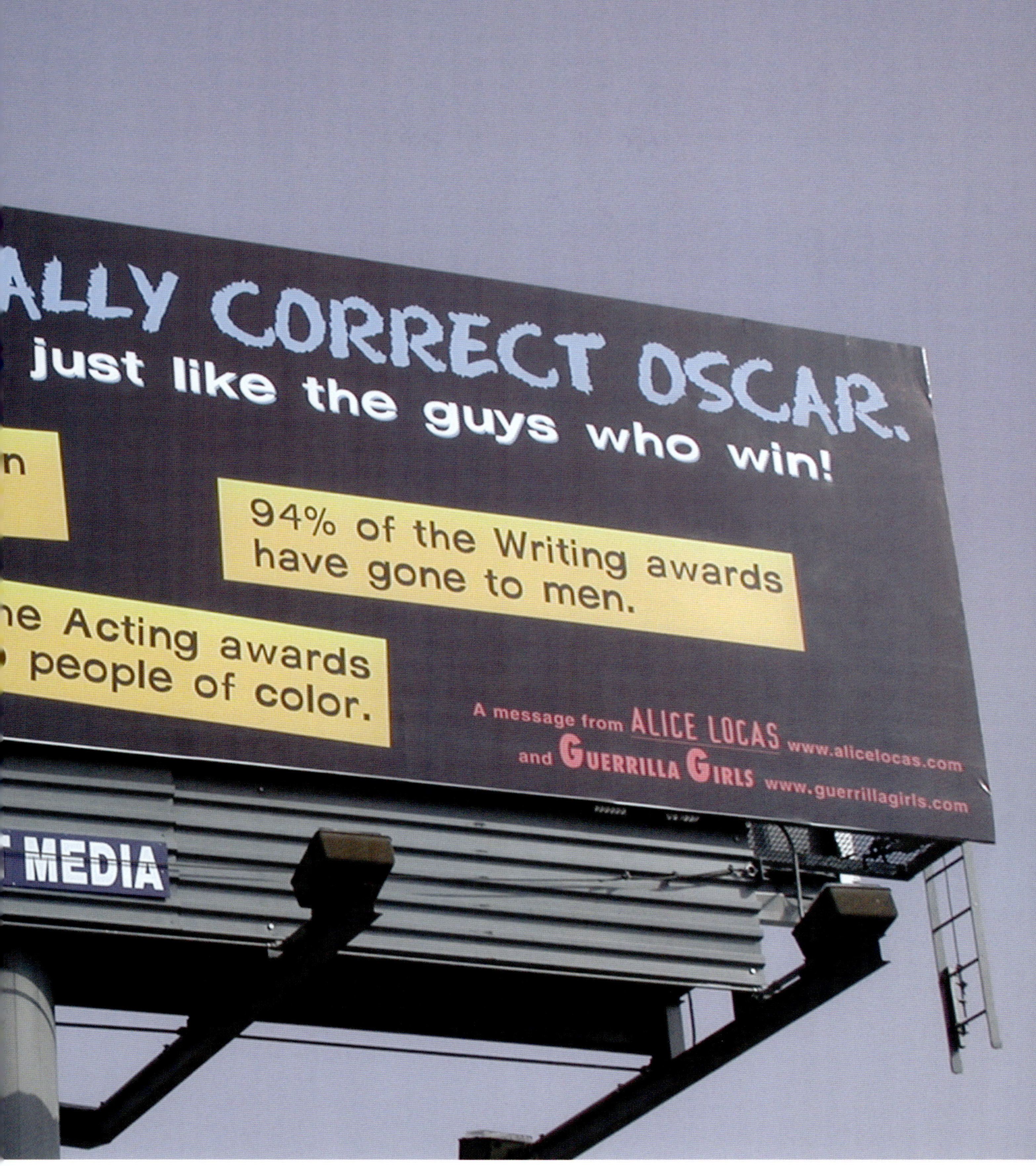

Billboard, Hollywood, 2002

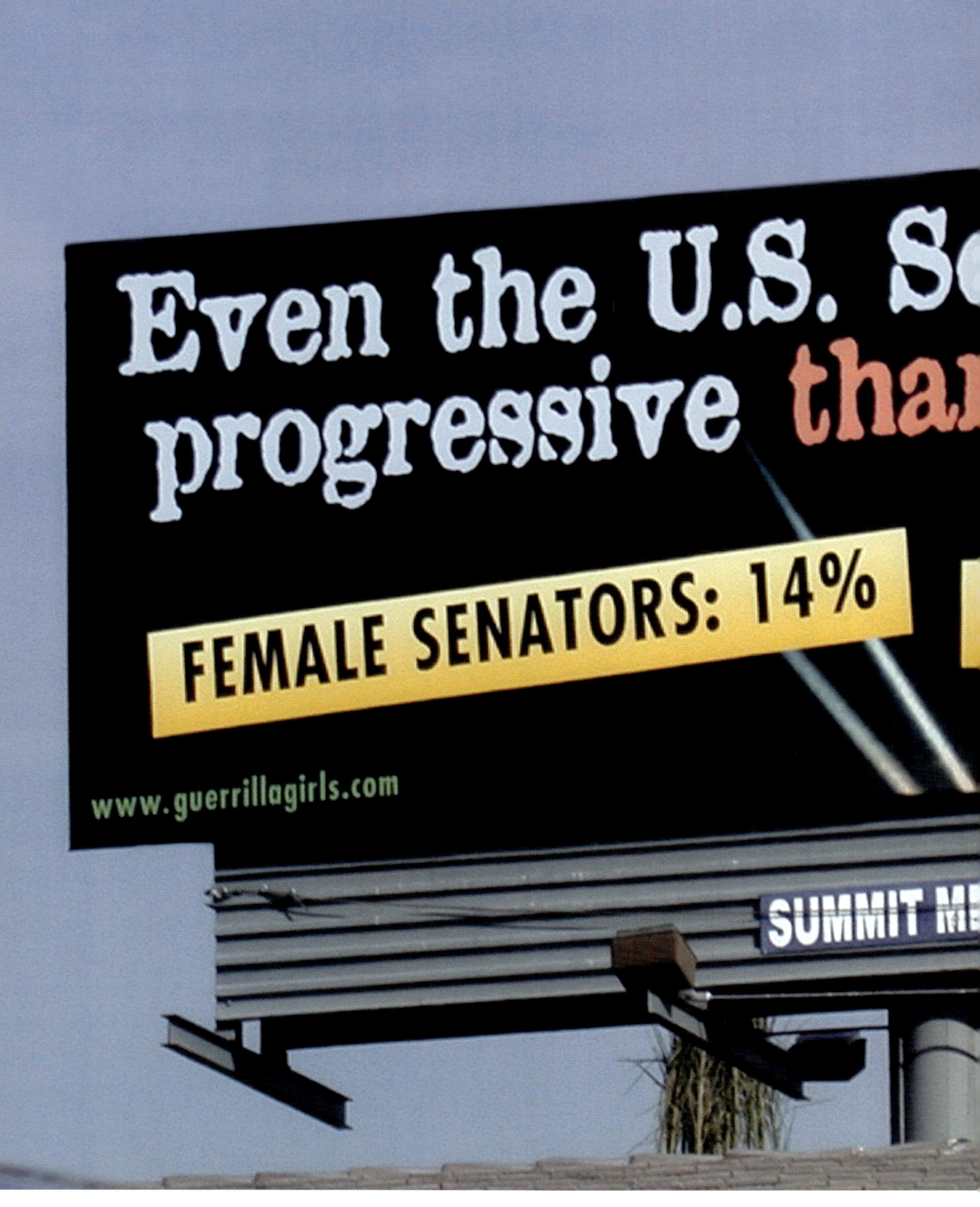

Even the U.S. Se
progressive than
FEMALE SENATORS: 14%
www.guerrillagirls.com
SUMMIT ME

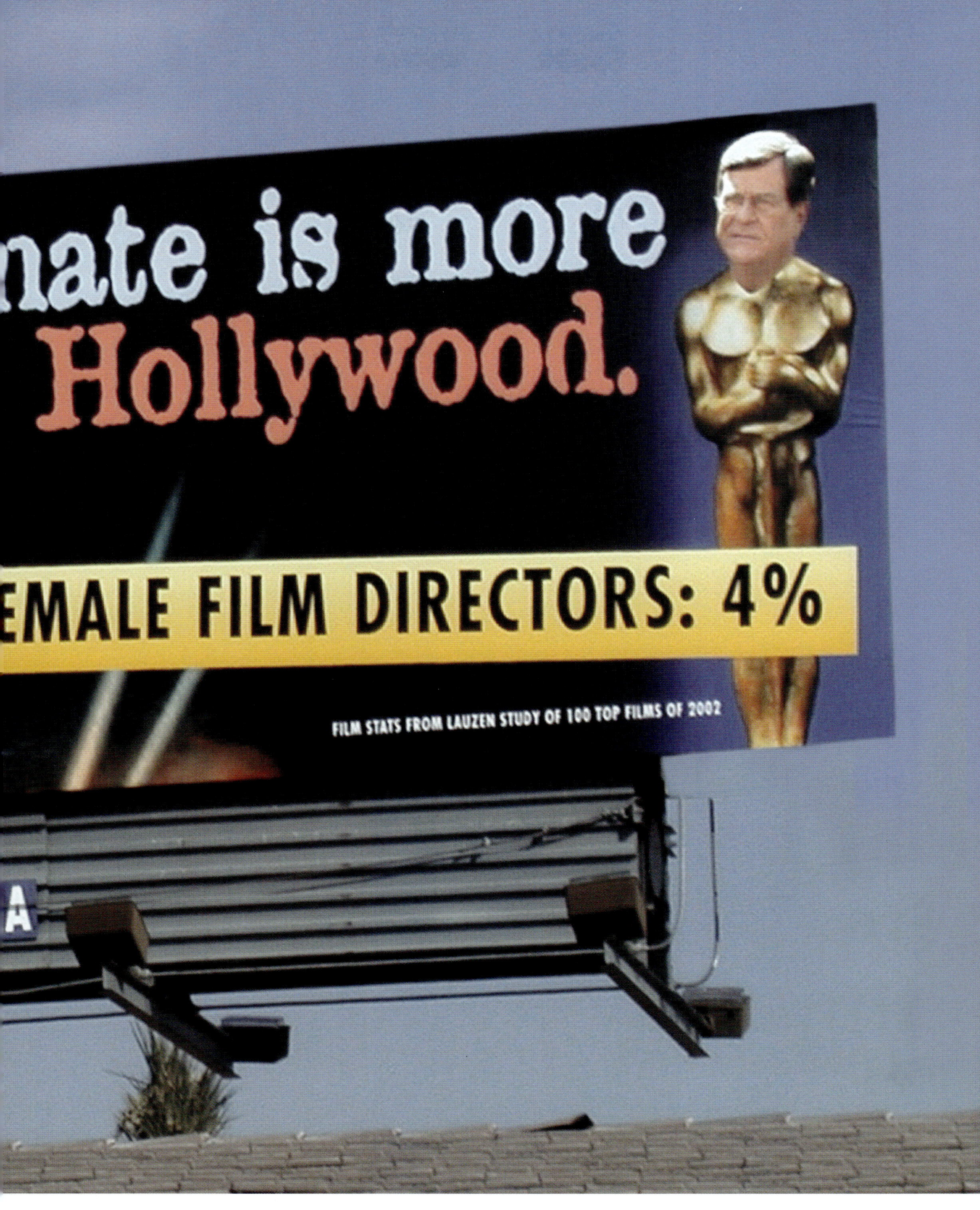

Billboard, Hollywood, 2003

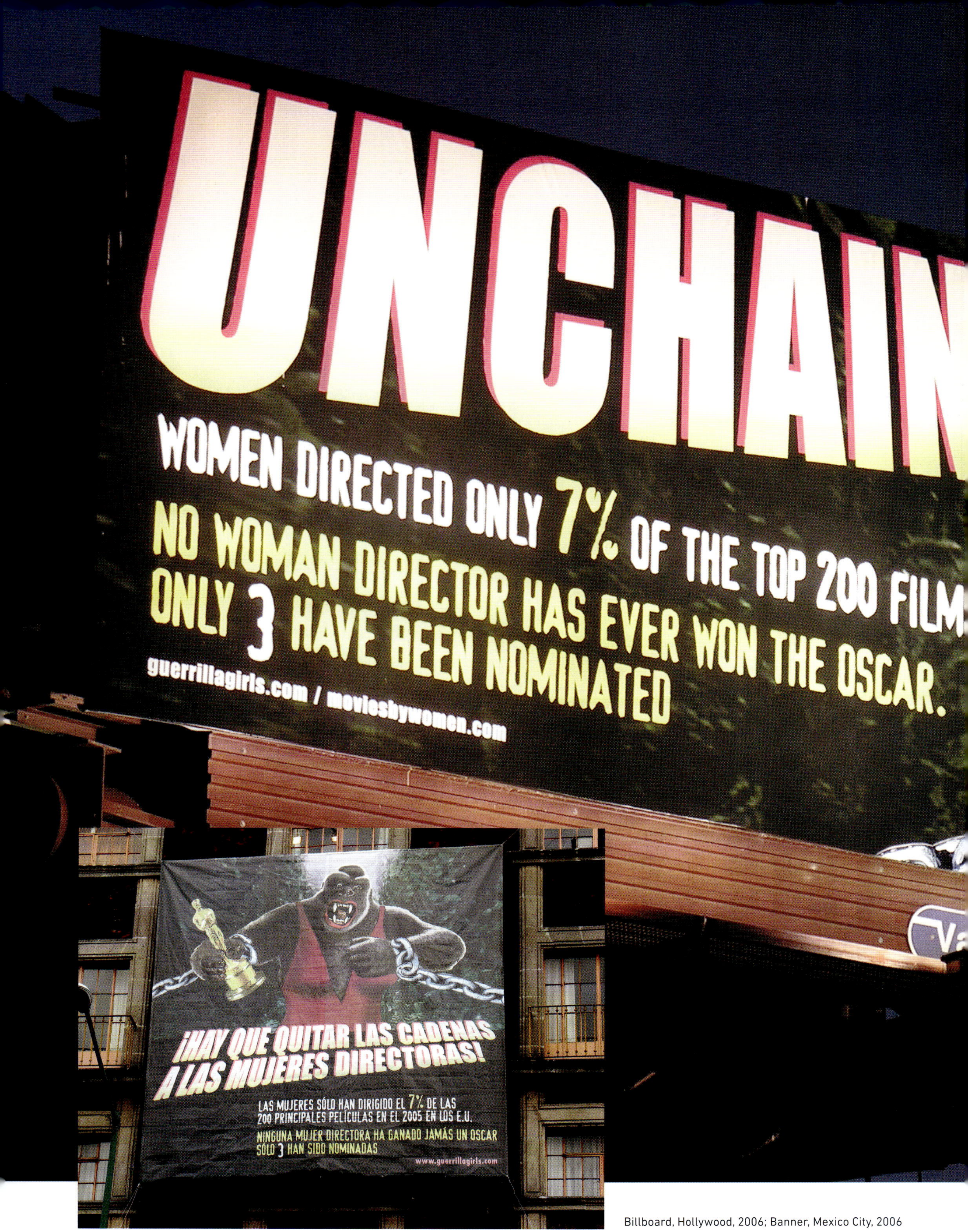

Billboard, Hollywood, 2006; Banner, Mexico City, 2006

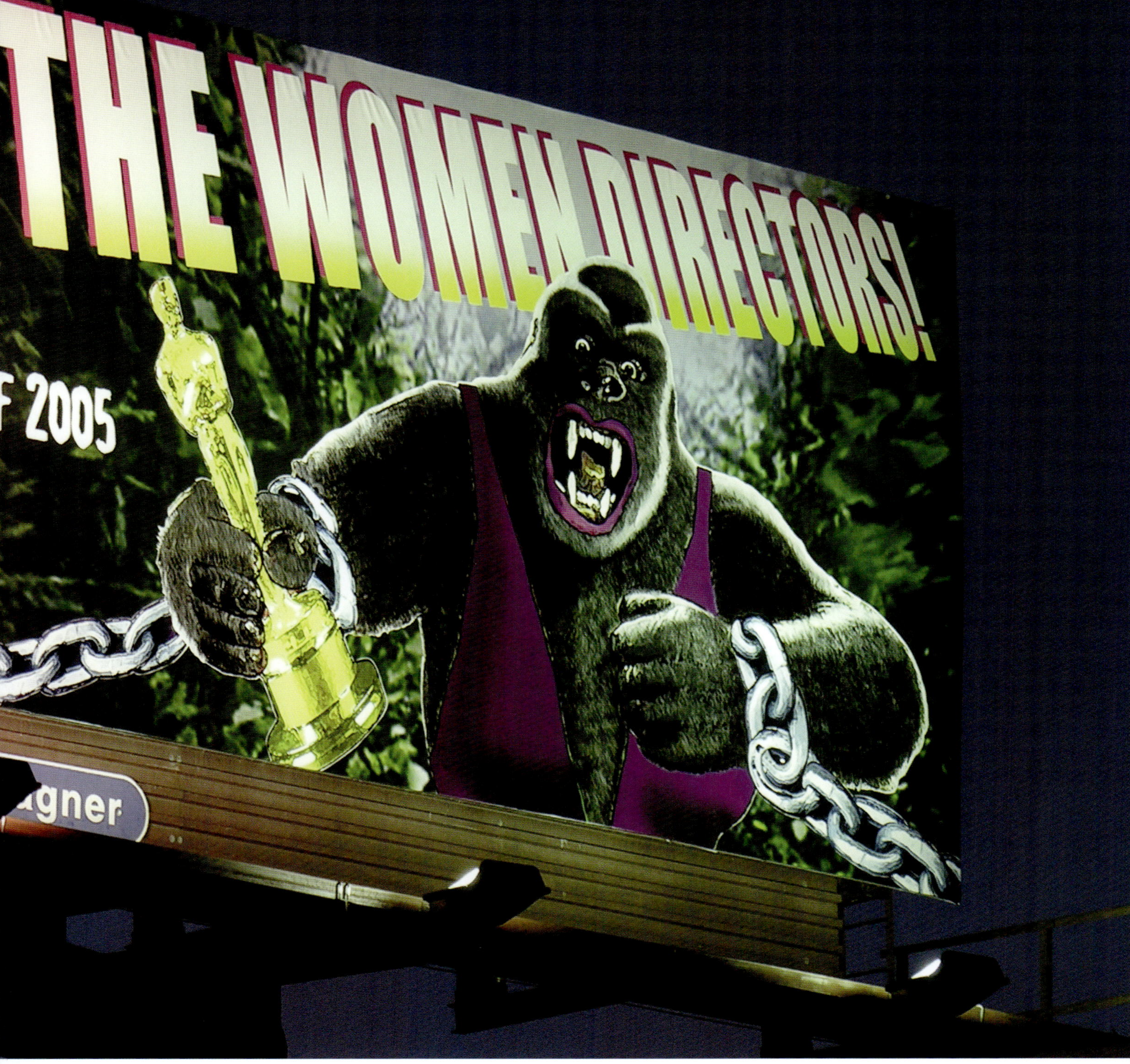
THE WOMEN DIRECTORS!
F 2005
gner

Thinking about film and pop culture drove us to investigate female stereotypes. How are they born? How do they evolve? How can we escape them?

Book, 2003. Cover and some interior pages

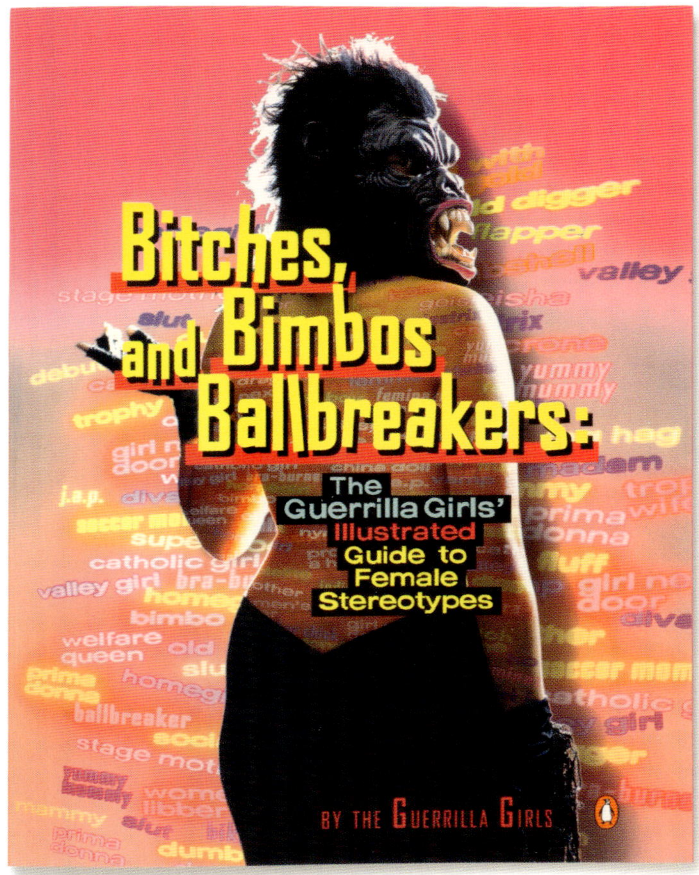

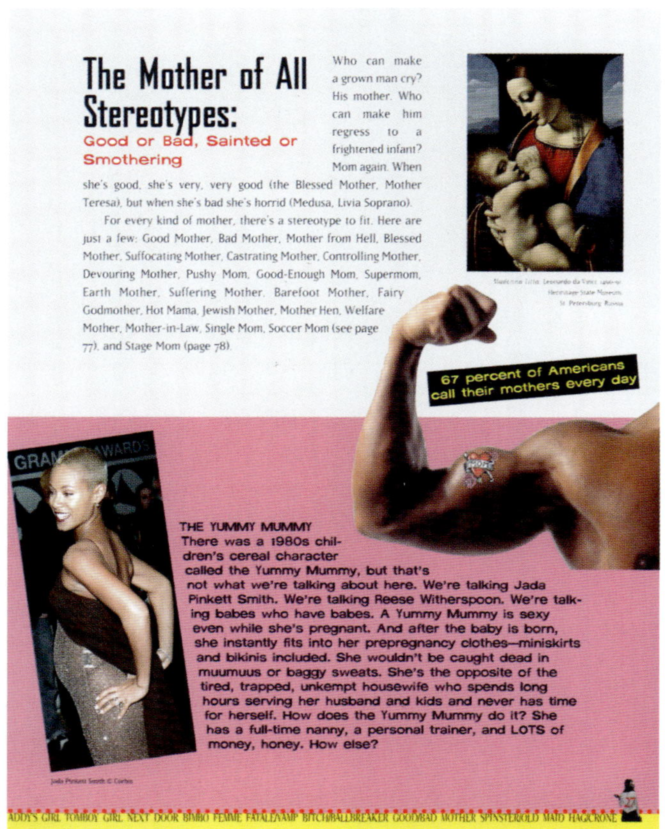

The Mother of All Stereotypes:
Good or Bad, Sainted or Smothering

Who can make a grown man cry? His mother. Who can make him regress to a frightened infant? Mom again. When she's good, she's very, very good (the Blessed Mother, Mother Teresa), but when she's bad she's horrid (Medusa, Livia Soprano).

For every kind of mother, there's a stereotype to fit. Here are just a few: Good Mother, Bad Mother, Mother from Hell, Blessed Mother, Suffocating Mother, Castrating Mother, Controlling Mother, Devouring Mother, Pushy Mom, Good-Enough Mom, Supermom, Earth Mother, Suffering Mother, Barefoot Mother, Fairy Godmother, Hot Mama, Jewish Mother, Mother Hen, Welfare Mother, Mother-in-Law, Single Mom, Soccer Mom (see page 77), and Stage Mom (page 78).

THE YUMMY MUMMY
There was a 1980s children's cereal character called the Yummy Mummy, but that's not what we're talking about here. We're talking Jada Pinkett Smith. We're talking Reese Witherspoon. We're talking babes who have babes. A Yummy Mummy is sexy even while she's pregnant. And after the baby is born, she instantly fits into her prepregnancy clothes—miniskirts and bikinis included. She wouldn't be caught dead in muumuus or baggy sweats. She's the opposite of the tired, trapped, unkempt housewife who spends long hours serving her husband and kids and never has time for herself. How does the Yummy Mummy do it? She has a full-time nanny, a personal trainer, and LOTS of money, honey. How else?

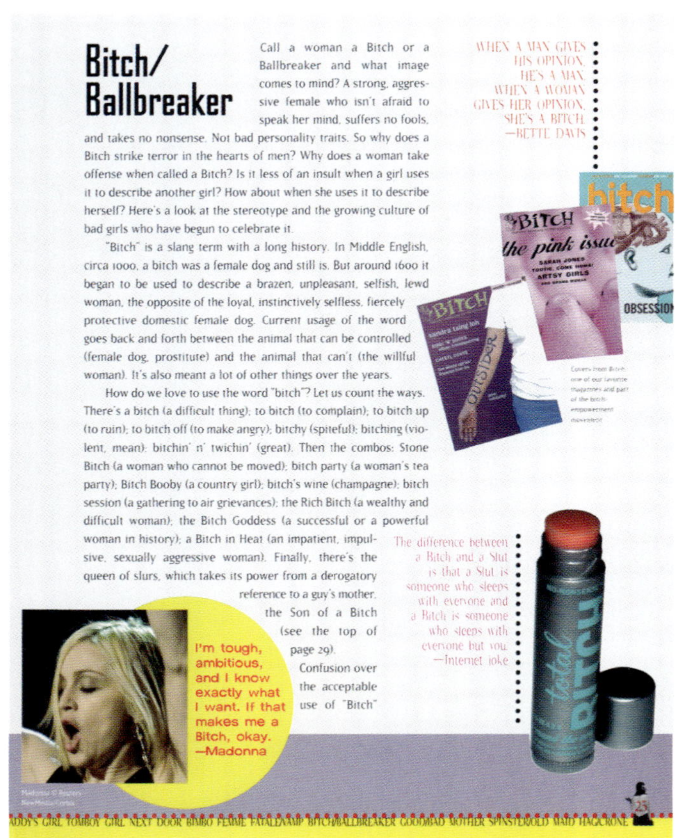

Bitch/ Ballbreaker

Call a woman a Bitch or a Ballbreaker and what image comes to mind? A strong, aggressive female who isn't afraid to speak her mind, suffers no fools, and takes no nonsense. Not bad personality traits. So why does a Bitch strike terror in the hearts of men? Why does a woman take offense when called a Bitch? Is it less of an insult when a girl uses it to describe another girl? How about when she uses it to describe herself? Here's a look at the stereotype and the growing culture of bad girls who have begun to celebrate it.

"Bitch" is a slang term with a long history. In Middle English, circa 1000, a bitch was a female dog and still is. But around 1600 it began to be used to describe a brazen, unpleasant, selfish, lewd woman, the opposite of the loyal, instinctively selfless, fiercely protective domestic female dog. Current usage of the word goes back and forth between the animal that can be controlled (female dog, prostitute) and the animal that can't (the willful woman). It's also meant a lot of other things over the years.

How do we love to use the word "bitch"? Let us count the ways. There's a bitch (a difficult thing); to bitch (to complain); to bitch up (to ruin); to bitch off (to make angry); bitchy (spiteful); bitching (violent, mean); bitchin' n' twichin' (great). Then the combos: Stone Bitch (a woman who cannot be moved); bitch party (a woman's tea party); Bitch Booby (a country girl); bitch's wine (champagne); bitch session (a gathering to air grievances); the Rich Bitch (a wealthy and difficult woman); the Bitch Goddess (a successful or a powerful woman in history); a Bitch in Heat (an impatient, impulsive, sexually aggressive woman). Finally, there's the queen of slurs, which takes its power from a derogatory reference to a guy's mother, the Son of a Bitch (see the top of page 29).

Confusion over the acceptable use of "Bitch"

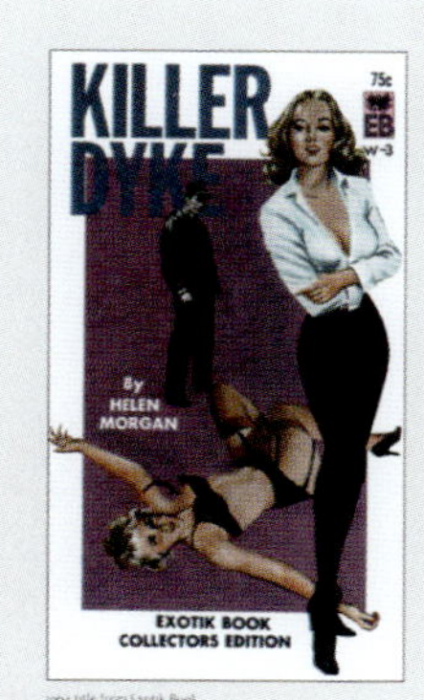

1964 title from Exotik Book.
courtesy Jaye Zimet, author of Strange Sisters

Girls Who Do Girls

When we get to Girls Who Do Girls, at last we find a few female stereotypes invented by, for, and about women. Here is a list: Amy-John, Androdyke, Cofeminator, Dandysette, Dutch Girl, Dykeosaurus, Etelle, Fairy Lady, Gay Lady, Goose Girl, He-She, Lady-Lover, Lemonade, Les-Be-Friends, Lesbyterian, Mandyke, Muffet, Ruffle, Sistagirl, Tinkerbell, Tootsie, Two Spirit, and Zami.

The words "Lesbian" and "Sapphist" hearken back to the Greek poet Sappho in the seventh century B.C. Like other women of her class, which was upper, Sappho's official job was to marry, bear children, and pass on her family legacy. That might have kept her home a lot of the time, but it didn't keep her from developing a unique form of poetry and gathering a group of female devotees around her. She returned their admiration by writing bridal odes and love poetry for them, like this:

I see he who sits near you as an equal of the gods
For he can closely listen to your delightful voice
And that seductive laugh
That makes the heart behind my breasts to tremble.

Whether or not Sappho ever consummated her passion with these women doesn't really matter. That she came to represent the transgressive idea that a woman can desire another woman does. Throughout Western history, romantic love between women has been tagged "Sapphist." But in the late 19th century, when a term

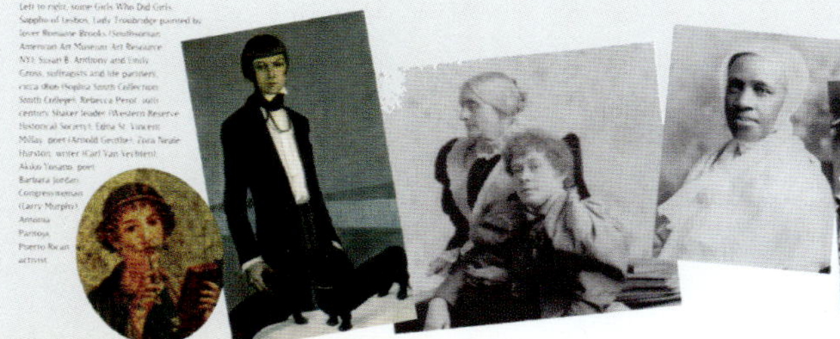

Left to right, some Girls Who Did Girls:
Sappho of lesbos; Lady Troubridge (painted by Janet Romaine Brooks; Hirschhorn Museum, Art Resource, NY); Susan B. Anthony and Emily Gross, suffragists and life partners (circa 1890, Regina Smith Collection; Smith College); Rebecca Primus (Rebecca Primus auto-letters; Shaker Seader, Weaters Reserve Historical Society); Edna St. Vincent Millay, poet (Arnold Genthe); Zora Neale Hurston, writer (Carl Van Vechten); Akiko Tanaka, poet; Barbara Jordan, Congresswoman (Garry Murphy); Amanita Pantoya, Puerto Rican activist.

In eras when women had few rights, to dress as a man and to be thought of as male was to have privilege. It meant freedom to get a job, to own property, to move about unaccosted, to love a woman, to be a father. If discovered or caught, it could mean disgrace, disenfranchisement, even jail. History is filled with tales of women who dressed as men, some for their entire lives, from Joan of Arc to the hundreds of women who fought as male soldiers in the Civil War. Their reasons were as varied as their backgrounds. Many might never have considered themselves Lesbians. Some were clearly not. Here are a few good stories:

When Dr. James Barry died in 1865, he was discovered to have been the first FEMALE physician in Great Britain. Historians suspect that a group of aristocrats in support of education for women helped the daughter of an Irish grocer get a place in an all-male medical school in Edinburgh. For that, she became James Barry and went on to be a highly respected doctor who traveled the world and transformed the practice of medicine and surgery. Dr Barry performed one of the earliest successful Caesarean sections. He was popular and well liked by women. How popular, we'll never know.

Mary Fields (1832–1914) kept her name and even wore a skirt over her trousers and boots, but everything else about her life on the frontier was macho. A patchwork of jobs took her from slavery in Tennessee to cowboy country. At one point she drove a stagecoach and was known as Stagecoach Mary. Formidable at 200 pounds, she wore a revolver strapped to her waist and was the only woman allowed to drink in the saloons of Cascade, Montana. Known as a brawler who used her gun to settle scores, Mary was also loved by her neighbors and their children, who took a school holiday on her birthday.

Luisa Capetillo's cross-dressing was immortalized by a folk song in her native Puerto Rico and led to an arrest during a trip to Cuba. Capetillo (1879–1922) was a socialist, union organizer, author, feminist, and single mother of three.

Ralph Kerwineo started life as Cora Anderson. A Native American, Ralph witnessed discrimination and genocide firsthand. He chose to pass as a man but he was a kind of feminist, too. He claimed he married one of his two wives to protect her from a sexist world. Here is a statement he made circa 1914: "The world is made for man...In the future centuries it is probable that woman will be the owner of her own body and the custodian of her own soul. But until that time you can expect the statutes [concerning] women will be all wrong. The well-cared-for woman is a parasite, and the woman who must work is a slave...Do you blame me for wanting to be a man?...Do you blame me for hating to again resume wearing a woman's clothes?"

Billy Tipton (1914–1989) was born Dorothy Tipton in Oklahoma City. At 19 she transformed herself into Billy Lee to get a job as a sax player in a jazz band. Billy stayed in drag the rest of his life, marrying five times, playing music, and later becoming a booking agent. When he died at age 74, his secret came out and was coast-to-coast news. It's not clear if all his wives knew the truth. To his adopted children, Bill was "just Dad."

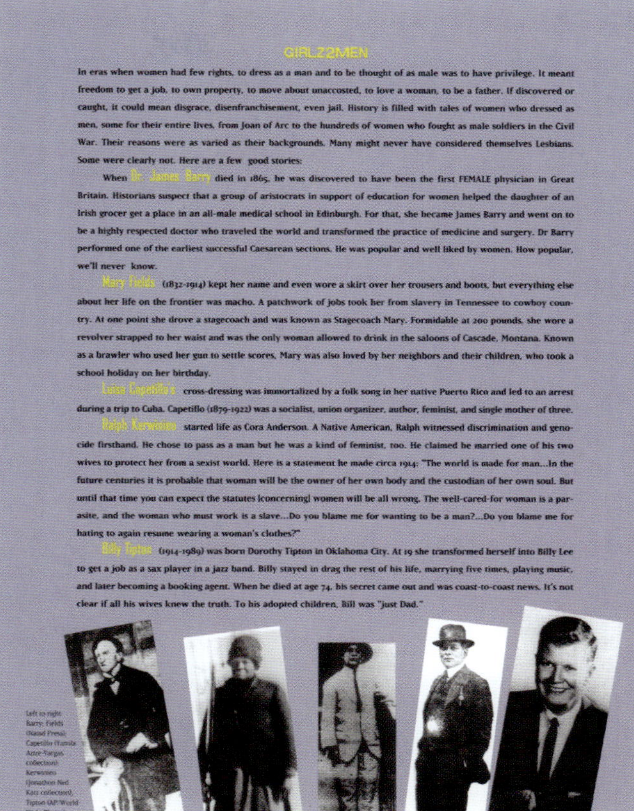

Left to right:
Barry, Fields (Hoand Press); Capetillo (Florida Aztec-Vargas collections); Kerwineo (Jonathan Ned Katz collection); Tipton (AP/World Wide Photos).

Aunt Jemima

Mention her name to white Americans and the aroma of fresh pancakes fills their senses, along with the image of a kindly, jovial black woman who wants nothing but to serve and dote on them. To African-Americans, another image comes to mind: an uneducated, servile black woman who doesn't realize slavery is over. She's an offensive racial stereotype fabricated by white businessmen to sell their product. One of the longest-lived icons in American advertising, Aunt Jemima is also one of the most controversial. Who is she and why, after all these years, can we still find her hanging out on grocery shelves trying to make us buy her pancake mix?

Aunt Jemima never was a real person. She was created by entrepreneurs Chris Rutt and Charles Underwood in the 1890s. They used the stereotype of the Southern black Mammy and a nostalgia for the antebellum South to sell their new invention: instant pancake mix. The false familiarity of the salutation "Aunt" mimicked the way black domestic slaves had been belittled in the South. Rutt and Underwood based her character on a minstrel show act, and on a popular song. They even hired a real person, Nancy Green, an African-American born in slavery in 1834, to flip thousands of pancakes at the Chicago World's Fair in 1894. She was a sensation and signed a lifelong contract to be the "spokes-mammy" for Aunt Jemima.

After Ms. Green's death in 1923, at least six other women were hired to appear as Aunt Jemima in public, giving demonstrations at state fairs, conventions, and on radio and TV. Quaker Oats, which owns the Aunt Jemima brand, went so far as to invent myths and legends to make people believe there really was an Aunt Jemima, even though at times three Aunt

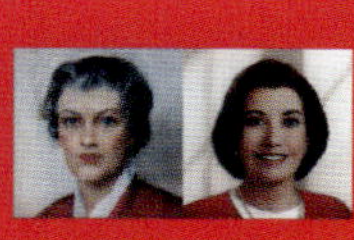

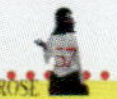

A CROCK OF BETTY

In 1921, a company that eventually became General Mills received so many letters from women with baking questions, it cooked up Betty Crocker to respond to them. Her official signature was selected from women employees' handwriting samples. The last name of a retiring exec was combined with a first name judged to be reassuring and homey. It worked! Women really believed there was a professional out there who could help them solve their cooking and homemaking problems. In 1945, Betty Crocker was the second most admired women in America after Eleanor Roosevelt!

Betty wrote over 200 cookbooks, starred in hundreds of radio programs and even taught Gracie Allen how to cook on TV! Naturally (or is it unnaturally?) all Betty's meal ideas include General Foods products, like Hamburger Helper, instant potatoes, fake bacon, artificially flavored cakes, aerosol frostings, and microwave popcorn.

Eighty years later, Betty is still at work and—miracle of miracles—actually getting younger! Her first image, created in 1936, shows her aging, gray, and stern-faced. At last sighting her skin had become olive-toned and her hair darkened in a gesture toward ethnic diversity. She's now a computer composite of a number of American female types. That's our Betty!

Above: Betty Crocker in 1936 and today.

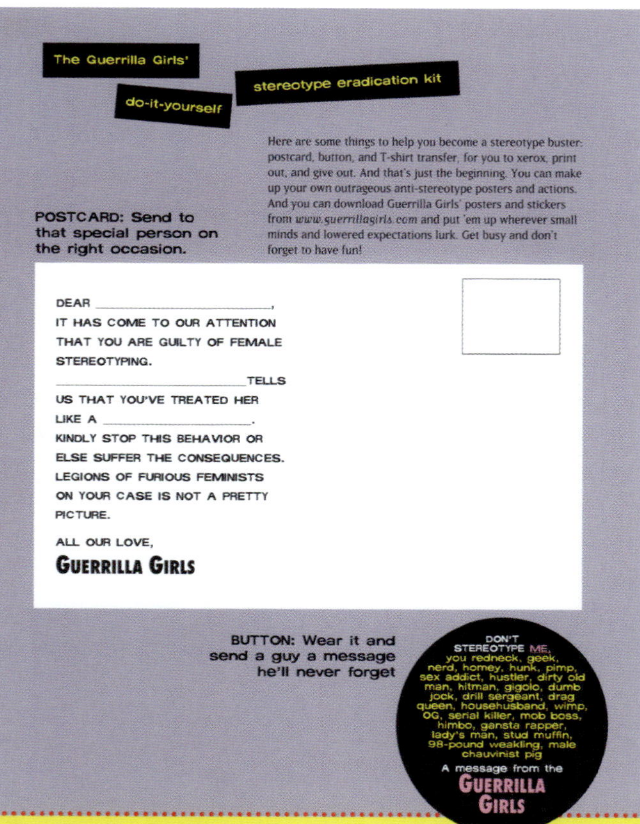

Here are some things to help you become a stereotype buster: postcard, button, and T-shirt transfer, for you to xerox, print out, and give out. And that's just the beginning. You can make up your own outrageous anti-stereotype posters and actions. And you can download Guerrilla Girls' posters and stickers from www.guerrillagirls.com and put 'em up wherever small minds and lowered expectations lurk. Get busy and don't forget to have fun!

POSTCARD: Send to that special person on the right occasion.

DEAR ________________,
IT HAS COME TO OUR ATTENTION
THAT YOU ARE GUILTY OF FEMALE
STEREOTYPING.
________________ TELLS
US THAT YOU'VE TREATED HER
LIKE A ________________.
KINDLY STOP THIS BEHAVIOR OR
ELSE SUFFER THE CONSEQUENCES.
LEGIONS OF FURIOUS FEMINISTS
ON YOUR CASE IS NOT A PRETTY
PICTURE.

ALL OUR LOVE,

GUERRILLA GIRLS

BUTTON: Wear it and send a guy a message he'll never forget

DON'T STEREOTYPE ME, you redneck, geek, nerd, homey, hunk, pimp, sex addict, hustler, dirty old man, hitman, gigolo, dumb jock, drill sergeant, drag queen, househusband, wimp, OG, serial killer, mob boss, himbo, gansta rapper, lady's man, stud muffin, 98-pound weakling, male chauvinist pig

A message from the **GUERRILLA GIRLS**

Museums sell books to teach kids how to appreciate art. We wrote a book to teach adults how to criticize museums.

Book, 2003. Cover and some interior pages

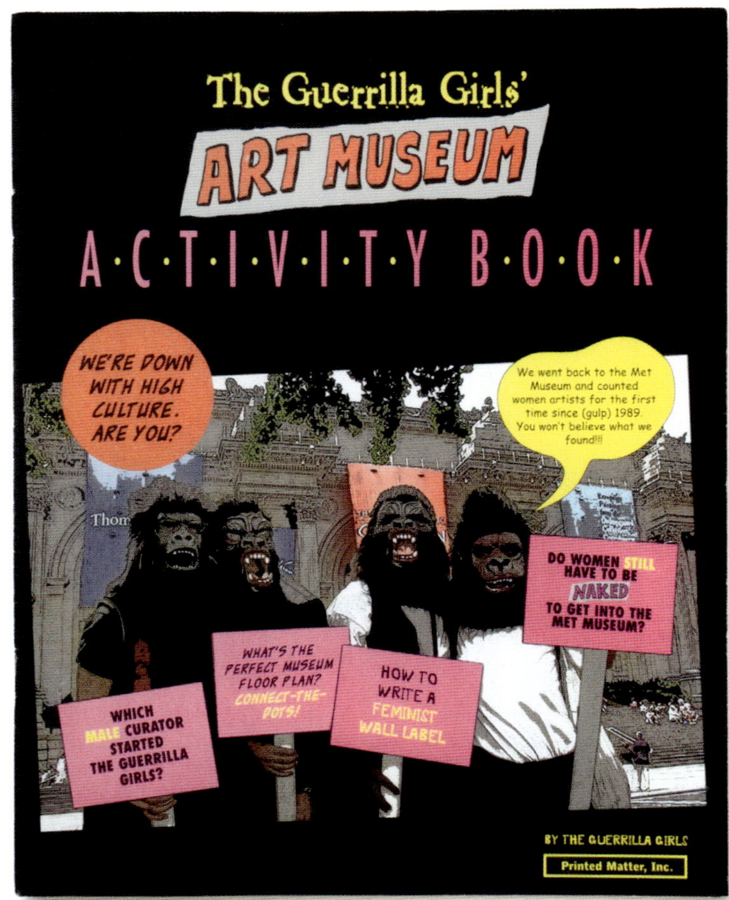

ACTIVITY #1: READING COMPREHENSION

A brief history of art museums . . . according to the Guerrilla Girls

We love museums so much, we worry about them. Are they fair to artists? Do they collect the things people will want to see a hundred years from now? How did museums come to be the way they are?

It all began because rich people have always had a lot of stuff. A few centuries ago, they ran out of space in their palaces and churches and needed new places to store it all. Bingo! They started art museums. In Europe, museums became part of the government and are run by bureaucrats and civil servants. In the US, most museums were—and still are—funded and overseen by the wealthy.

Lots of the art you see in European and American museums was originally stolen—sometimes from countries (the Greek friezes in the British museum), sometimes from indigenous peoples (Indian artifacts in US museums) and even from victims of the Holocaust. Some countries, native peoples and families are now trying to get their stuff back, but most museums won't give it up. Finders keepers!

Few museums collected art of their own time, until the Museum of Modern Art was founded in 1929. Today there are plenty of contemporary art museums and they have one big advantage over historical museums: the artists they exhibit are alive and can come to openings, so they have better parties!

Museums have lots of employees: directors, curators, educators, financial experts, marketing specialists, store executives and guards. The director is usually a guy from an elite background, with an education to match, who is good at running things and talking to rich people. Museum directors used to be underpaid but over the last 10 years their salaries have gone up, up up! Curators usually come from the same background, and you would think they would be as well paid, but the staff who direct finances, investments, sales and marketing get a lot more. (see page 6.) At the bottom of the food chain are curatorial assistants, guards and bookstore clerks. With a couple of exceptions, the few women who run museums are still paid a whole lot less than guys.

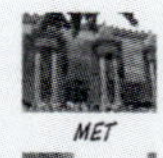

Museums are overseen by a board of trustees, consisting mostly of wealthy art collectors who donate money and artworks. Museum newsletters are full of photos of these trustees at museum functions, and bios of their illustrious careers—that is, until they go to jail for price fixing or running their compa-

3

ACTIVITY #2: FUN FACTS ABOUT MUSEUMS

What goes on behind the pretty pictures

WHAT MALE MUSEUM CURATOR IS RESPONSIBLE FOR STARTING THE GUERRILLA GIRLS?

Answer: In 1984, MoMA curator Kynaston MacShine opened a show called "An International Survey of Painting and Sculpture." Out of 169 artists, he chose only 13 women and then told the press any artist who wasn't in the show should rethink "his" career. That made a bunch of us really mad and we started making posters to expose racism and sexism in the artworld.

WHICH MUSEUM HAS THE MOST MONEY?

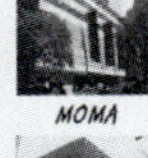
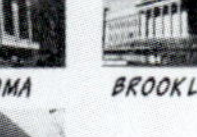

Answer: The richest art museum in New York is the Met with $2.3 billion in assets, not including the art. MoMA is in 2nd place with $1.2 billion. The Brooklyn Museum comes in a far 3rd at $148 million. The Guggenheim is fourth at $133 million and the Whitney is last at $89 million. (All stats 2001.)

**FILL IN THE BLANK:
THE ARTIST _ _ _ _ _ _ _ _ _ _ _ _ _ _ HAD TWO RETROSPECTIVES AT MOMA WHILE HIS ART DEALER WAS THE BROTHER OF THE CHIEF CURATOR.**

Answer: Frank Stella had two retrospectives in 1970 (age 34) and 1987 (age 51). Stella's dealer in Europe just happened to be Lawrence Rubin, the brother of curator Bill Rubin, who also wrote the catalogs. Bill Rubin retired in 1988 and Stella hasn't had a show since.

**WHO'S NOT ON THE BOARD OF ART MUSEUMS?
A. WELDERS
B. SCHOLARS
C. ARTISTS
D. ALL OF THE ABOVE**

Answer: D. All of the above. Our research shows that museum board members fall into four major categories: corporate execs, philanthropists, art collectors and socialites. Rare exceptions are artist Chuck Close and Professor Henry Louis Gates at the Whitney Museum and playwright/performer Anna Deveare Smith at MoMA.

ARTRAGEOUS FUN FACT

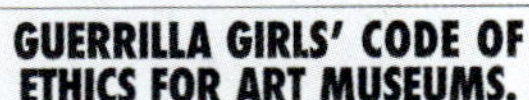
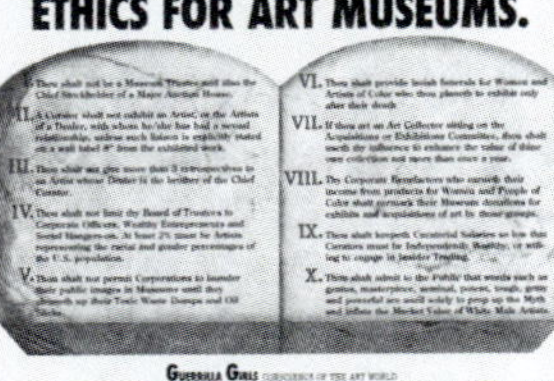

In 1989 Guerrilla Girls created the satirical "Code of Ethics" for art museums shown above. It took four more years and a couple of scandals for the American Association of Museums to adopt a real code of ethics in 1993.

TRUE OR FALSE: ART COLLECTORS CAN BE ON MORE THAN ONE MUSEUM BOARD. (EXTRA CREDIT: WHO HOLDS THE RECORD?)

True, of course! Peter Norton is on the Whitney and MoMA. Eugene Thaw is at the

5

ACTIVITY # 5: CORRECTING WALL LABELS

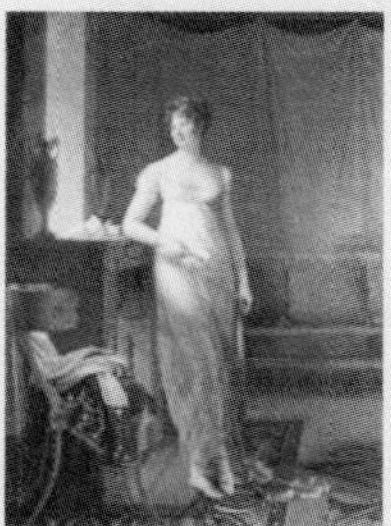

Those little labels next to the paintings tell as much about the person who wrote them as about the art they describe. Below is a wall label that hangs at the Metropolitan Museum in New York beside a portrait of Catherine Worlée (right), whose life it luridly describes.

Baron François-Pascal-Simon Gérard (French, 1770–1837)
Madame Charles-Maurice de Talleyrand-Périgord, Princesse de Bénévent
(née Catherine Noele Worlée, later Madame George Francis Grand,
1762–1835), ca. 1808

This painting portrays one of the celebrated beauties of her time, Catherine Worlée (1762–1835). By the age of fifteen she had seduced her future husband, the Englishman George Francis Grand, an employee of the Indian civil services (as Madame Grand she was portrayed by Vigée Lebrun in an oval portrait displayed in this gallery). This was the first of a series of liaisons that culminated in her becoming the mistress and then the wife of Talleyrand, whose portrait by Prud'hon hangs nearby. Talleyrand tired of his pretty but frivolous wife, whom he had sent away in 1817. After residing in London and Brussels, she returned to Paris, where, separated from her husband, she lived a quiet and devout life.

The author doesn't say much about the painting, but sure lets us know what a slut Catherine was at fifteen, what a bore she became after forty, and how she mended her wicked ways once her husband kicked her out. But there's another way to look at Catherine's life. On the next page is the same info rewritten feminist-style.

Baron François-Pascal-Simon Gérard (French, 1770–1837)
Catherine Noele Worlée (1762–1835), ca. 1808

Catherine Worlée (1762–1835) couldn't wait to get away from her parents! With little choice but to submit to sexual advances that would today be considered statutory rape, she was forced to marry an older Brit with the hope he would take her somewhere. Despite her married state she had a sexually liberated life in Calcutta and London, where she soon became bored with her civil servant husband. She found her way to the intellectual salons of revolutionary Paris where her beauty and intellect attracted the attention of powerful men. She became the mistress of statesman Talleyrand, who helped her dump her dull husband and figured out a way they could marry in 1802. The corrupt Talleyrand became a political turncoat several times over so Catherine dumped him, too, had fun in Brussels and London, and finally led the life of a wise crone in Paris.

Now it's your turn. Find some wall labels at your favorite museum that could use a face-lift! Rewrite and send 'em to us at gg@guerrillagirls.com. We'll post them on our website.

My new, improved (feminist) wall label:

ACTIVITY # 3: CONNECT-THE-DOTS
MUSEUM FLOOR PLAN

Museums are all competing to create the most unusual building. Attention famous architects: here's a concept for your next museum job. Follow the dots to create the perfect floor plan for today's art museum.

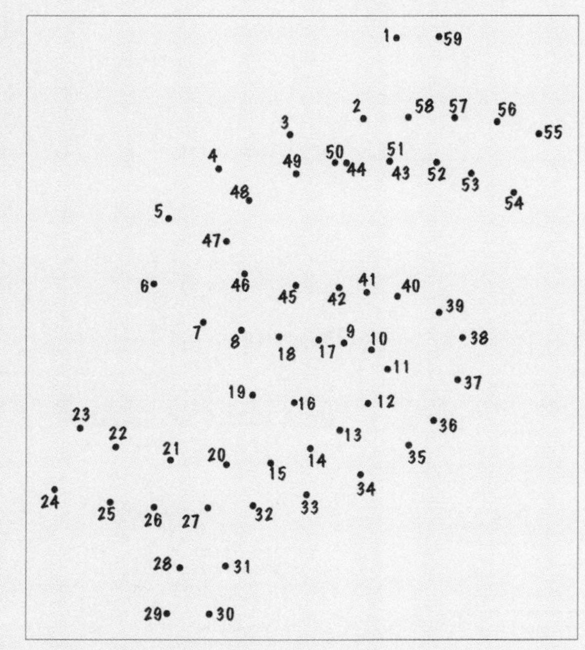

ACTIVITY # 7: CREATE YOUR OWN MUSEUM STORE

We can't go into a museum store without thinking of things we'd like to see there.
Check out some of our ideas and then design some products of your own.

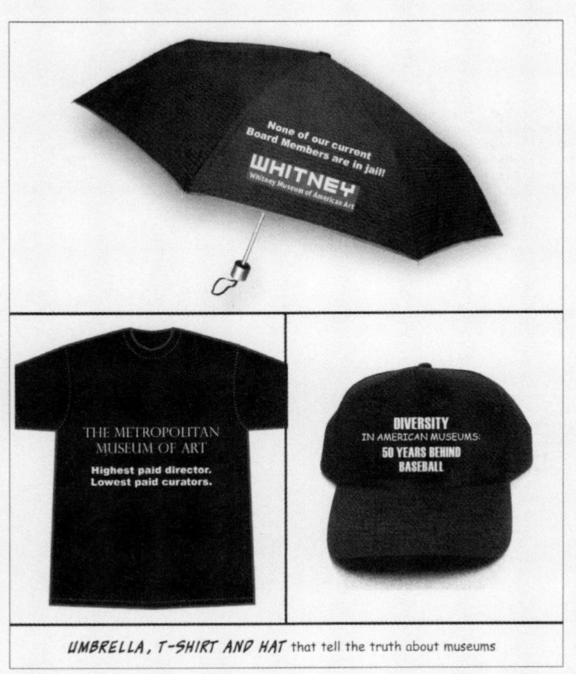

UMBRELLA, T-SHIRT AND HAT that tell the truth about museums

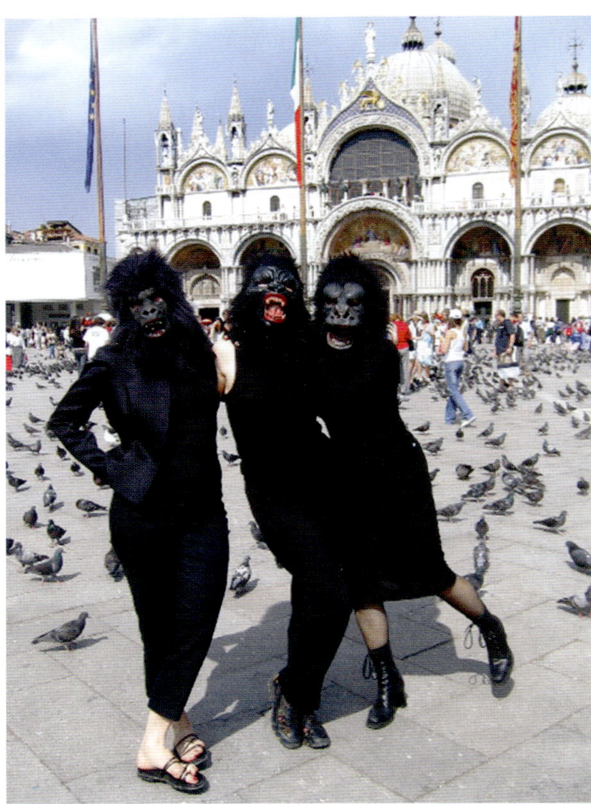
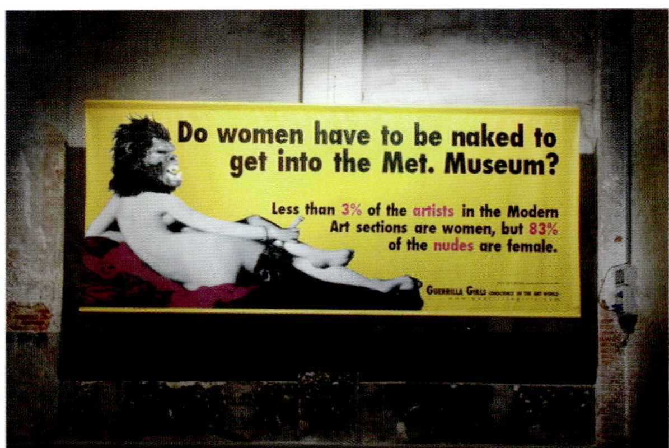

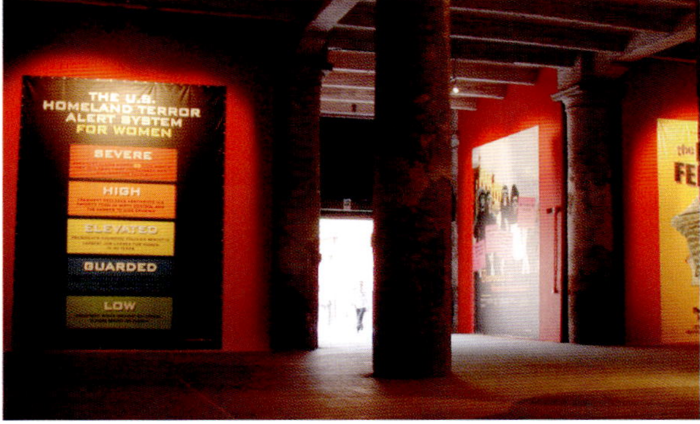

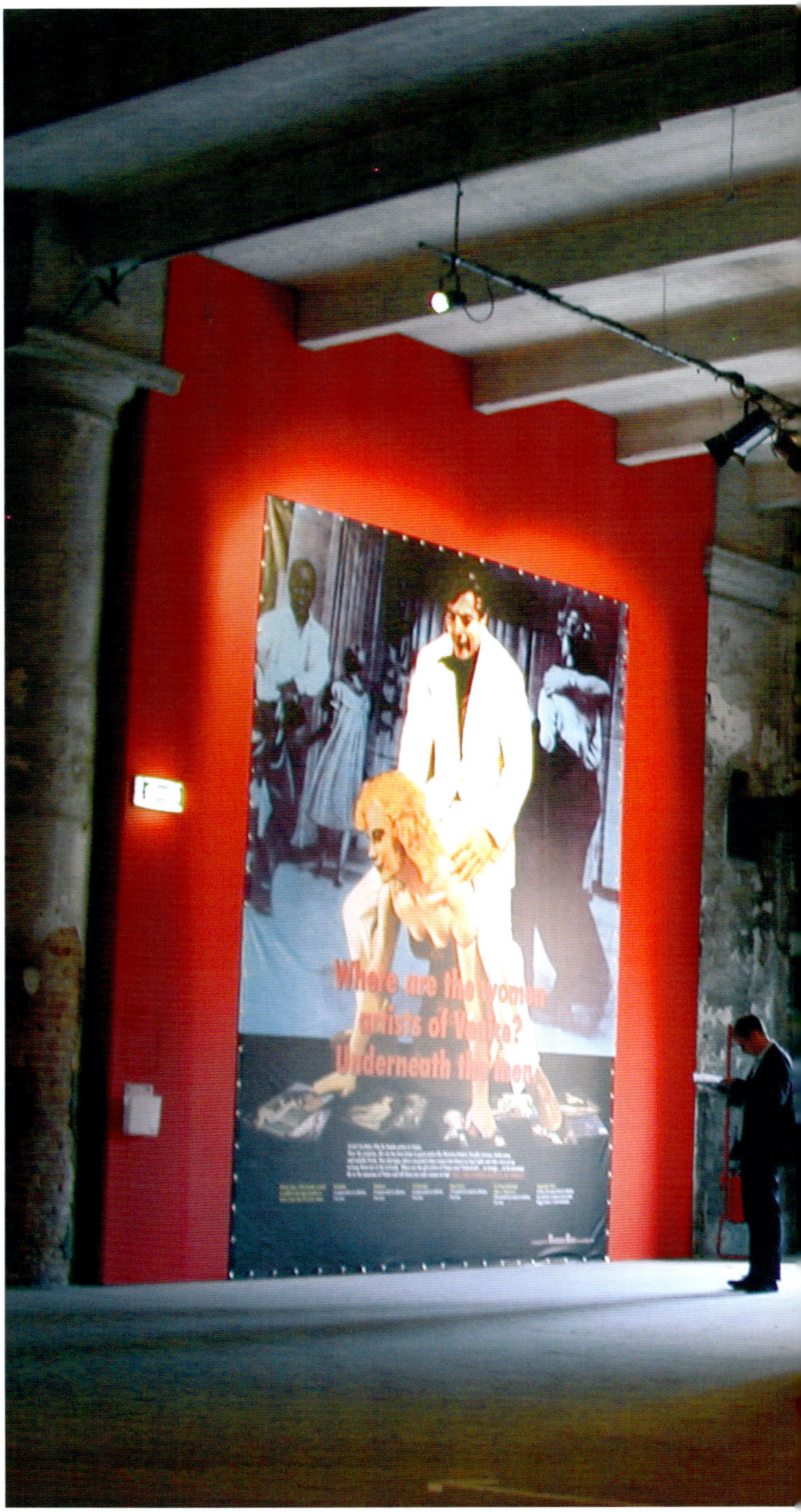

Our work was included in the first Venice Biennale ever directed by women. Unsurprisingly, the exhibition had the largest number of women artists ever.

Guerrilla Girls in Venice (photo by Jason Schmidt); Installation views and button giveaway, 2005

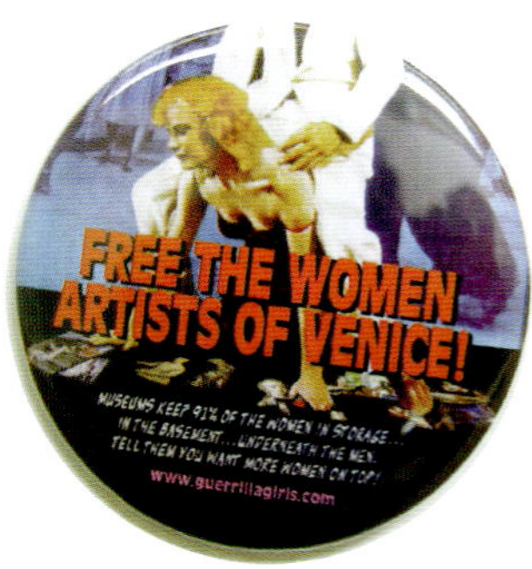

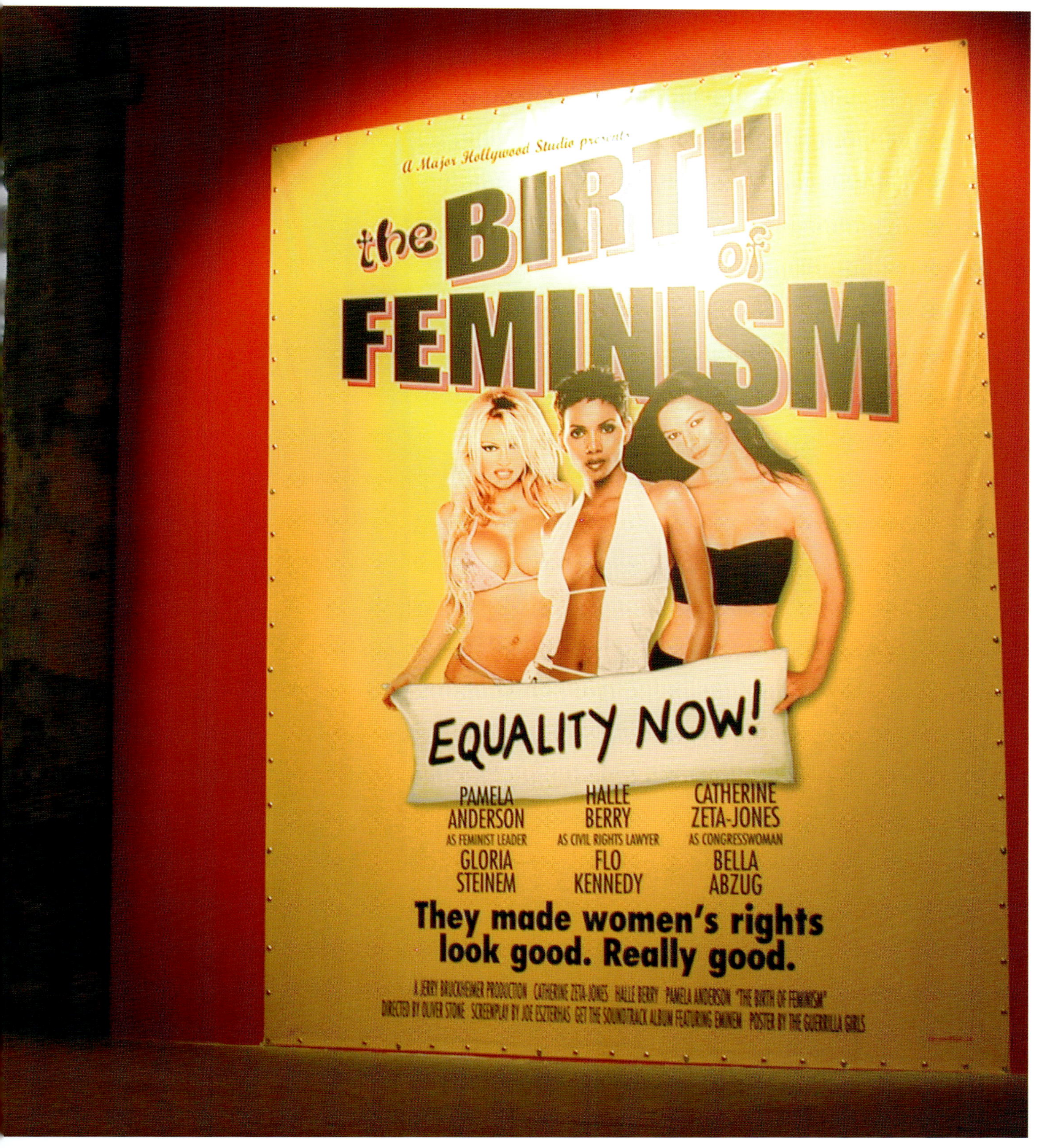

Page 94: Because of the number of women artists, we declared it the "Feminist Biennale." But we couldn't let the Biennale off the hook for its 110-year history of almost no diversity.

Page 95: We discovered that all the historical museums of Venice, except one, collected art by women, but kept it hidden in storage.

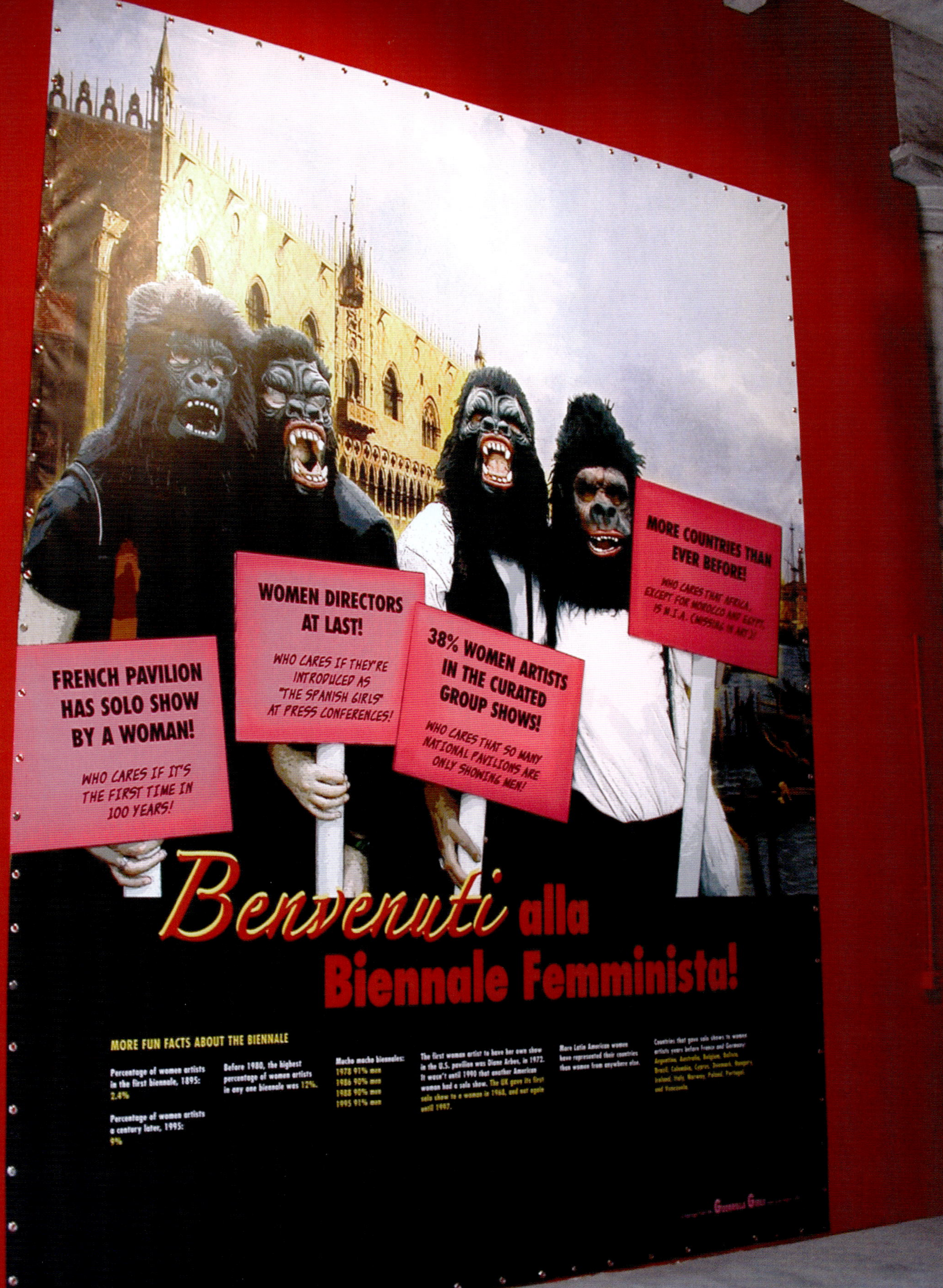

FRENCH PAVILION
HAS SOLO SHOW
BY A WOMAN!

WHO CARES IF IT'S
THE FIRST TIME IN
100 YEARS!

WOMEN DIRECTORS
AT LAST!

WHO CARES IF THEY'RE
INTRODUCED AS
"THE SPANISH GIRLS"
AT PRESS CONFERENCES!

38% WOMEN ARTISTS
IN THE CURATED
GROUP SHOWS!

WHO CARES THAT SO MANY
NATIONAL PAVILIONS ARE
ONLY SHOWING MEN!

MORE COUNTRIES THAN
EVER BEFORE!

WHO CARES THAT AFRICA,
EXCEPT FOR MOROCCO AND EGYPT,
IS M.I.A. (MISSING IN ART)!

Benvenuti alla
Biennale Femminista!

MORE FUN FACTS ABOUT THE BIENNALE

Percentage of women artists
in the first biennale, 1895:
2.4%

Percentage of women artists
a century later, 1995:
9%

Before 1980, the highest
percentage of women artists
in any one biennale was 12%.

Macho macho biennales:
1978 91% men
1986 90% men
1988 90% men
1995 91% men

The first woman artist to have her own show
in the U.S. pavilion was Diane Arbus, in 1972.
It wasn't until 1990 that another American
woman had a solo show. The UK gave its first
solo show to a woman in 1966, and not again
until 1997.

More Latin American women
have represented their countries
than women from anywhere else.

Countries that gave solo shows to women
artists years before France and Germany:
Argentina, Australia, Belgium, Bolivia,
Brazil, Colombia, Cyprus, Denmark, Hungary,
Ireland, Italy, Norway, Poland, Portugal,
and Venezuela.

GUERRILLA GIRLS

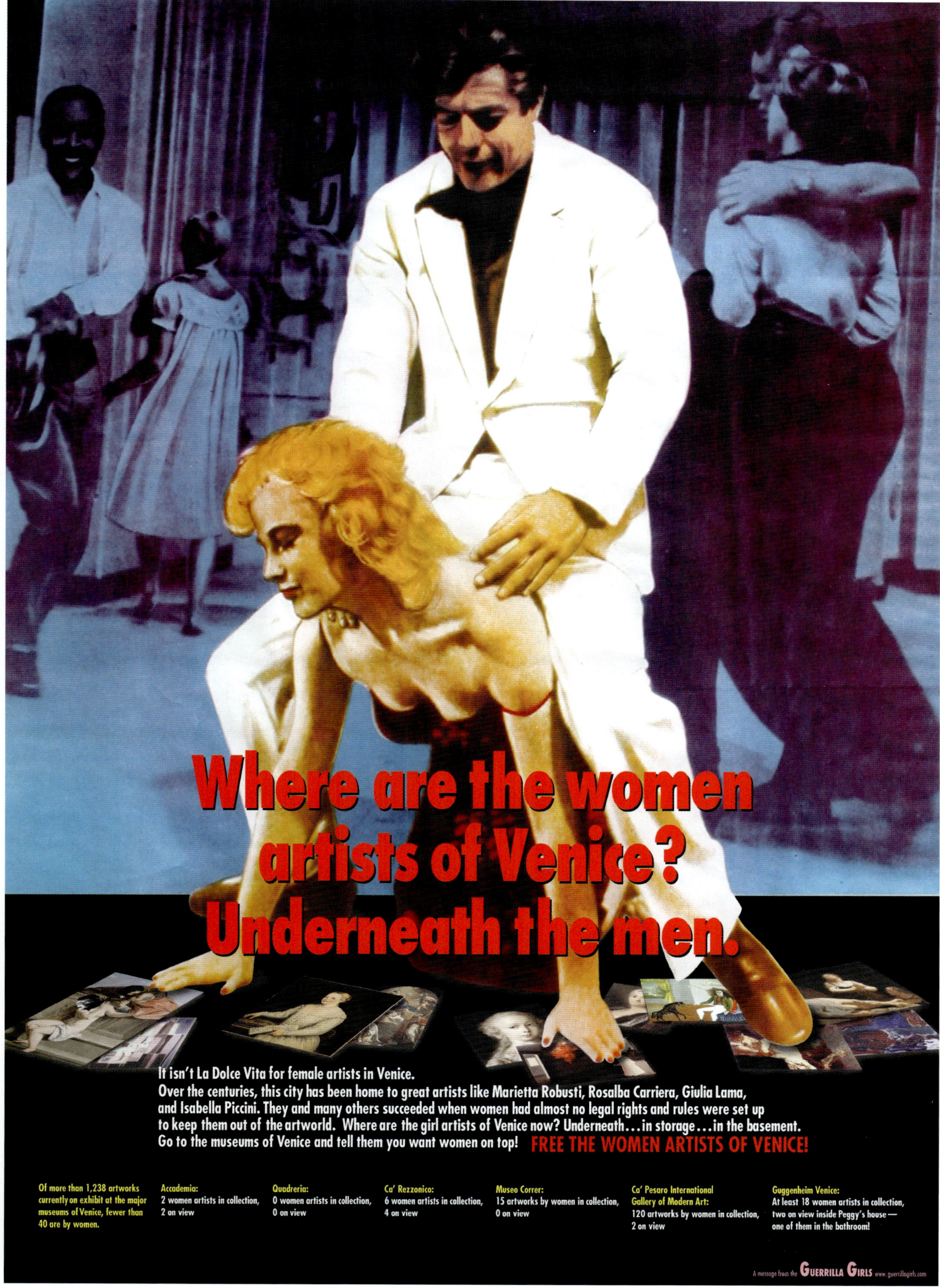

Installation views, 2005

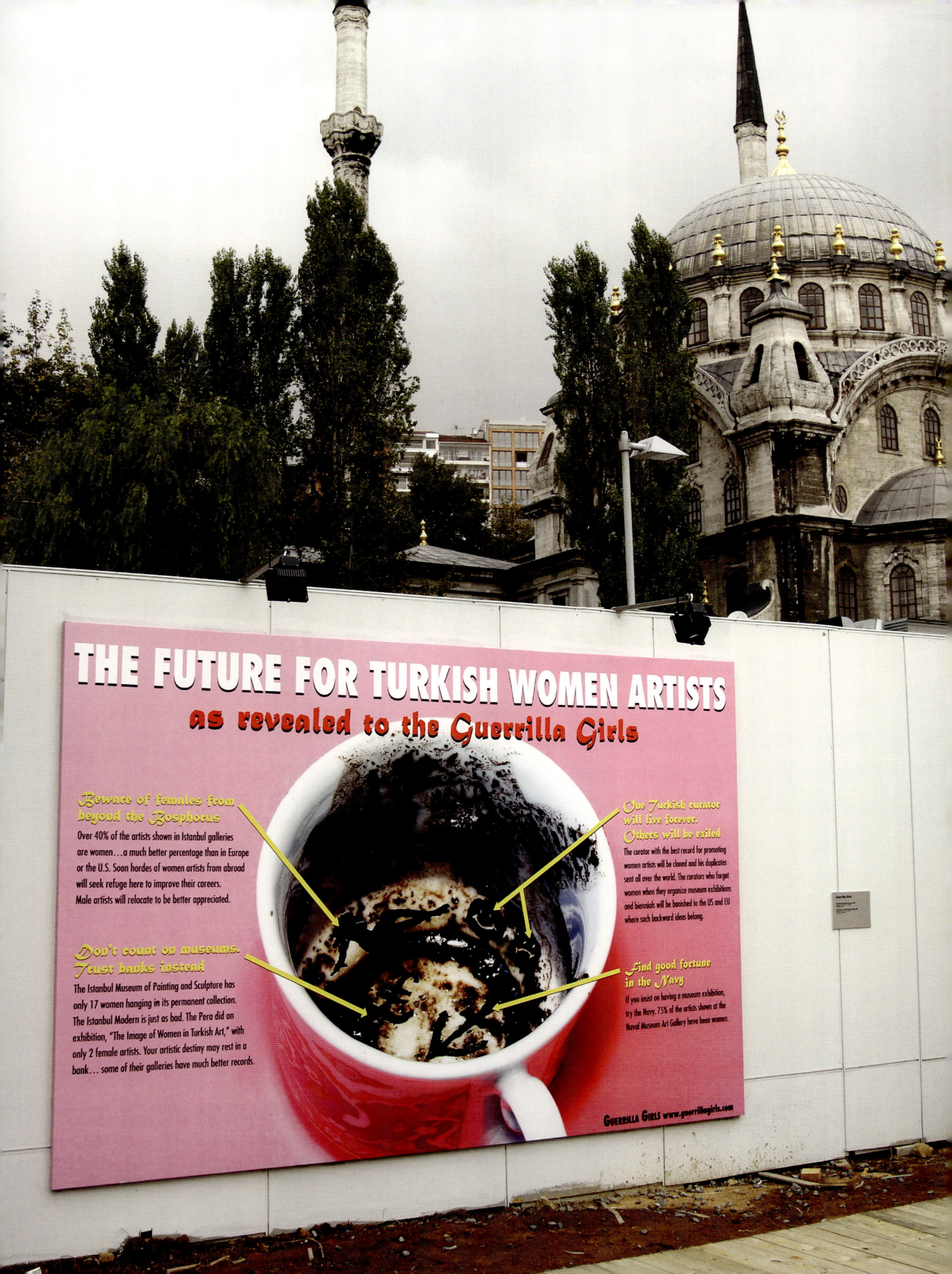

THE FUTURE FOR TURKISH WOMEN ARTISTS
as revealed to the Guerrilla Girls

Beware of females from beyond the Bosphorus
Over 40% of the artists shown in Istanbul galleries are women…a much better percentage than in Europe or the U.S. Soon hordes of women artists from abroad will seek refuge here to improve their careers. Male artists will relocate to be better appreciated.

Don't count on museums. Trust banks instead
The Istanbul Museum of Painting and Sculpture has only 17 women hanging in its permanent collection. The Istanbul Modern is just as bad. The Pera did an exhibition, "The Image of Women in Turkish Art," with only 2 female artists. Your artistic destiny may rest in a bank… some of their galleries have much better records.

One Turkish curator will live forever. Others will be exiled
The curator with the best record for promoting women artists will be cloned and his duplicates sent all over the world. The curators who forget women when they organize museum exhibitions and biennials will be banished to the US and EU where such backward ideas belong.

Find good fortune in the Navy
If you insist on having a museum exhibition, try the Navy. 75% of the artists shown at the Naval Museum Art Gallery have been women.

Guerrilla Girls www.guerrillagirls.com

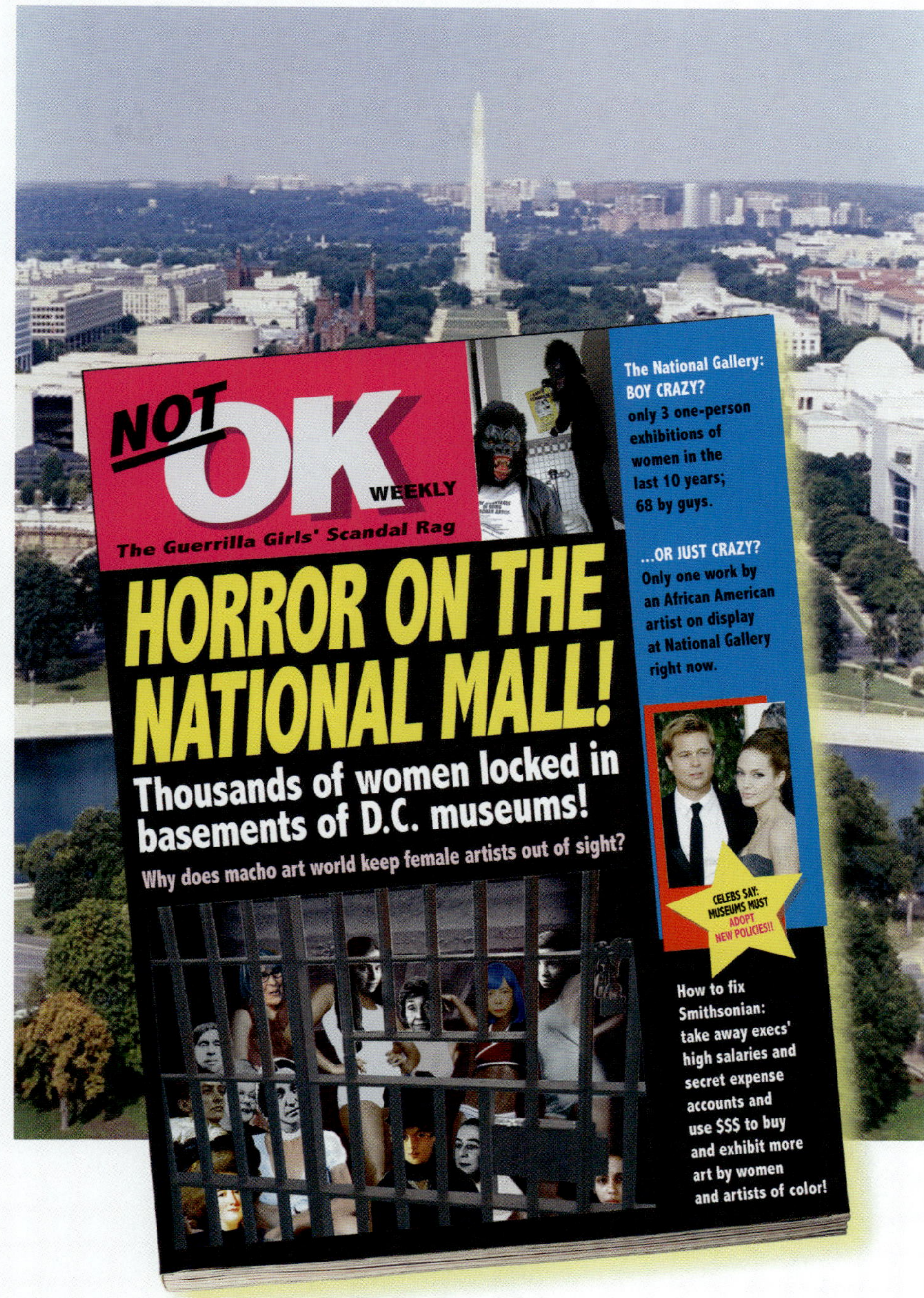

Left: We interviewed women artists in Istanbul, then predicted their fortunes. Our advice: avoid Europeanizing influences; things are better for women artists in Turkey.

Right: The Washington Post gave us a page in the paper, and we zeroed in on the atrocious lack of diversity in our taxpayer supported museums in the US capital.

Left: Instanbul Modern Museum, 2006;
Above: *Washington Post*, 2006

FREE THE WOMEN ARTISTS OF EUROPE!

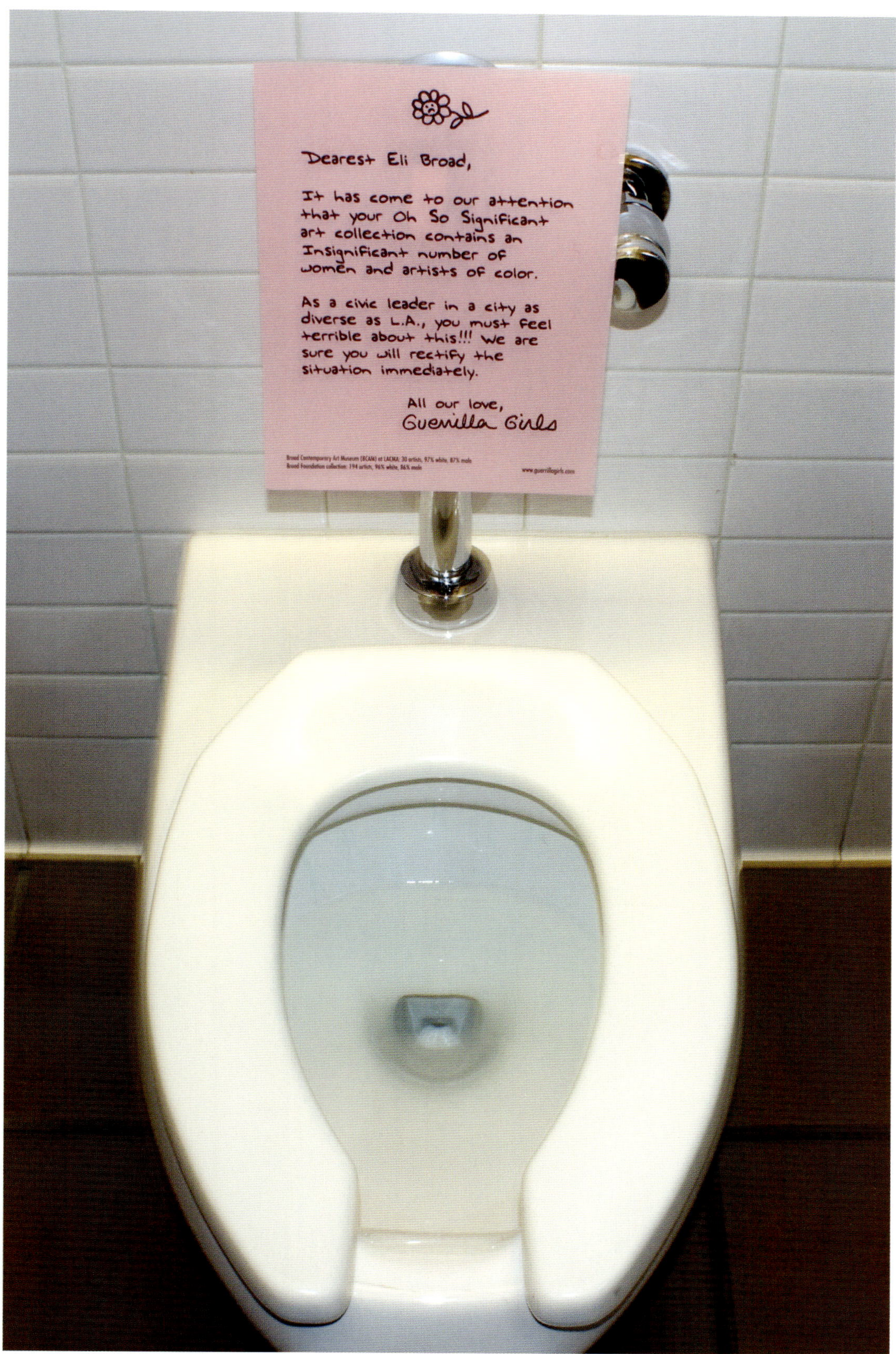

Left: All over Europe, women artists were being held captive.

Poster, 2008

Above: Art collector Eli Broad inaugurated his own museum wing at the Los Angeles County Museum of Art with an exhibition that was 97% white and 86% male. At the opening we left a message for him in the toilet stalls.

Flyer, Los Angeles County Museum of Art, 2008

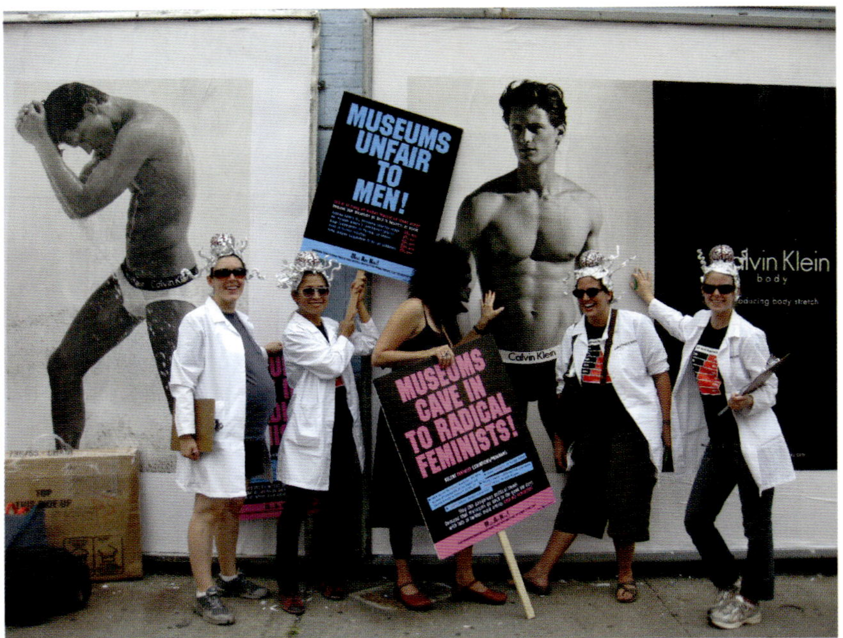

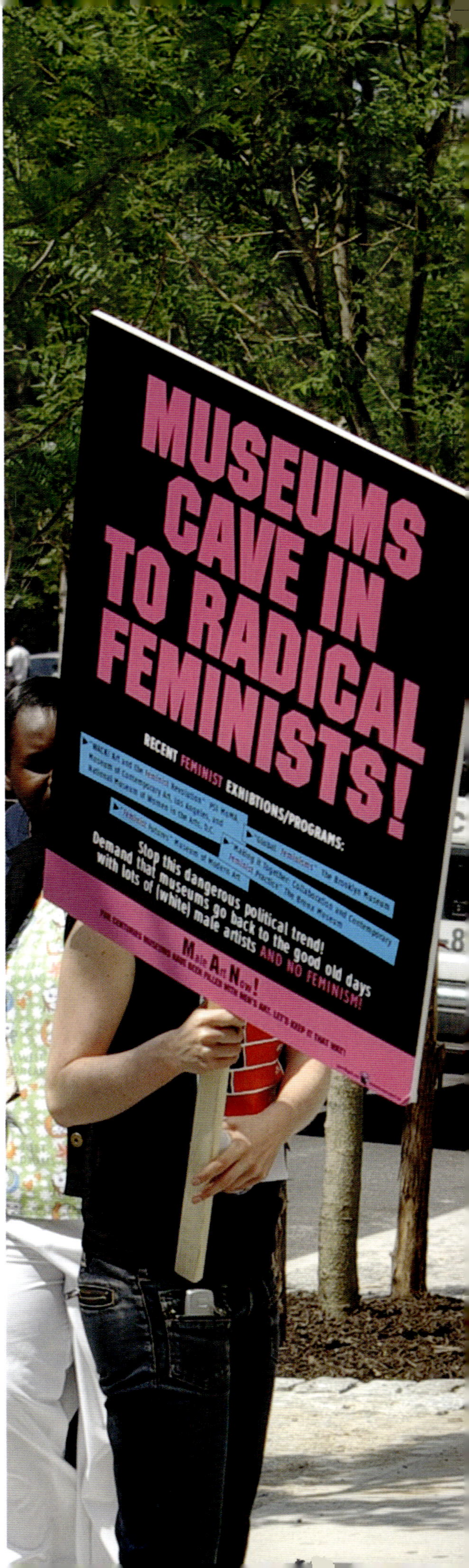

We staged a mock demonstration with the Brainstormers
collective, "protesting" the sudden increase of feminist
exhibitions at museums. Our action was actually part of
a show at the Bronx Museum about feminism. We restaged
the demo outside art galleries in Manhattan.

Left: Protest, Manhattan, 2008; Right: Protest, Bronx Museum, 2008
(photos by the Brainstormers)

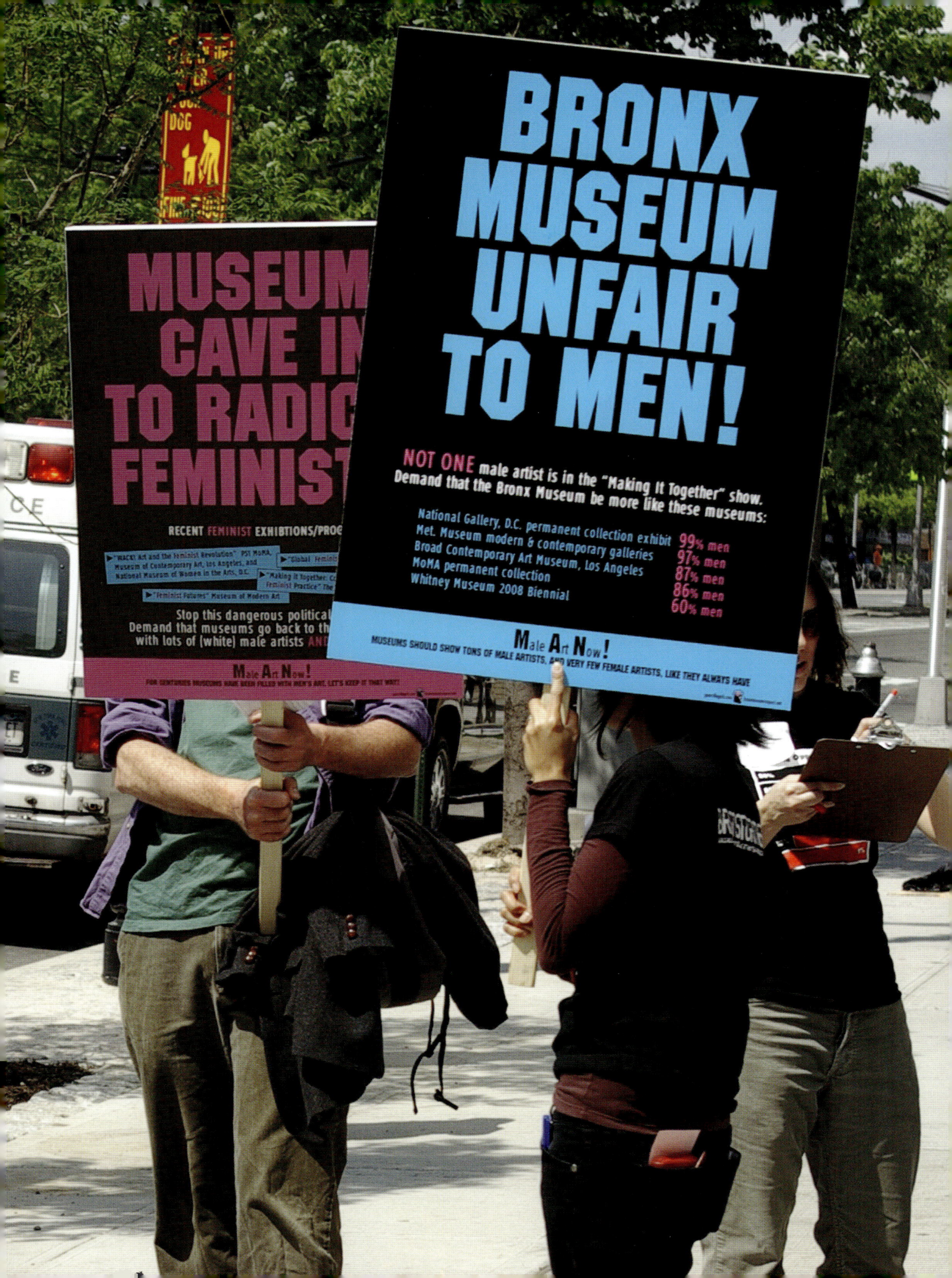
BRONX MUSEUM UNFAIR TO MEN !
NOT ONE male artist is in the "Making It Together" show.
Demand that the Bronx Museum be more like these museums:
National Gallery, D.C. permanent collection exhibit 99% men
Met. Museum modern & contemporary galleries 97% men
Broad Contemporary Art Museum, Los Angeles 87% men
MoMA permanent collection 86% men
Whitney Museum 2008 Biennial 60% men
Male Art Now!
MUSEUMS SHOULD SHOW TONS OF MALE ARTISTS, AND VERY FEW FEMALE ARTISTS, LIKE THEY ALWAYS HAVE
MUSEUMS CAVE IN TO RADICAL FEMINIST
RECENT FEMINIST EXHIBITIONS/PROG
"WACK! Art and the Feminist Revolution" PS1 MoMA, Museum of Contemporary Art, Los Angeles, and National Museum of Women in the Arts, D.C.
"Global Feminis
"Making It Together: Feminist Practice" The
"Feminist Futures" Museum of Modern Art
Stop this dangerous political
Demand that museums go back to th
with lots of (white) male artists AND
Male Art Now!
FOR CENTURIES MUSEUMS HAVE BEEN FILLED WITH MEN'S ART. LET'S KEEP IT THAT WAY!

The University of Quebec at Montreal asked us to commemorate the 20th anniversary of the Polytechnique Massacre, the worst mass murder in Canada. Fourteen women students studying engineering were killed by a gunman. Our street campaign showed how pervasive hate speech against women has been through the ages and connected violence and misogyny.

Right: Poster, 2009; Page 104: Posters on street, Montreal, 2009 (photo by Laurence N. Béland)

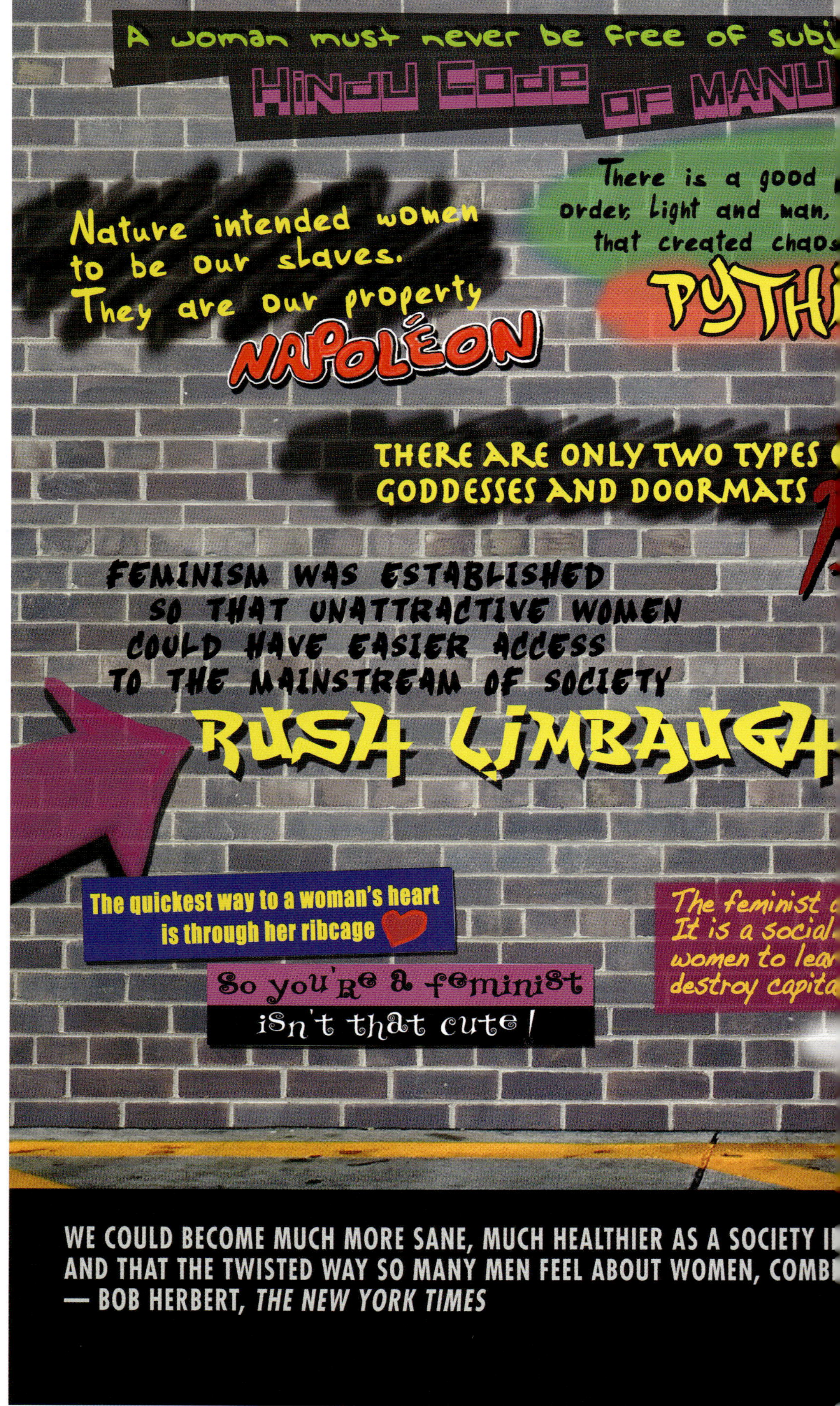

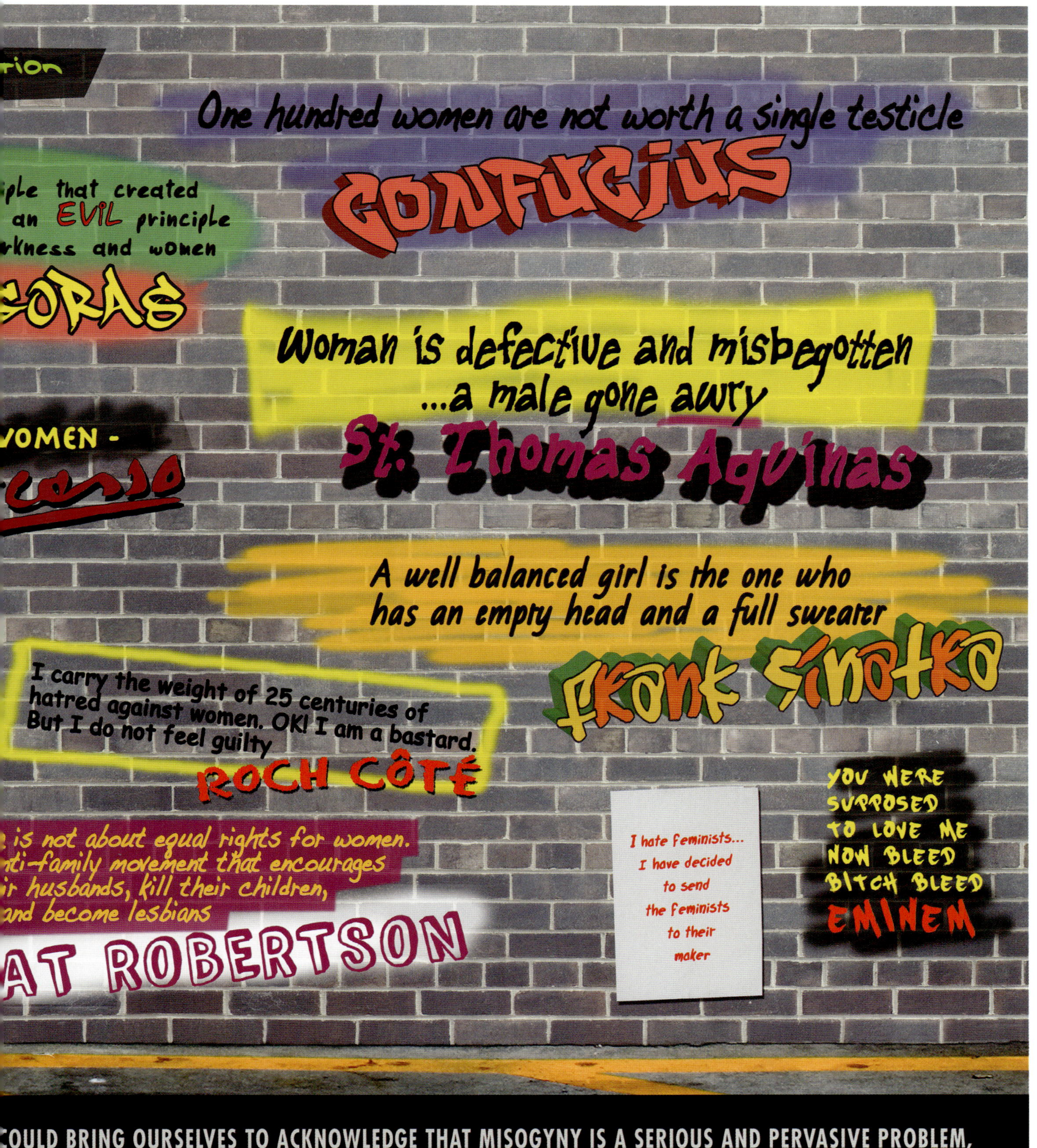
One hundred women are not worth a single testicle
CONFUCIUS
...ple that created an EVIL principle
...rkness and women
...ORAS
Woman is defective and misbegotten
...a male gone awry
St. Thomas Aquinas
...OMEN -
...erso
A well balanced girl is the one who
has an empty head and a full sweater
Frank Sinatra
I carry the weight of 25 centuries of
hatred against women. OK! I am a bastard.
But I do not feel guilty
ROCH CÔTÉ
...is not about equal rights for women.
...ti-family movement that encourages
...r husbands, kill their children,
...and become lesbians
...AT ROBERTSON
I hate feminists...
I have decided
to send
the feminists
to their
maker
YOU WERE
SUPPOSED
TO LOVE ME
NOW BLEED
BITCH BLEED
EMINEM
...COULD BRING OURSELVES TO ACKNOWLEDGE THAT MISOGYNY IS A SERIOUS AND PERVASIVE PROBLEM,
...WITH THE ABSURDLY EASY AVAILABILITY OF GUNS, IS A TOXIC MIX OF THE MOST TRAGIC PROPORTIONS
www.guerrillagirls.com

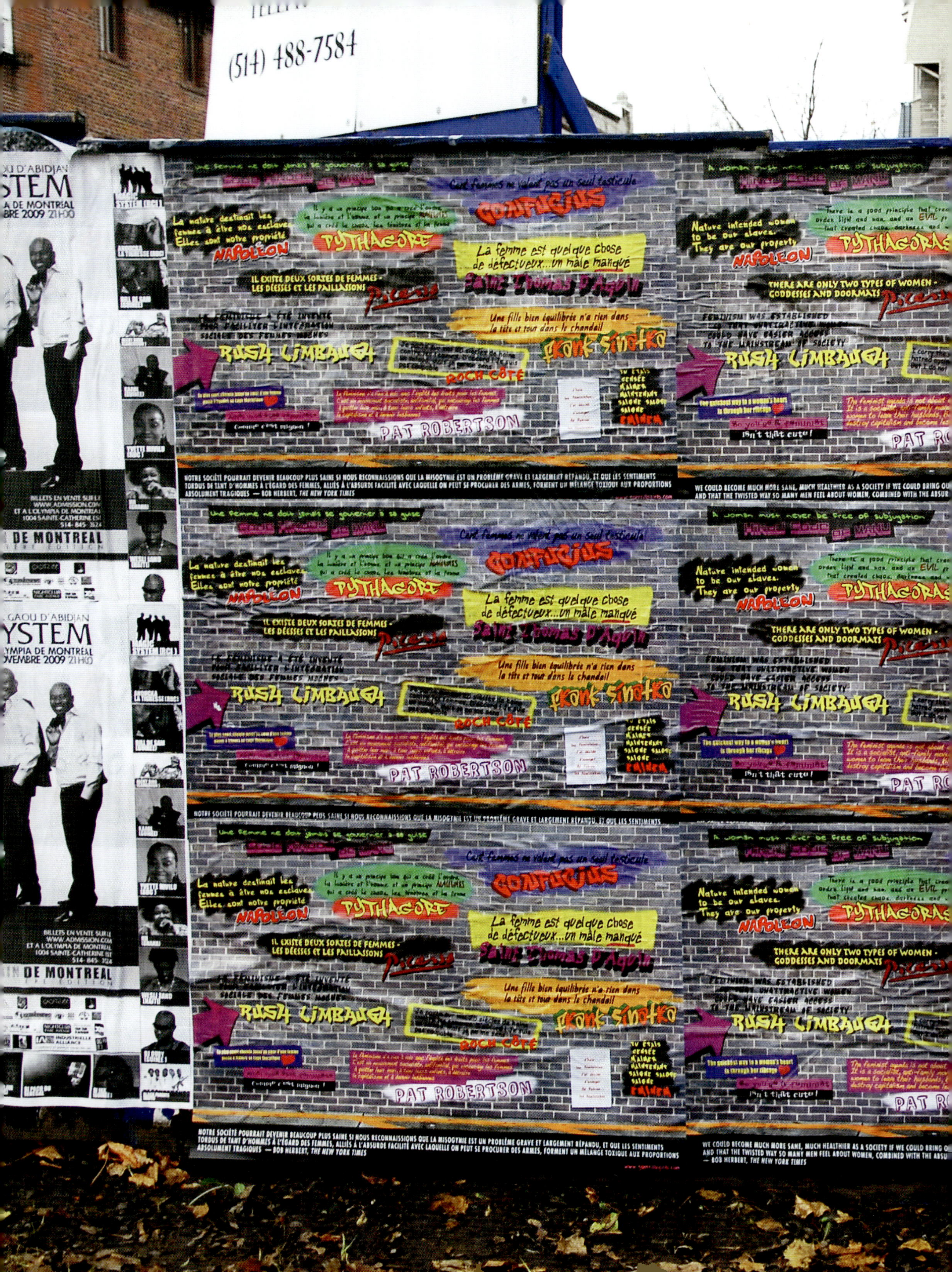

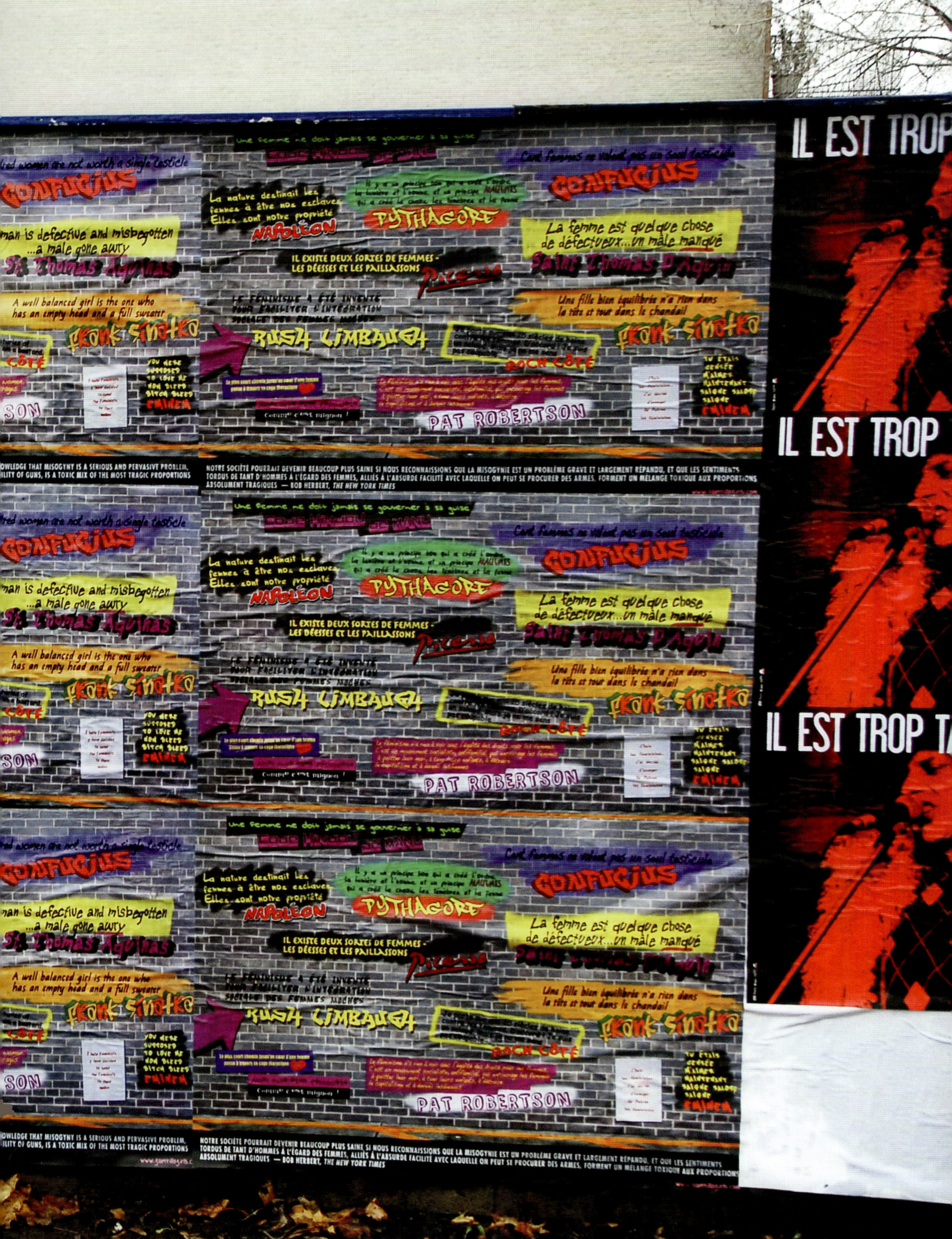
IL EST TROP
IL EST TROP
IL EST TROP TA
Une femme ne doit jamais se gouverner à sa guise
CONFUCIUS
Car femmes ne valent pas un seul testicule
CONFUCIUS
...red women are not worth a single testicle
La nature destinait les femmes à être nos esclaves. Elles sont notre propriété
NAPOLÉON
PYTHAGORE
La femme est quelque chose de défectueux...un mâle manqué
Saint Thomas D'Aquin
man is defective and misbegotten ...a male gone awry
St. Thomas Aquinas
IL EXISTE DEUX SORTES DE FEMMES - LES DÉESSES ET LES PAILLASSONS
Picasso
Une fille bien équilibrée n'a rien dans la tête et tout dans le chandail
A well balanced girl is the one who has an empty head and a full sweater
FRANK SINATRA
FRANK SINATRA
LE FÉMINISME A ÉTÉ INVENTÉ POUR FACILITER L'INTÉGRATION SOCIALE DES FEMMES MOCHES
RUSH LIMBAUGH
ROCH CÔTÉ
CÔTÉ
SON
EMINEM
PAT ROBERTSON
NOTRE SOCIÉTÉ POURRAIT DEVENIR BEAUCOUP PLUS SAINE SI NOUS RECONNAISSIONS QUE LA MISOGYNIE EST UN PROBLÈME GRAVE ET LARGEMENT RÉPANDU, ET QUE LES SENTIMENTS TORDUS DE TANT D'HOMMES À L'ÉGARD DES FEMMES, ALLIÉS À L'ABSURDE FACILITÉ AVEC LAQUELLE ON PEUT SE PROCURER DES ARMES, FORMENT UN MÉLANGE TOXIQUE AUX PROPORTIONS ABSOLUMENT TRAGIQUES — BOB HERBERT, THE NEW YORK TIMES
...OWLEDGE THAT MISOGYNY IS A SERIOUS AND PERVASIVE PROBLEM, ...ILITY OF GUNS, IS A TOXIC MIX OF THE MOST TRAGIC PROPORTIONS

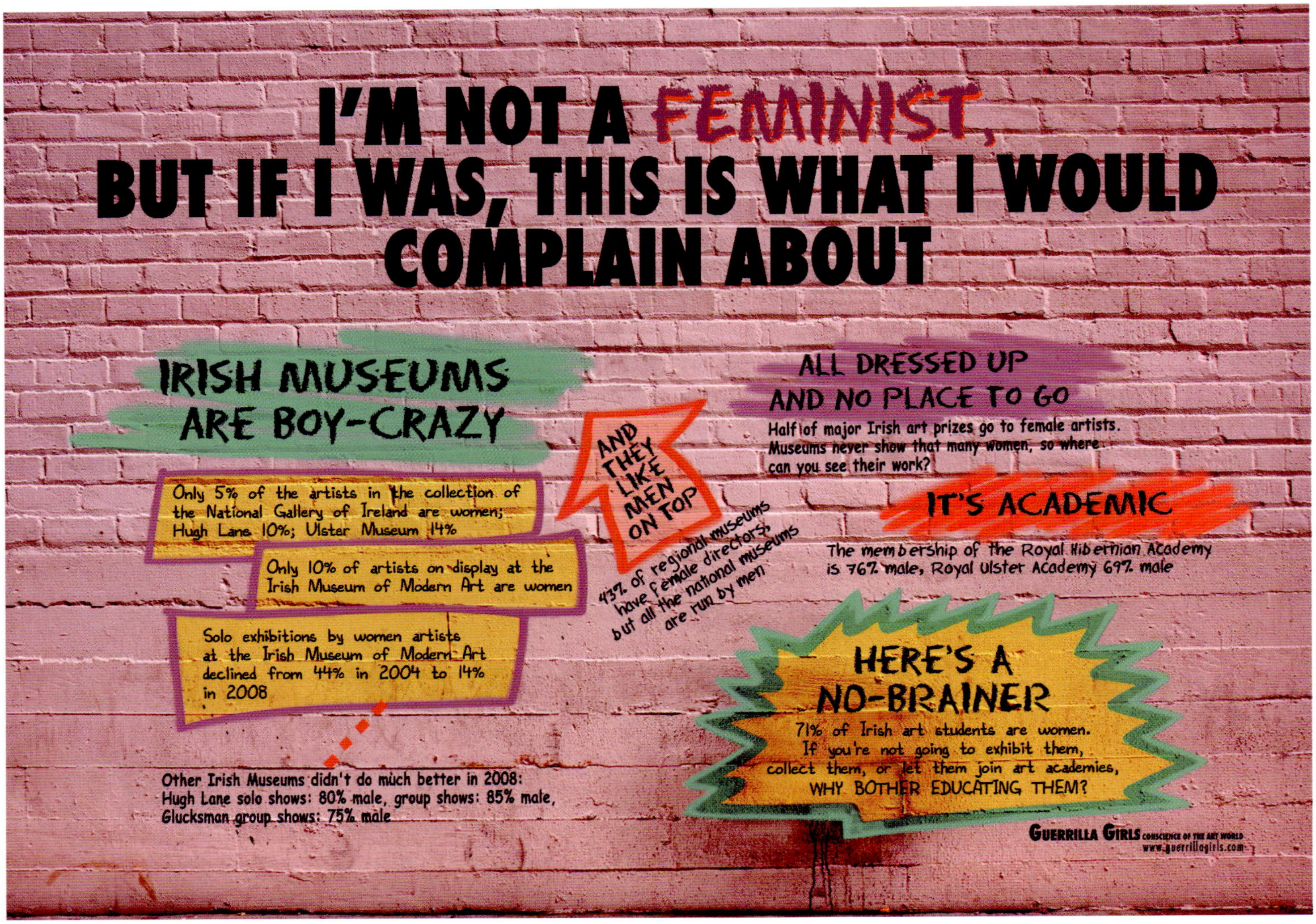

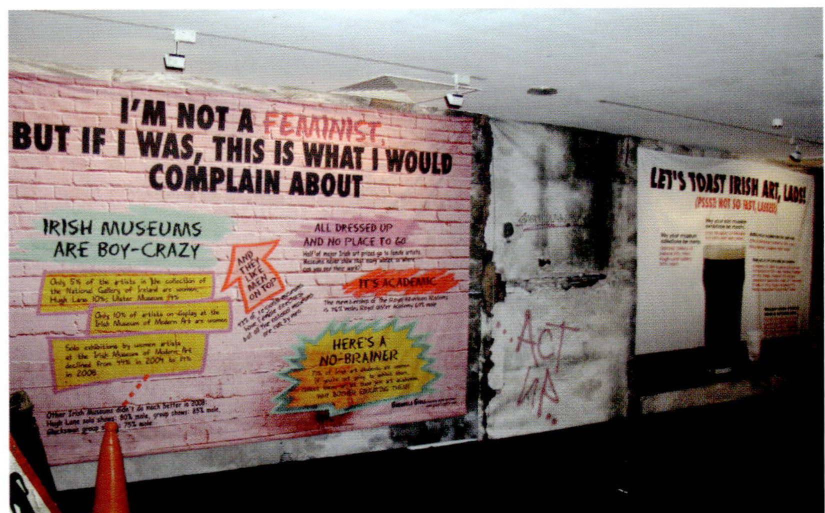

Poster, 2009; Installation view, Millennium Court Arts Centre, Belfast, 2009

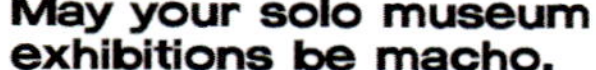

In Ireland, we interviewed women artists who didn't consider themselves feminists but had a lot to complain about. We gave them a chance to express themselves without the label and put their complaints on banners (left) that toured Belfast, Dublin, Cork and Kilkenny, and (above) concocted a special toast to their situation.

Poster, 2009

I'M NOT A FEMINIST, BUT IF I WAS, THIS IS WHAT I WOULD COMPLAIN ABOUT

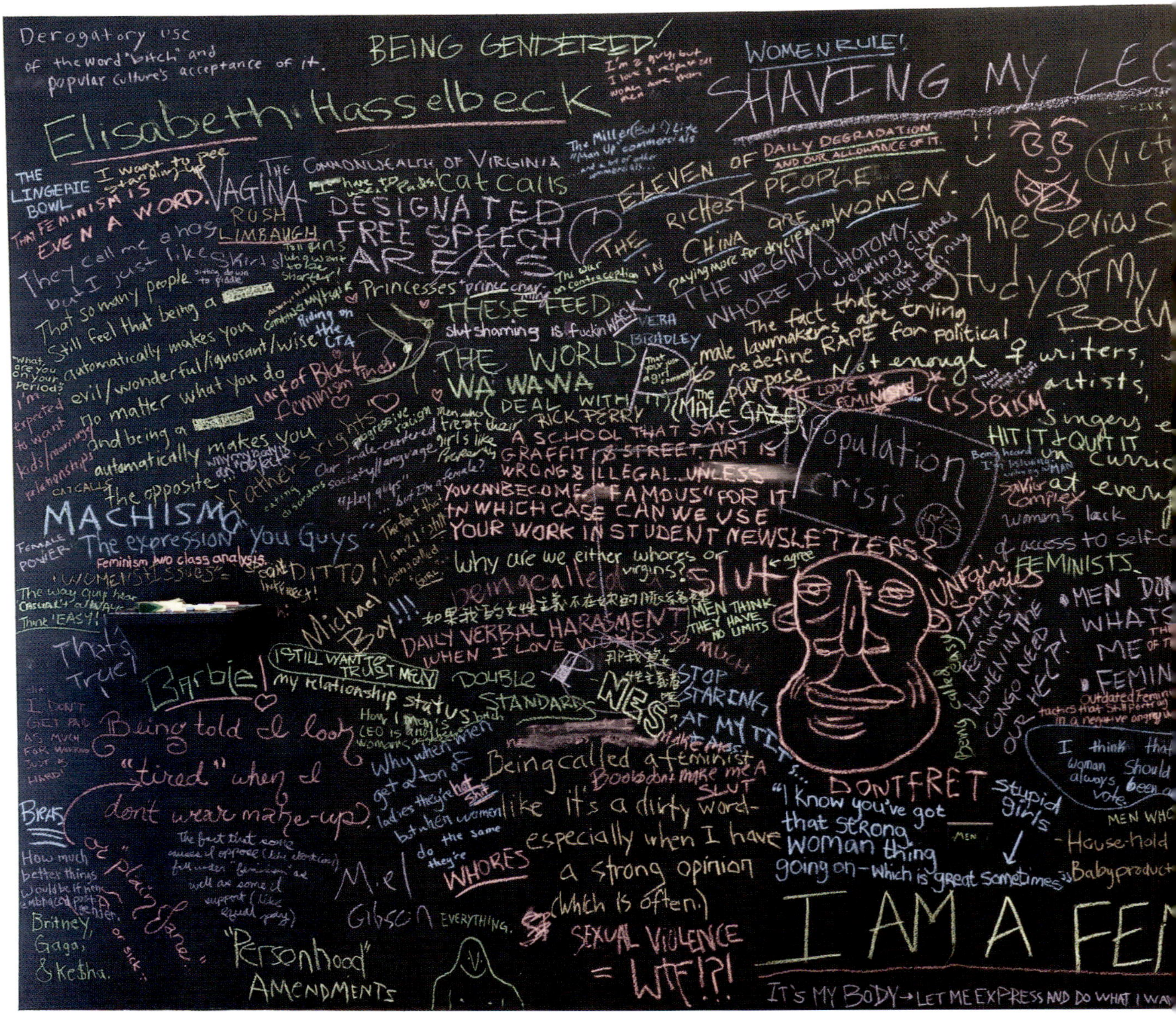

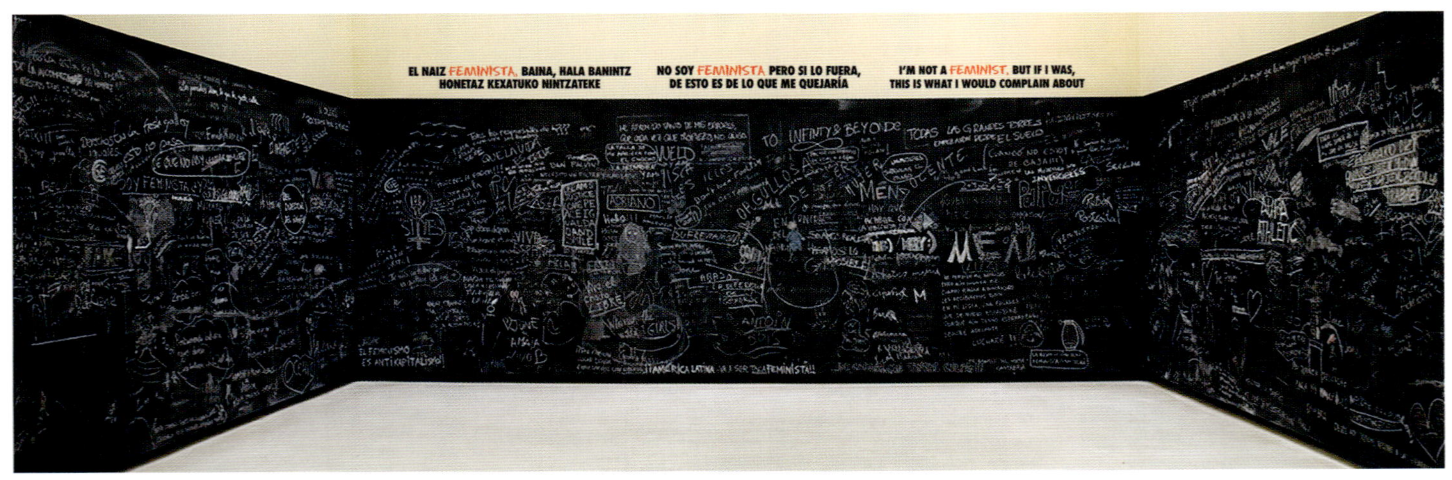

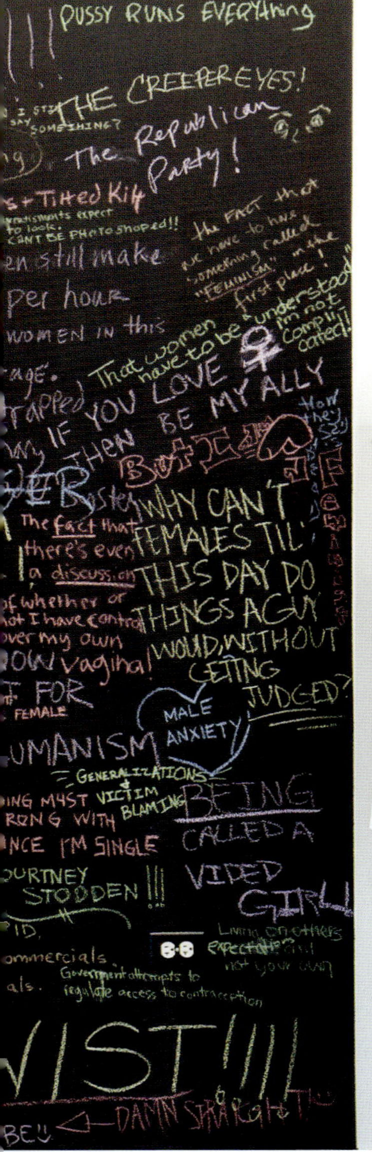

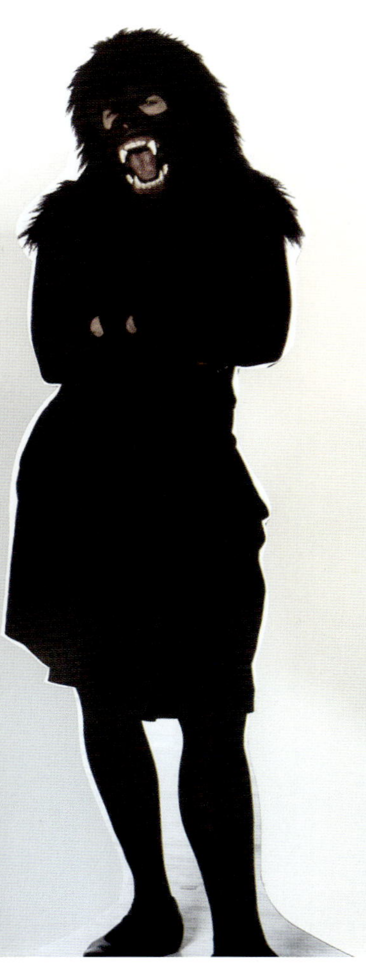

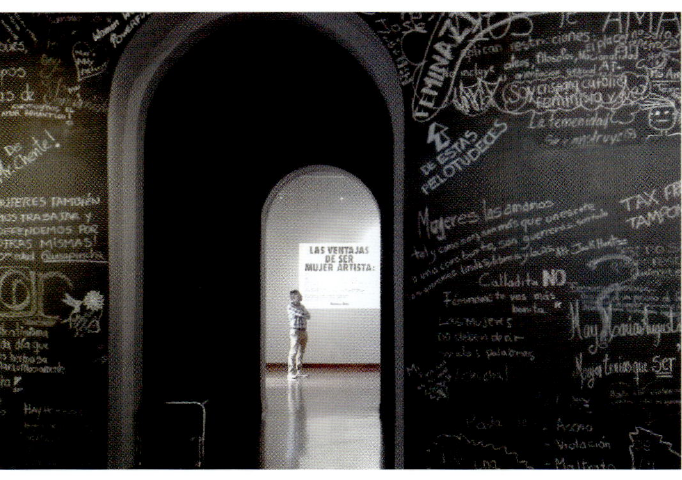

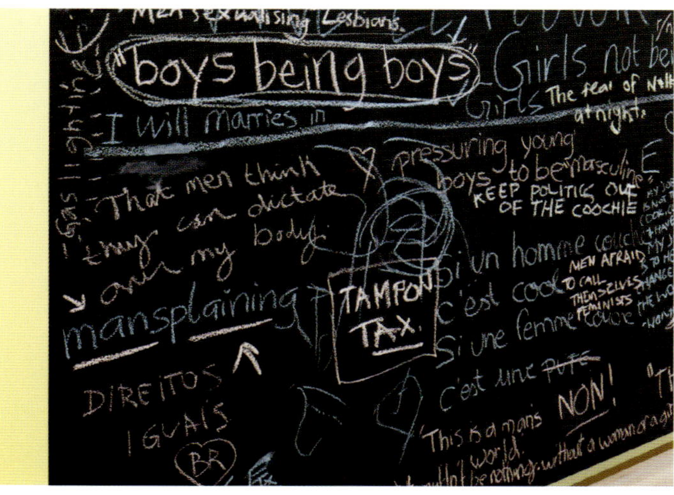

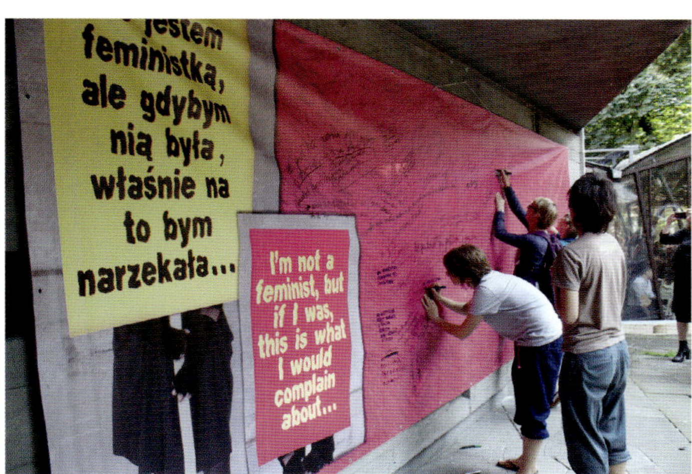

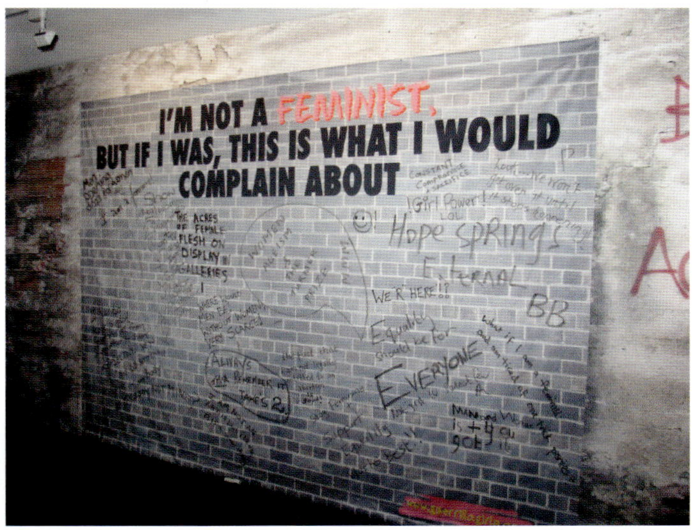

We first devised this participatory work for the *Guerrilla Girls All-Ireland Tour*, 2008–10. It has traveled to four continents—so far. Clockwise from top: Columbia College, Chicago, 2012; Auckland Art Gallery TOI O TĀMAKI, 2019; ArtBoom Festival, Krakow, 2012; Millennium Court Arts Centre, Belfast, 2010: Centro Cultural Metropolitano, Quito, 2017; Alhóndiga Bilbao, 2013

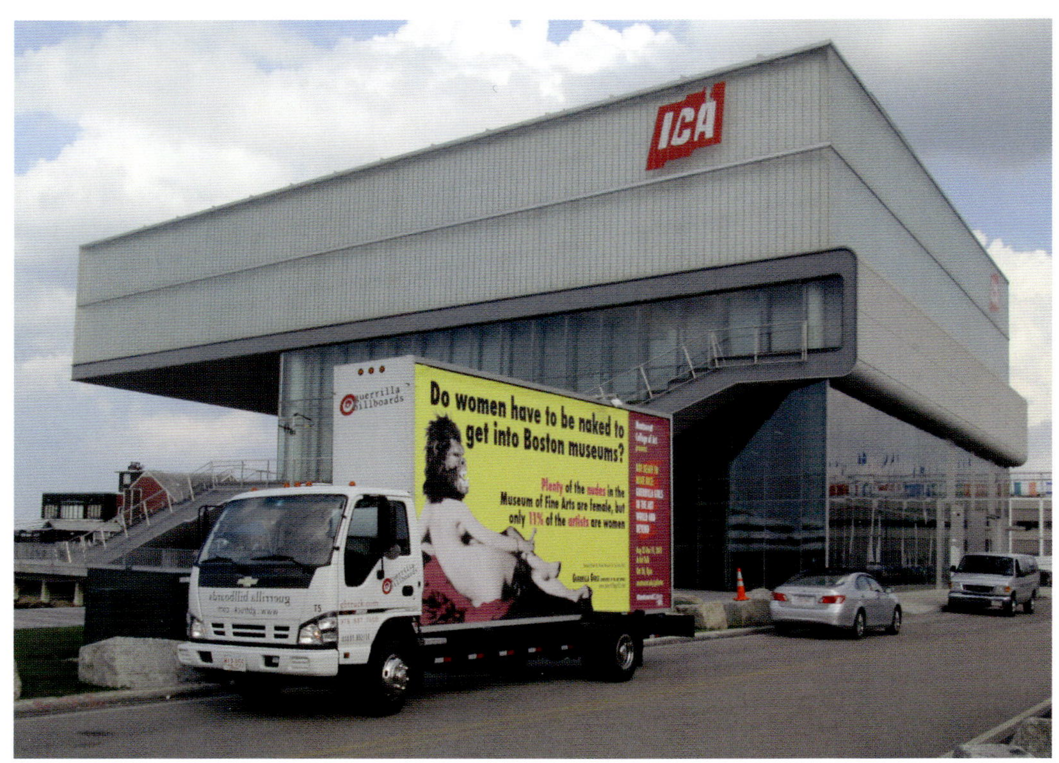
ICA
Do women have to be naked to get into Boston museums?
Plenty of the nudes in the Museum of Fine Arts are female, but only 11% of the artists are women
GUERRILLA GIRLS
Montserrat College of Art
Guerrilla Billboards

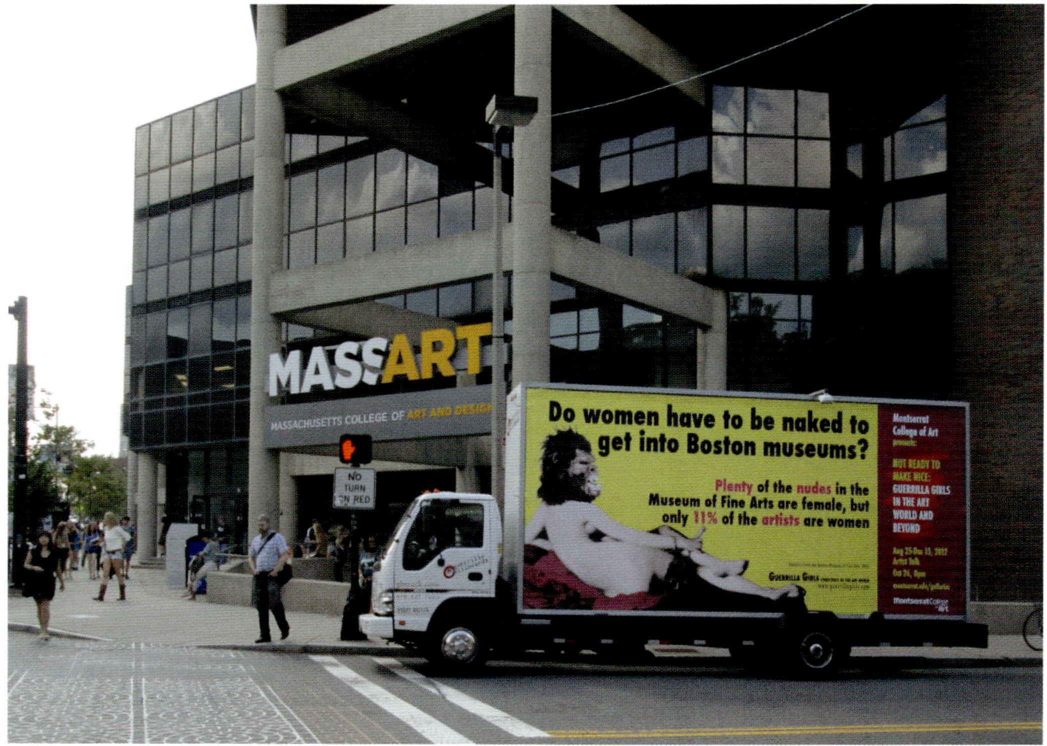
MASSART
MASSACHUSETTS COLLEGE OF ART AND DESIGN
NO TURN ON RED
Do women have to be naked to get into Boston museums?
Plenty of the nudes in the Museum of Fine Arts are female, but only 11% of the artists are women
GUERRILLA GIRLS
Montserrat College of Art present:
NOT READY TO MAKE NICE: GUERRILLA GIRLS IN THE ART WORLD AND BEYOND
Aug 25-Dec 15, 2015
Artist Talk
Oct 24, 8pm
montserrat.edu/gallerie

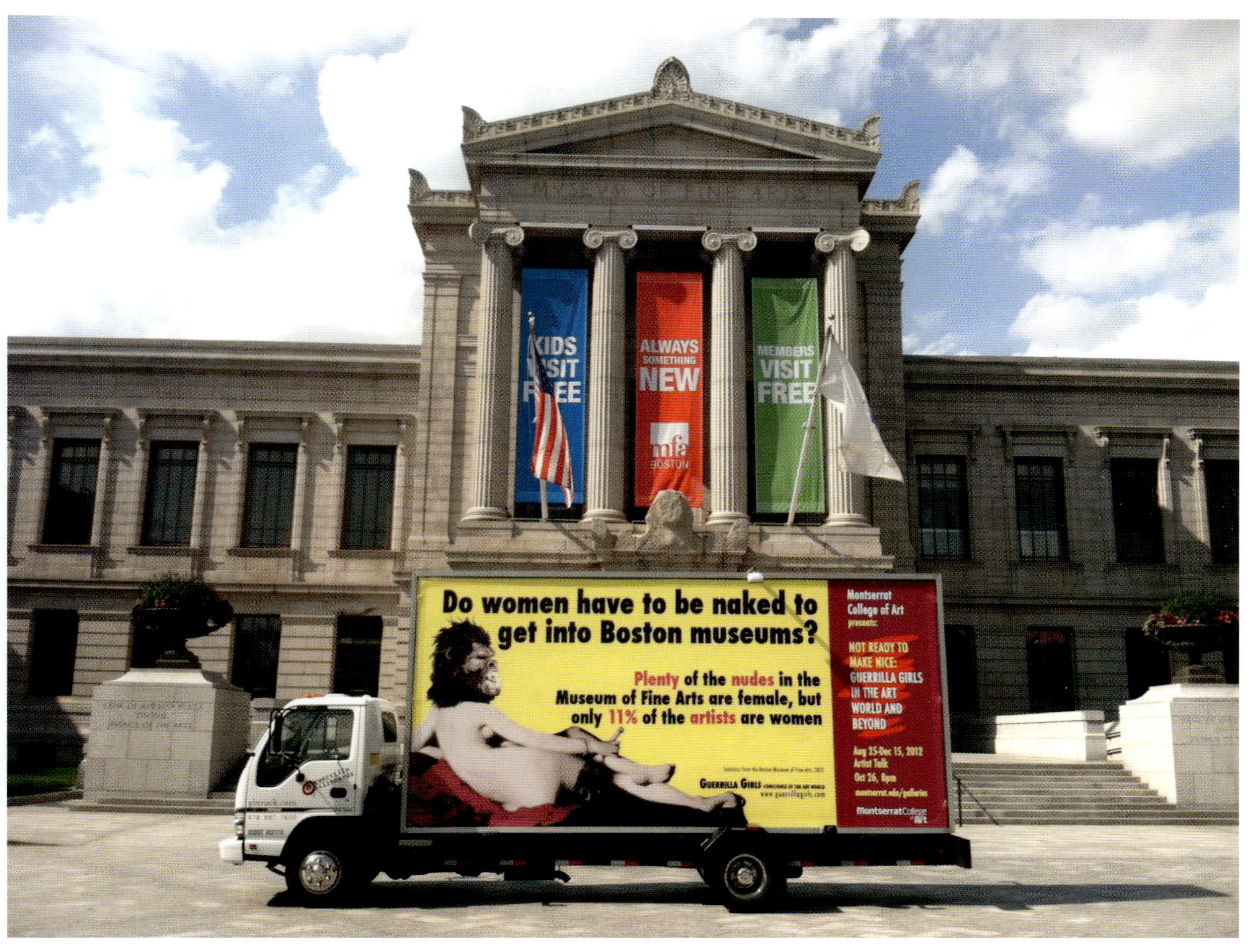

Students from Montserrat College of Art helped us conduct a gender count at the Boston Museum of Fine Art. A billboard truck then carried the results all over the city. After the truck stopped in front of the museum for a photo op, the curator called us and promised to do better.

Truck banner, Boston, 2012: Institute of Contemporary Art; Massachusetts College of Art and Design; Museum of Fine Art (Photos by Guerrilla Billboards, Boston)

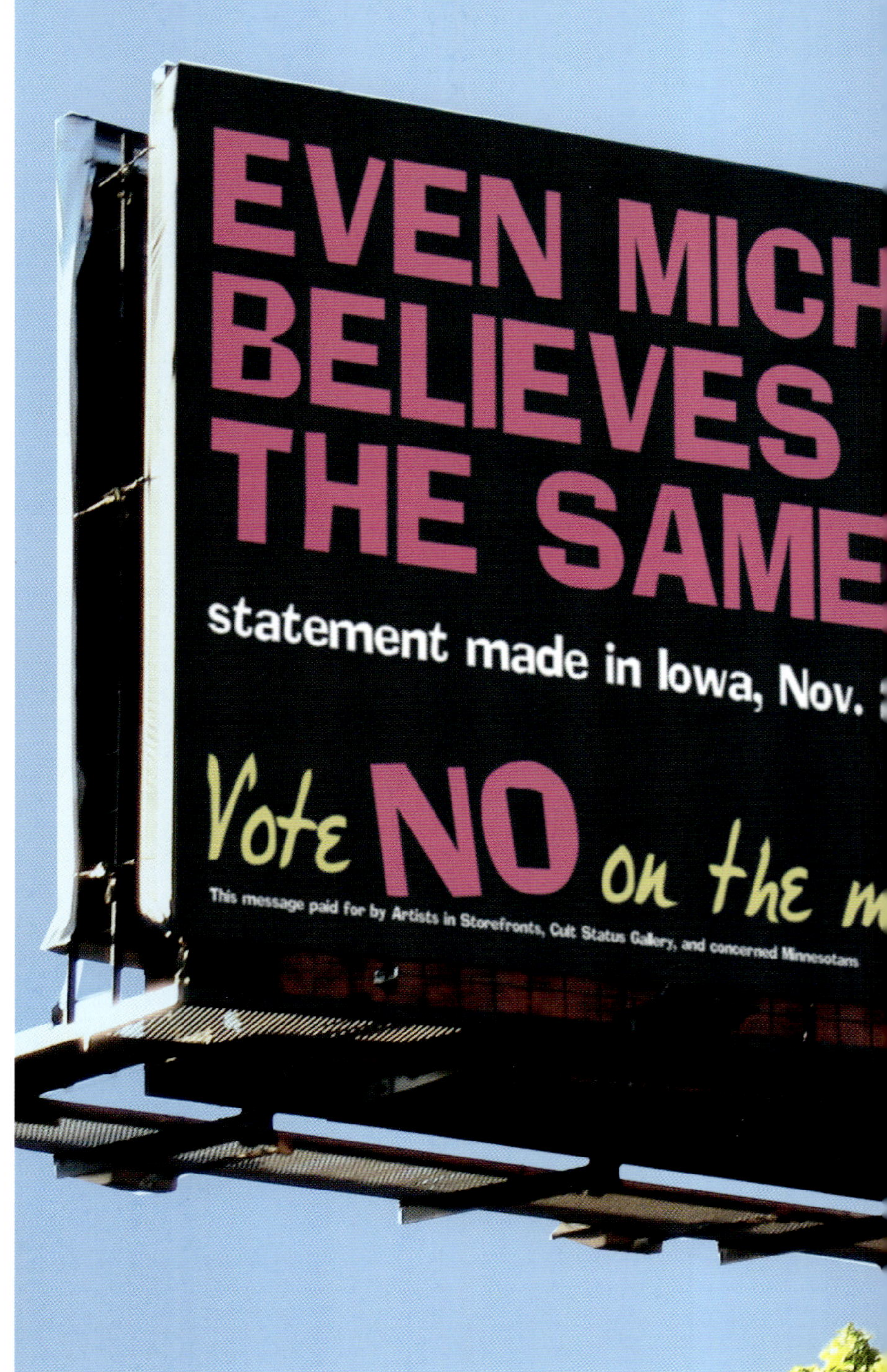

Above: We exposed the enormous cost of Voter IDs, a thinly disguised effort to suppress the vote. The result: Marriage equality triumphed. Voter ID lost. Right: It was election time in Minnesota. We used Michele Bachmann's own words to imply she supported marriage equality.

Billboard, Minneapolis, 2012; Poster, 2012

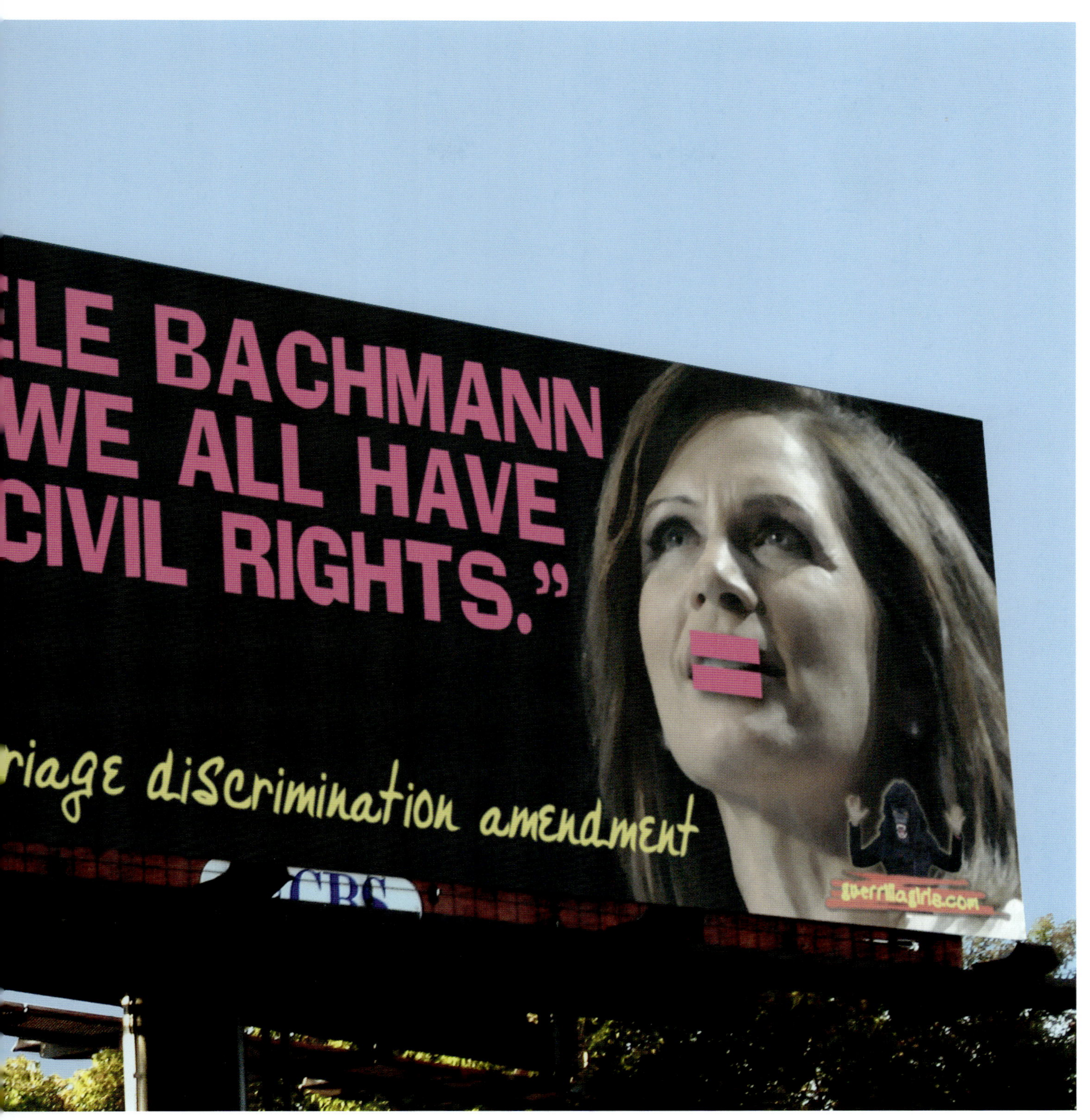
ELE BACHMANN
WE ALL HAVE
CIVIL RIGHTS."
riage discrimination amendment
guerrillagirls.com

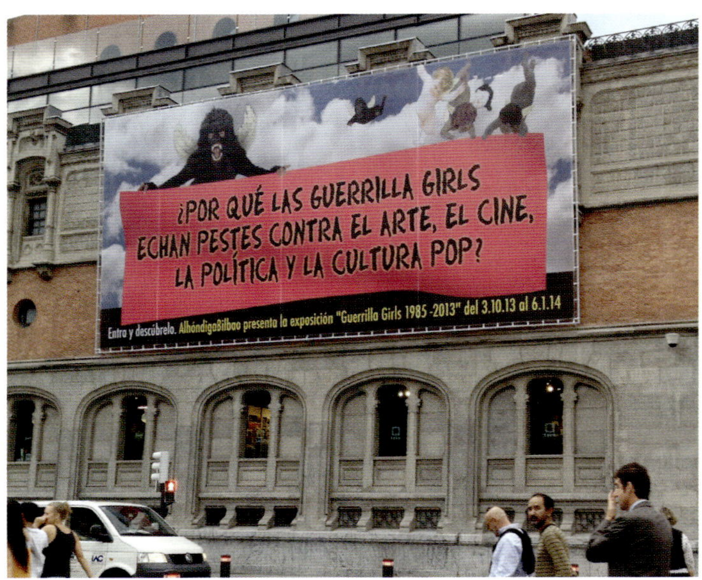
¿POR QUÉ LAS GUERRILLA GIRLS ECHAN PESTES CONTRA EL ARTE, EL CINE, LA POLÍTICA Y LA CULTURA POP?
Entra y descúbrelo. AlhóndigaBilbao presenta la exposición "Guerrilla Girls 1985 -2013" del 3.10.13 al 6.1.14

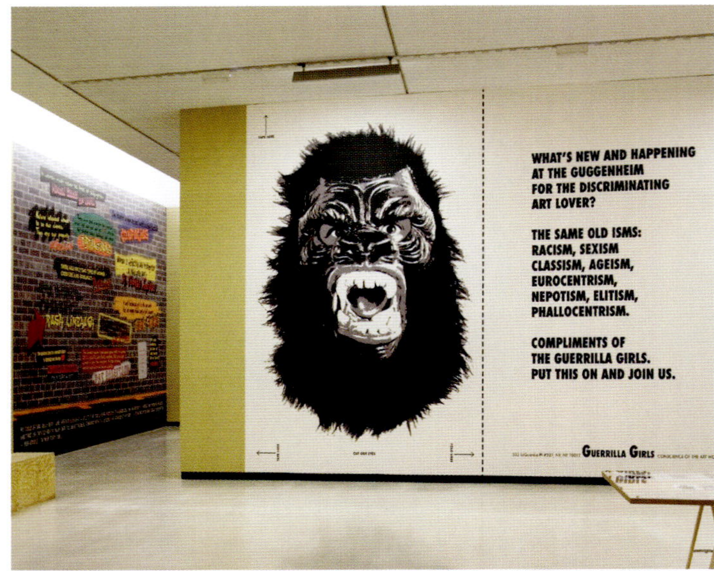
WHAT'S NEW AND HAPPENING AT THE GUGGENHEIM FOR THE DISCRIMINATING ART LOVER?
THE SAME OLD ISMS: RACISM, SEXISM CLASSISM, AGEISM, EUROCENTRISM, NEPOTISM, ELITISM, PHALLOCENTRISM.
COMPLIMENTS OF THE GUERRILLA GIRLS. PUT THIS ON AND JOIN US.
GUERRILLA GIRLS

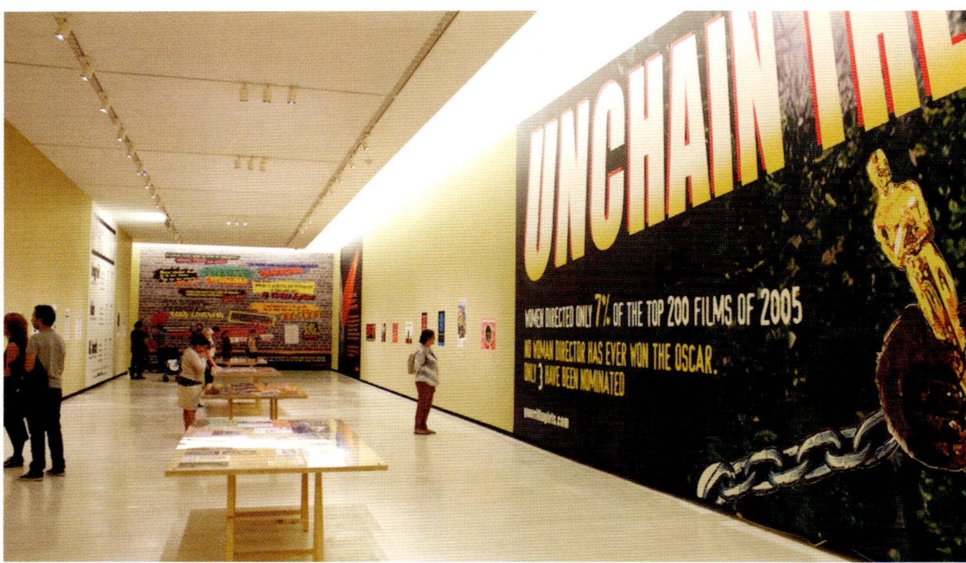
UNCHAIN
WOMEN DIRECTED ONLY 7% OF THE TOP 200 FILMS OF 2005
NO WOMAN DIRECTOR HAS EVER WON THE OSCAR. ONLY 3 HAVE BEEN NOMINATED

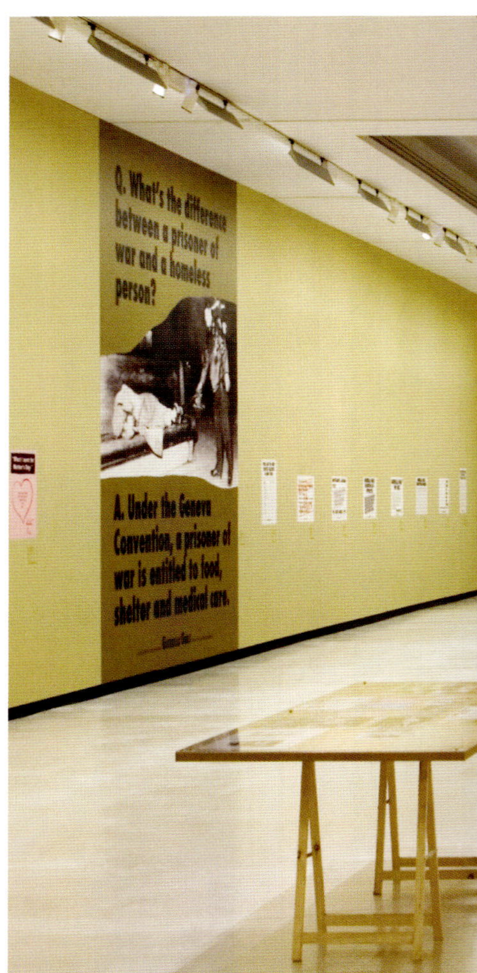
Q. What's the difference between a prisoner of war and a homeless person?
A. Under the Geneva Convention, a prisoner of war is entitled to food, shelter and medical care.

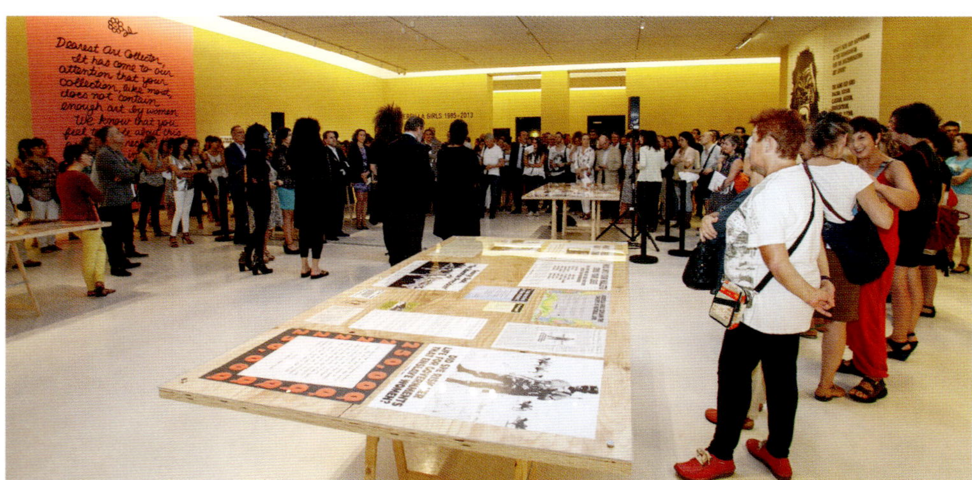

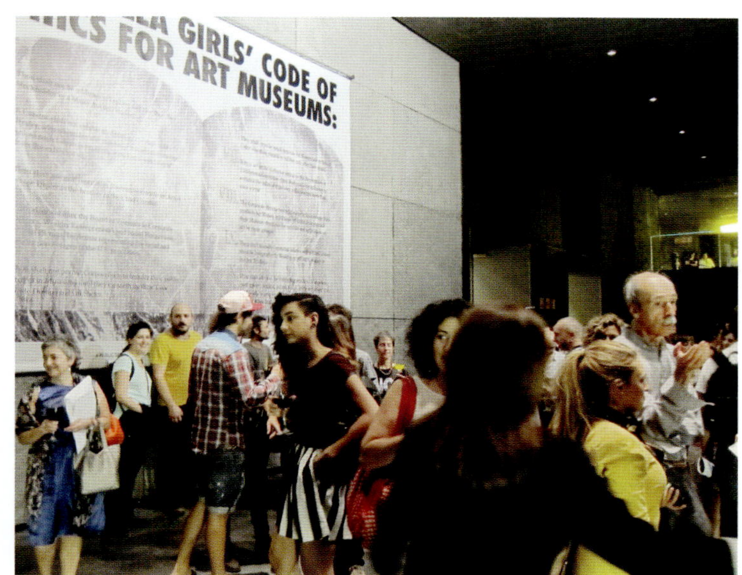

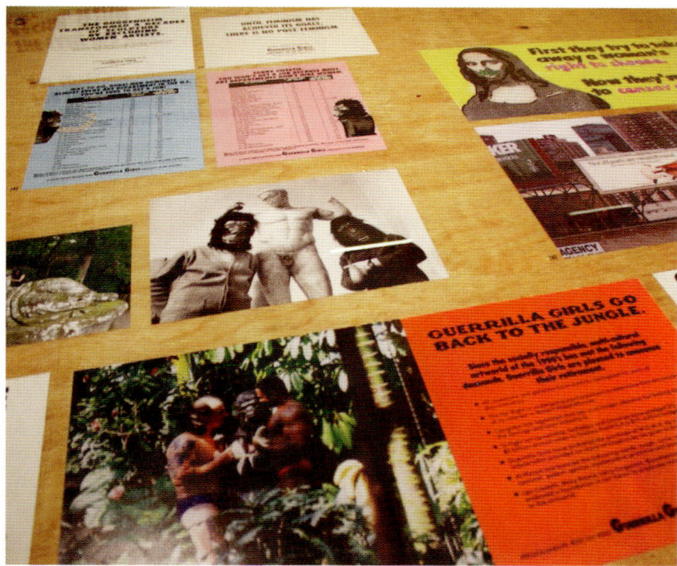

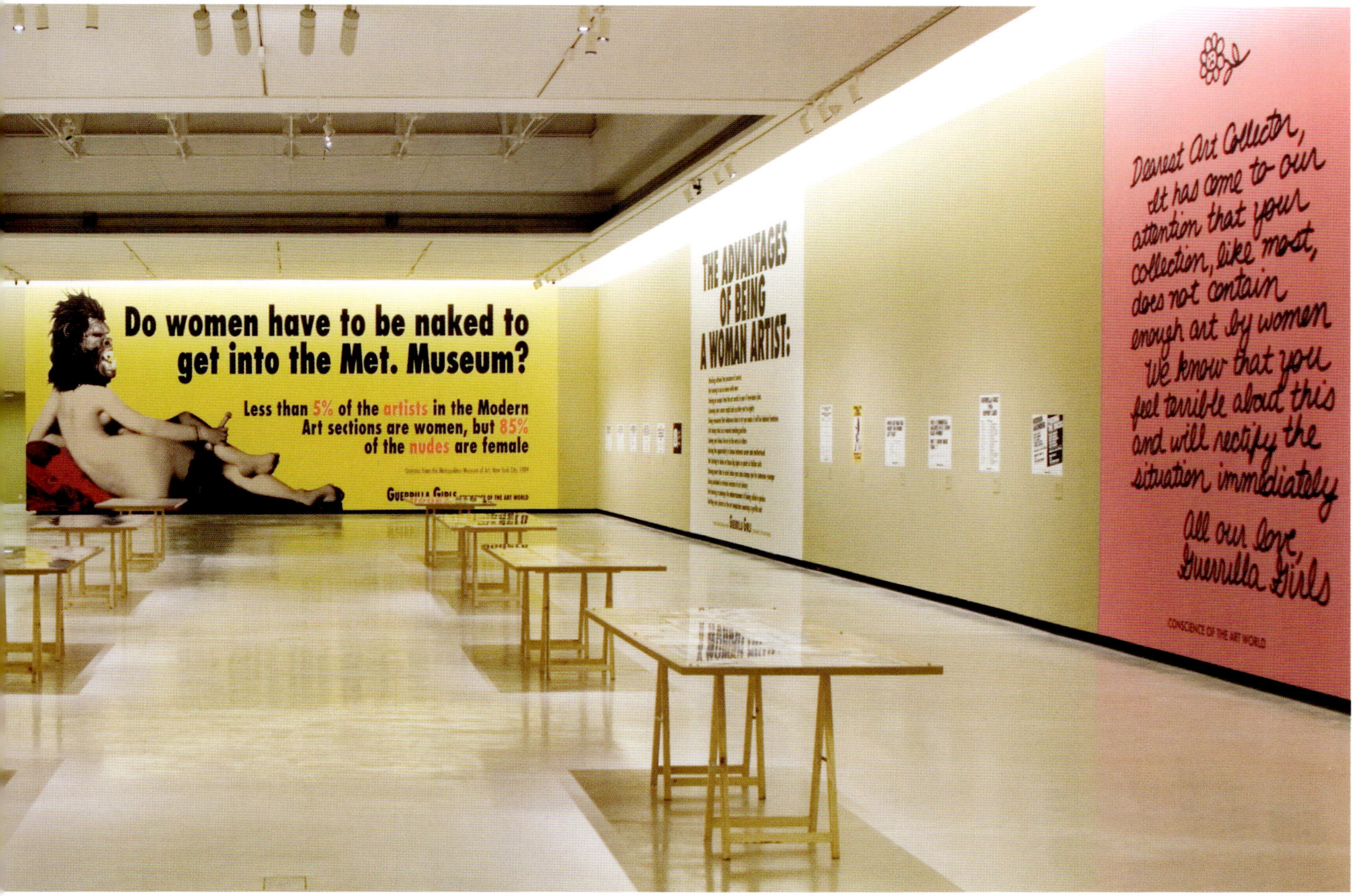

Xabier Arakistain curated our first retrospective at the Alhóndiga Bilbao, Spain. Over 70 posters, in chronological order, with Spanish translations, told the history of our work and how it evolved. There were 14 tables of archival material: snapshots, letters, notes, sketches, press and other goodies from our secret stash.

Installation views, Bilbao, 2013

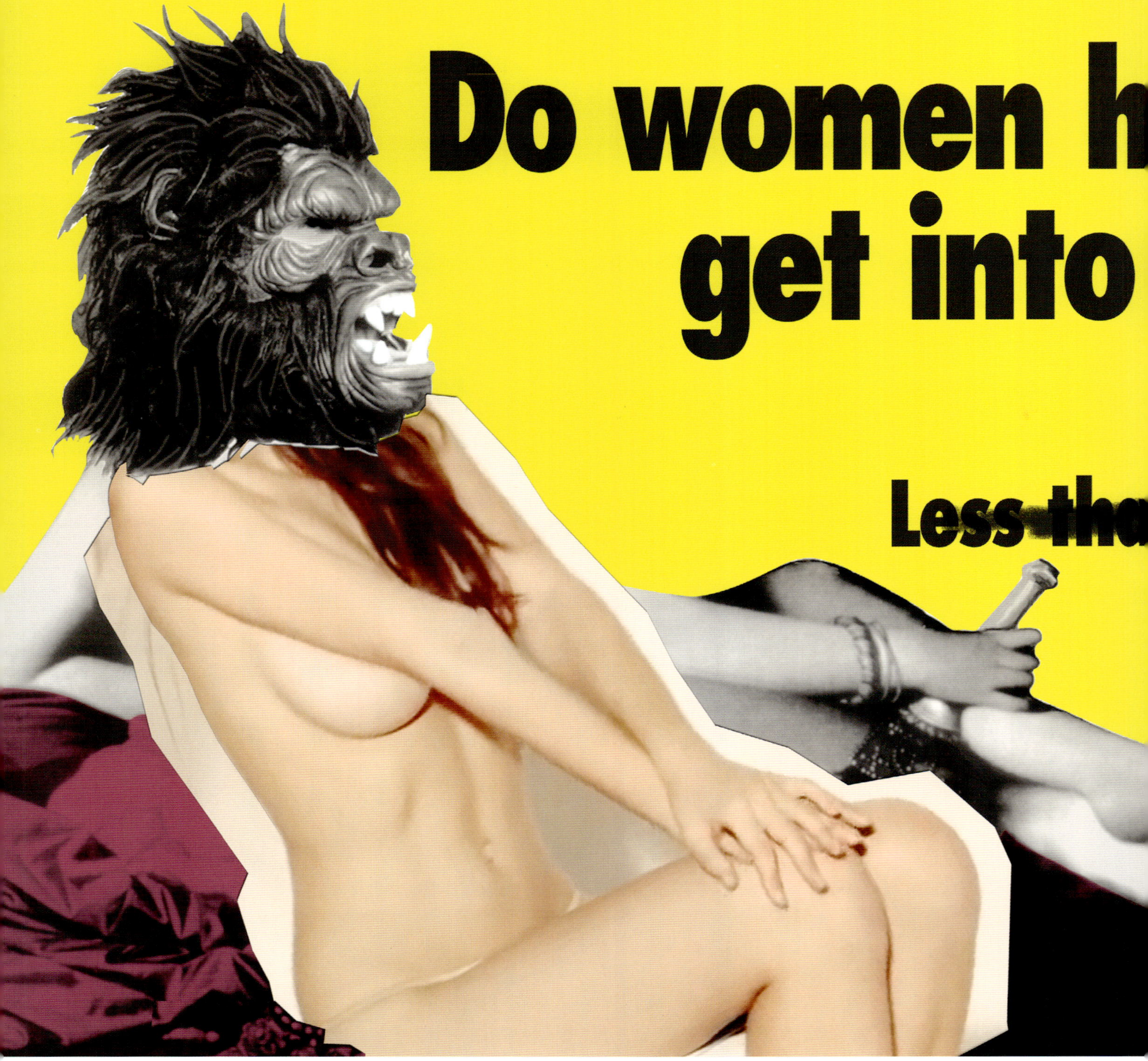

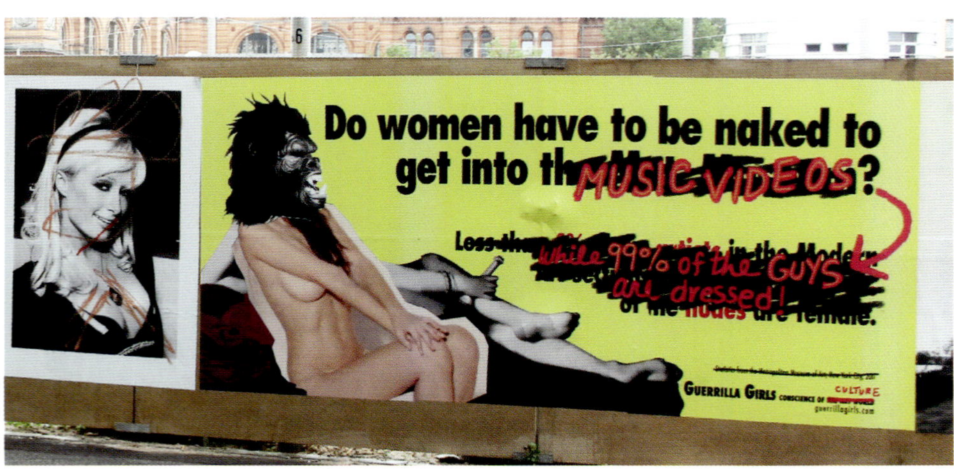
Do women have to be naked to get into the MUSIC VIDEOS?
while 99% of the GUYS are dressed!
GUERRILLA GIRLS CONSCIENCE OF CULTURE
guerrillagirls.com

Pharrell Williams invited us to be in an exhibition about "femininity" at a fancy art gallery in Paris. We accepted under the condition that we expose sexism in music videos. We graffitied over our iconic *Naked* poster and added an image of a nude performer from the problematic *Blurred Lines* video featuring Pharrell.

Poster, 2014; Banner, Bremen, Germany, 2018

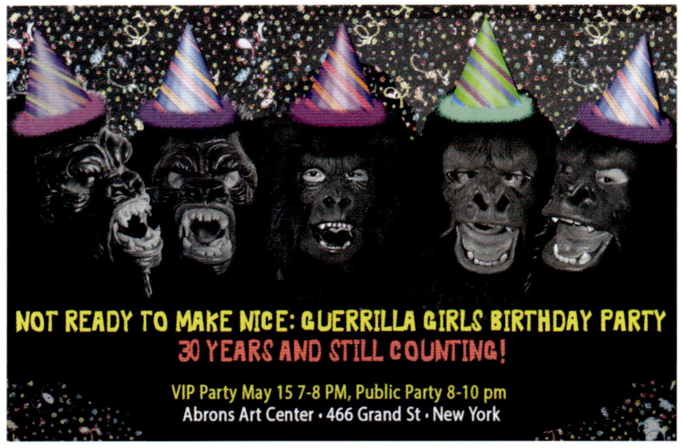

For our 30th anniversary, we got busy with a new street campaign about income inequality, a stealth projection on the Whitney Museum facade, and an exhibition and blowout party at Abrons Arts Center, where our work was on display 24/7.

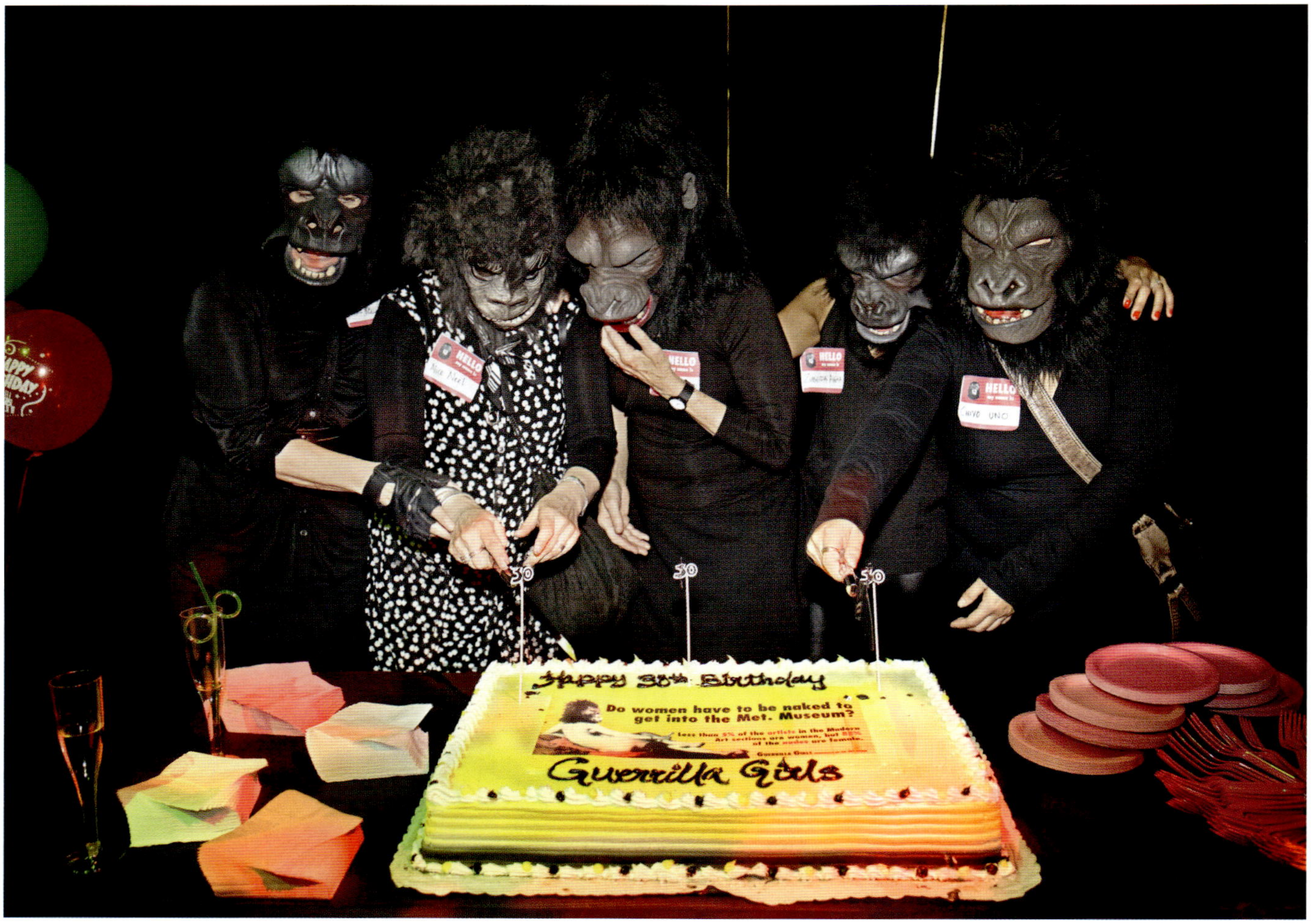

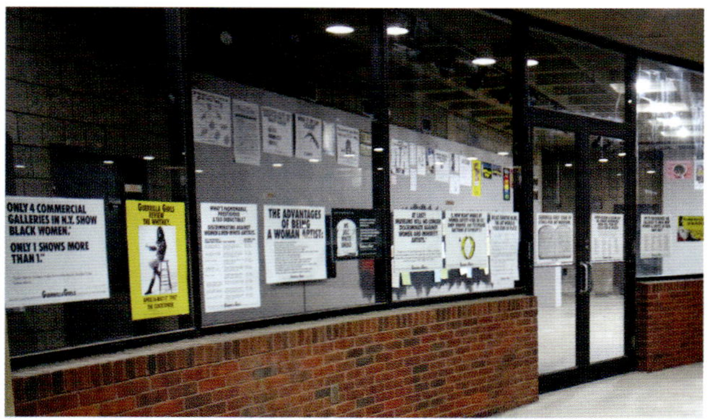

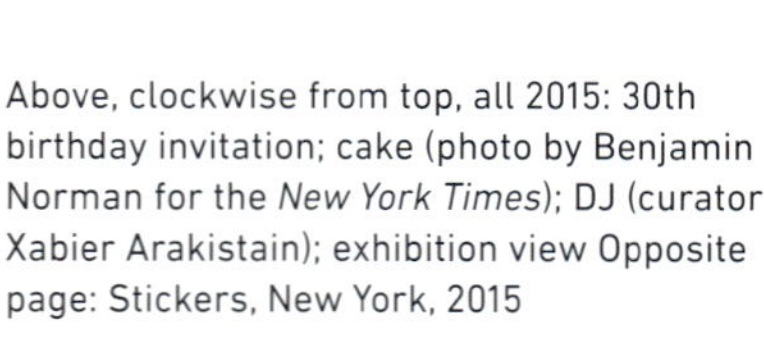

Above, clockwise from top, all 2015: 30th birthday invitation; cake (photo by Benjamin Norman for the *New York Times*); DJ (curator Xabier Arakistain); exhibition view Opposite page: Stickers, New York, 2015

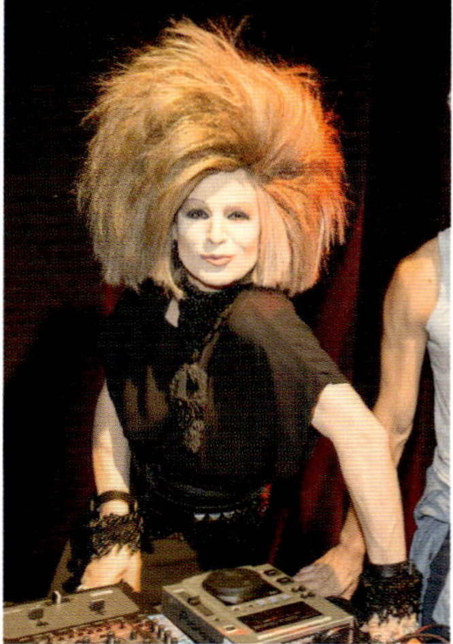

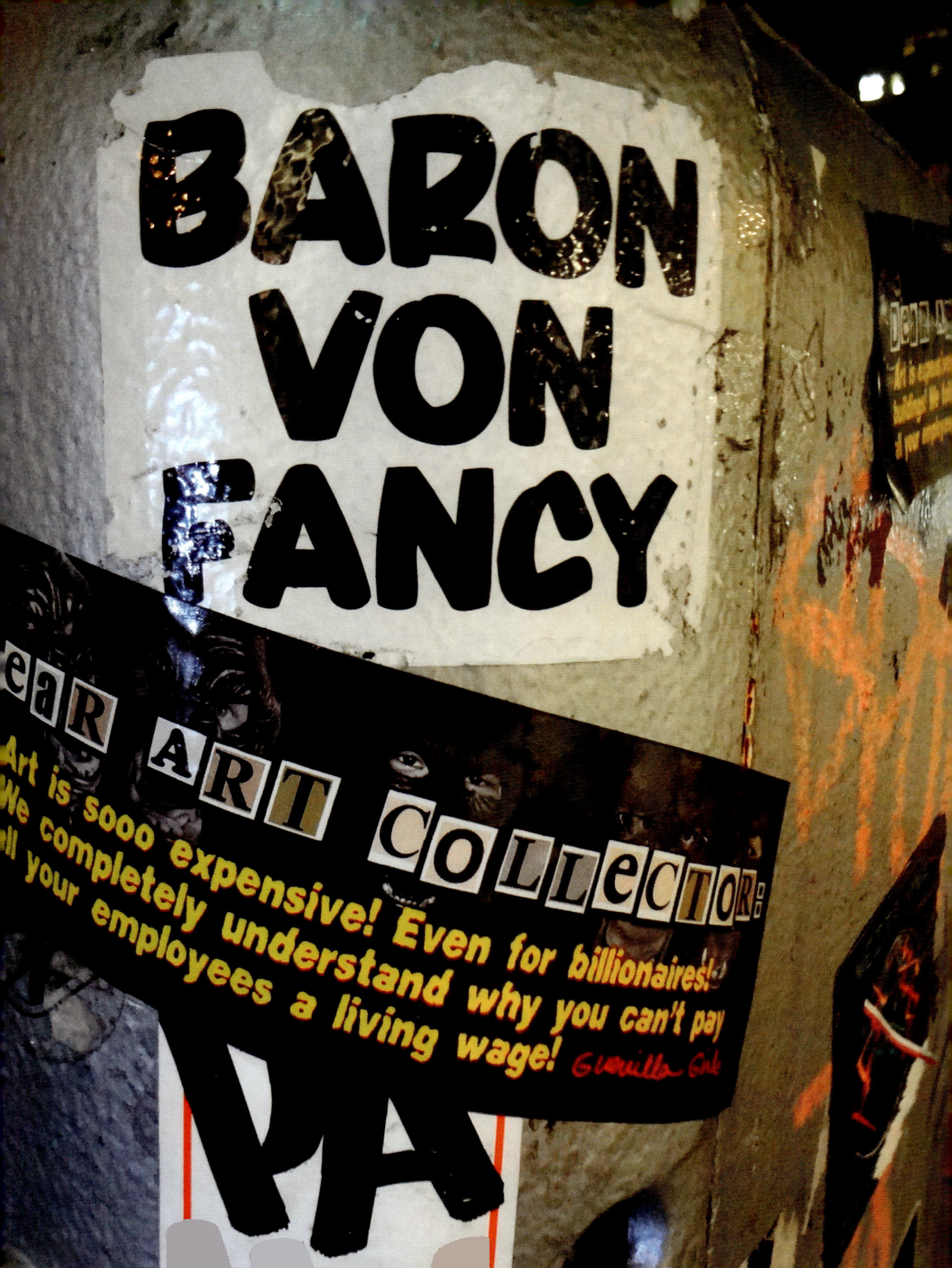
BARON VON FANCY
eaR ART COLLECTOR:
Art is sooo expensive! Even for billionaires!
We completely understand why you can't pay
your employees a living wage!
Guerilla Girls

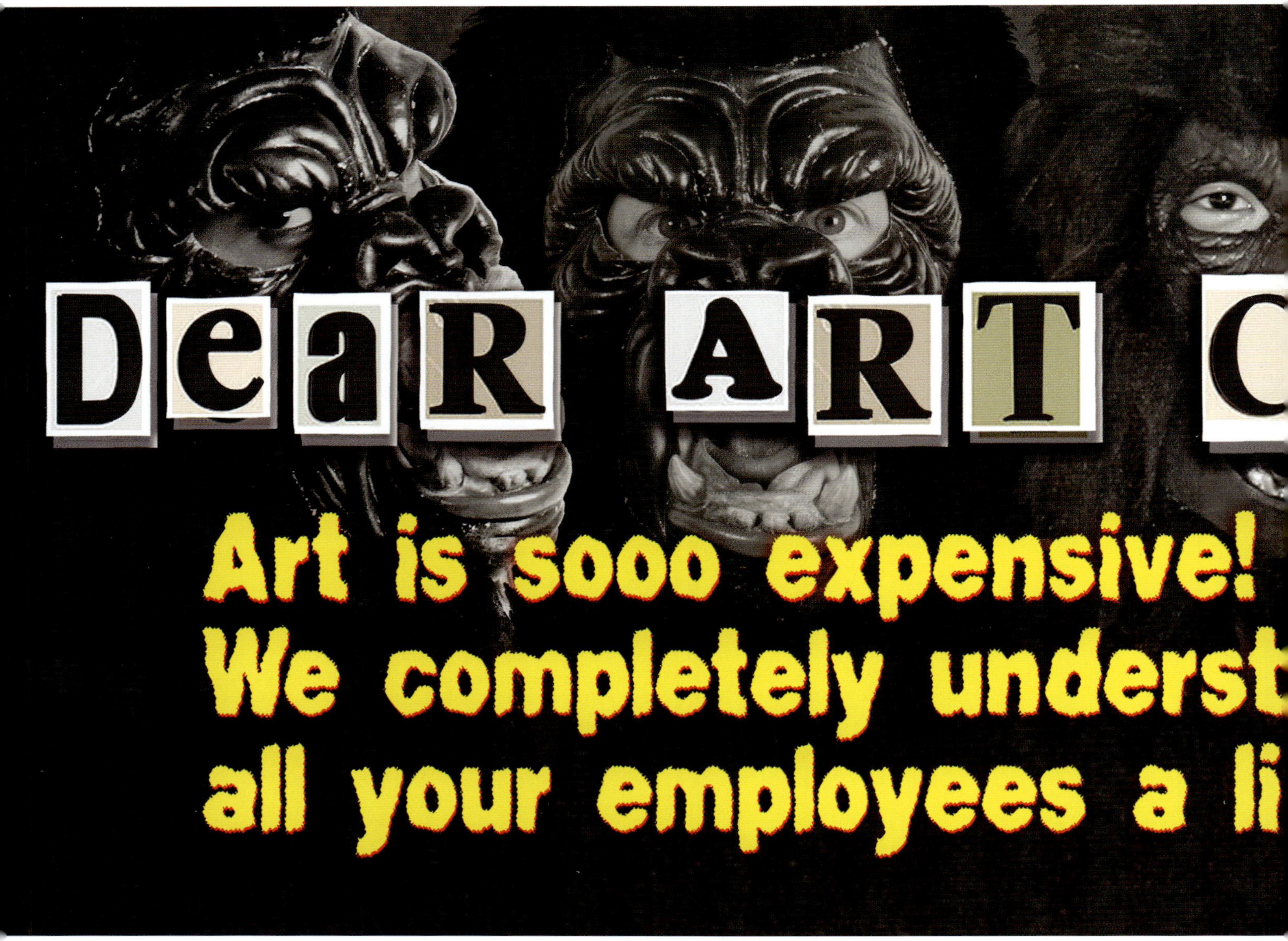

We took to the streets with a sticker campaign, fingering art collectors who spend a ton of money on art while exploiting their own workers.

Pages 122–23: Galleries and museums aren't the greatest employers either.

Poster, stickers, 2015

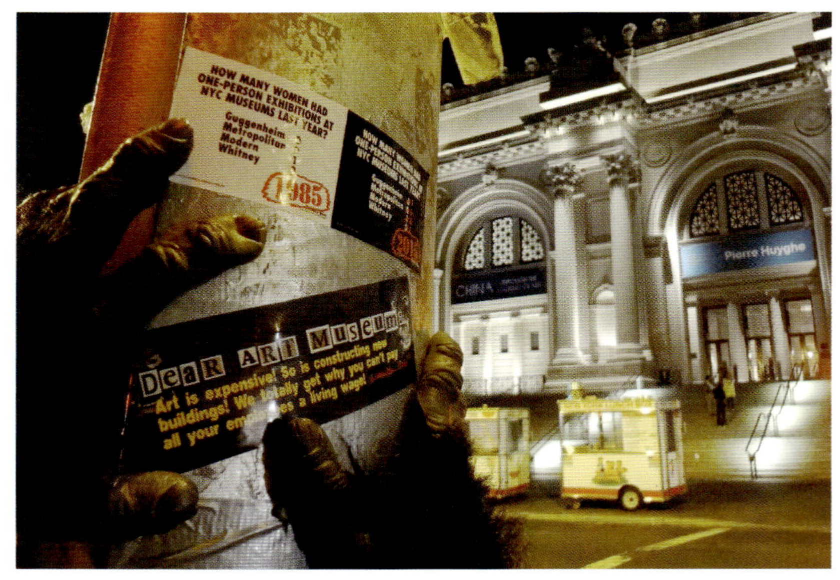

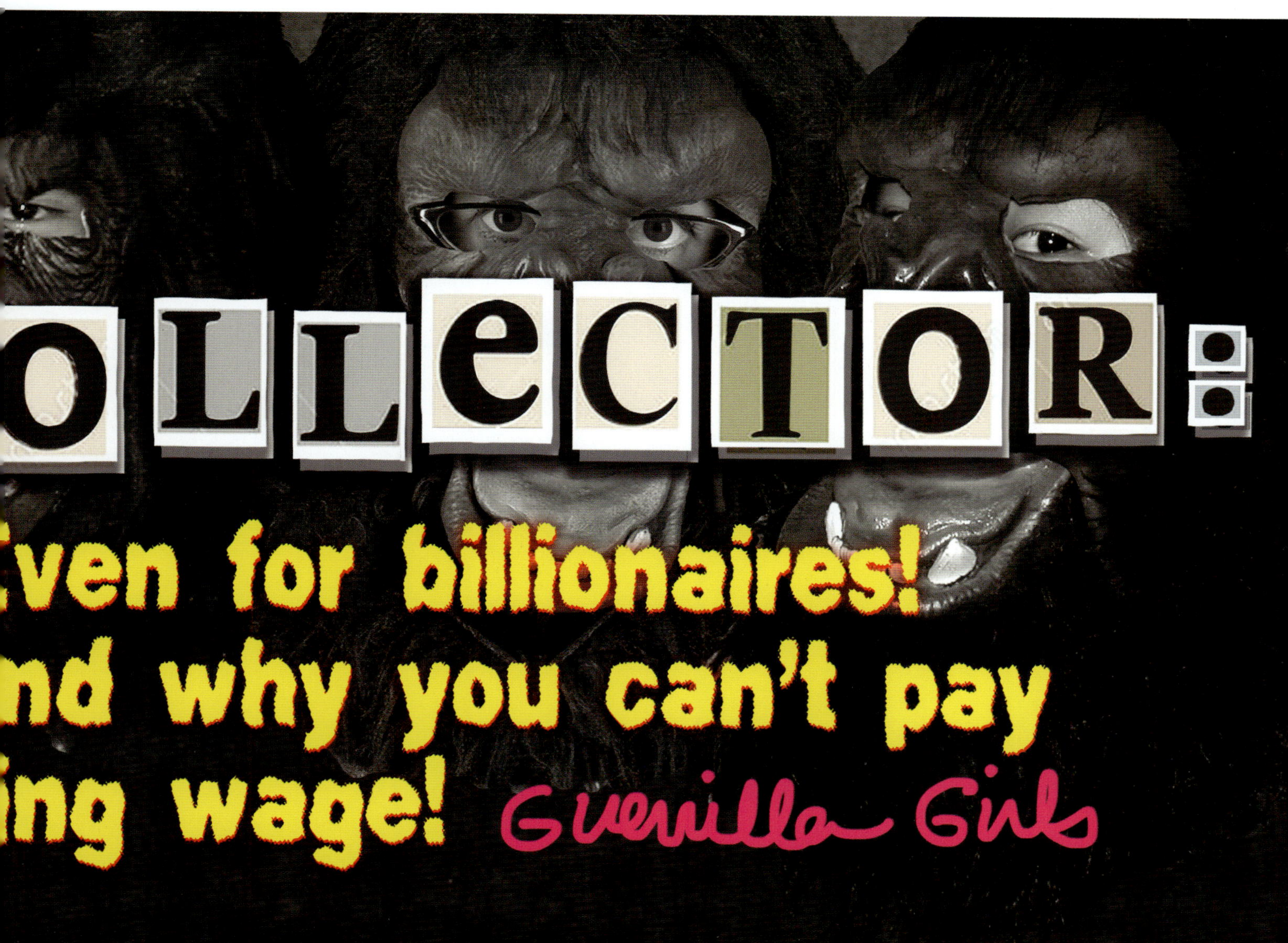
OLLECTOR:
ven for billionaires!
nd why you can't pay
ng wage!
Guerilla Girls

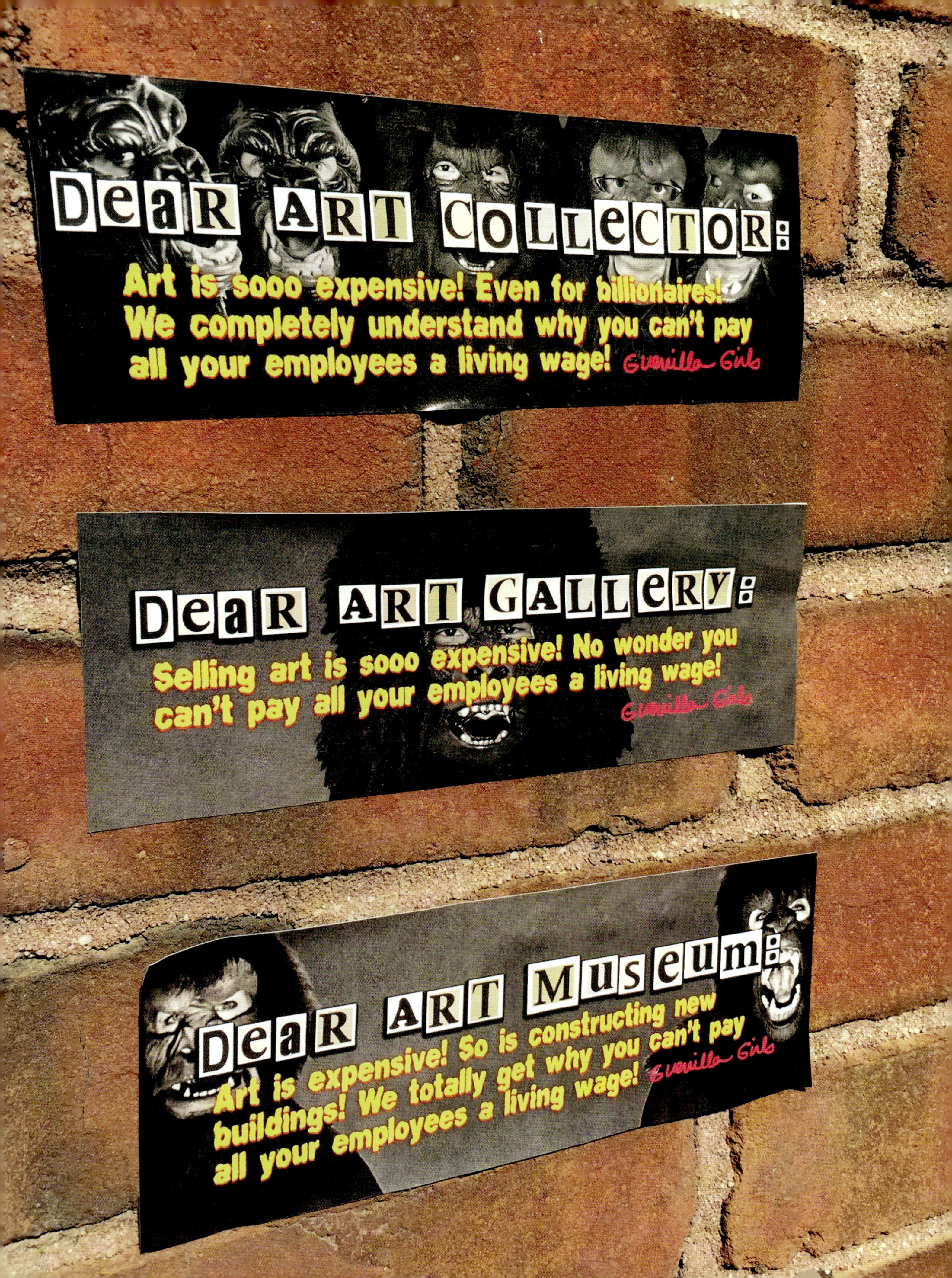
Dear Art Collector:
Art is sooo expensive! Even for billionaires! We completely understand why you can't pay all your employees a living wage!
Guerrilla Girls
Dear Art Gallery:
Selling art is sooo expensive! No wonder you can't pay all your employees a living wage!
Guerrilla Girls
Dear Art Museum:
Art is expensive! So is constructing new buildings! We totally get why you can't pay all your employees a living wage!
Guerrilla Girls

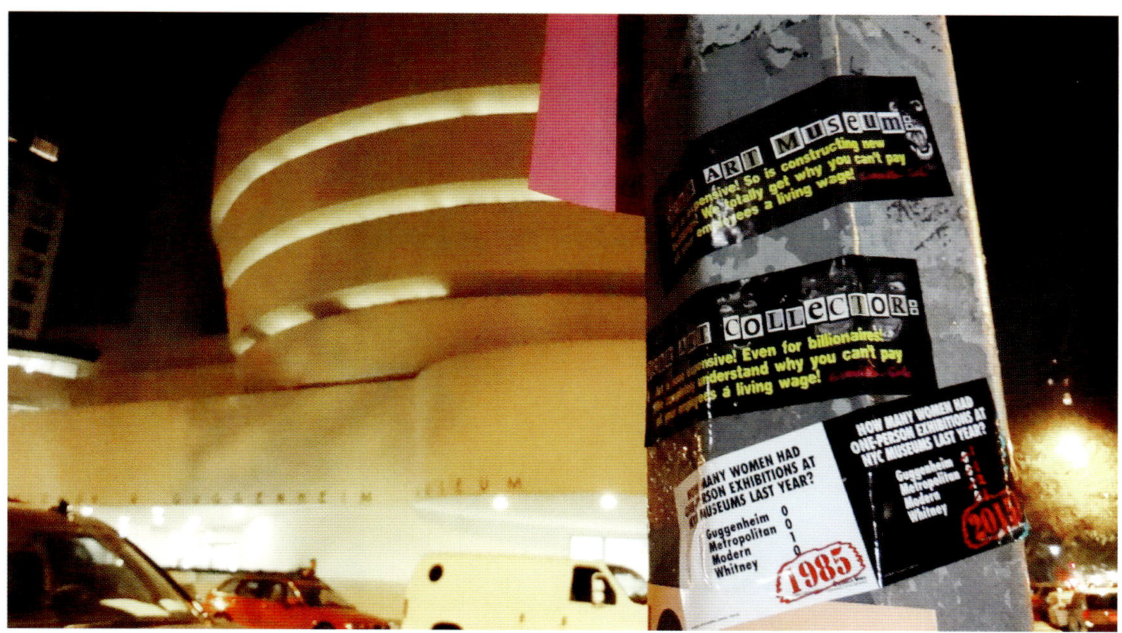

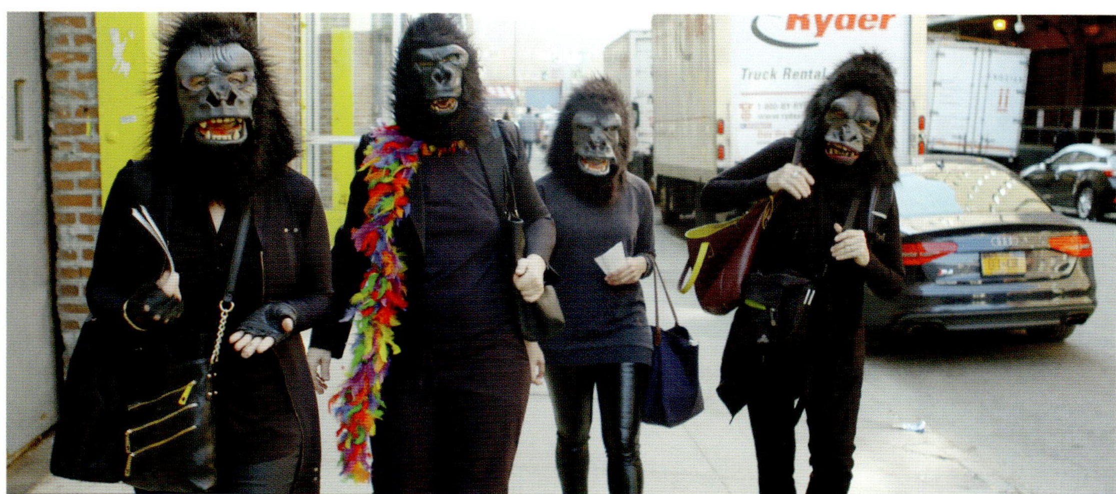

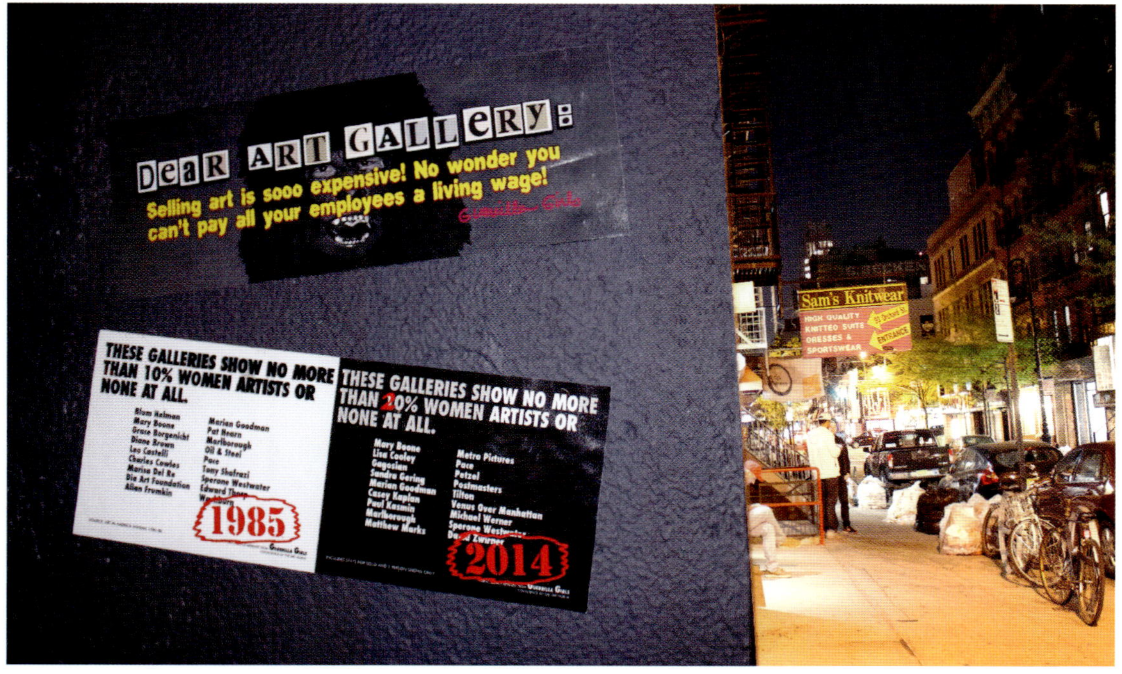

Top and bottom: stickers, New York, 2015,
Middle: film still, 22 Productions, 2015

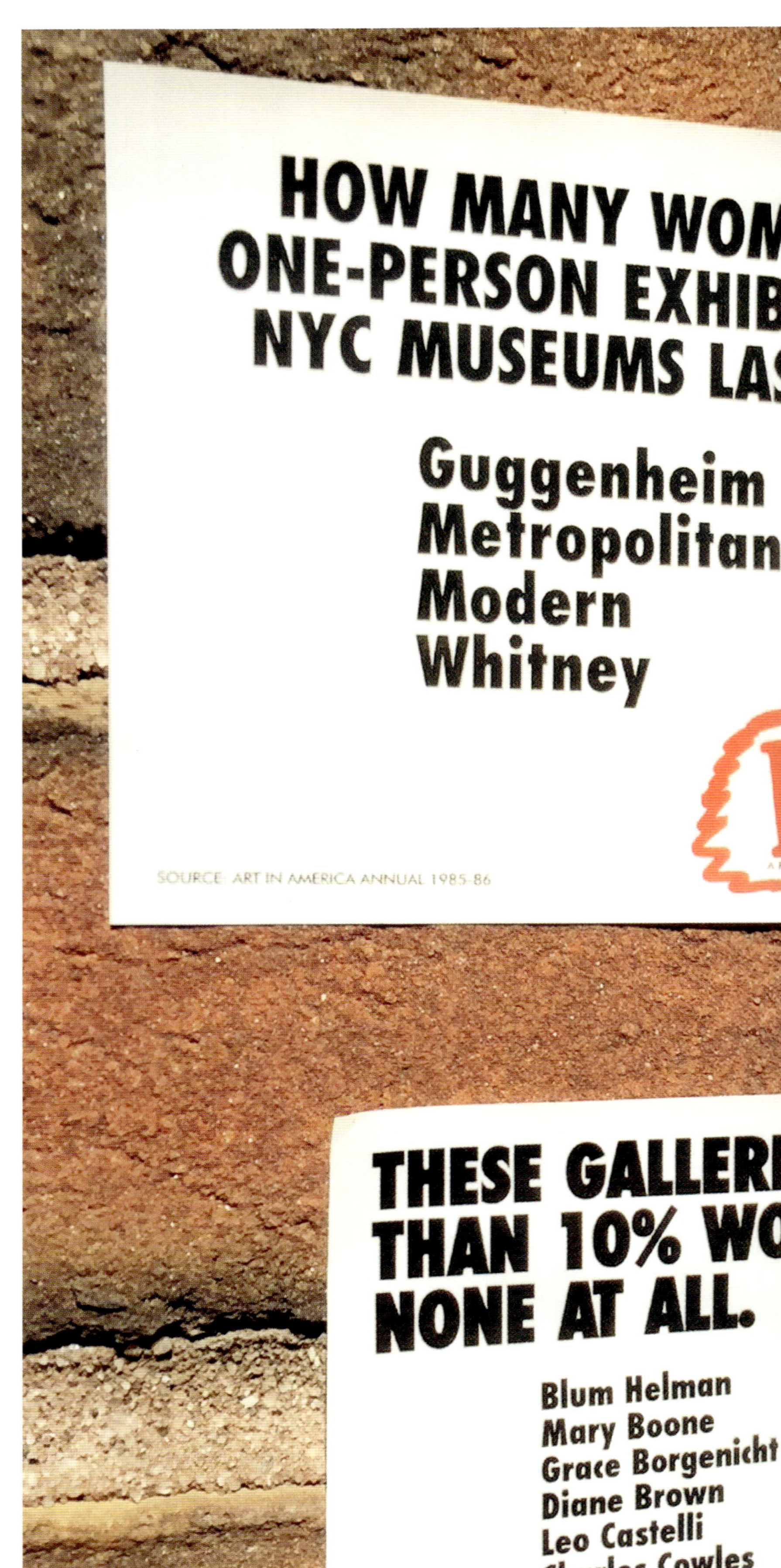

Our anniversary street campaign revisited two of
our early posters to see if anything had improved.
Some galleries were almost as bad in 2015 as in
1985. Museum exhibitions weren't much better.

Stickers, 2015

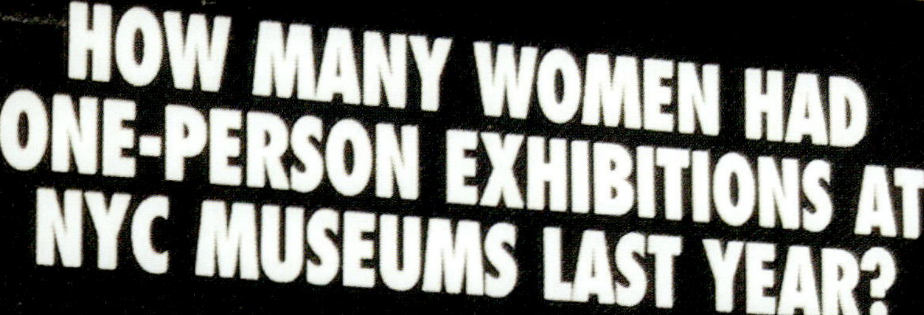
HAD
ONS AT
YEAR?
085
GUERRILLA GIRLS
CONSCIENCE OF THE ART WORLD
HOW MANY WOMEN HAD ONE-PERSON EXHIBITIONS AT NYC MUSEUMS LAST YEAR?
Guggenheim
Metropolitan
Modern
Whitney
0 1 1 2 3 4
2015
SOURCE: MUSEUM WEBSITES
A PUBLIC SERVICE MESSAGE FROM GUERRILLA GIRLS
CONSCIENCE OF THE ART WORLD

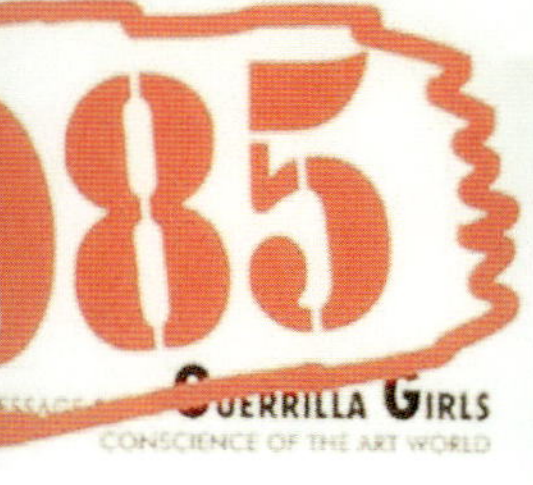

SHOW NO MORE
N ARTISTS OR
arian Goodman
t Hearn
arlborough
l & Steel
ce
ny Shafrazi
erone Westwater
ward Thorp
lburn
1985
GUERRILLA GIRLS

THESE GALLERIES SHOW NO MORE THAN 20% WOMEN ARTISTS OR NONE AT ALL.
Mary Boone
Lisa Cooley
Gagosian
Sandra Gering
Marian Goodman
Casey Kaplan
Paul Kasmin
Marlborough
Matthew Marks
Metro Pictures
Pace
Petzel
Postmasters
Tilton
Venus Over Manhattan
Michael Werner
Sperone Westwater
David Zwirner
2014
PUBLIC SERVICE MESSAGE FROM GUERRILLA GIRLS
CONSCIENCE OF THE ART WORLD
INCLUDES STATS FOR SOLO AND 2 PERSON SHOWS ONLY

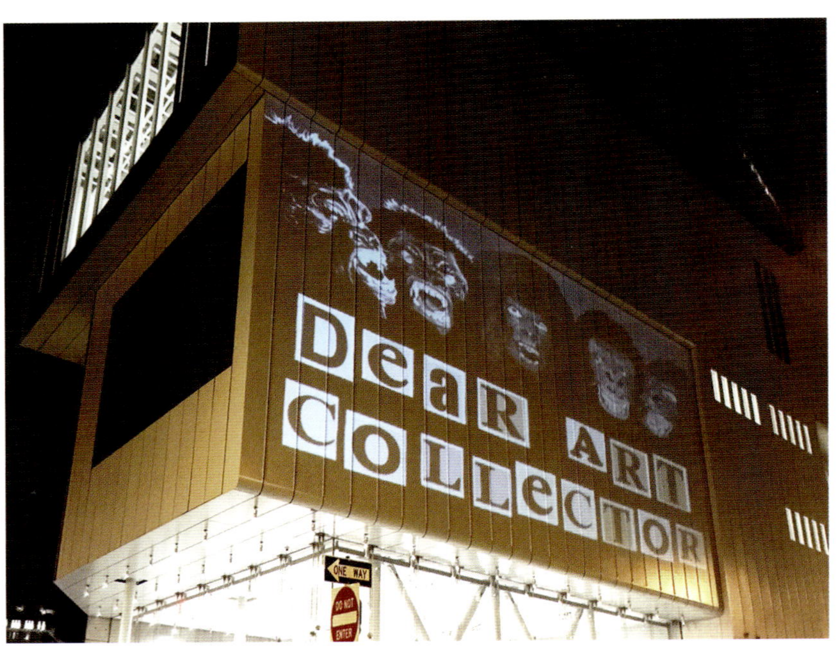

DEAR ART
COLLECTOR
ONE WAY
DO NOT ENTER

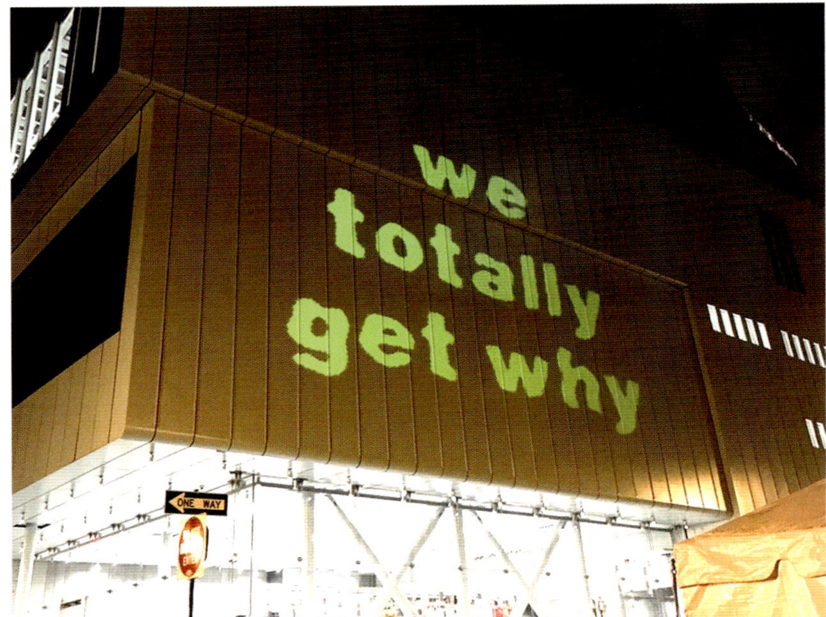

we
totally
get why
ONE WAY

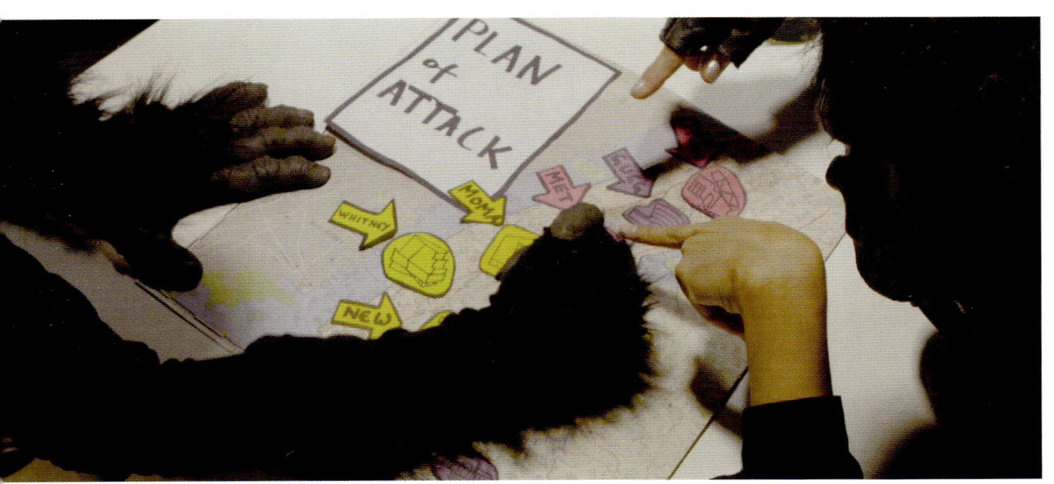

PLAN
of
ATTACK
WHITNEY
MOMA
MET
NEW

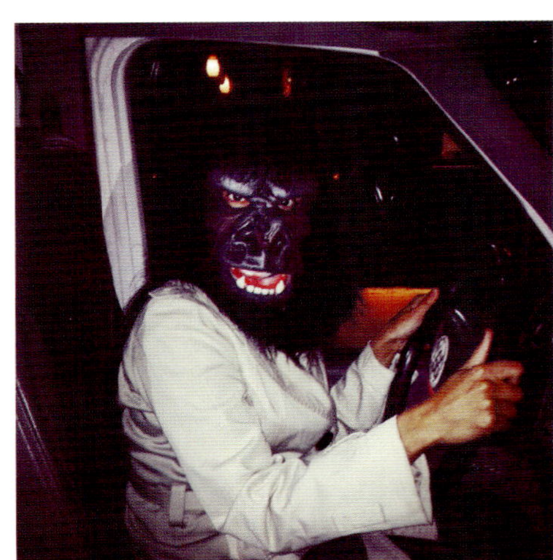

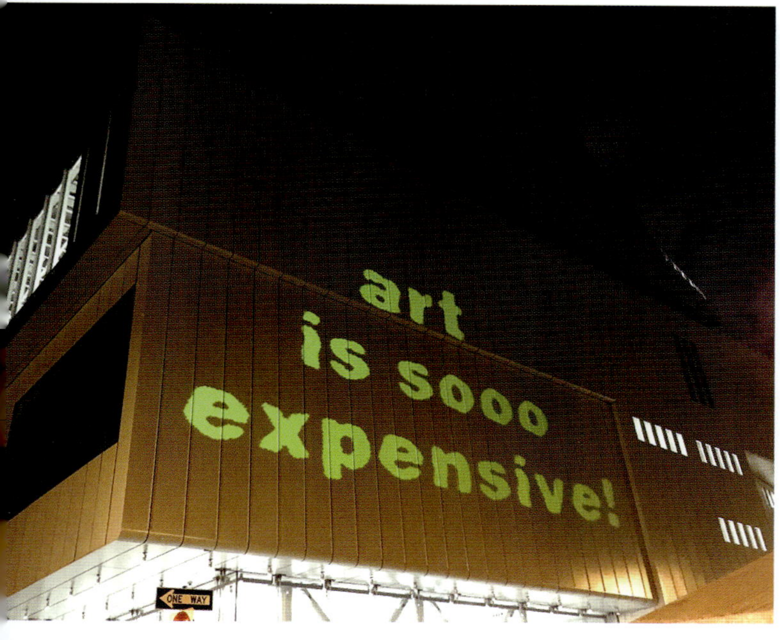

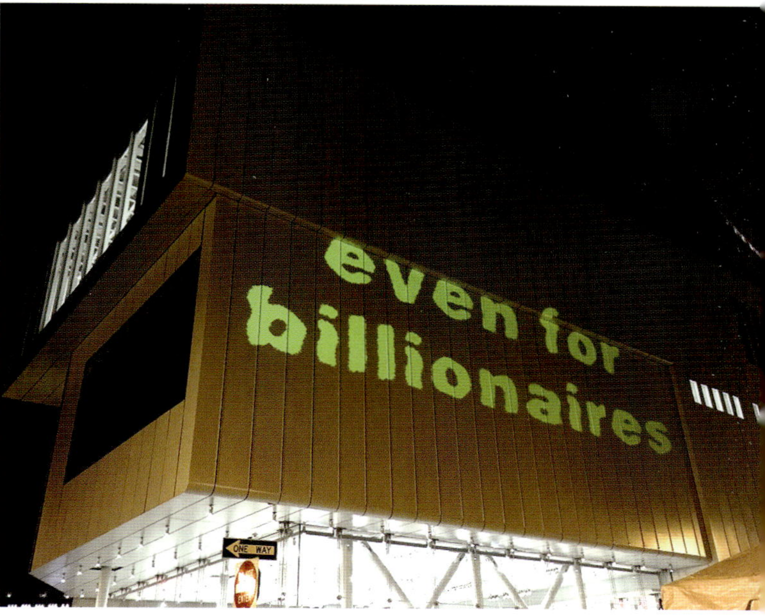

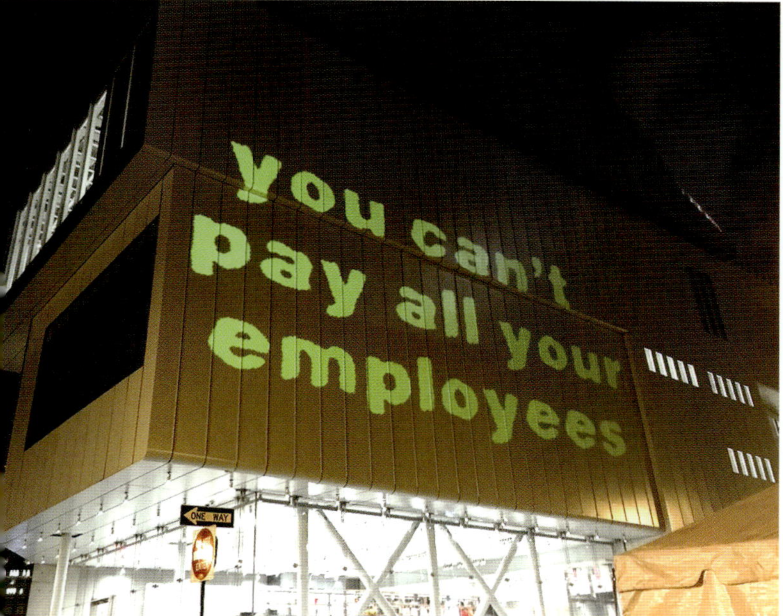

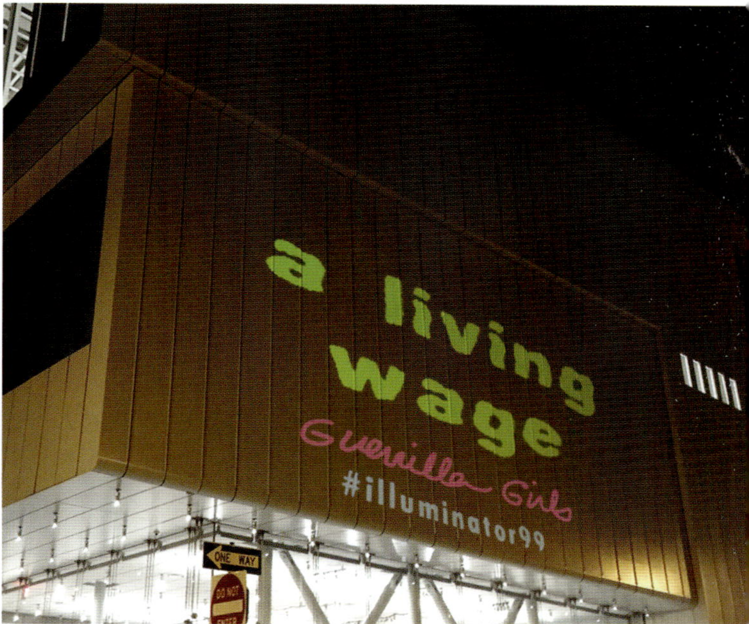

We projected a message, uninvited, onto the facade of the Whitney Museum, with the help of the Illuminator Collective. It was the night its new building opened to the public. 22 Productions turned our caper into a short film, *Guerrilla Girls: Not Ready to Make Nice*.

Top: Projection, 2015;
Bottom: Film stills, 22 Productions, 2015

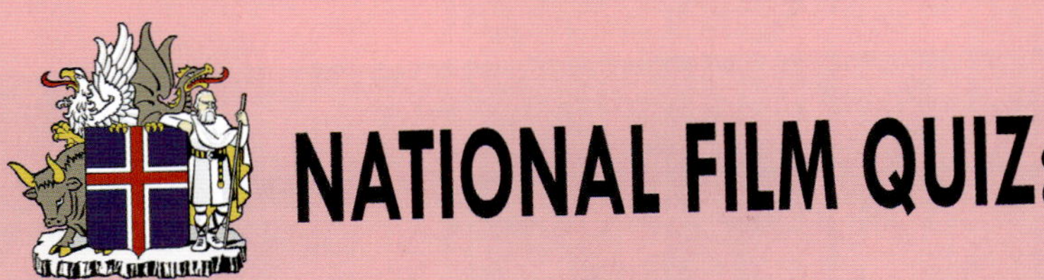

We celebrated the centennial of Icelandic women's suffrage at the Reykjavík Arts Festival. Our project revealed that even in a progressive country like Iceland, the film industry, like the U.S. film industry, lags way behind the rest of society in the treatment of women professionals.

Billboard, Reykjavík, 2015

ANDIC FILM CENTRE
N?

l big cameras.

s and running the government.

is way behind the rest of the country!

2000-2012 only 13% of films funded by Icelandic Film Centre were made by women. A message from the GUERRILLA GIRLS

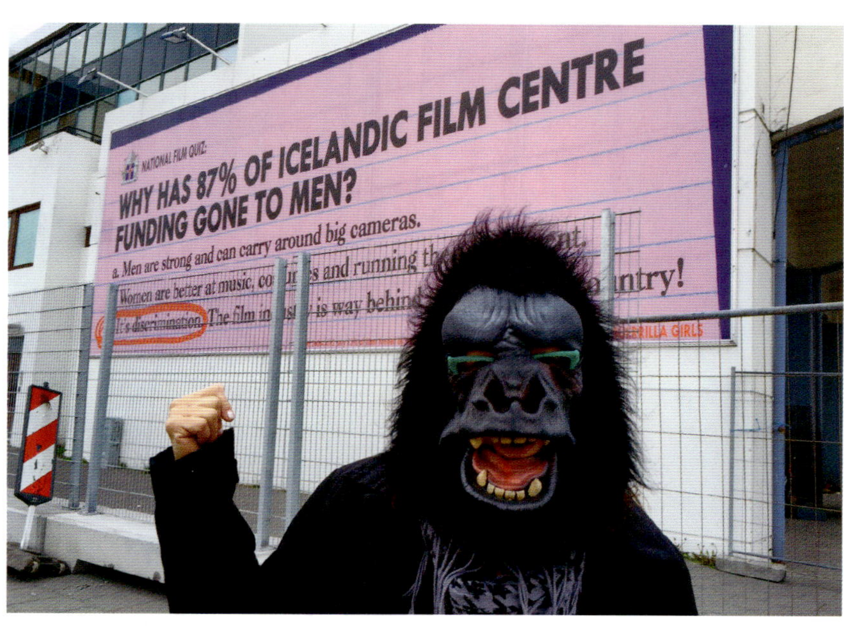

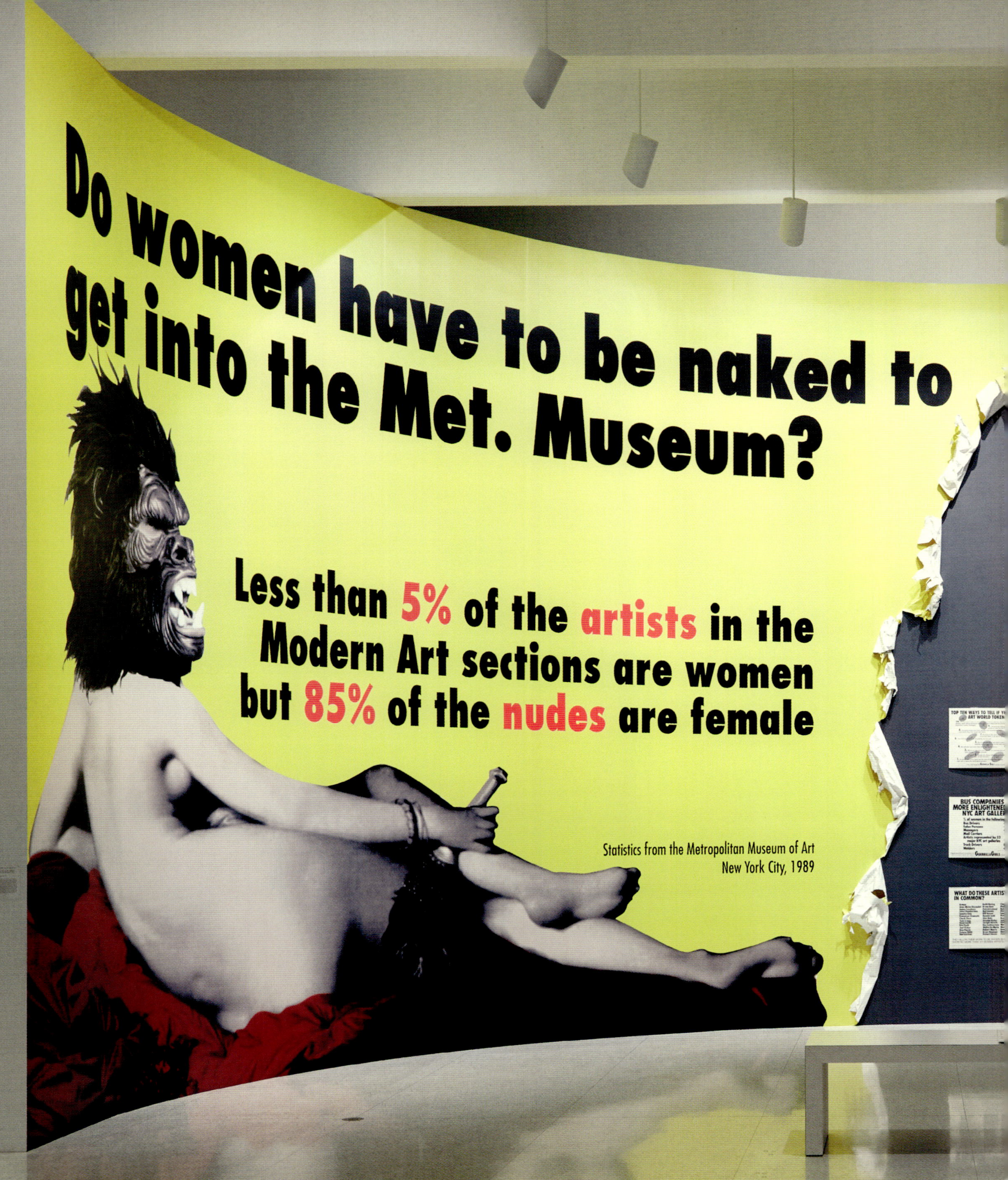

We came together with artists and arts organizations in Minnesota to present The Guerrilla Girls Twin Cities Takeover, a series of shows and public projects. We designed a unique exhibition of our work for the Walker Art Center.

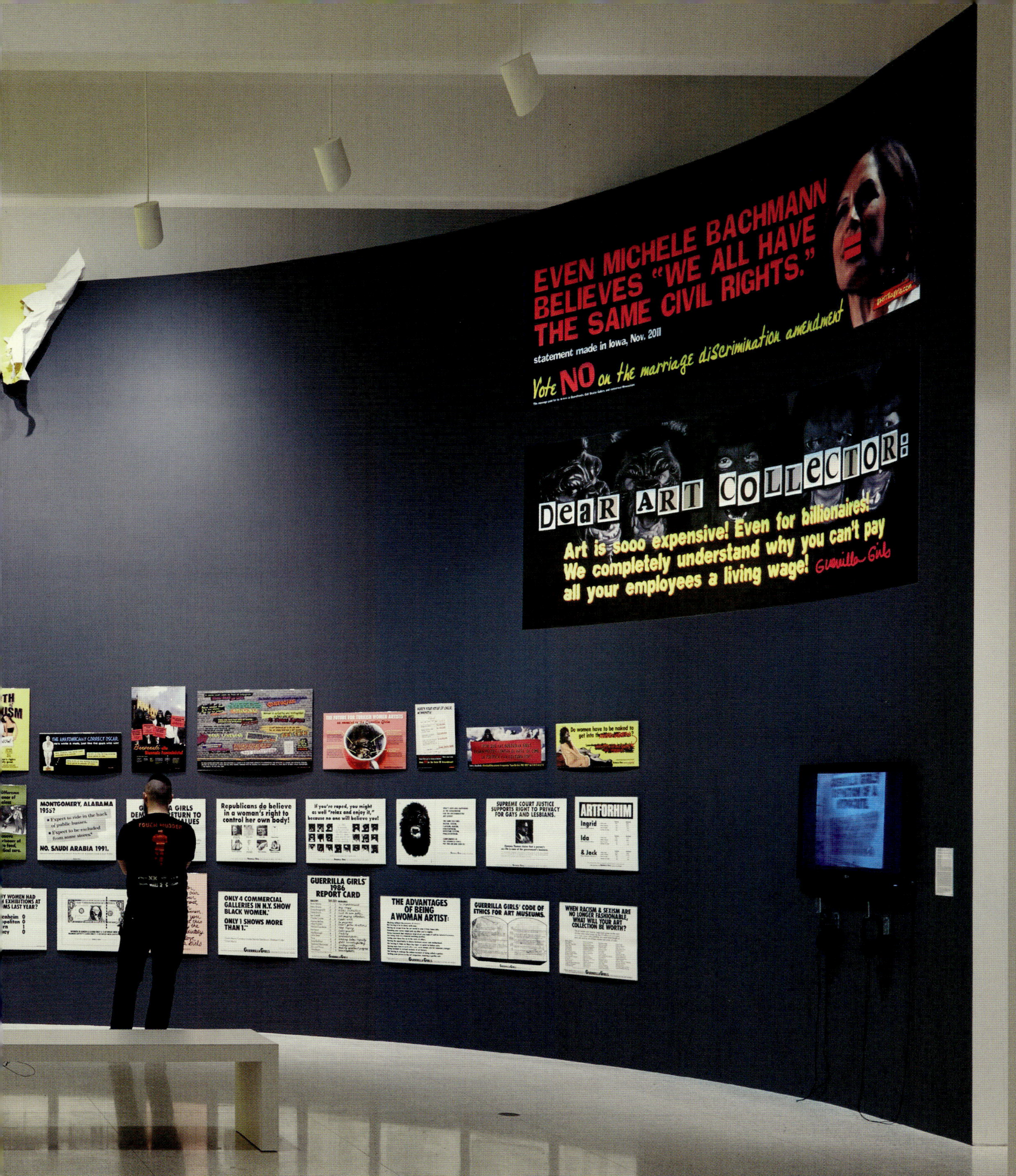

Installation view, 2015 (Photo by Gene Pittman)

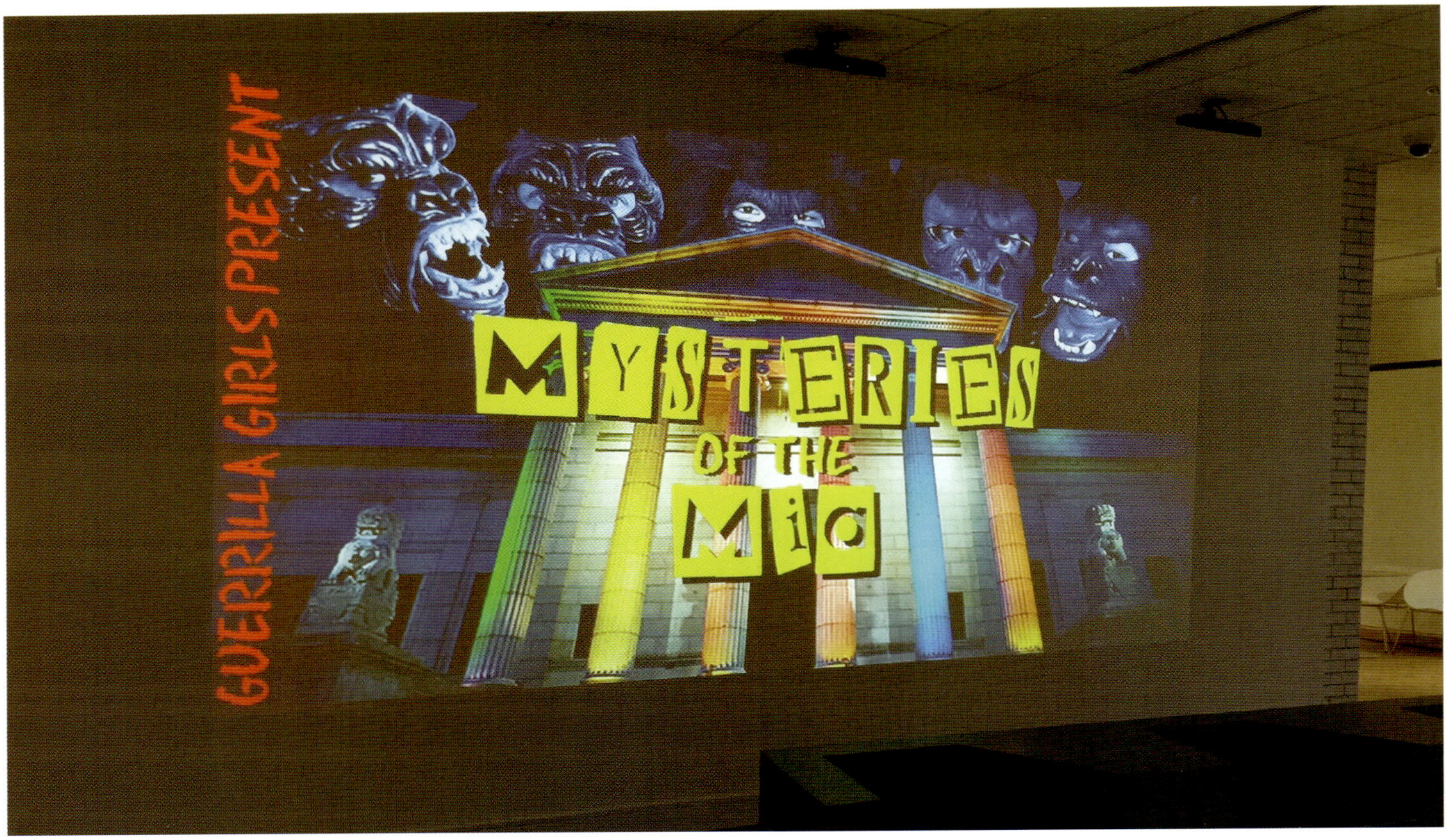

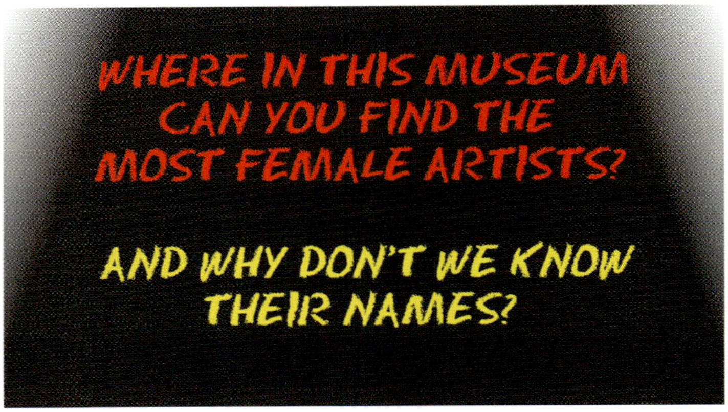

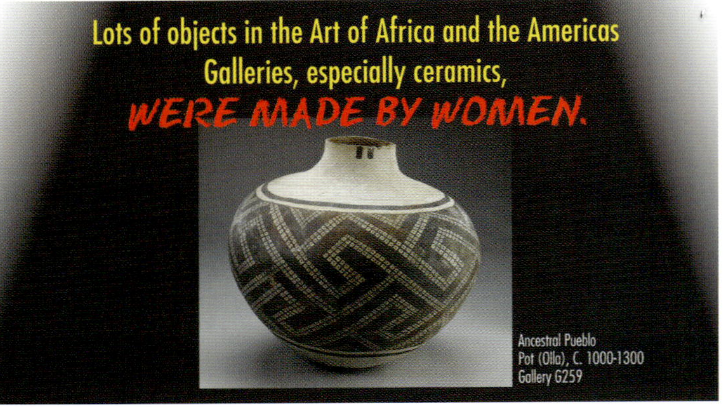

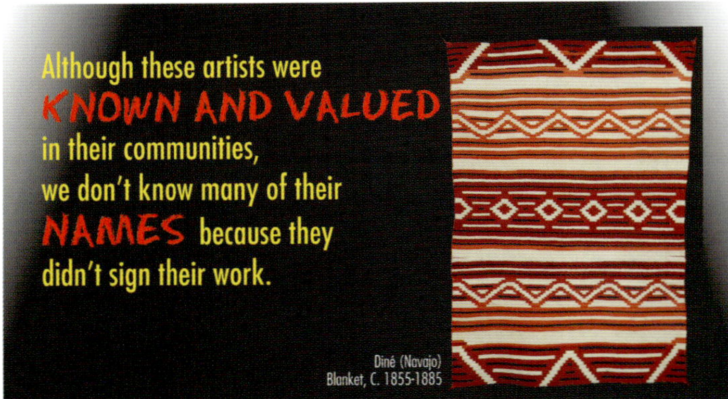

We examined the Minneapolis Institute of Art and discovered its collection wasn't diverse enough. We turned our findings into a video that played continuously in the main lobby.

Video stills, 2015

COULD YOU BE
GENDER NON-CONFORMING
AND SUCCEED AS AN ARTIST

IN 19TH CENTURY FRANCE?

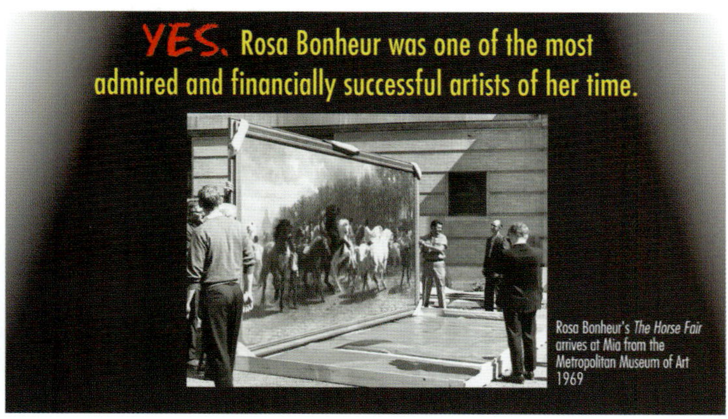

Rosa Bonheur's *The Horse Fair*
arrives at Mia from the
Metropolitan Museum of Art
1969

THERE ARE 90,000 ARTWORKS
IN Mia's COLLECTION.

HOW MANY ARE BY
AFRICAN-AMERICAN ARTISTS?

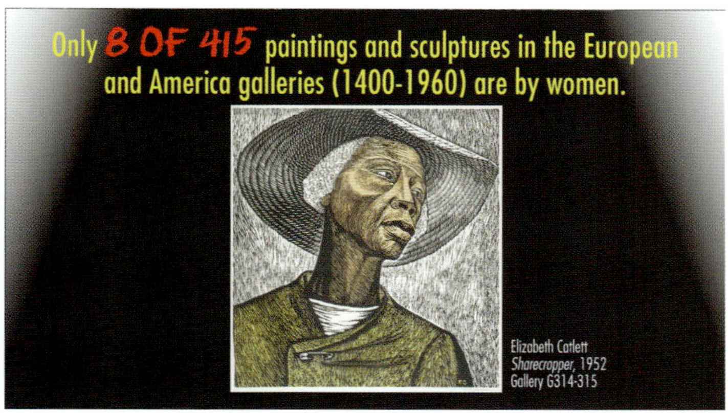

Elizabeth Catlett
Sharecropper, 1952
Gallery G314-315

MORE SOMALIS AND HMONG
LIVE IN MINNESOTA THAN
ANYWHERE ELSE IN THE U.S.

HOW MANY OF THEIR
ARTWORKS CAN BE FOUND
IN THE MUSEUM?

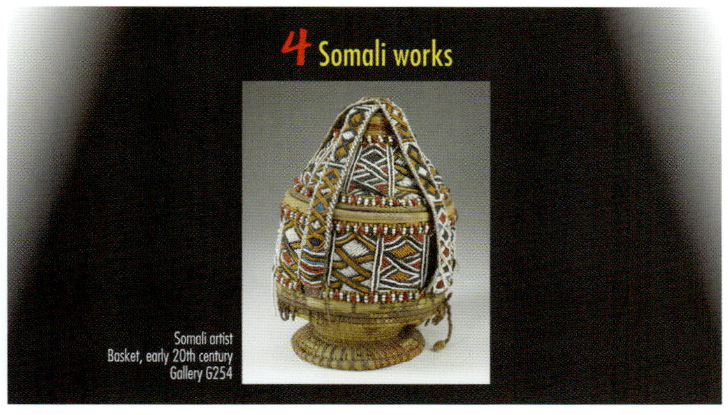

Somali artist
Basket, early 20th century
Gallery G254

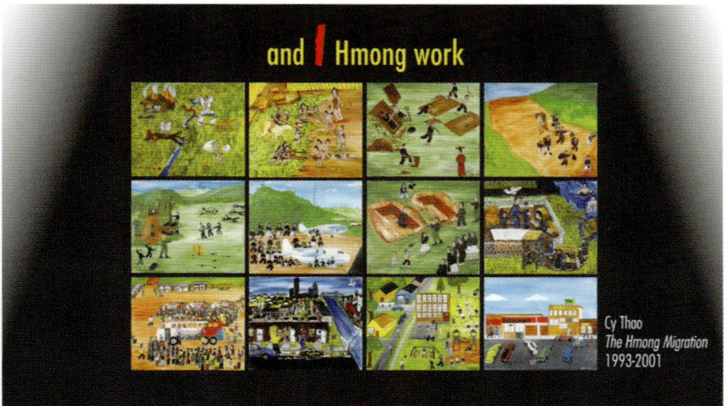

Cy Thao
The Hmong Migration
1993-2001

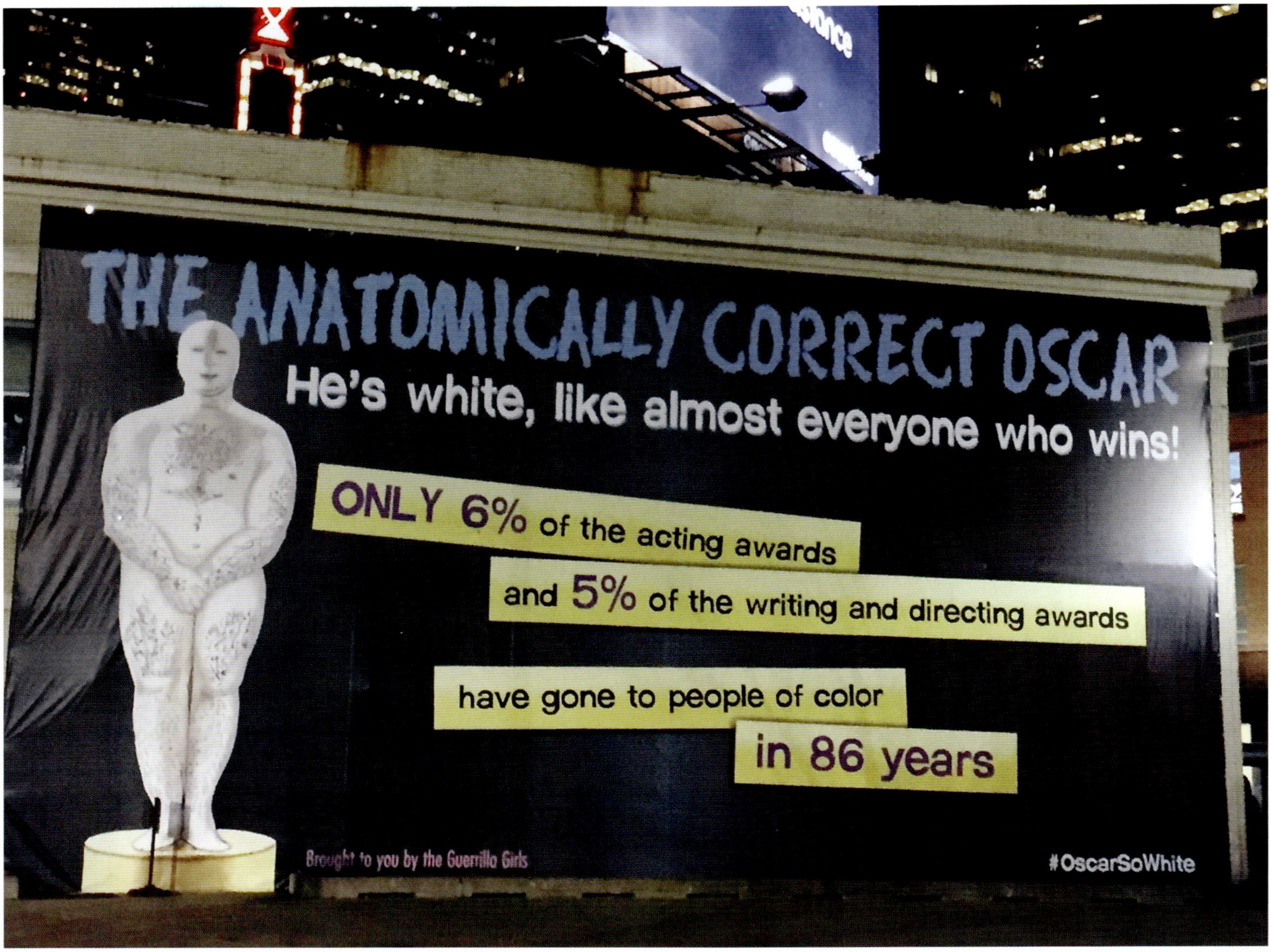

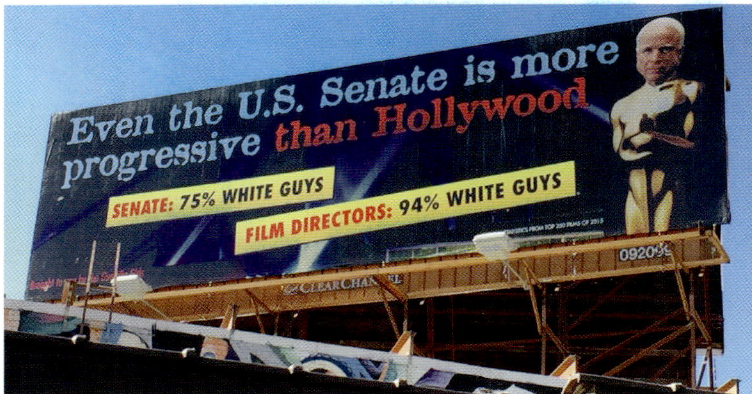

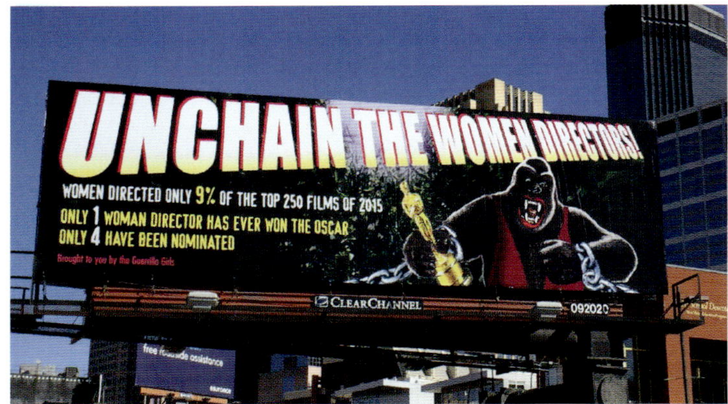

The Twin Cities Takeover coincided with #OscarsSoWhite protests of 2016. We updated our 2002–2006 billboards and slammed Hollywood with new statistics (pages 84, 86).

Billboards, Hennepin Avenue, Minneapolis, 2016

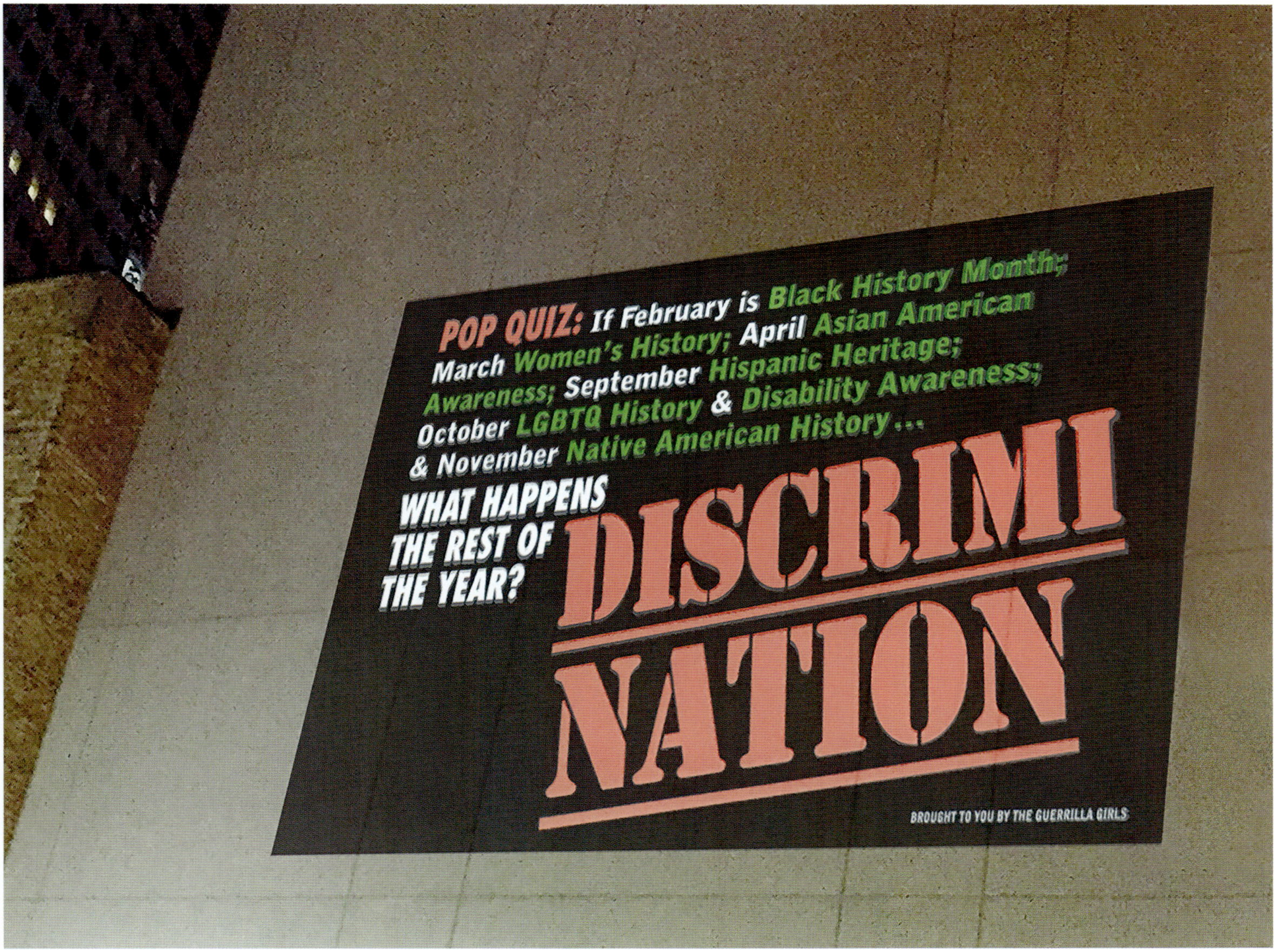

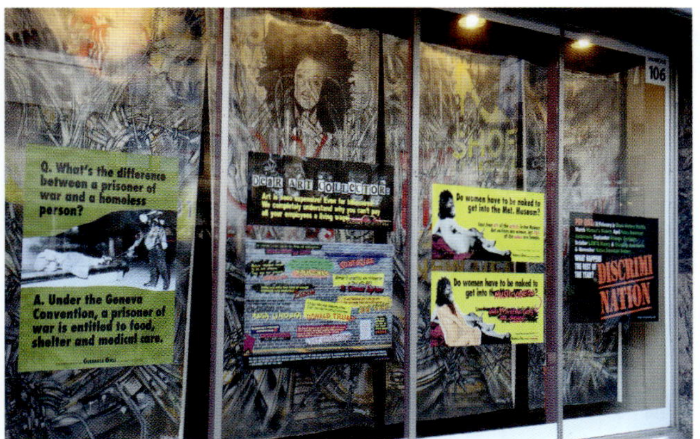

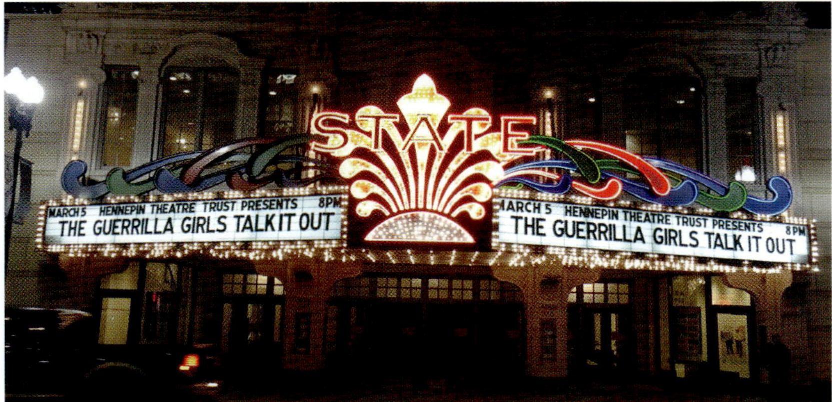

Our Twin Cities Takeover street projects included a video projection with an updated *Pop Quiz* (page 33), posters in storefronts and a gig at a downtown theatre.

Video still; Posters; Theatre marquee, 2016

GIRLSPLAINING MUSEUM LUDWIG

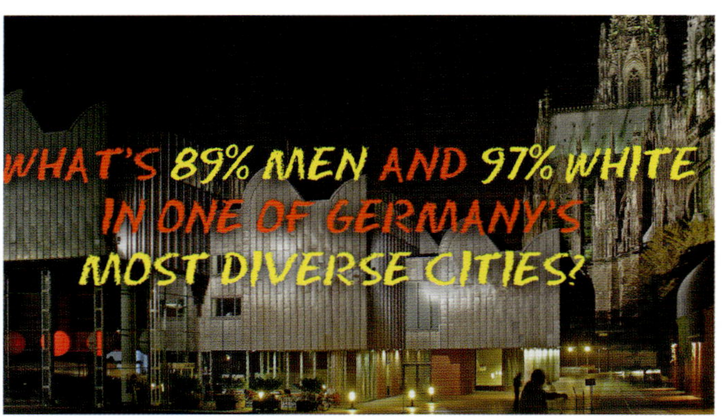

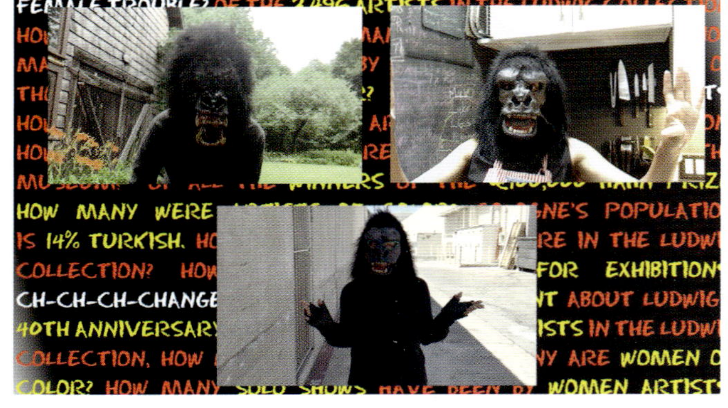

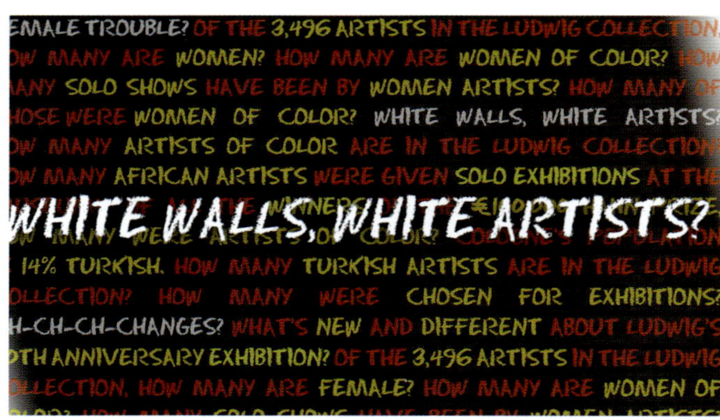

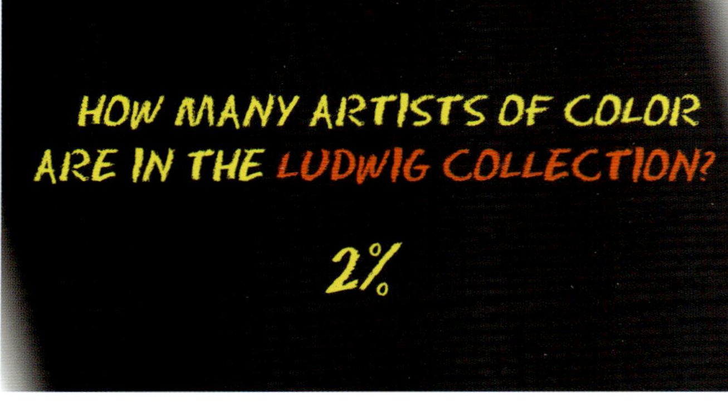

We took a look at the history of the not-so-diverse Museum Ludwig Cologne for its 40th anniversary exhibition. Then we made a video that played continuously during the show.

Video projection, 2016

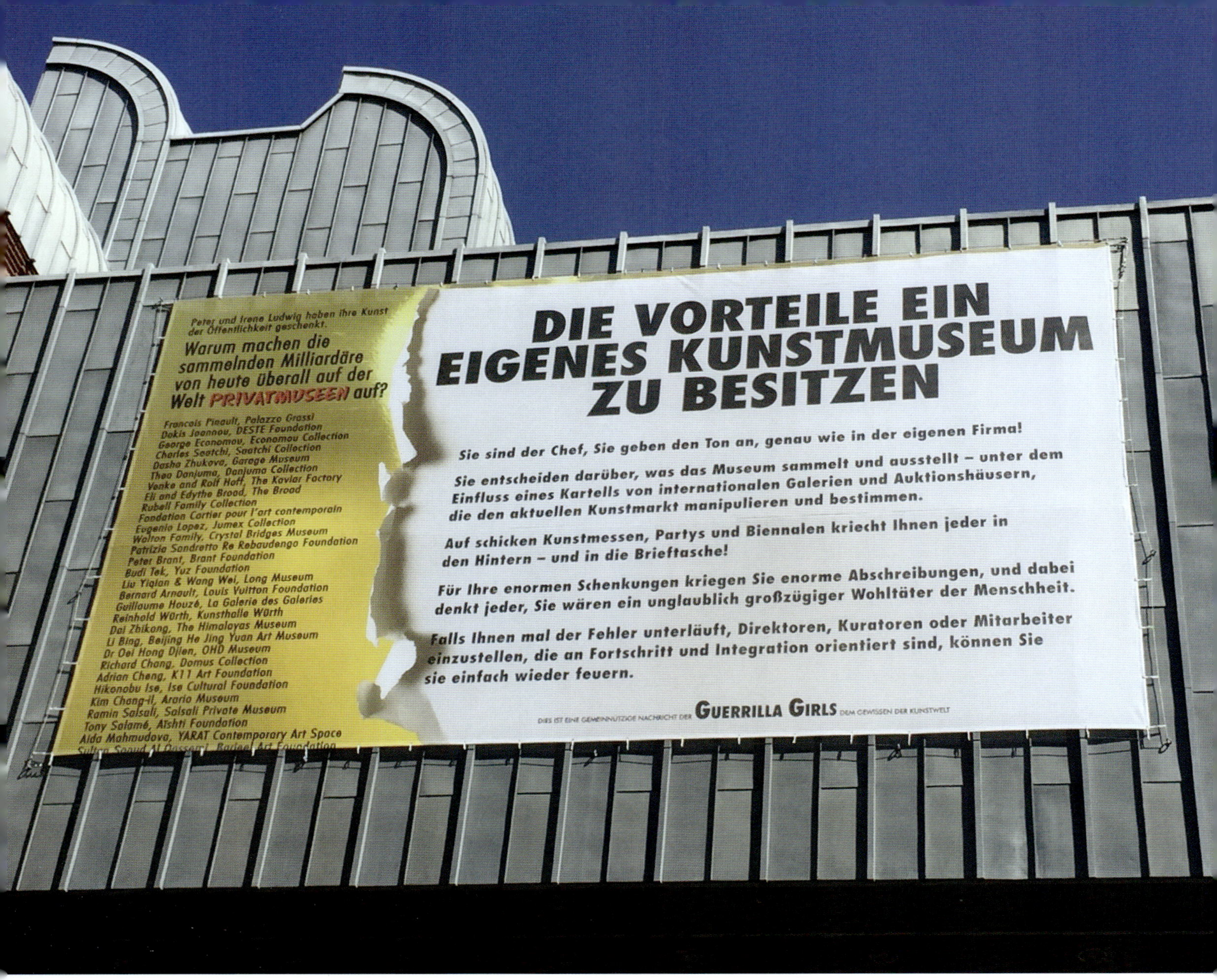

The advantages of owning your own art museum, 2015

Peter und Irene Ludwig haben ihre Kunst der Öffentlichkeit geschenkt.

Warum machen die sammelnden Milliardäre von heute überall auf der Welt PRIVATMUSEEN auf?

Francois Pinault, Palazzo Grassi
Dakis Joannou, DESTE Foundation
George Economou, Economou Collection
Charles Saatchi, Saatchi Collection
Dasha Zhukova, Garage Museum
Theo Danjuma, Danjuma Collection
Venke and Rolf Hoff, The Kaviar Factory
Eli and Edythe Broad, The Broad
Rubell Family Collection
Fondation Cartier pour l'art contemporain
Eugenio Lopez, Jumex Collection
Walton Family, Crystal Bridges Museum
Patrizia Sandretto Re Rebaudengo Foundation
Peter Brant, Brant Foundation
Budi Tek, Yuz Foundation
Liu Yiqian & Wang Wei, Long Museum
Bernard Arnault, Louis Vuitton Foundation
Guillaume Houzé, La Galerie des Galeries
Reinhold Würth, Kunsthalle Würth
Dai Zhikang, The Himalayas Museum
Li Bing, Beijing He Jing Yuan Art Museum
Dr Oei Hong Djien, OHD Museum
Richard Chang, Domus Collection
Adrian Cheng, K11 Art Foundation
Hikonobu Ise, Ise Cultural Foundation
Kim Chang-il, Arario Museum
Ramin Salsali, Salsali Private Museum
Tony Salamé, Aïshti Foundation
Aida Mahmudova, YARAT Contemporary Art Space
Sultan Sooud Al Qassemi, Barjeel Art Foundation

DIE VORTEILE EIN EIGENES KUNSTMUSEUM ZU BESITZEN

Sie sind der Chef, Sie geben den Ton an, genau wie in der eigenen Firma!

Sie entscheiden darüber, was das Museum sammelt und ausstellt — unter dem Einfluss eines Kartells von internationalen Galerien und Auktionshäusern, die den aktuellen Kunstmarkt manipulieren und bestimmen.

Auf schicken Kunstmessen, Partys und Biennalen kriecht Ihnen jeder in den Hintern — und in die Brieftasche.

Für Ihre enormen Schenkungen kriegen Sie enorme Abschreibungen, und dabei denkt jeder, Sie wären ein unglaublich großzügiger Wohltäter der Menschheit.

Falls Ihnen mal der Fehler unterläuft, Direktoren, Kuratoren oder Mitarbeiter einzustellen, die an Fortschritt und Integration orientiert sind, können Sie sie einfach wieder feuern.

DIES IST EINE GEMEINNÜTZIGE NACHRICHT DER **GUERRILLA GIRLS** DEM GEWISSEN DER KUNSTWELT

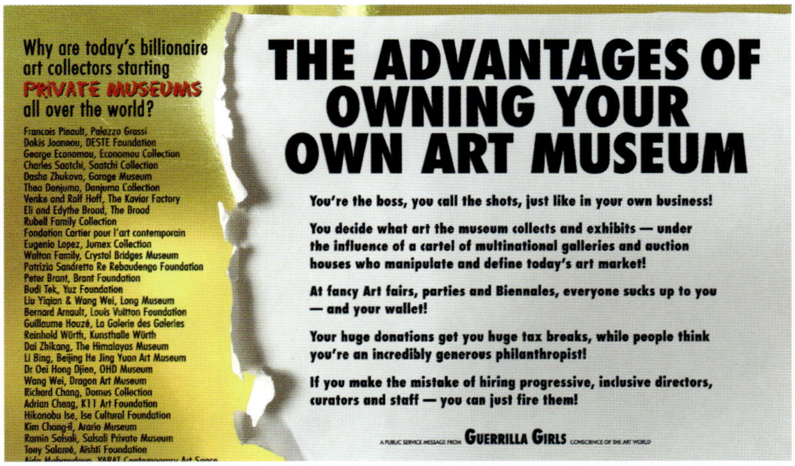

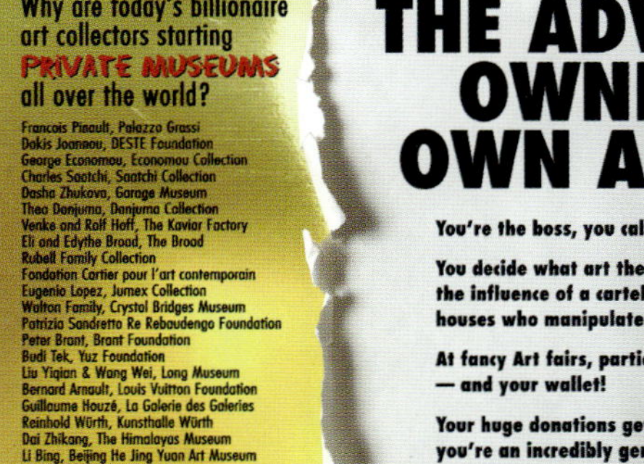

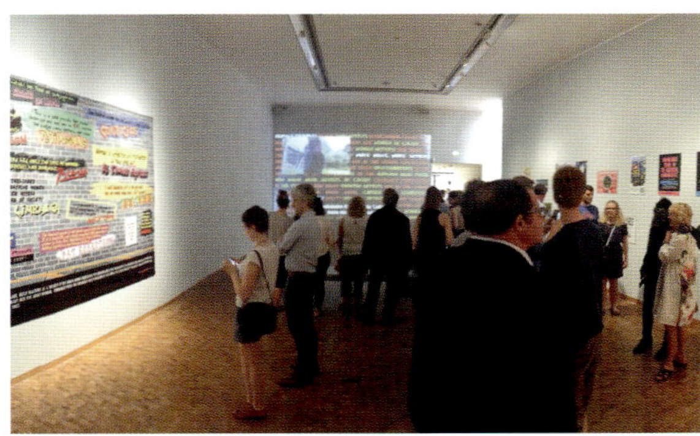

Today more and more super-rich collectors are creating their own private museums to house their valuable art, reap tax benefits, sugarcoat their involvement in inhumane industries and come out looking like generous philanthropists, kind of like chocolate baron Peter Ludwig.

Clockwise from top: Facade banner; Exhibition view with video; Poster, Cologne, 2016

The medical history of the vibrator inspired us to write a "children's book" about the mistreatment of women's bodies over the centuries, and how feminism is fighting back.

Book, 2016. Cover and some interior pages

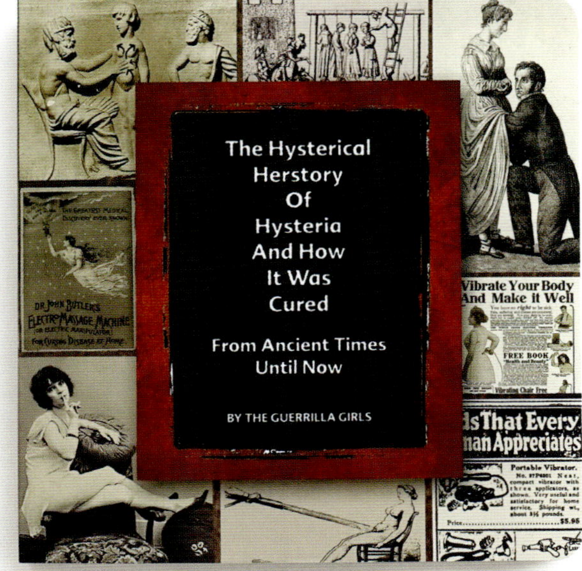

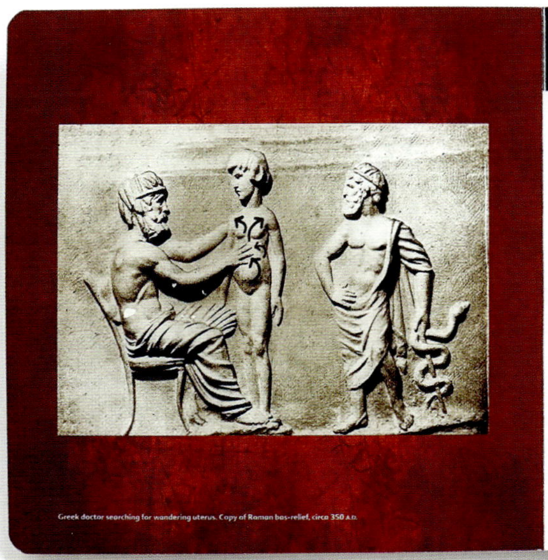

Greek doctor searching for wandering uterus. Copy of Roman bas-relief, circa 350 A.D.

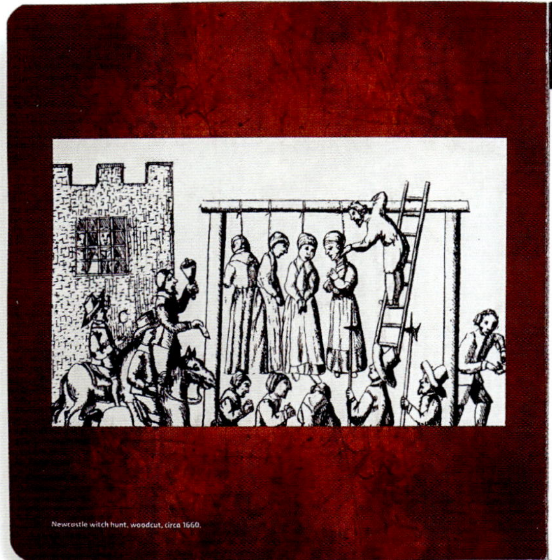

Newcastle witch hunt, woodcut, circa 1660.

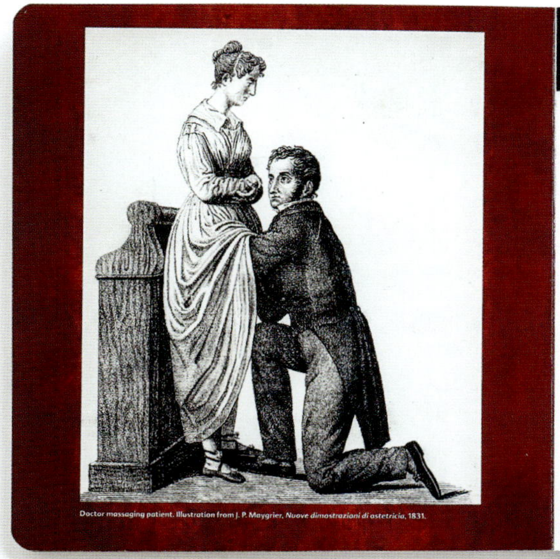

Doctor massaging patient. Illustration from J. P. Maygrier, *Nuove dimostrazioni di ostetricia*, 1831.

Another treatment for hysteria, if you could afford it, involved a physician massaging the inside edges of a patient's vagina with aromatic oils.

If the procedure was successful, the patient would fall into a frenzied state of groaning and moaning, sometimes over and over again. It was not unusual for the patient to lose consciousness or fall asleep. When revived, she was in a state of calm relaxation. Cured! Until her next episode of hysteria.

Some women had the procedure as often as once a week. It was especially effective on virgins, widows, and nuns. Sometimes the treatment would take minutes, sometimes hours. What a lot of work for doctors!

Reality check: Doctors gave women orgasms and got paid for it. Was this healthcare … or prostitution?

GIRLS JUST WANT TO HAVE FUN

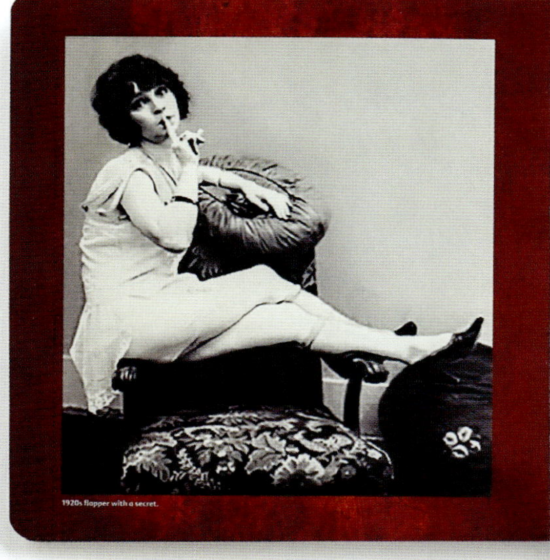

1920s flapper with a secret.

The porn industry discovered the vibrator in the 1920s. Psychiatrists were horrified to see, right there on the screen, a medical device used for sexual pleasure. Vibrators were declared lascivious and immoral. Stores stopped selling them. As late as 2008, it was a crime to sell vibrators in Texas. It's still illegal to sell them in Alabama.

R-E-S-P-E-C-T

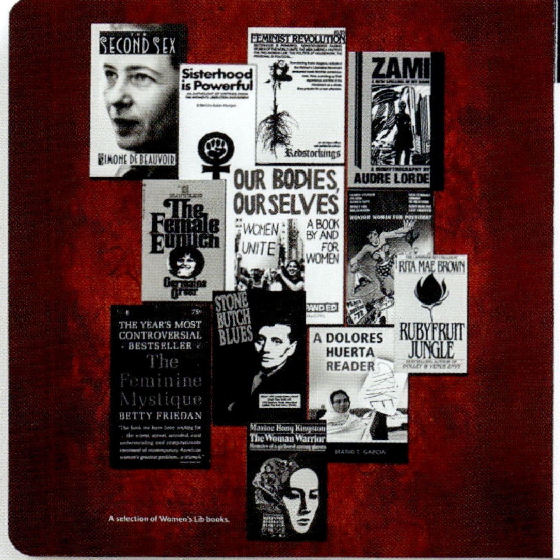

A selection of Women's Lib books.

By the second half of the 20th century, women's sexuality was no longer a big mystery. Female orgasm was identified, described, and encouraged for good mental and physical health. Vibrators became the best friend of many a girl and are still at the center of a thriving sex-toy industry.

In the early 1950s, the medical profession dropped hysteria as a credible female disease — right after Simone de Beauvoir published her manifesto, *The Second Sex*, which jump-started the Women's Liberation Movement. Coincidence?

Feminism helped everyone understand how society constrained, misunderstood and mistreated female bodies over the centuries. Was feminism the medicine that cured hysteria?

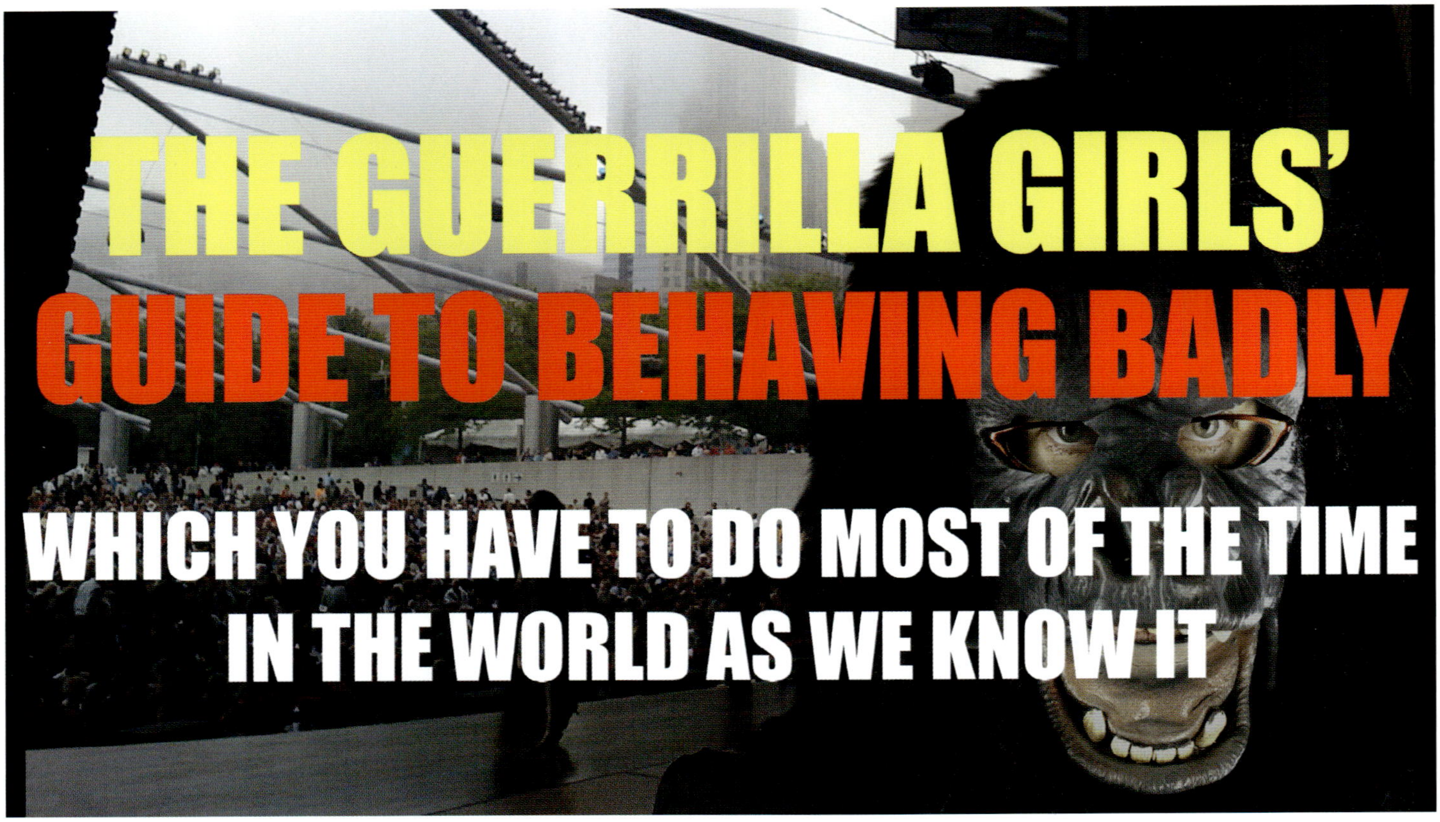

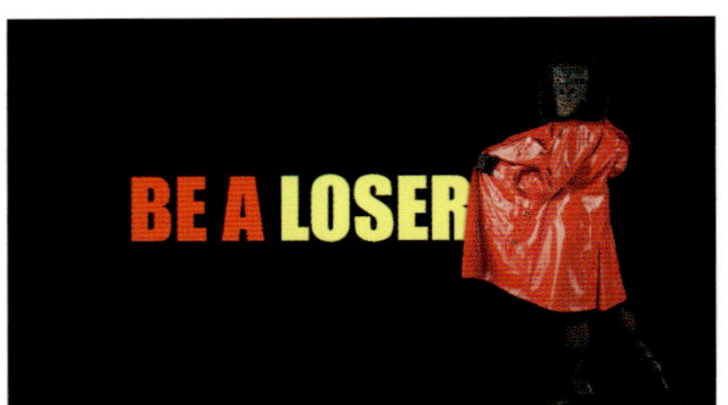

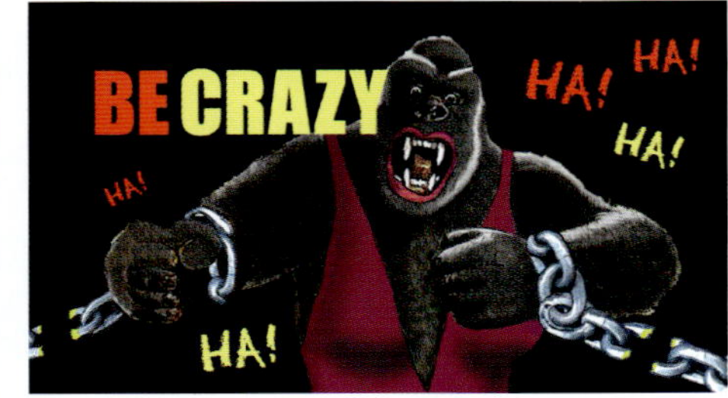

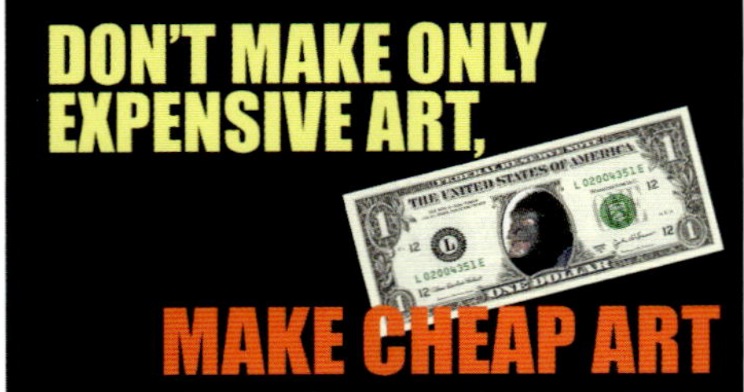

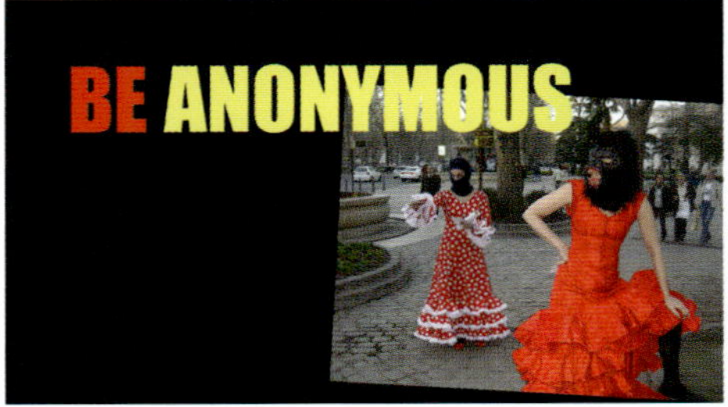

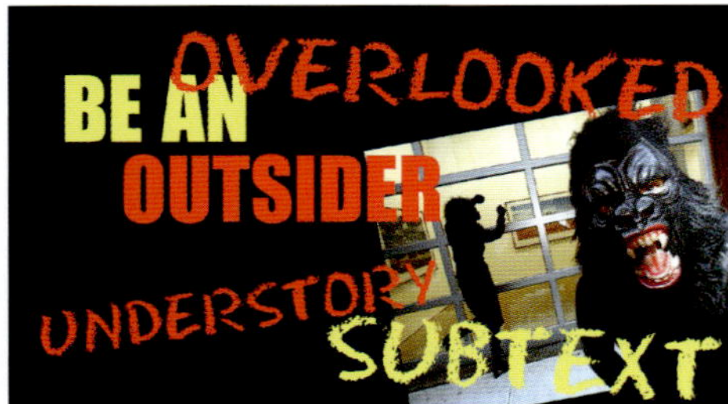

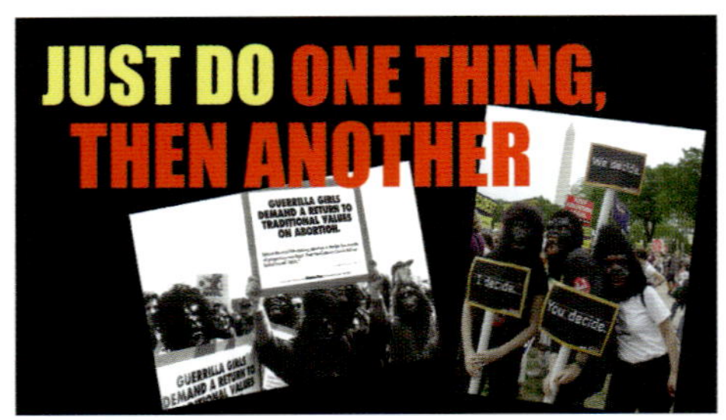

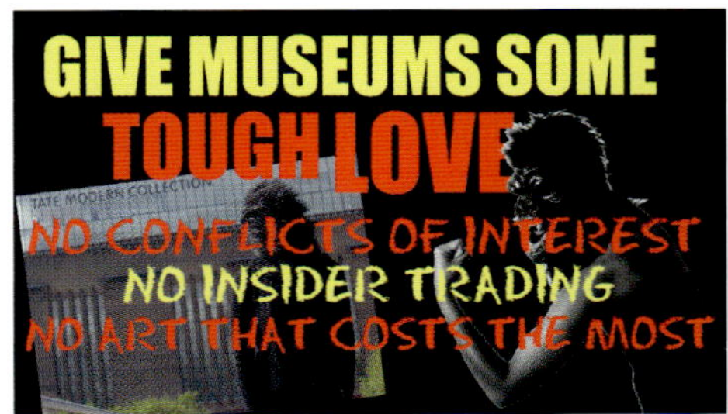

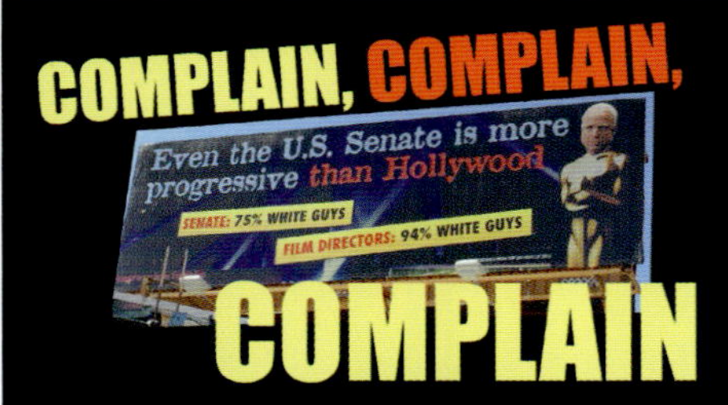

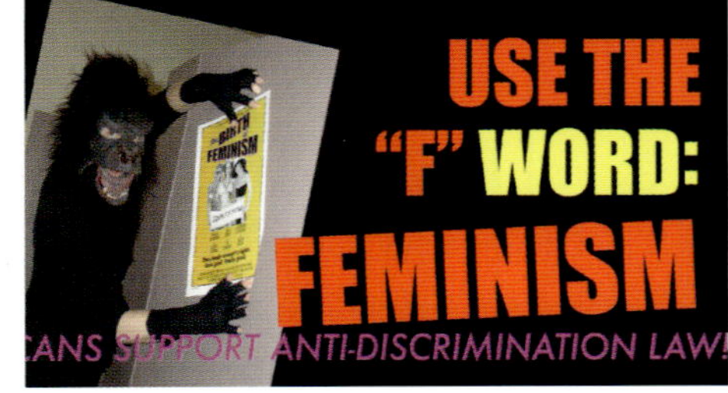

The School of the Art Institute of Chicago invited us to deliver the commencement address to the class of 2010, in front of a crowd of cheering students (and a few angry parents). Our advice was unconventional. Later we turned this rant into a video to show at gigs and appearances.

Video stills, 2016

THE GUERRILLA GIRLS' GUIDE TO BEHAVING BADLY (Which You Have to Do Most of the Time in the World as We Know It)

BE A LOSER. The world of art doesn't have to be an Olympics where a few win and everyone else is forgotten. The art market – and its hypercompetitive celebrity culture – makes everyone but the stars feel like failures. But there's another world out there that's not about raging egos – a world of artistic cooperation and collaboration. That's the one we joined, and we invite you to join it, too! Let's make trouble together!

BE CRAZY. Political art or activism that points to something and says, "This is bad" is just preaching to the converted. Instead, try to change people's minds, and do it in some unforgettable way. A trick we learned is humor helps you fly under the radar. If you can get people who disagree with you to laugh at an issue, you have a hook right into their brain. Once there, you have a much better chance to convert them.

BE ANONYMOUS. Sometimes you gotta speak out publicly, but sometimes it works even better to speak out anonymously. Now this has its disadvantages, like working your whole life without getting any credit, but it has lots of advantages, too. Our anonymity, for example, keeps the focus on the issues, and away from our personalities. The mystery of who we might be draws lots of attention to the issues we promote. Plus…you won't believe what comes out of your mouth while wearing a gorilla mask!

BE AN OUTSIDER. Even if you are working inside the system, we say act like an outsider. Seek out the understory, the subtext, the overlooked, and the downright unfair. Then expose it. Jam your culture. Remake your institution.

JUST DO ONE THING. If it works, do another. If it doesn't, do another anyway. Don't be paralyzed if you don't get it right every time. Just keep chipping away. We promise that, bit by bit, your efforts will add up to something effective.

ARTISTS: DON'T MAKE ONLY EXPENSIVE ART that only billionaire art collectors can afford. Curators: Don't exhibit only the expensive art your trustees donate! Let's have more cheap art that everyone can own…. like books, zines music and movies -- like our posters!

SHOW MUSEUMS TOUGH LOVE. It's unethical that wealthy art collectors who invest lots of money in art can become museum trustees, overseeing institutions that in turn validate their investments. It's a lousy way to write and preserve our history! Demand ethical standards inside museums. No more conflicts of interest or insider trading! No more cookie cutter collections of Art That Costs the Most. Convince art collectors their collections are inferior with only work by white male artists. Don't let museums perpetuate this version of art and power, with a few tokens thrown in. Make sure your favorite museum casts a wider net and collects the whole story of our culture. Whether you work in a museum or a classroom, don't teach an art history constructed by corrupt institutions. Do like we did, write your own!

COMPLAIN, COMPLAIN, COMPLAIN. Be a creative complainer. Be a professional complainer. Don't assume people know what's missing from museums – remind them how many modern and contemporary art collections still contain less than 15% females and artists of color.

USE THE F WORD – FEMINISM. We think it's crazy that so many people who believe in the tenets of feminism are still afraid to call themselves feminists. Feminism doesn't get the respect it deserves. Women's rights, civil rights, Lesbian, Gay, Bisexual and Transgender rights and Black Lives Matter are the great human rights movements of our time. Feminists like us who believe in intersectionality fight for all human rights. No one is free until everyone is free.

FEMINISM IS CHANGING THE WORLD, it's revolutionizing human thought and giving many people lives their great grandparents could never have imagined. But there is still so much work to do. There are so many countries worldwide where LGBTQ people and women have little or no human rights. 90% of transgender employees have faced discrimination or harassment at work. In the US, no federal law protects them, even though nearly 80% of voters support such a law. Then there's rampant sexism in the tech industry including the harassment of female gamers. And what about the gender earning gap that the US Congress refuses to move against.

Violence and abuse against women, GAY and transgender people is still a huge international problem – from gang rape in India, to kidnappings in Nigeria, to sexual slavery by ISIS, to the negligible punishment given out for domestic violence in America. Trans women are assaulted and even murdered in the US.

But despite all this bad news, feminist resistance movements are exploding all over the world. LET'S MAKE THE "F" WORD "FEMINISM" THE "F" WORD FOR THE FUTURE. LET'S ALL JOIN TOGETHER WITH FEMINISTS ON THE RIGHT SIDE OF HISTORY.

Video script, 2016

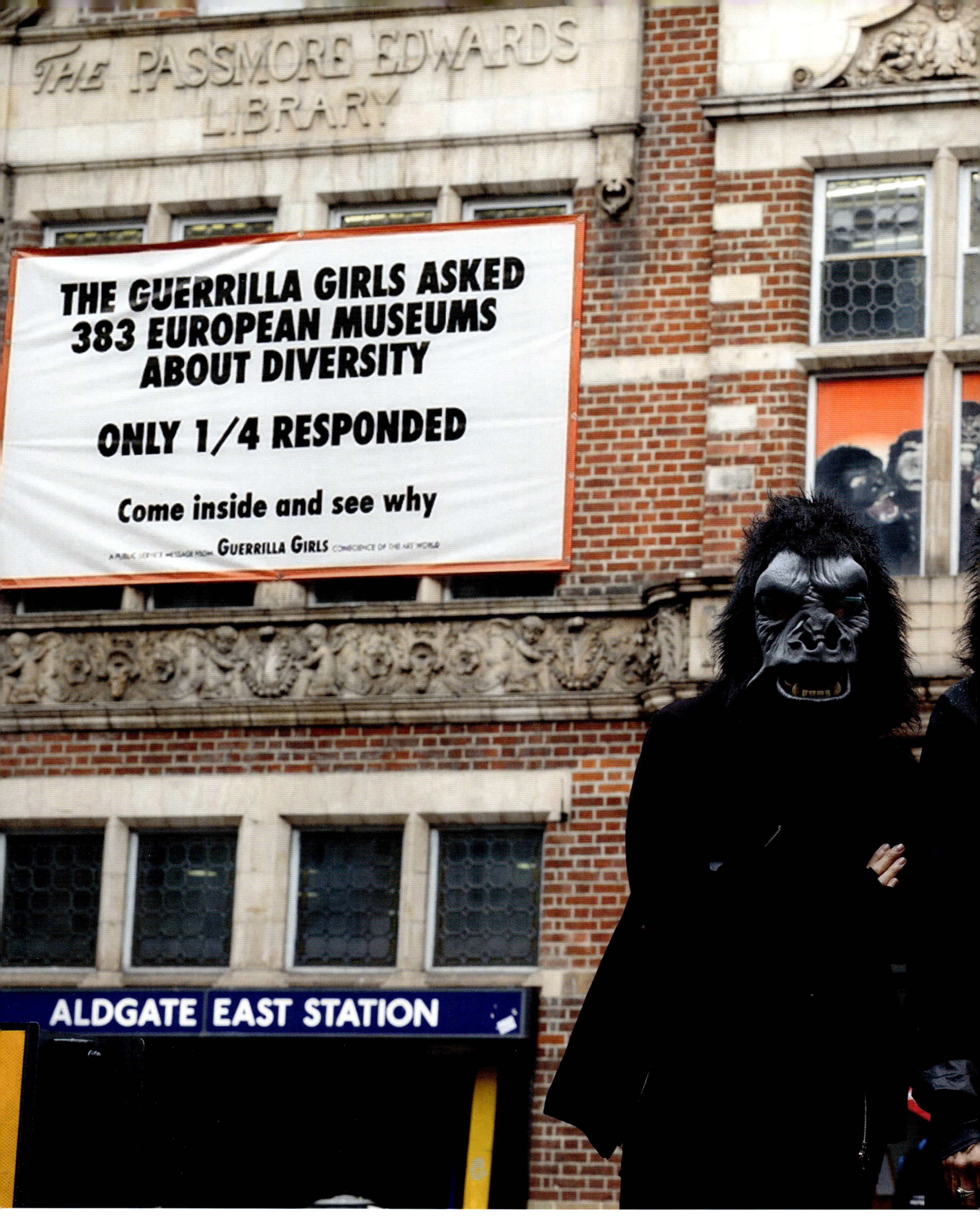

Is It Even Worse in Europe? facade installation, Whitechapel Gallery, London, 2016
(photo by David Parry/PA Wire)

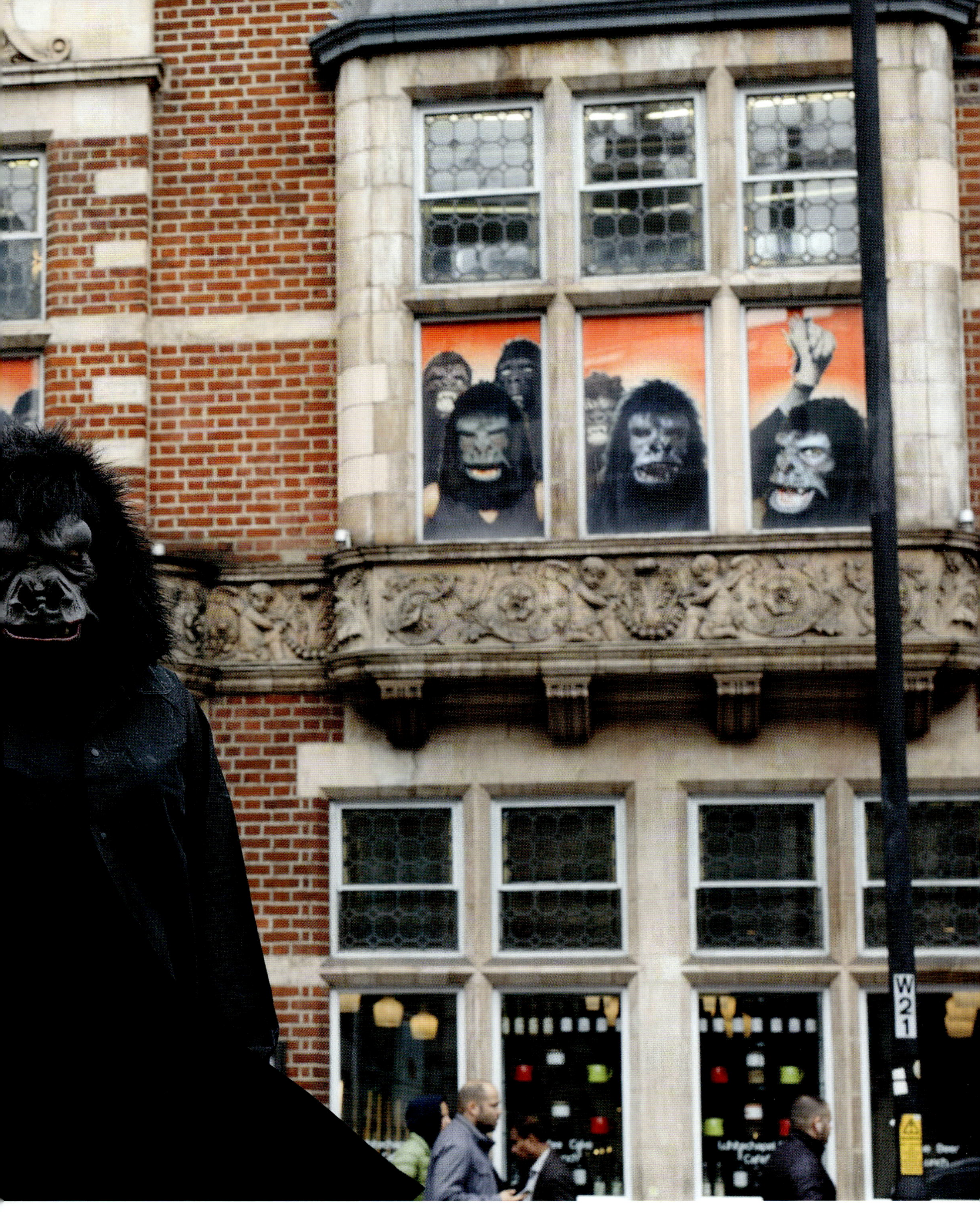

W21

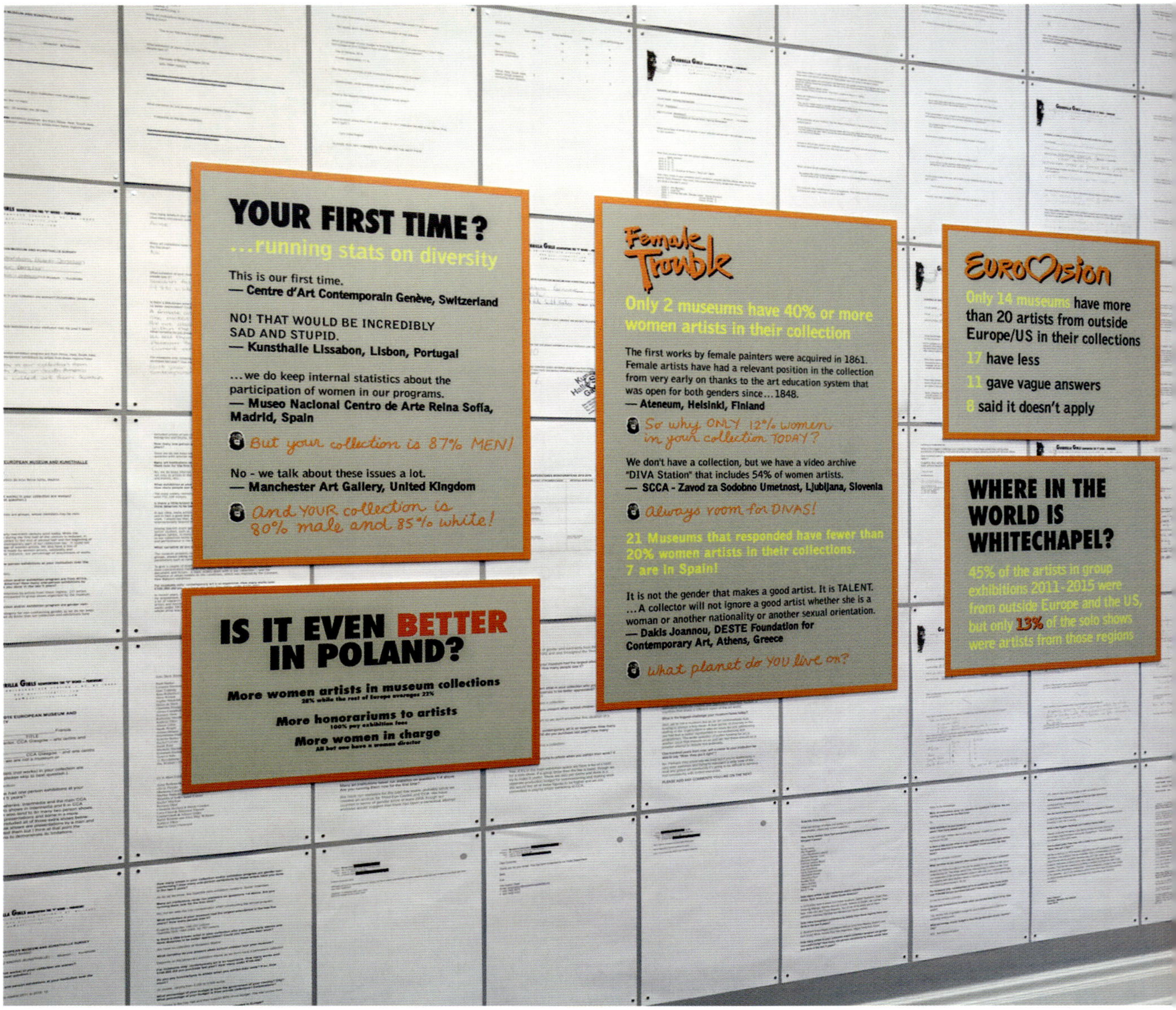

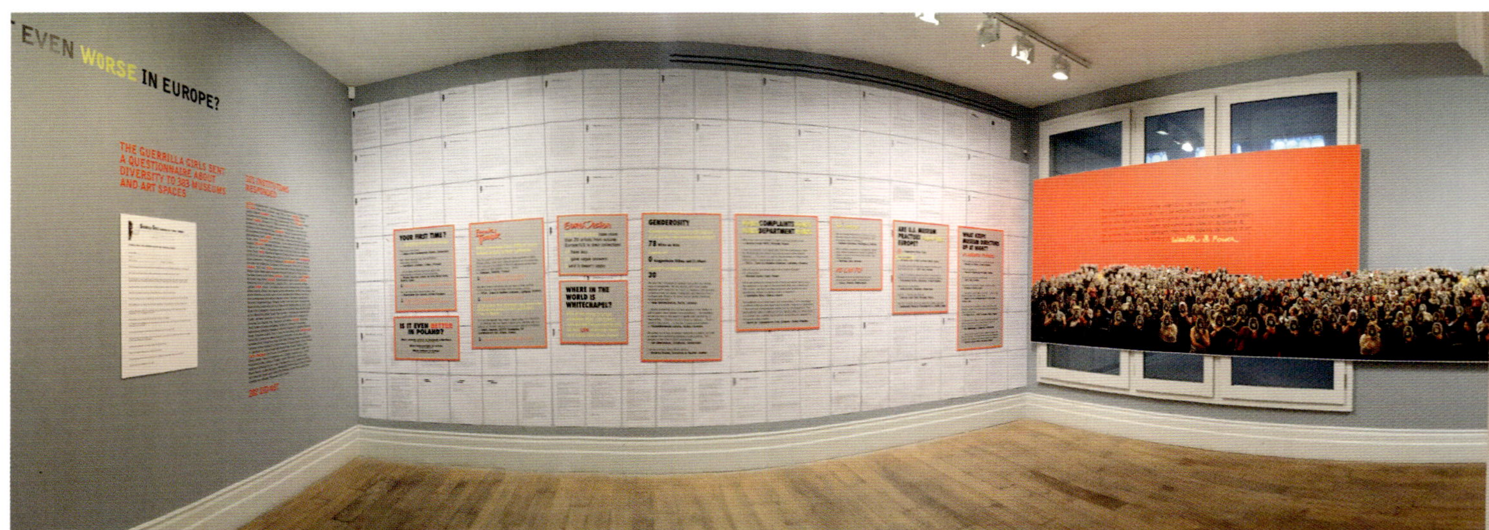

We sent diversity questionnaires to 383 museum directors all over Europe for an exhibition at Whitechapel Gallery and 101 replied. The museums that didn't were printed on the floor. What did we discover? Polish museums gave the most opportunities to women artists. The Reina Sofia "thinks about diversity all the time," but its collection is 87% male and overwhelmingly white. Billionaire art collector Dakis Joannou refused to examine his private museum because "the only thing that matters is 'pure' talent." Our question to him: What "pure" planet do you live on? The show, its title a riff on an early poster (page 13), ended with a rallying cry (page 146).

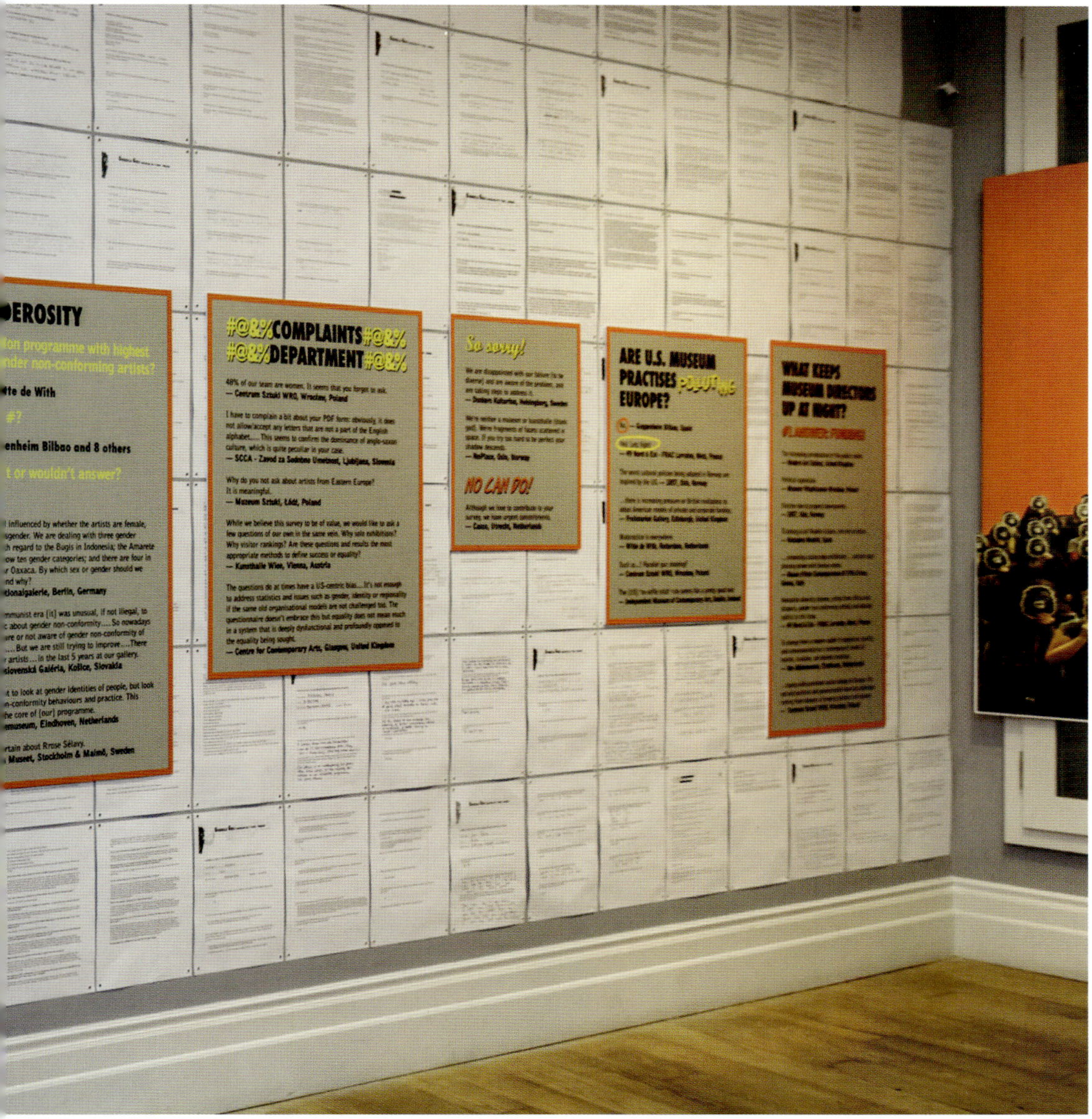

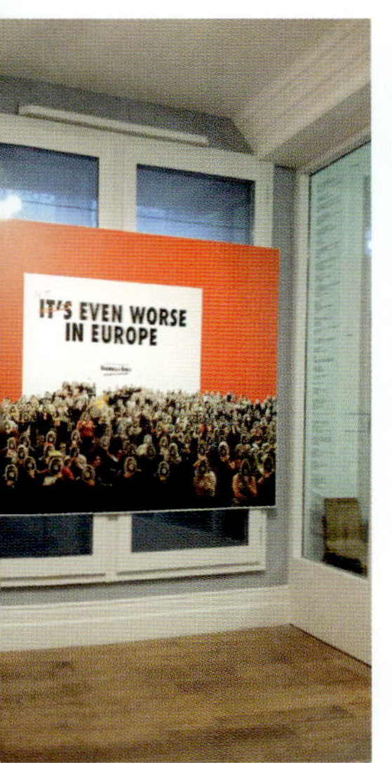

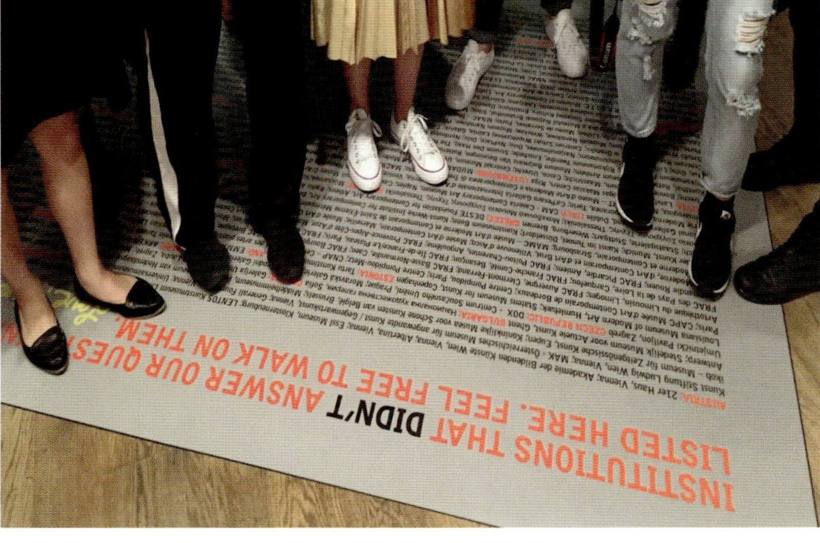

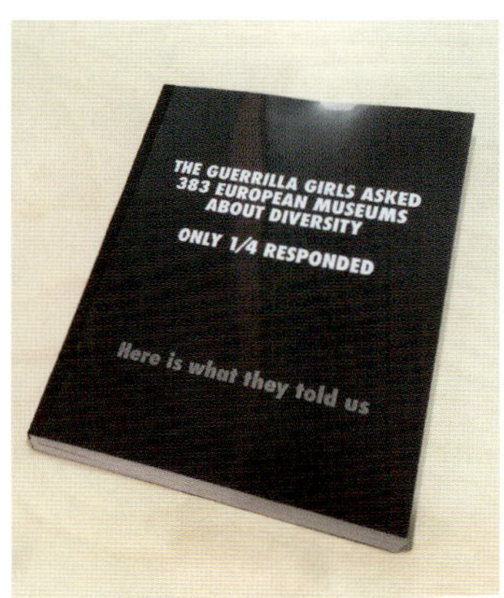

Installation views, *Is It Even Worse in Europe?*, Whitechapel Gallery, Whitechapel Gallery Archive, 2016. Top photo by Dan Weill

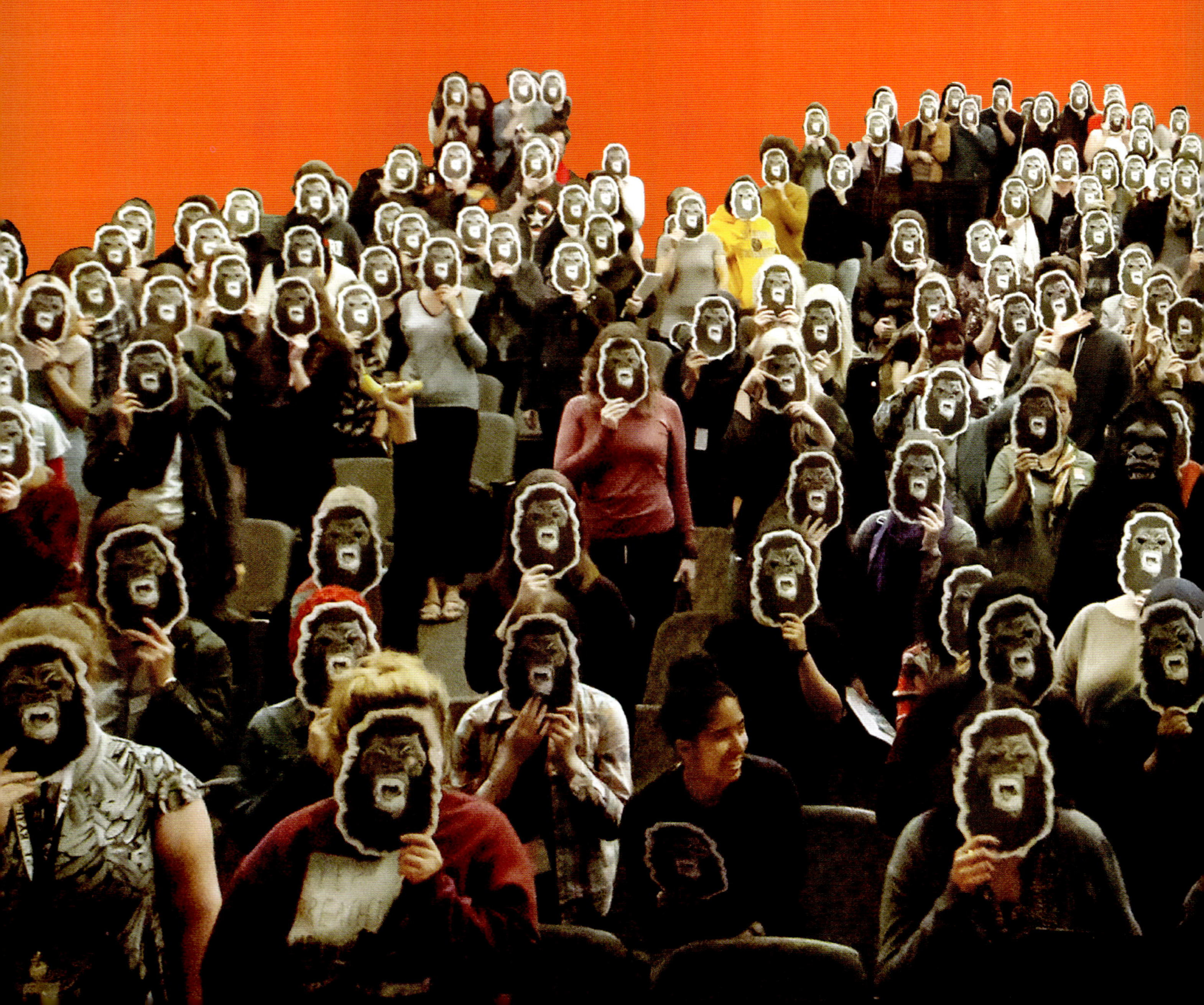

DON'T LET MUSEUMS reduce art to
won a popularity contest among big-ti
If museums don't show art as DIVERS
represent, TELL THEM they're not sh
just preserving the history of Wea

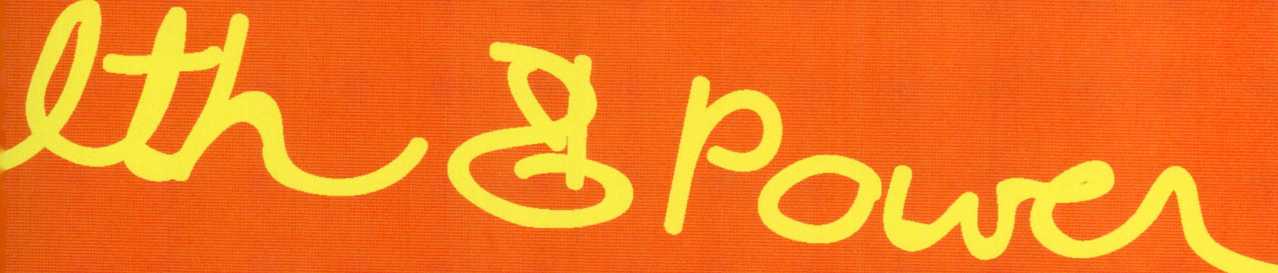
he small number of artists who have
dealers, curators and collectors.
as the cultures they claim to
ing the history of art, they are
lth & Power
Guerrilla Girls

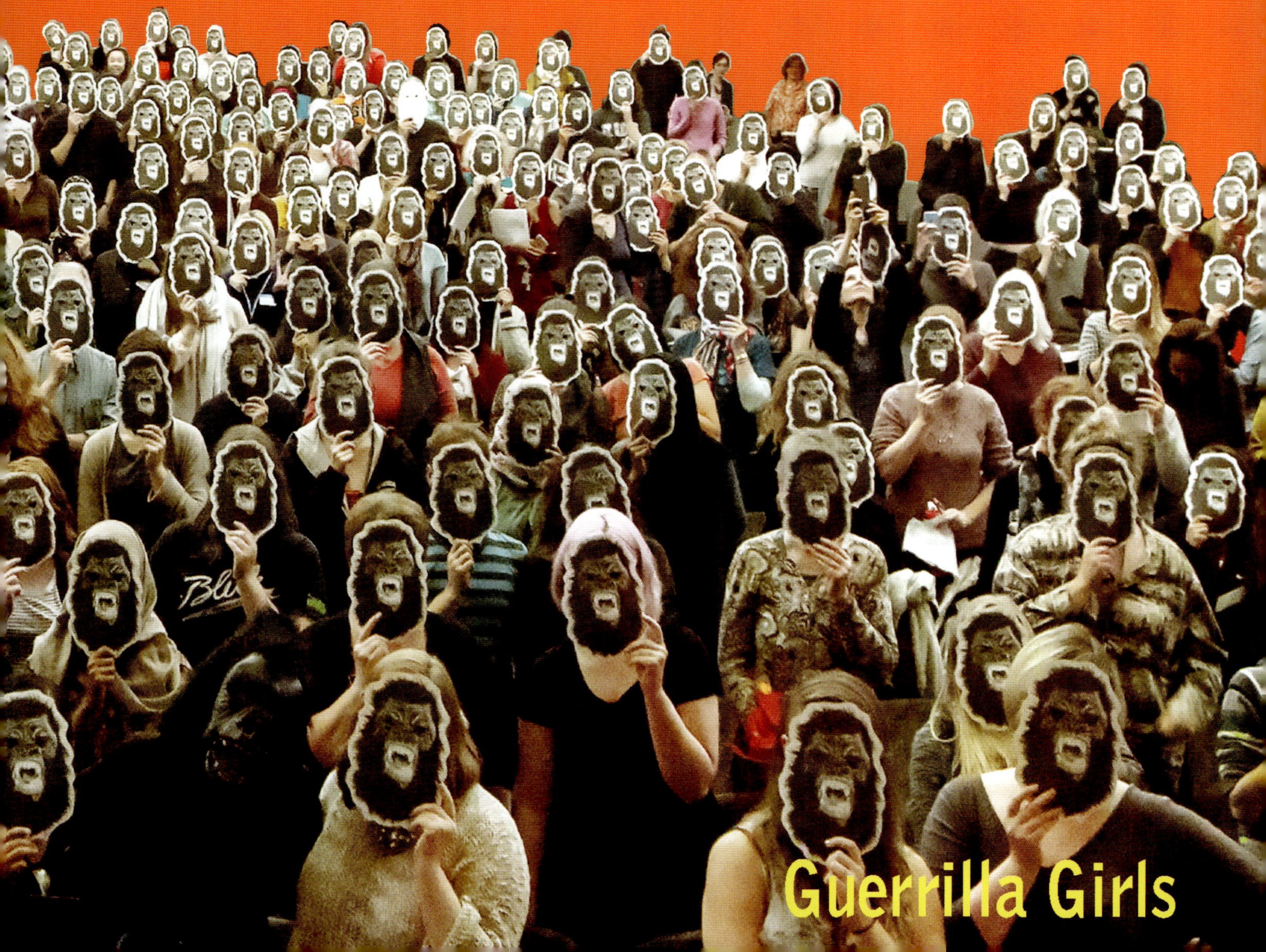

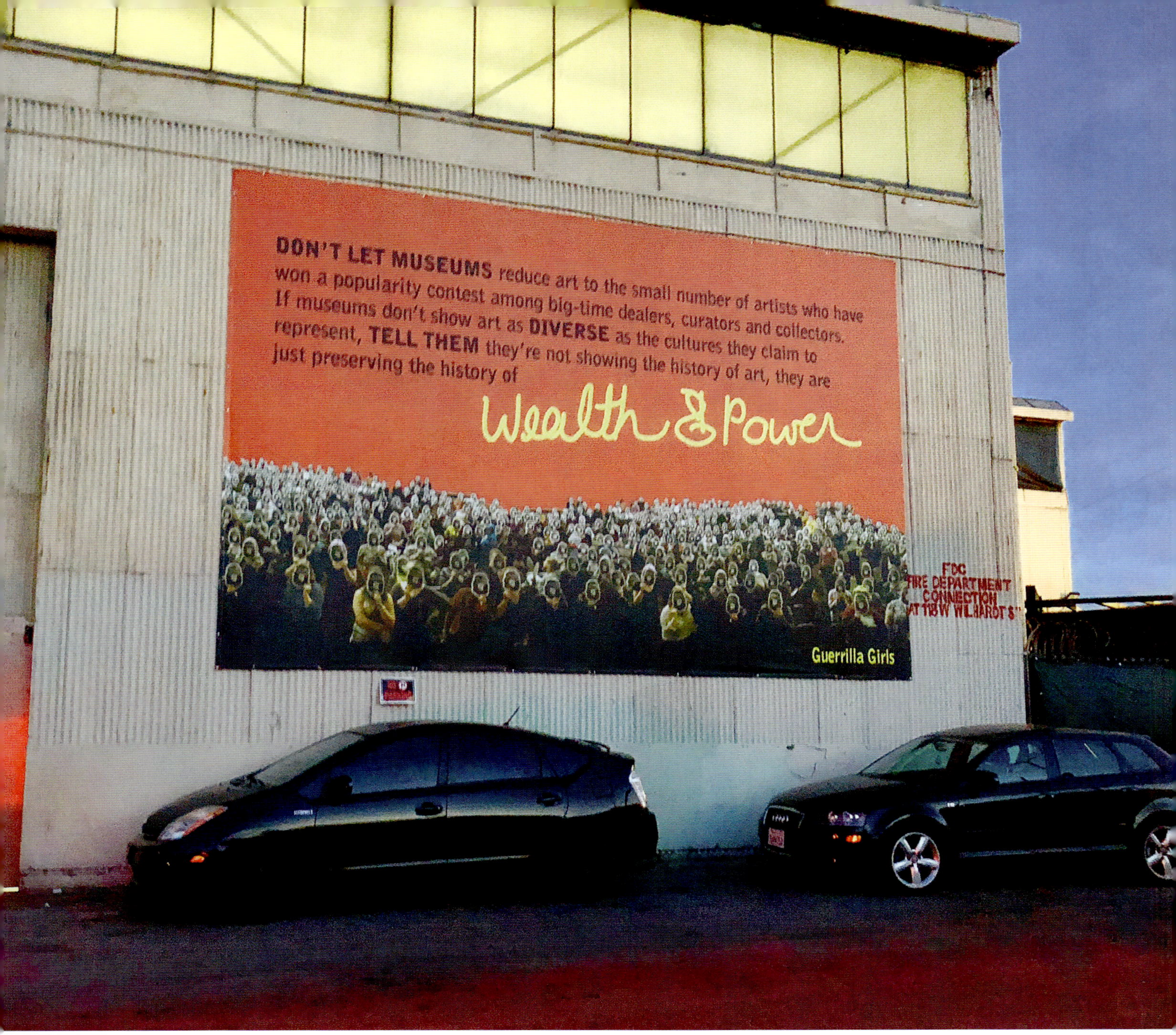

DON'T LET MUSEUMS reduce art to the small number of artists who have won a popularity contest among big-time dealers, curators and collectors. If museums don't show art as DIVERSE as the cultures they claim to represent, TELL THEM they're not showing the history of art, they are just preserving the history of
Wealth & Power
Guerrilla Girls

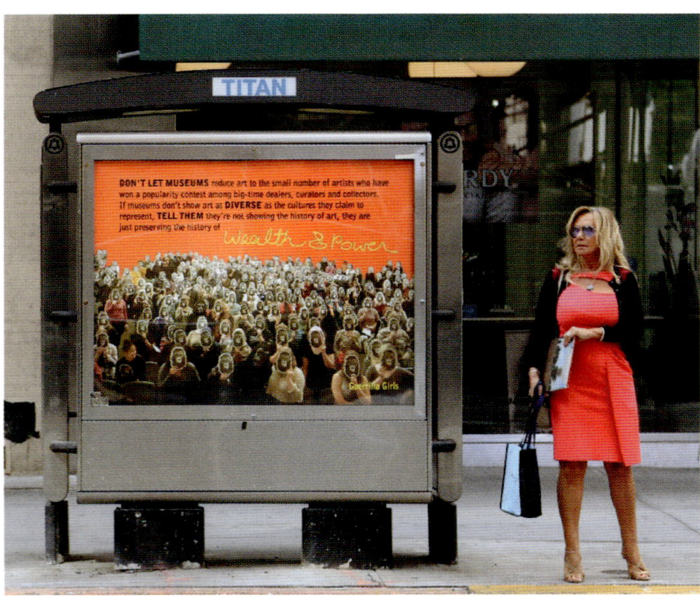
TITAN
DON'T LET MUSEUMS reduce art to the small number of artists who have won a popularity contest among big-time dealers, curators and collectors. If museums don't show art as DIVERSE as the cultures they claim to represent, TELL THEM they're not showing the history of art, they are just preserving the history of
Wealth & Power
Guerrilla Girls

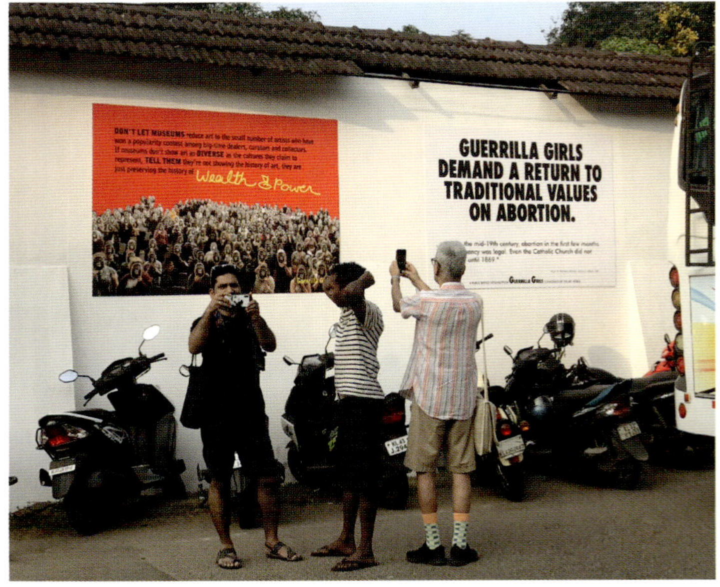
GUERRILLA GIRLS
DEMAND A RETURN TO
TRADITIONAL VALUES
ON ABORTION.

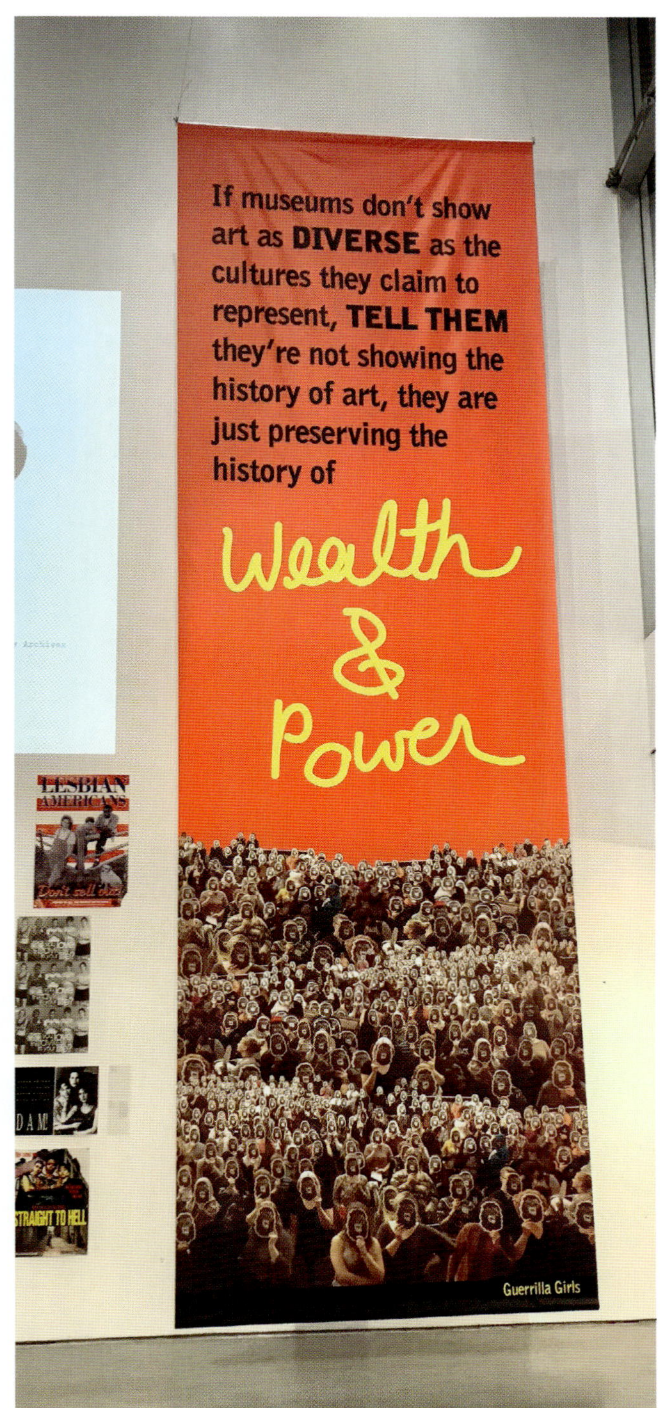

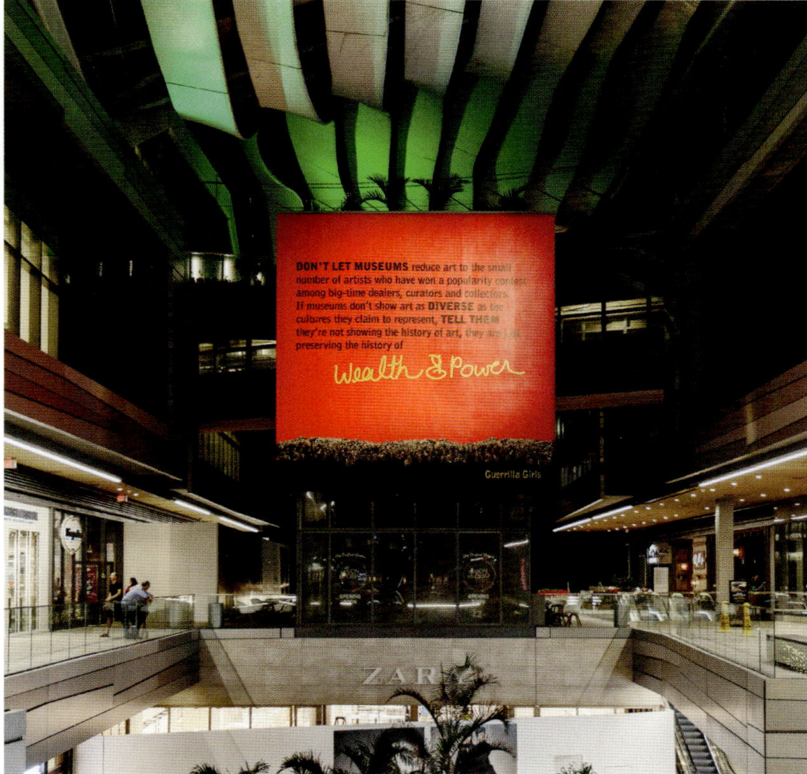

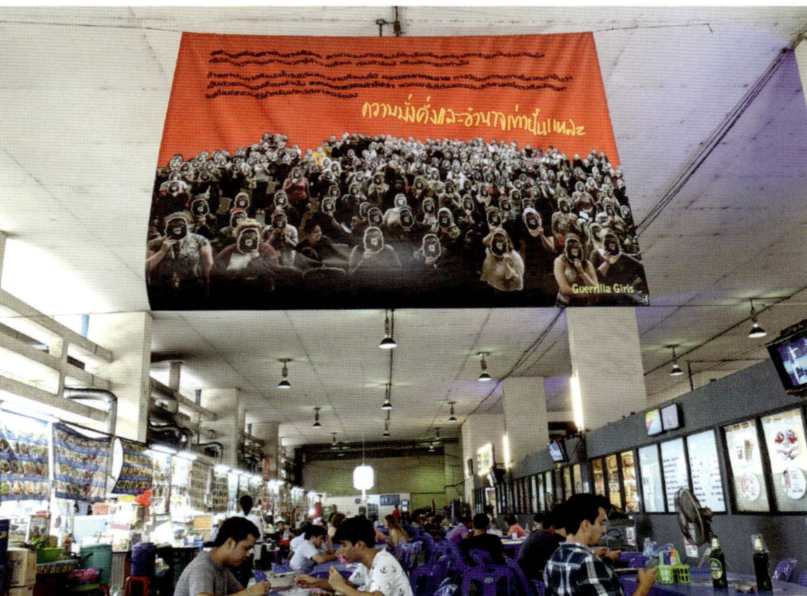

Wealth and Power has traveled all over the world, from Miami to Bangkok. It hits a raw nerve and elicits cheers wherever it goes.

Clockwise from top of facing page: *Beyond the Steets*, Los Angeles, 2018; *We Dissent*, The Cooper Union, NY, 2018; *FAIR*, Miami, 2017; Bangkok Biennale, 2018; Kochi-Muziris Biennale, 2018; Art in Ad Places bus shelter, NY, 2017, photo by Luna Park

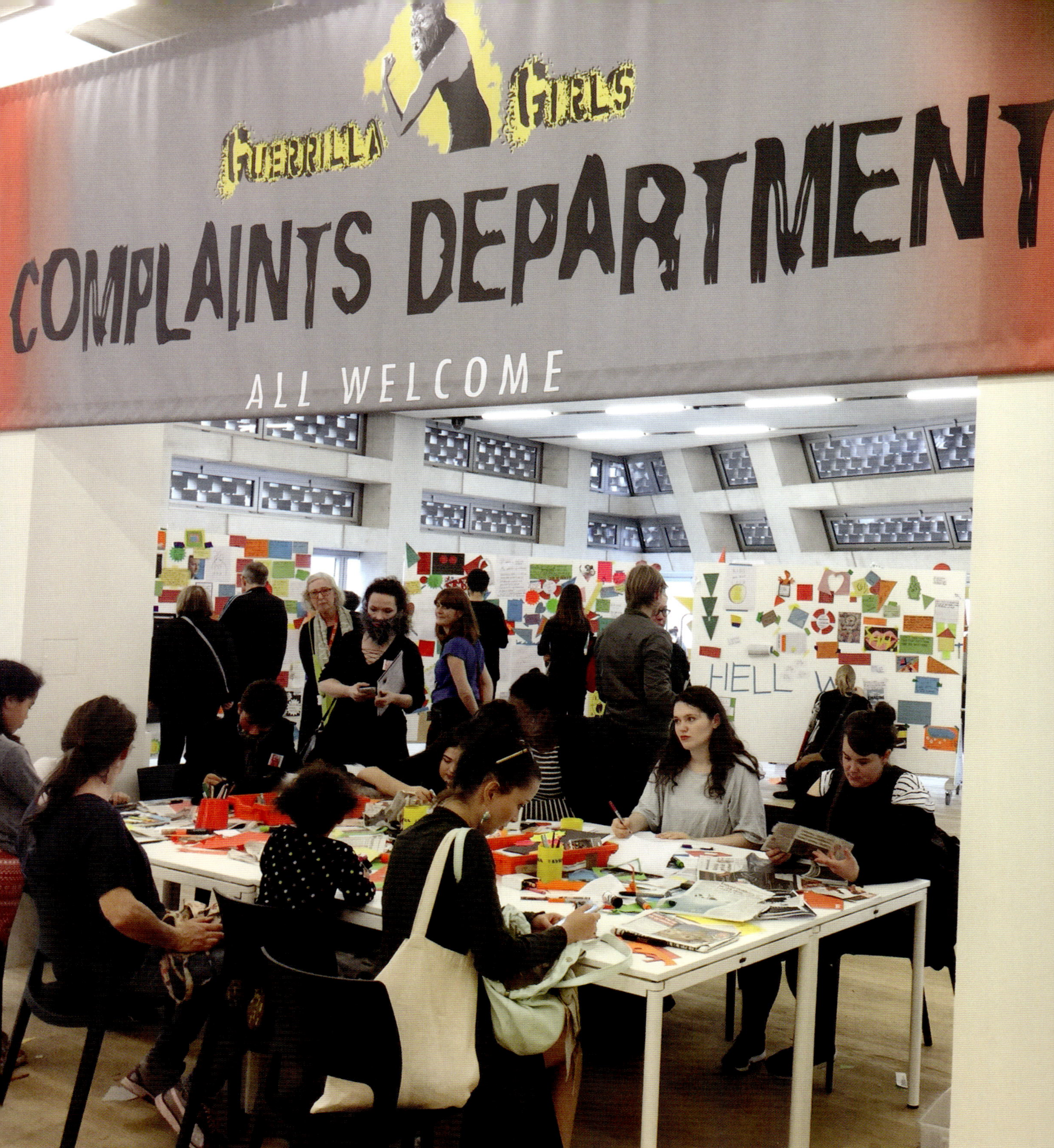

People who go to museums deserve the right to complain. We set up shop at Tate Modern for a week and thousands came to post their thoughts and grievances about everything, including the museum itself.

Above, opposite top, and opposite center left: Installation views, *Complaints Department*, 2016

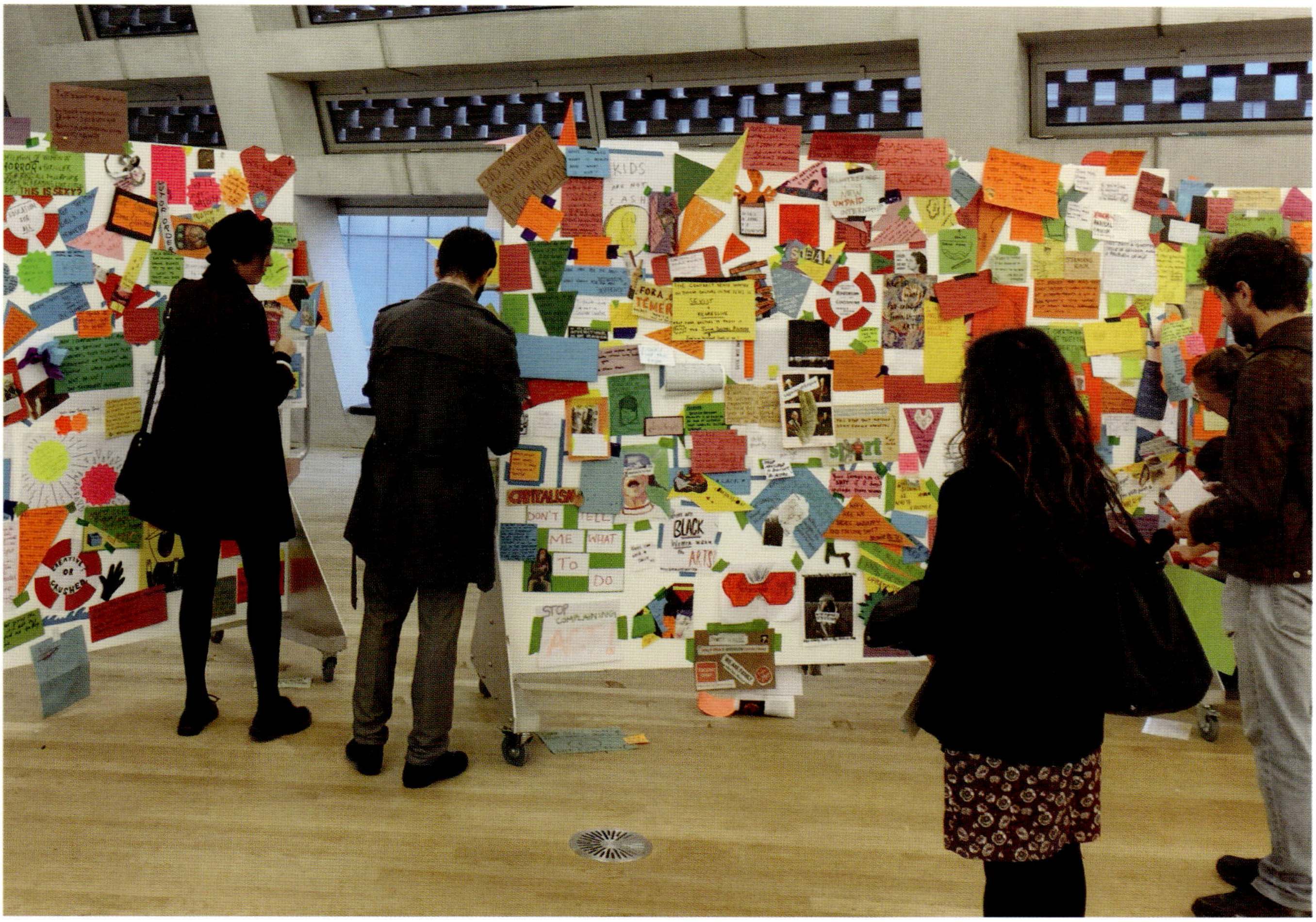

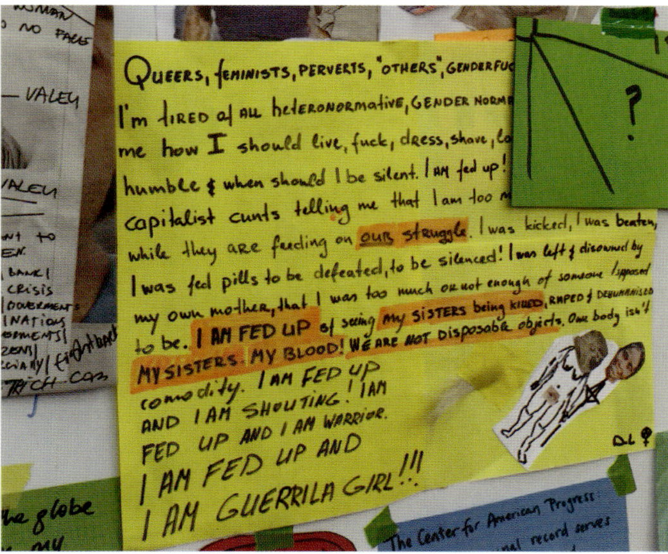

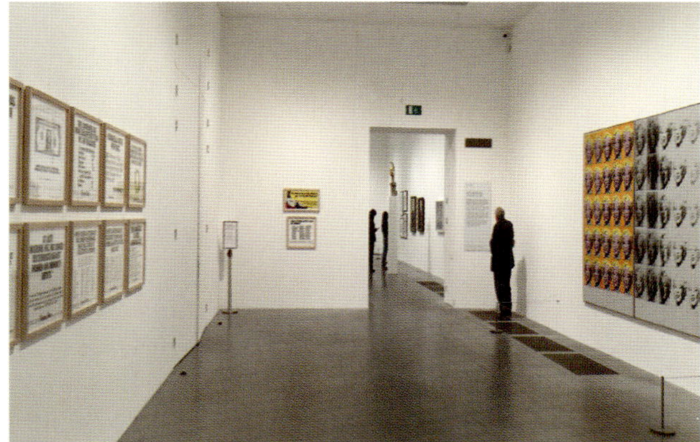

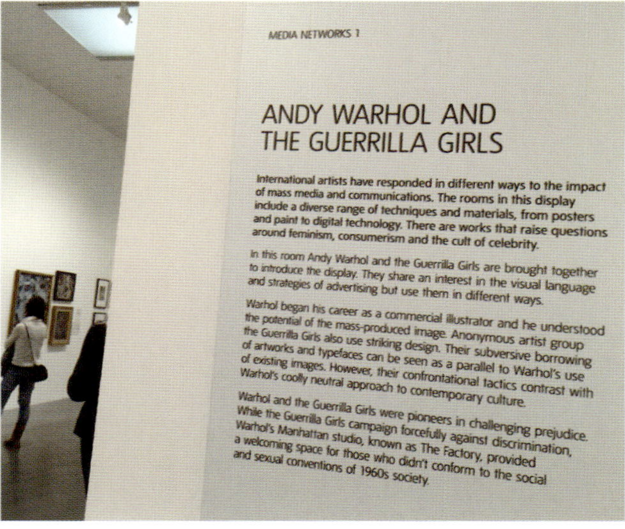

Above center right: Wall label, Tate Modern exhibition room

Right: One of the galleries at Tate Modern connects our media
strategies and support of LGBTQ issues with Andy Warhol's.
But Andy got top billing.

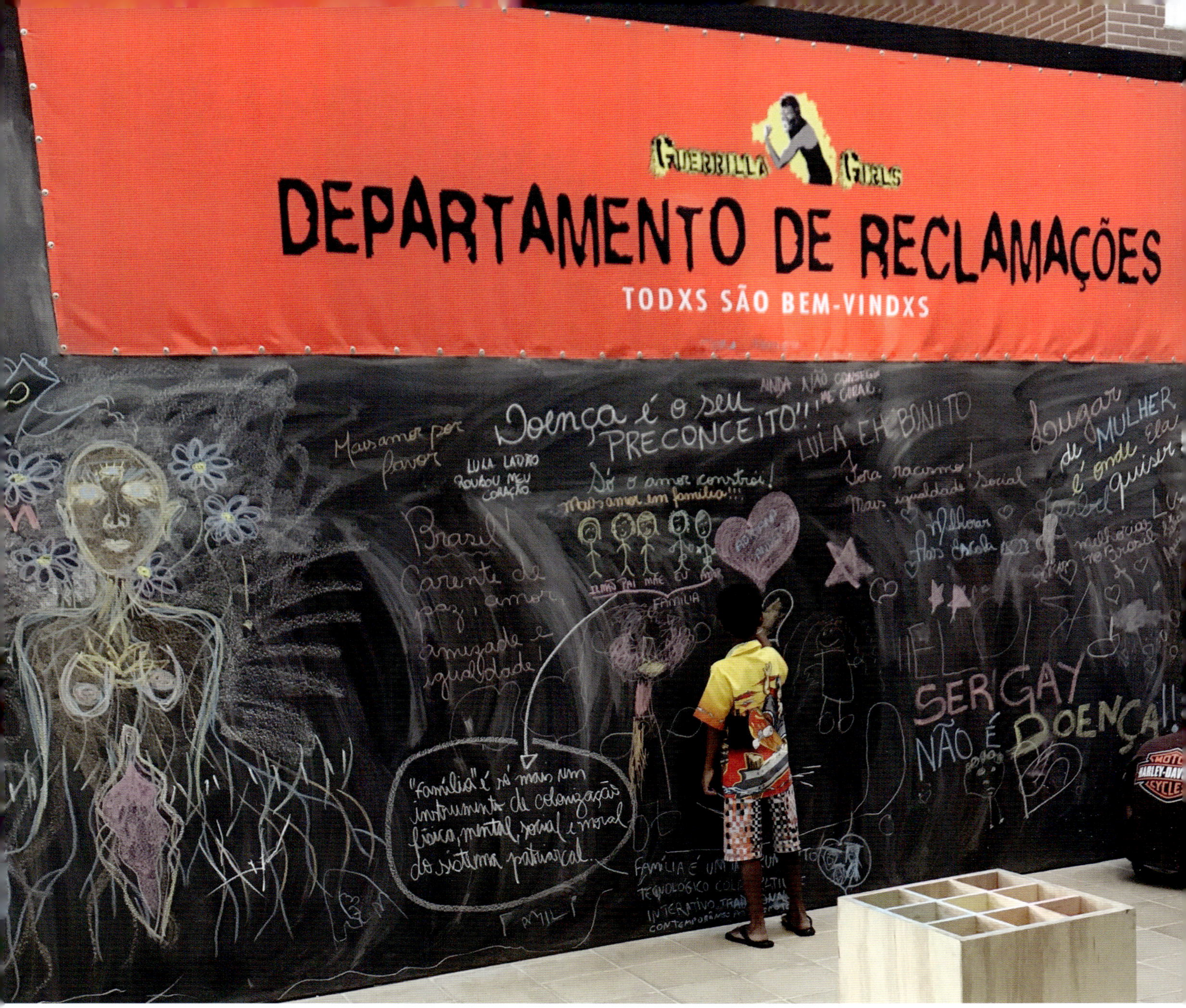

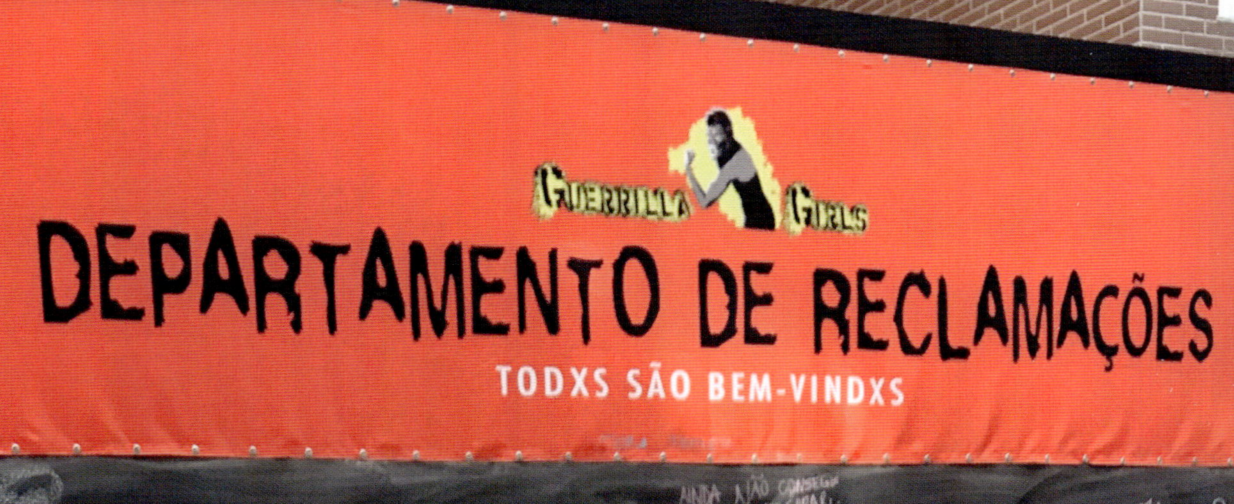

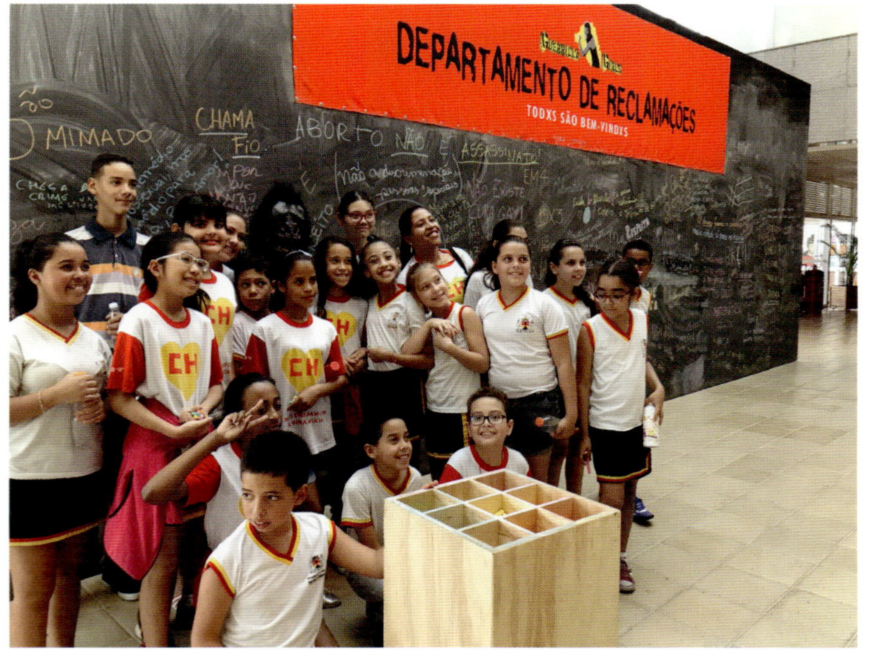

Times are tough in Brazil, so we sent the *Guerrilla Girls Complaints Department* to Sorocaba's *Frestas Triennial*.

Installation views, Sorocaba, 2017

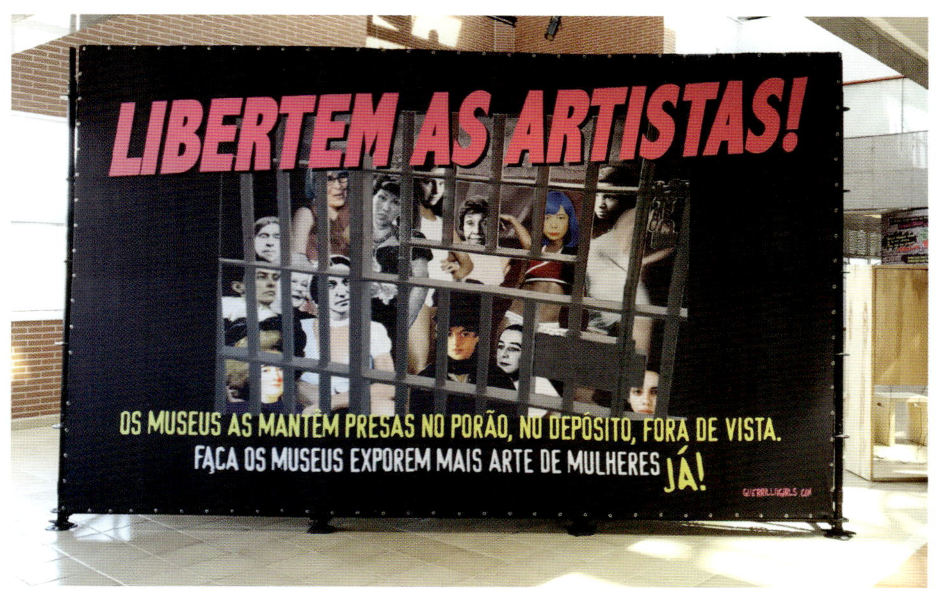

LIBERTEM AS ARTISTAS!
OS MUSEUS AS MANTÊM PRESAS NO PORÃO, NU DEPÓSITO, FORA DE VISTA.
FAÇA OS MUSEUS EXPOREM MAIS ARTE DE MULHERES JÁ!
GUERRILLAGIRLS.COM

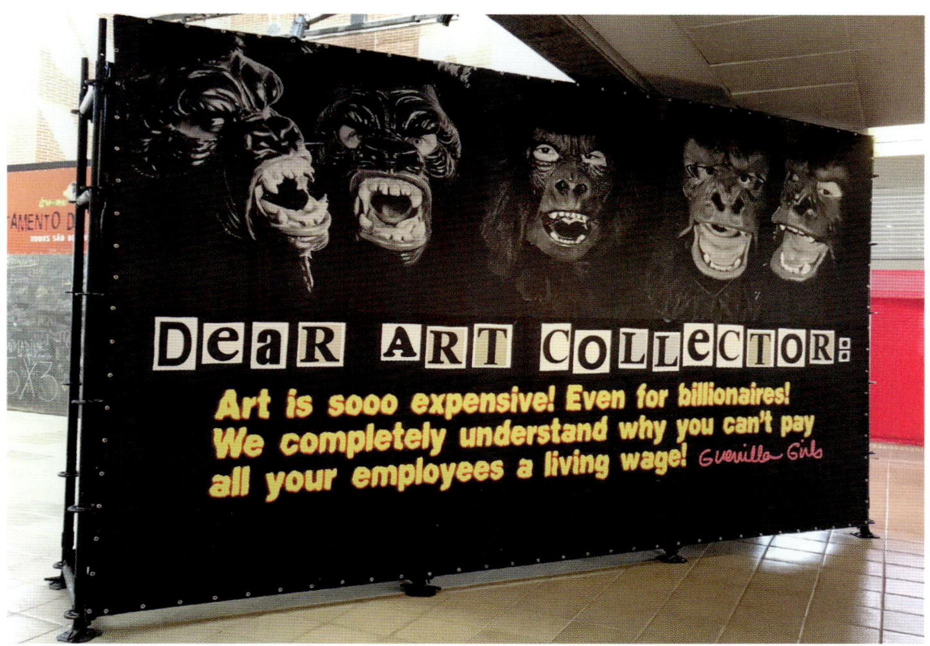

DEAR ART COLLECTOR:
Art is sooo expensive! Even for billionaires!
We completely understand why you can't pay
all your employees a living wage! Guerrilla Girls
guerrillagirls.com

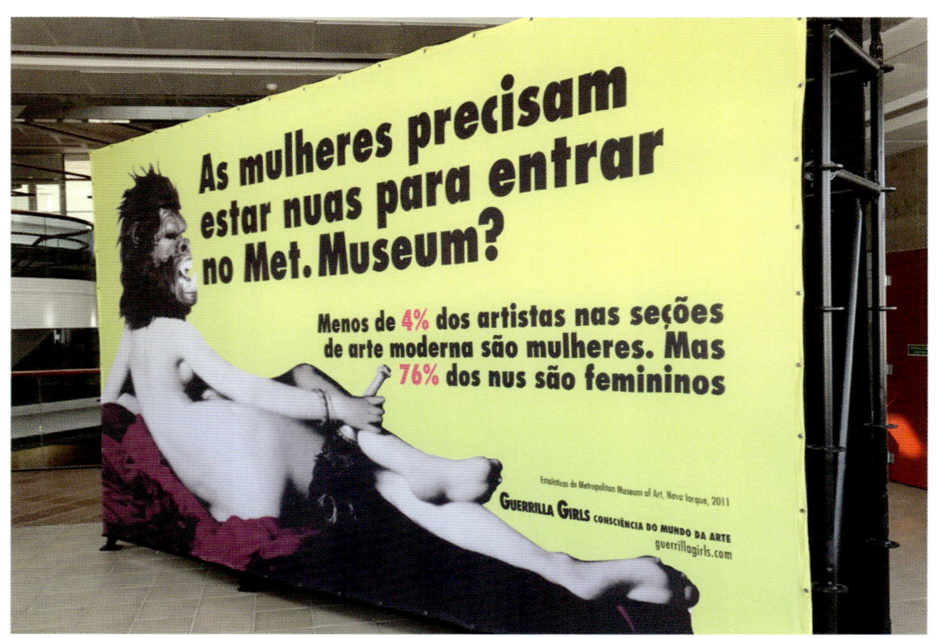

As mulheres precisam
estar nuas para entrar
no Met. Museum?
Menos de 4% dos artistas nas seções
de arte moderna são mulheres. Mas
76% dos nus são femininos
Estatísticas do Metropolitan Museum of Art, Nova Iorque, 2011
GUERRILLA GIRLS CONSCIÊNCIA DO MUNDO DA ARTE
guerrillagirls.com

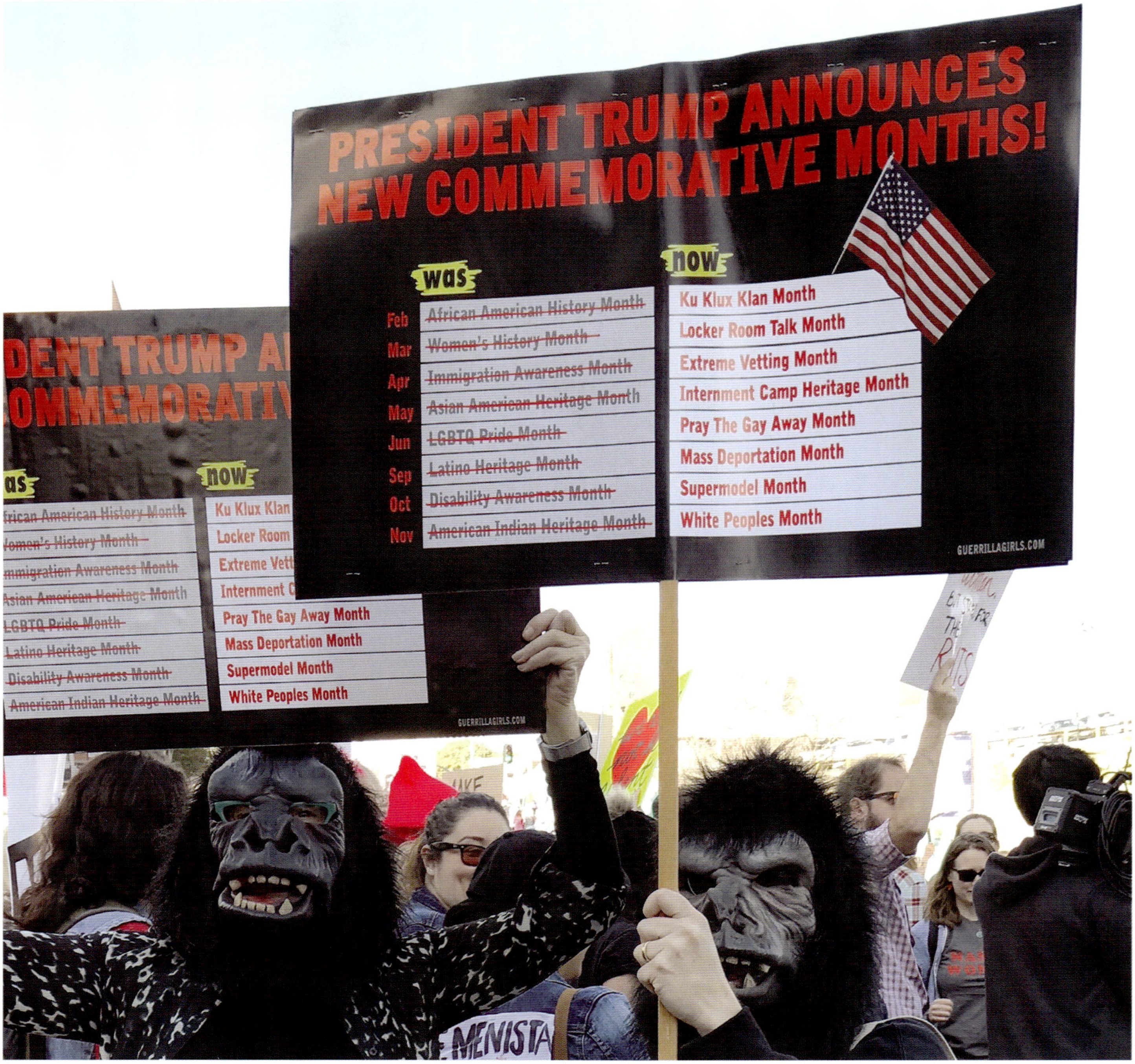

PRESIDENT TRUMP ANNOUNCES
NEW COMMEMORATIVE MONTHS!

was

Feb — African American History Month
Mar — Women's History Month
Apr — Immigration Awareness Month
May — Asian American Heritage Month
Jun — LGBTQ Pride Month
Sep — Latino Heritage Month
Oct — Disability Awareness Month
Nov — American Indian Heritage Month

now

Ku Klux Klan Month
Locker Room Talk Month
Extreme Vetting Month
Internment Camp Heritage Month
Pray The Gay Away Month
Mass Deportation Month
Supermodel Month
White Peoples Month

GUERRILLAGIRLS.COM

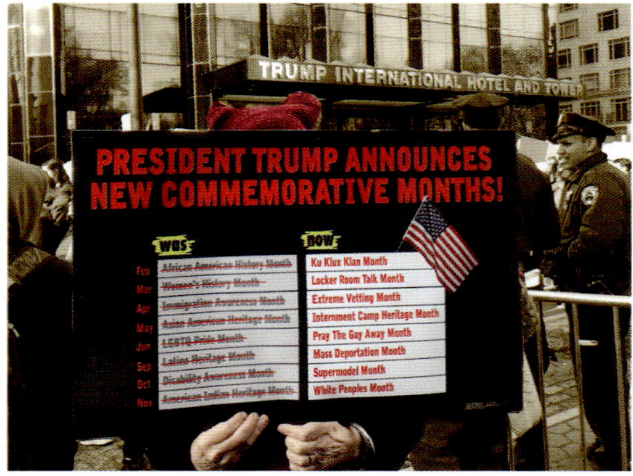

TRUMP INTERNATIONAL HOTEL AND TOWER
PRESIDENT TRUMP ANNOUNCES
NEW COMMEMORATIVE MONTHS!

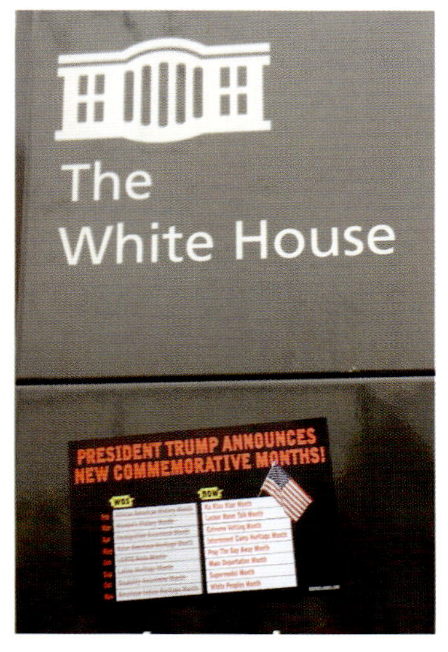

The
White House
PRESIDENT TRUMP ANNOUNCES
NEW COMMEMORATIVE MONTHS!

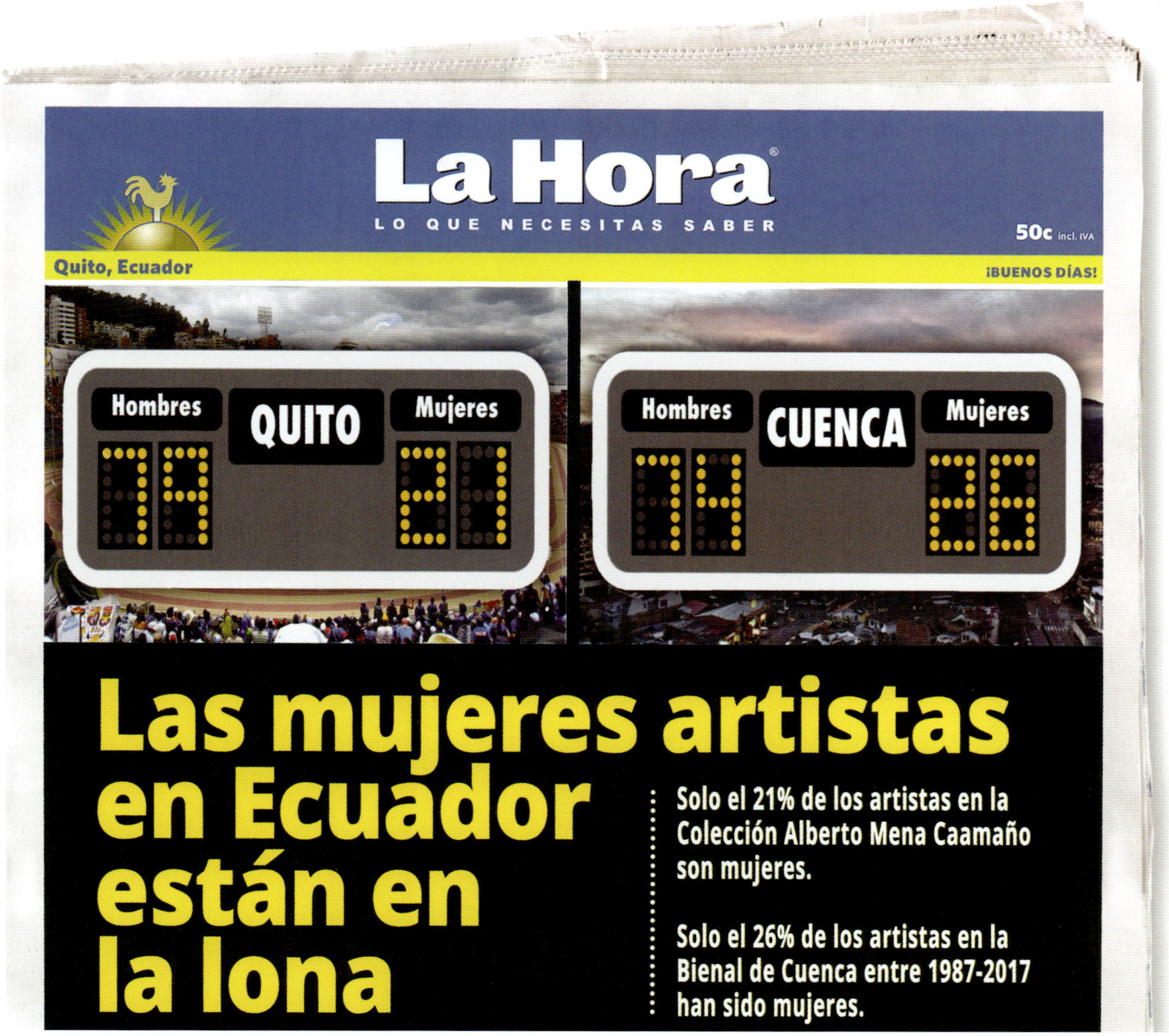

La Hora

LO QUE NECESITAS SABER

Quito, Ecuador

50¢ incl. IVA

¡BUENOS DÍAS!

Hombres	QUITO	Mujeres
19		21

Hombres	CUENCA	Mujeres
74		26

Las mujeres artistas en Ecuador están en la lona

Solo el 21% de los artistas en la Colección Alberto Mena Caamaño son mujeres.

Solo el 26% de los artistas en la Bienal de Cuenca entre 1987-2017 han sido mujeres.

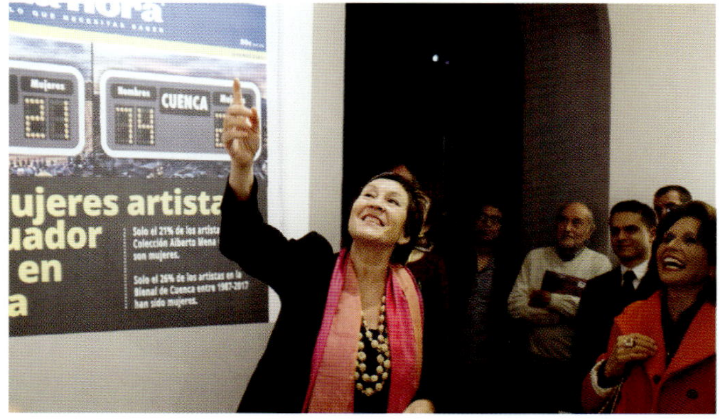

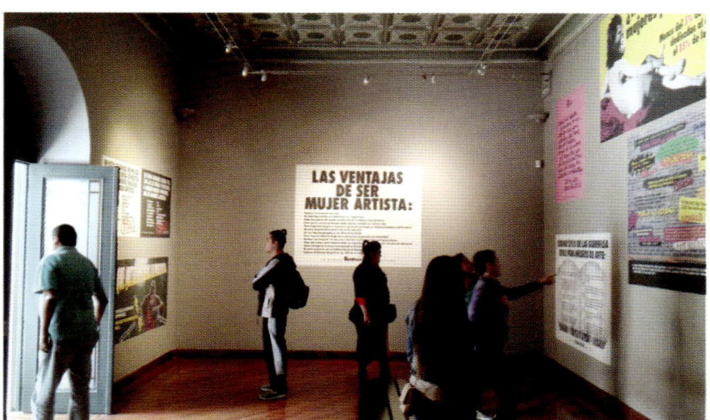

Left: After Donald Trump was elected, we carried this cringe-worthy poster in the Women's Marches, predicting what his presidency could do to marginalized communities in the U.S. Tragically, he has targeted one group after another.

Poster and Sticker, Women's March: Los Angeles, New York, Washington, D.C., 2016–17

Women artists lose big time in Ecuador! In Quito, we pitted two major art institutions against each other, as if they were sports teams. Both were losers when it came to showing female artists.

Poster; Exhbition views, Quito, 2017

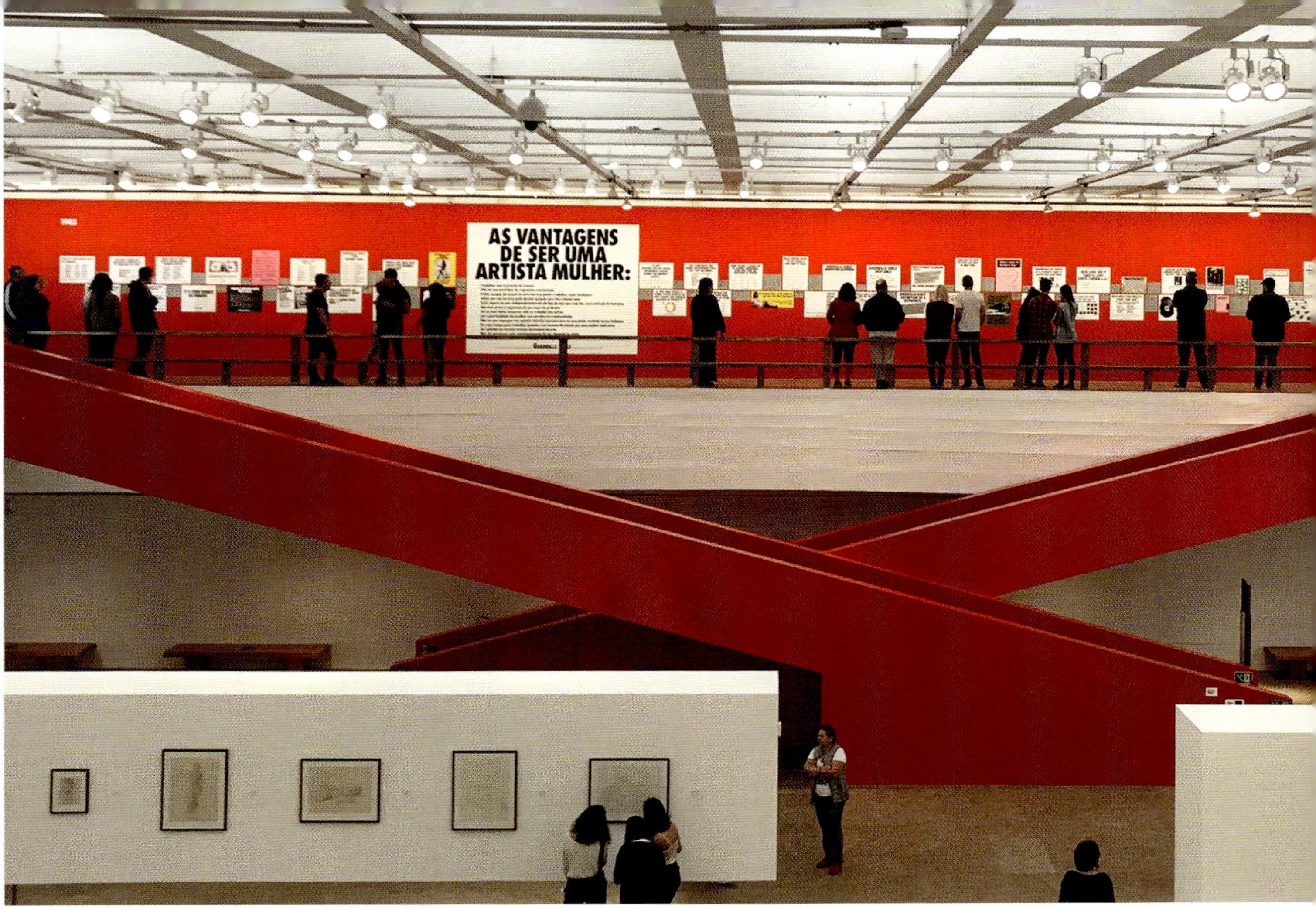

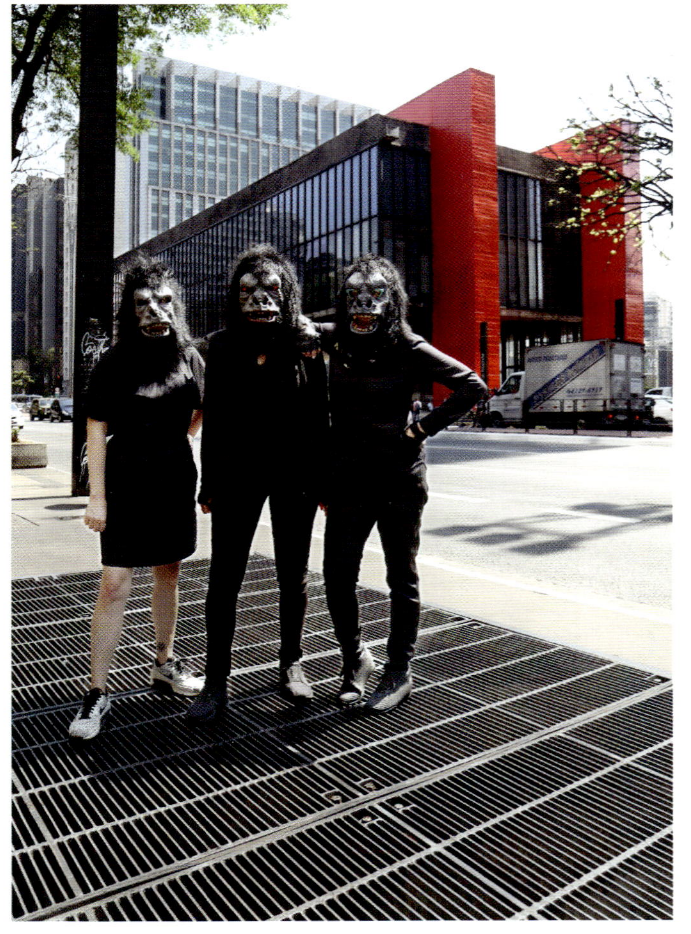

The Museum of Art São Paulo mounted our first South American retrospective with a radical installation. So far, all our major exhibitions have taken place abroad. What are U.S. museums waiting for?

Installation views, *Guerrilla Girls Gráphica 1985–2017*, Museum of Art São Paulo, 2017

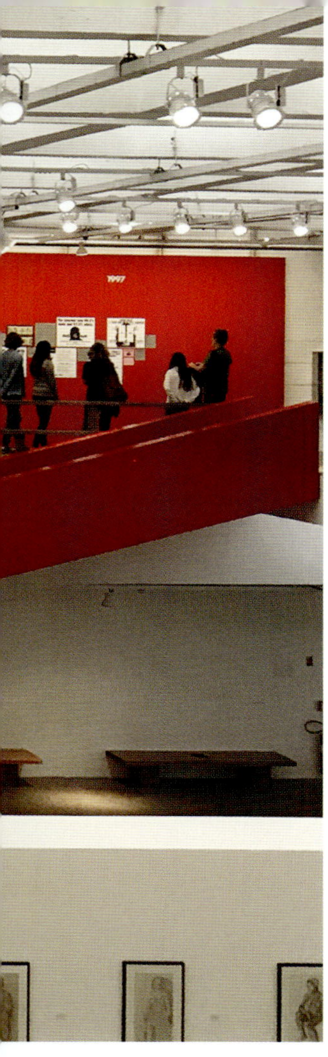

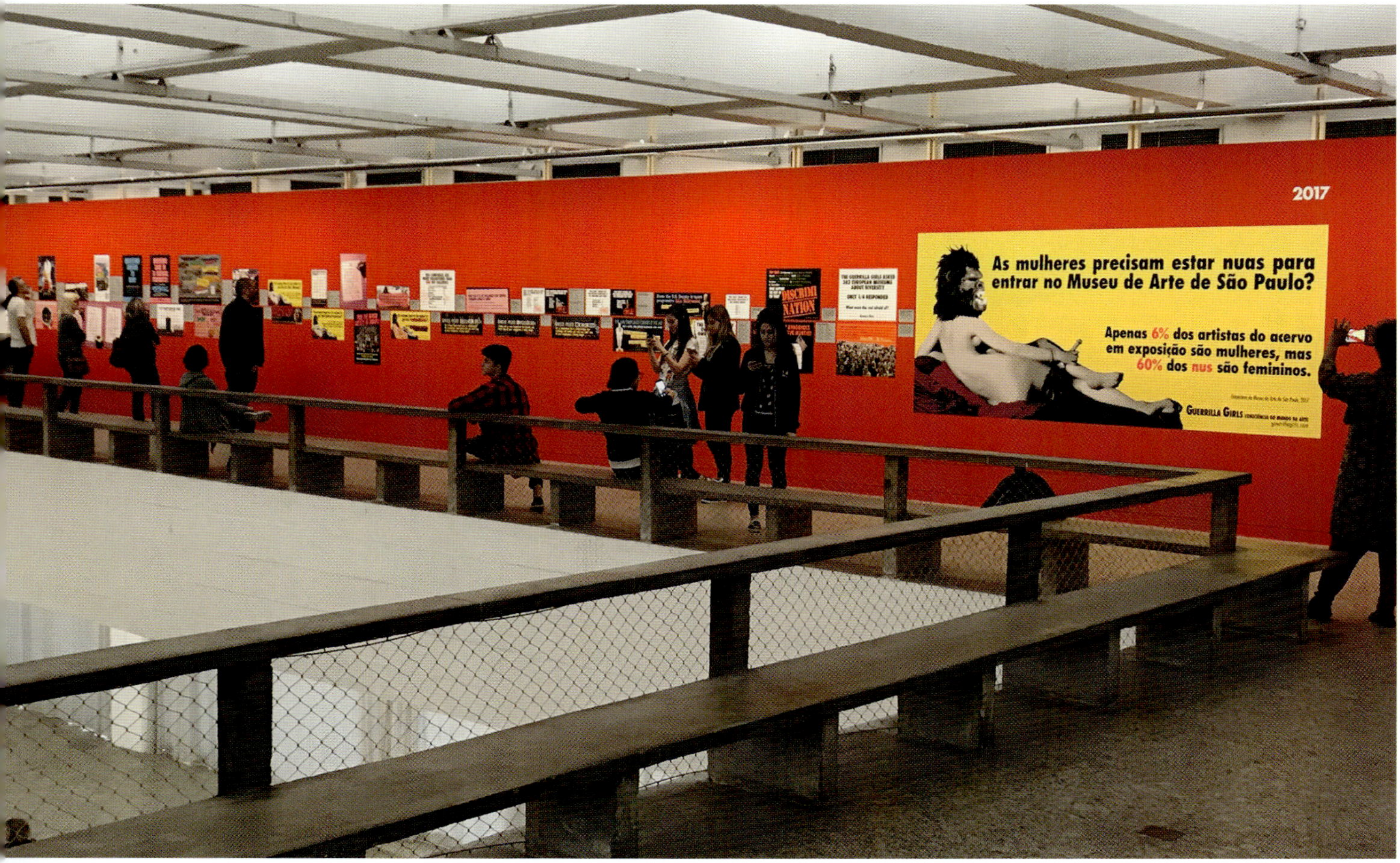

As mulheres precisam estar nuas para
entrar no Museu de Arte de São Paulo?

Apenas 6% dos artistas do acervo
em exposição são mulheres, mas
60% dos nus são femininos.

GUERRILLA GIRLS CONSCIÊNCIA DO MUNDO DA ARTE

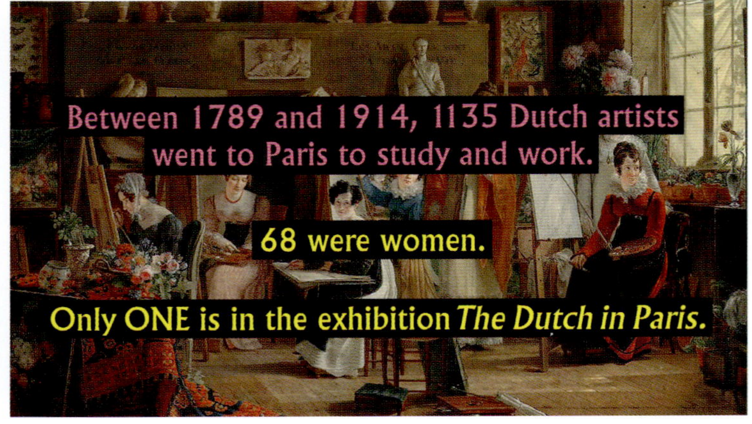

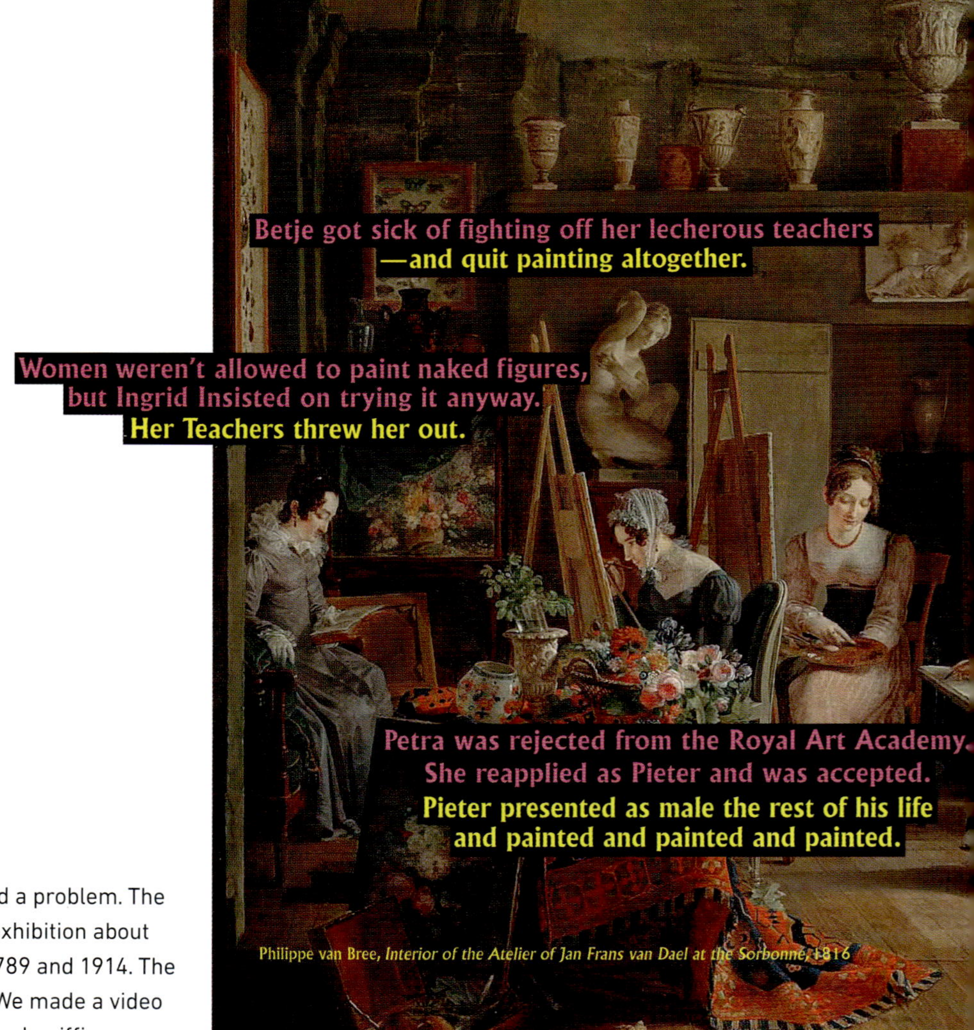

A Message From The
GUERRILLA GIRLS

Right: The Van Gogh Museum in Amsterdam had a problem. The curators chose one token woman artist for an exhibition about Dutch painters who worked in Paris between 1789 and 1914. The education department asked us to investigate. We made a video about the lives of women artists in the Netherlands, riffing on historic facts. We called out tokenism in the exhibition, and also in the museum collection.

Page 160: The Military History Museum in Dresden has a unique mandate: to document, not glorify, the horror and destruction of war. Our *Estrogen Bomb* poster, reproduced on a massive scale for an exhibition about gender and violence, poses the eternal question: If women were in charge, would there be world peace?

Video stills, *One Is Not Enough*, Van Gogh Museum, 2017

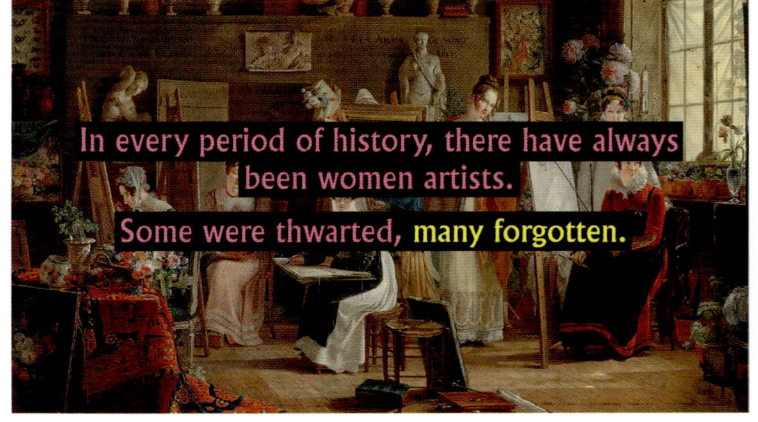

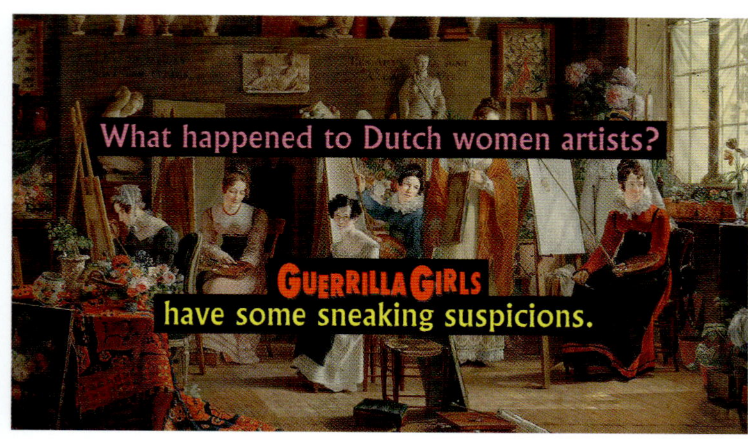

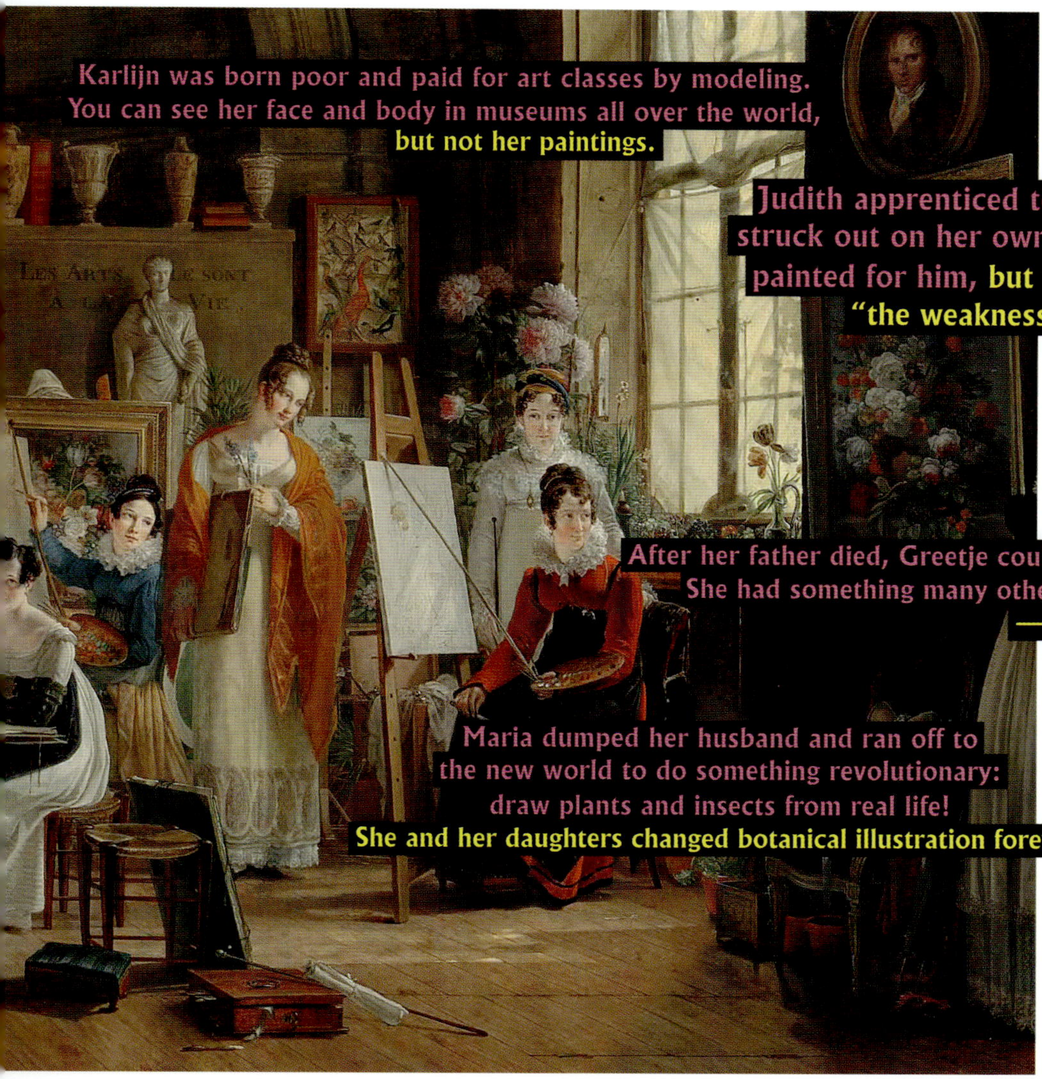

Karlijn was born poor and paid for art classes by modeling.
You can see her face and body in museums all over the world,
but not her paintings.

Judith apprenticed to a famous male painter, then
struck out on her own. Art historians loved what she
painted for him, but thought her own work showed
"the weakness of the feminine hand."

After her father died, Greetje could do whatever she wanted.
She had something many other women artists didn't
—a big inheritence.

Maria dumped her husband and ran off to
the new world to do something revolutionary:
draw plants and insects from real life!
She and her daughters changed botanical illustration forever.

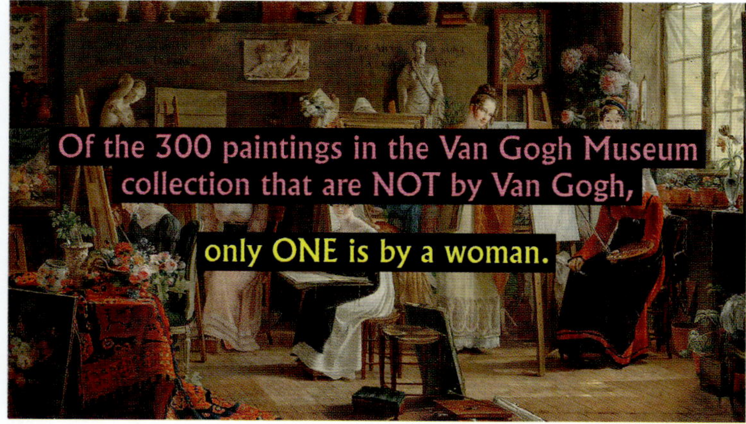

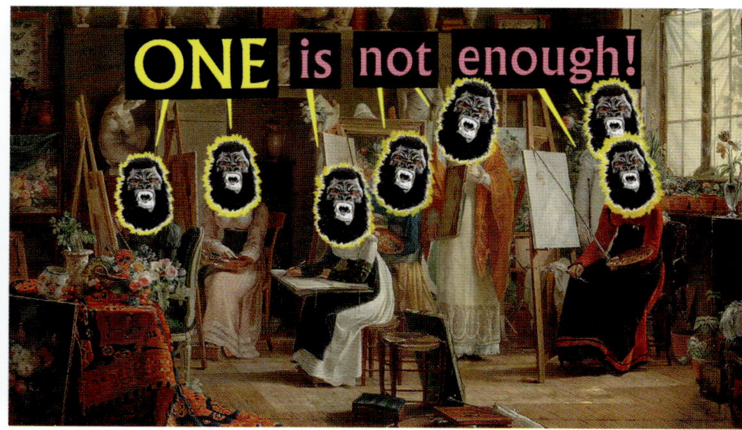

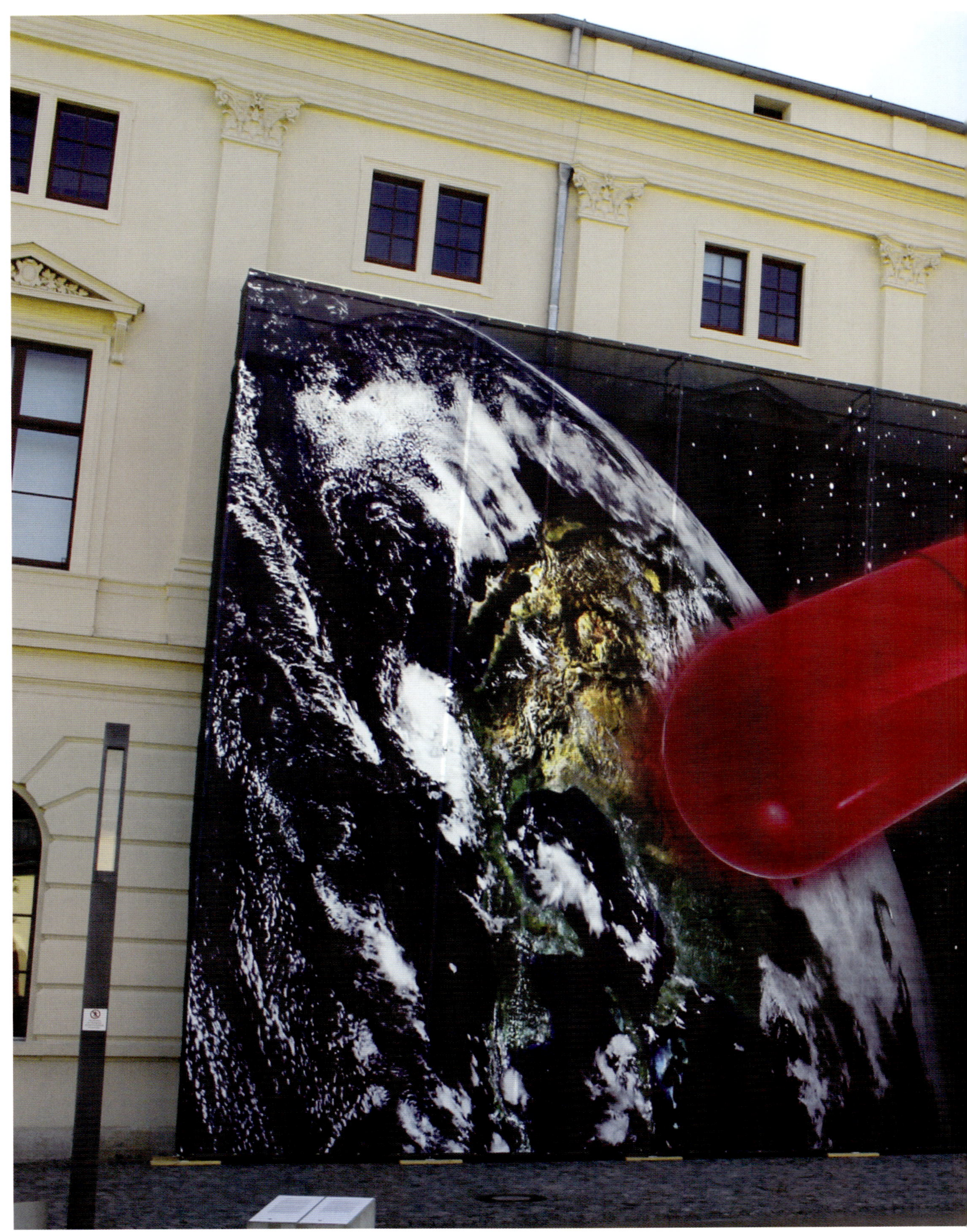

Banner, Militärhistorisches Museum der Bundeswehr, Dresden, 2018

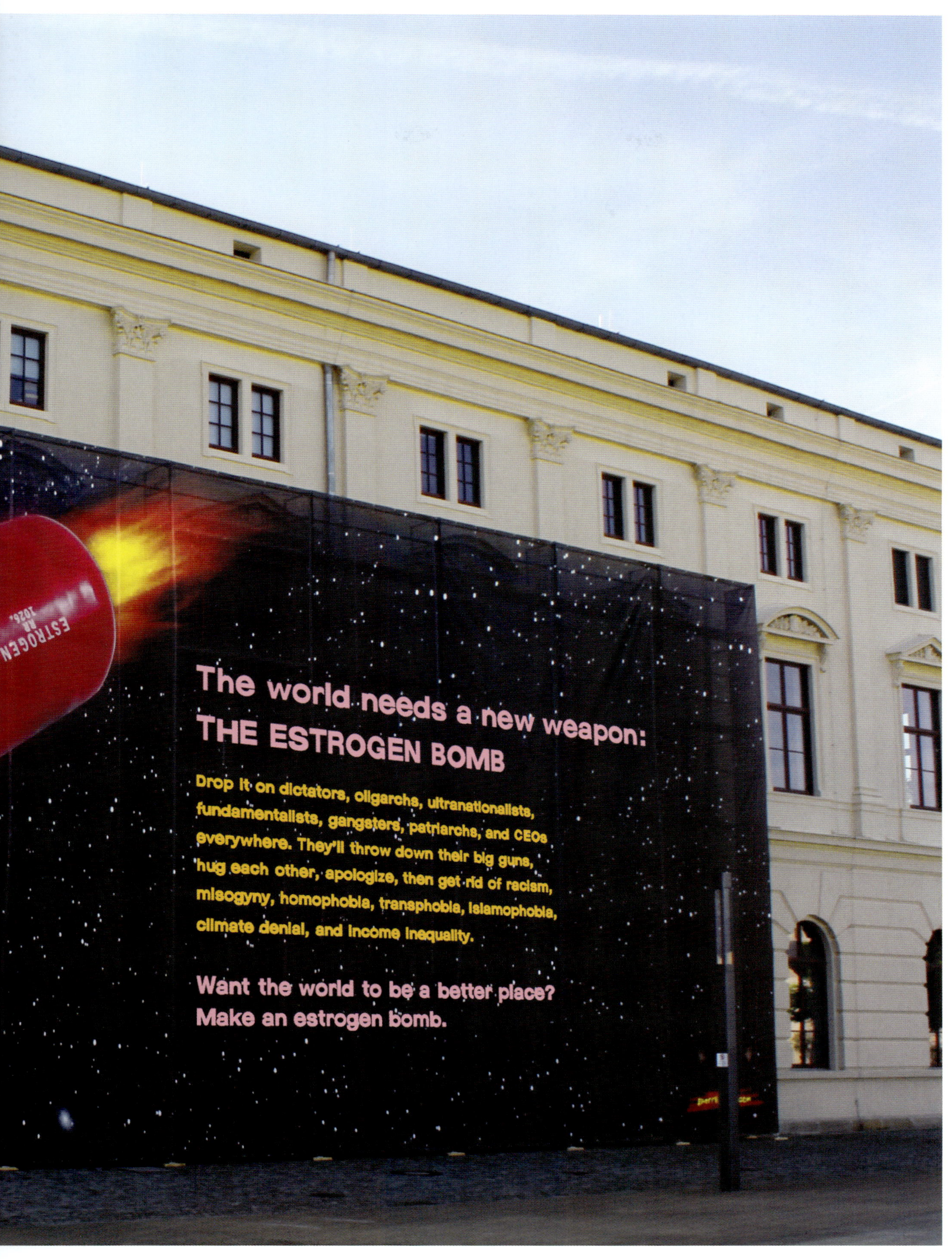
ESTROGEN
B14
1026.
The world needs a new weapon:
THE ESTROGEN BOMB
Drop it on dictators, oligarchs, ultranationalists, fundamentalists, gangsters, patriarchs, and CEOs everywhere. They'll throw down their big guns, hug each other, apologize, then get rid of racism, misogyny, homophobia, transphobia, Islamophobia, climate denial, and income inequality.

Want the world to be a better place?
Make an estrogen bomb.

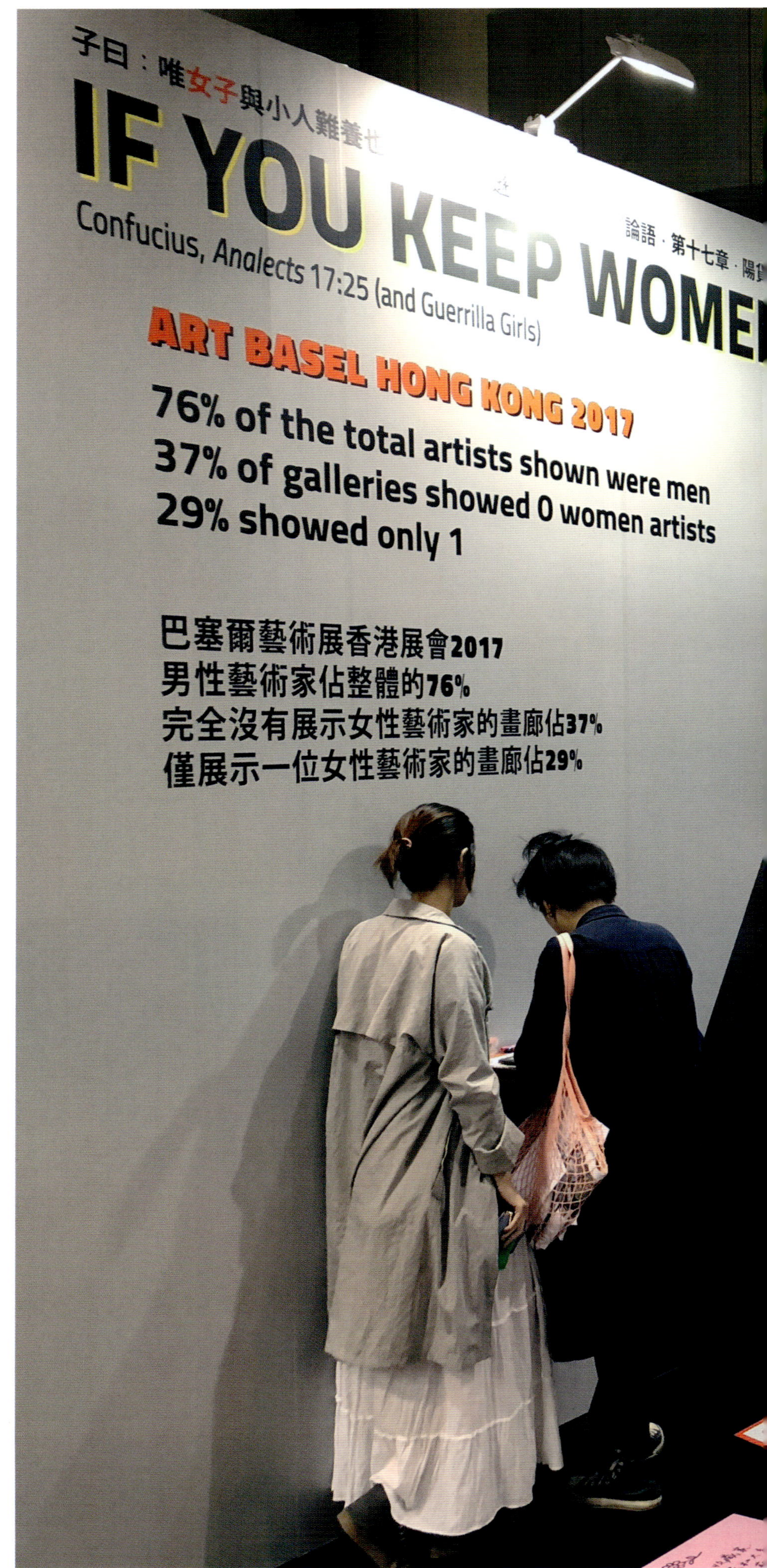

The Asia Art Archive asked us to infiltrate Art Basel Hong Kong. We quoted Confucius, displayed stats from the previous year's fair, then invited visitors to do a gender count inside the fair and post their results and comments. This did not make fair officials happy.

Women Get Resentful, installation view, 2018

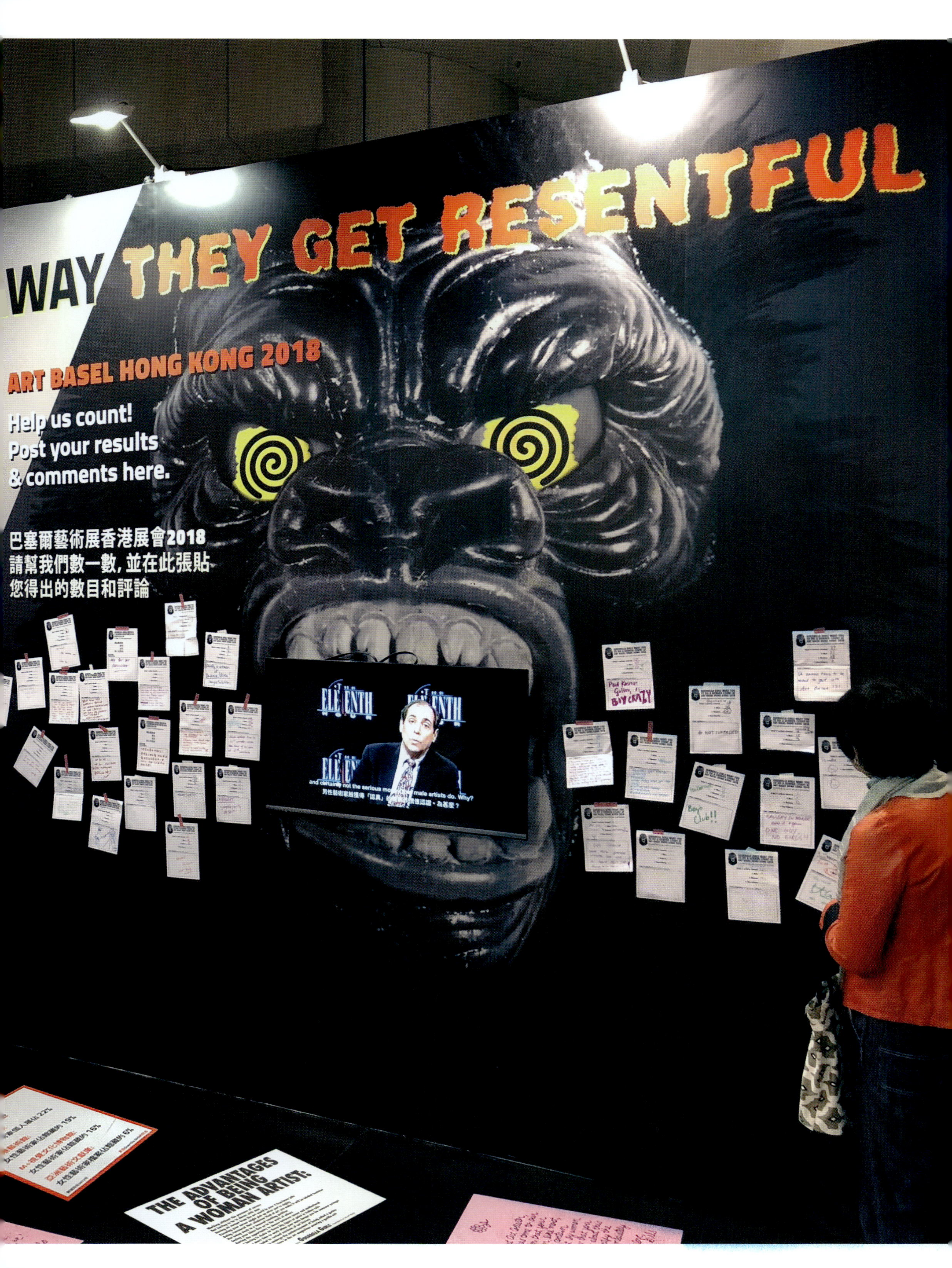

WAY THEY GET RESENTFUL
ART BASEL HONG KONG 2018
Help us count!
Post your results
& comments here.
巴塞爾藝術展香港展會2018
請幫我們數一數, 並在此張貼
您得出的數目和評論
ELEVENTH
and certainly not the serious money the male artists do. Why?
男性藝術家能獲得「認真」的金錢回報價值回報‧為甚麼？
Paul Kasmin Gallery is BUY CRAZY
NOT SURPRISED
Boys Club!!
THE ADVANTAGES OF BEING A WOMAN ARTIST:

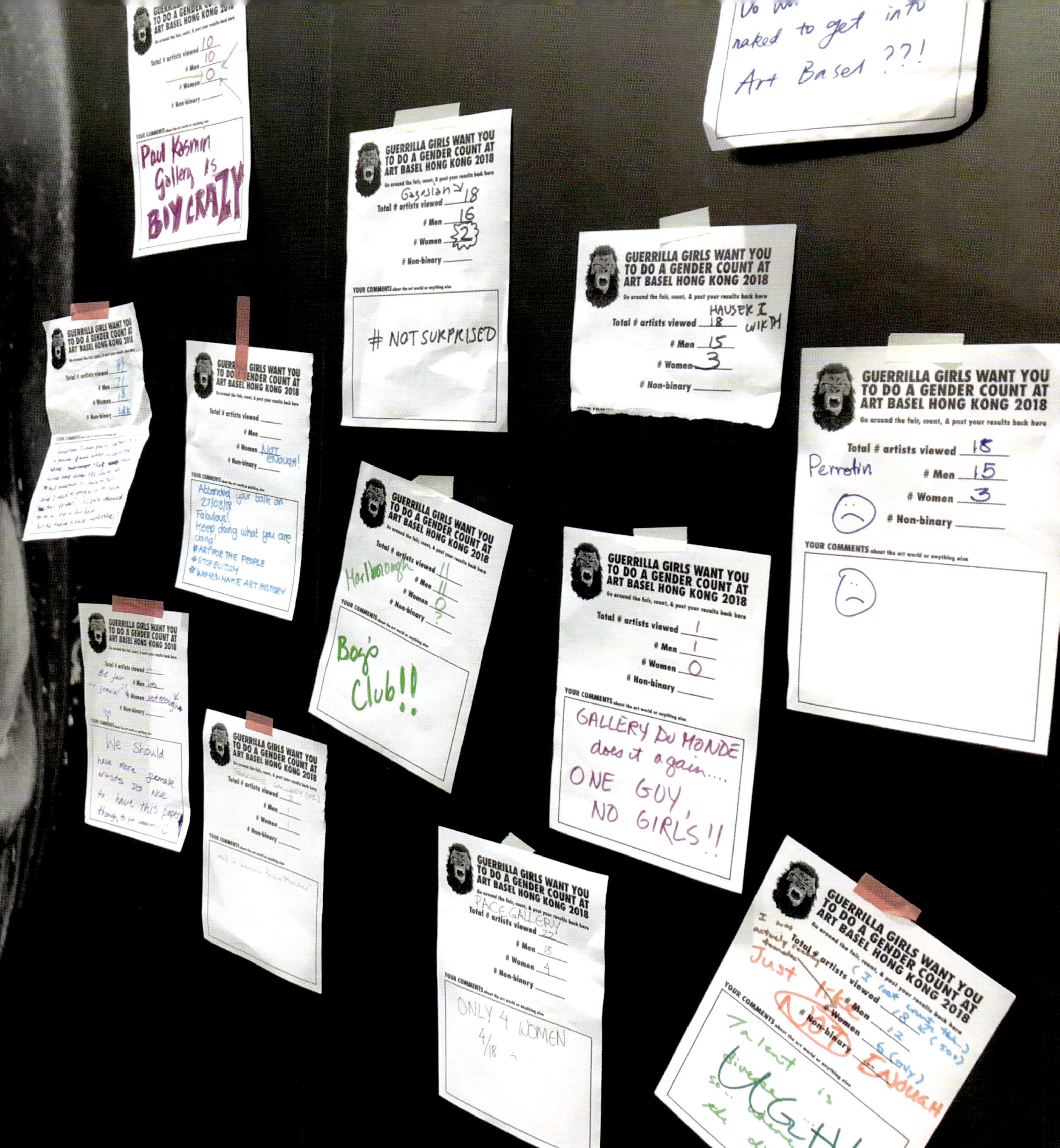

Gender counts posted by visitors to Art Basel Hong Kong, 2018

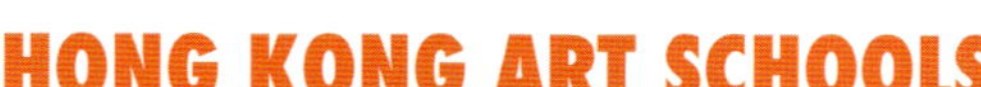

HONG KONG ART SCHOOLS
Women students = **<u>82%</u>**

HONG KONG ART GALLERIES
Women's solo exhibitions = **22%**

HONG KONG MUSEUM OF ART
Women in collection = **19%**

M+ MUSEUM OF VISUAL CULTURE
Women in collection = **16%**

ASIA ART ARCHIVE
Women artists' archives = **6%**

All statistics from 2017

A message from the **GUERRILLA GIRLS**

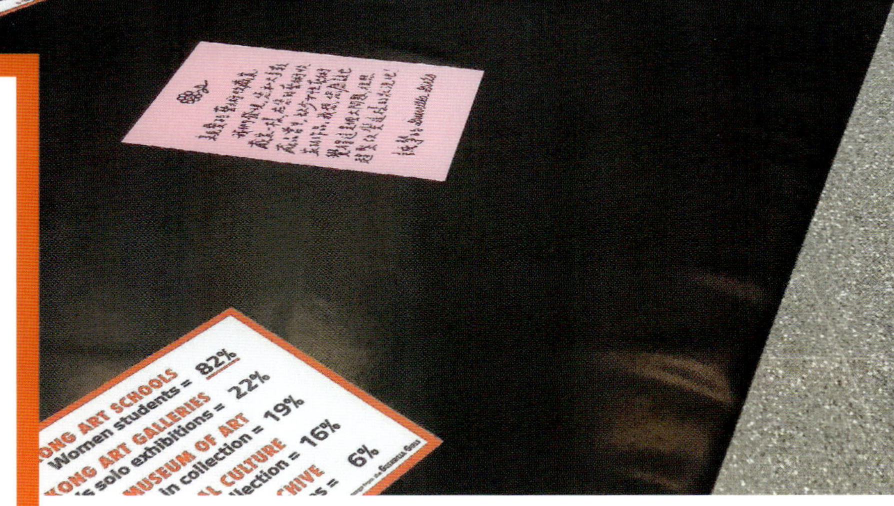

香港的藝術課程：
女性學生佔 **<u>82%</u>**

香港的畫廊：
女性藝術家個人展佔 **22%**

香港藝術館：
女性藝術家佔館藏的 **19%**

M+視覺文化博物館：
女性藝術家佔館藏的 **16%**

亞洲藝術文獻庫：
女性藝術家檔案佔館藏的 **6%**

數據取自2017年

來自 **Guerrilla Girls** 的訊息

We looked at life after art school for female artists in Hong Kong and found it similar to almost everywhere else. The majority of art students are women, but after graduation the professional opportunities go to men. The Asia Art Archive, which brought us to Hong Kong, did not escape scrutiny: only 6% of the artists in its collection are women.

Posters, 2018

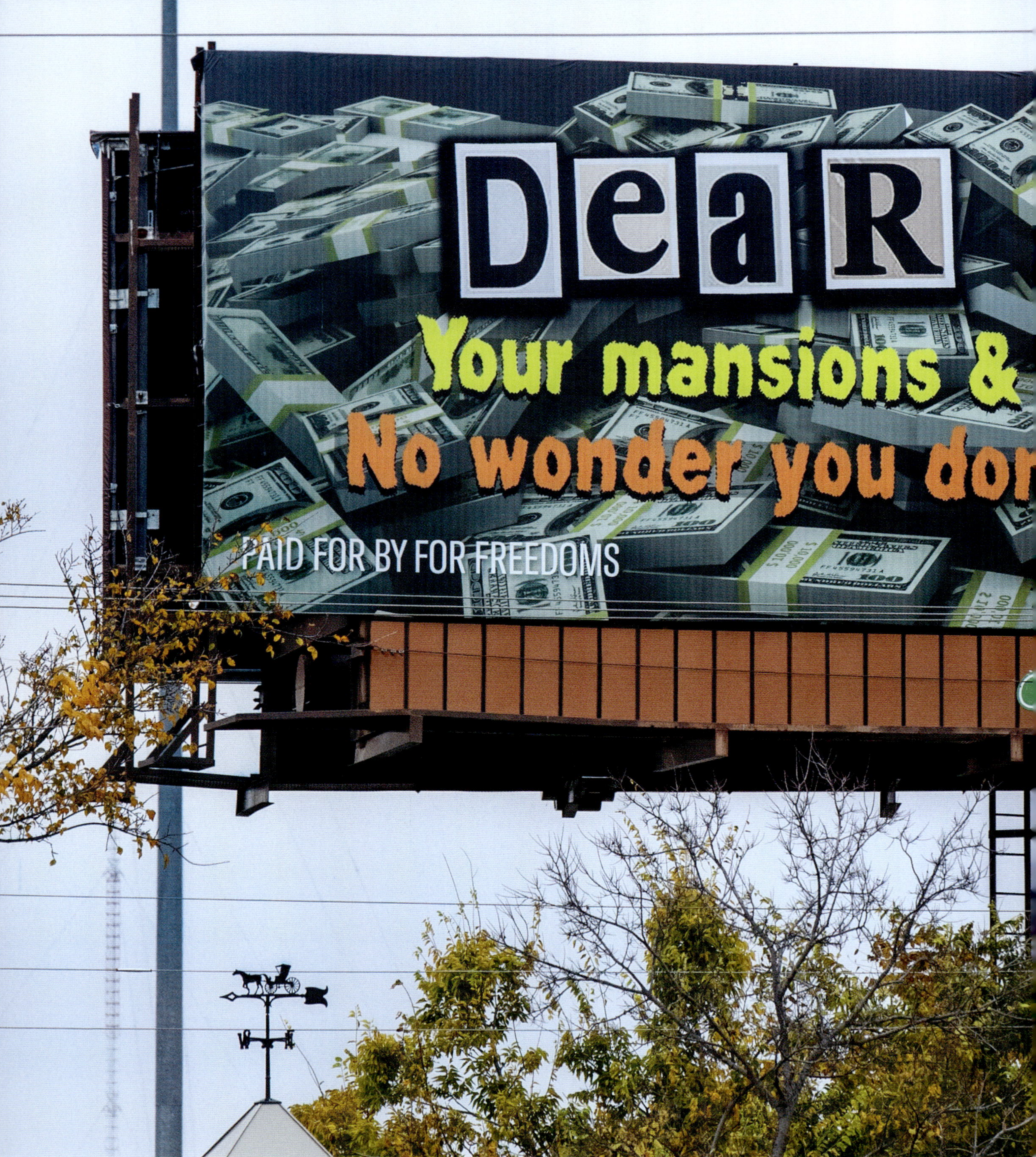

For Freedoms, an organization that uses art to provoke public
dialog, installed billboards all over the U.S. We sent a message
to bosses everywhere who perpetuate income inequality. It was
one of 50 billboards, one in each state.

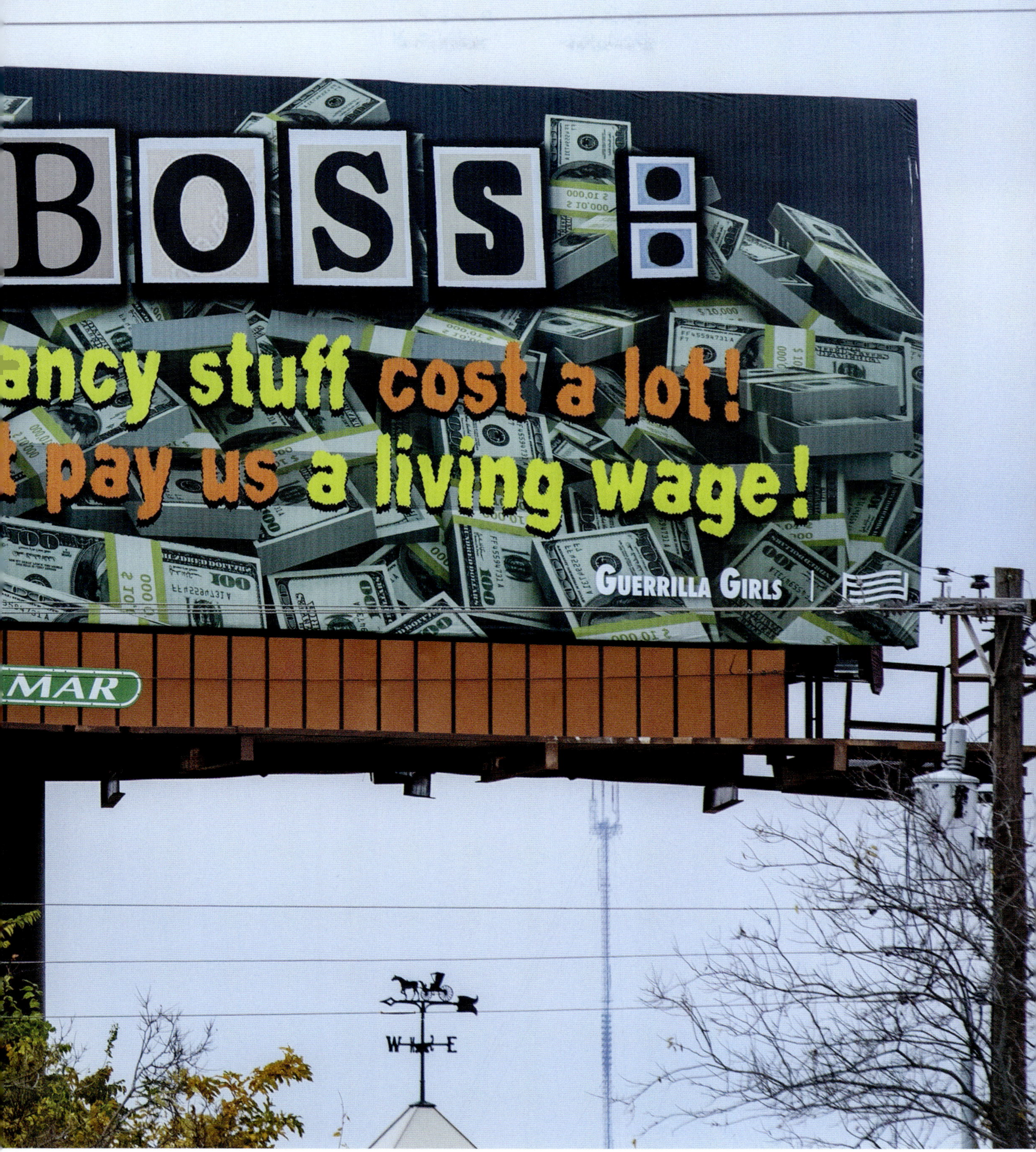

Billboard, Oklahoma City, 2018
(photo by David McNeese)

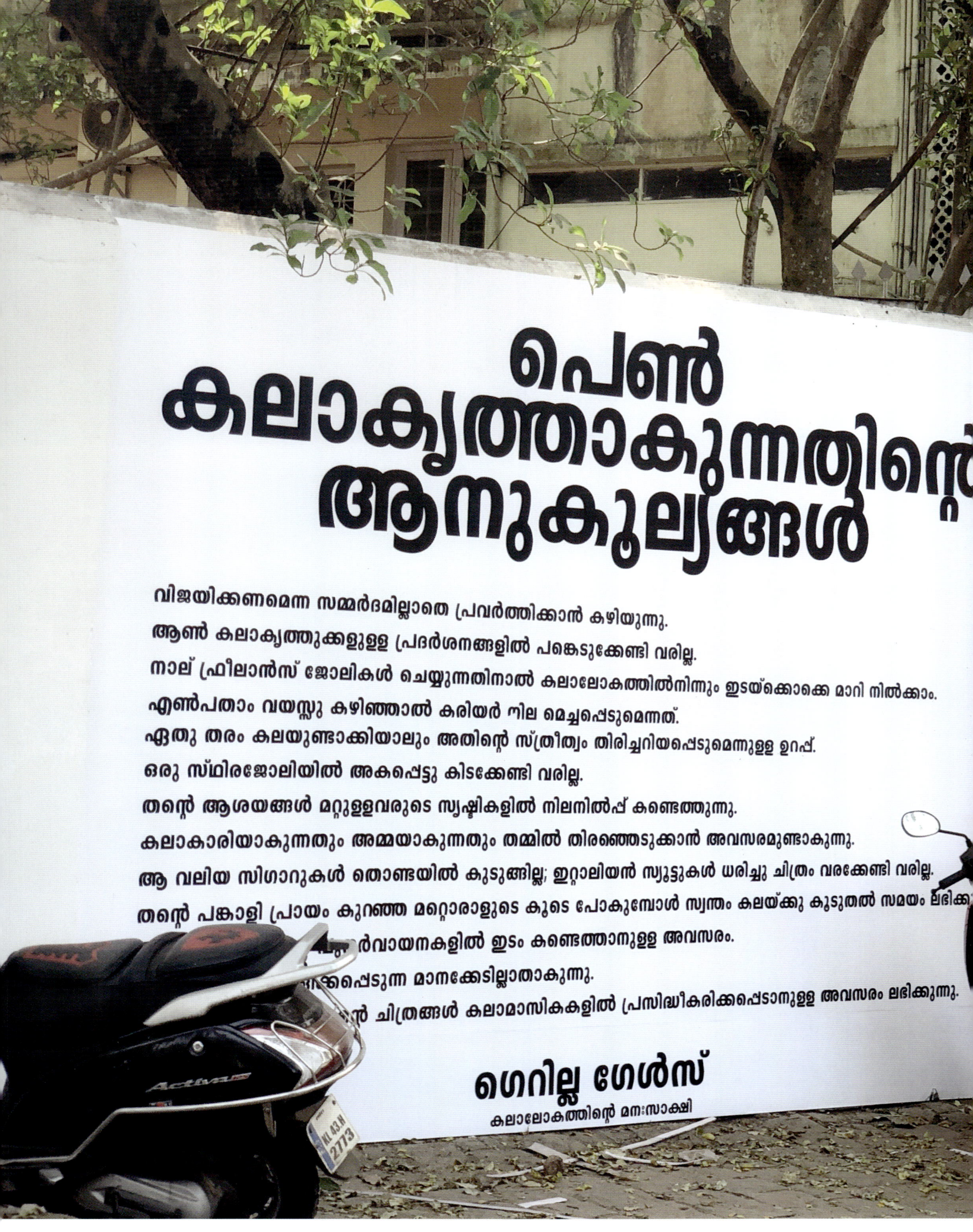
പെൺ
കലാകൃത്താകുന്നതിന്റെ
ആനുകൂല്യങ്ങൾ

വിജയിക്കണമെന്ന സമ്മർദമില്ലാതെ പ്രവർത്തിക്കാൻ കഴിയുന്നു.

ആൺ കലാകൃത്തുക്കളുളള പ്രദർശനങ്ങളിൽ പങ്കെടുക്കേണ്ടി വരില്ല.

നാല് ഫ്രീലാൻസ് ജോലികൾ ചെയ്യുന്നതിനാൽ കലാലോകത്തിൽനിന്നും ഇടയ്ക്കൊക്കെ മാറി നിൽക്കാം.

എൺപതാം വയസ്സു കഴിഞ്ഞാൽ കരിയർ നില മെച്ചപ്പെടുമെന്നത്.

ഏതു തരം കലയുണ്ടാക്കിയാലും അതിന്റെ സ്ത്രീത്വം തിരിച്ചറിയപ്പെടുമെന്നുള്ള ഉറപ്പ്.

ഒരു സ്ഥിരജോലിയിൽ അകപ്പെട്ടു കിടക്കേണ്ടി വരില്ല.

തന്റെ ആശയങ്ങൾ മറ്റുളളവരുടെ സൃഷ്ടികളിൽ നിലനിൽപ്പ് കണ്ടെത്തുന്നു.

കലാകാരിയാകുന്നതും അമ്മയാകുന്നതും തമ്മിൽ തിരഞ്ഞെടുക്കാൻ അവസരമുണ്ടാകുന്നു.

ആ വലിയ സിഗാറുകൾ തൊണ്ടയിൽ കുടുങ്ങില്ല; ഇറ്റാലിയൻ സ്യൂട്ടുകൾ ധരിച്ചു ചിത്രം വരക്കേണ്ടി വരില്ല.

തന്റെ പങ്കാളി പ്രായം കുറഞ്ഞ മറ്റൊരാളുടെ കൂടെ പോകുമ്പോൾ സ്വന്തം കലയ്ക്കു കൂടുതൽ സമയം ലഭിക്ക

ർവായനകളിൽ ഇടം കണ്ടെത്താനുള്ള അവസരം.

പ്പെടുന്ന മാനക്കേടില്ലാതാകുന്നു.

ൻ ചിത്രങ്ങൾ കലാമാസികകളിൽ പ്രസിദ്ധീകരിക്കപ്പെടാനുള്ള അവസരം ലഭിക്കുന്നു.

ഗെറില്ല ഗേൾസ്
കലാലോകത്തിന്റെ മനഃസാക്ഷി

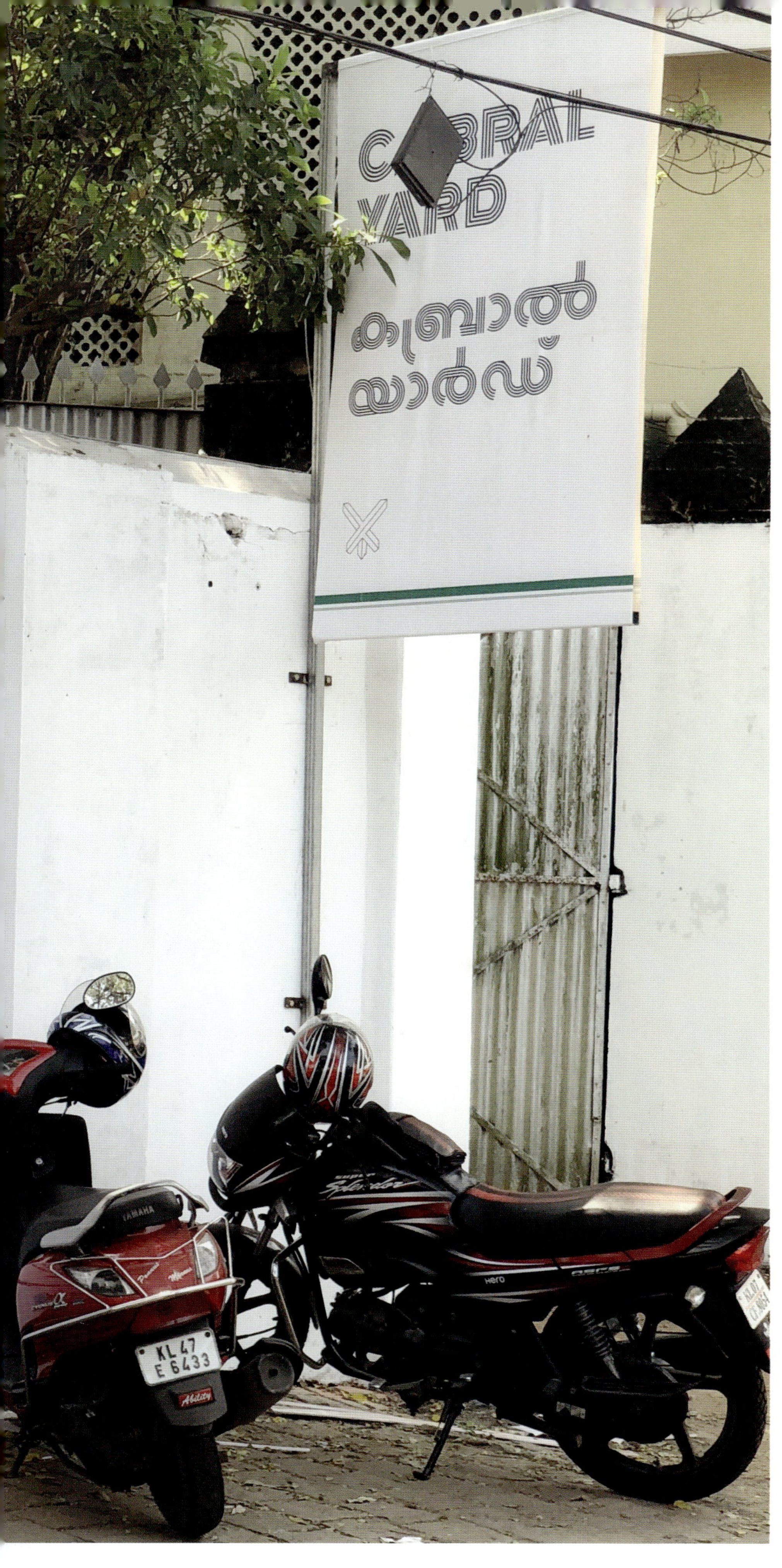

The Kochi-Muziris Biennale in India was majority Asian and South Asian artists and over 50% women. Our Advantages poster was translated into the local language, Malayalam. A huge crowd came to our gig, and a group of activists read their manifesto about sexual harassment within the Biennale organization. The #MeToo movement has taken off in India.

Installation view, 2018

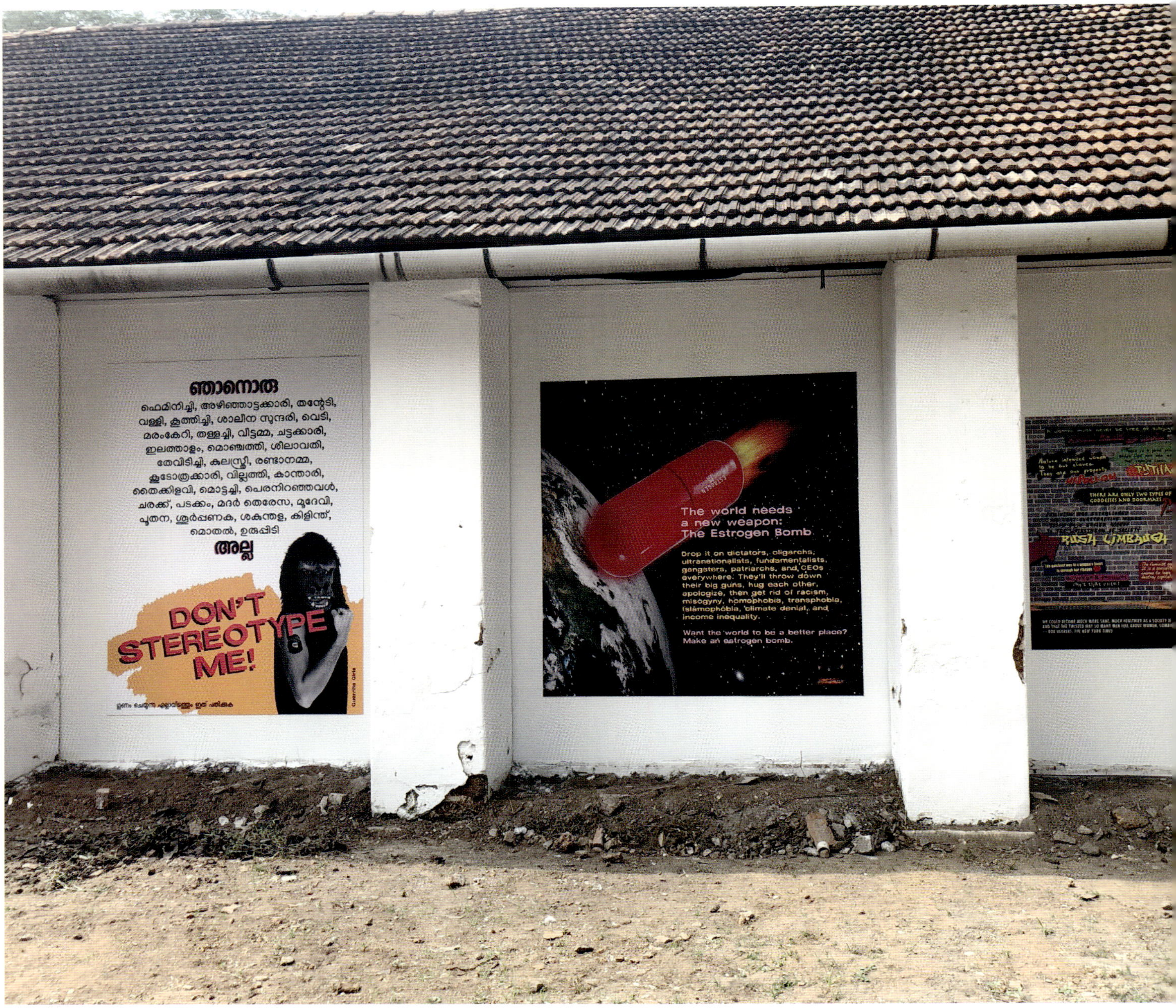

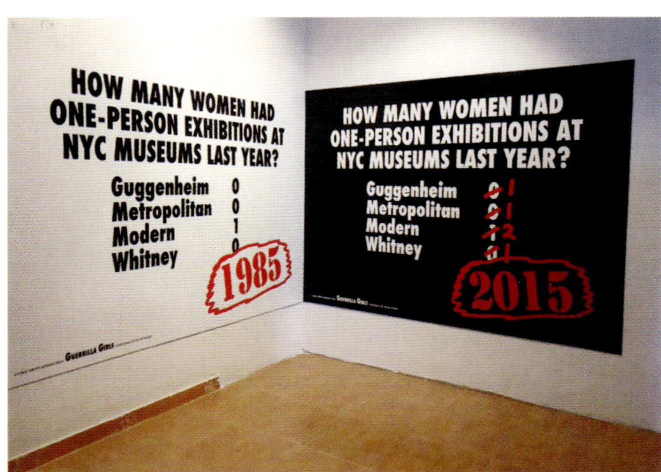
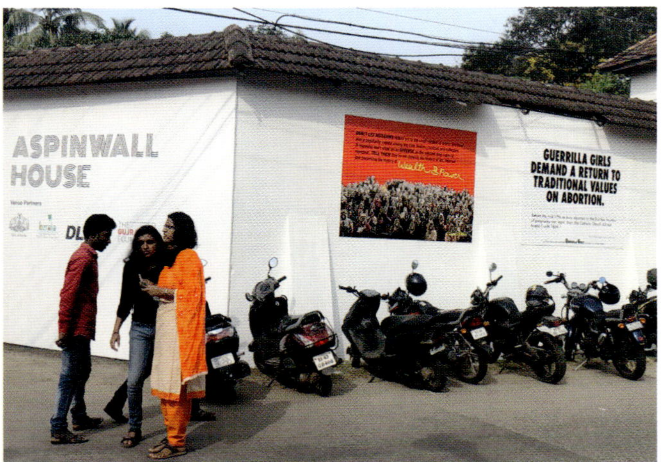

Installation views, Kochi, 2018

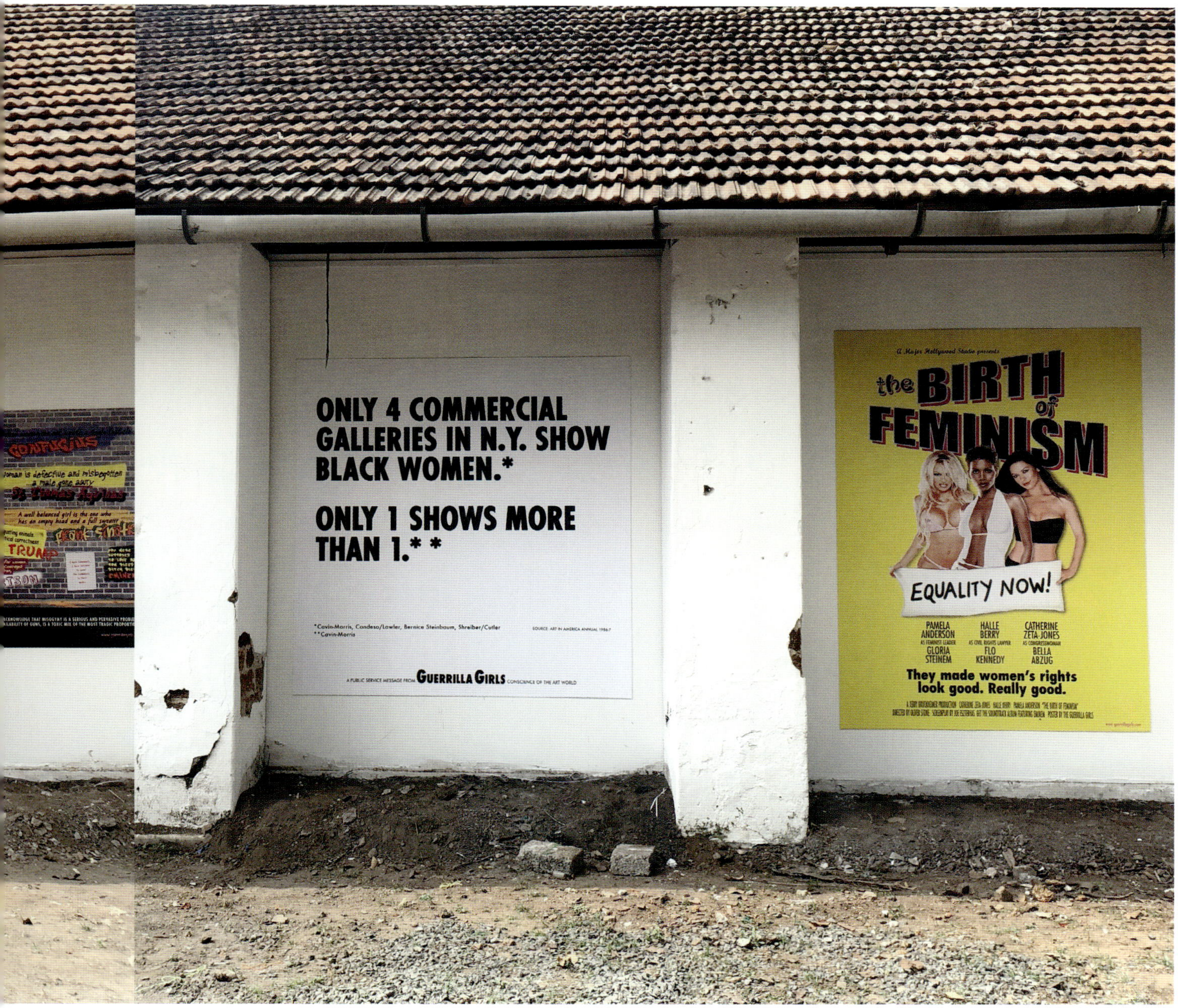

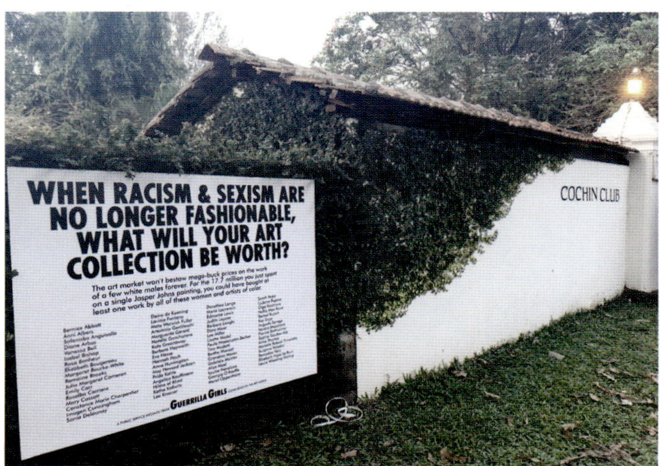
WHEN RACISM & SEXISM ARE
NO LONGER FASHIONABLE,
WHAT WILL YOUR ART
COLLECTION BE WORTH?
COCHIN CLUB
GUERRILLA GIRLS

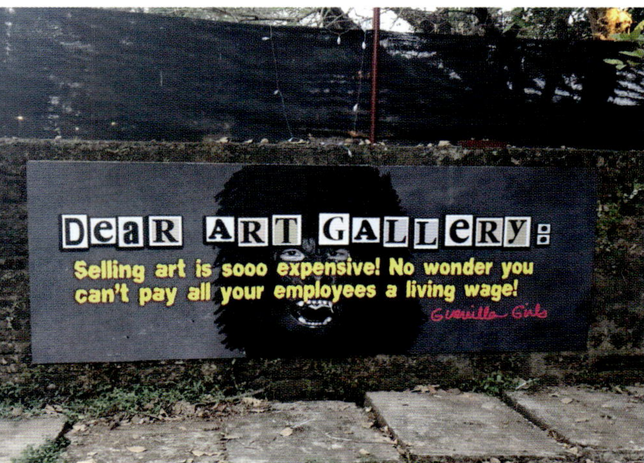
Dear ART GALLERY,
Selling art is sooo expensive! No wonder you
can't pay all your employees a living wage!
Guerrilla Girls

3 WAYS TO WI
WHEN THE AR

For museums afraid of alienating billionaire trustees and collectors who donated the artist's work

Chuck Close
American, born 1940 Monroe, Ohio

Portrait of President Bill Clinton, 1992
oil on canvas
National Portrait Gallery, Washington DC

Chuck Close is one of the most important artists of his generation, and the creator of a new kind of portraiture consisting of patterns of color.

A PUBLIC SERVICE MESSAGE FROM 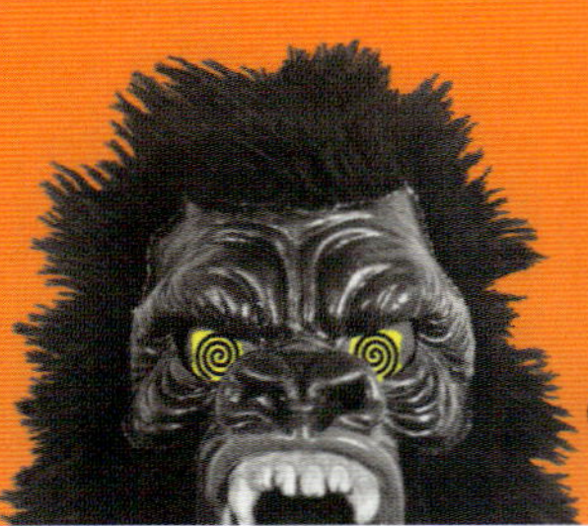 CONS

What should museums do about artists who behave badly? We decided to help them figure it out.

Poster, 2018

For museums conflicted about disclosing an artist's abuse next to his art

For museums who need help from the Guerrilla Girls

Chuck Close

American, born 1940 Monroe, Ohio

Portrait of President Bill Clinton, 1992
oil on canvas
National Portrait Gallery, Washington DC

Chuck Close is one of the most important artists of his generation, and the creator of a new kind of portraiture consisting of patterns of color. Like many artists, he has had a few disgruntled employees.

Chuck Close

American, born 1940 Monroe, Ohio

Portrait of President Bill Clinton, 1992
oil on canvas
National Portrait Gallery, Washington DC

Chuck Close has had a huge career with prices to match. He has been accused of sexually abusing models, and students he picked up at fancy art schools. How fitting and ironic that he painted the official portrait of Bill Clinton. The art world tolerates abuse because it believes art is above it all, and rules don't apply to "genius" white male artists. WRONG!

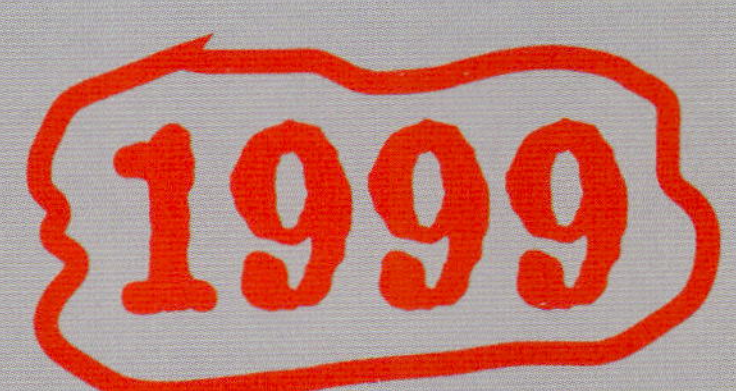

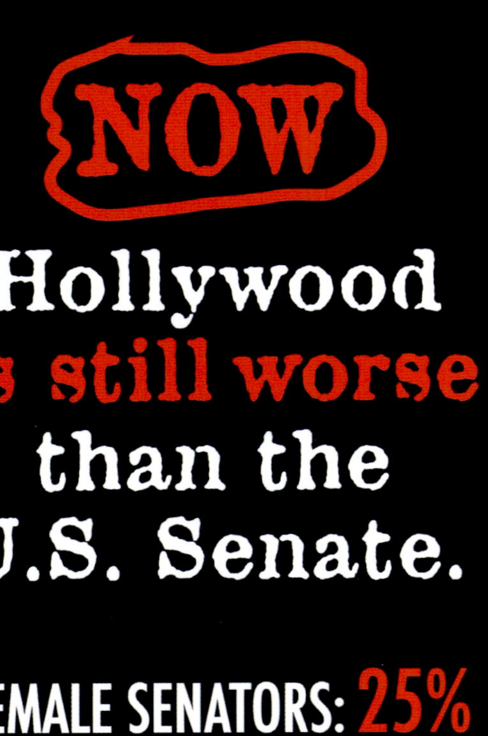

We've been confronting the film industry since 1999. Hollywood thinks it's liberal and progressive, but women still have a better chance of becoming a United States senator than a Hollywood film director.

Poster, 2019

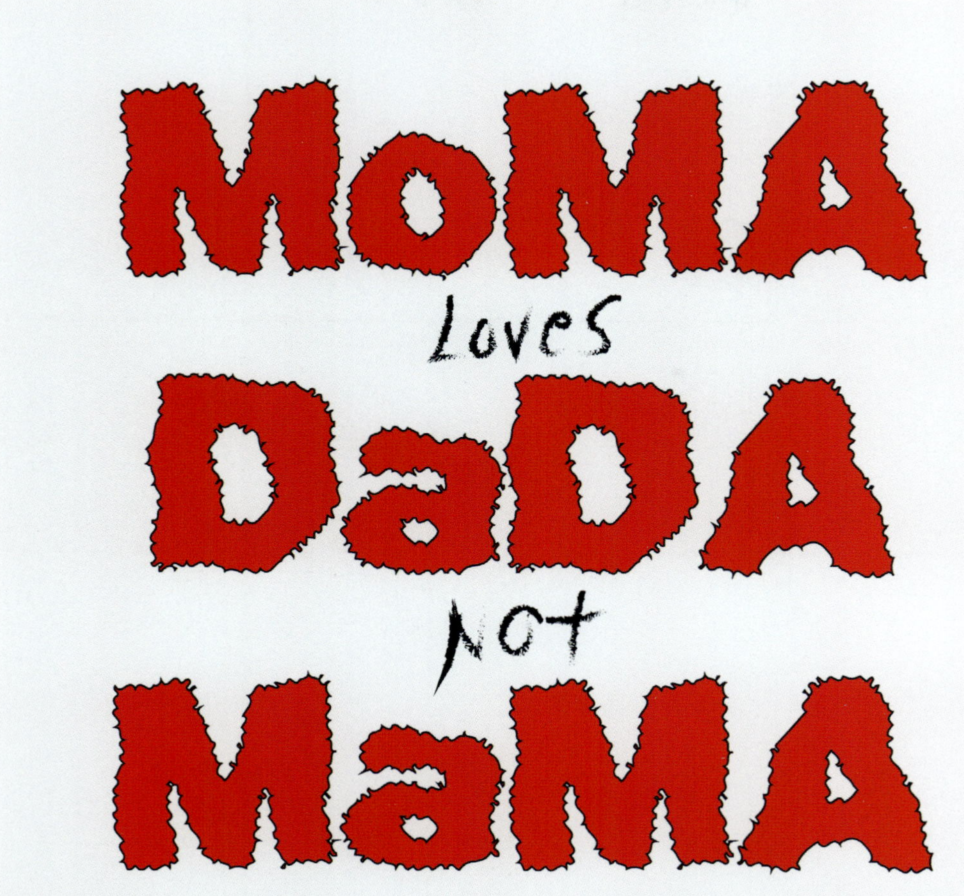

Discrimination against working mothers happens everywhere in the U.S., even at big-time museums.

Poster, 2019

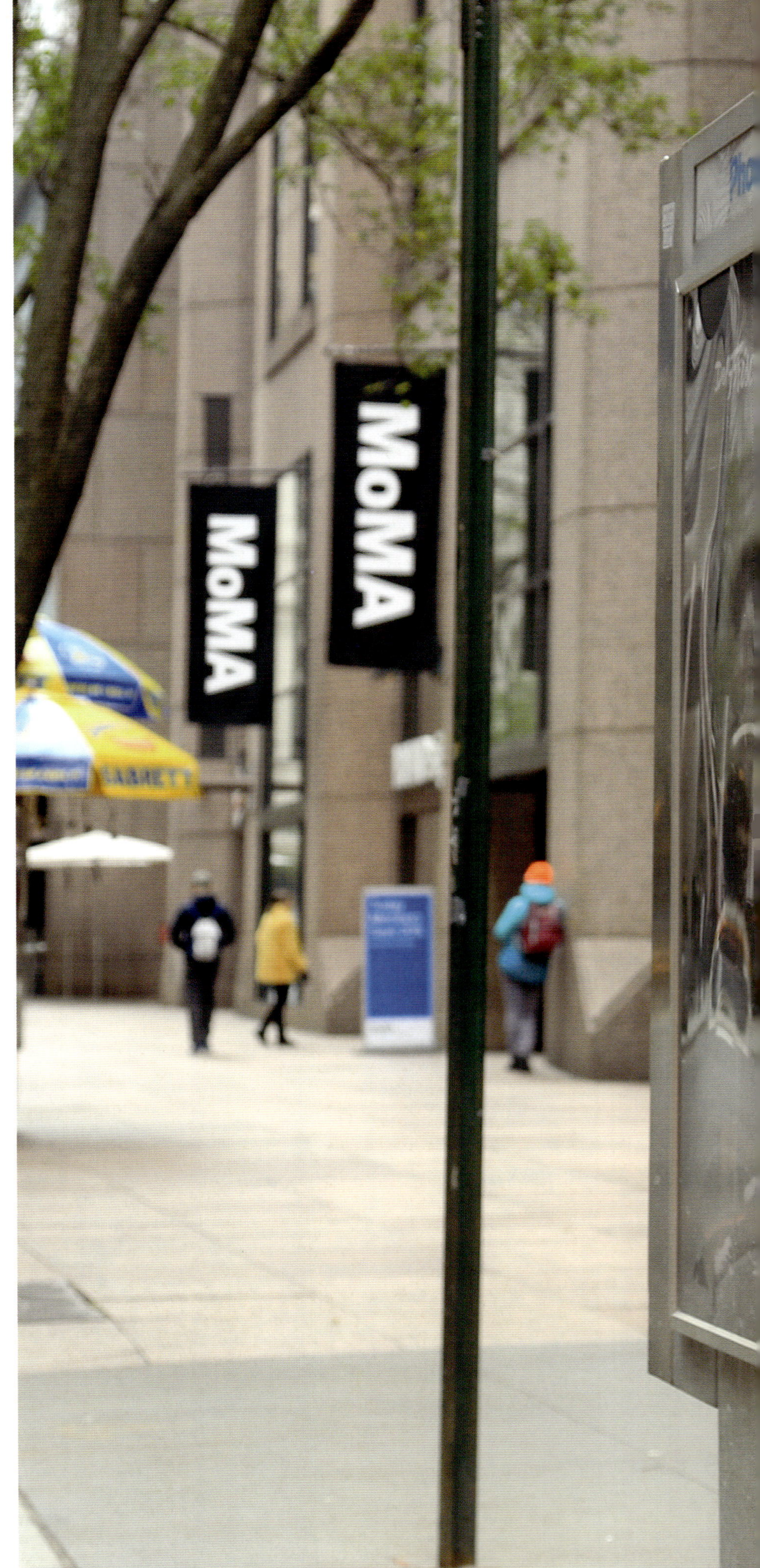

After a billion dollar renovation, the Museum of Modern Art reopened with a more diverse collection — and two new galleries named for close associates of pedophile Jeffrey Epstein: MoMA board chairman Leon Black and donor Glenn Dubin. We declared the galleries an insult to the public, especially to survivors of sexual assault. Our poster appeared on a phone booth in front of the museum.

Posters, 2019. Phone booth photo courtesy of Art in Ad Places, photo by Luna Park

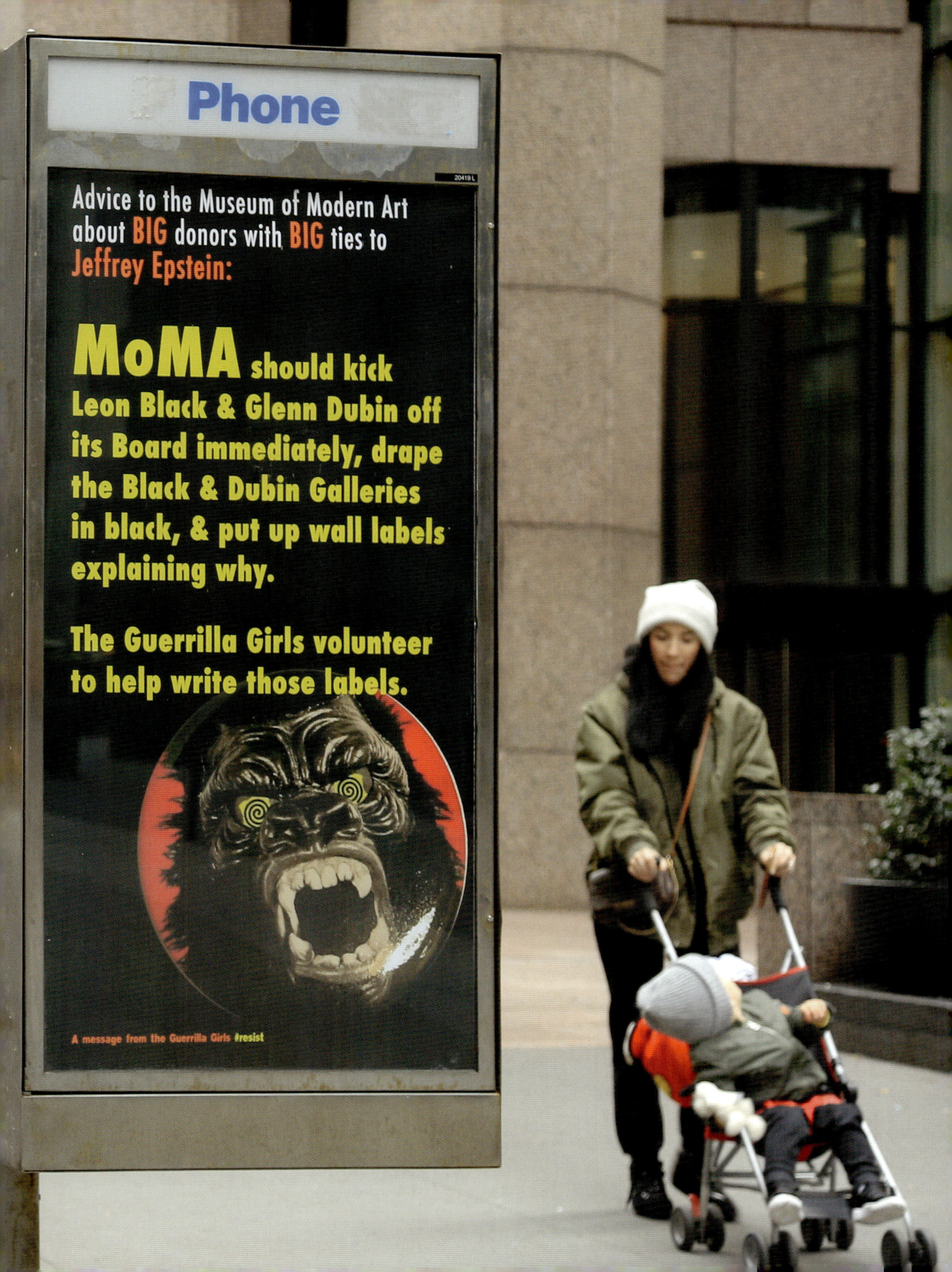

Phone
Advice to the Museum of Modern Art
about BIG donors with BIG ties to
Jeffrey Epstein:
MoMA should kick
Leon Black & Glenn Dubin off
its Board immediately, drape
the Black & Dubin Galleries
in black, & put up wall labels
explaining why.
The Guerrilla Girls volunteer
to help write those labels.
A message from the Guerrilla Girls #resist

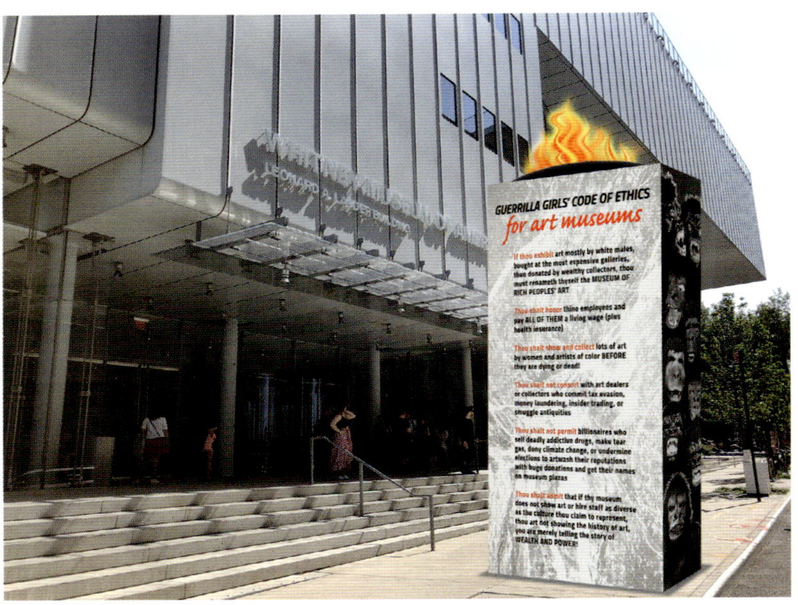

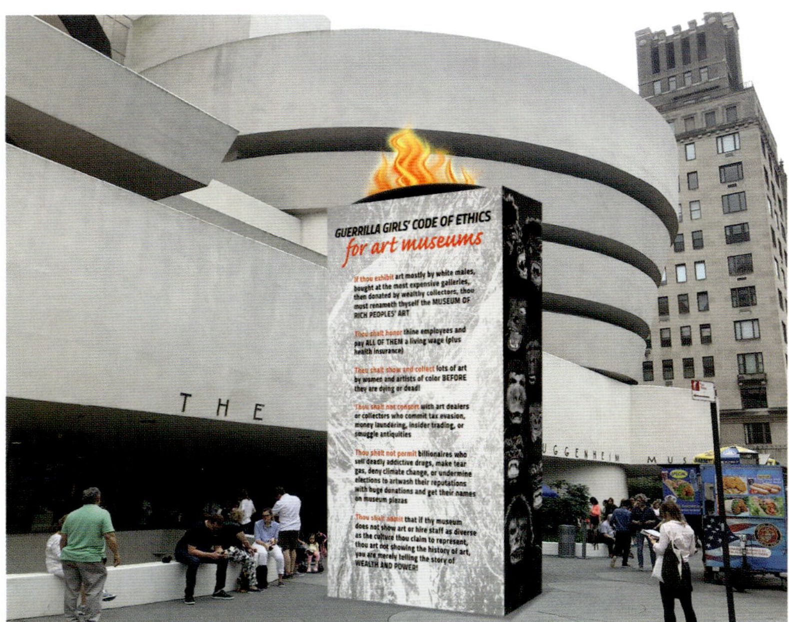

It's an outrage that museums in a wealthy country like the U.S. must rely on billionaires to exist. If that's the system we're stuck with, Guerrilla Girls believe museums have an ethical responsibility to accept money only from donors whose whose business and investments make the world a better place, not a worse one.

Our first *Code of Ethics* appeared in 1990 (page 34). Museums still have a long way to go. This monument belongs in front of every one of them.

Above, top to bottom: Posters showing *Code of Ethics* at the Whitney, Guggenheim, and MoMA; Facing page: poster for for the Highline, NY, showing Metropolitan Museum of Art

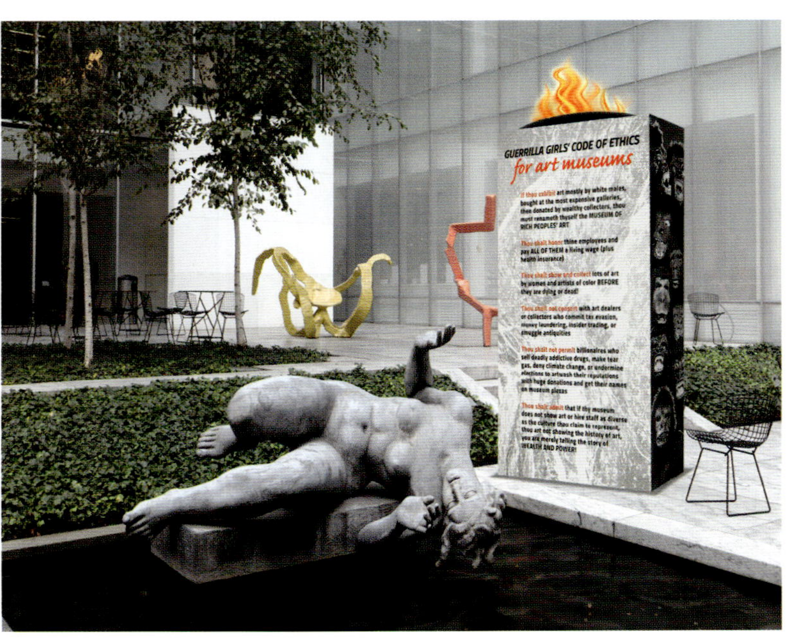

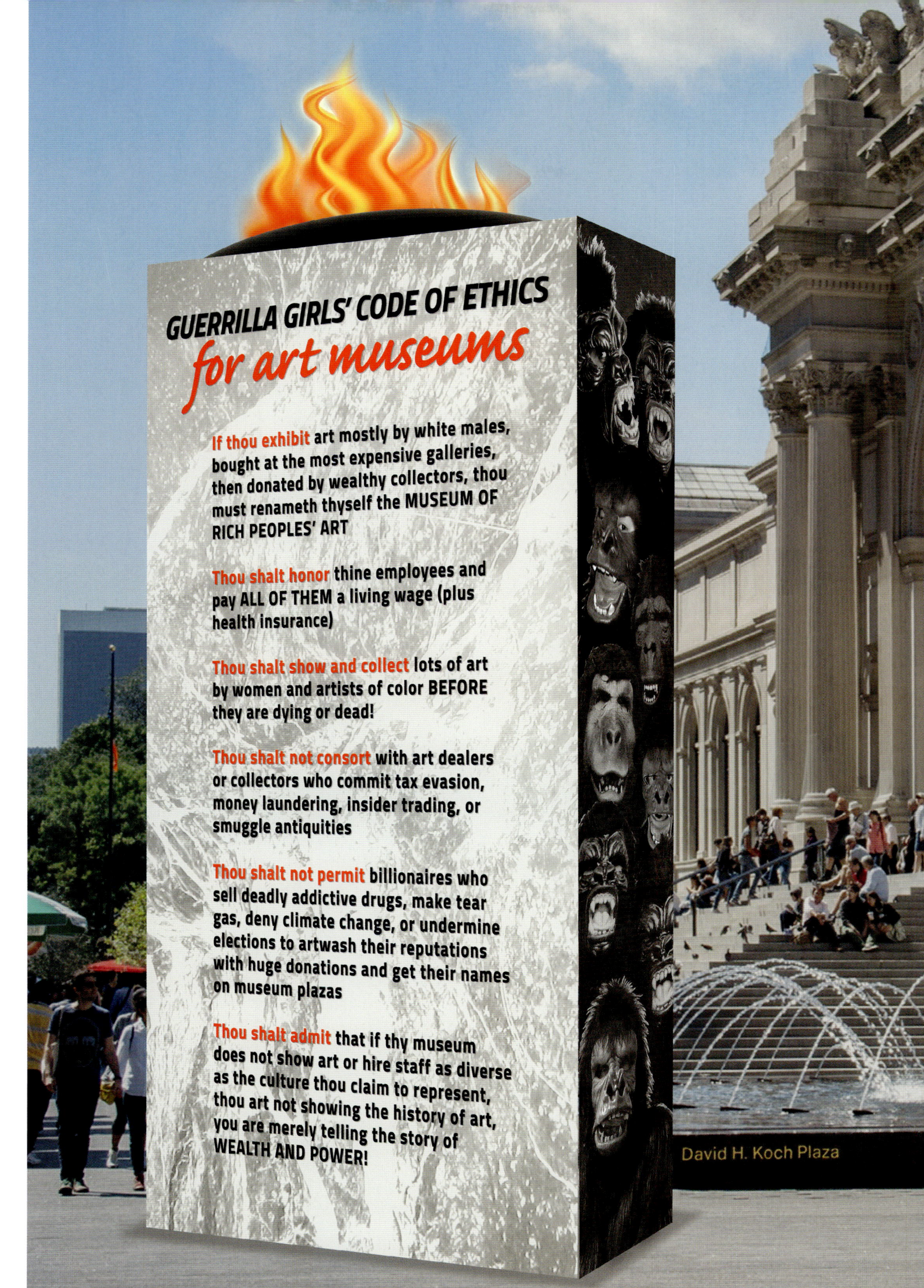

GUERRILLA GIRLS' CODE OF ETHICS
for art museums

If thou exhibit art mostly by white males, bought at the most expensive galleries, then donated by wealthy collectors, thou must renameth thyself the MUSEUM OF RICH PEOPLES' ART

Thou shalt honor thine employees and pay ALL OF THEM a living wage (plus health insurance)

Thou shalt show and collect lots of art by women and artists of color BEFORE they are dying or dead!

Thou shalt not consort with art dealers or collectors who commit tax evasion, money laundering, insider trading, or smuggle antiquities

Thou shalt not permit billionaires who sell deadly addictive drugs, make tear gas, deny climate change, or undermine elections to artwash their reputations with huge donations and get their names on museum plazas

Thou shalt admit that if thy museum does not show art or hire staff as diverse as the culture thou claim to represent, thou art not showing the history of art, you are merely telling the story of WEALTH AND POWER!

David H. Koch Plaza

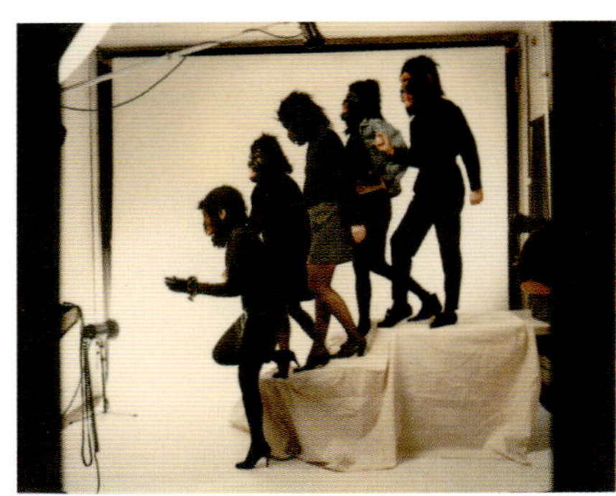
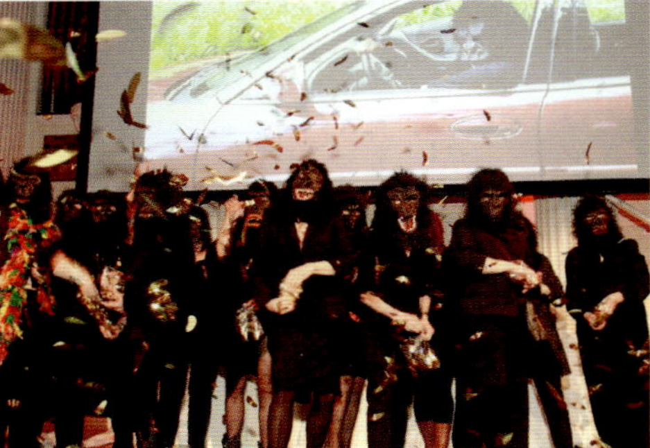
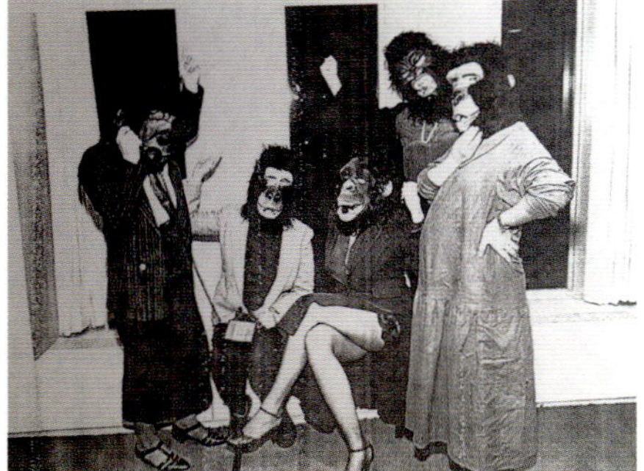
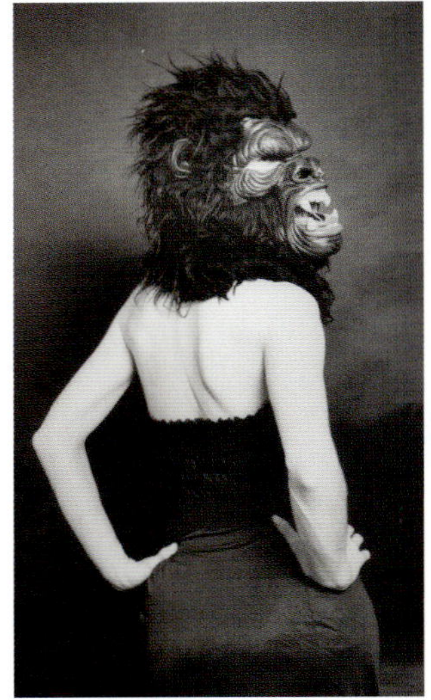
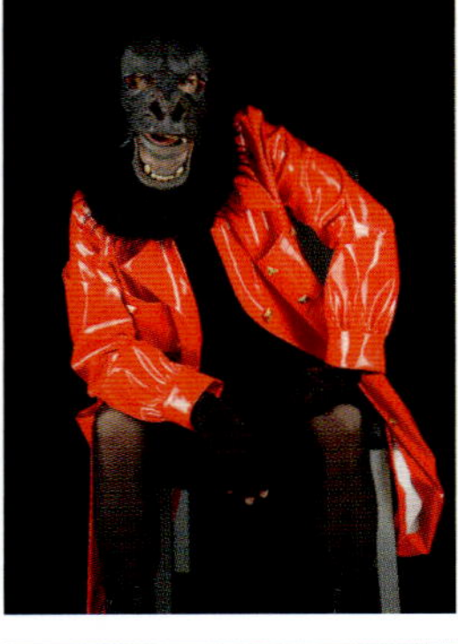
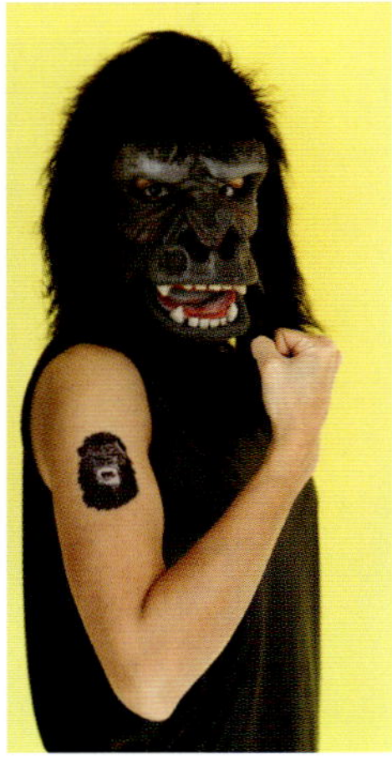
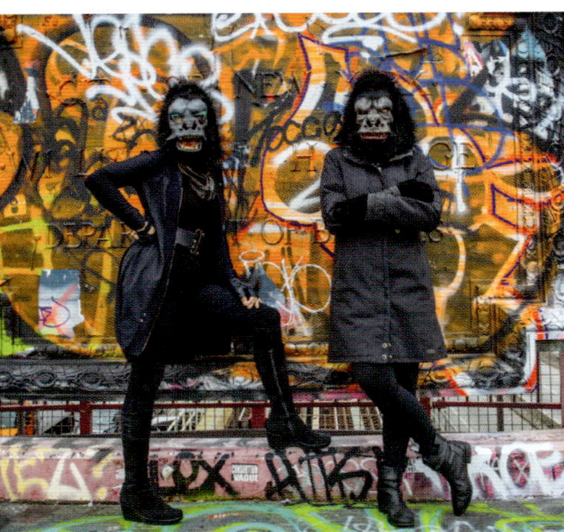
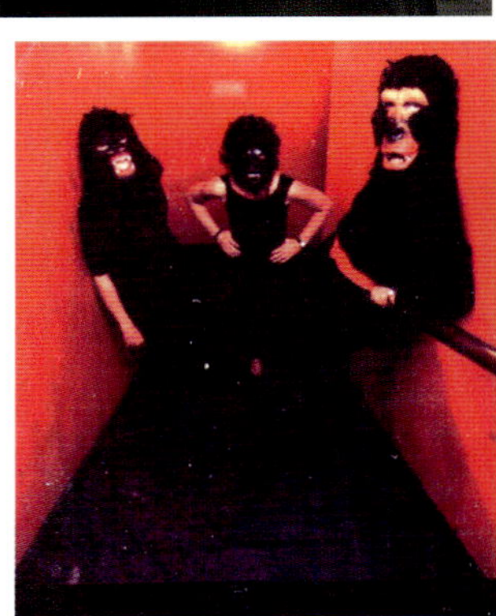
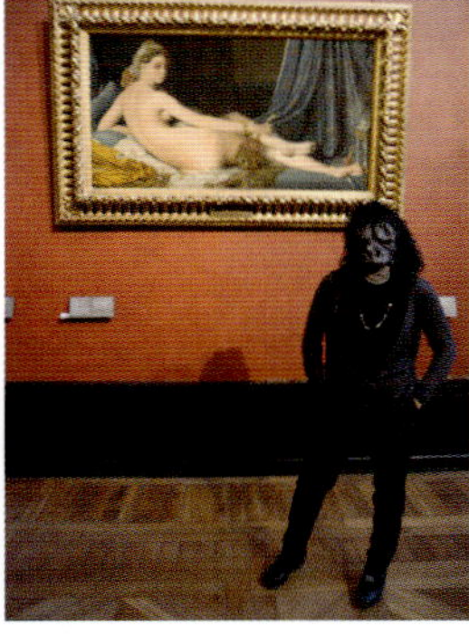
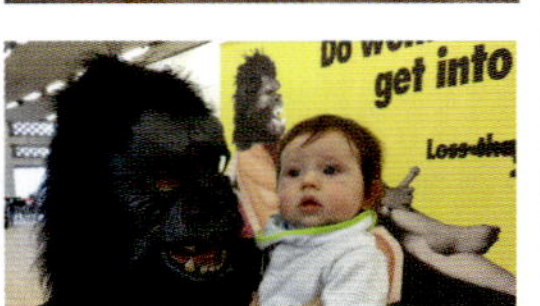

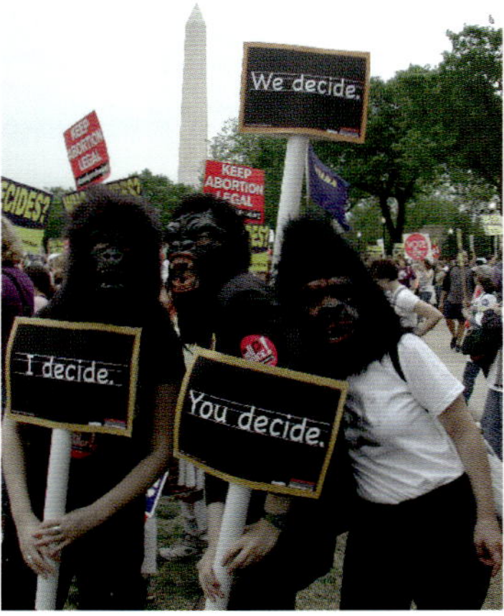
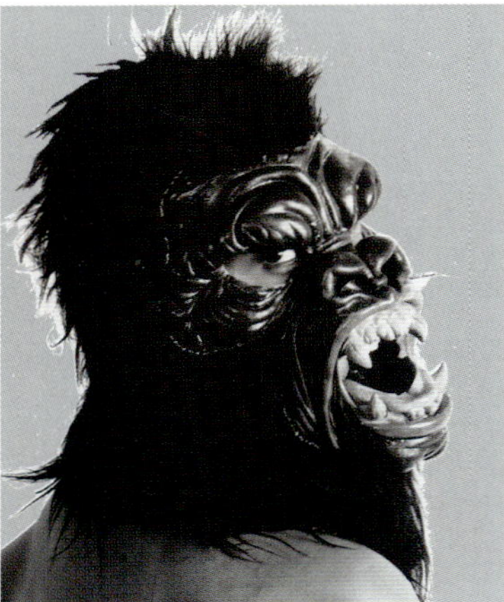

Photos this page by: top row center, Teri Slotkin; middle row starting with red coat, Lynn Hershman; Tattly; Katie Booth/Women in the World; bottom row right Richard Ross. Next page: top row left to right: *Esquire* magazine, Jason Schmidt, Jonathan Herman; middle row left and bottom row left and right, 22 Productions"

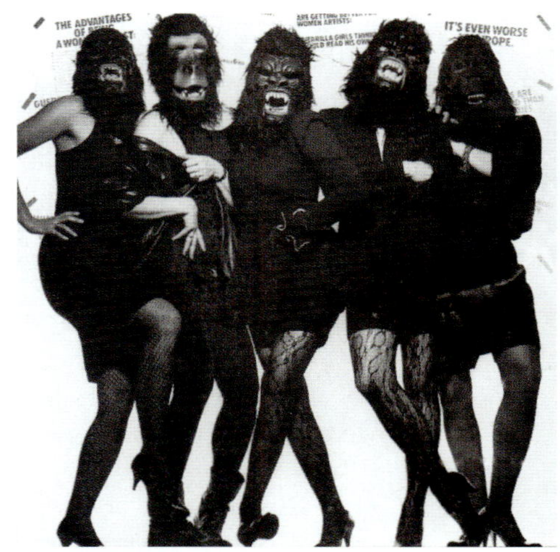
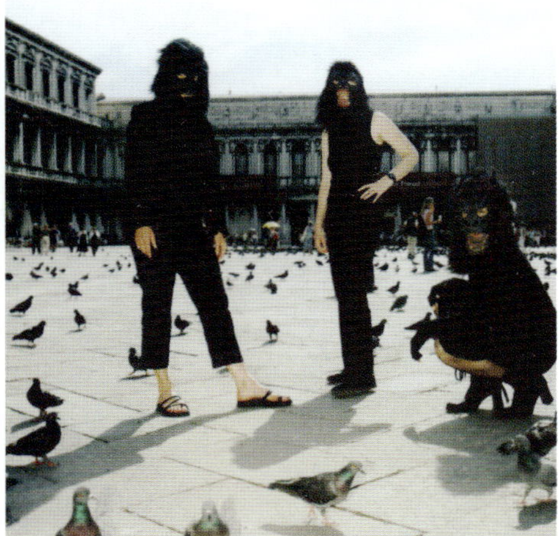
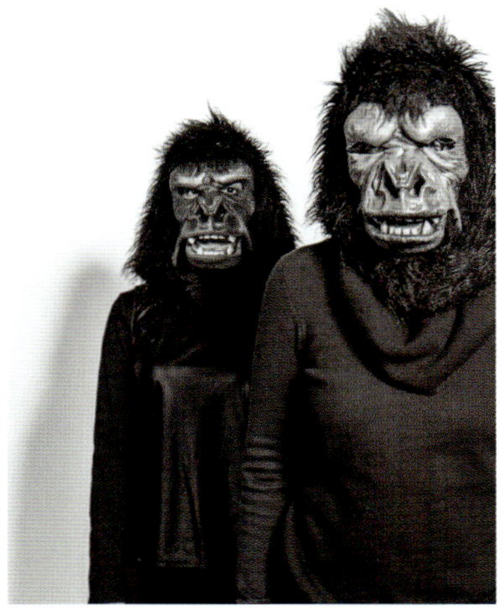
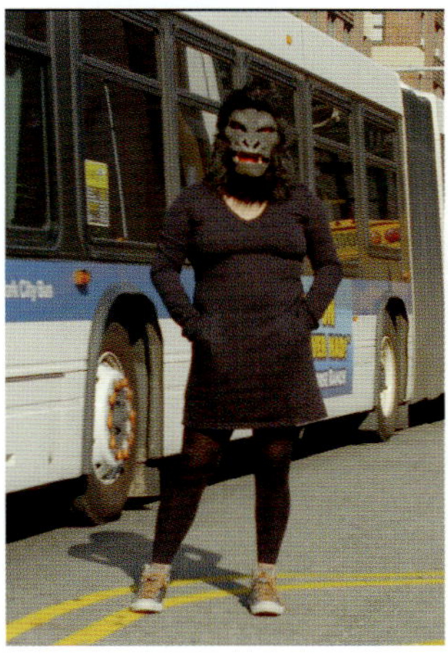
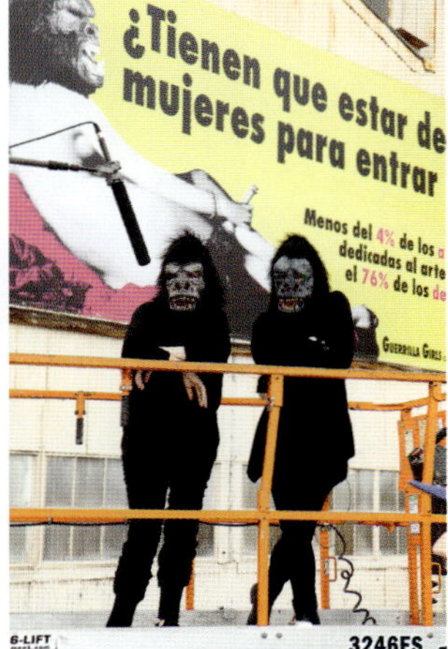
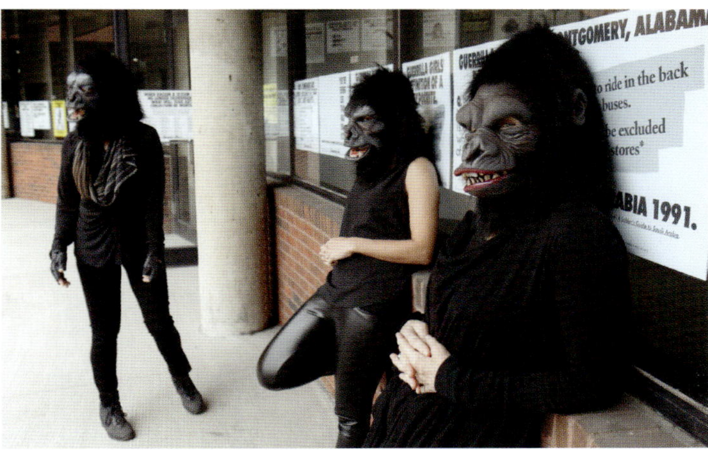
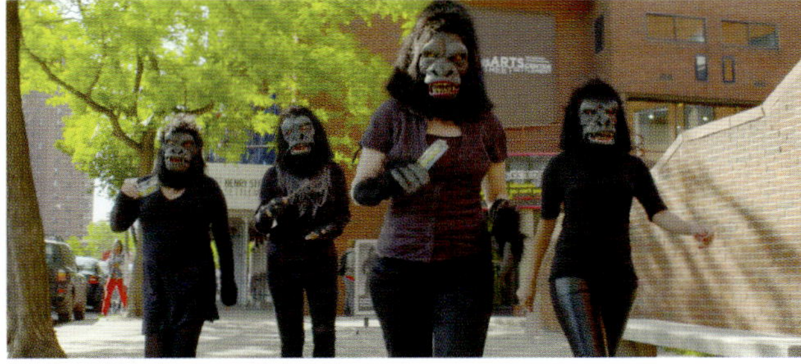
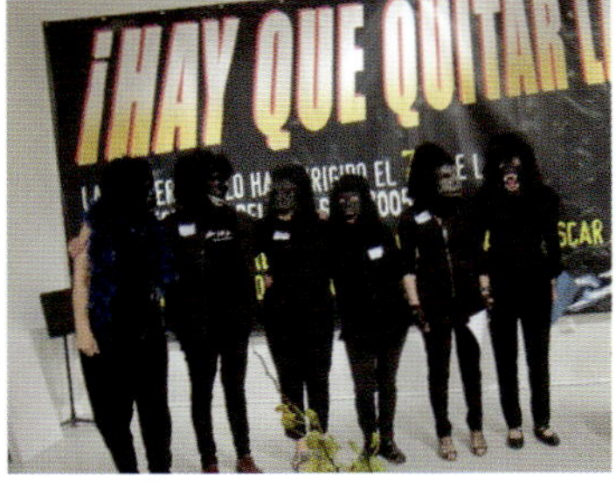
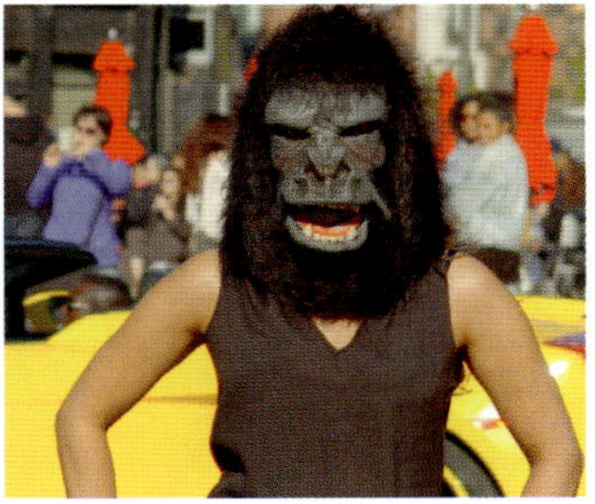

We're still anonymous and still committed to taking action. Our work together is complicated, exhilarating and something we just can't stop. We promise to continue making trouble in the artworld and beyond, and hope that you will too. Our motto: do one thing. If it works, do another. If it doesn't, do another anyway. Just keep chipping away.

Guerrilla Girls

LIST OF INCLUDED WORKS

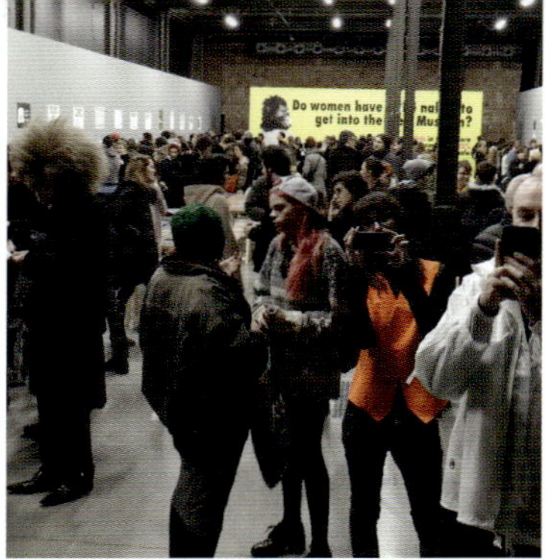

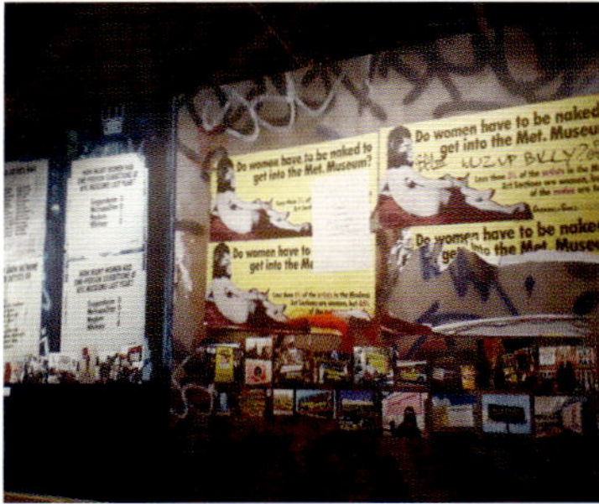

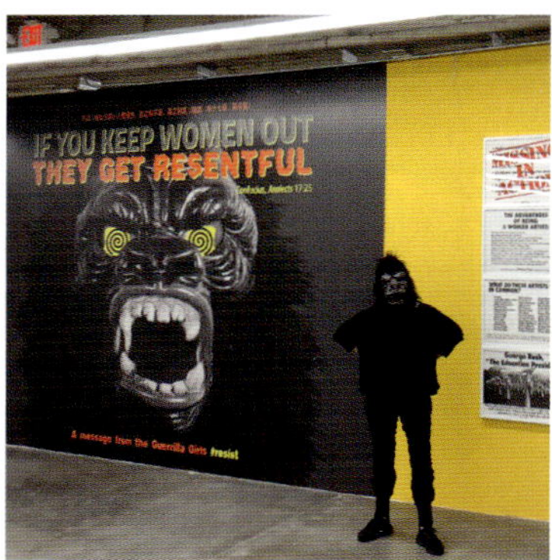

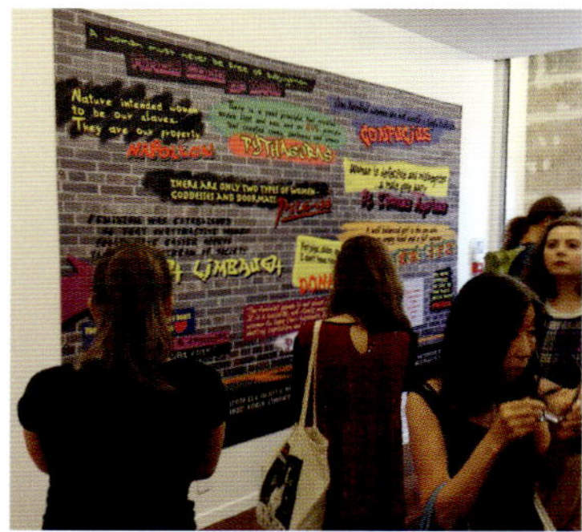

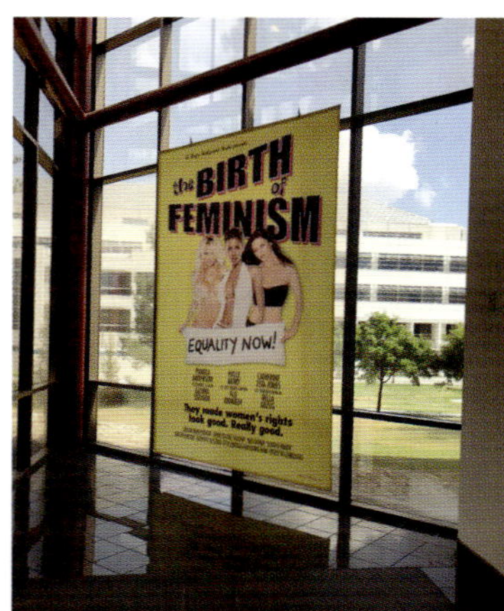

From top: Madrid, 2015; Helsinki, 2018; Beyond the Streets, Los Angeles, 2019; Paris, 2016; Fullerton, California, 2017

EXHIBITIONS

Exhibitions take our message to a global audience, and in return we gain a broader perspective. Plus, it's a thrill to criticize a museum or gallery right on its own walls.

•denotes solo show or Biennale

2020 (partial)

Wellin Museum of Art at Hamilton College, *SUM Artists*, Clinton, NY

•Utah Museum of Contemporary Art, *Guerrilla Girls*, Salt Lake City

Moss Arts Center, Virginia Tech Univ., *Fierce Women*, Richmond, VA

2019

Susan Inglett Gallery, *By / Buy Me*, New York

Dusseldorf Art Fair, Dusseldorf, Germany

MoMA PS1, *Theater of Operations: The Gulf Wars 1991-2011*, New York

Festival Les Créatives, Geneva

Bangalore International Center, Under the Raintree: Women's Cultural Festival, Bangalore, India

•Samek Art Gallery at Bucknell Univ., *The Art of Behaving Badly*, Lewisburg, PA

Museum Dr. Guislain, *Unhinged*, Ghent, Belgium

•Millbrook School, *The Art of Behaving Badly*, Millbrook, NY

Maverick Projects, *Art the Arms Fair 2019*, Peckham, England

Swedish National Museum, *1989 Culture and Politics*, Stockholm

The High Line, *New Monuments for New Cities*, New York

Chao Artcenter, *Ways of Seeing*, Beijing, China

OpenART Biennale, Örebro, Sweden

Stadtgalerie Saarbrücken, Strong Pieces—*Feminisms and Geographies*, Saarbrücken, Germany

Haus Ungarn, *FREEDOM TRANSMISSIONS: Interventions on the Protection and Promotion of Artistic Freedom*, Berlin

Heidelberger Kunstverein, *Act Up! Political Poster & Artistic Activism*, Heidelberg, Germany

Guts Gallery, London

Galeria Monumental, *Nasty Women Exhibition*, Lisbon

Bob Rauschenberg Gallery at Florida Southwestern State College, *Guerrilla Girls: A Public Service Message*, Fort Myers, Florida

•Auckland Art Gallery Toi o Tāmaki, Aukland, New Zealand

Beyond the Streets, Brooklyn, NY

The British Museum, *The World Exists to Be Put on a Postcard*, London

Gracie Mansion Mayoral Residence, *She Persists: A Century of Women Artists in New York*, 1919–2019, New York

Hirshhorn Museum, *Manifesto*, Washington, D.C.

Heist Gallery at the 58th Venice Biennale, *She Persists*, Venice

Arts Santa Mònica, Barcelona

Centro Andaluz de Arte Contemporáneo, *Us Girls*, *Again*, Seville, Spain

Protein Studios, *Man-Made Disaster: Patriarchy and the Planet*, London

Schinkel Pavillon, *Straying from the Line*, Berlin

•Västerås Konstmuseum, Västerås, Sweden

Backlit Gallery, *Familiar Machines*, Nottingham, England

Galleri Kit, *Sorry for the Inconvenience*, Trondheim, Norway

2018

•Kochi-Muziris Bienniale, Kochi, India

•Art Basel Hong Kong, Asia Art Archive, Hong Kong

•La Usina del Arte, Buenos Aires

•Bangkok Biennale, Bangkok, Thailand

•National Gallery of Victoria, Melbourne, Australia

41 Cooper Gallery at the Cooper Union, *We Dissent…Design of the Women's Movement in New York*, New York

•Mjellby Konstmuseum, *Guerrilla Girls*, Hamlstad, Sweden

•Cydonia Gallery, *Battle Cry*, Dallas

•Ringel Gallery, Purdue Univ., *Guerrilla Girls: The Art of Behaving Badly*, West Lafayette, IN

Brooklyn Museum, *Half the Picture: A Feminist Look at the Collection*, Brooklyn, NY

For Freedoms, *50 States, 50 Billboards*, Oklahoma City

Centrale for Contemporary Art, *Resistance*, Brussels

Fundacja Nośna, *Do It (Her)self*, Kracow, Poland

•Kestnergesellschaft, *Guerrilla Girls: The Art of Behaving Badly*, Hanover, Germany

•Amar Gallery, *Eve*, London

Pierogi Gallery, *Under Erasure*, New York

Cohen Gallery, Brown Univ., *On Protest, Art and Activism*, Providence, RI

Barcelona Museum of Contemporary Art, *A Shrt Century*, Barcelona

Design Museum, *Hope to Nope: Graphics and Politics 2008–18*, London

Faction Art Projects, *Visual Language*, New York

Subliminal Projects, *Visual Language*, Los Angeles

Shiva Gallery at John Jay College, *The Un-Heroic Act*, New York

Carnegie Museum, *Crossroads*, Pittsburgh

National Gallery of Art, *Sense of Humor*, Washington, D.C.

Queer Arts Festival, *DECADEnce*, Vancouver, BC

Serralves Museum of Contemporary Art, *Zéro de Conduite*, Porto, Portugal

RISD Museum, *The Phantom of Liberty*, Providence, RI

Beyond the Streets, Los Angeles

Military History Museum, *Targeted Interventions*, Dresden, Germany

Helsinki Art Museum, *Graffiti*, Helsinki

Coreana Museum of Art, *Hidden Workers*, Seoul, South Korea

Art Center College of Design, *Feminae: Typographic Voices of Women by Women*, Los Angeles

Hirshhorn Museum, *Brand New: Art and Commodity in the 1980s*, Washington, D.C.

•Muscarelle Museum of Art at College of William & Mary, *Guerrilla Girls: Conscience of the Artworld*, Williamsburg, VA

Fashion and Textile Museum, *T-Shirt: Cult—Culture—Subversion*, London

Paul Robeson Galleries, *Mirror Mirror*, Newark, NJ

2017

•Museo de Arte de São Paulo, *Guerrilla Girls: Gráfica, 1985–2017*, São Paulo, Brazil

•Van Gogh Museum, *One Is Not Enough!*, Amsterdam

•Frestas Trienal de Artes, *Guerrilla Girls: Departamento de Reclamações*, Sorocaba, Brazil

• Gaia Gallery, *Is It Even Worse in Europe?*, Istanbul

Whitney Museum, *An Incomplete History of Protest*, New York

Antiguo Colegio de San Ildefonso, *Three Centuries of American Prints*, Mexico City

Barnes Foundation, *Person of the Crowd: The Contemporary Art of Flânerie*, Philadelphia

Frac Normandie, *Scénario fantôme: Collection Frac Normandie*, Caen, France

CHEAP Festival, Bologna, Italy

Hofstra Univ. Museum, *Converging Voices: Gender and Identity*, Hempstead, NY

Museum of Reclaimed Urban Space, *Taking it to the Streets! The Art + Design of Posters + Flyers on the Lower East Side in the 80s + 90s*, New York

Dallas Museum of Art, *Visions of America: Three Centuries of Prints from the National Gallery of Art*, Dallas

Kunsthaus Zürich, *Action!*, Zürich

Centro Cultural Metropolitano, *Intimacy is Political: Sex, Gender, Language, Power*, Quito, Peru

Kunsthalle Bern and Kunsthaus Glarus, *Comedy of Being: Art and Humour from Antiquity until Today*, Switzerland

•Denison Museum, *The Art of Behaving Badly*, Granville, OH

2016

•Whitechapel Gallery, *Is it Still Worse in Europe?*, London

•Tate Modern, *Guerrilla Girls' Complaints Department*, London

Tate Modern, Permanent Collection Exhibition, London

•Galerie mfc-michèle didier, *Guerrilla Girls and La Barbe*, Paris

Harn Museum of Art, *Intra-Action: Women Artists from the Harn Collection*, Gainesville, FL

•The Baltimore Museum of Art, Guerrilla Girls, Baltimore

Museum of Fine Art, *Political Intent*, Boston

49 Nord 6 Est - FRAC Lorraine, *Guerrilla Girls: Not Ready to Make Nice, 30 Years and Still Counting*, Metz, France

Offenes Kulturhaus, *Skandal Normal?*, Linz, Austria

2015

Brooklyn Museum, *Agitprop!*, Brooklyn, NY

•Abrons Arts Center, *Guerrilla Girls: Not Ready To Make Nice: 30 Years and Still Counting*, New York

•Matadero Madrid, *Guerrilla Girls 1985–2015*, Madrid

•Pomona College Museum of Art, *Guerrilla Girls: Art in Action*, Claremont, CA

Rubin Museum, *When Artists Speak Truths*, New York

Center for Book Arts, *Archive Bound*, New York

Art Center Dos de Mayo of the Community of Madrid, *PUNK. Its Traces in Contemporary Art*. Traveled 2015–17, Madrid

Nathan Cummings Foundation Center, *Public Art, Intervention and Performance in Lower Manhattan from 1978–1993*, New York

Mills College Art Museum, *Public Works: Artists' Interventions 1970s - Now*, Oakland, CA

Westbeth Gallery, *Triacontagon: A Celebration of 30 Years of the Artists' Fellowship Program*, New York

Station 16 Gallery, *Woman x Women*, Montreal

In the City, Street exhibition, Bremen, Germany

Lower Manhattan Cultural Council, *Public Art, Intervention & Performance in Lower Manhattan from 1978–1993*, New York

Cooper Hewitt Museum, *How Posters Work*, New York

2014

•The Univ. of Paris VIII, *Guerrilla Girls*, Saint-Denis, France

Asian Youth in Action/CAAAV, *Asian Youth in Art Exhibit*, New York

Victoria and Albert Museum, *Disobedient Objects*, London

Kleine Humboldt Galerie at Humboldt Universität zu Berlin, *Female Intervention*, Berlin

Galerie Perrotin, *G I R L –curated by Pharrell Williams*, Paris

20 Jay Street, *Whitney Houston Biennial: I'm Every Woman*, Brooklyn, NY

La Panacée Centre de Culture Contemporaine Montpellier, *Infinite Jest*, France

Begovich Gallery at California State Univ., *Seeing the Invisible: Life on the Street*, Fullerton, CA

Bremen Archive, *Archive slivers: women, men, power*, Bremen, Germany

DOX Centre for Contemporary Art, *The Medium and the Message: The Poster in the Clash of Ideologies 1914–2014*, Prague

Maison du livre, de l'image et du son, Villeurbanne, France

2013

•Alhóndiga Bilbao, *Guerrilla Girls 1985–2013*, Bilbao, Spain

Tate Liverpool, *Art Turning Left: How Values Changed Making 1789–2013*, Liverpool, England

•Southbank Centre, *Yoko Ono's Meltdown*, London

Museo Reina Sofía, *Minimal Resistance. Between Late Modernism and Globalization: Artistic Practices during the 80s and 90s,*, Madrid

•GDM Tokyo Gallery at Palais de Tokyo, *Guerrilla Girls*, Paris

•Göteborgs Konsthall, *Göteborg International Biennial*, Sweden

Centro Cultural Banco do Brasil, *Elles: Women Artists from the Centre Pompidou*, Rio de Janeiro

Worker and Collective Farm Girl, *Feminism: from avant-garde to the present day*, Moscow

Maison de la Catalanité, *Qui Aurait Pu Imaginer Une Chose Pareille?* Perpignan, France

Paula Modersohn-Becker Museum, *Merciless - Female artists and the funny*, Bremen, Germany; Städtische Museen Heilbronn-Kunsthalle Vogelmann, Heilbronn, Germany

Hessel Museum of Art, *Object Permanence*, Bard College, New York

Margaret Lawrence Gallery Univ. of Melbourne, *Backflip: Feminism and Humour in Contemporary Art*, Melbourne, Australia

Clifford Chance LLP, *Art/Activism: Annual Pride Art Exhibition*, New York

•Peter Fingesten Gallery at Pace Univ., *Guerrilla Girls 1985–2000*, New York

Freedman Gallery at Albright College, *Canceled: Alternative Manifestations & Productive Failures*, Reading, PA

2012

Museum of Contemporary Art Chicago, *This Will Have Been: Art, Love & Politics in the 1980's*, Chicago. Traveled to the Institute of Contemporary Art, Boston; Walker Art Center, Minneapolis

Kulturhuset, *SUPERMARKET 2012 - Stockholm Independent Art Fair*, Stockholm

•Glass Curtain and A+D Galleries, Columbia College of Chicago, *Guerrilla Girls : Not Ready to Make Nice*. Traveled 2012–2018 to Montserrat College of Art, Beverly, MA; Moore College, Philadelphia; Robert and Frances Fullerton Museum of Art at California State Univ., San Bernardino; Verge Center for the Arts, Sacramento, CA; Zuccaire Gallery, SUNY Stony Brook, NY; The Richard E. Peeler Art Center at DePauw Univ., Greencastle, IN; Georgia Museum of Art at Univ. of Georgia, Athens; Thomas J. Walsh Art Gallery at Fairfield Univ., CT; Krannert Art Museum at Univ. of Illinois Urbana-Champaign

Museo Reina Sofia, *Indomitable Women, a (his)tory of Women in Audiovisual Art (1944–2009)*, Madrid

The Center for Book Arts, *Canceled: Alternative Manifestations and Productive Failures*, New York

The Greenhouse Innovation Hub, Honolulu

Art Boom Festival, *I'm Not A Feminist, But If I Was, This Is What I Would Complain About... Interactive Street Project*, Krakow, Poland

The Univ. Library Art Gallery Sonoma State Univ., *Agents of Change: Artists As Activists*, Rohnert Park, CA

• *Guerrilla Girls Billboard Truck Project*, Boston

National Gallery of Art, *Shock of the News*, Washington, D.C.

•Marriage Equality Billboard Project, Minneapolis

Seattle Museum of Art, *Elles: Women Artists from the Centre Pompidou*, Seattle

Museum Dr. Guislain, *Nervous Women*, Ghent, Belgium

Contemporary Wing, *Of the People*, Washington, D.C.

2011

Museum of Modern Art, *Contemporary Art from the Collection*, New York

Centre Pompidou, *elles@centrepompidou*, Paris

Alsdorf Gallery and Mary & Leigh Block Museum of Art at Northwestern Univ., *The Satirical Edge in Contemporary Prints and Graphics*, Evanston, IL

Meyers Place Art Space, Melbourne, Australia

•Mason Gross School of the Arts Galleries at Rutgers Univ., *Feminist Masked Avengers*, New Brunswick, NJ

•National Museum of Women in the Arts, *The Guerrilla Girls Talk Back*, Washington, D.C.

Künstlerhaus Vienna, *Beziehungsarbeit: Kunst und Institution*, Vienna

Nasher Museum of Art at Duke Univ., *The Deconstructive Impulse: Women Artists Reconfigure the Signs of Power, 1973–1991*, Durham, NC. Traveled to Neuberger Museum of Art, New York

Burnaby Art Gallery, *One Vision/Multiple Hands*, Burnaby, BC

White Space, *Ready-To-Print*, Zurich

Teatro Teresa Careeño, *El Encuentro Mundial de Arte Corporal*, Caracas, Venezuela

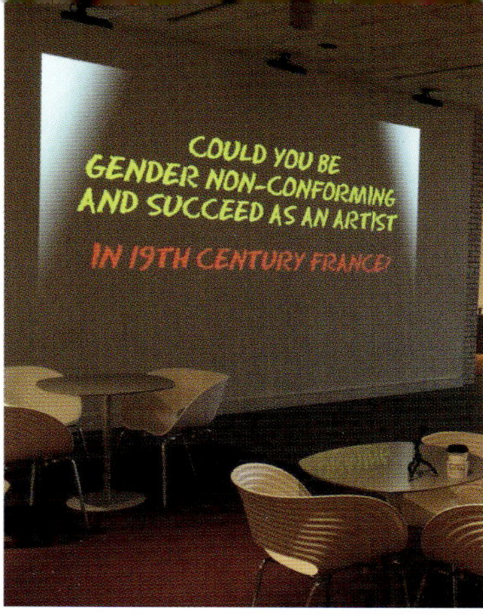

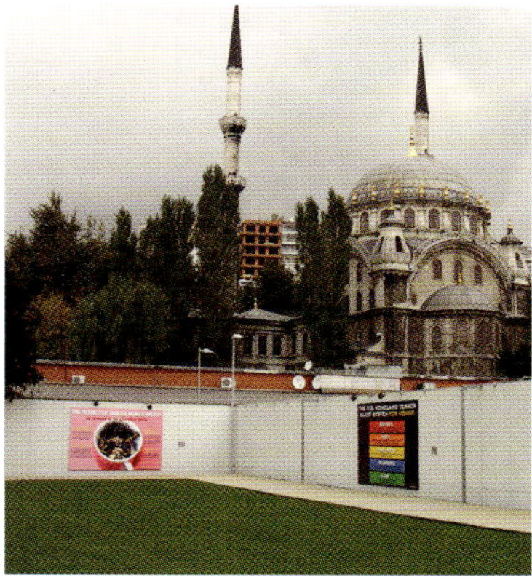

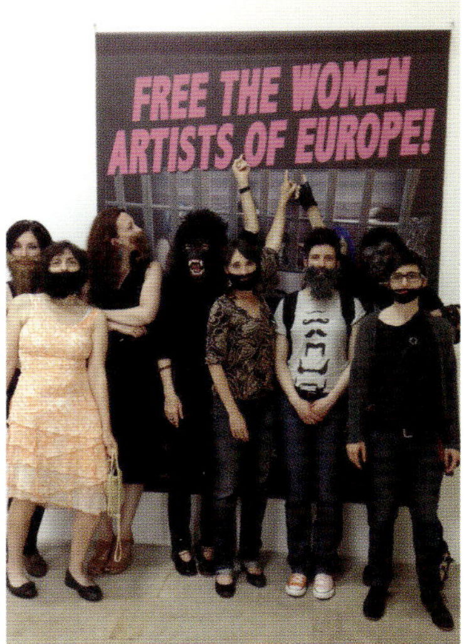

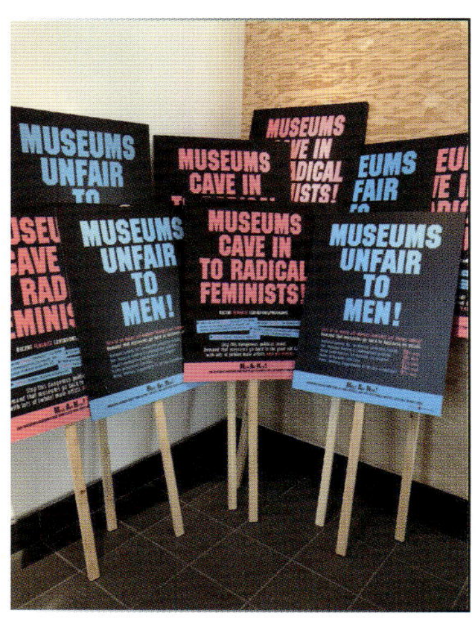

From top: Minneapolis, 2016; Istanbul, 2006; Paris, 2016; Chicago, 2012

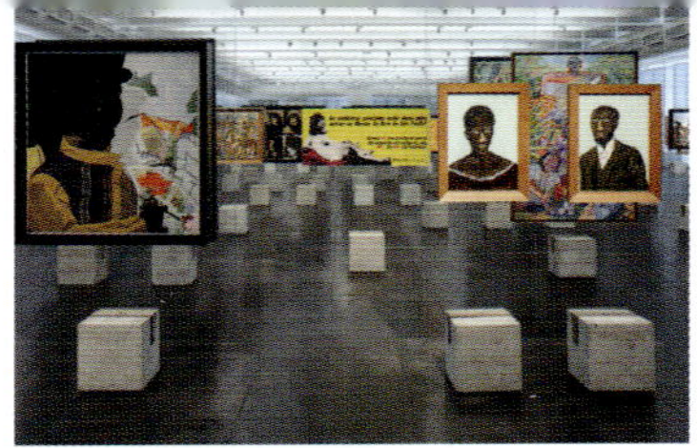

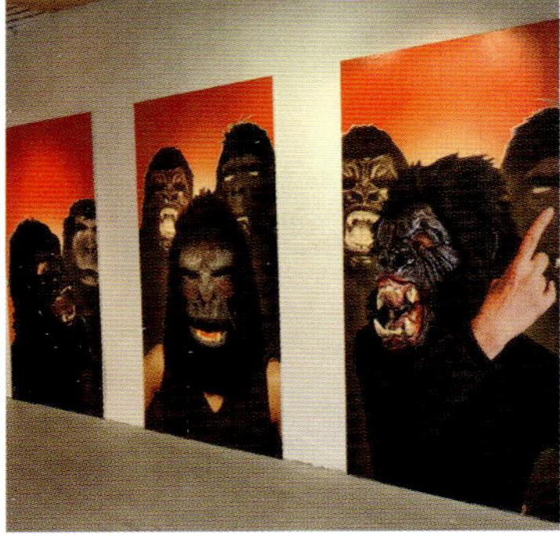

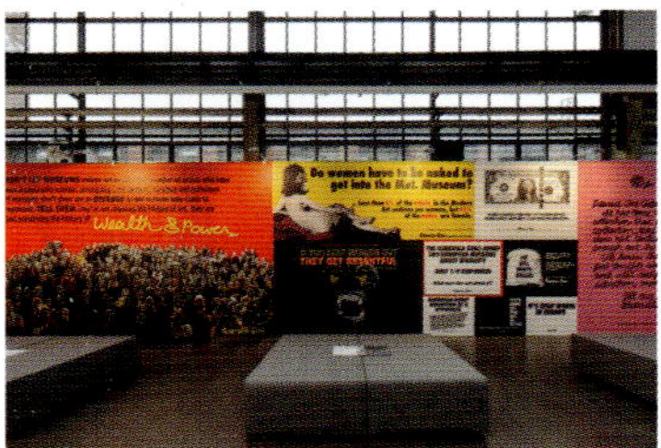

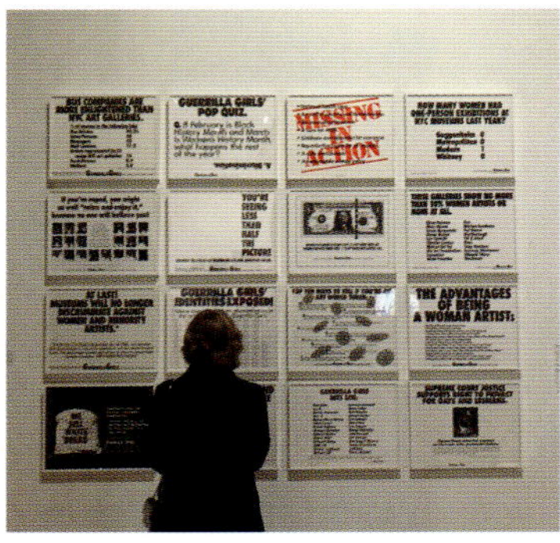

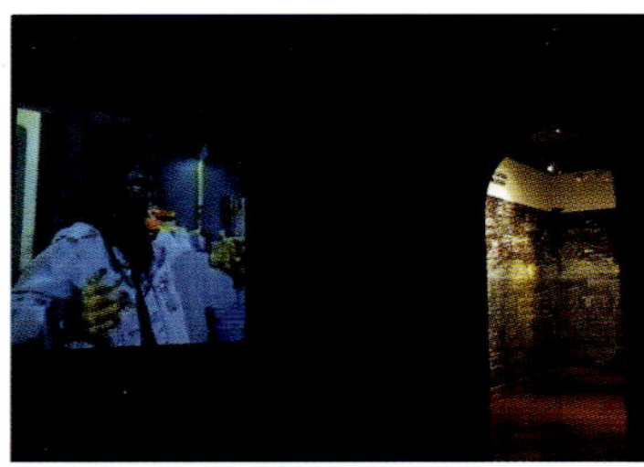

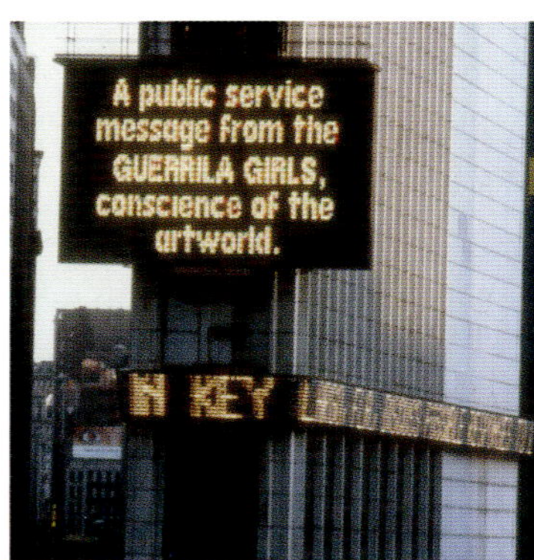

From top: Bilbao, 2013; Mjellby, Sweden 2018; Madrid, 2015; GDM at Palais de Tokyo, Paris, 2013; Whitney Museum, New York, 2018; Quito, 2018; Times Square, New York, 1992

2010

•National College of Art and Design, *Guerrilla Girls' All Ireland Project*, Dublin: traveled to The Glucksman Museum, Cork, Ireland; No. 76 John Street, Kilkenny, Ireland

Citilab Corneliá, *L'Observatori de les Dones en els Mitjans de Comunicació*, Catalonia, Spain

Francis M. Naumann Fine Art, *The Visible Vagina*, New York

Hood Museum of Art at Dartmouth College, *Fresh Perspectives on the Permanent Collection from Dartmouth's Students*, Hanover, NH

Whitney Museum of American Art, *2010 Whitney Biennial*, New York

Los Angeles Contemporary Exhibitions, *Art Against Empire: Graphic Responses to U.S. Interventions Since W.W. II.*, Los Angeles

Gerrit Rietveld Academie, *Becoming Bitch, Becoming Outcast*, Amsterdam

Centro Cultural y de Convenciones Teatro los Fundadores, *IX Festival Internacional de la Imagen*, Manizales, Colombia

LA BONNE-Centre Cultura de Dones Francesca Bonnemaison, *Indomitable Women*, Barcelona

Artrang Gallery, *2010 BITT Festival*, Seoul, South Korea

Museum of Modern Art, *Contemporary Art from the Collection*, New York

National Museum of Art, Architecture and Design, *Goddesses*, Oslo

ONE Archives Gallery & Museum, *Out of the Closet & into the Street: Posters of LGBTQ Struggles & Celebration*, West Hollywood, CA

Tallinn, Estonia

Le Pont Organization, *Aleppo 8th International Women Art Festival*, Aleppo, Syria

Harlem PoP, *ANARCHY: In Search of a New World Order*, New York

Gallery LOOP, *The 1st Public Discourse Sphere-After Effects of Neo-liberalism*, Seoul, South Korea

2009

Centre Pompidou, *elles@centrepompidou*, Paris

•Millenium Court Arts Centre, *Guerrilla Girls New Work*, Portadown, Northern Ireland

Berardo Museum, *She is a Femme Fatale*, Lisbon

•Galerie de l'UQAM, *Guerrilla Girls: Troubler le repos / Disturbing the Peace*, Montreal

Paul Robeson Gallery at Rutgers Univ., *Hysteria: Past yet Present*, Newark, NJ

Ivan Dougherty Gallery at Univ. of New South Wales, *Bushwhacked*, Sydney, Australia

•Acadia Univ. Art Gallery, *Guerrilla Girls*, Nova Scotia

The Storefront Artist Project, *Radical Detour and the 1st Annual Berkshire Festival of Women in the Arts*, Pittsfield, MA

Museum voor Moderne Kunst, *REBELLE: Art and Feminism 1969–2009*, Arnhem, Netherlands

The Lesbian, Gay, Bisexual & Transgender Community Center, *Then and Now: 20th Anniversary of the Center Show*, New York

Da Vinci Gallery Los Angeles City College, *MasterPeaces—High Art for Higher Purpose*, Los Angeles

Musée Ingres, *Ingres et les Modernes*, Montauban, France

Museu d'Art Contemporani de Barcelona, *On the Margins of Art—Creation and Political Engagement*, Barcelona

Galleri Box, *KÅT A4 (Horny)*, Gothenburg, Sweden

Albin O. Kuhn Gallery at Univerisity of Maryland, *The Art of Persuasion: Poster Design from 1896 through 2008*, Baltimore

2008

Neuberger Museum of Art, *Person of The Crowd: The Contemporary Art of Flânerie*, Purchase, NY

DeYoung Museum of San Francisco, *Lynne Hershman Leeson: No Body Special*, San Francisco

Museo de Arte Contemporáneo Rosario, *Subjected Culture*, Rosario, Argentina

ARC Gallery, *Are We There Yet?: 40 Years of Feminism*, Chicago

National Gallery of Art, *Medieval to Modern: Recent Acquisitions*, Washington, D.C.

Leslie-Lohman Museum, *Pink & Bent: Art of Queer Women*, New York

Mike Curb College of Arts, Media, and Communication at CSUN, *Reclaiming the 'F' Word: Posters on International Feminism*, Northridge, CA

The Madison Museum of Contemporary Art, *Girls and Company: Feminist Works from MMoCA's Permanent Collection*, Madison, WI

Fotomuseum Winterthur, *DARKSIDE: Photographic Desire and Sexuality Photographed*, Zurich

Espace Le Carré, *Over the Rainbow*, Lille, France

Brooklyn Museum, *Burning Down the House: Building a Feminist Art Collection*, Brooklyn, NY

•Salem College Elberson Fine Arts Center, *The Activist Art of the Guerrilla Girls*, Winston-Salem, NC

516 Arts, *Speak Out: Art, Design & Politics*, Albuquerque, NM

2007

Museum of Modern Art, *Documenting a Feminist Past: Artworld Critique*, New York

Museum of Modern Art, *Feedback: The Video Data Bank, Video Art, and Artist Interviews*, New York

•Hellenic American Union Galleries, *Guerrilla Girls*, Athens

Art Athina International Contemporary Art Fair, *Art Athina 2007*, Athens

Museo de Bellas Artes de Bilbao, *Kiss Kiss Bang Bang: 45 Years of Art and Feminism*, Bilbao, Spain

SH Contemporary Art Fair, Public Viewing, Shanghai, China

Witte de With Center for Contemporary Arts, *BODYPOLITICX*, Rotterdam, the Netherlands

Ceres Gallery, *AGENTS OF CHANGE: Women, Art and Intellect*, New York

Autonomous Women's Center, *Do You See the Violence Against Women?*, Belgrade, Serbia

2006

•Hotel Virreyes, Mexico City

•The Istanbul Museum of Modern Art, *Venice-Istanbul*, Turkey

BilbaoArte Fundazioa, *Para Todos Los Públicos*, Bilbao, Spain

Boston Women's Film Festival, Boston

Centraal Museum, *This Is America: Visions of the American Dream*, Utrecht, the Netherlands

Créteil International Women's Film Festival, Paris

Univ. of Tennessee, Knoxville, TN

Participant Inc., *Ridykeulous*, New York

Timoteo Navarro Provincial Museum of Fine Arts, *Subjected Culture – Interruptions and Resistances on Femaleness*, Tucumán, Argentina

Dyer Arts Center, Rochester Institute of Technology, *Poster Art*, Rochester, NY

Altered Esthetics, *Guerrilla Art, Art As Activism*, Minneapolis

The Museum of Television & Radio and Museum of the City of New York, *Until the Violence Stops: NYC Women's Vday Film Festival*, New York

Walter Phillips Gallery Banff Centre for the Arts, *Conceptual Comics, Plan B*, Banff, AB

Centre d'Art Santa Mònica, *Merch & Promo*, Barcelona

National Gallery of Canada, *Witness to the Passing Time: The Art Metropole Collection*, Ottawa, ON

2005

•51st Venice Biennale, *Always a Little Further*, Venice

Museo Nacional Centro de Arte Reina Sofia, *Violencia Sin Cuerpos (Violence without Bodies)*, Madrid

School of Visual Arts, *The Design of Dissent*, New York

Museo de Zaragoza, *Gender Frontiers*, Zaragoza, Spain

Citywide in Dún Laoghaire, *The Festival of World Cultures*, Dublin

Centre of Attention, *On Demand, A Group Show Brought to 1 Person at a Time*, London

Amnesty International, *Imagine a World Without Violence Against Girls and Women*, Bargehouse, London

Casa elle Culture i Roma, *Disarming Images: Picturing Dissent in America, 2001–2005*, Rome

•CUNY Kingsborough Community College Art Gallery, *Guerrilla Girls: Graphic Activism*, Brooklyn, NY

Heuser Art Gallery at Bradley Univ., Peoria, IL

UCLA Student Exhibit, Los Angeles

Lentos Kunstmuseum, *Just Do It! The Subversion of Signs from Marcel Duchamp to Prada Meinhof*, Linz, Austria

Sandra and David Bakalar Gallery at Massachusetts College of Art, *The Graphic Imperative: International Posters for Peace, Social Justice and the Environment 1965–2005*, Boston. Traveled 2006–2010

Boston Bargehouse, *Imagine a World: Amnesty International's Stop Violence Against Women Campaign,* London

Transport Gallery, *Yo! What Happened to Peace?,* Los Angeles

Borderland Museum, *DETOX,* Kirkenes, Norway

CSUN Art Galleries, *Reel to Real: A Political Reflection of Hollywood Film Posters,* produced by the Center for the Study of Political Graphics, Northridge, CA

Chisholm Gallery, *Peace Signs—Posters of the Anti-War Movement,* New York

NiSource Gallery at Indiana State Museum, *Some things Happening: 25 Years of Contemporary Art at the Heron Gallery,* Indianapolis

Citywide in Chicago, *Estrojam,* 2004, Chicago

2004

Tate Modern, *States of Flux,* London

•Printed Matter, *The Guerrilla Girls' Art Museum Activity Book,* New York

•Melvin Art Gallery, Florida Southern College, *The Guerrilla Girls: 25 Years of Revolutionary Art Posters,* Lakeland, FL

2003

Track 16 Gallery, *The Anti-War Show: U.S. Interventions from Korea to Iraq,* Santa Monica, CA

Citywide Philadelphia, *LadyFest Philly 2003,* Philadelphia

Espai d'Art Contemporani de Castelló, *Micropolitics: Art and Everyday Life (2001–1968) Part 2,* Castellón, Spain

IT Space, *Art during Wartime,* New York

David Zwirner, *Bright Lights, Big City,* New York

Aeroplastics Gallery, *Female Turbulence,* Brussels

Hogeschool West-Vlaanderen, *Logo!/No Logo?,* Brugge, Belgium

2002

Robert Miller Gallery, *Art and Outrage,* New York

Riot Grrrls Festival, Belgium

National Women's Conference 25th Anniversary Show, Dallas

Bilbao Arte Fundazioa, *The Guerrilla Girls,* Bilbao, Spain

National Museum of Women in the Arts, *Feminism and Art: Selections from the permanent Collection,* Washington, D.C.

Festival internacional de cine sobre derechos humanos, Santiago, Chile

Staatliche Kunsthalle Baden-Baden, *Prophets of Boom,* Baden-Baden, Germany

Watts Towers Art Center, *No Place Like Home: Graphics on the Crisis of Housing and Homelessness,* produced by Center for the Study of Political Graphics, Los Angeles

Center Gallery at Fordham Univ., *What's Your Problem?: Graphic Design with Conscience,* New York

2001

Barcelona Museum of Contemporary Art, *Image, Contemporary Art and Ideology,* Barcelona

Independent Media Center, *PhenomANON: Two Decades of Ephemeral Urban Guerrilla Artfare,* Seattle

Moderna Museet, *The Path of Resistance: MoMA Meets Moderna 1960–2000,* Stockholm

2000

•The Print Center, *Girls on Politics: Posters by the Guerrilla Girls,* Philadelphia

1999

Massachusetts Museum of Contemporary Art, *Billboard: Art on the Road,* North Adams, MA

1998

New Museum, *Urban Encounters,* New York

1997

Exit Art, P*UBLIC NOTICE: Art and Activist Posters 1951–1997,* New York

1996

Museum of Modern Art, *Thinking Print: Books to Billboards, 1980–95,* New York

The Richard F. Brush Art Gallery & Permanent Collection at St. Lawrence Univ., *A Candle in the Wilderness: Selections from the Permanent Collection,* Canton, NY

1995

•Printed Matter, *Guerrilla Girls Bear All,* New York

New Museum, *Temporarily Possessed: The Semi-Permanent Collection,* New York

1994

Centre d'Art Santa Mònica, *Public Domain,* Barcelona

New Museum, *Bad Girls (Part 1),* New York

•East Fine Arts Gallery at Texas Woman's Univ., *Guerrilla Girls Talk Back: The First Five Years, A Retrospective: 1985–1990,* Denton, TX

Cleveland Center for Contemporary Art, *Outside the Frame: Performance and the Object, A Survey History of Performance Art in the USA since 1950,* Cleveland

1993

•Armand Hammer Museum of Art and Cultural Center, *The Art of Attack: Social Commentary and Its Effect,* Los Angeles

1992

Bennington College, *The Poster Show,* Bennington, VT

•Kunstforening, *The Guerrilla Girls,* Oslo

John Michael Kohler Arts Center, *Hair,* Sheboygan, WI

The Institute of Contemporary Art, *Public Interventions,* Boston

Whitney Museum of American Art at Equitable Center, *Dirt and Domesticity: Constructions of the Feminine,* New York

Musée de la Poste, *Les Couleurs de l'argent (The Color of Money),* Paris

El Camino College Art Gallery, *Courageous Voices: An International Poster Exhibition on Racism, Sexism and Human Rights,* produced by Center for Political Graphics, Torrance, CA

1991

•Billboards, sponsored by the Public Art Fund, *Now They're Trying to Censor Art,* New York

•Falkirk Cultural Center, *Guerrilla Girls Talk Back: The First Five Years, A Retrospective: 1985–1990,* San Rafael, CA

•Fordham Univ., *The Guerrilla Girls,* New York

Independent Curators International, *No Laughing Matter,* USA and Canada

Aldrich Museum, *The Art of Advocacy,* Ridgefield, CT

The New York Public Library, *Documents of Dissent,* New York

Key Gallery, *Counter Media,* Richmond, VA

Gallery 1199, *Images of Labor, A Bread & Roses Cultural Project,* New York

Franklin Furnace, *Burning in Hell,* New York

San Francisco Art Institute, *Transactions in the Post-Industrial Era,* San Francisco

Spencer Museum of Art, Univ. of Kansas, Lawrence, KS

1990

Whitney Museum of American Art, *Image World: Art Media and Culture,* New York

Atlanta College of Art Gallery, *Oh! Those Four White Walls!: The Gallery as Context,* Atlanta

Studio Museum in Harlem, *The Decade Show: Frameworks of Identity in the 1980s,* New York

Arts and Other Fields, Women Working in Sciences, Basel, Switzerland

•Kulturhuset, *Guerrilla Girls: Poster Installation,* Stockholm

1989

•Lower Manhattan Cultural Council Outdoor Installation, *Guerrilla Girls Grace Wall Street,* New York

Federal Reserve Plaza, *Desire of the Whitney Museum Branch,* New York

First Bank Collection, Minneapolis

1988

Goddard Riverside Community Center, *Unity: A Collaborative Process,* New York

Akron Art Museum, *All the News That's Fit to Print,* Akron, OH

The Print Club, Philadelphia

1987

•The Clocktower, *Guerrilla Girls Review the Whitney,* New York

The Anchorage, *Creative Time's Art in the Anchorage 4: Guerrilla Girl Retrospective,* Brooklyn, New York

1985

The Palladium Club, *The Night the Palladium Apologized: An Exhibit of 100 Contemporary Women Artists Curated by Guerrilla Girls,* New York

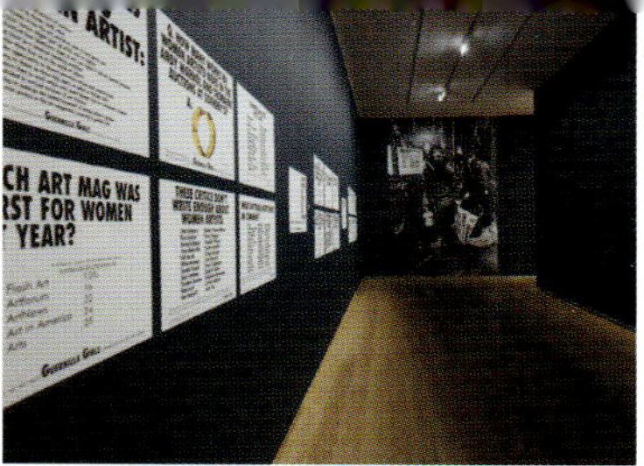
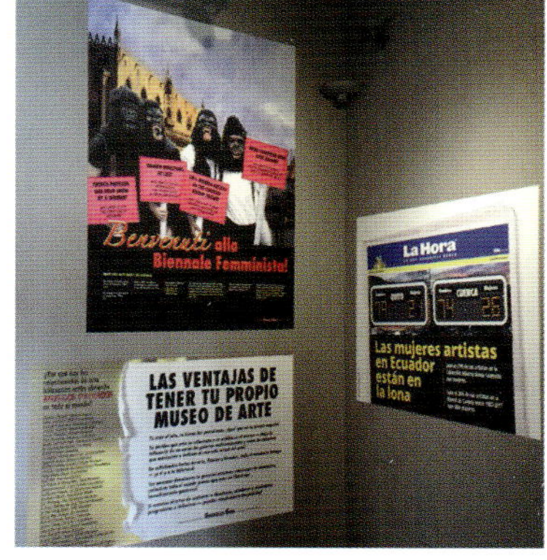
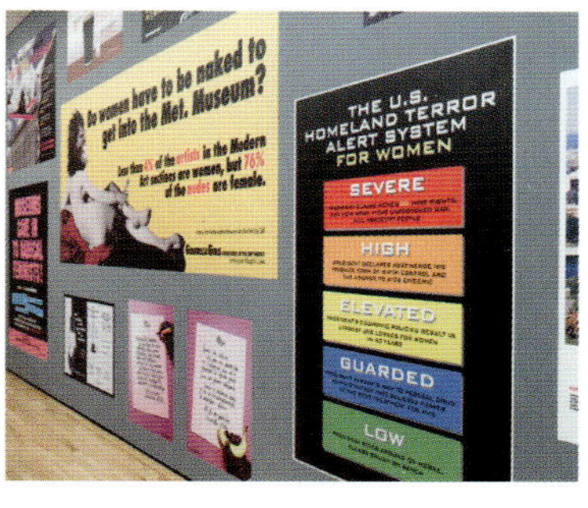
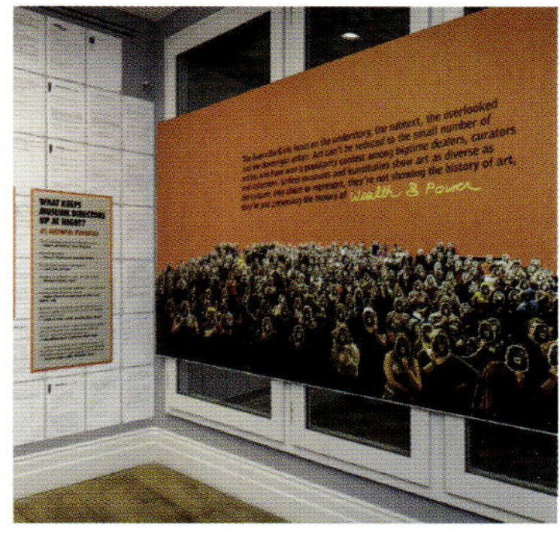
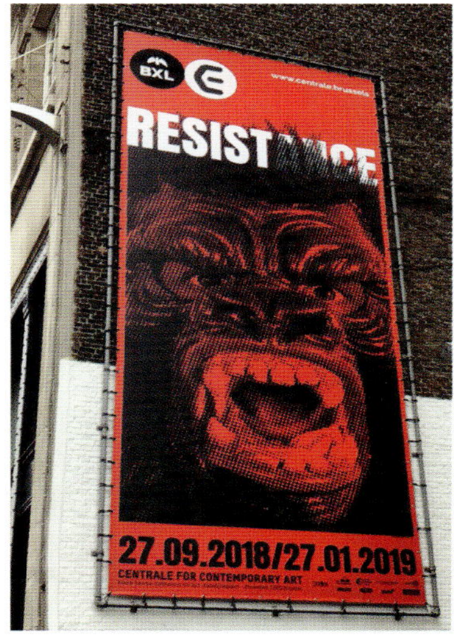

From top: Auckland, 2019; Quito, 2018, Baltimore, 2017; London, 2016; Brussels, 2018

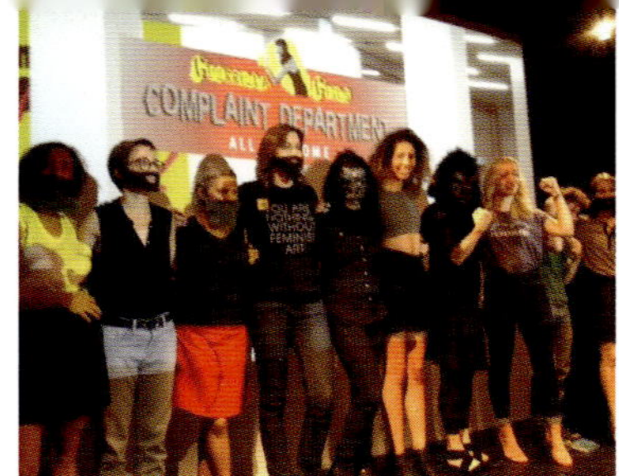

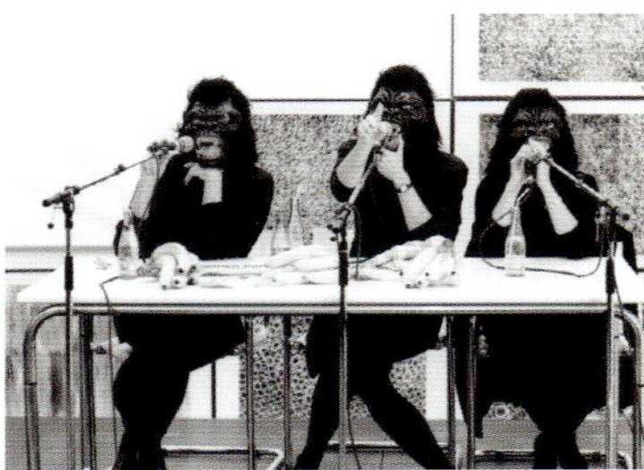

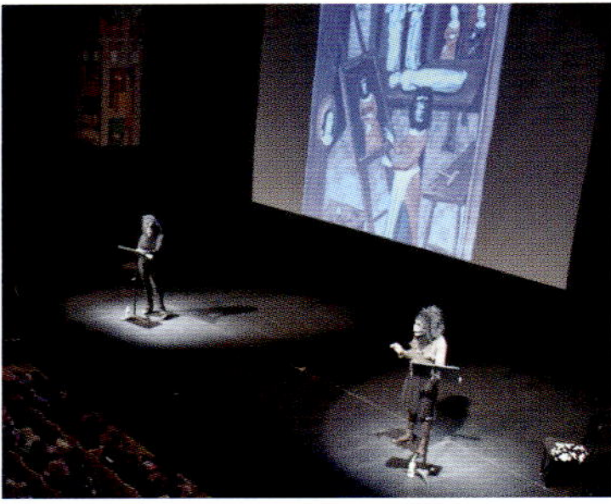

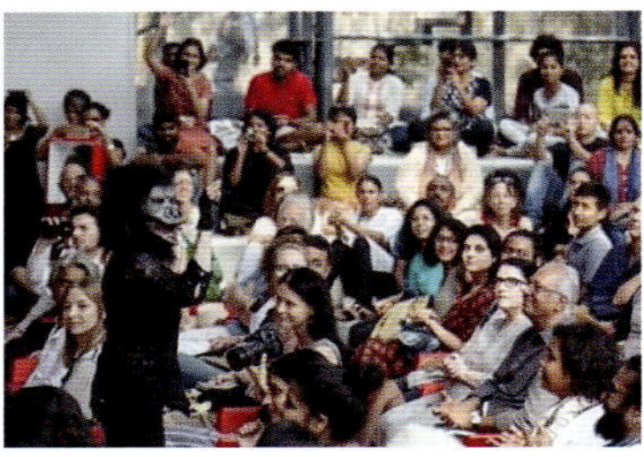

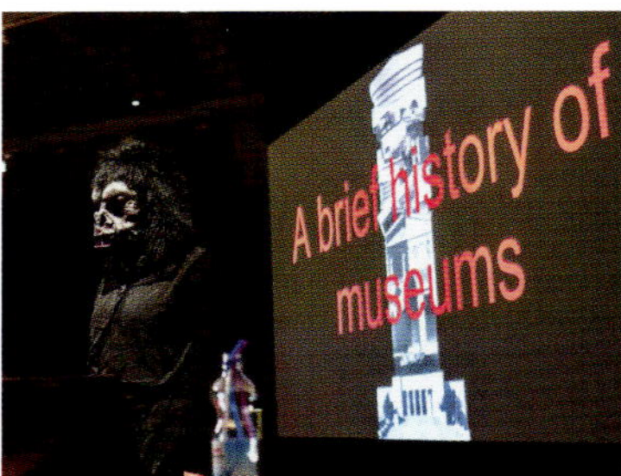

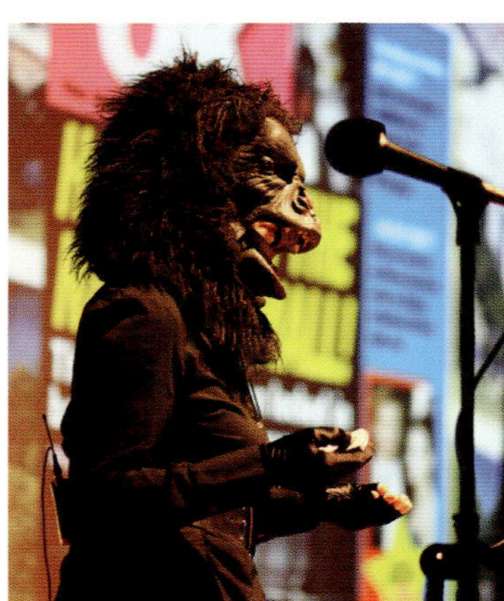

From top: New York City, 2015; Vienna, 1991; Albuquerque, 2010; Kochi, 2018; Helsinki, 2018

GIGS

Students, artists and activists come to our multi-media performances and workshops. We show them what we do and how they can do it, too.

2020 (partial)
ArtHyve, Denver
CajasCanarias, Tenerife, Spain
Utah Museum of Contemporary Art, Salt Lake City
Washington & Lee Univ., Lexington, VA

2019
Beyond the Streets, Brooklyn, NY
Brown Univ., Providence, RI
Bucknell Univ., Lewisburg, PA
Columbia Univ., New York
Festival Les Créatives, MAMCO Genève, Switzerland
Haus der Kunst, Munich, Germany
Kunstmuseum Basel, Basel, Switzerland
National Gallery of Art, Auckland, New Zealand
North Carolina Museum of Art, Raleigh, NC
Sarah Lawrence College, Bronxville, NY
Sotheby's Pre-College Institute, New York
State Univ. of New York at Plattsburgh, Plattsburgh, NY

2018
ABC No Rio, W.A.G.E. Panel, New York
Beyond the Streets, Los Angeles
Centrale for Contemporary Art, Brussels
Fashion Institute of Technology, New York
Hellerau Zentrum der Künste, Dresden, Germany
Helsinki Art Museum, Helsinki
Hong Kong Univ., Hong Kong
Kestnergesellschaft, Hannover, Germany
Kochi Biennial, Kochi, India
MAMA Cash, Stedelijk Museum, Amsterdam
McNay Art Museum, San Antonio
Minnesota Street Project, San Francisco
Mjellby Museum, Halmstad, Sweden
Moore College of Art & Design, Philadelphia
Purdue Univ., West Lafayette, IN
San Diego State Univ., San Diego
Stanford Univ., Stanford, CA
St. Ann's School, Brooklyn, NY

2017
Augustana College, Rock Island, IL
Baltimore Museum of Art, Baltimore
Bluestockings Bookstore, New York
California State Univ., Sacramento, CA
Dallas Museum of Art, Dallas
Frestas Trienal de Artes, Sorocaba, Brazil
Fullerton Museum, Fullerton, CA
Harn Museum, Gainesville, FL
Jule Collins Smith Museum, Auburn, AL
Milwaukee Institute of Art and Design, Milwaukee
Museum of Art São Paulo, São Paulo, Brazil
Norton Museum of Art, West Palm Beach, FL
Onassis Cultural Center, Athens
Regis College, Denver
Univ. of California, Santa Barbara, CA

2016
Arizona State Univ., Scottsdale, AZ
Arts Westchester, White Plains, NY
Bruce Museum, Greenwich, CT
Bowdoin College, Brunswick, ME
Center for Book Arts, New York
Hennepin Theatre Trust, Minneapolis
Maison des Auteurs, Paris
SMOCA Scottsdale, Scottsdale, AZ
Museum Ludwig, Cologne, Germany
Murray Edwards College, Cambridge, UK
National Gallery of Art, Ontario, Canada
Neuberger Museum, SUNY Purchase, Harrison, NY
New Hall College, Cambridge, UK
St Lawrence Univ., Canton, NY
Univ. of Connecticut, Storrs, Connecticut
Univ. of Indianapolis, Indianapolis
Univ. of Iowa, Iowa City, IA
Univ. of Minnesota, Duluth, MN
Weisman Art Museum, Minneapolis
Whitechapel Gallery, London

2015
Academy of Fine Arts Vienna, Vienna
Georgia Museum of Art, Athens, GA
Matadero Madrid, Madrid
Minneapolis College of Art and Design, Minneapolis
Minneapolis Institute of Art, Minneapolis
Museum of Fine Arts, St. Petersburg, FL
Museum of the City of New York, New York
New York County Lawyers Association, New York
PitchWise Festival, Sarajevo, Bosnia and Herzegovina

Pomona College Museum of Art, Claremont, CA
Reykjavik Arts Festival, Reykjavik, Iceland
Smith College, Northampton, MA
Stanford Univ., Stanford, CA
St Ann's School, Brooklyn, NY
St. Catherine's College, St. Paul, MN
Texas Woman's Univ., Denton, TX

2014
Ball State Univ., Muncie, IN
Blackburn College, Carlinville, IL
City College of New York, Spitzer School, New York
East Central Univ., Ada, OK
Fairfield Univ., Fairfield, CT
Google Cultural Institute, Paris
Krannert Art Museum Champaign, Champaign, IL
Middlebury College, Middlebury, VT
Purdue Univ., Fort Wayne, IN
Tacoma Art Museum, Tacoma, WA
Univ. of California, Santa Barbara, CA
Univ. of Denver, Denver
Univ. of Tennessee, Knoxville, TN
Univ. of Virginia, Charlottesville, VA
Victoria and Albert Museum, London

2013
Carnegie Natural History Museum, Pittsburgh
Chaffey College, Rancho Cucamonga, CA
Chapman Univ., Orange, CA
Davis Museum, Wellesley College, Wellesley, MA
East Carolina Univ., Greenville, NC
Gallery Knipsu, Kunsthall Bergen, Norway
Hunter College, New York
Iberoamericana y MUAC, Mexico City
Princeton Univ. School of Architecture, Princeton, NJ
Skowhegan Awards Dinner, New York
Univ. of Pennsylvania, Philadelphia
Utah Museum of Art, Salt Lake City
Utah State Univ., Logan, UT
Vanderbilt Univ., Nashville, TN
Warren County Community College, Washington, NJ
Weber State Univ., Ogden, UT
Yoko Ono Meltdown Festival, London

2012
Alhóndiga Bilbao, Bilbao, Spain
ArtBoom Festival, Krakow, Poland
Brooklyn Museum, Brooklyn, NY
Coastal Carolina Univ., Conway, SC
Columbia College Chicago, Chicago
Cornell Univ., Ithaca, NY
Fordham Univ., Bronx, NY
Hood Museum of Art, Dartmouth College, Hannover, NH
Lake Forest College, Lake Forest, IL
Montserrat College of Art, Beverly, MA
North Country Community College, Saranac Lake, NY
Princeton Univ. Art Museum, Princeton, NJ
Printed Matter, New York
St. Francis College, Brooklyn, NY
Tompkins Cortland Community College, Dryden, NY
Univ. of Hartford, West Hartford, CT

2011
College Art Association, New York
Colby College, Waterville, ME
College of Charleston, Charleston, SC
Göteborgs Konsthall, Göteborgs, Sweden
IFC Center, New York
Kutztown Univ., Kutztown, PA
Miami Univ. of Ohio, Hamilton, OH
Nasher Museum, Duke Univ., Durham, NC
Neuberger Museum of Art, Purchase, NY
Northern Michigan Univ., Marquette, MI
Rowan Univ., Glassboro, NJ
Rutgers Univ., New Brunswick, NJ
The Café Santropol, Montréal
Työväenmuseo Werstas, Tampere, Finland
Univ. of Arizona, Tucson, AZ
Univ. of California, Riverside, CA
Univ. of Helsinki, Helsinki
Univ. of Illinois at Chicago, Chicago
Univ. of Wisconsin, Milwaukee
White Space, Zurich

2010
Augsburg College, Minneapolis
Bienal de São Paulo, São Paulo, Brazil
California Univ. of Pennsylvania, California, PA
Central Missouri State Univ., Warrensburg, MS
Centre Pompidou, Paris
Centro Cultural Montehermoso, Vitoria-Gasteiz, Spain
Gender International Encounters, Seville, Spain
Institute for Art, Religion and Social Justice, New York

Loyola Marymount Univ., Los Angeles
New Mexico State Univ., Las Cruces, NM
Oi Futuro, Rio de Janeiro
Pittsburgh Creative and Performing Arts School, Pittsburgh
Rhode Island School of Design, Providence, RI
Sage College of Albany, Albany, NY
San Diego Mesa College, San Diego
School of the Art Institute of Chicago, Chicago
SESC São Paulo, São Paulo, Brazil
Shippensburg Univ., Shippensburg, PA
Univ. of California, Santa Barbara, CA

2009
Acadia Univ., Wolfville, NS
Atlantic Theatre Festival, Wolfville, NS
Bitch Magazine Lecture, Portland State Univ., Portland, OR
Butler Gallery, Kilkenny, Ireland
Chicago Humanities Festival, MCA, Chicago
Glucksman Gallery, Cork, Ireland
Grinnell College, Grinnell, IA
Illinois State Univ., Normal, IL
Iowa State Univ., Ames, IA
Los Angeles County Museum of Art, Los Angeles
Michigan Art Education Conference, Kalamazoo
Millennium Court Arts Centre, Portadown, Northern Ireland
National College of Art and Design, Dublin
National Women's Studies Conference, Atlanta
Rutgers Univ., New Brunswick, NJ
Univ. College, Dublin
Univ. of California, Santa Barbara, CA
Univ. of Chicago, Chicago
Univ. of North Texas, Denton, TX
Univ. of Ulster, Belfast, North Ireland
West Virginia State Univ., Institute

2008
516 Arts, Albuquerque, NM
Asheville Art Museum, Ashville, NC
College Art Association, Dallas
Hamilton College, Clinton, NY
Housatonic Museum of Art, Bridgeport, CT
Indiana Univ. of Pennsylvania, Indiana, PA
Longwood Univ., Farmville, VA
MacMurray College, Jacksonville, IL
Oakton Community College, Des Plaines, IL
Ohio Wesleyan Univ., Delaware, OH
Randolph College, Lynchburg, VA
Ryerson Univ., Toronto, ON
Salem College, Winston-Salem, NC
Syracuse Univ., Syracuse, NY
Univ. of California, Los Angeles
Univ. of Connecticut at Storrs, Storrs, CT
Wilson College, Chambersburg, PA
YWCA Kansas City, Kansas City, MO

2007
Art Educators of Indiana Conference, Indianapolis Museum of Art, Indianapolis
Brentwood School, Los Angeles
Chatham Univ., Pittsburgh
Dickinson College, Carlisle, PA
Feminist Futures Symposium, Museum of Modern Art, New York
Grand Valley State Univ., Allendale, MI
Hellenic American Union, Athens
Illinois Wesleyan Univ., Bloomington, IL
Intercollege, Nicosia, Cyprus
MacMurray College, Jacksonville, IL
Miami Univ., Hamilton, OH
Midwestern State Univ., Wichita Falls, TX
Muskegon Museum of Art, Muskegon, MI
National Art Educators Association Annual Conference, New York
National Museum of Women in the Arts, Washington, D.C.
Networking 2007, Tuscany, Italy
New Museum High School Program, New York
New York City Art Teachers Artist-of-the-Year Award Ceremony, New York
Northern Arizona Univ., Flagstaff, AZ
Oakland Univ., Rochester, MI
Old Dominion Univ., Norfolk, VA
Pacific Univ., Forest Grove, OR
PitchWise Festival, Bosnia Herzegovina
Queens College, Queens, NY
Scottsdale Museum of Contemporary Art, Scottsdale, AZ
Seton Hill Univ., Greensburg, PA
Springside School, Philadelphia
Swarthmore College, Swarthmore, PA
Tekniart, Paphos, Cyprus
Univ. of Illinois, Springfield, IL
Univ. of Leeds, Leeds, UK
Univ. of Rochester, Rochester, NY
Wellesley College, Wellesley, MA

2006

American Cinematheque, Los Angeles
Barnard College, New York
Boston Women's Fund Benefit and Women's
    Film Festival, Cambridge, MA
Centraal Museum, Utrecht, Netherlands
Center for Inquiry, Los Angeles
East Tennessee State Univ., Johnson City, TN
Oakwood School, North Hollywood, CA
Smith College, Northampton, MA
Tate Modern, London
Univ. of Maryland, College Park, MD
Univ. of Minnesota, Minneapolis
Univ. of Tennessee, Knoxville, TN
Univ. of Wisconsin, Stevens Point, WI
Yale Univ., New Haven, CT

2005

Amnesty International, London
ARCO, Madrid
Arizona State Univ., Tempe, AZ
Bradley Univ., Peoria, IL
California State Univ., Sacramento, CA
Clemson Univ., Clemson, SC
Florida State Univ., Tallahassee, FL
Goucher College, Baltimore
Los Angeles Valley College, Van Nuys, CA
St. Louis Museum of Contemporary Art,
    St. Louis
Pennsylvania State Univ., State College, PA
Quilt Conference, Lincoln, NE
Reed College Arts Festival, Portland, OR
Stetson Univ., DeLand, FL
Triple Candie, New York
Univ. of Tulsa, Tulsa, OK
Univ. of Wisconsin, Whitewater, WI
Univ. of Wyoming, Laramie, WY
Western Kentucky Univ., Bowling Green, KY

2004

Albion College, Albion, MI
ARCO, Madrid
Binghamton Univ., Birmingham, NY
Boston Univ., Boston
Columbia Univ., New York
Eastern Connecticut State Univ., Willimantic,
    CT
Florida Southern College, Lakeland, FL
Furman Univ., Greenville, SC
Idaho State Univ., Pocatello, ID
Iowa State Univ., Ames, IA
Our Bodies, Ourselves, Boston
Polk Museum, Lakeland, FL
Radcliffe Institute, Harvard Univ., Cambridge,
    MA
Radcliffe Union of Students, Harvard Univ.,
    Cambridge, MA
Skidmore College, Saratoga Springs, NY
Univ. of Kansas, Lawrence, KS
Univ. of Louisville, Louisville, KY
Univ. of Maine, Orono, ME
Univ. of Memphis, Memphis, TN
Utah Art Educators Conference, St. George, UT
Wabash College, Crawfordsville, IN
Washington and Lee Univ., Lexington, VA

2003

92nd Street Y, New York
Allegheny College, Meadville, PA
Barnes & Noble, New York
Bates College, Lewiston, ME
California State Univ., Long Beach, CA
California State Univ., San Marcos, CA
Carnegie Mellon Univ., Pittsburgh
Case Western Reserve Univ., Cleveland
Clarion Univ., Clarion, PA
Chemeketa Community College, Salem, OR
College of New Jersey, Ewing, NJ
Corcoran Gallery of Art, Washington, D.C.
Diesel Bookstore, Oakland, CA
Drury College, Springfield, MO
El Sereno Middle School, Los Angeles
Philadelphia Free Library, Philadelphia
Harry W. Schwartz Bookshop, Milwaukee
Hollins Univ., Roanoke, VA
LaSalle Univ., Philadelphia
Lewis & Clark College, Portland, OR
Mark Taper Auditorium, Los Angeles Public
    Library, Los Angeles
Modern Times Bookstore, San Francisco
Ohio Northern Univ., Ada, OH
Piscataway High School, Piscataway, NJ
Powell's Books, Portland, OR
Queens College, Queens, NY
Roger Williams Univ., Bristol, RI
Saint Mary's College, Notre Dame, IN
Slippery Rock Univ., Slippery Rock, PA
Texas Art Education Assn. Conference, Dallas
Vassar College, Poughkeepsie, NY
The Ellis School, Pittsburgh
The Mama Gathering, Los Angeles
Towson Univ., Towson, MD

Track 16 Gallery, Santa Monica, CA
Univ. of California, Los Angeles
Univ. of Missouri, St. Louis
Univ. of Nebraska, Omaha, NE
Walker Art Center, Minneapolis

2002

Boise State Univ., Boise, ID
Butler Univ., Indianapolis
College of Creative Studies, Detroit
Cornell Univ., Ithaca, NY
Emory Univ., Atlanta
Fundación Bilbao Arte Fundazioa, Bilbao
George Mason Univ., Fairfax, VA
Gettysburg College, Gettysburg, PA
Kutztown Univ., Kutztown, PA
Loyola Univ., New Orleans
McColl Center for Visual Art, Charlotte, NC
Ringling College of Art, Sarasota, FL
Towson Univ., Towson, MD
Tufts Univ., Boston
Univ. of California, Irvine, CA
Univ. of Michigan, Ann Arbor, MI
Univ. of South Florida, Tampa, FL
The Transparent Space, Vienna
Washington State Univ., Pullman, WA
Westminster College, Salt Lake City
Whitman College, Walla Walla, WA

2001

A.S.K. Theatre Festival, Los Angeles
ATHE Conference, Chicago
Center for Political Graphics Benefit, El Rey
    Theater, Los Angeles
Columbia Univ. School of Journalism, New
    York
Pennsylvania State Univ., State College, PA
Smith College, Northampton, MA
State Univ. of New York, Oswego, NY

2000

Barnes & Noble, Astor Place, New York
Encuentro Nacional de Escritoras, Buenos
    Aires
Ms. Millennium Conference, New York
New School, New York
Northern Illinois Univ., Dekalb, IL
Ohio Wesleyan Univ., Delaware, OH
Scripps College, Claremont, CA
Skowhegan School of Painting & Sculpture,
    Madison, ME
The Stanley Theatre, Vancouver, BC
Univ. of Florida, Gainesville, FL

1999

Eastern Michigan Univ., Ypsilanti, MI
Georgetown Univ., Washington, D.C.
Kenyon College, Gambier, OH
Red Planet, Melbourne, Australia
New York Univ., New York
Queen's Univ., Ontario, ON
Univ. of Chicago, Chicago
Univ. of Maine, Orono, ME
Vanderbilt Univ., Nashville, TN

1998

Florida State Univ., Tallahassee, FL
Indiana Univ., Bloomington, IN
St Michael's College, Burlington, VT
Univ. of Redlands, Redlands, CA
Univ. of Wisconsin, WI
Washington Univ., St. Louis

1997

Arteleku, San Sebastián, Spain
Dennison Univ., Granville, OH
College of Charleston, Charleston, SC
College of Santa Fe, Santa Fe, NM
Hampshire College, Amherst, MA
Iowa State, Ames, IA
Kent State Univ., Kent, OH
Old Dominion Univ., Norfolk, VA
Truman State Univ., Kirksville, MO
Univ. of California, Santa Barbara, CA
William Patterson Univ., Wayne, NJ
Williams College, Williamstown, MA

1996

Bard College, Annandale-on-Hudson, NY
Central Michigan Univ., Mt. Pleasant, MI
Hobart and William Smith College, Geneva,
    NY
Internationale Sommerakademie für
    Bildende Kunst, Salzburg, Austria
Newcomb College, Tulane Univ., New Orleans
NYU Tisch School for the Arts, New York
Pratt Univ., New York
Univ. of Minnesota, Minneapolis

1995

Albright-Knox Art Gallery, Buffalo, NY
California State Univ., Fresno, CA
Centre International D'Arts Visuels, Marseille,
    France
Douglass College, New Brunswick, NJ

Monroe Community College, Rochester, NY
Philadelphia Museum of Art, Philadelphia
San Francisco Museum of Modern Art,
    San Francisco
School of Visual Arts, New York
Univ. of Redlands, Redlands, CA
Wadsworth Atheneum, Hartford, CT

1994

Centre d'Art, Santa Monica, Barcelona
DeCordova Museum, Lincoln, MA
Guild Hall, East Hampton, NY
Mary Washington Univ., Fredericksburg, VA
New School for Social Research, New York
Northwestern Univ., Evanston, IL
SUNY College at Brockport, NY
Texas Woman's Univ., Denton, TX
Univ. of New Hampshire, Durham, NH
Univ. of South Florida, Tampa, FL

1985–1993

Adelaide Festival, South Australia
Alberta College of Art, Calgary, AB
Alfred Univ., Alfred, NY
Armand Hammer Museum, Los Angeles
Art Institute of Chicago, Chicago
Baltimore Museum of Art, Baltimore
Bard College, Annandale-on-Hudson, NY
Bennington College, Bennington, VT
Berlin Univ. of the Arts, Berlin
Book Works, London
Bryn Mawr College, Bryn Mawr, MA
California Institute of the Arts, Valencia, CA
Cincinnati Art Museum, Cincinnati
College Art Association, New York
Delta College, Midland, MI
Denison Univ., Granville, OH
Detroit Institute of Arts, Detroit
Falkirk Cultural Center, San Rafael, CA
Franklin and Marshall College, Lancaster, PA
Gettysburg College, Gettysburg, PA
Graz, Austria
Headlands Center for the Arts, Sausalito, CA
Herron Gallery, Univ. of Iowa, Iowa City, IA
IAWA Symposium, Dublin
Indiana State Univ., Terre Haute, IN
Isabella Stewart Gardner Museum, Boston
MacKenzie Art Gallery, Regina, SK
Miami Dade Community College, Miami
Miami Univ., Oxford, OH
Mills College, Oakland, CA
Milwaukee Art Museum, Milwaukee
Montgomery Museum of Fine Arts,
    Montgomery, AL
Museum of Fine Arts, Boston
Nassau Community College, Garden City, NY
National Association of Arts Organizations
NCECA Conference, Arizona State Univ.,
    Tempe, AZ
New Mexico State Univ., Las Cruces, NM
Nike, Inc., Beaverton, OR
Ontario College of Art, Toronto, ON
Oslo Kunstforening, Oslo
Princeton Univ., Princeton, NJ
Purchase College, State Univ. of New York,
    Purchase, NY
R.C.A.A.O. Montreal
Radcliffe Institute, Harvard Univ., Cambridge,
    MA
Reed College, Portland, OR
Rhode Island School of Design, Providence, RI
Sackler Museum, Washington, D.C.
San Francisco State Univ., San Francisco
San José State Univ., San Jose, CA
Symposium 1990, Kunstmuseum, Basel,
    Switzerland
Skidmore College, Saratoga Springs, NY
Sonoma State Univ., Rohnert Park, CA
Spencer Museum of Art, Lawrence, KS
St. Lawrence Univ., Canton, NY
Kulturhuset, Stockholm
Virginia Tech, Blacksburg, VA
Ulmer Museum, Ulm, Germany
Univ. of California, Los Angeles
Univ. of California, Davis, CA
Univ. of California, Santa Cruz, CA
Univ. of Colorado at Boulder, Boulder, CO
Univ. of Texas, Austin, TX
Akademie der bildenden Künste, Vienna
Wadsworth Atheneum, Hartford, CT
Wellesley College, Wellesley, MA
Wichita State Univ., Witchita, KS
Williams College, Williamstown, MA

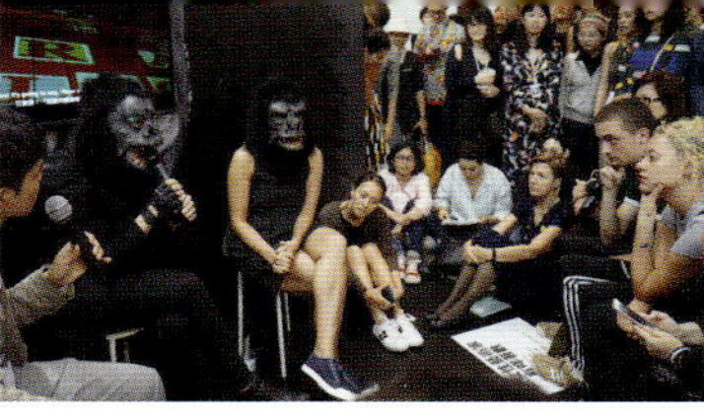

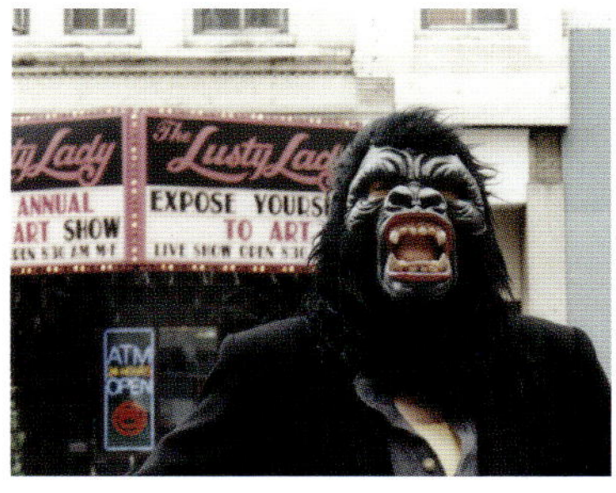

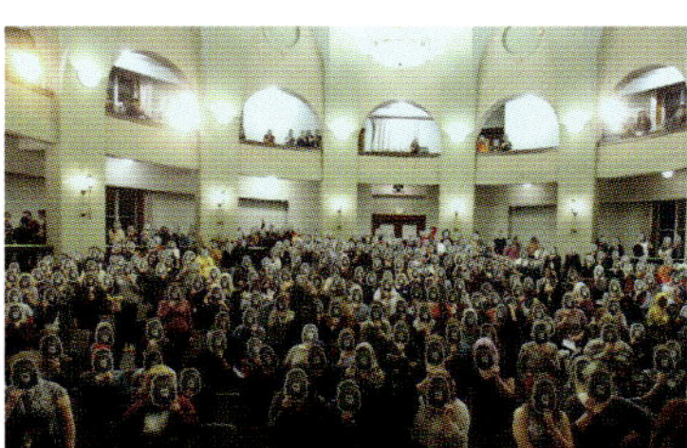

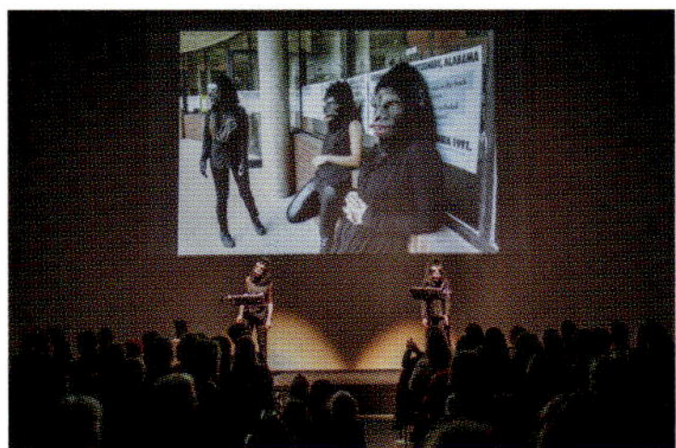

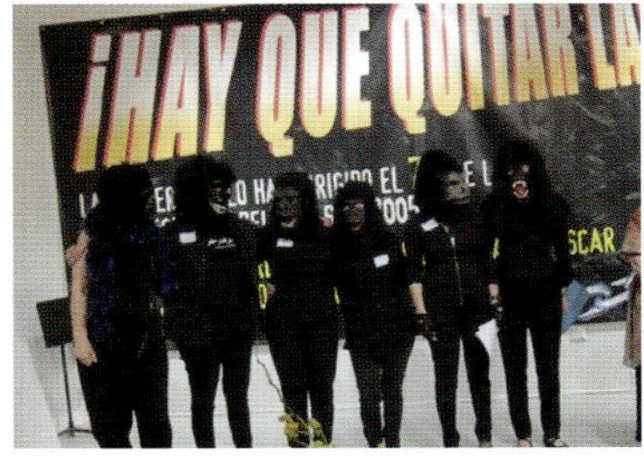

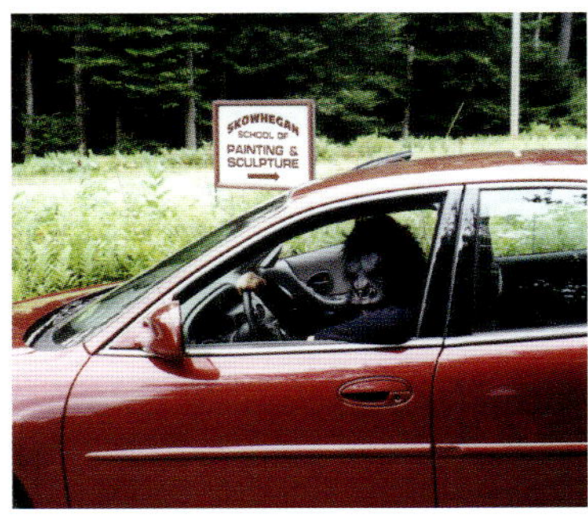

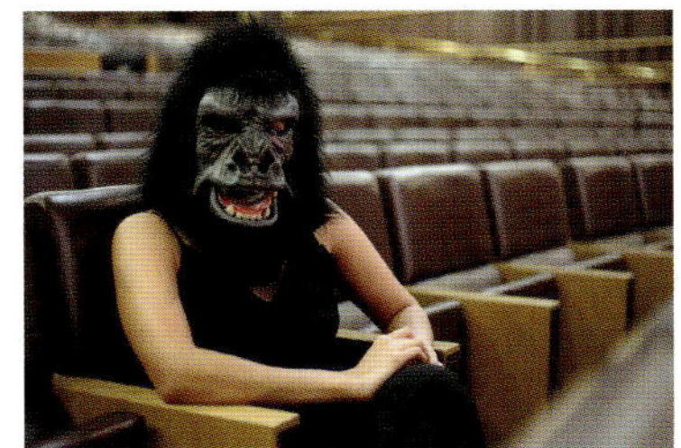

From top: Hong Kong, 2018; Seattle, 1995;
Amsterdam, 2018; New Brunswick, NJ,
2011; Skowhegan, 2000; Athens, 2017

INDEX

Library of Congress Cataloging-in-Publication Data

Names: Guerrilla Girls (Group of artists), author.
Title: Guerrilla Girls : the art of behaving badly / Guerrilla Girls.
Description: San Francisco, California : Chronicle Books, [2020] | Includes index. |
Identifiers: LCCN 2020015720 | ISBN 9781452175812 (hardback)
Subjects: LCSH: Guerrilla Girls (Group of artists)-- Themes, motives. | Feminimism and art--Pictorial works. | Political art--Pictorial works.
Classification: LCC N6512.5.G83 A4 2020 | DDC 704/.042--dc23
LC record available at https://lccn.loc.gov/2020015720

Manufactured in China.

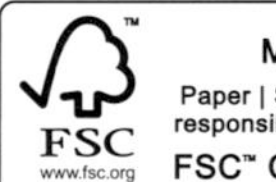

10 9 8 7 6

Chronicle books and gifts are available at special quantity discounts to corporations, professional associations, literacy programs, and other organizations. For details and discount information, please contact our premiums department at corporatesales@chroniclebooks.com or at 1-800-759-0190.

Chronicle Books LLC
680 Second Street
San Francisco, California 94107
www.chroniclebooks.com

Page 1: Photograph by Lori Grinker © 1985 Lori Grinker/Contact Press Images.

More about the Guerrilla Girls:
guerrillagirls.com
facebook.com/guerrillagirls | youtube.com/c/GUERRILLAGIRLS
instagram.com/guerrillagirls | #guerrillagirls

Special thanks to all Guerrilla Girls past and present (and future), Xabier Arakistain, Manu Arregui, Art in Ad Places, Artists and Homeless Collaborative, Muge Özbay Aydoğan, Angela Bailey, Mirka Balazy, Nia Belton, Avis Berman, Tamar Bessinger, Melanie Boucher, Leonie Bradbury, Brainstormers, Michael Brand, Carol Brode, Judith Brodsky, A.A. Bronson, Tina Brown, Tanya Brugrera, Michelle Brunnick, Deborah Buck, Sarah Burney, Maris Bustamante, Natalie Butterfield, Laura Castagnini, Theo Cheng, Melissa Chiu, Marco Daniel, Louise Déry, Michèle Didier, Kaleta Doolin, Anita Dube, Jonathan Durham, Yilmaz Dziewior, Susan Faludi, Lourdes Fernández, Christian Fillipone, Tom Finkelpearl, Noah Fisher, For Freedoms, Julia Friedrich, Coco Fusco, Roger Gastman, Eliza Gluckman, Blake Gopnik, Sarah Urist Green, Amy Harrison, Paolo Herkenhoff, Lynn Hershman, Phoebe Hoban, Claire Hsu, Laura Hurtado, The Illuminator, Emma Jameson, Misa Jeffries, Megan Johnston, Karen Jones, Caitlin Kirkpatrick, Yeewan Koon, Kathryn Kramer, Daniela Labra, Martha Lauzen, Carrie Lederer, Robert Lewetzky, Albert Litewka, Clea Litewka, Dan Mandel, Rosa Martinez, Vikki McInnes, Lourdes Mendez, Claudine Meredith-Gougon, Ivo Mesquita, Monica Meyer, Kerry Morgan, Robin Morgan, Camille Morineau, Rebecca Morrill, Frances Morris, Tom Muller, Helen Nesbit, Occupy Museums, Ferris Olin, Yoko Ono, Neysa Page-Lieberman, Joanne Paradise, Adriano Pedroso, Lucrezia Perrig, Sarah Peter, David Platzker, Mark Pomeroy, Josefina Posch, Artemis Potamianou, Jennifer Ramkalawon, Helena Reckitt, Marcia Reed, Maura Reilly, Chris Rogy, Casey Ruble, Melena Ryzik, Dimitri Salmon, Lora Sariaslan, Elke Schmidt, Elmas Senol, Max Schumann, Sarah Sigmund, Peter Silverman, Kira Sjöberg, Kit-Yin Snyder, Nicole Soukup, Gloria Steinem, Kim Stephens, Hanna Styrmisdóttir, John Tain, Maija Tanninen, Francis Terpak, Maite Vissault, Olga Viso, Joan Vorderbruggen, Margaret Washington, Jay Wegman, Valerie Westcott, Roos Wijnen, Fred Wilson, Wendy Wolf, Nayia Yiakoumaki, Lynn Zelevansky